STONEWALL JACKSON

AND THE

AMERICAN CIVIL WAR

BY

LIEUT.-COL. G. F. R. HENDERSON, C.B.

AUTHOR OF 'THE BATTLE OF SPICHEREN, A TACTICAL STUDY'
AND 'THE CAMPAIGN OF FREDERICKSBURG'

WITH AN INTRODUCTION BY FIELD-MARSHAL
THE RIGHT HON. VISCOUNT WOLSELEY, K.P., G.C.B., G.C.M.G. &c.

IN TWO VOLUMES—VOL. II.

WITH PORTRAITS, MAPS, AND PLANS

THE
BLUE AND GREY
PRESS

Published by The Blue and Grey Press, a division of Book Sales, Inc.,
110 Enterprise Avenue, Secaucus, N.J. 07094.

89   9 8 7 6 5 4 3 2

Printed and bound in the United States of America.
ISBN: 1-55521-190-9

CONTENTS

OF

THE SECOND VOLUME

——◦◦——

ILLUSTRATIONS IN VOL. II

———◆◆◆———

MAPS

STONEWALL JACKSON

CHAPTER XIII

THE SEVEN DAYS. GAINES' MILL

The region whither the interest now shifts is very different from the Valley. From the terraced banks of the Rappa-

1862.   hannock, sixty miles north of Richmond, to the shining reaches of the James, where the capital of the Confederacy stands high on her seven hills, the lowlands of Virginia are clad with luxuriant vegetation. The roads and railways run through endless avenues of stately trees; the shadows of the giant oaks lie far across the rivers, and ridge and ravine are mantled with the unbroken foliage of the primeval forest. In this green wilderness the main armies were involved. But despite the beauty of broad rivers and sylvan solitudes, gay with gorgeous blossoms and fragrant with aromatic shrubs, the eastern, or 'tidewater,' counties of Virginia had little to recommend them as a theatre of war. They were sparsely settled. The wooden churches, standing lonely in the groves where the congregations hitched their horses; the solitary taverns, half inns and half stores; the court-houses of the county justices, with a few wooden cottages clustered round them, were poor substitutes for the market-towns of the Shenandoah. Here and there on the higher levels, surrounded by coppice and lawn, by broad acres of corn and clover, the manors of the planters gave life and brightness to the landscape. But the men were fighting in Lee's ranks, their families had fled to Richmond, and these hospitable homes showed signs of poverty and neglect. Neither food nor forage was to be drawn from the country, and the difficulties of supply and shelter were not the worst obstacles to military operations. At this season of the year the climate and the soil were persistent foes. The roads were mere tracks, channels which served as drains for the interminable forest. The deep meadows, fresh and green to the eye, were damp and unwholesome camping-grounds. Turgid streams, like the Chickahominy and its affluents, winding sluggishly through rank jungles, spread in swamp and morass across the valleys, and the languid atmosphere, surcharged with vapour, was redolent of decay.

Through this malarious region the Federal army had been pushing its slow way forward for more than six weeks, June. and 105,000 men, accompanied by a large siege train, lay intrenched within sight of the spires of Richmond. 30,000 were north of the Chickahominy, covering the York River Railway and waiting the coming of McDowell. The remainder, from Woodbury's Bridge to the Charles City road, occupied the line of breastworks which stood directly east of the beleaguered city. So nearly was the prize within their grasp that the church bells, and even the clocks striking the hour, were heard in the camps; and at Mechanicsville Bridge, watched by a picket, stood a sign-post which bore the legend : ' To Richmond, 4½ miles.' The sentries who paced that beat were fortunate. For the next two years they could boast that no Federal soldier, except as a prisoner, had stood so close as they had to the rebel stronghold. But during these weeks in June not a single soul in McClellan's army, and few in the Confederacy, suspected that the flood of invasion had reached high-water mark. Richmond, gazing night after night at the red glow which throbbed on the eastern vault, the reflection of countless camp-fires, and listening with strained ears to the far-off call of hostile bugles, seemed in perilous case. No formidable position protected the approaches. Earthworks, indeed, were in process of construction; but, although the left flank at New Bridge was covered by the

Chickahominy, the right was protected by no natural obstacle, as had been the case at Yorktown; and the lines occupied no commanding site. Nor had the Government been able to assemble an army of a strength sufficient to man the whole front. Lee, until Jackson joined him, commanded no more than 72,500 men. Of these a large portion were new troops, and their numbers had been reduced by the 7,000 dispatched under Whiting to the Valley.

But if the Federal army was far superior in numbers, it was not animated by an energy in proportion to its strength. The march from the White House was more sluggish than the current of the Chickahominy. From May 17 to June 26 the Army of the Valley had covered four hundred miles. Within the same period the Army of the Potomac had covered twenty. It is true that the circumstances were widely different. McClellan had in front of him the lines of Richmond, and his advance had been delayed by the rising of the Chickahominy. He had fought a hard fight at Seven Pines; and the constant interference of Jackson had kept him waiting for McDowell. But, at the same time, he had displayed an excess of caution which was perfectly apparent to his astute opponent. He had made no attempt to use his superior numbers; and Lee had come to the conclusion that the attack on Richmond would take the same form as the attack on Yorktown,—the establishment of great batteries, the massing of heavy ordnance, and all the tedious processes of a siege. He read McClellan like an open book. He had personal knowledge both of his capacity and character, for they had served together on the same staff in the Mexican war. He knew that his young adversary was a man of undoubted ability, of fascinating address, and of courage that was never higher than when things were at their worst. But these useful qualities were accompanied by marked defects. His will was less powerful than his imagination. Bold in conception, he was terribly slow in execution. When his good sense showed him the opportunity, his imagination whispered, 'Suppose the enemy has reserves of which I know nothing! Is it not more prudent to wait until I receive more accurate information?' And so 'I dare not,'

June 11.

B 2

inevitably waited on 'I would.' He forgot that in war it is impossible for a general to be absolutely certain. It is sufficient, according to Napoleon, if the odds in his favour are three to two; and if he cannot discover from the attitude of his enemy what the odds are, he is unfitted for supreme command.

Before Yorktown McClellan's five army corps had been held in check, first by 15,000 men, then by 53,000, protected by earthworks of feeble profile.[1] The fort at Gloucester Point was the key of the Confederate lines.[2] McClellan, however, although a division was actually under orders to move against it, appears to have been unwilling to risk a failure.[3] The channel of the York was thus closed both to his transports and the gunboats, and he did nothing whatever to interfere with Johnston's long line of communications, which passed at several points within easy reach of the river bank. Nor had he been more active since he had reached West Point. Except for a single expedition, which had dispersed a Confederate division near Hanover Court House, north of the Chickahominy, he had made no aggressive movement. He had never attempted to test the strength of the fortifications of Richmond, to hinder their construction, or to discover their weak points. His urgent demands for reinforcements had appeared in the Northern newspapers, and those newspapers had found their way to Richmond. From the same source the Confederates were made aware that he believed himself confronted by an army far larger than his own; and when, on the departure of Whiting's division for the Valley, he refused to take advantage of the opportunity to attack Lee's diminished force, it became abundantly clear, if further proof were wanting, that much might be ventured against so timid a commander.

From his knowledge of his adversary's character, and

---

[1] 'No one but McClellan would have hesitated to attack.' Johnston to Lee, April 22, 1862. O. R., vol. xi., part iii., p. 456.

[2] *Narrative of Military Operations*, General J. E. Johnston, pp. 112, 113

[3] The garrison consisted only of a few companies of heavy artillery, and the principal work was still unfinished when Yorktown fell. Reports of Dr. Comstock, and Colonel Cabell, C.S.A. O. R., vol. xi., part i.

still more from his attitude, Lee had little difficulty in discovering his intentions. McClellan, on the other hand, failed to draw a single correct inference. And yet the information at his disposal was sufficient to enable him to form a fair estimate of how things stood in the Confederate camp. He had been attacked at Seven Pines, but not by superior numbers; and it was hardly likely that the enemy had not employed their whole available strength in this battle; otherwise their enterprise was insensate. Furthermore, it was clearly to the interests of the Confederates to strike at his army before McDowell could join him. They had not done so, and it was therefore probable that they did not feel themselves strong enough to do so. It is true that he was altogether misled by the intelligence supplied as to the garrison of Richmond by his famous detective staff. 200,000 was the smallest number which the chief agent would admit. But that McClellan should have relied on the estimate of these untrained observers rather than on the evidence furnished by the conduct of the enemy is but a further proof that he lacked all power of deduction.[1]

It may well be questioned whether he was anxious at heart to measure swords with Lee. His knowledge of his adversary, whose reputation for daring, for ability, for strength of purpose, had been higher than any other in the old army, must needs have had a disturbing influence on his judgment. Against an enemy he did not know McClellan might have acted with resolution. Face to face with Lee, it can hardly be doubted that the weaker will was dominated by the stronger. Vastly different were their methods of war. McClellan made no effort whatever either to supplement or to corroborate the information supplied by his detectives. Since he had reached West Point his cavalry had done little.[2] Lee, on the other hand, had found

[1] In one sense McClellan was not far wrong in his estimate of the Confederate numbers. In assuming control of the Union armies Lincoln and Stanton made their enemies a present of at least 50,000 men.

[2] It must be admitted that his cavalry was very weak in proportion to the other arms. On June 20 he had just over 5,000 sabres (O. R., vol. xi., part iii., p. 238), of which 3,000 were distributed among the army corps. The

means to ascertain the disposition of his adversary's troops, and had acquired ample information of the measures which had been taken to protect the right wing, north of the Chickahominy, the point he had determined to attack.

Early on June 12, with 1,200 horsemen and a section of artillery, Stuart rode out on an enterprise of a
June 12. kind which at that time was absolutely unique, and which will keep his memory green so long as cavalry is used in war. Carefully concealing his march, he encamped that night near Taylorsville, twenty-two miles north of Richmond, and far beyond the flank of the Federal intrenchments. The next morning he turned
June 13. eastward towards Hanover Court House. Here he drove back a picket, and his advanced-guard, with the loss of one officer, soon afterwards charged down a squadron of regulars. A few miles to the south-east, near Old Church, the enemy's outposts were finally dispersed; and then, instead of halting, the column pushed on into the very heart of the district occupied by the Federals, and soon found itself in rear of their encampments. Stuart had already gained important information. He had learned that McClellan's right flank extended but a short way north of the Chickahominy, that it was not fortified, and that it rested on neither swamp nor stream, and this was what Lee had instructed him to discover. But it was one thing to obtain the information, another to bring it back. If he returned by the road he had come, it was probable he would be cut off, for the enemy was thoroughly roused, and the South Anna River, unfordable from recent rains, rendered a *détour* to the north impracticable. To the south and west of him lay the Federal army, some of the infantry camps not five miles distant. It was about

Confederates appear to have had about 3,000, but of superior quality, familiar, more or less, with the country, and united under one command. It is instructive to notice how the necessity for a numerous cavalry grew on the Federal commanders. In 1864 the Army of the Potomac was accompanied by a cavalry corps over 13,000 strong, with 32 guns. It is generally the case in war, even in a close country, that if the cavalry is allowed to fall below the usual proportion of one trooper to every six men of the other arms the army suffers.

four o'clock in the afternoon. He could hardly reach Hanover Court House before dark, and he might find it held by the enemy. To escape from the dilemma he determined on a plan of extraordinary daring, which involved nothing less than the passage of the Chickahominy in rear of the enemy, and a circuit of the entire Federal army.

The audacity of the design proved the salvation of his command. The enemy had assembled a strong force of both cavalry and infantry at Hanover Court House, under Stuart's father-in-law, General Cooke; but, misled by the reports brought in, and doubtless perplexed by the situation, the latter pursued but slowly and halted for the night at Old Church. Stuart, meanwhile, had reached Tunstall's Station on the York River Railway, picking up prisoners at every step. Here, routing the guard, he tore up the rails, destroyed a vast amount of stores and many waggons, broke down the telegraph and burnt the railway bridge, his men regaling themselves on the luxuries which were found in the well-stored establishments of the sutlers. Two squadrons, despatched to Garlick's Landing on the Pamunkey, set fire to two transports, and rejoined with a large number of prisoners, horses, and mules. Then, led by troopers who were natives of the country, the column marched south-east by the Williamsburg road, moving further and still further away from Richmond. The moon was full, and as the troops passed by the forest farms, the women, running to the wayside, wept with delight at the unexpected apparition of the grey jackets, and old men showered blessings on the heads of their gallant countrymen. At Talleysville, eight miles east, Stuart halted for three hours; and shortly after midnight, just as a Federal infantry brigade reached Tunstall's Station in hot pursuit, he turned off by a country road to the Chickahominy. At Forge Bridge, where he arrived at daylight, he should have found a ford; June 14. but the river had overflowed its banks, and was full of floating timber. Colonel Fitzhugh Lee, not the least famous member of a famous family, accompanied by a few men, swam his horse at imminent peril over to the

other bank ; but, although he re-crossed the swollen waters
in the same manner, the daring young officer had to report
that the passage was impracticable. It was already light.
The enemy would soon be up, and the capture of the whole
column seemed absolutely certain. Hitherto the men,
exhilarated by the complete success of the adventure, had
borne themselves as gaily as if they were riding through
the streets of Richmond. But the danger of their situation
was now forcibly impressed upon them, and the whole
command became grave and anxious. Stuart alone was
unmoved, and at this juncture one of his scouts informed
him that the skeleton of an old bridge spanned the stream
about a mile below. An abandoned warehouse furnished
the materials for a footway, over which the troopers
passed, holding the bridles of their horses as they swam
alongside. Half the column thus crossed, while the remainder strengthened the bridge so as to permit the passage of
the artillery. By one o'clock the whole force was over
the Chickahominy, unmolested by the enemy, of whom only
small parties, easily driven back by the rear-guard, had
made their appearance.

Thirty-five miles now to Richmond, in rear of the left
wing of the Northern army, and within range, for some
portion of the march, of the gunboats on the James River !
Burning the bridge, with a wave of the hand to the
Federal horsemen who covered the heights above Stuart
plunged into the woods, and without further misadventure
brought his troops at sunset to the neighbourhood of
Charles City Court House. Leaving his men sleeping,
after thirty-six hours in the saddle, he rode to Richmond to
June 15.   report to Lee. Before dawn on the 15th, after
          covering another thirty miles, over a road which
was patrolled by the enemy, he reached head-quarters. His
squadrons followed, marching at midnight, and bringing
with them 165 prisoners and 260 captured horses and mules.

This extraordinary expedition, which not only effected
the destruction of a large amount of Federal property,
and broke up, for the time being, their line of supplies, but
acquired information of the utmost value, and shook the con-

fidence of the North in McClellan's generalship, was accomplished with the loss of one man. These young Virginia soldiers marched one hundred and ten miles in less than two days. 'There was something sublime,' says Stuart, 'in the implicit confidence and unquestioning trust of the rank and file in a leader guiding them straight, apparently, into the very jaws of the enemy, every step appearing to them to diminish the hope of extrication.'[1] Nor was the influence of their achievement on the *moral* of the whole Confederate army the least important result attained. A host of over 100,000 men, which had allowed a few squadrons to ride completely round it, by roads which were within hearing of its bugles, was no longer considered a formidable foe.

On receiving Stuart's information, Lee drew up the plan of operations which had been imparted to Jackson on the 22nd.

It was a design which to all appearance was almost foolhardy. The Confederate army was organised as follows :—

Longstreet .	9,000
A. P. Hill .	14,000
Magruder .	13,000
Huger	9,000
Holmes	6,500
D. H. Hill .	10,000
Jackson	18,500
Cavalry	3,000
Reserve Artillery	3,500
	86,500[2]

On the night of June 24 the whole of these troops, with the exception of the Valley army, were south of the Chickahominy, holding the earthworks which protected Richmond. Less than two miles eastward, strongly intrenched, lay four of McClellan's army corps, in round numbers 75,000 officers and men.[3]

June 24.

To attack this force, even after Jackson's arrival,

[1] Stuart's Report, O. R., vol. xi., part i.

[2] This estimate is rather larger than that of the Confederate historians (Allan, W. H. Taylor, &c., &c.), but it has been arrived at after a careful examination of the strength at different dates and the losses in the various engagements.

[3] Return of June 20, O. R., vol. xi., part i., p. 238.

was to court disaster. The right was protected by the Chickahominy, the left rested on White Oak Swamp, a network of sluggish streams and impassable swamps, screened everywhere by tangled thickets. It needed not the presence of the siege ordnance, placed on the most commanding points within the lines, to make such a position absolutely impregnable.

North of the Chickahominy, however, the Federals were less favourably situated. The Fifth Army Corps, 25,000 strong,[1] under General FitzJohn Porter, had been pushed forward, stretching a hand to McDowell and protecting the railway, in the direction of Mechanicsville; and although the tributaries of the Chickahominy, running in from the north, afforded a series of positions, the right flank of these positions, resting, as Stuart had ascertained, on no natural obstacle, was open to a turning movement. Furthermore, in rear of the Fifth Corps, and at an oblique angle to the front, ran the line of supply, the railway to West Point. If Porter's right were turned, the Confederates, threatening the railway, would compel McClellan to detach largely to the north bank of the Chickahominy in order to recover or protect the line.

On the north bank of the Chickahominy, therefore, Lee's attention had been for some time fixed. Here was his adversary's weak point, and a sudden assault on Porter, followed up, if necessary, by an advance against the railway, would bring McClellan out of his intrenchments, and force him to fight at a disadvantage. To ensure success, however, in the attack on Porter it was necessary to concentrate an overwhelming force on the north bank; and this could hardly be done without so weakening the force which held the Richmond lines that it would be unable to resist the attack of the 75,000 men who faced it. If McClellan, while Lee was fighting Porter, boldly threw forward the great army he had on the south bank, the rebel capital might be the reward of his resolution. The danger

---

[1] The Fifth Army Corps included McCall's division, which had but recently arrived by water from Fredericksburg. Report of June 20, O. R., vol. xi., part i., p. 238.

was apparent to all, but Lee resolved to risk it, and his audacity has not escaped criticism. It has been said that he deliberately disregarded the contingency of McClellan either advancing on Richmond, or reinforcing Porter. The truth is, however, that neither Lee, nor those generals about him who knew McClellan, were in the least apprehensive that their over-cautious adversary, if the attack were sudden and well sustained, would either see or utilise his opportunity.

From Hannibal to Moltke there has been no great captain who has neglected to study the character of his opponent, and who did not trade on the knowledge thus acquired, and it was this knowledge which justified Lee's audacity.

The real daring of the enterprise lay in the inferiority of the Confederate armament. Muskets and shot-guns, still carried by a large part of the army, were ill-matched against rifles of the most modern manufacture; while the smooth-bore field-pieces, with which at least half the artillery was equipped, possessed neither the range nor the accuracy of the rifled ordnance of the Federals.

That Lee's study of the chances had not been patient and exhaustive it is impossible to doubt. He was no hare-brained leader, but a profound thinker, following the highest principles of the military art. That he had weighed the disconcerting effect which the sudden appearance of the victorious Jackson, with an army of unknown strength, would produce upon McClellan, goes without saying. He had omitted no precaution to render the surprise complete, and although the defences of Richmond were still too weak to resist a resolute attack, Magruder, the same officer who had so successfully imposed upon McClellan at Yorktown, was such a master of artifice that, with 28,000 men and the reserve artillery,[1] he might be relied upon to hold Richmond until Porter had been dis-

---

[1] Magruder's division, 13,000; Huger's division, 9,000; reserve artillery, 3,000; 5 regiments of cavalry, 2,000. Holmes' division, 6,500, was still retained on the south bank of the James.

posed of. The remainder of the army, 2,000 of Stuart's
cavalry, the divisions of Longstreet and the two Hills, 35,000
men all told, crossing to the north bank of the Chickahominy
and combining with the 18,500 under Jackson, would be
sufficient to crush the Federal right.

The initial operations, however, were of a somewhat
complicated nature. Four bridges [1] crossed the river on
Lee's left. A little more than a mile and a half from
Mechanicsville Bridge, up stream, is Meadow Bridge,
and five and a half miles further up is another passage
at the Half Sink, afterwards called Winston's Bridge.
Three and a half miles below Mechanicsville Bridge
is New Bridge. The northern approaches to Mechanicsville, Meadow, and New Bridge, were in possession of the
Federals ; and it was consequently no simple operation to
transfer the troops before Richmond from one bank of the
Chickahominy to the other. Only Mechanicsville and
Meadow Bridges could be used. Winston's Bridge was too
far from Richmond, for, if Longstreet and the two Hills
were to cross at that point, not only would Magruder be
left without support during their march, but McClellan,
warned by his scouts, would receive long notice of the
intended blow and have ample time for preparation. To
surprise Porter, to give McClellan no time for reflection,
and at the same time to gain a position which would
bring the Confederates operating on the north bank into
close and speedy communication with Magruder on the
south, another point of passage must be chosen. The
position would be the one commanding New Bridge, for
the Confederate earthworks, held by Magruder, ran due
south from that point. But Porter was already in possession of the coveted ground, with strong outposts at
Mechanicsville. To secure, then, the two centre bridges
was the first object. This, it was expected, would be
achieved by the advance of the Valley army, aided by
a brigade from the Half Sink, against the flank and
rear of the Federals at Mechanicsville. Then, as soon

[1] Lee's bridge, shown on the map, had either been destroyed or was not
yet built.

as the enemy fell back, Longstreet and the two Hills would cross the river by the Meadow and Mechanicsville Bridges, and strike Porter in front, while Jackson attacked his right. A victory would place the Confederates in possession of New Bridge, and the troops north of the Chickahominy would be then in close communication with Magruder.

Lee's orders were as follows :—' Headquarters, Army of Northern Virginia, June 24, 1862. General Orders, No. 75.

'I.—General Jackson's command will proceed to-morrow (June 25) from Ashland towards the Slash (Merry Oaks) Church, and encamp at some convenient point west of the Central Railroad. Branch's brigade of A. P. Hill's division will also, to-morrow evening, take position on the Chickahominy, near Half Sink. At three o'clock Thursday morning, 26th instant, General Jackson will advance on the road leading to Pole Green Church, communicating his march to General Branch, who will immediately cross the Chickahominy, and take the road leading to Mechanicsville. As soon as the movements of these columns are discovered, General A. P. Hill, with the rest of his division, will cross the Chickahominy at Meadow Bridge, and move direct upon Mechanicsville. To aid his advance the heavy batteries on the Chickahominy will at the proper time open upon the batteries at Mechanicsville. The enemy being driven from Mechanicsville and the passage of the bridge being opened, General Longstreet, with his division and that of General D. H. Hill, will cross the Chickahominy at or near that point ; General D. H. Hill moving to the support of General Jackson, and General Longstreet supporting General A. P. Hill ; the four divisions keeping in communication with each other, and moving en échelon on separate roads if practicable ; the left division in advance, with skirmishers and sharp-shooters extending in their front, will sweep down the Chickahominy, and endeavour to drive the enemy from his position above New Bridge, General Jackson bearing well to his left, turning Beaver Dam Creek, and taking the direction towards

Cold Harbour. They will then press forward towards the York River Railroad, closing upon the enemy's rear, and forcing him down the Chickahominy. An advance of the enemy towards Richmond will be prevented by vigorously following his rear, and crippling and arresting his progress.

'II.—The divisions under Generals Huger and Magruder will hold their position in front of the enemy against attack, and make such demonstrations, Thursday, as to discover his operations. Should opportunity offer, the feint will be converted into a real attack. . . . .

'IV.—General Stuart, with the 1st, 4th, and 9th Virginia Cavalry, the cavalry of Cobb's Legion, and the Jeff Davis Legion, will cross the Chickahominy to-morrow (Wednesday, June 25), and take position to the left of General Jackson's line of march. The main body will be held in reserve, with scouts well extended to the front and left. General Stuart will keep General Jackson informed of the movements of the enemy on his left, and will co-operate with him in his advance. . . . .'

On the 25th Longstreet and the two Hills moved towards the bridges; and although during the movement McClellan drove back Magruder's pickets to their trenches, and pushed his own outposts nearer Richmond, Lee held firmly to his purpose. As a matter of fact, there was little to be feared from McClellan. With a profound belief in the advantages of defensive and in the strength of a fortified position, he expected nothing less than that the Confederates would leave the earthworks they had so laboriously constructed, and deliberately risk the perils of an attack. He seems to have had little idea that in the hands of a skilful general intrenchments may form a 'pivot of operations,' [1] the means whereby he covers his most vulnerable point, holds the enemy in front, and sets his main body free for offensive action. Yet

June 25.

---

[1] 'The meaning of this term is clearly defined in Lee's report. ' It was therefore determined to construct defensive lines, so as to enable a part of the army to defend the city, and leave the other part free to operate on the north bank.' O. R., vol. xi., part i., p. 490.

McClellan was by no means easy in his mind. He knew Jackson was approaching. He knew his communications were threatened. Fugitive negroes, who, as usual, either exaggerated or lied, had informed him that the Confederates had been largely reinforced, and that Beauregard, with a portion of the Western army, had arrived in Richmond. But that his right wing was in danger he had not the faintest suspicion. He judged Lee by himself. Such a plan as leaving a small force to defend Richmond, and transferring the bulk of the army to join Jackson, he would have at once rejected as overdaring. If attack came at all, he expected that it would come by the south bank; and he was so far from anticipating that an opportunity for offensive action might be offered to himself that, on the night of the 25th, he sent word to his corps commanders that they were to regard their intrenchments as 'the true field of battle.'[1]

Lee's orders left much to Jackson. The whole operation which Lee had planned hinged upon his movements. On the morning of the 24th he was at Beaver Dam Station. The same night he was to reach Ashland, eighteen miles distant as the crow flies. On the night of the 25th he was to halt near the Slash Church, just west of the Virginia Central Railway, and six miles east of Ashland. At three o'clock,

June 26. however, on the morning of the 26th, the Army of
3 A.M. the Valley was still at Ashland, and it was not till nine that it crossed the railroad. Branch, on hearing
10.30 A.M. that Jackson was at last advancing, passed the Chickahominy by Winston's Bridge, and driving the Federal pickets before him, moved on Mechanicsville. General A. P. Hill was meanwhile near Meadow Bridge, waiting until the advance of Jackson and Branch should turn the flank of the Federal force which blocked his
3 P.M. passage. At 3 P.M., hearing nothing from his colleagues, and apprehensive that longer delay might hazard the failure of the whole plan, he ordered his advanced-guard to seize the bridge. The enemy, already threatened in rear by Branch, at once fell back. Hill followed

[1] O. R., vol. xi., part iii., p. 252.

the retiring pickets towards Beaver Dam Creek, and after a short march of three miles found himself under fire of the Federal artillery. Porter had occupied a position about two miles above New Bridge.

The rest of the Confederate army was already crossing the Chickahominy; and although there was no sign of Jackson, and the enemy's front was strong, protected by a long line of batteries, Hill thought it necessary to order an attack. A message from Lee, ordering him to postpone all further movement, arrived too late.[1] There was no artillery preparation, and the troops, checked unexpectedly by a wide abattis, were repulsed with terrible slaughter, the casualties amounting to nearly 2,000 men.[2] The Union loss was 360.[3]

Jackson, about 4.30 P.M., before this engagement had begun, had reached Hundley's Corner, three miles north 4.30 P.M. of the Federal position, but separated from it by dense forest and the windings of the creek. On the opposite bank was a detachment of Federal infantry, supported by artillery. Two guns, accompanied by the 6 P.M. advanced-guard, sufficed to drive this force to the shelter of the woods; and then, establishing his outposts, Jackson ordered his troops to bivouac.

It has been asserted by more than one Southern general that the disaster at Beaver Dam Creek was due to Jackson's indifferent tactics; and, at first sight, the bare facts would seem to justify the verdict. He had not reached his appointed station on the night of the 25th, and on the 26th he was five hours behind time. He should have crossed the Virginia Central Railway at sunrise, but at nine o'clock he was still three miles distant. His advance against the Federal right flank and rear should have been made in co-operation with the remainder of the army. But his whereabouts was unknown when Hill attacked; and although the cannonade was distinctly heard at Hundley's Corner, he made no effort to lend assistance, and his troops were encamping when their comrades, not three miles

---

[1] Letter from Capt. T. W. Sydnor, 4th Va. Cavalry, who carried the message.
[2] So General Porter. *Battles and Leaders*, vol. ii., p. 331.
[3] O. R., vol. xi., part i., pp. 38, 39.

away, were rushing forward to the assault. There would seem to be some grounds, then, for the accusation that his delay thwarted General Lee's design; some reason for the belief that the victor of the Valley campaign, on his first appearance in combination with the main army, had proved a failure, and that his failure was in those very qualities of swiftness and energy to which he owed his fame.

General D. H. Hill has written that ' Jackson's genius never shone when he was under the command of another. It seemed then to be shrouded or paralysed. . . . MacGregor on his native heath was not more different from MacGregor in prison than was Jackson his own master from Jackson in a subordinate position. This was the keynote to his whole character. The hooded falcon cannot strike the quarry.' [1]

The reader who has the heart to follow this chronicle to the end will assuredly find reason to doubt the acumen, however he may admire the eloquence, of Jackson's brother-in-law. When he reads of the Second Manassas, of Harper's Ferry, of Sharpsburg and of Chancellorsville, he will recall this statement with astonishment; and it will not be difficult to show that Jackson conformed as closely to the plans of his commander at Mechanicsville as elsewhere.

The machinery of war seldom runs with the smoothness of clockwork. The course of circumstances can never be exactly predicted. Unforeseen obstacles may render the highest skill and the most untiring energy of no avail; and it may be well to point out that the task which was assigned to Jackson was one of exceeding difficulty. In the first place, his march of eight-and-twenty miles, from Frederickshall to Ashland, on June 23, 24, and 25, was made over an unmapped country, unknown either to himself or to his staff, which had lately been in occupation of the Federals. Bridges had been destroyed and roads obstructed. The Valley army had already marched far and fast; and although Dabney hints that inexperienced and sluggish subordinates were the chief cause of delay,

---

[1] *Battles and Leaders*, vol. ii., pp. 389, 390.

there is hardly need to look so far for excuse.[1]   The march
from Ashland to Hundley's Corner, sixteen miles, was little
less difficult.   It was made in two columns, Whiting and the
Stonewall division, now under Winder, crossing the railway
near Merry Oaks Church, Ewell moving by Shady Grove
Church ; but this distribution did not accelerate the march.
The midsummer sun blazed fiercely down on the dusty
roads ; the dense woods on either hand shut out the air, and
interruptions were frequent.   The Federal cavalry held a
line from Atlee's Station to near Hanover Court House.
The 8th Illinois, over 700 strong, picketed all the woods
between the Chickahominy and the Totopotomoy Creek.
Two other regiments prolonged the front to the Pamunkey,
and near Hundley's Corner and Old Church were posted
detachments of infantry.   Skirmishing was constant.   The
Federal outposts contested every favourable position.   Here
and there the roads were obstructed by felled trees ; a
burned bridge over the Totopotomoy delayed the advance for
a full hour, and it was some time before the enemy's force
at Hundley's Corner was driven behind Beaver Dam Creek.

At the council of war, held on the 23rd, Lee had left
it to Jackson to fix the date on which the operation against
the Federal right should begin, and on the latter deciding on
the 26th, Longstreet had suggested that he should make
more ample allowance for the difficulties that might be presented by the country and by the enemy, and give himself
more time.[2]   Jackson had not seen fit to alter his decision,
and it is hard to say that he was wrong.

Had McClellan received notice that the Valley army
was approaching, a day's delay would have given him a
fine opportunity.   More than one course would have been
open to him.   He might have constructed formidable intrenchments on the north bank of the Chickahominy and

---

[1] Dr. White, in his excellent *Life of Lee*, states that the tardiness of the
arrival of the provisions sent him from Richmond had much to do with the
delay of Jackson's march.

[2] 'Lee's Attacks North of the Chickahominy.'   By General D. H. Hill.
Battles and Leaders, vol. ii., p. 347.   General Longstreet, however, *From
Manassas to Appomattox*, says Jackson appointed the morning of the 25th,
but, on Longstreet's suggestion, changed the date to the 26th.

have brought over large reinforcements of men and guns; or he might have turned the tables by a bold advance on Richmond. It was by no means inconceivable that if he detected Lee's intention and was given time to prepare, he might permit the Confederates to cross the Chickahominy, amuse them there with a small force, and hurl the rest of his army on the works which covered the Southern capital. It is true that his caution was extreme, and to a mind which was more occupied with counting the enemy's strength than with watching for an opportunity, the possibility of assuming the offensive was not likely to occur. But, timid as he might be when no enemy was in sight, McClellan was constitutionally brave; and when the chimeras raised by an over-active imagination proved to be substantial dangers, he was quite capable of daring resolution. Time, therefore, was of the utmost importance to the Confederates. It was essential that Porter should be overwhelmed before McClellan realised the danger; and if Jackson, in fixing a date for the attack which would put a heavy tax on the marching powers of his men, already strained to the utmost, ran some risks, from a strategical point of view those risks were fully justified.

In the second place, an operation such as that which Lee had devised is one of the most difficult manœuvres which an army can be called upon to execute. According to Moltke, to unite two forces on the battle-field, starting at some distance apart, at the right moment, is the most brilliant feat of generalship. The slightest hesitation may ruin the combination. Haste is even more to be dreaded. There is always the danger that one wing may attack, or be attacked, while the other is still far distant, and either contingency may be fatal. The Valley campaign furnishes more than one illustration. In their pursuit of Jackson, Shields and Frémont failed to co-operate at Strasburg, at Cross Keys, and at Port Republic. And greater generals than either Shields or Frémont have met with little better success in attempting the same manœuvre. At both Eylau and Bautzen Napoleon was deprived of decisive victory by his failure to ensure the co-operation of his widely separated columns.

Jackson and A. P. Hill, on the morning of the 26th, were nearly fifteen miles apart. Intercommunication at the outset was ensured by the brigade under Branch; but as the advance progressed, and the enemy was met with, it became more difficult. The messengers riding from one force to the other were either stopped by the Federals, or were compelled to make long *détours*; and as they approached the enemy's position, neither Hill nor Jackson was informed of the whereabouts of the other.

The truth is, that the arrangements made by the Confederate headquarter staff were most inadequate. In the first place, the order of the 24th, instructing Jackson to start from Slash Church at 3 A.M. on the 26th, and thus leading the other generals to believe that he would certainly be there at that hour, should never have been issued. When it was written Jackson's advanced-guard was at Beaver Dam Station, the rear brigades fifteen miles behind; and to reach Slash Church his force had to march forty miles through an intricate country, in possession of the enemy, and so little known that it was impossible to designate the route to be followed. To fix an hour of arrival so long in advance was worse than useless, and Jackson cannot be blamed if he failed to comply with the exact letter of a foolish order. As it was, so many of the bridges were broken, and so difficult was it to pass the fords, that if Dr. Dabney had not found in his brother, a planter of the neighbourhood, an efficient substitute for the guide headquarters should have provided, the Valley army would have been not hours but days too late. In the second place, the duty of keeping up communications should not have been left to Jackson, but have been seen to at headquarters. Jackson had with him only a few cavalry, and these few had not only to supply the necessary orderlies for the subordinate generals, and the escorts for the artillery and trains, but to form his advanced-guard, for Stuart's squadrons were on his left flank, and not in his front. Moreover, his cavalry were complete strangers to the country, and there were no maps. In such circumstances the only means of ensuring constant communication was to have detached two of Stuart's squadrons, who knew the ground, to establish a series of posts between Jackson's line of march and the Chickahominy; and to have detailed a staff officer, whose sole duty would have been to furnish the Commander-in-Chief with hourly reports of the progress made, to join the Valley army.[1] It may be remarked, too, that Generals Branch and Ewell, following converging roads, met near Shady Grove Church about 3 P.M. No report appears to have been sent by the latter to General A. P. Hill; and although Branch a little later received a message to the effect that Hill had crossed the Chickahominy and was moving on Mechanicsville,[2] the information was not passed on to Jackson.

Neglect of these precautions made it impracticable to arrange a simultaneous attack, and co-operation depended solely on the judgment of Hill and Jackson. In the action which ensued on Beaver Dam Creek there was no co-operation whatever. Hill attacked and was repulsed. Jackson had halted at Hundley's Corner, three miles distant from the battle-field. Had the latter come down on the Federal rear while Hill moved against their front an easy success would in all probability have been the result.

Nevertheless, the responsibility for Hill's defeat cannot be held to rest on Jackson's shoulders. On August 18, 1870, the Prussian Guards and the Saxon Army Corps

[1] Of the events of June 26 Dr. Dabney, in a letter to the author, writes as follows :—' Here we had a disastrous illustration of the lack of an organised and intelligent general staff. Let my predicament serve as a specimen. As chief of Jackson's staff, I had two assistant adjutant-generals, two men of the engineer department, and two clerks. What did I have for orderlies and couriers? A detail from some cavalry company which happened to bivouac near. The men were sent to me without any reference to their local knowledge, their intelligence, or their courage ; most probably they were selected for me by their captain on account of their lack of these qualities. Next to the Commander-in-Chief, the Chief of the General Staff should be the best man in the country. The brains of an army should be in the General Staff. The lowest orderlies attached to it should be the very best soldiers in the service, for education, intelligence, and courage. Jackson had to find his own guide for his march from Beaver Dam Station. He had not been furnished with a map, and not a single orderly or message reached him during the whole day.'

[2] Branch's Report, O. R., vol. xi., part ii., p. 882.

were ordered to make a combined attack on the village
of St. Privat, the Guards moving against the front, the
Saxons against the flank. When the order was issued the
two corps were not more than two miles apart. The tract
of country which lay between them was perfectly open, the
roads were free, and inter-communication seemed easy in
the extreme. Yet, despite their orders, despite the facilities
of communication, the Guards advanced to the attack an
hour and a half too soon ; and from six o'clock to nearly
seven their shattered lines lay in front of the position,
at the mercy of a vigorous counterstroke, without a single
Saxon regiment coming to their aid. But the Saxons were
not to blame. Their march had been unchecked ; they had
moved at speed. On their part there had been no hesitation ; but on the part of the commander of the Guards
there had been the same precipitation which led to the premature attack on the Federal position at Beaver Dam
Creek. It was the impatience of General Hill, not the
tardiness of Jackson, which was the cause of the Confederate repulse.

We may now turn to the question whether Jackson was
justified in not marching to the sound of the cannon.
Referring to General Lee's orders, it will be seen that as soon
as Longstreet and D. H. Hill had crossed the Chickahominy
the four divisions of the army were to move forward *in communication with each other* and drive the enemy from his
position, Jackson, in advance upon the left, 'turning Beaver
Dam Creek, and taking the direction of Cold Harbour.'

When Jackson reached Hundley's Corner, and drove the
Federal infantry behind the Creek, the first thing to do, as
his orders indicated, was to get touch with the rest of the
army. It was already near sunset ; between Hundley's
Corner and Mechanicsville lay a dense forest, with no roads
in the desired direction ; and it was manifestly impossible, under ordinary conditions, to do more that evening
than to establish connection ; the combined movement
against the enemy's position must be deferred till the
morning. But the sound of battle to the south-west introduced a complication. 'We distinctly heard,' says Jackson,

'the rapid and continued discharges of cannon.'[1]   What did this fire portend?   It might proceed, as was to be inferred from Lee's orders, from the heavy batteries on the Chickahominy covering Hill's passage.   It might mean a Federal counterstroke on Hill's advanced-guard ; or, possibly, a premature attack on the part of the Confederates.   General Whiting, according to his report, thought it 'indicated a severe battle.'[2]   General Trimble, marching with Ewell, heard both musketry and artillery ; and in his opinion the command should have moved forward ;[3] and whatever may have been Jackson's orders, it was undoubtedly his duty, if he believed a hot engagement was in progress, to have marched to the assistance of his colleagues.   He could not help them by standing still.   He might have rendered them invaluable aid by pressing the enemy in flank.   But the question is, What inference did the cannonade convey to Jackson's mind ?   Was it of such a character as to leave no doubt that Hill was in close action, or might it be interpreted as the natural accompaniment of the passage of the Chickahominy ?   The evidence is conflicting.   On the one hand we have the evidence of Whiting and Trimble, both experienced soldiers ; on the other, in addition to the indirect evidence of Jackson's inaction, we have the statement of Major Dabney.   'We heard no signs,' says the chief of the staff, 'of combat on Beaver Dam Creek until a little while before sunset.   The whole catastrophe took place in a few minutes about that time ; and in any case our regiments, who had gone into bivouac, could not have been reassembled, formed up, and moved forward in time to be of any service.   A night attack through the dense, pathless, and unknown forest was quite impracticable.'[4]   It seems probable, then—and the Federal reports are to the same effect[5]—that the firing was only really heavy for a very short period, and that Jackson believed it

[1] Jackson's Report, O. R., vol. xi., part i., p. 553.
[2] Whiting's Report, O. R., vol. xi., part i., p. 562.
[3] Trimble's Report, O. R., vol. xi., part i., p. 614.
[4] Letter to the author.
[5] Porter's Report, O. R., vol. xi., part i., p. 222.   *Battles and Leaders,* vol. ii., p. 330.

to be occasioned by Hill's passage of the Chickahominy, and the rout of the Federals from Mechanicsville. Neither Trimble nor Whiting were aware that Lee's orders directed that the operation was to be covered by a heavy cannonade.

Obeying orders very literally himself, Jackson found it difficult to believe that others did not do the same. He knew that the position he had taken up rendered the line of Beaver Dam Creek untenable by the Federals. They would never stand to fight on that line with a strong force established in their rear and menacing their communications, nor would they dare to deliver a counterstroke through the trackless woods. It might confidently be assumed, therefore, that they would fall back during the night, and that the Confederate advance would then be carried out in that concentrated formation which Lee's orders had dictated. Such, in all probability, was Jackson's view of the situation; and that Hill, in direct contravention of those orders, would venture on an isolated attack before that formation had been assumed never for a moment crossed his mind.[1]

Hill, on the other hand, seems to have believed that if the Federals were not defeated on the evening of the 26th they would make use of the respite, either to bring up reinforcements, or to advance on Richmond by the opposite bank of the Chickahominy. It is not impossible that he thought the sound of his cannon would bring Jackson to his aid. That it would have been wiser to establish communication, and to make certain of that aid before attacking, there can be no question. It was too late to defeat Porter the same evening. Nothing was to be gained by immediate attack, and much would be risked. The last assault, in which the heaviest losses were incurred, was made just as night fell. It was a sacrifice of life as unnecessary as that of the Prussian Guard before St. Privat. At the same time, that General Hill did wrong in crossing the Chickahominy before he heard of his colleague's approach is not a fair

[1] Longstreet, on p. 124 of his *From Manassas to Appomattox*, declares that 'Jackson marched by the fight without giving attention, and went into camp at Hundley's Corner, *half a mile in rear* of the enemy's position.' A reference to the map is sufficient to expose the inaccuracy of this statement.

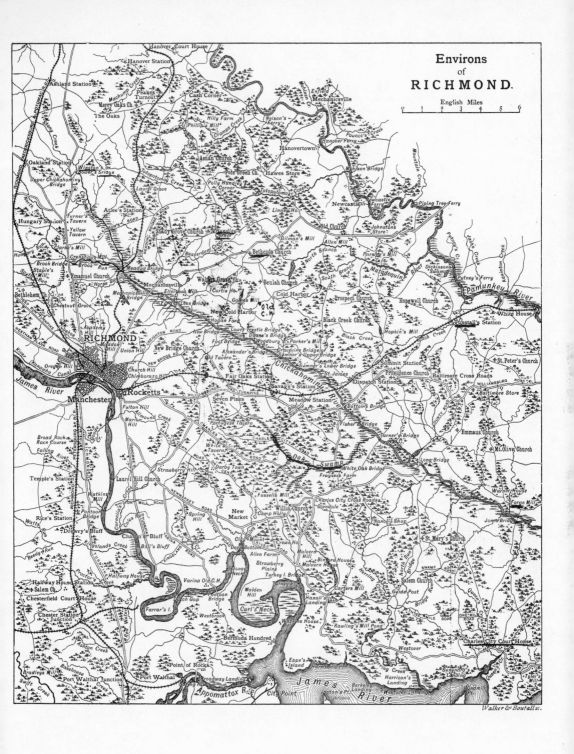

Environs
of
RICHMOND.

English Miles
0 1 2 3 4 5 6

Walker & Boutall sc.

accusation. To have lingered on the south bank would have
been to leave Jackson to the tender mercies of the Federals
should the turn against him in the forest. Moreover,
it was Hill's task to open a passage for the remaining
divisions, and if that passage had been deferred to a later
hour, it is improbable that the Confederate army would
have been concentrated on the north bank of the Chickahominy until the next morning. It must be admitted,
too, that the situation in which Hill found himself,
after crossing the river, was an exceedingly severe
test of his self-control. His troops had driven in the
Federal outposts; infantry, cavalry, and artillery were
retiring before his skirmishers. The noise of battle filled
the air. From across the Chickahominy thundered the
heavy guns, and his regiments were pressing forward with
the impetuous ardour of young soldiers. If he yielded to the
excitement of the moment, if eagerness for battle overpowered his judgment, if his brain refused to work calmly
in the wild tumult of the conflict, he is hardly to be blamed.
The patience which is capable of resisting the eagerness
of the troops, the imperturbable judgment which, in the
heat of action, weighs with deliberation the necessities of
the moment, the clear vision which forecasts the result of
every movement—these are rare qualities indeed.

During the night Porter fell back on Gaines' Mill.
While the engagement at Beaver Dam Creek was still in
progress vast clouds of dust, rising above the forests to the
north-west and north, had betrayed the approach of
Jackson, and the reports of the cavalry left no doubt
that he was threatening the Federal rear.

The retreat was conducted in good order, a strong
rear-guard, reinforced by two batteries of horse-artillery,
holding the Confederates in check, and before morning a
second position, east of Powhite Creek, and covering two
bridges over the Chickahominy, Alexander's and Grapevine,
was occupied by the Fifth Army Corps.

New Bridge was now uncovered, and Lee's army was in
motion shortly after sunrise, Jackson crossing Beaver Dam
Creek and moving due south in the direction of Walnut

Grove Church.[1]   The enemy, however, had already passed
June 27, eastward ; and the Confederates, well concentrated
5 A.M.   and in hand, pushed forward in pursuit ; A. P. Hill,
with Longstreet on his right, moving on Gaines' Mill, while
Jackson, supported by D. H. Hill, and with Stuart covering
his left, marched by a more circuitous route to Old Cold
Harbour.   Near Walnut Grove Church Jackson met the
Commander-in-Chief, and it is recorded that the staff officers
of the Valley army, noting the eagerness displayed by
General Lee's suite to get a glimpse of ' Stonewall,' then for
the first time realised the true character and magnitude
of the Valley campaign.

About noon, after a march of seven miles, A. P. Hill's
scouts reported that the Federals had halted behind
12 noon.   Powhite Creek.   The leading brigade was sent
across the stream, which runs past Gaines'
Mill, and pressing through the thick woods found the
enemy in great strength on a ridge beyond.   Hill formed
his division for attack, and opened fire with his four
batteries.   The enemy's guns, superior in number, at
once responded, and the skirmish lines became actively
engaged.   The Confederate general, despite urgent messages from his subordinates, requesting permission to
attack, held his troops in hand, waiting till he should be
supported, and for two and a half hours the battle was no
more than an affair of ' long bowls.'

The position held by the defence was emphatically one
to impose caution on the assailants.   To reach it the
Confederates were confined to three roads, two from
Mechanicsville, and one from Old Cold Harbour.   These
roads led each of them through a broad belt of forest,
and then, passing through open fields, descended into a

---

[1] Jackson's division—so-called in Lee's order—really consisted of three
divisions:

| | | Whiting's Division | { | Hood's Brigade Law's | " |
| Jackson's [Winder] Division | { Stonewall Brigade Cunningham's " Fulkerson's " Lawton's " | | | Ewell's Division | { B. T. Johnson's Brigade Elzey's " Trimble's " Taylor's " |

winding valley, from five hundred to a thousand yards
in breadth.   Rising near McGehee's House, due south
of Old Cold Harbour, a sluggish creek, bordered by
swamps and thick timber, and cutting in places a deep
channel, filtered through the valley to the Chickahominy.
Beyond this stream rose an open and undulating plateau,
admirably adapted to the movement of all arms, and with
a slight command of the opposite ridge.   On the plateau,
facing west and north, the Federals were formed up.   A
fringe of trees and bushes along the crest gave cover and
concealment to the troops.   60 feet below, winding darkly
through the trees, the creek covered the whole front ; and
in the centre of the position, east of New Cold Harbour, the
valley was completely filled with tangled wood.

Towards Old Cold Harbour the timber on the Confederate side of the ravine was denser than elsewhere.   On
the Federal left flank the valley of the Chickahominy was
open ground, but it was swept by heavy guns from
the right bank of the river, and at this point the creek
became an almost impassable swamp.

Porter, who had been reinforced by 9,000 men under
General Slocum, now commanded three divisions of
infantry, four regiments of cavalry, and twenty-two
batteries, a total of 36,000 officers and men.   The *moral*
of the troops had been strengthened by their easy victory
of the previous day.   Their commander had gained
their confidence; their position had been partially intrenched, and they could be readily supported by way of
Alexander's and Grapevine Bridges from the south bank of
the Chickahominy.

The task before the Confederates, even with their
superior numbers, was formidable in the extreme.   The
wooded ridge which encircled the position afforded scant
room for artillery, and it was thus impracticable to prepare
the attack by a preliminary bombardment.   The ground
over which the infantry must advance was completely
swept by fire, and the centre and left were defended by
three tiers of riflemen, the first sheltered by the steep
banks of the creek, the second halfway up the bluff,

covered by a breastwork, the third on the crest, occupying
a line of shelter-trenches; and the riflemen were supported by a dozen batteries of rifled guns.[1]

But Lee had few misgivings. In one respect the
Federal position seemed radically defective. The line of
retreat on White House was exposed to attack from Old
Cold Harbour. In fact, with Old Cold Harbour in possession of the Confederates, retreat could only be effected by
one road north of the Chickahominy, that by Parker's
Mill and Dispatch Station; and if this road were threatened,
Porter, in order to cover it, would be compelled to bring
over troops from his left and centre, or to prolong his line
until it was weak everywhere. There was no great reason to
fear that McClellan would send Porter heavy reinforcements.
To do so he would have to draw troops from his intrenchments
on the south bank of the Chickahominy, and Magruder had
been instructed to maintain a brisk demonstration against
this portion of the line. It was probable that the Federal
commander, with his exaggerated estimate of the numbers
opposed to him, would be induced by this means to anticipate a general attack against his whole front, and would
postpone moving his reserves until it was too late.

While Hill was skirmishing with the Federals, Lee was
anxiously awaiting intelligence of Jackson's arrival at Old
Cold Harbour. Longstreet was already forming up for
battle, and at 2.30 Hill's regiments were slipped to the
attack. A fierce and sanguinary conflict now
2.30 P.M. ensued. Emerging in well-ordered lines from the
cover of the woods, the Confederates swept down the open
slopes. Floundering in the swamps, and struggling
through the abattis which had been placed on the banks
of the stream, they drove in the advanced line of hostile
riflemen, and strove gallantly to ascend the slope which
lay beyond. 'But brigade after brigade,' says General
Porter, 'seemed almost to melt away before the concentrated fire of our artillery and infantry; yet others pressed
on, followed by supports daring and brave as their prede-
cessors, despite their heavy losses and the disheartening

---

[1] The remainder of the guns were in reserve.

effect of having to clamber over many of their disabled and
dead, and to meet their surviving comrades rushing back
in great disorder from the deadly contest.' [1] For over
an hour Hill fought on without support. There were
no signs of Jackson, and Longstreet, whom it was not
intended to employ until Jackson's appearance should have
caused the Federals to denude their left, was then sent in to
save the day.

As on the previous day, the Confederate attack had
failed in combination. Jackson's march had been again
delayed. The direct road from Walnut Grove Church to
Old Cold Harbour, leading through the forest, was found
to be obstructed by felled timber and defended by sharp-
shooters, and to save time Jackson's division struck off
into the road by Bethesda Church. This threw it in rear of
D. H. Hill, and it was near 2 P.M. when the latter's
advanced-guard reached the tavern at the Old Cold Harbour cross roads. No harm, however, had been done.
A. P. Hill did not attack till half an hour later. But when
he advanced there came no response from the left. A battery
of D. H. Hill's division was brought into action, but was soon
silenced, and beyond this insignificant demonstration the
Army of the Valley made no endeavour to join the battle.
The brigades were halted by the roadside. Away to the right,
above the intervening forest, rolled the roar of battle, the
crash of shells and the din of musketry, but no orders
were given for the advance.

Nor had Jackson's arrival produced the slightest consternation in the Federal ranks. Although from his
position at Cold Harbour he seriously threatened their line
of retreat to the White House, they had neither denuded
their left nor brought up their reserves. Where he was
now established he was actually nearer White House than
any portion of Porter's army corps, and yet that general
apparently accepted the situation with equanimity.

Lee had anticipated that Jackson's approach would
cause the enemy to prolong their front in order to cover
their line of retreat to the White House, and so weaken

[1] *Battles and Leaders of the Civil War*, vol. ii., p. 337.

that part of the position which was to be attacked by
Longstreet; and Jackson had been ordered [1] to draw
up his troops so as to meet such a contingency. 'Hoping,'
he says in his report, 'that Generals A. P. Hill
and Longstreet would soon drive the Federals towards
me, I directed General D. H. Hill to move his division to
the left of the wood, so as to leave between him and the
wood on the right an open space, across which I hoped
that the enemy would be driven.' But Lee was deceived.
The Federal line of retreat ran not to the White House,
but over Grapevine Bridge. McClellan had for some time
foreseen that he might be compelled to abandon the York
River Railway, and directly he suspected that Jackson was
marching to Richmond had begun to transfer his line of
operations from the York to the James, and his base of
supply from the White House to Harrison's Landing.

So vast is the amount of stores necessary for the
subsistence, health, and armament of a host like
McClellan's that a change of base is an operation which
can only be effected under the most favourable circumstances.[2] It is evident, then, that the possibility of the
enemy shifting his line of operations to the James,
abandoning the York River Railroad, might easily have

[1] This order was verbal; no record of it is to be found, and Jackson
never mentioned, either at the time or afterwards, what its purport
was. His surviving staff officers, however, are unanimous in declaring
that he must have received direct instructions from General Lee. 'Is it
possible,' writes Dr. McGuire, 'that Jackson, who knew nothing of the
country, and little of the exact situation of affairs, would have taken the
responsibility of stopping at Old Cold Harbour for an hour or more, unless
he had had the authority of General Lee to do so? I saw him that
morning talking to General Lee. General Lee was sitting on a log, and
Jackson standing up. General Lee was evidently giving him instructions
for the day.' In his report (O. R., vol. xi., part i., p. 492) Lee says : 'The
arrival of Jackson on our left was momentarily expected ; it was supposed
that his approach would cause the enemy's extension in that direction.'

[2] The Army of the Potomac numbered 105,000 men, and 25,000
animals. 600 tons of ammunition, food, forage, medical and other supplies
had to be forwarded each day from White House to the front ; and at one
time during the operations from fifty to sixty days' rations for the
entire army, amounting probably to 25,000 tons, were accumulated at the
depôt. 5 tons daily per 1,000 men is a fair estimate for an army operating
in a barren country.

escaped the penetration of either Lee or Jackson. They
were not behind the scenes of the Federal administrative
system. They were not aware of the money, labour,
and ingenuity which had been lavished on the business of
supply. They had not seen with their own eyes the
fleet of four hundred transports which covered the reaches
of the York. They had not yet realised the enormous
advantage which an army derives from the command of
the sea.

Nor were they enlightened by the calmness with which
their immediate adversaries on the field of battle regarded
Jackson's possession of Old Cold Harbour. Still, one fact
was manifest : the Federals showed no disposition whatever to weaken or change their position, and it was clear that
the success was not to be attained by mere manœuvre. Lee,
seeing Hill's division roughly handled, ordered Longstreet
forward, while Jackson, judging from the sound and
direction of the firing that the original plan had failed,
struck in with vigour. Opposed to him was Sykes' division
of regulars, supported by eighteen guns, afterwards
increased to twenty-four ; and in the men of the United
States Army the Valley soldiers met a stubborn foe. The
position, moreover, occupied by Sykes possessed every
advantage which a defender could desire. Manned even
by troops of inferior mettle it might well have proved
impregnable. The valley was wider than further west,
and a thousand yards intervened between the opposing
ridges. From either crest the cornfields sloped gently to
the marshy sources of the creek, hidden by tall timber
and dense undergrowth. The right and rear of the
position were protected by a second stream, running south
to the Chickahominy, and winding through a swamp which
Stuart, posted on Jackson's left, pronounced impassable for
horsemen. Between the head waters of these two streams
rose the spur on which stands McGehee's house, facing
the road from Old Cold Harbour, and completely commanding the country to the north and north-east. The flank,
therefore, was well secured ; the front was strong, with a
wide field of fire ; the Confederate artillery, even if it could

make its way through the thick woods on the opposite crest, would have to unlimber under fire at effective range, and the marsh below, with its tangled undergrowth and abattis, could hardly fail to throw the attacking infantry into disorder. Along the whole of Sykes' line only two weak points were apparent. On his left, as already described, a broad tract of woodland, covering nearly the whole valley, and climbing far up the slope on the Federal side, afforded a covered approach from one crest to the other; on his right, a plantation of young pines skirted the crest of McGehee's Hill, and ran for some distance down the slope. Under shelter of the timber it was possible that the Confederate infantry might mass for the assault; but once in the open, unaided by artillery, their further progress would be difficult. Under ordinary circumstances a thorough reconnaissance, followed by a carefully planned attack, would have been the natural course of the assailant. The very strength of the position was in favour of the Confederates. The creek which covered the whole front rendered a counterstroke impracticable, and facilitated a flank attack. Holding the right bank of the creek with a portion of his force, Jackson might have thrown the remainder against McGehee's Hill, and, working round the flank, have repeated the tactics of Kernstown, Winchester, and Port Republic.

But the situation permitted no delay. A. P. Hill was hard pressed. The sun was already sinking. McClellan's reserves might be coming up, and if the battle was to be won, it must be won by direct attack. There was no time for further reconnaissance, no time for manœuvre.

Jackson's dispositions were soon made. D. H. Hill, eastward of the Old Cold Harbour road, was to advance against McGehee's Hill, overlapping, if possible, the enemy's line. Ewell was to strike in on Hill's right, moving through the tract of woodland; Lawton, Whiting, and Winder, in the order named, were to fill the gap between Ewell's right and the left of A. P. Hill's division, and the artillery was ordered into position opposite McGehee's Hill.

D. H. Hill, already in advance, was the first to move. Pressing forward from the woods, under a heavy fire of

artillery, his five brigades, the greater part in first line,
$\quad$ descended to the creek, already occupied by his skir-
4 P.M.$\quad$ mishers. In passing through the marshy thickets,
where the Federal shells were bursting on every hand, the
confusion became great. The brigades crossed each other's
march. Regiments lost their brigades, and companies their
regiments. At one point the line was so densely crowded that
whole regiments were forced to the rear; at others there were
wide intervals, and effective supervision became impossible.
Along the edge of the timber the fire was fierce, for the Union
regulars were distant no more than four hundred yards; the
smoke rolled heavily through the thickets, and on the right
and centre, where the fight was hottest, the impetuosity of
both officers and men carried them forward up the slope. An
attempt to deliver a charge with the whole line failed in combination, and such portion of the division as advanced,
scourged by both musketry and artillery, fell back before
the fire of the unshaken Federals.

In the wood to the right Ewell met with even fiercer
opposition. So hastily had the Confederate line been formed,
and so difficult was it for the brigades to maintain touch and
direction in the thick covert, that gaps soon opened along
the front; and of these gaps, directly the Southerners gained
the edge of the timber, the Northern brigadiers took
quick advantage. Not content with merely holding their
ground, the regular regiments, changing front so as to
strike the flanks of the attack, came forward with the
bayonet, and a vigorous counterstroke, delivered by five
battalions, drove Ewell across the swamp. Part of Trimble's
brigade still held on in the wood, fighting fiercely; but
the Louisiana regiments were demoralised, and there were
no supports on which they might have rallied.

Jackson, when he ordered Hill to the front, had sent
verbal instructions—always dangerous—for the remainder
of his troops to move forward in line of battle.[1] The young

---

[1] The instructions, according to Dr. Dabney, ran as follows:—

'The troops are standing at ease along our line of march. Ride back
rapidly along the line and tell the commanders to advance instantly *en
échelon* from the left. Each brigade is to follow as a guide the right

staff officer to whom these instructions were entrusted, misunderstanding the intentions of his chief, communicated the message to the brigadiers with the addition that 'they were to await further orders before engaging the enemy.' Partly for this reason, and partly because the rear regiments of his division had lost touch with the leading brigades, Ewell was left without assistance. For some time the error was undiscovered. Jackson grew anxious. From his station near Old Cold Harbour little could be seen of the Confederate troops. On the ridge beyond the valley the dark lines of the enemy's infantry were visible amongst the trees, with their well-served batteries on the crests above. But in the valley immediately beneath, and as well as in the forest to the right front, the dense smoke and the denser timber hid the progress of the fight. Yet the sustained fire was a sure token that the enemy still held his own; and for the first time and the last his staff beheld their leader riding restlessly to and fro, and heard his orders given in a tone which betrayed the storm within.[1] 'Unconscious,' says Dabney, ' that his veteran brigades were but now reaching the ridge of battle, he supposed that all his strength had been put forth, and (what had never happened before) the enemy was not crushed.'[2] Fortunately, the error of the aide-de-camp had already been corrected by the vigilance of the chief of the staff, and the remainder of the Valley army was coming up.

Their entry into battle was not in accordance with the

regiment of the brigade on the left, and to keep within supporting distance. Tell the commanders that if this formation fails at any point, to form line of battle and move to the front, pressing to the sound of the heaviest firing and attack the enemy vigorously wherever found. As to artillery, each commander must use his discretion. If the ground will at all permit tell them to take in their field batteries and use them. If not, post them in the rear.' Letter to the author.

[1] It may be noted that Jackson's command had now been increased by two divisions, Whiting's and D. H. Hill's, but there had been no increase in the very small staff which had sufficed for the Valley army. The mistakes which occurred at Gaines' Mill, and Jackson's ignorance of the movements and progress of his troops, were in great part due to his lack of staff officers. A most important message, writes Dr. Dabney, involving tactical knowledge, was carried by a non-combatant.

[2] Dabney, vol. ii., p. 194.

intentions of their chief. Whiting should have come in on Ewell's right, Lawton on the right of Whiting, and Jackson's division on the right of Lawton. Whiting led the way; but he had advanced only a short distance through the woods when he was met by Lee, who directed him to support General A. P. Hill.[1] The brigades of Law and of Hood were therefore diverted to the right, and, deploying on either side of the Gaines' Mill road, were ordered to assault the commanding bluff which marked the angle of the Federal position. Lawton's Georgians, 3,500 strong, moved to the support of Ewell; Cunningham and Fulkerson, of Winder's division, losing direction in the thickets, eventually sustained the attack of Longstreet, and the Stonewall Brigade reinforced the shattered ranks of D. H. Hill. Yet the attack was strong, and in front of Old Cold Harbour six batteries had forced their way through the forest.

As this long line of guns covered McGehee's Hill with a storm of shells, and the louder crash of musketry told him that his lagging brigades were coming into line, Jackson sent his last orders to his divisional commanders: 'Tell them,' he said, 'this affair must hang in suspense no longer; let them sweep the field with the bayonet.' But there was no need for further urging. Before the messengers arrived the Confederate infantry, in every quarter of the battlefield, swept forward from the woods, and a vast wave of men converged upon the plateau. Lee, almost at the same moment as Jackson, had given the word for a general advance. As the supports came thronging up the shout was carried down the line, ' The Valley men are here ! ' and with the cry of ' Stonewall Jackson ! ' for their slogan, the Southern army dashed across the deep ravine. Whiting, with the eight regiments of Hood and Law, none of which had been yet engaged, charged impetuously against the centre. The brigades of A. P. Hill, spent with fighting but clinging stubbornly to their ground, found strength for a final effort. Longstreet threw in his last reserve against the triple line which had already decimated his division. Lawton's Georgians bore back the regulars. D. H. Hill, despite the

[1] Whiting's Report, O. R., vol. xi., part i., p. 563.

fire of the batteries on McGehee's Hill, which, disregarding
the shells of Jackson's massed artillery, turned with canister
on the advancing infantry, made good his footing on the
ridge; and as the sun, low on the horizon, loomed blood-red
through the murky atmosphere, the Confederate colours
waved along the line of abandoned breastworks.

As the Federals retreated, knots of brave men, hastily
collected by officers of all ranks, still offered a fierce resistance, and, supported by the batteries, inflicted terrible losses
on the crowded masses which swarmed up from the ravine;
but the majority of the infantry, without ammunition and
with few officers, streamed in disorder to the rear. For a
time the Federal gunners stood manfully to their work.
Porter's reserve artillery, drawn up midway across the
upland, offered a rallying point to the retreating infantry.
Three small squadrons of the 5th United States Cavalry
made a gallant but useless charge, in which out of seven
officers six fell; and on the extreme right the division of
regulars, supported by a brigade of volunteers, fell back
fighting to a second line. As at Bull Run, the disciplined
soldiers alone showed a solid front amid the throng of
fugitives. Not a foot of ground had they yielded till their
left was exposed by the rout of the remainder. Of the
four batteries which supported them only two guns were
lost, and on their second position they made a determined effort to restore the fight. But their stubborn
valour availed nothing against the superior numbers which
Lee's fine strategy had concentrated on the field of battle.

Where the first breach was made in the Federal line is
a matter of dispute. Longstreet's men made a magnificent charge on the right, and D. H. Hill claimed to have
turned the flank of the regulars; but it is abundantly
evident that the advent of Jackson's fresh troops, and the
vigour of their assault, broke down the resistance of the
Federals.[1] When the final attack developed, and along the
whole front masses of determined men, in overwhelming

---

[1] Porter himself thought that the first break in his line was made by
Hood, ' at a point where he least expected it.'—*Battles and Leaders*, vol. ii.,
pp. 335 and 340.

numbers, dashed against the breastworks, Porter's troops were well-nigh exhausted, and not a single regiment remained in reserve. Against the very centre of his line the attack was pushed home by Whiting's men with extraordinary resolution. His two brigades, marching abreast, were formed in two lines, each about 2,000 strong. Riding along the front, before they left the wood, the general had enjoined his men to charge without a halt, in double time, and without firing. 'Had these orders,' says General Law, 'not been strictly obeyed the assault would have been a failure. No troops could have stood long under the withering storm of lead and iron that beat in their faces as they became fully exposed to view from the Federal line.'[1] The assault was met with a courage that was equally admirable.[2] But the Confederate second line reinforced the first at exactly the right moment, driving it irresistibly forward; and the Federal regiments, which had been hard pressed through a long summer afternoon, and had become scattered in the thickets, were ill-matched with the solid and ordered ranks of brigades which had not yet fired a shot. It was apparently at this point that the Southerners first set foot on the plateau, and sweeping over the intrenchments, outflanked the brigades which still held out to right and left, and compelled them to fall back. Inspired by his soldierly enthusiasm for a gallant deed, Jackson himself has left us a vivid description of the successful charge. 'On my extreme right,' he says in his report, 'General Whiting advanced his division through the dense forest and swamp, emerging from the wood into the field near the public road and at the head of the deep ravine which covered the enemy's left. Advancing thence through a number of retreating and disordered regiments he came within range of the enemy's fire, who, concealed in an open wood and protected by breastworks, poured a destructive fire for a quarter of a mile into his advancing

---

[1] *Battles and Leaders*, vol. ii., p. 363.
[2] 'The Confederates were within ten paces when the Federals broke cover, and leaving their log breastworks, swarmed up the hill in rear, carrying the second line with them in their rout.'—General Law, *Battles and Leaders*, vol. ii., p. 363.

line, under which many brave officers and men fell.
Dashing on with unfaltering step in the face of these
murderous discharges of canister and musketry, General
Hood and Colonel Law, at the heads of their respective
brigades, rushed to the charge with a yell. Moving down
a precipitous ravine, leaping ditch and stream, clambering
up a difficult ascent, and exposed to an incessant and
deadly fire from the intrenchments, those brave and
determined men pressed forward, driving the enemy from
his well-selected and fortified position. In this charge,
in which upwards of 1,000 men fell killed and wounded
before the fire of the enemy, and in which 14 pieces of
artillery and nearly a whole regiment were captured, the
4th Texas, under the lead of General Hood, was the first
to pierce these strongholds and seize the guns.' [1]

How fiercely the Northern troops had battled is told in
the outspoken reports of the Confederate generals. Before
Jackson's reserves were thrown in the first line of the Confederate attack had been exceedingly roughly handled.
A. P. Hill's division had done good work in preparing the
way for Whiting's assault, but a portion of his troops had
become demoralised. Ewell's regiments met the same fate;
and we read of them ' skulking from the front in a shameful
manner ; the woods on our left and rear full of troops in
safe cover, from which they never stirred ; ' of ' regiment
after regiment rushing back in utter disorder ; ' of others
which it was impossible to rally ; and of troops retiring in
confusion, who cried out to the reinforcements, ' You need
not go in ; we are whipped, we can't do anything ! ' It is
only fair to say that the reinforcements replied, ' Get out of
our way, we will show you how to do it ; ' [2] but it is not to
be disguised that the Confederates at one time came near
defeat. With another division in reserve at the critical
moment, Porter might have maintained his line unbroken.
His troops, had they been supported, were still capable of
resistance.

[1] Jackson's Report, O. R., vol. xi., part i., pp. 555, 556.
[2] Reports of Whiting, Trimble, Rodes, Bradley T. Johnson, O. R., vol. xi.,
part i.

McClellan, however, up to the time the battle was lost, had sent but one division (Slocum's) and two batteries to Porter's support. 66,000 Federals, on the south bank of the Chickahominy, had been held in their intrenchments, throughout the day, by the demonstrations of 28,000 Confederates. Intent on saving his trains, on securing his retreat to the river James, and utterly regardless of the chances which fortune offered, the 'Young Napoleon' had allowed his rearguard to be overwhelmed. He was not seen on the plateau which his devoted troops so well defended, nor even at the advanced posts on the further bank of the Chickahominy. So convinced was he of the accuracy of the information furnished by his detective staff that he never dreamt of testing the enemy's numbers by his own eyesight. Had he watched the development of Lee's attack, noted the small number of his batteries, the long delay in the advance of the supports, the narrow front of his line of battle, he would have discovered that the Confederate strength had been greatly exaggerated. There were moments, too, during the fight when a strong counterstroke, made by fresh troops, would have placed Lee's army in the greatest peril. But a general who thinks only of holding his lines and not of annihilating the enemy is a poor tactician, and McClellan's lack of enterprise, which Lee had so accurately gauged, may be inferred from his telegram to Lincoln : ' I have lost this battle because my force is too small.' [1]

Porter was perhaps a more than sufficient substitute for the Commander-in-Chief. His tactics, as fighting a waiting battle, had been admirable ; and, when his front was broken, strongly and with cool judgment he sought to hold back the enemy and cover the bridges. The line of batteries he established across the plateau—80 guns in all—proved at first an effective barrier. But the retreat of the infantry, the waning light, and the general dissolution of all order, had its effect upon the gunners. When the remnant of the 5th Cavalry was borne back in flight, the greater part of the batteries had already limbered up, and over the bare surface of the upland the Confederate infantry, shooting down

[1] Report of Committee on the Conduct of the War.

the terrified teams, rushed forward in hot pursuit. 22 guns, with a large number of ammunition waggons, were captured on the field, prisoners surrendered at every step, and the fight surged onward towards the bridges. But between the bridges and the battlefield, on the slopes falling to the Chickahominy, the dark forest covered the retreat of the routed army. Night had already fallen. The confusion in the ranks of the Confederates was extreme, and it was impossible to distinguish friend from foe. All direction had been lost. None knew the bearings of the bridges, or whether the Federals were retreating east or south. Regiments had already been exposed to the fire of their comrades, and in front of the forest a perceptible hesitation seized on both officers and men. At this moment, in front of D. H. Hill's division, which was advancing by the road leading directly to the bridges, loud cheers were heard. It was clear that Federal reinforcements had arrived; the general ordered his troops to halt, and along the whole line the forward movement came quickly to a standstill. Two brigades, French's and Meagher's, tardily sent over by McClellan, had arrived in time to stave off a terrible disaster. Pushing through the mass of fugitives with the bayonet, these fine troops had crossed the bridge, passed through the woods, and formed line on the southern crest of the plateau. Joining the regulars, who still presented a stubborn front, they opened a heavy fire, and under cover of their steadfast lines Porter's troops withdrew across the river.

Notwithstanding this strong reinforcement of 5,000 or 6,000 fresh troops, it is by no means impossible, had the Confederates pushed resolutely forward, that the victory would have been far more complete. 'Winder,' says General D. H. Hill, 'thought that we ought to pursue into the woods, on the right of the Grapevine Bridge road; but not knowing the position of our friends, nor what Federal reserves might be awaiting us in the woods, I thought it advisable not to move on. General Lawton concurred with me. I had no artillery to shell the woods in front, as mine had not got through the swamp. Winder,' he adds, ' was right; even a show of pressure must have been attended with great result.' [1] Had Jackson been at hand the pressure would in all probability have been applied. The contagion of defeat soon spreads; and whatever reserves a flying enemy may possess, if they are vigorously attacked whilst the fugitives are still passing through their ranks, history tells us, however bold their front, that, unless they are intrenched, their resistance is seldom long protracted. More than all, when night has fallen on the field, and prevents all estimate of the strength of the attack, a resolute advance has peculiar chances of success. But when his advanced line halted Jackson was not yet up; and before he arrived the impetus of victory had died away; the Federal reserves were deployed in a strong position, and the opportunity had already passed.

It is no time, when the tide of victory bears him forward, for a general ' to take counsel of his fears.' It is no time to count numbers, or to conjure up the phantoms of possible reserves; the sea itself is not more irresistible than an army which has stormed a strong position, and which has attained, in so doing, the exhilarating consciousness of superior courage. Had Stuart, with his 2,000 horsemen, followed up the pursuit towards the bridges, the Federal reserves might have been swept away in panic. But Stuart, in common with Lee and Jackson, expected that the enemy would endeavour to reach the White House, and when he saw that their lines were breaking he had dashed down a lane which led to the river road, about three miles distant. When he reached that point, darkness had already fallen, and finding no traces of the enemy, he had returned to Old Cold Harbour.

On the night of the battle the Confederates remained where the issue of the fight had found them. Across the Grapevine road the pickets of the hostile forces were in close proximity, and men of both sides, in search of water, or carrying messages, strayed within the enemy's lines. Jackson himself, it is said, came near capture. Riding forward in the darkness, attended by only a few staff

[1] *Battles and Leaders*, vol. ii., p. 357.

officers, he suddenly found himself in presence of a Federal picket. Judging rightly of the enemy's *moral*, he set spurs to his horse, and charging into the midst, ordered them to lay down their arms; and fifteen or twenty prisoners, marching to the rear, amused the troops they met on the march by loudly proclaiming that they had the honour of being captured by Stonewall Jackson. These men were not without companions. 2,830 Federals were reported either captured or missing; and while some of those were probably among the dead, a large proportion found their way to Richmond; 4,000, moreover, had fallen on the field of battle.[1]

The Confederate casualties were even a clearer proof of the severity of the fighting. So far as can be ascertained, 8,000 officers and men were killed or wounded.

Longstreet	1,850
A. P. Hill	2,450
Jackson	3,700

Jackson's losses were distributed as follows :—

Jackson's own Division	600
Ewell	650
Whiting	1,020
D. H. Hill	1,430

The regimental losses, in several instances, were exceptionally severe. Of the 4th Texas, of Hood's brigade, the first to pierce the Federal line, there fell 20 officers and 230 men. The 20th North Carolina, of D. H. Hill's division, which charged the batteries on McGehee's Hill, lost 70 killed and 200 wounded; of the same division the 3rd Alabama lost 200, and the 12th North Carolina 212; while two of Lawton's regiments, the 31st and the 38th Georgia, had each a casualty list of 170. Almost every single regiment north of the Chickahominy took part in the action. The cavalry did nothing, but at least 48,000 infantry were engaged, and seventeen batteries are mentioned in the reports as having participated in the battle.

[1] O. R., vol. xi., part i., pp. 40-2.

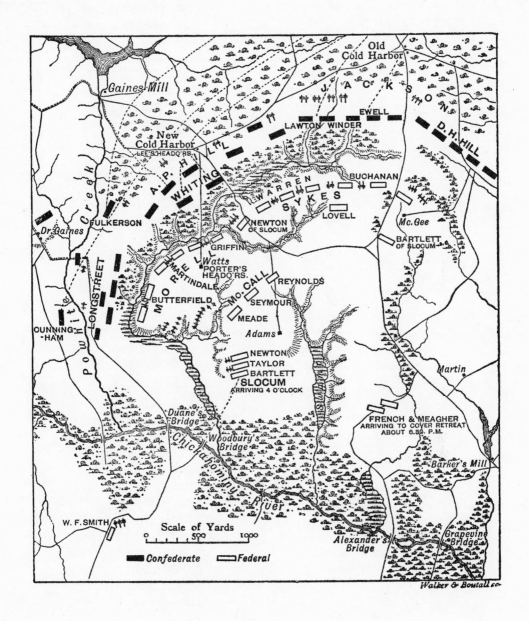

Old
Cold Harbor

J A C K S O N

Gaines Mill

EWELL

LAWTON WINDER

New
Cold Harbor

LEE'S HEAD Q'RS.

A. P. HILL

WHITING

D. H. HILL

BUCHANAN

WARREN

SYKES

Mc. Gee

Dr. Gaines

FULKERSON

Powite Creek

LOVELL

NEWTON
OF SLOCUM

BARTLETT
OF SLOCUM

GRIFFIN

MORELL

Watts
PORTER'S
HEAD Q'RS.

REYNOLDS

LONGSTREET

MARTINDALE

Mc. CALL

SEYMOUR

BUTTERFIELD

MEADE

Adams

Martin

OUNNING
-HAM

NEWTON
TAYLOR
BARTLETT
SLOCUM
ARRIVING 4 O'CLOCK

Duane's
Bridge

FRENCH & MEAGHER
ARRIVING TO COVER RETREAT
ABOUT 6.30. P.M.

Woodbury's
Bridge

Chickahominy River

Barker's Mill

W. F. SMITH

Scale of Yards
0   500   1000

Alexander's
Bridge

Grapevine
Bridge

■ Confederate ☐ Federal

Walker & Boutall sc.

CHAPTER XIV

THE SEVEN DAYS. FRAYSER'S FARM AND MALVERN HILL

THE battle of Gaines' Mill, although the assailants suffered heavier losses than they inflicted, was a long step towards June 28, accomplishing the deliverance of Richmond. One 1862. of McClellan's five army corps had been disposed of, a heavy blow had been struck at the *moral* of his whole army, and his communications with the White House and the Pamunkey were at the mercy of his enemies. Still the Confederate outlook was not altogether clear. It is one thing to win a victory, but another to make such use of it as to annihilate the enemy. Porter's defeat was but a beginning of operations; and although Lee was convinced that McClellan would retreat, he was by no means so certain that his escape could be prevented. Yet this was essential. If the Federal army were suffered to fall back without incurring further loss, it would be rapidly reinforced from Washington, and resuming the advance, this time with still larger numbers, might render Gaines' Mill a barren victory. How to compass the destruction of McClellan's host was the problem that now confronted the Confederate leader; and before a plan could be devised it was necessary to ascertain the direction of the retreat.

On the morning of June 28 it was found that no formed body of Federal troops remained north of the Chickahominy. French, Meagher, and Sykes, the regulars forming the rear-guard, had fallen back during the night and destroyed the bridges. Hundreds of stragglers were picked up, and one of the most gallant of the Northern brigadiers [1] was found asleep in the woods, unaware that his troops had crossed the stream. No further fighting was to be expected on the plateau. But it was possible that the enemy might still endeavour to preserve his communications, marching by the south bank of the river and recrossing by the railway and Bottom's Bridges. Stuart, supported by Ewell, was at once ordered to seize the former; but when the cavalry reached Dispatch Station, a small Federal detachment retreated to the south bank of the Chickahominy and fired the timbers.

Meanwhile, from the field of Gaines' Mill, long columns of dust, rising above the forests to the south, had been descried, showing that the enemy was in motion; and when the news came in that the railway bridge had been destroyed, and that the line itself was unprotected, it was at once evident that McClellan had abandoned his communications with White House.

This was valuable information, but still the line of retreat had not yet been ascertained. The Federals might retreat to some point on the James River, due south, there meeting their transports, or they might march down the Peninsula to Yorktown and Fortress Monroe. 'In the latter event,' says Lee, ' it was necessary that our troops should continue on the north bank of the river, and until the intention of General McClellan was discovered it was deemed injudicious to change their disposition. Ewell was therefore ordered to proceed to Bottom's Bridge, and the cavalry to watch the bridges below. No certain indications of a retreat to the James River were discovered by our forces (Magruder) on the south side of the Chickahominy, and late in the afternoon the enemy's works were reported to be fully manned. Below (south of) the enemy's works the country was densely wooded and intersected by impassable swamps, at once concealing his movements and precluding reconnaissances except by the regular roads, all of which were strongly guarded. The bridges over the Chickahominy in rear of the enemy were destroyed, and their reconstruction impracticable in the presence of

[1] General Reynolds.

his whole army and powerful batteries. We were therefore compelled to wait until his purpose should be developed.' [1]

During the day, therefore, the Confederate army remained on the battle-field, waiting for the game to bolt. In the evening, however, signs of a general movement were reported in rear of the intrenchments at Seven Pines; and as nothing had been observed by the cavalry on the Chickahominy, Lee, rightly concluding that McClellan was retreating to the James, issued orders for the pursuit to be taken up the next morning.

But to intercept the enemy before he could fortify a position, covered by the fire of his gunboats, on the banks of the James, was a difficult operation. The situation demanded rapid marching, close concert, and delicate manœuvres. The Confederate army was in rear of the Federals, and separated from them by the Chickahominy, and, to reach the James, McClellan had only fourteen miles to cover. But the country over which he had to pass was still more intricate, and traversed by even fewer roads, than the district which had hitherto been the theatre of operations. Across his line of march ran the White Oak Swamp, bordered by thick woods and a wide morass, and crossed by only one bridge. If he could transfer his whole army south of this stream, without molestation, he would find himself within six miles of his gunboats; and as his left flank was already resting on the Swamp, it was not easy for Lee's army to prevent his passage.

But 28,000 Confederates were already south of the Chickahominy, on the flank of McClellan's line of march, and it was certainly possible that this force might detain the Federals until A. P. Hill, Longstreet, and Jackson should come up. Magruder and Huger were therefore ordered to advance early on the 29th, and moving, the one by the Williamsburg, the other by the Charles City road, to strike the enemy in flank.

A. P. Hill and Longstreet, recrossing the Chickahominy at New Bridge, were to march by the Darbytown road in the

[1] Lee's Report, O. R., vol. xi., part i., pp. 493, 494.

direction of Charles City cross roads, thus turning the head
waters of the White Oak Swamp, and threatening the
Federal rear.

Jackson, crossing Grapevine Bridge, was to move down
the south bank of the Chickahominy, cross the Swamp by
the bridge, and force his way to the Long Bridge road.

The Confederate army was thus divided into four
columns, moving by four different roads; each column at
starting was several miles distant from the others, and a
junction was to be made upon the field of battle. The
cavalry, moreover, with the exception of a few squadrons,
was far away upon the left, pursuing a large detachment
which had been observed on the road to the White
House.[1]

McClellan had undoubtedly resolved on a most hazardous manœuvre. His supply and ammunition train
consisted of over five thousand waggons. He was en-
cumbered with the heavy guns of the siege artillery. He
had with him more than fifty field batteries; his army was
still 95,000 strong; and this unwieldy multitude of men,
horses, and vehicles, had to be passed over White Oak
Swamp, and then to continue its march across the front
of a powerful and determined enemy.

But Lee also was embarrassed by the nature of the
country.[2] If McClellan's movements were retarded by the
woods, swamps, and indifferent roads, the same obstacles
would interfere with the combination of the Confederate
columns; and the pursuit depended for success on their
close co-operation.

---

[1] This detachment, about 3,500 strong, consisted of the outposts that had
been established north and north-east of Beaver Dam Creek on June 27, of
the garrison of the White House, and of troops recently disembarked.

[2] Strange to say, while the Confederates possessed no maps whatever,
McClellan was well supplied in this respect. ' Two or three weeks before
this,' says General Averell (*Battles and Leaders*, vol. ii., p. 431), ' three
officers of the 3rd Pennsylvania Cavalry, and others, penetrated the region
between the Chickahominy and the James, taking bearings and making
notes. Their fragmentary sketches, when put together, made a map which
exhibited all the roadways, fields, forests, bridges, the streams, and houses,
so that our commander knew the country to be traversed far better than
any Confederate commander.'

The first day's work was hardly promising. The risks of unconnected manœuvres received abundant illustration. Magruder, late in the afternoon, struck the enemy's rear-guard near Savage's Station, but was heavily repulsed by two Federal army corps. Huger, called by Magruder to his assistance, turned aside from the road which had been assigned to him, and when he was recalled by an urgent message from Lee, advanced with the timidity which almost invariably besets the commander of an isolated force in the neighbourhood of a large army. Jackson, whose line of march led him directly on Savage's Station, was delayed until after nightfall by the necessity of rebuilding the Grapevine Bridge.[1] Stuart had gone off to the White House, bent on the destruction of the enemy's supply depôt. Longstreet and Hill encamped south-west of Charles City cross roads, but saw nothing of the enemy. Holmes, with 6,500 men, crossed the James during the afternoon and encamped on the north bank, near Laurel Hill Church. During the night the Federal rear-guard fell back, destroying the bridge over White Oak Swamp ; and although a large quantity of stores were either destroyed or abandoned, together with a hospital containing 2,500 wounded, the whole of McClellan's army, men, guns, and trains, effected the passage of this dangerous obstacle.

June 29.

The next morning Longstreet, with Hill in support, moved forward, and found a Federal division in position near Glendale. Bringing his artillery into action, he held his infantry in hand until Huger should come up on his left, and Jackson's guns be heard at White Oak Bridge. Holmes, followed by Magruder, was marching up the Newmarket road to Malvern House ; and when the sound of Jackson's artillery became audible to the northwards, Lee sent Longstreet forward to the attack. A sanguinary conflict, on ground covered with heavy timber, and cut up by deep ravines, resulted in the Federals holding

June 30.

---

[1] Jackson had with him a gang of negroes who, under the superintendence of Captain Mason, a railroad contractor of long experience, performed the duties which in regular armies appertain to the corps of engineers. They had already done useful service in the Valley.

their ground till nightfall; and although many prisoners and several batteries were captured by the Confederates, McClellan, under cover of the darkness, made good his escape.

The battle of Glendale or Frayser's Farm was the crisis of the 'Seven Days.' Had Lee been able to concentrate his whole strength against the Federals it is probable that McClellan would never have reached the James. But Longstreet and Hill fought unsupported. As the former very justly complained, 50,000 men were within hearing of the guns but none came to co-operate, and against the two Confederate divisions fought the Third Federal Army Corps, reinforced by three divisions from the Second, Fifth, and Sixth. Huger's march on the Charles City road was obstructed by felled trees. When he at last arrived in front of the enemy, he was held in check by two batteries, and he does not appear to have opened communication with either Lee or Longstreet. Magruder had been ordered to march down from Savage Station to the Darbytown road, and there to await orders. At 4.30 P.M. he was ordered to move to Newmarket in support of Holmes. This order was soon countermanded, but he was unable to join Longstreet until the fight was over. Holmes was held in check by Porter's Army Corps, minus McCall's division, on Malvern Hill; and the cavalry, which might have been employed effectively against the enemy's left flank and rear, was still north of the Chickahominy, returning from a destructive but useless raid on the depôt at the White House. Nor had the conduct of the battle been unaffected by the complicated nature of the general plan. Longstreet attacked alone, Hill being held back, in order to be fresh for the pursuit when Jackson and Huger should strike in. The attack was successful, and McCall's division, which had shared the defeat at Gaines' Mill, was driven from its position. But McCall was reinforced by other divisions; Longstreet was thrown on to the defensive by superior numbers, and when Hill was at length put in, it was with difficulty that the fierce counterblows of the Federals were beaten off.

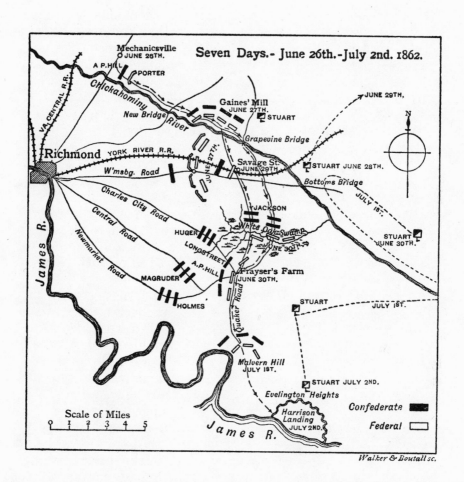

Seven Days.- June 26th.-July 2nd. 1862.

Mechanicsville
JUNE 26TH.

A.P.HILL
PORTER

VA. CENTRAL R.R.

Chickahominy

New Bridge River

Gaines' Mill
JUNE 27TH.

STUART

JUNE 29TH.

Grapevine Bridge

Richmond YORK RIVER R.R.

W'msbg. Road

JUNE 27TH.

Savage St.
JUNE 29TH.

STUART JUNE 28TH.

Bottoms Bridge

JULY 1ST.

STUART
JUNE 30TH.

Charles City Road

Central Road

Newmarket Road

JACKSON

White Oak Swamp

HUGER

LONGSTREET

JUNE 30TH.

A.P.HILL

Frayser's Farm
JUNE 30TH.

STUART JULY 1ST.

MAGRUDER

HOLMES

Quaker Road

James R.

Malvern Hill
JULY 1ST.

STUART JULY 2ND.

Evelington Heights

Harrison
Landing
JULY 2ND.

James R.

Confederate

Federal

Scale of Miles
0 1 2 3 4 5

N

Walker & Boutall sc.

Jackson had been unable to participate in the conflict. When night fell he was still north of the White Oak Swamp, seven miles distant from his morning bivouac, and hardly a single infantry man in his command had pulled a trigger. According to his own report his troops reached White Oak Bridge about noon. 'Here the enemy made a determined effort to retard our advance and thereby to prevent an immediate junction between General Longstreet and myself. We found the bridge destroyed, the ordinary place of crossing commanded by their batteries on the other side, and all approach to it barred by detachments of sharp-shooters concealed in a dense wood close by. . . . A heavy cannonading in front announced the engagement of General Longstreet at Frayser's Farm (Glendale) and made me eager to press forward; but the marshy character of the soil, the destruction of the bridge over the marsh and creek, and the strong position of the enemy for defending the passage, prevented my advancing until the following morning.' [1]

Such are Jackson's reasons for his failure to co-operate with Longstreet. It is clear that he was perfectly aware of the importance of the part he was expected to play; and he used every means which suggested itself as practicable to force a crossing. The 2nd Virginia Cavalry, under Colonel Munford, had now joined him from the Valley, and their commanding officer bears witness that Jackson showed no lack of energy.

'When I left the general on the preceding evening, he ordered me to be at the cross-roads (five miles from White Oak Bridge) at sunrise the next morning, ready to move in advance of his troops. The worst thunderstorm came up about night I ever was in, and in that thickly wooded country one could not see his horse's ears. My command scattered in the storm, and I do not suppose that any officer had a rougher time in any one night than I had to endure. When the first grey dawn appeared I started off my adjutant and officers to bring up the scattered regiment; but at sunrise I had not more than fifty men,

[1] O. R., vol. xi., part i., pp. 556, 557.

and I was half a mile from the cross-roads. When I
arrived, to my horror there sat Jackson waiting for me.
He was in a bad humour, and said, " Colonel, my orders
to you were to be here at sunrise." I explained my
situation, telling him that we had no provisions, and that
the storm and the dark night had conspired against me.
When I got through he replied, " Yes, sir. But, Colonel,
I ordered you to be here at sunrise. Move on with your
regiment. If you meet the enemy drive in his pickets, and
if you want artillery, Colonel Crutchfield will furnish you."

'I started on with my little handful of men. As others
came straggling on to join me, Jackson noticed it, and sent
two couriers to inform me that "my men were straggling
badly." I rode back and went over the same story, hoping
that he would be impressed with my difficulties. He
listened to me, but replied as before, " Yes, sir. But I
ordered you to be here at sunrise, and I have been waiting
for you for a quarter of an hour."

' Seeing that he was in a peculiar mood, I determined
to make the best of my trouble, sent my adjutant back,
and made him halt the stragglers and form my men as
they came up; and with what I had, determined to give
him no cause for complaint. When we came upon the
enemy's picket we charged, and pushed the picket every
step of the way into their camp, where there were a large
number of wounded and many stores. It was done so
rapidly that the enemy's battery on the other side of White
Oak Swamp could not fire on us without endangering their
own friends.

' When Jackson came up he was smiling, and he at
once (shortly after noon) ordered Colonel Crutchfield to
bring up the artillery, and very soon the batteries were at
work. After the lapse of about an hour my regiment had
assembled, and while our batteries were shelling those of
the enemy, Jackson sent for me and said, " Colonel, move
your regiment over the creek, and secure those guns. I
will ride with you to the Swamp. When we reached the
crossing we found that the enemy had torn up the bridge,
and had thrown the timbers into the stream, forming a

tangled mass which seemed to prohibit a crossing. I said to General Jackson that I did not think that we could cross. He looked at me, waved his hand, and replied, "Yes, Colonel, try it." In we went and floundered over, and before I formed the men, Jackson cried out to me to move on at the guns. Colonel Breckenridge started out with what we had over, and I soon got over the second squadron, and moved up the hill. We reached the guns, but they had an infantry support which gave us a volley; at the same time a battery on our right, which we had not seen, opened on us, and back we had to come. I moved down the Swamp about a quarter of a mile, and re-crossed with great difficulty by a cow-path.' [1]

The artillery did little better than the cavalry. The ground on the north bank of the Swamp by no means favoured the action of the guns. To the right of the road the slopes were clear and unobstructed, but the crest was within the forest; while to the left a thick pine wood covered both ridge and valley. On the bank held by the Federals the ground was open, ascending gently to the ridge; but the edge of the stream, immediately opposite the cleared ground on the Confederate right, was covered by a belt of tall trees, in full leaf, which made observation, by either side, a matter of much difficulty. This belt was full of infantry, while to the right rear, commanding the ruined bridge, stood the batteries which had driven back the cavalry.

After some time spent in reconnaissance, it was determined to cut a track through the wood to the right of the road. This was done, and thirty-one guns, moving forward simultaneously ready-shotted, opened fire on the position. The surprise was complete. One of the Federal batteries dispersed in confusion; the other disappeared, and the infantry supports fell back. Jackson immediately ordered two guns to advance down the road, and shell the belt of trees which harboured the

---

[1] 'Jackson himself,' writes Dr. McGuire, 'accompanied by three or four members of his staff, of whom I was one, followed the cavalry across the Swamp. The ford was miry and deep, and impracticable for either artillery or infantry.'

enemy's skirmishers. These were driven back; the divisions of D. H. Hill and Whiting were formed up in the pine wood on the left, and a working party was sent forward to repair the bridge. Suddenly, from the high ground behind the belt of trees, by which they were completely screened, two fresh Federal batteries—afterwards increased to three—opened on the line of Confederate guns. Under cover of this fire their skirmishers returned to the Swamp, and their main line came forward to a position whence it commanded the crossing at effective range. The two guns on the road were sent to the right-about. The shells of the Federal batteries fell into the stream, and the men who had been labouring at the bridge ran back and refused to work. The artillery duel, in which neither side could see the other, but in which both suffered some loss, continued throughout the afternoon.

Meantime a Confederate regiment, fording the stream, drove in the hostile skirmishers, and seized the belt of trees; Wright's brigade, of Huger's division, which had joined Jackson as the guns came into action, was sent back to force a passage at Brackett's Ford, a mile up stream; and reconnaissances were pushed out to find some way of turning the enemy's position. Every road and track, however, was obstructed by felled trees and abattis, and it was found that a passage was impracticable at Brackett's Ford. Two companies were pushed over the creek, and drove back the enemy's pickets. 'I discovered,' says Wright, 'that the enemy had destroyed the bridge, and had completely blockaded the road through the Swamp by felling trees in and across it. . . . I ascertained that the road debouched from the Swamp into an open field (meadow), commanded by a line of high hills, all in cultivation and free from timber. Upon this ridge of hills the enemy had posted heavy batteries of field-artillery, strongly supported by infantry, which swept the meadow by a direct and cross fire, and which could be used with terrible effect upon my column while struggling through the fallen timber in the wood through the Swamp.'[1]

[1] O R., vol. xi., part i., pp. 810, 811.

Having ascertained that the enemy was present in great strength on the further bank, that every road was obstructed, and that there was no means of carrying his artillery over the creek, or favourable ground on which his infantry could act, Jackson gave up all hope of aiding Longstreet.

That the obstacles which confronted him were serious there can be no question. His smooth-bore guns, although superior in number, were unable to beat down the fire of the rifled batteries. The enemy's masses were well hidden. The roads were blocked, the stream was swollen, the banks marshy, and although infantry could cross them, the fords which had proved difficult for the cavalry would have stopped the artillery, the ammunition waggons, and the ambulances; while the Federal position, on the crest of a long open slope, was exceedingly strong. Jackson, as his report shows, maturely weighed these difficulties, and came to the conclusion that he could do no good by sending over his infantry alone. It was essential, it is true, to detain as many as possible of the enemy on the banks of the Swamp, while Longstreet, Hill, Huger, and Magruder dealt with the remainder; and this he fully realised, but it is by no means improbable that he considered the heavy fire of his guns and the threatening position of his infantry would have this effect.

It is interesting to note how far this hope, supposing that he entertained it, was fulfilled. Two divisions of Federal infantry and three batteries—a total of 22,000 men—defended the passage at White Oak Bridge against 27,000 Confederates, including Wright; and a detached force of infantry and guns was posted at Brackett's Ford.[1] On the Confederate artillery opening fire, two

[1] General Heintzleman, commanding the Federal 3rd Corps, reports that he had placed a force at Brackett's Ford (O. R., vol. xi., part ii., p. 100). General Slocum (6th Corps) sent infantry and a 12-pounder howitzer (O. R., vol. xi., part ii., p. 435) to the same point; and Seeley's battery of the 3rd Corps was also engaged here (O. R., vol. xi., part ii., p. 106). The force at White Oak Bridge was constituted as follows:—

Smith's Division	. . . . . of the	6th Corps.
Richardson's Division	. . . . „	2nd Corps.
Dana's Brigade } Sedgwick's Division	„	2nd Corps.
Sully's Brigade		
Naglee's Brigade, Peck's Division	„	4th Corps.

brigades were sent up from near Glendale, but when it was found that this fire was not followed up by an infantry attack, these brigades, with two others in addition, were sent over to reinforce the troops which were engaged with Longstreet. When these facts became known; when it was clear that had Jackson attacked vigorously, the Federals would hardly have dared to weaken their line along White Oak Swamp, and that, in these circumstances, Longstreet and A. P. Hill would probably have seized the Quaker road, his failure to cross the creek exposed him to criticism. Not only did his brother-generals complain of his inaction, but Franklin, the Federal commander immediately opposed to him, writing long afterwards, made the following comments :—

'Jackson seems to have been ignorant of what General Lee expected of him, and badly informed about Brackett's Ford. When he found how strenuous was our defence at the bridge, he should have turned his attention to Brackett's Ford also. A force could have been as quietly gathered there as at the bridge ; a strong infantry movement at the ford would have easily overrun our small force there, placing our right at Glendale, held by Slocum's division, in great jeopardy, and turning our force at the bridge by getting between it and Glendale. In fact, it is likely that we should have been defeated that day had General Jackson done what his great reputation seems to make it imperative he should have done.'[1] But General Franklin's opinion as to the ease with which Brackett's Ford might have been passed is not justified by the facts. In the first place, General Slocum, who was facing Huger, and had little to do throughout the day, had two brigades within easy distance of the crossing ; in the second place, General Wright reported the ford impassable ; and in the third place, General Franklin himself admits that directly Wright's scouts were seen near the ford two brigades of Sedgwick's division were sent to oppose their passage.

General Long, in his life of Lee, finds excuse for Jackson in a story that he was utterly exhausted, and that

[1] *Battles and Leaders*, **vol. ii., p. 381.**

his staff let him sleep until the sun was high. Apart from the unlikelihood that a man who seems to have done without sleep whenever the enemy was in front should have permitted himself to be overpowered at such a crisis, we have Colonel Munford's evidence that the general was well in advance of his columns at sunrise, and the regimental reports show that the troops were roused at 2.30 A.M.

Jackson may well have been exhausted. He had certainly not spared himself during the operations. On the night of the 27th, after the battle of Gaines' Mill, he went over to Stuart's camp at midnight, and a long conference took place. At 3.30 on the morning of the 29th he visited Magruder, riding across Grapevine Bridge from McGehee's House, and his start must have been an early one. In a letter to his wife, dated near the White Oak Bridge, he says that in consequence of the heavy rain he rose 'about midnight' on the 30th. Yet his medical director, although he noticed that the general fell asleep while he was eating his supper the same evening, says that he never saw him more active and energetic than during the engagement;[1] and Jackson himself, neither in his report nor elsewhere, ever admitted that he was in any way to blame.

It is difficult to conceive that his scrupulous regard for truth, displayed in every action of his life, should have yielded in this one instance to his pride. He was perfectly aware of the necessity of aiding Longstreet; and if, owing to the obstacles enumerated in his report, he thought the task impossible, his opinion, as that of a man who as difficulties accumulated became the more determined to overcome them, must be regarded with respect. The critics, it is possible, have forgotten for the moment that the condition of the troops is a factor of supreme importance in military operations. General D. H. Hill has told us that 'Jackson's own corps was worn out by long and exhausting marches, and reduced in numbers by numerous sanguinary battles;'[2] and he records his conviction that pity for his

[1] Letter from Dr. Hunter McGuire to the author.
[2] *Battles and Leaders*, vol. ii., p. 389.

troops had much to do with the general's inaction. Hill would have probably come nearer the truth if he had said that the tired regiments were hardly to be trusted in a desperate assault, unsupported by artillery, on a position which was even stronger than that which they had stormed with such loss at Gaines' Mill.

Had Jackson thrown two columns across the fords— which the cavalry, according to Munford, had not found easy, —and attempted to deploy on the further bank, it was exceedingly probable that they would have been driven back with tremendous slaughter. The refusal of the troops to work at the bridge under fire was in itself a sign that they had little stomach for hard fighting.

It may be argued that it was Jackson's duty to sacrifice his command in order to draw off troops from Glendale. But on such unfavourable ground the sacrifice would have been worse than useless. The attack repulsed—and it could hardly have gone otherwise—Franklin, leaving a small rear-guard to watch the fords, would have been free to turn nearly his whole strength against Longstreet. It is quite true, as a tactical principle, that demonstrations, such as Jackson made with his artillery, are seldom to be relied upon to hold an enemy in position. When the first alarm has passed off, and the defending general becomes aware that nothing more than a feint is intended, he will act as did the Federals, and employ his reserves else-where. A vigorous attack is, almost invariably, the only means of keeping him to his ground. But an attack which is certain to be repulsed, and to be repulsed in quick time, is even less effective than a demonstration. It may be the precursor of a decisive defeat.

But it is not so much for his failure to force the passage at White Oak Swamp that Jackson has been criti-cised, as for his failure to march to Frayser's Farm on finding that the Federal position was impregnable. 'When, on the forenoon of the 30th,' writes Longstreet, 'Jack-son found his way blocked by Franklin, he had time to march to the head of it (White Oak Swamp), and across to the Charles City road, in season for the engagement at

Frayser's Farm [Glendale], the distance being about four miles.' [1]

Without doubt this would have been a judicious course to pursue, but it was not for Jackson to initiate such a movement. He had been ordered by General Lee to move along the road to White Oak Swamp, to endeavour to force his way to the Long Bridge road, to guard Lee's left flank from any attack across the fords or bridges of the lower Chickahominy, and to keep on that road until he received further orders. These further orders he never received; and it was certainly not his place to march to the Charles City road until Lee, who was with Longstreet, sent him instructions to do so. ' General Jackson,' says Dr. McGuire, ' demanded of his subordinates implicit, blind obedience. He gave orders in his own peculiar, terse, rapid way, and he did not permit them to be questioned. He obeyed his own superiors in the same fashion. At White Oak Swamp he was looking for some message from General Lee, but he received none, and therefore, as a soldier, he had no right to leave the road which had been assigned to him. About July 13, 1862, the night before we started to Gordonsville, Crutchfield, Pendleton (assistant-adjutant-general), and myself were discussing the campaign just finished. We were talking about the affair at Frayser's Farm, and wondering if it would have been better for Jackson with part of his force to have moved to Longstreet's aid. The general came in while the discussion was going on, and curtly said : " If General Lee had wanted me he could have sent for me." It looked the day after the battle, and it looks to me now, that if General Lee had sent a staff officer, who could have ridden the distance in forty minutes, to order Jackson with three divisions to the cross roads, while D. H. Hill and the artillery watched Franklin, we should certainly have crushed McClellan's army. If Lee had wanted Jackson to give direct support to Longstreet, he could have had him there in under three hours. The staff officer was not sent, and the evidence is that General Lee believed Longstreet strong enough to defeat the Federals without

[1] *From Manassas to Appomattox*, p. 150.

direct aid from Jackson.'[1] Such reasoning appears incontrovertible. Jackson, be it remembered, had been directed to guard the left flank of the army 'until further orders.' Had these words been omitted, and he had been left free to follow his own judgment, it is possible that he would have joined Huger on the Charles City road with three divisions. But in all probability he felt himself tied down by the phrase which Moltke so strongly reprobates. Despite Dr. McGuire's statement Jackson knew well that disobedience to orders may sometimes be condoned. It may be questioned whether he invariably demanded 'blind' obedience. 'General,' said an officer, 'you blame me for disobedience of orders, but in Mexico you did the same yourself.' 'But I was successful,' was Jackson's reply; as much as to say that an officer, when he takes upon himself the responsibility of ignoring the explicit instructions of his superior, must be morally certain that he is doing what that superior, were he present, would approve. Apply this rule to the situation at White Oak Swamp. For anything Jackson knew it was possible that Longstreet and Hill might defeat the Federals opposed to them without his aid. In such case, Lee, believing Jackson to be still on the left flank, would have ordered him to prevent the enemy's escape by the Long Bridge. What would Lee have said had his 'further orders' found Jackson marching to the Charles City road, with the Long Bridge some miles in rear? The truth is that the principle of 'marching to the sound of the cannon,' though always to be borne in mind, cannot be invariably followed. The only fair criticism on Jackson's conduct is that he should have informed Lee of his inability to force the passage across the Swamp, and have held three divisions in readiness to march to Glendale. This, so far as can be ascertained, was left undone, but the evidence is merely negative.

Except for this apparent omission, it cannot be fairly said that Jackson was in the slightest degree responsible for the failure of the Confederate operations. If the truth be told, Lee's design was by no means

[1] Letter to the author.

perfect. It had two serious defects. In the first place, it depended for success on the co-operation of several converging columns, moving over an intricate country, of which the Confederates had neither accurate maps nor reliable information. The march of the columns was through thick woods, which not only impeded inter-communication, but provided the enemy with ample material for obstructing the roads, and Jackson's line of march was barred by a formidable obstacle in White Oak Swamp, an admirable position for a rear-guard. In the second place, concentration at the decisive point was not provided for. The staff proved incapable of keeping the divisions in hand. Magruder was permitted to wander to and fro after the fashion of D'Erlon between Quatre Bras and Ligny. Holmes was as useless as Grouchy at Waterloo. Huger did nothing, although some of his brigades, when the roads to the front were found to be obstructed, might easily have been drawn off to reinforce Longstreet. The cavalry had gone off on a raid to the White House, instead of crossing the Chickahominy and harassing the enemy's eastward flank; and at the decisive point only two divisions were assembled, 20,000 men all told, and these two divisions attacked in succession instead of simultaneously. Had Magruder and Holmes, neither of whom would have been called upon to march more than thirteen miles, moved on Frayser's Farm, and had part of Huger's division been brought over to the same point, the Federals would in all probability have been irretrievably defeated. It is easy to be wise after the event. The circumstances were extraordinary. An army of 75,000 men was pursuing an army of 95,000, of which 65,000, when the pursuit began, were perfectly fresh troops. The problem was, indeed, one of exceeding difficulty; but, in justice to the reputation of his lieutenants, it is only fair to say that Lee's solution was not a masterpiece.

During the night which followed the battle of Frayser's Farm the whole Federal army fell back on Malvern Hill—a strong position, commanding the country for many miles, and very difficult of access, on which the reserve artillery, supported by the Fourth and Fifth Corps, was already posted.

July 1. The Confederates, marching at daybreak, passed over roads which were strewn with arms, blankets, and equipments. Stragglers from the retreating army were picked up at every step. Scores of wounded men lay untended by the roadside. Waggons and ambulances had been abandoned; and with such evidence before their eyes it was difficult to resist the conviction that the enemy was utterly demoralised. That McClellan had seized Malvern Hill, and that it was strongly occupied by heavy guns, Lee was well aware. But, still holding to his purpose of annihilating his enemy before McDowell could intervene from Fredericksburg, he pushed forward, determined to attack; and with his whole force now well in hand the result seemed assured. Three or four miles south of White Oak Swamp Jackson's column, which was leading the Confederate advance, came under the fire of the Federal batteries. The advanced-guard deployed in the woods on either side of the road, and Lee, accompanied by Jackson, rode forward to reconnoitre.

Malvern Hill, a plateau rising to the height of 150 feet above the surrounding forests, possessed nearly every requirement of a strong defensive position. The open ground on the top, undulating and unobstructed, was a mile and a half in length by half a mile in breadth. To the north, north-west, and north-east it fell gradually, the slopes covered with wheat, standing or in shock, to the edge of the woods, which are from eight to sixteen hundred yards distant from the commanding crest. The base of the hill, except to the east and south-east, was covered with dense forest; and within the forest, at the foot of the declivity, ran a tortuous and marshy stream. The right flank was partially protected by a long mill-dam. The left, more open, afforded an excellent artillery position overlooking a broad stretch of meadows, drained by a narrow stream and deep ditches, and flanked by the fire of several gunboats. Only three approaches, the Quaker and the river roads, and a track from the north-west, gave access to the heights.

The reconnaissance showed that General Porter, commanding the defence, had utilised the ground to the best advantage. A powerful artillery, posted just in rear of the crest, swept the entire length of the slopes, and under cover in rear were dense masses of infantry, with a strong line of skirmishers pushed down the hill in front.

Nevertheless, despite the formidable nature of the Federal preparations, orders were immediately issued for attack. General Lee, who was indisposed, had instructed Longstreet to reconnoitre the enemy's left, and to report whether attack was feasible. Jackson was opposed to a frontal attack, preferring to turn the enemy's right. Longstreet, however, was of a different opinion. 'The spacious open,' he says, 'along Jackson's front appeared to offer a field for play of a hundred or more guns. . . . I thought it probable that Porter's batteries, under the cross-fire of the Confederates' guns posted on his left and front, could be thrown into disorder, and thus make way for the combined assaults of the infantry. I so reported, and General Lee ordered disposition accordingly, sending the pioneer corps to cut a road for the right batteries.' [1]

It was not till four o'clock that the line of battle was formed. Jackson was on the left, with Whiting to the left of the Quaker road, and D. H. Hill to the right; Ewell's and Jackson's own divisions were in reserve. Nearly half a mile beyond Jackson's right came two of Huger's brigades, Armistead and Wright, and to Huger's left rear was Magruder. Holmes, still on the river road, was to assail the enemy's left. Longstreet and A. P. Hill were in reserve behind Magruder, on the Long Bridge road.

4 P.M.

The deployment of the leading divisions was not effected without loss, for the Federal artillery swept all the roads and poured a heavy fire into the woods; but at length D. H. Hill's infantry came into line along the edge of the timber.

The intervening time had been employed in bringing the artillery to the front; and now were seen the tremendous difficulties which confronted the attack. The swamps

[1] *From Manassas to Appomattox*, p. 143.

and thickets through which the batteries had to force
their way were grievous impediments to rapid or orderly
movement, and when they at last emerged from the cover,
and unlimbered for action, the concentrated fire of the
Federal guns overpowered them from the outset.   In front
of Huger four batteries were disabled in quick succession,
the enemy concentrating fifty or sixty guns on each of them
in turn; four or five others which Jackson had ordered to
take post on the left of his line, although, with two exceptions, they managed to hold their ground, were powerless
to subdue the hostile fire.   'The obstacles,' says Lee in his
report, 'presented by the woods and swamp made it impracticable to bring up a sufficient amount of artillery to oppose
successfully the extraordinary force of that arm employed by
the enemy, while the field itself afforded us few positions
favourable for its use and none for its proper concentration.'

According to Longstreet, when the inability of the
batteries to prepare the way for the infantry was demonstrated by their defeat, Lee abandoned the original plan of
attack.   'He proposed to me to move "round to the left
with my own and A. P. Hill's division, and turn the Federal
right."   I issued my orders accordingly for the two divisions to go around and turn the Federal right, when in
some way unknown to me the battle was drawn on.'[1]

Unfortunately, through some mistake on the part of
Lee's staff, the order of attack which had been already
issued was not rescinded.   It was certainly an extraordinary
production.   'Batteries,' it ran, 'have been established
to rake the enemy's line.   If it is broken, as is probable, Armistead, who can witness the effect of the fire,
has been ordered to charge with a yell. Do the same.'[2]   This
was to D. H. Hill and to Magruder, who had under his
command Huger's and McLaws' divisions as well as his own.

So, between five and six o'clock, General D. H. Hill,
5.30 P.M.   believing that he heard the appointed signal, broke
               forward from the timber, and five brigades, in one
irregular line, charged full against the enemy's front.   The

---

[1] *Battles and Leaders*, vol. ii., p. 403.
[2] O. R., vol. xi., part i., p. 677.

Federals, disposed in several lines, were in overwhelming strength. Their batteries were free to concentrate on the advancing infantry. Their riflemen, posted in the interval between the artillery masses, swept the long slopes with a grazing fire, while fence, bank, and ravine, gave shelter from the Confederate bullets. Nor were the enormous difficulties which confronted the attack in any way mitigated by careful arrangement on the part of the Confederate staff. The only hope of success, if success were possible, lay in one strong concentrated effort ; in employing the whole army ; in supporting the infantry with artillery, regardless of loss, at close range ; and in hurling a mass of men, in several successive lines, against one point of the enemy's position. It is possible that the Federal army, already demoralised by retreat, might have yielded to such vigorous pressure. But in the Confederate attack there was not the slightest attempt at concentration. The order which dictated it gave an opening to misunderstanding ; and, as is almost invariably the case when orders are defective, misunderstanding occurred. The movement was premature. Magruder had only two brigades of his three divisions, Armistead's and Wright's, in position. Armistead, who was well in advance of the Confederate right, was attacked by a strong body of skirmishers. D. H. Hill took the noise of this conflict for the appointed signal, and moved forward. The divisions which should have supported him had not yet crossed the swamp in rear ; and thus 10,500 men, absolutely unaided, advanced against the whole Federal army. The blunder met with terrible retribution. On that midsummer evening death reaped a fearful harvest. The gallant Confederate infantry, nerved by their success at Gaines' Mill, swept up the field with splendid determination. 'It was the onset of battle,' said a Federal officer present, 'with the good order of a review.' But the iron hail of grape and canister, laying the ripe wheat low as if it had been cut with a sickle, and tossing the shocks in air, rent the advancing lines from end to end. Hundreds fell, hundreds swarmed back to the woods, but still the brigades pressed on, and through the smoke of battle

F 2

the waving colours led the charge. But the Federal infantry had yet to be encountered. Lying behind their shelter they had not yet fired a shot; but as the Confederates reached close range, regiment after regiment, springing to their feet, poured a devastating fire into the charging ranks. The rush was checked. Here and there small bodies of desperate men, following the colours, still pressed onward, but the majority lay down, and the whole front of battle rang with the roar of musketry. But so thin was the Confederate line that it was impossible to overcome the sustained fire of the enemy. The brigade reserves had already been thrown in; there was no further support at hand; the Federal gunners, staunch and resolute, held fast to their position, and on every part of the line Porter's reserves were coming up. As one regiment emptied its cartridge-boxes it was relieved by another. The volume of fire never for a moment slackened; and fresh batteries, amongst which were the 32-prs. of the siege train, unlimbering on the flanks, gave further strength to a front which was already impregnable.

Jackson, meanwhile, on receiving a request for reinforcements, had sent forward three brigades of his own division and a brigade of Hill's. But a mistake had been committed in the disposition of these troops. The order for attack had undoubtedly named only D. H. Hill's division. But there was no good reason that it should have been so literally construed as to leave the division unsupported. Whiting was guarding the left flank, and was not available; but Ewell and Winder were doing nothing, and there can be no question but that they should have advanced to the edge of the woods directly D. H. Hill moved forward, and have followed his brigades across the open, ready to lend aid directly his line was checked. As it was, they had been halted within the woods and beyond the swamp, and the greater part, in order to avoid the random shells, had moved even further to the rear. It thus happened that before the reinforcements arrived Hill's division had been beaten back, and under the tremendous fire of the Federal artillery it was with difficulty that the border of the forest was maintained.

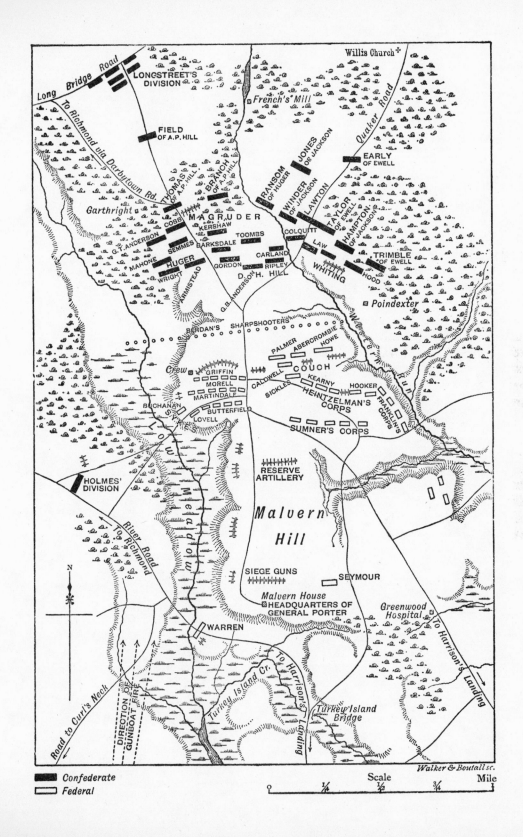

Willis Church

French's Mill

Long Bridge Road

LONGSTREET'S DIVISION

To Richmond via Darbytown Rd.

FIELD OF A.P. HILL

THOMAS OF A.P. HILL

BRANCH OF A.P. HILL

RANSOM OF HUGER

JONES OF JACKSON

WINDER OF JACKSON

LAWTON

EARLY OF EWELL

Garthright

COBB

MAGRUDER

KERSHAW

COLQUITT

TAYLOR OF EWELL

HAMPTON OF JACKSON

Quaker Road

G.T. ANDERSON

SEMMES

TOOMBS

MAHONE

HUGER

BARKSDALE

CARLAND

LAW

TRIMBLE OF EWELL

WRIGHT

ARMISTEAD

GORDON

RIPLEY

D.H. HILL

WHITING

HOOD

Poindexter

G.B. ANDERSON

BERDAN'S SHARPSHOOTERS

PALMER

ABERCROMBIE

HOWE

Crew

GRIFFIN

MORELL

COUCH

CALDWELL

KEARNY

HOOKER

BUCHANAN

MARTINDALE

SICKLES

HEINTZELMAN'S CORPS

FRANKLIN'S CORPS

Low

BUTTERFIELD

LOVELL

SUMNER'S CORPS

Meadow

HOLMES' DIVISION

RESERVE ARTILLERY

Malvern Hill

To Richmond

River Road

SIEGE GUNS

SEYMOUR

Malvern House

HEADQUARTERS OF GENERAL PORTER

Greenwood Hospital

To Harrison's Landing

N

WARREN

Road to Curl's Neck

DIRECTION OF GUNBOAT FIRE

To Harrison's Landing

Turkey Island Cr.

Turkey Island Bridge

To Harrison's Landing

Walker & Boutall sc.

■ Confederate
□ Federal

Scale

0   ¼   ½   ¾   1   Mile

While Hill was retiring, Huger, and then Magruder, came into action on the right. It had been reported to Lee that the enemy was beginning to fall back. This report originated, there can be little doubt, in the withdrawal of the Federal regiments and batteries which had exhausted their ammunition and were relieved by others; but, in any case, it was imperative that D. H. Hill should be supported, and the other divisions were ordered forward with all speed. Huger's and Magruder's men attacked with the same determination as had been displayed by Hill's, but no better success attended their endeavours. The brigades were not properly formed when the order arrived, but scattered over a wide front, and they went in piecemeal. Magruder's losses were even greater than Hill's; and with his defeat the battle ceased.

Had the Federals followed up the repulse with a strong counter-attack the victory of Malvern Hill might have been more decisive than that of Gaines' Mill. It is true that neither Longstreet nor A. P. Hill had been engaged, and that three of Jackson's divisions, his own, Whiting's and Ewell's, had suffered little. But Magruder and D. H. Hill, whose commands included at least 30,000 muskets, one half of Lee's infantry, had been completely crushed, and Holmes on the river road was too far off to lend assistance. The fatal influence of a continued retreat had paralysed, however, the initiative of the Federal generals. Intent only on getting away unscathed, they neglected, like McClellan at Gaines' Mill, to look for opportunities, forgetting that when an enemy is pursuing in hot haste he is very apt to expose himself. Jackson had acted otherwise at Port Republic.

The loss of over 5,000 men was not the worst which had befallen the Confederates. 'The next morning by dawn,' says one of Ewell's brigadiers, 'I went off to ask for orders, when I found the whole army in the utmost disorder— thousands of straggling men were asking every passer-by for their regiments; ambulances, waggons, and artillery obstructing every road, and altogether, in a drenching rain, presenting a scene of the most woeful and disheartening confusion.'[1] The reports of other officers corroborate General Trimble's statement, and there can be no question that demoralisation had set in. Whether, if the Federals had used their large reserves with resolution, and, as the Confederates fell back down the slopes, had followed with the bayonet, the demoralisation would not have increased and spread, must remain in doubt. Not one of the Southern generals engaged has made public his opinion. There is but one thing certain, that with an opponent so blind to opportunity as McClellan a strong counterstroke was the last thing to be feared. After witnessing the opening of the attack, the Federal commander, leaving the control of the field to Porter, had ridden off to Harrison's Landing, eight miles down the James, whither his trains, escorted by the Fourth Army Corps, had been directed, and where he had determined to await reinforcements. The Federal troops, moreover, although they had withstood the charge of the Confederate infantry with unbroken ranks, had not fought with the same spirit as they had displayed at Gaines' Mill. General Hunt, McClellan's chief of artillery, to whose admirable disposition of the batteries the victory was largely due, wrote that ' the battle was desperately contested, and frequently trembled in the balance. The last attack . . . was nearly successful; but we won from the fact that we had kept our reserves in hand.'[2] Nor had McClellan much confidence in his army. 'My men,' he wrote to Washington on the morning of the battle, ' are completely exhausted, and I dread the result if we are attacked to-day by fresh troops. If possible, I shall retire to-night to Harrison's Landing, where the gunboats can render more aid in covering our position. Permit me to urge that not an hour should be lost in sending me fresh troops. More gunboats are much needed. . . . I now pray for time. My

---

[1] Trimble's Report, O. R., vol. xi., part i., p. 619.

[2] Three horse-batteries and eight 32-pr. howitzers were ' brought up to the decisive point at the close of the day, thus bringing every gun of this large artillery force (the artillery reserve) into the most active and decisive use. Not a gun remained unemployed: not one could have been safely spared. —Hunt's Report, O. R., vol. xi., part ii., p. 239.

men have proved themselves the equals of any troops in the world, but they are worn out. Our losses have been very great, we have failed to win only because overpowered by superior numbers.'[1]

Surely a more despairing appeal was never uttered. The general, whose only thought was 'more gunboats and fresh troops,' whatever may have been the condition of his men, had reached the last stage of demoralisation.

The condition to which McClellan was reduced seems to have been realised by Jackson. The crushing defeat of his own troops failed to disturb his judgment. Whilst the night still covered the battle-field, his divisional generals came to report the condition of their men and to receive instructions. 'Every representation,' says Dabney, 'which they made was gloomy.' At length, after many details of losses and disasters, they concurred in declaring that McClellan would probably take the aggressive in the morning, and that the Confederate army was in no condition to resist him. Jackson had listened silently, save when he interposed a few brief questions, to all their statements; but now he replied: 'No; he will clear out in the morning.'

The forecast was more than fulfilled. When morning dawned, grey, damp, and cheerless, and the Confederate sentinels, through the cold mist which rose from the sodden woods, looked out upon the battle-field, they saw that Malvern Hill had been abandoned. Only a few cavalry patrols rode to and fro on the ground which had been held by the Federal artillery, and on the slopes below, covered with hundreds of dead and dying men, the surgeons were quietly at work. During the night the enemy had fallen back to Harrison's Landing, and justification for Lee's assault at Malvern Hill may be found in the story of the Federal retreat. The confusion of the night march, following on a long series of fierce engagements, told with terrible effect on the *moral* of the men, and stragglers increased at every step. 'It was like the retreat,' said one of McClellan's generals, 'of a whipped army. We retreated like a parcel of sheep, and a

July 2.

[1] O. R., vol. xi., part iii., p. 282.

few shots from the rebels would have panic-stricken the whole command.'[1] At length, through blinding rain, the flotilla of gunboats was discovered, and on the long peninsula between Herring Run and the James the exhausted army reached a resting-place. But so great was the disorder, that during the whole of that day nothing was done to prepare a defensive position; a ridge to the north, which commanded the whole camp, was unoccupied; and, according to the Committee of Congress which took evidence on the conduct of the war, 'nothing but a heavy rain, thereby preventing the enemy from bringing up their artillery, saved the army from destruction.'[2] McClellan's own testimony is even more convincing. 'The army,' he wrote on July 3, the second day after the battle, 'is thoroughly worn out and requires rest and very heavy reinforcements. . . . I am in hopes that the enemy is as completely worn out as we are. . . . The roads are now very bad; for these reasons I hope we shall have enough breathing space to reorganise and rest the men, and get them into position before the enemy can attack again. . . . It is of course impossible to estimate as yet our losses, but I doubt whether there are to-day more than 50,000 men with the colours.'[3]

As his army of 105,000 men, during the whole of the Seven Days, lost only 16,000, the last admission, if accurate, is most significant. Nearly half the men must either have been sick or straggling.

It was not because the Confederates were also worn out that the Federals were given time to reorganise and to establish themselves in a strong position. Jackson, the moment it was light, rode through the rain to the front. Learning that the enemy had evacuated their position, he ordered his chief of staff to get the troops under arms, to form the infantry in three lines of battle, and then to allow the men to build fires, cook their rations, and dry their clothes. By 11 o'clock the ammunition had been

[1] Report on the Conduct of the War, p. 580. General Hooker's evidence.
[2] Report on the Conduct of the War, p. 27.
[3] O. R., vol. xi., part i., pp. 291, 292.

replenished, and his four divisions were formed up. Longstreet's brigades had pushed forward a couple of miles, but no orders had reached the Valley troops, and Major Dabney rode off to find his general. 'I was told,' he writes, 'that he was in the Poindexter House, a large mansion near Willis' Church. Lee, Jackson, Dr. McGuire, and Major Taylor of Lee's staff, and perhaps others, were in the dining-room. Asking leave to report to General Jackson that his orders had been fulfilled, I was introduced to General Lee, who, with his usual kindness, begged me to sit by the fire and dry myself. Here I stayed much of the day, and witnessed some strange things. Longstreet, wet and muddy, was the first to enter. He had ridden round most of the battle-field, and his report was not particularly cheerful. Jackson was very quiet, never volunteering any counsel or suggestion, but answering when questioned in a brief, deferential tone. His countenance was very serious, and soon became very troubled. After a time the clatter of horses' hoofs was heard, and two gentlemen came in, dripping. They were the President and his nephew. Davis and Lee then drew to the table, and entered into an animated military discussion. Lee told the President the news which the scouts were bringing in, of horrible mud, and of abandoned arms and baggage-waggons. They then debated at length what was to be done next. McClellan was certainly retiring, but whether as beaten or as only manœuvring was not apparent, nor was the direction of his retreat at all clear. Was he aiming for some point on the lower James where he might embark and get away? or at some point on the upper James—say Shirley, or Bermuda Hundred—where he could cross the river (he had pontoons and gunboats) and advance on Richmond from the south? Such were the questions which came up, and at length it was decided that the army should make no movement until further information had been received. The enemy was not to be pursued until Stuart's cavalry, which had arrived the previous evening at Nance's Shop, should obtain reliable information.

'Jackson, meanwhile, sat silent in his corner. I

watched his face. The expression, changing from surprise to dissent, and lastly to intense mortification, showed clearly the tenor of his thoughts. He knew that McClellan was defeated, that he was retreating and not manœuvring. He knew that his troops were disorganised, that sleeplessness, fasting, bad weather, and disaster must have weakened their *moral*. He heard it said by General Lee that the scouts reported the roads so deep in mud that the artillery could not move, that our men were wet and wearied. But Jackson's mind reasoned that where the Federals could march the Confederates could follow, and that a decisive victory was well worth a great effort.' [1]

The decision of the council of war was that the army should move the next morning in the direction of
July 3.   Harrison's Landing. Longstreet, whose troops had not been engaged at Malvern Hill, was to lead the way. But the operations of this day were without result. The line of march was by Carter's Mill and the river road. But after the troops had been set in motion, it was found that the river road had been obstructed by the enemy, and Lee directed Longstreet to countermarch to the Charles City cross roads and move on Evelington Heights.[2] But ignorance of the country and inefficient guides once more played into the enemy's hands, and when night closed the troops were still some distance from the Federal outposts.

The delay had been exceedingly unfortunate. At 9 A.M. Stuart's cavalry had occupied the Evelington Heights, and, believing that Longstreet was close at hand, had opened fire with a single howitzer on the camps below. The consternation caused by this unlooked-for attack was great. But the Federals soon recovered from their surprise, and, warned as to the danger of their situation, sent out infantry and artillery to drive back the enemy and secure the heights. Stuart, dismounting his troopers, held on for some time; but at two o'clock, finding that the Confederate infantry was still six or seven miles distant,

---

[1] Letter to the author. Dr. McGuire writes to the same effect.
[2] Evelington Heights are between Rawling's Mill Pond and Westover.

and that his ammunition was failing, he gave up the Heights, which were immediately fortified by the enemy. Had the cavalry commander resisted the temptation of spreading panic in the enemy's ranks, and kept his troops under cover, infantry and artillery might possibly have been brought up to the Heights before they were occupied by the Federals. In any case, it was utterly useless to engage a whole army with one gun and a few regiments of cavalry, and in war, especially in advanced-guard operations, silence is often golden.[1] It was not till they were warned by the fire of Stuart's howitzer that the Federals realised the necessity of securing and intrenching the Evelington Heights, and it is within the bounds of possibility, had they been left undisturbed, that they might have neglected them altogether. McClellan, according to his letters already quoted, believed that the condition of the roads would retard the advance of the enemy; and, as is evident from a letter he wrote the same morning, before the incident took place, he was of opinion that there was no immediate need for the occupation of a defensive position.[2]

During this day the Valley divisions, crawling in rear of Longstreet, had marched only three miles; and such sluggish progress, at so critical a moment, put the climax to Jackson's discontent. His wrath blazed forth with unwonted vehemence. 'That night,' says Dabney,[3] 'he was quartered in a farmhouse a mile or two east of Willis' Church. The soldier assigned to him as a guide made a most stupid report, and admitted that he knew nothing of the road. Jackson turned on him in fierce anger, and ordered him from his presence with threats of the severest punishment. On retiring, he said to his staff, " Now, gentlemen, Jim will have breakfast for you punctually at dawn. I expect you to be up, to eat immediately, and be in the saddle without delay. We must burn no more daylight." About daybreak I heard him tramping down the stairs. I alone went out to meet him. All the rest were asleep. He addressed me in

---

[1] The military student will compare the battles of Weissembourg, Vionville, and Gravelotte in 1870, all of which began with a useless surprise.
[2] O. R., vol. xi., part iii., pp. 291-2.   [3] Letter to the author.

stern tones : " Major, how is it that this staff never will be punctual ? " I replied : " I am in time ; I cannot control the others.". Jackson turned in a rage to the servant : " Put back that food into the chest, have that chest in the waggon, and that waggon moving in two minutes." I suggested, very humbly, that he had better at least take some food himself. But he was too angry to eat, and repeating his orders, flung himself into the saddle, and galloped off. Jim gave a low whistle, saying : " My stars, but de general is just mad dis time ; most like lightnin' strike him ! " '

With the engagement on the Evelington Heights the fighting round Richmond came to an end. When Lee

July 4. came up with his advanced divisions on the morning of the 4th, he found the pickets already engaged, and the troops formed up in readiness for action. He immediately rode forward with Jackson, and the two, dismounting, proceeded without staff or escort to make a careful reconnaissance of the enemy's position. Their inspection showed them that it was practically impregnable. The front, facing westward, was flanked from end to end by the fire of the gunboats, and the Evelington Heights, already fortified, and approached by a single road, were stronger ground than even Malvern Hill. The troops were therefore withdrawn to the forest, and for the next three days, with the exception of those employed in collecting the arms and

July 8. stores which the Federals had abandoned, they remained inactive. On July 8, directing Stuart to watch McClellan, General Lee fell back to Richmond.

The battles of the Seven Days cost the Confederates 20,000 men. The Federals, although defeated, lost no more than 16,000, of whom 10,000, nearly half of them wounded, were prisoners. In addition, however, 52 guns and 35,000 rifles became the prize of the Southerners ; and vast as was the quantity of captured stores, far greater was the amount destroyed.

But the defeat of McClellan's army is not to be measured by a mere estimate of the loss in men and in *matériel*. The discomfited general sought to cover his failure by a lavish employment of strategic phrases. The retreat to the James, he declared, had been planned before the battle of Mechanicsville. He had merely manœuvred to get quit of an inconvenient line of supply, and to place his army in a more favourable position for attacking Richmond. He congratulated his troops on their success in changing the line of operations, always regarded as the most hazardous of military expedients. Their conduct, he said, ranked them among the most celebrated armies of history. Under every disadvantage of numbers, and necessarily of position also, they had in every conflict beaten back their foes with enormous slaughter. They had reached the new base complete in organisation and unimpaired in spirit.[1]

It is possible that this address soothed the pride of his troops. It certainly deluded neither his own people nor the South. The immediate effect of his strategic manœuvre was startling.

5,000 men, the effective remnant of Shields' division, besides several new regiments, were sent to the Peninsula from the army protecting Washington. General Burnside, who had mastered a portion of the North Carolina coast, was ordered to suspend operations, to leave a garrison in New Berne, and to bring the remainder of his army to Fortress Monroe. Troops were demanded from General Hunter, who had taken the last fort which defended Savannah, the port of Georgia.[2] The Western army of the Union was asked to reinforce McClellan, and Lincoln called on the Northern States for a fresh levy. But although 300,000 men were promised him, the discouragement of the Northern people was so great that recruits showed no alacrity in coming forward. The South, on the other hand, ringing with the brilliant deeds of Lee and Jackson, turned with renewed vigour to the task of resisting the invader. Richmond, the beleaguered capital, although the enemy was in position not more than twenty miles away, knew that her agony was over. The city was one vast hospital. Many of the best and bravest of the Confederacy had fallen in the Seven Days, and the voice of mourning hushed all sound

[1] O. R., vol. xi., part iii., p. 299.
[2] The forces under Burnside and Hunter amounted to some 35,000 men.

of triumph. But the long columns of prisoners, the captured cannon, the great trains of waggons, piled high with spoil, were irrefragable proof of the complete defeat of the invader.

When the army once more encamped within sight of the city it was received as it deserved. Lee and Jackson were the special objects of admiration. All recognised the strategic skill which had wrought the overthrow of McClellan's host ; and the hard marches and sudden blows of the campaign on the Shenandoah, crowned by the swift transfer of the Valley army from the Blue Ridge to the Chickahominy, took fast hold of the popular imagination. The mystery in which Jackson's operations were involved, the dread he inspired in the enemy, his reticence, his piety, his contempt of comfort, his fiery energy, his fearlessness, and his simplicity aroused the interest and enthusiasm of the whole community. Whether Lee or his lieutenant was the more averse to posing before the crowd it is difficult to say. Both succeeded in escaping all public manifestation of popular favour ; both went about their business with an absolute absence of ostentation, and if the handsome features of the Commander-in-Chief were familiar to the majority of the citizens, few recognised in the plainly dressed soldier, riding alone through Richmond, the great leader of the Valley, with whose praises not the South only, but the whole civilised world, was already ringing.

CHAPTER XV

CEDAR RUN

THE victories in the Valley, the retreat of Banks, Shields, and Frémont, followed by the victory of Gaines' Mill, had raised the hopes of the South to the highest pitch.

When McClellan fell back to the James the capture or destruction of his army seemed a mere matter of time, and it was confidently expected that a disaster of such magnitude would assuredly bring the North to terms. But the slaughter of the Confederates at Malvern Hill, the unmolested retreat of the enemy to Harrison's Landing, the fortification of that strong position, induced a more sober mood. The Northern soldiers had displayed a courage for which the South had not yet given them credit. On the last of the Seven Days they had fought almost as stubbornly as on the first. Their losses had been heavy, but they had taught their adversaries that they were no longer the unmanageable levies of Bull Run, scattered by the first touch of disaster to the four winds. It was no frail barrier which stood now between the South and her independence, but a great army of trained soldiers, seasoned by experience, bound together by discipline, and capable of withstanding a long series of reverses. And when it became clear that McClellan, backed by the fleet, had no intention of losing his grip on Richmond; when the news came that Lincoln had asked for 300,000 fresh troops; and that the Federal Army of the West, undisturbed by Lee's victories, was still advancing through Tennessee,[1] the power and persistency of the North were revealed in all their huge proportions.

[1] After the repulse of the Confederates at Malvern Hill, and the unmolested retreat of the Army of the Potomac to Harrison's Landing, Lincoln cancelled his demand for troops from the West.

But the disappointment of the Southern people in no way abated their gratitude. The troops drank their fill of praise. The deeds of the Valley regiments were on every tongue. The Stonewall Brigade was the most famous organisation in the Confederacy. To have marched with Jackson was a sure passport to the good graces of every citizen. Envied by their comrades, regarded as heroes by the admiring crowds that thronged the camps, the ragged soldiers of the Shenandoah found ample compensation for their labours. They had indeed earned the rest which was now given them. For more than two months they had been marching and fighting without cessation. Since they left Elk Run, on April 29, until they fell back to the capital on July 8, their camps had never stood in the same spot for more than four days in succession.

But neither they nor their general looked forward to a long sojourn within the works round Richmond. The men pined for the fresh breezes of their native highlands. The tainted atmosphere of a district which was one vast battle-ground told upon their health, and the people of Richmond, despite their kindness, were strangers after all. Nor was Jackson less anxious to leave the capital. The heavy rain which had deluged the bivouac on the Chicka-hominy had chilled him to the bone. During the whole of the pursuit, from White Oak Swamp to Westover, he had suffered from fever. But his longing for a move westward was dictated by other motives than the restoration of his health. No sooner had it become evident that McClellan's position was impregnable than he turned his thoughts to some more vulnerable point. He would allow the enemy no respite. In his opinion there should be no 'letting up' in the attack. The North should be given no leisure to reorganise the armies or to train recruits. A swift succession of fierce blows, delivered at a vital point, was the only means of bringing the colossus to its knees, and that vital point was far from Richmond.

Before the Confederate troops marched back to Rich-

mond he laid his views before the member of Congress
for the Winchester district, and begged Mr. Boteler to
impress them on the Government. 'McClellan's army,'
he said, 'was manifestly thoroughly beaten, incapable of
moving until it had been reorganised and reinforced.
There was danger,' he foresaw, 'that the fruits of victory
would be lost, as they had been lost after Bull Run. The
Confederate army should at once leave the malarious
district round Richmond, and moving northwards, carry
the horrors of invasion across the border. This,' he
said, 'was the only way to bring the North to its senses,
and to end the war. And it was within the power of
the Confederates, if they were to concentrate their resources, to make a successful bid for victory. 60,000 men
might march into Maryland and threaten Washington.
But while he was anxious that these views should
be laid before the President, he would earnestly disclaim
the charge of self-seeking. He wished to follow, and
not to lead. He was willing to follow anyone—Lee, or
Ewell, or anyone who would fight.' 'Why do you not
urge your views,' asked Mr. Boteler, 'on General Lee?'
'I have done so,' replied Jackson. 'And what does he say
to them?' 'He says nothing,' was the answer; 'but do
not understand that I complain of this silence; it is proper
that General Lee should observe it. He is wise and
prudent. He feels that he bears a fearful responsibility,
and he is right in declining a hasty expression of his
purpose to a subordinate like me.' [1]

Jackson was perfectly right in his estimate of the
Federal army. McClellan had 90,000 men, but 16,000
were sick, and he was still under the delusion that he had
been defeated by more than twice his numbers. His letters
to the President, it is true, betrayed no misgiving. He
was far from admitting that he had been defeated. His
army, he wrote, was now so favourably placed that an
advance on Richmond was easy. He was full of confidence.
He was watching carefully for any fault committed by the
enemy, and would take advantage of it. The spirit of his

[1] Dabney, vol. ii., pp. 230, 231.

army, he declared, was such that he felt unable to restrain it
from speedily assuming the offensive. He had determined
not to fall back unless he was absolutely forced to do so.
He was ready for a rapid and heavy blow at Richmond.
But to strike that blow he required heavy reinforcements,
and while waiting their arrival he was unwilling to leave
his strong position. [1]

Jackson's views were considered by Mr. Davis. For
the present, however, they were disregarded. The situation, in the opinion of the Government, was still critical.
McClellan might be reinforced by sea. He might be superseded by a more energetic commander, and the Federals
might then cross to the right bank of the James, cut the
railways which connected Richmond with the South,
and turn the line of fortifications. The losses of the
Seven Days had reduced the Confederate strength to
60,000. Under such circumstances it was not considered
safe to remove the army from the capital. Jackson,
however, was entrusted with a more congenial duty
than watching an enemy who, he was absolutely
convinced, had no intention of leaving his intrenchments. His longing for active work was gratified
by an order to march westward. Lee, finding
July 13.   McClellan immovable, had recourse to his former
strategy. He determined to play once more on Lincoln's
fears. The Army of Virginia, under the command of
Pope, defended Washington. Would the Northern Government, when the news came that Stonewall Jackson
was returning to the Shenandoah, deem this force
sufficient to protect the capital? Would they not
rather think it necessary to recall McClellan? The
experiment was worth trying. After some delay in
recovering from the disorganisation caused by the
disasters in the Valley, Pope had assembled his army
east of the Blue Ridge, near the sources of the Rappahannock. Sperryville, his advanced post, was no more than
forty miles north of the Virginia Central Railway, and his
cavalry was already advancing. It was essential that

[1] O. R., vol. xi., part ii., p. 306.

the railway, the chief line of supply of the Confederate army, should be protected; and Jackson was instructed July 16. to halt near Gordonsville. On the 16th his leading brigades reached their destination. Their arrival was opportune. The Federal cavalry, with a strong infantry support, was already threatening Gordonsville. On learning, however, that the town was occupied they at once fell back.

Jackson, as soon as his command was up, and he had had time to ascertain the Federal strength, applied for reinforcements. His own numbers were very small. The divisions of D. H. Hill and Whiting had remained at Richmond. The Army of the Valley, reduced to its original elements, was no more than 11,000 strong. Pope's army consisted of 47,000 men.[1] But the Federals were scattered over a wide front. Sigel, a German who had succeeded Frémont, was near Sperryville, and Banks lay close to Sigel. Each of these officers commanded an army corps of two divisions. Of McDowell's army corps, Ricketts' division held Warrenton, twenty-five miles east of Banks; while King's division was retained at Fredericksburg, forty miles south-east of Ricketts'. Such dispersion seemed to invite attack. Lee, however, found it impossible to comply with his lieutenant's request for such aid as would enable him to assume the offensive. The army covering Richmond was much smaller than McClellan's, and the Confederates were aware that a large reinforcement for the latter, under General Burnside, had landed in the Peninsula. But assistance was promised in case Pope advanced so far south that troops could be detached without risk to Richmond. Pope, in fact, was too far off, and Jackson was to entice him forward.

A week, however, passed away without any movement on the part of McClellan. He knew that Lee's army was diminished; and it was believed at his headquarters that 'Jackson had started towards the Valley with 60,000 to 80,000 troops.'[2] He knew that there was no large force

[1] Sigel, 13,000; Banks, 11,000; McDowell, 18,000; Bayard's and Buford's cavalry, 5,000.
[2] O. R., vol. xi., part iii., p. 334.

within ten miles of his outposts, and if the President would send him 20,000 or 30,000 more men he said that he was ready to march on Richmond. But, as yet, he had not observed the opportunity for which, according to his own account, he was so carefully watching. Pope was far more enterprising. His cavalry had burned the railway depôt at Beaver Dam, destroyed some Confederate stores, cut the line at several points, and threatened Hanover Junction. Stuart, with his cavalry division, was immediately sent northwards, and Lee ordered A. P. Hill to Gordonsville.

Jackson's letters to headquarters at this period are missing. But Lee's answers indicate the tenor of the views therein expressed. On July 27 the Commander-in-Chief wrote :—

'I have received your dispatch of the 26th instant. I will send A. P. Hill's division and the Second Brigade of Louisiana volunteers to you. . . . I want Pope to be suppressed. . . . A. P. Hill you will, I think, find a good officer, with whom you can consult, and by advising with your division commanders as to your movements, much trouble will be saved you in arranging details, and they can act more intelligently. I wish to save you trouble from my increasing your command. *Cache* your troops as much as possible till you can strike your blow, and be prepared to return to me when done, if necessary. I will endeavour to keep General McClellan quiet till it is over, if rapidly executed.'

This letter, besides containing a delicate hint that extreme reticence is undesirable, evidently refers to some plan proposed by Jackson. Whatever this may have been, it is certain that both he and Lee were in close accord. They believed that the best method of protecting the railway was, in Lee's words, 'to find the main body of the enemy and drive it,' and they were agreed that there should be no more Malvern Hills. 'You are right,' says Lee on August 4, 'in not attacking them in their strong and chosen positions. They ought always to be turned as you propose, and thus force them on to more favourable ground.'

At the end of July, about the same time that Hill

joined Jackson, Pope, under instructions from Washington, moved forward. His cavalry occupied the line of Robertson River, within twenty miles of the Confederate lines, and it became clear that he intended advancing on Gordonsville. His infantry, however, had not yet crossed Hazel Run, and Jackson, carefully concealing his troops, remained on the watch for a few days longer. His anxiety, however, to bring his enemy to battle was even greater than usual. Pope had already gained an unenviable notoriety. On taking over command he had issued an extraordinary address. His bombast was only equalled by his want of tact. Not content with extolling the prowess of the Western troops, with whom he had hitherto served, he was bitterly satirical at the expense of McClellan and of McClellan's army. 'I have come to you,' he said to his soldiers, ' from the West, where we have always seen the backs of our enemies—from an army whose business it has been to seek the adversary, and beat him when found, whose policy has been attack and not defence. . . . I presume that I have been called here to pursue the same system, and to lead you against the enemy. It is my purpose to do so, and that speedily. . . . Meantime, I desire you to dismiss from your minds certain phrases, which I am sorry to find much in vogue amongst you. I hear constantly of taking strong positions and holding them—of lines of retreat and of bases of supplies. Let us discard such ideas. . . . Let us study the probable line of retreat of our opponents, and leave our own to take care of themselves. Let us look before and not behind. Success and glory are in the advance. Disaster and shame lurk in the rear.' [1]

Even the Northern press made sport of Pope's ' 'Ercles vein,' and the Confederates contrasted his noisy declamation with the modesty of Lee and Jackson. To the South the new commander was peculiarly obnoxious. He was the first of the Federal generals to order that the troops should subsist upon the country, and that the people should be held responsible for all damage done to roads, railways, and

[1] O. R., vol. xii., part iii., p. 474.

telegraphs by guerillas. His orders, it is true, were
warranted by the practice of war. But 'forced requisitions,'
unless conducted on a well-understood system, must inevitably degenerate into plunder and oppression ; and Pope,
in punishing civilians, was not careful to distinguish between
the acts of guerillas and those of the regular Confederate
cavalry. 'These orders,' says a Northern historian, 'were
followed by the pillaging of private property, and by insults
to females to a degree unknown heretofore during the war.'
But in comparison with a third edict they were mild
and humane. On July 23 Pope's generals were instructed
to arrest every Virginian within the limits of their
commands, to administer the oath of allegiance to the
Union, and to expel from their homes all those who
refused to take it. This order was preceded by one from
General von Steinwehr, a German brigadier, directing the
arrest of five prominent citizens, to be held as hostages,
and to suffer death in the event of any soldiers being shot
by bushwhackers. The Confederate Government retaliated
by declaring that Pope and his officers were not entitled to
be considered as soldiers. If captured they were to be
imprisoned so long as their orders remained unrepealed ;
and in the event of any unarmed Confederate citizens being
tried and shot, an equal number of Federal prisoners were
to be hanged. It need hardly be added that the operations
north of Gordonsville were watched with peculiar interest
by the South. 'This new general,' it was said to Jackson,
' claims your attention.' 'And, please God, he shall have
it,' was the reply.

Nevertheless, with all his peculiar characteristics,
Pope was no despicable foe. The Federal cavalry were
employed with a boldness which had not hitherto been
seen. Their outposts were maintained twenty miles in
advance of the army. Frequent reconnaissances were
made. A regiment of Jackson's cavalry was defeated
at Orange Court House, with a loss of 60 or 70 men,
and scouting parties penetrated to within a few miles of
Gordonsville. Even Banks was spurred to activity, and
learned at last that information is generally to be obtained

if it is resolutely sought.[1] Very little that occurred within the Confederate lines escaped the vigilance of the enemy; and although Jackson's numbers were somewhat overestimated, Pope's cavalry, energetically led by two able young officers, Generals Buford and Bayard, did far better service than McClellan's detectives. Jackson had need of all his prudence. Including the Light Division, his force amounted to no more than 24,000 men; and if Pope handled his whole army with as much skill as he used his cavalry, it would go hard with Gordonsville. 24,000 men could hardly be expected to arrest the march of 47,000 unless the larger force should blunder.

During the first week in August events began to thicken. Stuart made a strong reconnaissance towards Fredericksburg, and administered a check to the Federal scouting parties in that quarter. But McClellan threw forward a division and occupied Malvern Hill, and it became evident that Pope also was meditating a further advance.

Jackson, for the purpose of luring him forward, and also of concealing Hill's arrival, had drawn back his cavalry, and moved his infantry south of Gordonsville. Pope was warned from Washington that this was probably a ruse. His confidence, however, was not to be shaken. ' Within ten days,' he reported, ' unless the enemy is heavily reinforced from Richmond, I shall be in possession of Gordonsville and Charlottesville.'

Although such an operation would carry Pope far from Washington there was no remonstrance from headquarters. Lincoln and Stanton, mistrustful at last of their ability as strategists, had called to their councils General Halleck, who had shown some evidence of capacity while in command of the Western armies. The new Commander-in-Chief had a difficult problem to work out. It is impossible to determine how far Jackson's movement to Gordonsville influenced the Federal authorities, but immediately on Halleck's arrival

---

[1] ' We must constantly feel the enemy, know where he is, and what he is doing. Vigilance, activity, and a precaution that has a considerable mixture of audacity in it will carry you through many difficulties.' Such were his instructions to an officer of the regular army! It was unfortunate he had not acted on those sound principles in the Valley.

at Washington, about the same date that the movement
was reported, he was urged, according to his own account,
to withdraw McClellan from the Peninsula. 'I delayed
my decision,' he says, ' as long as I dared delay it ; ' but on
August 3 his mind was made up, and McClellan, just after
Hill joined Jackson, was ordered to embark his army at
Fortress Monroe, sail to Aquia Creek, near Fredericksburg,
and join Pope on the Rappahannock. The proposed
combination, involving the transfer by sea of 90,000 men,
with all their artillery and trains, was a manœuvre full of
danger.[1] The retreat and embarkation of McClellan's troops
would take time, and the Confederates, possessing ' the
interior lines,' had two courses open to them :—

1. Leaving Jackson to check Pope, they might attack
McClellan as soon as he evacuated his intrenched position
at Harrison's Landing.

2. They might neglect McClellan and concentrate
against Pope before he could be reinforced.

Halleck considered that attack on McClellan was the
more likely, and Pope was accordingly instructed to threaten
Gordonsville, so as to force Lee to detach heavily from
Richmond, and leave him too weak to strike the Army of
the Potomac.

On August 6 Pope commenced his advance. Banks
had pushed a brigade of infantry from Sperryville to
Aug. 6.   Culpeper Court House, and Ricketts' division (of
McDowell's corps) was ordered to cross the Rappahannock at Waterloo Bridge and march to the same spot.
Jackson, whose spies had informed him of the enemy's dispositions, received early intelligence of Banks' movement, and
the next afternoon his three divisions were ordered forward,
marching by roads where there was no chance of their being
seen. ' He hoped,' so he wrote to Lee, ' through the blessing
of Providence, to defeat the advanced Federal detachment
before reinforcements should arrive.' This detachment was

---

[1] McClellan had received no further reinforcements than those sent from
Washington. Burnside, with 14,000 men, remained at Fortress Monroe
until the beginning of August, when he embarked for Aquia Creek,
concentrating on August 5. Hunter's troops were withheld.

his first objective; but he had long since recognised the strategic importance of Culpeper Court House. At this point four roads meet, and it was probable, from their previous dispositions, that the Federal army corps would use three of these in their advance. Pope's right wing at Sperryville would march by Woodville and Griffinsburg. His centre had already moved forward from Warrenton. His left wing at Falmouth, north of Fredericksburg, would march by Bealeton and Brandy Station, or by Richardsville and Georgetown. As all these roads were several miles apart, and the lateral communications were indifferent, the three columns, during the movement on Culpeper Court House, would be more or less isolated; and if the Confederates could seize the point at which the roads met, it might be possible to keep them apart, to prevent them combining for action, and to deal with them in detail. Pope, in fact, had embarked on a manœuvre which is always dangerous in face of a vigilant and energetic enemy. Deceived by the passive attitude which Jackson had hitherto maintained, and confident in the strength of his cavalry, which held Robertson River, a stream some ten miles south of Culpeper Court House, he had pushed a small force far in advance, and was preparing to cross Hazel Run in several widely separated columns. He had no apprehension that he might be attacked during the process. Most generals in Jackson's situation, confronted by far superior numbers, would have been content with occupying a defensive position in front of Gordonsville, and neither Pope nor Halleck had gauged as yet the full measure of their opponent's enterprise. So confident was the Federal Commander-in-Chief that General Cox, with 11,000 men, was ordered to march from Lewisburg, ninety miles southwest of Staunton, to join Pope at Charlottesville.[1]

Jackson's force was composed as follows:—

Jackson's Own Division (commanded by Winder)	3,000
Ewell	7,550
A. P. Hill (The Light Division) . . .	12,000
Cavalry	1,200
	23,750

[1] *Battles and Leaders*, vol. ii., p. 281.

Jackson was by no means displeased when he learned who was in command of the Federal advance. 'Banks is in front of me,' he said to Dr. McGuire, 'he is always ready to fight;' and then, laughing, he added as if to himself, 'and he generally gets whipped.'

The Confederate regiments, as a rule, were very weak. The losses of the Seven Days, of Winchester, of Cross Keys, and of Port Republic had not yet been replaced. Companies had dwindled down to sections. Brigades were no stronger than full battalions, and the colonel was happy who could muster 200 muskets. But the waste of the campaign was not altogether an evil. The weak and sickly had been weeded out. The faint-hearted had disappeared, and if many of the bravest had fallen before Richmond, those who remained were hardy and experienced soldiers. The army that lay round Gordonsville was the best that Jackson had yet commanded. The horses, which had become almost useless in the Peninsula, had soon regained condition on the rich pastures at the foot of the South-west Mountains. Nearly every man had seen service. The officers were no longer novices. The troops had implicit confidence in their leaders, and their *moral* was high. They had not yet tasted defeat. Whenever they had met the enemy he had abandoned the field of battle. With such troops much might be risked, and if the staff was not yet thoroughly trained, the district in which they were now operating was far less intricate than the Peninsula. As the troops marched westward from Richmond, with their faces towards their own mountains, the country grew more open, the horizon larger, and the breezes purer. The dark forests disappeared. The clear streams, running swiftly over rocky beds, were a welcome change from the swamps of the Chickahominy. North of Gordonsville the spurs of the Blue Ridge, breaking up into long chains of isolated hills, towered high above the sunlit plains. The rude tracks of the Peninsula, winding through the woods, gave place to broad and well-trodden highways. Nor did the marches now depend upon the guidance of some casual rustic or terrified negro. There were many in the Confederate ranks who were familiar with the country; and the quick pencil of Captain Hotchkiss, Jackson's trusted engineer, who had rejoined from the Valley, was once more at his disposal. Information, moreover, was not hard to come by. The country was far more thickly populated than the region about Richmond, and, notwithstanding Pope's harsh measures, he was unable to prevent the people communicating with their own army. If the men had been unwilling to take the risk, the women were quite ready to emulate the heroines of the Valley, and the conduct of the Federal marauders had served only to inflame their patriotism. Under such circumstances Jackson's task was relieved of half its difficulties. He was almost as much at home as on the Shenandoah, and although there were no Massanuttons to screen his movements, the hills to the north, insignificant as they might be when compared with the great mountains which divide the Valley, might still be turned to useful purpose.

On August 7, starting late in the afternoon, the Confederates marched eight miles by a country track, and halted Aug. 7. at Orange Court House. Culpeper was still twenty miles distant, and two rivers, the Rapidan and Robertson, barred the road. The Robertson was held by 5,000 or 6,000 Federal cavalry; five regiments, under General Buford, were near Madison Court House; four, under General Bayard, near Rapidan Station. East of the railway two more regiments held Raccoon Ford; others watched the Rappahannock as far as Fredericksburg, and on Thoroughfare Mountain, ten miles south-west of Culpeper, and commanding a view of the surrounding country as far as Orange Court House, was a signal station. Aug. 8. Early on the 8th, Ewell's division crossed the Rapidan at Liberty Mills, while the other divisions were ordered to make the passage at Barnett's Ford, six miles below. A forced march should have carried the Confederates to within striking distance of Culpeper, and a forced march was almost imperative. The cavalry had been in contact; the advance must already have been reported to Pope, and within twenty-four hours

the whole of the Federal army, with the exception of the
division at Fredericksburg, might easily be concentrated in
a strong position.

Still there were no grounds for uneasiness. If the
troops made sixteen miles before nightfall, they would be
before Culpeper soon after dawn, and sixteen miles was no
extraordinary march for the Valley regiments. But to
accomplish a long march in the face of the enemy, something is demanded more than goodwill and endurance on
the part of the men. If the staff arrangements are faulty,
or the subordinate commanders careless, the best troops
in the world will turn sluggards. It was so on August 8.
Jackson's soldiers never did a worse day's work during the
whole course of his campaigns. Even his energy was
powerless to push them forward. The heat, indeed, was
excessive. Several men dropped dead in the ranks; the
long columns dragged wearily through the dust, and the
Federal cavalry was not easily pushed back. Guns and
infantry had to be brought up before Bayard's dismounted
squadrons were dislodged. But the real cause of delay is
to be found elsewhere. Not only did General Hill misunderstand his orders, but, apparently offended by Jackson's
reticence, he showed but little zeal. The orders were
certainly incomplete. Nothing had been said about the
supply trains, and they were permitted to follow their divisions, instead of moving in rear of the whole force.
Ewell's route, moreover, was changed without Hill being
informed. The lines of march crossed each other, and
Hill was delayed for many hours by a long column of
ambulances and waggons. So tedious was the march
that when the troops halted for the night, Ewell had
made eight miles, Hill only two, and the latter was still
eighteen miles from Culpeper. Chagrined by the delay,
Jackson reported to Lee that 'he had made but little progress, and that the expedition,' he feared, 'in consequence
of his tardy movements, would be productive of little
good.'

How the blame should be apportioned it is difficult to
say. Jackson laid it upon Hill, and that officer's conduct

was undoubtedly reprehensible. The absence of Major
Dabney, struck down by sickness, is a possible explanation
of the faulty orders. But that Jackson would have done
better to have accepted Lee's hint, to have confided his
intentions to his divisional commanders, and to have
trusted something to their discretion, seems more than
clear. In war, silence is not invariably a wise policy. It
was not a case in which secresy was all-important. The
movement had already been discovered by the Federal
cavalry, and in such circumstances the more officers that
understood the intention of the general-in-chief the better.
Men who have been honoured with their leader's confidence,
and who grasp the purpose of the efforts they are called
upon to make, will co-operate, if not more cordially, at least
more intelligently, than those who are impelled by the sense
of duty alone.

As it was, so much time had been wasted that Jackson
would have been fully warranted in suspending the movement, and halting on the Rapidan. The Federals were
aware he was advancing. Their divisions were not so far
apart that they could not be concentrated within a few
hours at Culpeper, and, in approaching so close, he was
entering the region of uncertainty. Time was too pressing
to admit of waiting for the reports of spies. The enemy's
cavalry was far more numerous than his own, and screened
the troops in rear from observation. The information
brought in by the country people was not to be implicitly
relied on ; their estimate of numbers was always vague,
and it would be exceedingly difficult to make sure that the
force at Culpeper had not been strongly reinforced. It was
quite on the cards that the whole of Pope's army might
reach that point in the course of the next day, and in that
case the Confederates would be compelled to retreat, followed by a superior army, across two bridgeless rivers.

Nevertheless, the consideration of these contingencies
had no effect on Jackson's purpose. The odds, he decided,
were in his favour ; and the defeat of Pope's army in
detail, with all the consequences that might follow, was
worth risking much to bring about. It was still possible

that Pope might delay his concentration; it was still possible that an opportunity might present itself; and, as he had done at Winchester in March, when threatened by a force sevenfold stronger than his own, he resolved to look for that opportunity before he renounced his enterprise.

In speed and caution lay the only chance of success. The start on the 9th was early. Hill, anxious to redeem his shortcomings, marched long before daylight, and soon caught up with Ewell and Winder.
Aug. 9.
Half of the cavalry covered the advance; the remainder, screening the left flank, scouted west and in the direction of Madison Court House. Two brigades of infantry, Gregg's and Lawton's, were left in rear to guard the trains, for the Federal horsemen threatened danger, and the army, disembarrassed of the supply waggons, pressed forward across the Rapidan. Pushing the Federal cavalry before them, the troops reached Robertson River. The enemy's squadrons, already worn out by incessant reconnaissance and picket duty, were unable to dispute the passage, and forming a single column, the three divisions crossed the Locustdale Ford. Climbing the northern bank, the high-road to Culpeper, white with dust, lay before them, and to their right front, little more than two miles distant, a long wooded ridge, bearing the ominous name of Slaughter Mountain, rose boldly from the plain.

Ewell's division led the march, and shortly before noon, as the troops swept past the western base of Slaughter Mountain, it was reported that the Federal cavalry, massed in some strength, had come to a halt a mile or two north, on the bank of a small stream called Cedar Run.

The Confederate guns opened, and the hostile cavalry fell back; but from a distant undulation a Federal battery came into action, and the squadrons, supported by this fire, returned to their old position. Although Cedar Run was distant seven miles from Culpeper, it was evident, from the attitude of the cavalry, that the enemy was inclined to make a stand, and that in all probability Banks' army corps was in support.[1] Early's brigade, forming the advanced-

[1] This was the case. Banks had reached Culpeper on the 8th. On the

guard, which had halted in a wood by the roadside, was now ordered forward. Deploying to the right of the highway, it drove in the enemy's vedettes, and came out on the open ground which overlooks the stream. Across the shallow valley, covered with the high stalks and broad leaves of Indian corn, rose a loftier ridge, twelve hundred yards distant, and from more than one point batteries opened on the Confederate scouts. The regiments of the advanced-guard were immediately withdrawn to the reverse slope of the ridge, and Jackson galloped forward to the sound of the guns. His dispositions had been quickly made. A large force of artillery was ordered to come into action on either flank of the advanced-guard. Ewell's division was ordered to the right, taking post on the northern face of Slaughter Mountain; Winder was ordered to the left, and Hill, as soon as he came up, was to form the reserve, in rear of Winder. These movements took time. The Confederate column, 20,000 infantry and fifteen batteries, must have occupied more than seven miles of road; it would consequently take over two hours for the whole force to deploy for battle.

Before three o'clock, however, the first line was formed. On the right of the advanced-guard, near a clump of 2.45 P.M. cedars, were eight guns, and on Slaughter Mountain eight more. Along the high-road to the left six guns of Winder's division were soon afterwards 3 P.M. deployed, reinforced by four of Hill's. These twenty-six pieces, nearly the whole of the long-range ordnance which the Confederates possessed, were turned on the opposing batteries, and for nearly two hours the artillery thundered across the valley. The infantry, meanwhile, awaiting Hill's arrival, had come into line. Ewell's brigades, Trimble's, and the Louisianians (commanded by Colonel Forno) had halted in the woods on the extreme right, at the base of the mountain, threatening the enemy's flank. Winder had come up on the left, and had posted the Stonewall Brigade in rear of his guns; Campbell's

same day his advanced brigade was sent forward to Cedar Run, and was followed by the rest of the army corps on the 9th.

brigade, under Lieut.-Colonel Garnett, was stationed in front, west, and Taliaferro's brigade east, of the road. The 10,000 men of the Light Division, however, were still some distance to the rear, and the position was hardly secure against a counterstroke. The left of the line extended along a skirt of woodland, which ran at right angles to the road, overlooking a wheat-field but lately reaped, on the further side of which, and three hundred yards distant, was dense wood. This point was the most vulnerable, for there was no support at hand, and a great tract of forest stretched away westward, where cavalry was useless, but through which it was quite possible that infantry might force its way. Jackson ordered Colonel Garnett, commanding the brigade on this flank, 'to look well to his left, and to ask his divisional commander for reinforcements.' The brigadier sent a staff officer and an orderly to reconnoitre the forest to the left, and two officers were dispatched to secure the much-needed support.

But at this juncture General Winder was mortally wounded by a shell; there was some delay in issuing orders, and before the weak place in the line could be strengthened the storm broke. The enemy's batteries, five in number, although the concentrated fire of the Confederates had compelled them to change position, had not yet been silenced. No large force of Federal infantry had as yet appeared; skirmishers only had pushed forward through the corn; but the presence of so many guns was a clear indication that a strong force was not far off, and Jackson had no intention of attacking a position which had not yet been reconnoitred until his rear division had closed up, and the hostile artillery had lost its sting. About five o'clock, however, General

5 P.M.   Banks, although his whole force, including Bayard's cavalry, did not exceed 9,000 officers and men,[1] and Ricketts' division, in support, was four miles distant, gave orders for a general attack.[2] Two brigades, crossing the rise which formed the Federal position,

---

[1] 3,500 of Banks' army corps had been left at Winchester, and his sick were numerous.

[2] Banks had received an order from Pope which might certainly be understood to mean that he should take the offensive if the enemy approached.—*Report of Committee of Congress*, vol. iii., p. 45.

bore down on the Confederate centre, and strove to cross the stream. Early was hard pressed, but, Taliaferro's brigade advancing on his left, he held his own ; and on the highroad, raked by a Confederate gun, the enemy was unable to push forward. But within the wood to the left, at the very point where Jackson had advised precaution, the line of defence was broken through. On the edge of the timber commanding the wheat-field only two Confederate regiments were posted, some 500 men all told, and the 1st Virginia, on the extreme left, was completely isolated. The Stonewall Brigade, which should have been placed in second line behind them, had not yet received its orders; it was more than a half-mile distant, in rear of Winder's artillery, and hidden from the first line by the trees and undergrowth. Beyond the wheat-field 1,500 Federals, covered by a line of skirmishers, had formed up in the wood. Emerging from the covert with fixed bayonets and colours flying, their long line, overlapping the Confederate left, moved steadily across the three hundred yards of open ground. The shocks of corn, and some ragged patches of scrub timber, gave cover to the skirmishers, but in the closed ranks behind the accurate fire of the Southern riflemen made fearful ravages. Still the enemy pressed forward ; the skirmishers darted from bush to bush ; the regiments on the right swung round, enveloping the Confederate line ; and the 1st Virginia, despite the entreaties of its officers, broke and scattered.[1] Assailed in front from the field and in flank from the forest, the men would stand no longer, and flying back through the woodland, left the way open to the very rear of the position. The 42nd Virginia, outflanked in turn, was compelled to give ground ; and the Federals, without waiting to reform, swept rapidly through the wood, and bore down upon the flank of Taliaferro's brigade and Winder's batteries.

And now occurred a scene of terrible confusion. So swift was the onslaught that the first warning received by the Confederates on the highroad was a sudden storm

[1] O. R., vol. xii., part ii., p. 201.

H 2

of musketry, the loud cheers of the enemy, and the rush of
fugitives from the forest. Attacked simultaneously in front,
flank and rear, with the guns and limbers entangled among
the infantry, Winder's division was subjected to an ordeal of
which it was without experience. The batteries, by Jackson's order, were at once withdrawn, and not a gun was
lost. The infantry, however, did not escape so lightly. The
Federals, emboldened by the flight of the artillery, charged
forward with reckless courage. Every regimental commander in Garnett's brigade was either killed or wounded.
Taliaferro's brigade was driven back, and Early's left was
broken. Some regiments attempted to change front, others
retreated in disorder. Scattered groups, plying butt and
bayonet, endeavoured to stay the rout. Officers rushed into
the *mêlée*, and called upon those at hand to follow. Men
were captured and recaptured, and, for a few moments, the
blue and grey were mingled in close conflict amid the smoke.
But the isolated efforts of the Confederates were of no avail.
The first line was irretrievably broken; the troops were
mingled in a tumultuous mass, through which the shells
tore shrieking; the enemy's bayonets were surging forward
on every side, and his well-served batteries, firing over the
heads of their own infantry, played heavily on the road.
But fortunately for the Virginians the Federal right wing
was unsupported; and although the Light Division was
still at some distance from the field, the Stonewall Brigade
was already advancing. Breaking through the rout to the
left of the highroad, these five staunch regiments, undis-
mayed by the disaster, opened a heavy fire. The Federals,
although still superior in numbers at the decisive point, had
lost all order in their successful charge; to meet this fresh
onset they halted and drew together, and then Jackson,
with wonderful energy, restored the battle.

Sending orders for Ewell and A. P. Hill to attack at
once, he galloped forward, unattended by either staff
officer or orderly, and found himself in the midst of his
own men, his soldiers of the Valley, no longer presenting the
stubborn front of Bull Run or Kernstown, but an ungovern-
able mob, breaking rapidly to the rear, and on the very

verge of panic. Drawing his sword, for the first time in the war, his voice pealed high above the din ; the troops caught the familiar accents, instinct with resolution, and the presence of their own general acted like a spell. 'Rally, men,' he shouted, 'and follow me !' Taliaferro, riding up to him, emphatically insisted that the midst of the *mêlée* was no place for the leader of an army. He looked a little surprised, but with his invariable ejaculation of ' Good, good,' turned slowly to the rear. The impulse, however, had already been given to the Confederate troops. With a wild yell the remnant of the 21st Virginia rushed forward to the front, and received the pursuers with a sudden volley. The officers of other regiments, inspired by the example of their commander, bore the colours forward, and the men, catching the enthusiasm of the moment, followed in the path of the 21st. The Federals recoiled. Taliaferro and Early, reforming their brigades, again advanced upon the right ; and Jackson, his front once more established, turned his attention to the counterstroke he had already initiated.

Ewell was ordered to attack the Federal left. Branch, leading the Light Division, was sent forward to support the Stonewall Brigade, and Lane to charge down the highroad. Thomas was to give aid to Early. Archer and Pender, following Branch, were to outflank the enemy's right, and Field and Stafford were to follow as third line.

Ewell was unable to advance at once, for the Confederate batteries on Slaughter Mountain swept the whole field, and it was some time before they could be induced to cease fire. But on the left the mass of fresh troops, directed on the critical point, exerted a decisive influence. The Federal regiments, broken and exhausted, were driven back into the wood and across the wheat-field by the charge of the Stonewall Brigade. Still they were not yet done with. Before Hill's troops could come into action, Jackson's old regiments, as they advanced into the open, were attacked in front and threatened on the flank. The 4th and 27th Virginia were immediately thrown back to meet the more pressing danger, forming to the left within

the wood; but assailed in the confusion of rapid movement, they gave way and scattered through the thickets.
But the rift in the line was rapidly closed up. Jackson,
riding in front of the Light Division, and urging the
men to hold their fire and use their bayonets, rallied
the 27th and led them to the front; while Branch's
regiments, opening their ranks for the fugitives to pass
through, and pressing forward with unbroken line, drove
back the Northern skirmishers, and moving into the wheat-
field engaged their main body in the opposite wood.

Lane, meanwhile, was advancing astride the road.
Archer and Pender, in accordance with Jackson's orders,
were sweeping round through the forest, and Field and
Stafford were in rear of Branch. A fresh brigade had come
up to sustain the defeated Federals; but gallantly as
they fought, the Northerners could make no head against
overwhelming numbers. Outflanked to both right and
left, for Early and Ewell were now moving forward,
they began to yield. Jackson rode forward to the
wheat-field, and just at this moment Banks made a
despairing effort to extricate his infantry. Two squadrons, hitherto concealed by the woods, appeared suddenly on
the road, and, deploying into two lines, charged full against
the Confederate centre. The skirmishers were ridden
down; but the troops in rear stood firm, and several
companies, running to a fence along the highway, poured
a devastating fire into the mass of horsemen. Out of 174
officers and men only 71 rode back.[1]

This brilliant but useless exploit brought no respite to
the Federals. Archer and Pender had turned their right;
Ewell was pressing forward against their left,
6.30 P.M. scaling the ridge on which their batteries had been
posted; Early and Lane were pressing back their centre,
and their guns had already limbered up. Jackson, galloping
to the front, was received with the cheers of his victorious
troops. In every quarter of the field the enemy was in
full retreat, and as darkness began to fall the whole
Confederate line crossed Cedar Run and swept up the

[1] O. R., vol. xii., part ii., p. 141.

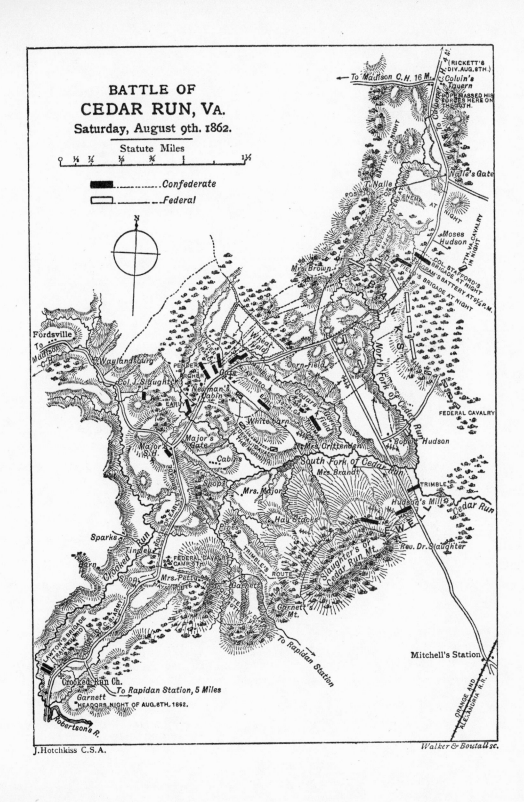

BATTLE OF
CEDAR RUN, VA.

Saturday, August 9th. 1862.

Statute Miles

▬▬▬ ....Confederate
▭ ....Federal

N

(RICKETT'S DIV. AUG. 8TH.)

Colvin's Tavern

POPE MASSED HIS FORCES HERE ON THE 9TH.

← To Madison C.H. 16 M.

To Culpeper C.H. 4 M.

Nalle's Gate

T. Nalle

Moses Hudson

FEDERAL BATTERY AT NIGHT

POSITION OF THE ENEMY AT NIGHT

7TH. VA. CAVALRY IN NIGHT

COL. STAFFORD'S BRIGADE AT NIGHT

PEGRAM'S BATTERY AT 9½ P.M.

Mrs. Brown

FIELD'S BRIGADE AT NIGHT

Wheat Field

Corn-field

Fordsville

To Madison C.H.

Waylandsburg

PENDER

ARCHER

GATE

Col. J. Slaughter

Newman's Cabin

EARLY

White Barn

Major's Gate

CEDAR CH'H.

Cedar's Field

Mrs. Crittenden

Robert Hudson

FEDERAL CAVALRY

North Fork of Cedar Run

Major's S.H.

Cabins

Shop

Mrs. Major

South Fork of Cedar Run

Mrs. Brandt

TRIMBLE

Hudson's Mill

Cedar Run

Hay Stacks

Pines

W. E.

Sparks

Tinsley's

Crooked Run

FEDERAL CAMP

Mrs. Petty

Garnett

TRIMBLE'S ROUTE

ROUTE OF GEN. EARLY

Slaughter's or Cedar Run Mt.

Rev. Dr. Slaughter

Mitchell's Station

LAWTON'S BRIGADE (TRANS'D) FORWARD

Garnett's Mt.

To Rapidan Station

Crooked Run Ch.

Garnett

HEADQRS. NIGHT OF AUG. 8TH. 1862.

→ To Rapidan Station, 5 Miles

Robertson's R.

ORANGE AND ALEXANDRIA R.R.

J. Hotchkiss C.S.A.

Walker & Boutall sc.

slopes beyond. Every yard of ground bore witness to the severity of the fighting. The slaughter had been very heavy. Within ninety minutes 3,000 men had fallen. The woods were a shambles, and among the corn the dead lay thick. Scores of prisoners surrendered themselves, and hundreds of discarded muskets bore witness to the demoralisation of the Northerners. Nevertheless, the pursuit was slow. The impetuosity of the Confederates, eager to complete their triumph, was checked with a firm hand. The infantry were ordered to reform before they entered the dense forest which lay between them and Culpeper. The guns, unable to cross Cedar Run except by the road, were brought over in a single column, and two fresh brigades, Field's and Stafford's, which had not yet fired a shot, were brought forward as advanced-guard. Although Jackson had been careful to bring guides who knew the woodland tracks, there was need for prudence. The light was failing; the cavalry could find no space to act; and, above all, the whereabouts of Pope's main body was still uncertain. The Federals had fought with fine courage. Their resolute attack, pressed home with extraordinary dash, had rolled up the choicest of the Valley regiments. And yet it was evident that only a small portion of the Northern army had been engaged. The stirring incidents of the battle had been crowded into a short space of time. It was five o'clock when the Federals left their covert. An hour and a half later they had abandoned the field. Their precipitate retreat, the absence of a strong rear-guard, were sure tokens that every regiment had been employed in the attack, and it was soon discovered by the Confederate soldiers that these regiments were old opponents of the Valley army. The men who had surprised and outflanked Jackson's old division were the same men that had been surprised at Front Royal and outflanked at Winchester. But Banks' army corps formed only a third part of Pope's army. Sigel and McDowell were still to be accounted for.

It was possible, however, that no more formidable enemies than the troops already defeated would be found between Cedar Run and Culpeper, and Jackson, intent upon securing that strategic point before morning,[1] pushed steadily forward. Of the seven miles that intervened between the battle-field and the Court House only one-and-a-half had been passed, when the scouts brought information that the enemy was in position a few hundred yards to the front. A battery was immediately sent forward to develop the situation. The moon was full, and on the far side of the glade where the advanced-guard, acting under Jackson's orders, had halted and deployed, a strong line of fire marked the hostile front. Once more the woodland avenues reverberated to the crash of musketry, and when the guns opened a portion of the Federal line was seen flying in disorder. Pope himself had arrived upon the scene, but surprised by the sudden salvo of Jackson's guns, he was constrained to do what he had never done in the West—to turn his back upon the enemy, and seek a safer position. Yet despite the disappearance of the staff the Union artillery made a vigorous reply. Two batteries, hidden by the timber, concentrated on the four guns of the advanced-guard, and about the same moment the Confederate cavalry on the extreme right reported that they had captured prisoners belonging to Sigel's army corps. ' Believing it imprudent,' says Jackson, ' to continue to move forward during the darkness, I ordered a halt for the night.'

Further information appears to have come to hand after midnight; and early the next morning General Stuart, who had arrived on a tour of inspection, having been placed in charge of the cavalry, ascertained beyond all question that the greater part of Pope's army had come up. The Confederates were ordered to withdraw, and before noon nearly the whole force had regained their old position on Cedar Run. They were not followed, save by the Federal cavalry; and for two days they remained in position, ready to receive attack. The enemy, however, gave no sign of aggressive intentions. On the morning of the 11th a flag of truce was received, and Pope was permitted to bury the dead which had not already been interred. The same

Aug. 10.

Aug. 11.

---

[1] Report. O. R., vol. xii., part ii., p. 184.

night, his wounded, his prisoners, and the captured arms
having already been removed, Jackson returned
to his old camps near Gordonsville. His position on Cedar Run, tactically strong, was strategically
unsound. The intelligence he had obtained was sub-
stantially correct. With the exception of five regiments
of McDowell's cavalry, only Banks' army corps had been
engaged at Cedar Run. But during the evening both Sigel
and McDowell had reached the field, and it was their
troops which had checked the Confederate pursuit. In fact,
on the morning of the 10th, Pope, besides 5,000 cavalry,
had 22,000 fresh troops in addition to those which had
been defeated, and which he estimated at 5,000 effectives,
wherewith to bar the way to Culpeper. McDowell's second
division, 10,000 strong, on the march from Fredericksburg, was not more than twenty miles east of Slaughter
Mountain.

In front, therefore, Jackson was confronted by superior
numbers. At the least estimate, 32,000 men were posted
beyond Cedar Run, and 10,000 under King were coming
up from Fredericksburg. Nor was a preponderance
of numbers the only obstacle with which Jackson had to
deal. A direct attack on Pope was impossible, but a turning movement, by way of James City, might have found him
unprepared, or a swift advance might have crushed King.
But for the execution of either manœuvre a large force of
cavalry was absolutely essential. By this means alone
could the march be concealed and a surprise effected.
In view, however, of the superior strength of the Federal
horsemen such a project was unfeasible, and retreat
was manifestly the only alternative. Nevertheless, it
was not till he was assured that no further opportunity
would be given him that Jackson evacuated his position.
For two days he remained on Cedar Run, within two
miles of the Federal outposts, defying his enemy to
battle. If an attack on the Federals promised nothing
but defeat, it was not so sure that Pope with 27,000 infantry,
of whom a considerable number had just tasted defeat,
would be able to oust Jackson with 22,000 from a position

which the latter had selected ; and it was not till King's approach gave the Federals an overwhelming superiority that the Confederates withdrew behind the Rapidan.

With sublime audacity, as soon as his enemy had disappeared, Pope claimed the battle of Cedar Run as a Federal success. Carried away by enthusiasm he ventured to forecast the future. 'It is safe to predict,' he declared in a general order, 'that this is only the first of a series of victories which shall make the Army of Virginia famous in the land.' That such language, however, was the natural result of intense relief at Jackson's retreat may be inferred from his telegrams, which, unfortunately for his reputation, have been preserved in the archives of Washington. Nor was his attitude on the 10th and 11th that of a victorious commander. For two days he never stirred from his position. He informed Halleck that the enemy was in very superior force, that Stuart and Longstreet had joined Jackson, and while the Confederates were withdrawing he was telegraphing that he would certainly be attacked the next morning.

Halleck's reply to Pope's final dispatch, which congratulated the defeated army corps on a ' hard-earned but brilliant success,' must have astonished Banks and his hapless troops. They might indeed be fairly considered to have 'covered themselves with glory.' [1] 9,000 men, of which only 7,000 were infantry, had given an enemy of more than double their strength a hard fight. They had broken some of the best troops in the Confederate army, under their most famous leader; and if they had been overwhelmed by numbers, they had at least fought to the last man. Jackson himself bore witness to the vigour of their onslaught, to their 'temporary triumph,' and to the 'impetuous valour' of their cavalry. The Federal defeat was more honourable than many victories. But that it was a crushing defeat can hardly be disputed. The two divisions which had been engaged were completely shattered, and Pope reported that they were no longer fit for service. The casualties amongst the infantry amounted to a third

[1] O. R., vol. xii., part ii., p. 135.

of the total strength. Of the brigade that had driven
in the Confederate left the 28th New York lost the
whole of its company officers ; the 5th Connecticut 17 officers
out of 20, and the 10th Maine had 170 killed or wounded.
In two brigades nearly every field-officer and every adjutant
was struck down. The 2nd Massachusetts, employed in
the last effort to hold back Jackson's counterstroke, lost 16
officers out of 23, and 147 men out of 451. The Ohio regiments, which had been with Shields at Kernstown and Port
Republic, and had crossed Cedar Run opposite the Confederate centre, were handled even more roughly. The 5th
lost 118 men out of 275, the 7th 10 officers out of 14, and
170 men out of 293. Two generals were wounded and one
captured. 400 prisoners, three stand of colours, 5,000
rifles and one gun were taken by the Southerners, and,
including those suffered by Sigel and McDowell in the
night action, the sum of losses reached 2,380. The Confederates by no means came off scatheless. General
Winder died upon the field, and the two brigades that
stood the brunt of the attack, together with Early's,
suffered heavily. But the number of killed and wounded
amounted to no more than 1,314, and many of the brigades
had few losses to report. The spirit of the Valley troops
was hardly to be tamed by such punishment as this.
Nevertheless, Northern historians have not hesitated to
rank Cedar Run as a battle unfavourable to the Confederates. Swinton declares that Jackson undertook the pursuit of Banks, ' *under the impression* that he had gained
a victory.' [1] Southern writers, on the other hand, have
classed Cedar Run amongst the most brilliant achievements of the war, and an unbiassed investigation goes
far to support their view.

During the first week in August Jackson, protecting the
Virginia Central Railroad, was confronted by a much
superior force. He could expect no further reinforcements,

[1] I may here express my regret that in the first edition I should have
classed Mr. Ropes amongst the adverse critics of Jackson's operations at this
period. How I came to fall into the error I cannot explain. I should certainly
have remembered that Mr. Ropes' writings are distinguished as much by
impartiality as by ability.

for McClellan was still near Richmond, and according to
the latest information was actually advancing. On the
7th he heard that Pope also was moving forward from
Hazel Run, and had pushed a portion of his army as far
as Culpeper. In face of the overwhelming strength of
the Federal cavalry it was impossible, if he occupied a defensive position, that he could protect the railroad; for
while their infantry and artillery held him in front, their
swarming squadrons would operate at their leisure on
either flank. Nor could a defensive position have been
long maintained. There were no natural obstacles, neither
river nor mountains, to protect Jackson's flanks; and
the railroad—his line of supply—would have been parallel
to his front. In a vigorous offensive, then, should opportunity offer, lay his best chance of success. That
opportunity was offered by the unsupported advance
of the Federal detachment under Banks. It is true that
Jackson hoped to achieve more than the defeat of this
comparatively small force. If he could have seized Culpeper he might have been able to deal with Pope's army
in detail; he saw before him another Valley campaign,
and he was fully justified in believing that victory on
the Rapidan would bring McClellan back to Washington.

His anticipations were not altogether realised. He
crushed the detachment immediately opposed to him, but he
failed to seize Culpeper, and McClellan had already been
ordered, although this was unknown to the Confederates, to
evacuate the Peninsula. But it cannot be fairly said that
his enterprise was therefore useless. Strategically it was a
fine conception. The audacity of his manœuvre was not the
least of its merits. For an army of 24,000 men, weak in
cavalry, to advance against an army of 47,000, including
5,000 horsemen, was the very height of daring. But it was
the daring of profound calculation. As it was, Jackson ran
little risk. He succeeded in his immediate object. He
crushed Pope's advanced-guard, and he retreated unmolested, bearing with him the prisoners, the colours, and the
arms which he had captured. If he did not succeed in
occupying Culpeper, it was not his fault. Fortune was against

him. On the very day that he had moved forward Pope had done the same. Banks and McDowell were at Culpeper on the 8th, and Sigel received orders to move the same day.

Nevertheless the expedition was far from barren in result. If Jackson failed to defeat Pope altogether, he at least 'singed his beard.' It was well worth the loss of 1,300 men to have destroyed two whole divisions under the very eyes of the general commanding a superior army. A few days later Pope was to feel the want of these gallant regiments,[1] and the confidence of his troops in their commander was much shaken. Moreover, the blow was felt at Washington. There was no more talk of occupying Gordonsville. Pope was still full of ardour. But Halleck forbade him to advance further than the Rapidan, where Burnside would reinforce him ; and McClellan was ordered to hasten the departure of his troops from the Peninsula.

Jackson's tactics have been criticised as severely as his strategy. Because his first line was broken it is asserted that he narrowly escaped a serious defeat, and that had the two forces been equally matched Banks would have won a decisive victory. This is hardly sound criticism. In the first place, Jackson was perfectly well aware that the two forces were not equally matched. If he had had no more men than Banks, would he have disposed his forces as he did ? He would scarcely have occupied the same extent of ground with 9,000 men that he did with 20,000. His actual front, when Banks attacked, was two miles long. With smaller numbers he would have occupied a smaller front, and would have retained a sufficient force in reserve. In the second place, it is generally possible for an inferior force, if it puts every man into the fighting-line, to win some measure of success. But such success, as was shown at Kernstown, can seldom be more than temporary ; and if the enemy makes good use of his reserves must end in defeat.

[1] So late as August 23, Pope reported that Banks' troops were much demoralised. O. R., vol. xii., part iii., p. 653.

So far from Jackson's tactics being indifferent, it is very easy to show that they were exactly the contrary. Immediately he came upon the field he sent Ewell to occupy Slaughter Mountain, a mile distant from his line of march; and the huge hill, with batteries planted on its commanding terraces, not only secured his flank, but formed a strong pivot for his attack on the Federal right. The preliminary operations were conducted with due deliberation. There was no rushing forward to the attack while the enemy's strength was still uncertain. The ridge occupied by the enemy, so far as possible, was thoroughly reconnoitred, and every rifled gun was at once brought up. The artillery positions were well selected, for, notwithstanding their superiority of ordnance, the Federal batteries suffered far more heavily than the Confederates. The one weak point was the extreme left, and to this point Jackson in person directed the attention of his subordinates. 'Had reinforcements,' says Colonel Garnett, who commanded the troops that first gave way, 'momentarily expected, arrived ten minutes sooner no disaster would have happened.'[1] That the point was not strengthened, that the Stonewall Brigade was not posted in second line behind the 1st Virginia, and that only a staff officer and an orderly were sent to patrol the forest to the westward, instead of several companies of infantry, was in no way due to the general-in-chief.

Nor was the position of A. P. Hill's division, which, in conjunction with the Stonewall Brigade, averted the disaster and won the victory, a fortuitous circumstance. Before the attack began it had been directed to this point, and the strong counterstroke which was made by these fresh troops was exactly the manœuvre which the situation demanded. At the time it was ordered the Confederate left and centre were hard pressed. The Stonewall Brigade had checked the troops which had issued from the forest, but the whole Confederate line was shaken. The normal, though less brilliant, course would have been to have re-established the front, and not

[1] O. R., vol. xii., part ii., p. 201.

till that had been done to have ventured on the counterstroke. Jackson, with that quick intuition which is possessed by few, saw and seized his opportunity while the
Federals were still pressing the attack. One of Hill's brigades was sent to support the centre, and, almost in the
same breath, six others, a mass of 7,000 or 8,000 men, were
ordered to attack the enemy's right, to outflank it, and to
roll back his whole line upon Ewell, who was instructed at
the same moment to outflank the left. Notwithstanding
some delay in execution, Ewell's inability to advance, and
the charge of the Federal cavalry, this vigorous blow changed
the whole aspect of the battle within a short half-hour.
Conceived in a moment, in the midst of wild excitement
and fierce tumult, delivered with all the strength available, it cannot be judged otherwise than as the mark
of a great captain. Few battles, indeed, bear the impress
of a single personality more clearly than Cedar Run.
From the first cannon-shot of the advanced-guard until
the last volley in the midnight forest, one will directed
every movement. The field was no small one. The fight
was full of startling changes. It was no methodical
conflict, but a fierce struggle at close quarters, the lines
swaying to and fro, and the ground covered with confused
masses of men and guns, with flying batteries and broken
regiments. But the turmoil of battle found a master. The
strong brain was never clearer than when the storm raged
most fiercely. Wherever his presence was most needed
there Jackson was seen, rallying the fugitives, reinforcing
the centre, directing the counterstroke, and leading the
pursuit. And he was well supported. His subordinate
generals carried out their orders to the letter. But every
order which bore upon the issue of the battle came from
the lips of one man.

If Northern writers have overlooked the skill with which
Jackson controlled the fight, they have at the same time
misunderstood his action two days later. His retreat to
Gordonsville has been represented as a flight. He is said to
have abandoned many wounded and stragglers, and to have
barely saved his baggage. In all this there is not one word

of truth. We have, indeed, the report of the Federal officer who conducted the pursuit. ' The flight of the enemy after Saturday's fight was most precipitate and in great confusion. His old camp was strewn with dead men, horses, and arms. . . . A good many (Federal) prisoners, wounded in Saturday's fight, were found almost abandoned. Major Andrews, chief of artillery to General Jackson, was found, badly wounded, at Crooked Run, in charge of an assistant surgeon.' It is hardly necessary to say that General Buford, the officer thus reporting, had not been present at the battle. He had been cut off with his four regiments by the advance of the Confederate cavalry, and had retired on Sperryville. He may accordingly be excused for imagining that a retreat which had been postponed for two days was precipitate. But dead men, dead horses, and old arms which the Confederates had probably exchanged for those which were captured, several wounded Federals, who had been prisoners in the enemy's hands, and one wounded Confederate, a major of horse-artillery and not a staff-officer at all, are hardly evidences of undue haste or great confusion. Moreover, in the list of Confederate casualties only thirty-one men were put down as missing.

It is true that Jackson need not have retreated so far as Gordonsville. He might have halted behind the Rapidan, where the bluffs on the south bank overlook the level country to the north. But Jackson's manœuvres, whether in advance or retreat, were invariably actuated by some definite purpose, and what that purpose was he explains in his dispatches.[1] ' I remained in position until the night of the 11th, when I returned to the vicinity of Gordonsville, in order to avoid being attacked by the vastly superior force in front of me, *and with the hope that by thus falling back, General Pope would be induced to follow me until I should be reinforced.*' That Pope, had he been left to his own judgment, would have crossed the Rapidan is certain. 'The enemy,' he reported, 'has retreated to Gordonsville. . . . I shall move forward on Louisa Court House as soon as Burnside arrives.' He was restrained, however,

[1] O. R., vol. xii., part ii., p. 185.

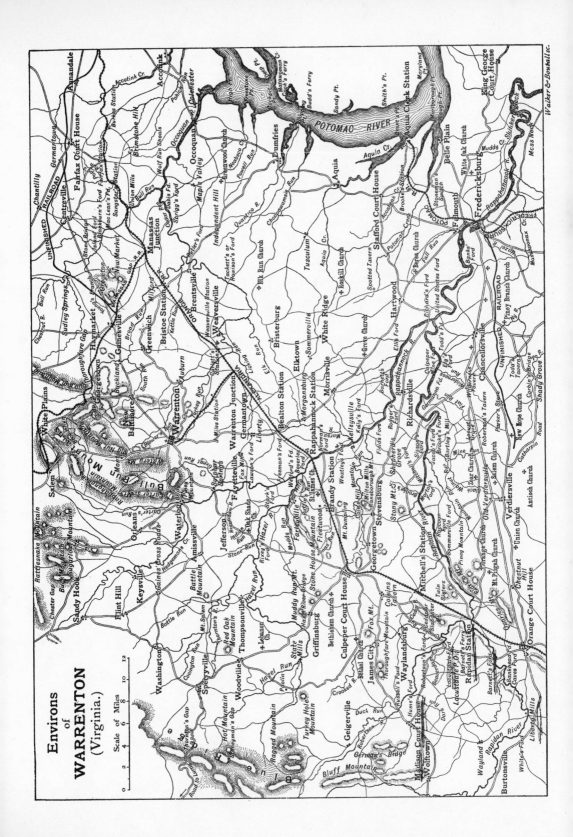

Environs
of
WARRENTON
(Virginia.)

Scale of Miles

Walker & Boutall sc.

by the more wary Halleck. 'Beware of a snare,' wrote the Commander-in-Chief. 'Feigned retreats are "Secesh" tactics.' How wise was this warning, and what would have been the fate of Pope had he recklessly crossed the Rapidan, the next chapter will reveal.

CHAPTER XVI

GROVETON AND THE SECOND MANASSAS

DURING the summer of 1862 the stirring events in the Western hemisphere attracted universal attention. All eyes were fixed on Richmond. The fierce fighting on the Chickahominy, and the defeat of the invaders, excited Europe hardly less than it did the North. The weekly mails were eagerly awaited. The newspapers devoted many columns to narrative, criticism, and prediction. The strategy and tactics of the rival armies were everywhere discussed, and the fact that almost every single item of intelligence came from a Northern source served only as a whet to curiosity. The vast territory controlled by the Confederacy was so completely cut off from the outer world that an atmosphere of mystery enveloped the efforts of the defence. 'The Southern States,' it has been said, 'stood in the attitude of a beleaguered fortress. The war was in truth a great siege; the fortress covered an area of more than 700,000 square miles, and the lines of investment around it extended over more than 10,000 miles.' Within the circle of Federal cannon and Federal cruisers only the imagination could penetrate. At rare intervals some daring blockade-runner brought a budget of Southern newspapers, or an enterprising correspondent succeeded in transmitting a dispatch from Richmond. But such glimpses of the situation within the cordon did little more than tantalise. The news was generally belated, and had often been long discounted by more recent events. Still, from Northern sources alone, it was abundantly clear that the weaker of the two belligerents was making a splendid struggle. Great names and great achievements loomed large through the darkness. The war at the outset, waged by ill-trained and ill-disciplined volunteers, commanded by officers unknown to fame, had attracted small notice from professional soldiers. After the Seven Days' battles it assumed a new aspect. The men, despite their shortcomings, had displayed undeniable courage, and the strategy which had relieved Richmond recalled the master-strokes of Napoleon. It was evident that the Southern army was led by men of brilliant ability, and the names of Lee's lieutenants were on every tongue. Foremost amongst these was Stonewall Jackson. Even the Northern newspapers made no scruple of expressing their admiration, and the dispatches of their own generals gave them constant opportunities of expatiating on his skill. During the first weeks of August, the reports from the front, whether from Winchester, from Fredericksburg, or from the Peninsula, betrayed the fear and uneasiness he inspired. The overthrow of Pope's advanced-guard at Cedar Run, followed by the unaccountable disappearance of the victorious army, was of a piece with the manœuvres in the Valley. What did this disappearance portend? Whither had the man of mystery betaken himself? Where would the next blow fall? 'I don't like Jackson's movements,' wrote McClellan to Halleck; 'he will suddenly appear when least expected.' This misgiving found many echoes. While Jackson was operating against Pope, McClellan had successfully completed the evacuation of Harrison's Landing. Embarking his sick, he marched his five army corps to Fortress Monroe, observed by Lee's patrols, but otherwise unmolested. The quiescence of the Confederates, however, brought no relief to the North. Stocks fell fast, and the premium on gold rose to sixteen per cent. For some days not a shot had been fired along the Rapidan. Pope's army rested in its camps. Jackson had completely vanished. But the silence at the front was not considered a reassuring symptom.

If the Confederates had allowed McClellan to escape, it was very generally felt that they had done so only because they were preparing to crush Pope before he could be reinforced. 'It is the fear of this operation,' wrote the *Times* Special Correspondent in the Northern States, 'conducted by the redoubtable Stonewall Jackson, that has filled New York with uneasy forebodings. Wall Street does not ardently believe in the present good fortune or the future prospects of the Republic.'[1]

Neither the knowledge which McClellan possessed of his old West Point comrade, nor the instinct of the financiers, proved misleading. Jackson had already made his plans. Even before he had lured Pope forward to the Rapidan he had begun to plot his downfall. 'When we were marching back from Cedar Run,' writes Major Hotchkiss, 'and had passed Orange Court House on our way to Gordonsville, the general, who was riding in front of the staff, beckoned me to his side. He at once entered into conversation, and said that as soon as we got back to camp he wished me to prepare maps of the whole country between Gordonsville and Washington, adding that he required several copies—I think five. This was about noon on Sunday, and as we were near camp I asked him

Aug. 13. if the map was to be begun immediately, knowing his great antipathy to doing anything on Sunday which was not a work of necessity. He replied that it was important to have it done at once.'[2] The next day,

Aug. 14. August 14, the exact position of the Federal army was ascertained. The camps were north and east of Slaughter Mountain, and Jackson instructed Captain Boswell, his chief engineer, who had lived in the neighbourhood, to report on the best means of turning the enemy's left flank and reaching Warrenton, thus intervening between Pope and Washington, or between Pope and Aquia Creek. The line of march recommended by Boswell led through Orange Court House to Pisgah Church, and crossing the Rapidan at Somerville Ford, ran by Lime Church and Stevensburg to Brandy Station.

Aug. 15. On the night of the 15th, after two days' rest, the three divisions moved from Gordonsville to Pisgah Church, and there halted to await reinforcements.

---

[1] The *Times*, September 4, 1862.   [2] Letter to the author.

These were already on their way. On the 13th General Lee had learned that Burnside, who had already left the Peninsula for Aquia Creek on the Potomac, was preparing to join Pope, and it was reported by a deserter that part of McClellan's army had embarked on the transports at Harrison's Landing. Inferring that the enemy had relinquished all active operations in the Peninsula, and that Pope would soon be reinforced by the Army of the Potomac, Lee resolved to take the offensive without delay. The campaign which Jackson had suggested more than a month before, when McClellan was still reeling under the effects of his defeat, and Pope's army was not yet organised, was now to be begun. The same evening the railway conveyed Longstreet's advanced brigade to Gordonsville, and with the exception of D. H. Hill's and McLaws' divisions, which remained to watch McClellan, the whole army followed.

On the 15th Lee met his generals in council. The map drawn by Captain Hotchkiss was produced, and the manœuvre which had suggested itself to Jackson was definitely ordered by the Commander-in-Chief. The Valley army, at dawn on the 18th, was to cross the Rapidan at Somerville Ford. Longstreet, preceded by Stuart, who was to cut the Federal communications in rear of Culpeper Court House, was to make the passage at Raccoon Ford. Jackson's cavalry was to cover the left and front, and Anderson's division was to form a general reserve. The movement was intended to be speedy. Only ambulances and ammunition waggons were to follow the troops. Baggage and supply trains were to be parked on the south side of the Rapidan, and the men were to carry three days' cooked rations in their haversacks.

On Clark's Mountain, a high hill near Pisgah Church, Jackson had established a signal station. The view from the summit embraced an extensive landscape. The ravages of war had not yet effaced its tranquil beauty, nor had the names of its bright rivers and thriving villages become household words. It was still unknown to history, a peaceful and pastoral district, remote from the beaten tracks of trade and travel, and inhabited by a quiet and industrious people.   To-day there are few regions which boast sterner or more heroic memories.   To the right, rolling away in light and shadow for a score of miles, is the great forest of Spotsylvania, within whose gloomy depths lie the fields of Chancellorsville; where the breast-works of the Wilderness can still be traced ; and on the eastern verge of which stand the grass-grown batteries of Fredericksburg.   Northward, beyond the woods which hide the Rapidan, the eye ranges over the wide and fertile plains of Culpeper, with the green crest of Slaughter Mountain overlooking Cedar Run, and the dim levels of Brandy Station, the scene of the great cavalry battle,[1] just visible beyond.   Far away to the north-east the faint outline of a range of hills marks the source of Bull Run and the Manassas plateau, and to the west, the long rampart of the Blue Ridge, softened by distance, stands high above the Virginia plains.

On the afternoon of August 17, Pope's forces seemed doomed to inevitable destruction.   The Confederate army, Aug. 17.   ready to advance the next morning, was con-centrated behind Clark's Mountain, and Lee and Jackson, looking toward Culpeper, saw the promise of victory in the careless attitude of the enemy.   The day was hot and still.   Round the base of Slaughter Mountain, fifteen miles northward, clustered many thousands of tents, and the blue smoke of the camp-fires rose straight and thin in the sultry air.   Regiments of infantry, just discernible through the glare, were marching and countermarching in various directions, and long waggon-trains were creeping slowly along the dusty roads.   Near at hand, rising above the tree-tops, the Union colours showed that the outposts still held the river, and the flash of steel at the end of some woodland vista betrayed the presence of scouting party or vedette.   But there were no symptoms of unusual excitement, no sign of working parties, of reinforcements for the advanced posts, of the construction of earthworks or abattis.   Pope's camps were scattered over a wide tract of

[1] June 9, 1863.

country, his cavalry was idle, and it seemed absolutely
certain that he was unconscious of the near neighbourhood
of the Confederate army.

The inference was correct.   The march to Pisgah
Church had escaped notice.   The Federals were unaware
that Lee had arrived at Gordonsville, and they had as yet
no reason to believe that there was the smallest danger of
attack.

Between Raccoon and Locustdale fords, and stretching
back to Culpeper Court House, 52,500 men—for Reno,with
two divisions of Burnside's army, 8,000 strong, had arrived
from Fredericksburg—were in camp and bivouac. The front
was protected by a river nearly a hundred yards wide, of
which every crossing was held by a detachment, and Pope
had reported that his position was so strong that it would
be difficult to drive him from it.   But he had not made
sufficient allowance for the energy and ability of the Confederate leaders.   His situation, in reality, was one of
extreme danger.   In ordering Pope to the Rapidan, and bid-
ding him 'fight like the devil' [1] until McClellan should come
up, Halleck made the same fatal error as Stanton, when
he sent Shields up the Luray Valley in pursuit of Jackson.
He had put an inferior force within reach of an enemy
who held the interior lines, and had ordered two armies,
separated by several marches, to effect their concentration
under the fire of the enemy's guns. And if Pope's strategical
position was bad, his tactical position was even worse.   His
left, covering Raccoon and Somerville Fords, was very
weak.   The main body of his army was massed on the
opposite flank, several miles distant, astride the direct road
from Gordonsville to Culpeper Court House, and he remained without the least idea, so late as the morning of
the 18th, that the whole Confederate army was concentrated
behind Clark's Mountain, within six miles of his most
vulnerable point.   Aware that Jackson was based on
Gordonsville, he seems to have been convinced that if
he advanced at all, he would advance directly on Culpeper

---

[1] O. R., vol. xii., part ii., p. 57.   'It may have been fortunate for the Confederates,' says Longstreet, 'that he was not instructed to *fight like Jackson*.'

Court House ; and the move to Pisgah Church, which left Gordonsville unprotected, never entered into his calculations.   A sudden attack against his left was the last contingency that he anticipated ; and had the Confederates moved as Lee intended, there can be no question but that the Federal army, deprived of all supplies, cut off from Washington, and forced to fight on ground where it was unprepared, would have been disastrously defeated.

But it was not to be.   The design was thwarted by one of those petty accidents which play so large a part in war. Stuart had been instructed to lead the advance.   The only brigade at his disposal had not yet come up into line, but a message had been sent to appoint a rendezvous, and it was expected to reach Verdiersvílle, five miles from Raccoon Ford, on the night of the 17th.   Stuart's message, however, was not sufficiently explicit.   Nothing was said of the exigencies of the situation ; and the brigadier, General Fitzhugh Lee, not realising the importance of reaching Verdiersville on the 17th, marched by a circuitous route in order to replenish his supplies.   At nightfall he was still absent, and the omission of a few words in a simple order cost the Confederates dear.   Moreover, Stuart himself, who had ridden to Verdiersville with a small escort, narrowly escaped capture.   His plumed hat, with which the whole army was familiar, as well as his adjutant-general and his dispatch-box, fell into the hands of a Federal reconnoitring party ; and among the papers brought to Pope was found a letter from General Lee, disclosing the fact that Jackson had been strongly reinforced.

In consequence of the absence of Fitzhugh Lee's brigade, the movement was postponed until the morning of the 20th.   The Commander-in-Chief was of opinion that the horses, exhausted by their long march, would require some rest before they were fit for the hard work he proposed for them.   Jackson, for once in opposition, urged that the movement should go forward.   His signal officer on Clark's Mountain reported that the enemy was quiet, and even extending his right up stream.   The location of the Federal divisions had been already ascertained.   The cavalry was not required to get information. There was no need, therefore, to wait till Fitzhugh Lee's brigade was fit for movement. Jackson had, with his own command, a sufficient number of squadrons to protect the front and flanks of the whole army ; and the main object was not to cut the enemy's communications, but to turn his left and annihilate him. Pope was still isolated, still unconscious of his danger, and the opportunity might never return.

The suggestion, however, was overruled, and 'it was fortunate,' says one of Pope's generals, 'that Jackson was not in command of the Confederates on the night of August 17 ; for the superior force of the enemy must have overwhelmed us, if we could not have escaped, and escape on that night was impossible.'[1]

It is probable, however, that other causes induced General Lee to hold his hand. There is good reason to believe that it was not only the cavalry that was unprepared. The movement from Richmond had been rapid, and both vehicles and supplies had been delayed. Nor were all the generals so avaricious of time as Jackson. It was impossible, it was urged, to move without some food in the waggons. Jackson replied that the enemy had a large magazine at Brandy Station, which might easily be captured, and that the intervening district promised an abundance of ripening corn and green apples. It was decided, however, that such fare, on which, it may be said, the Confederates learned afterwards to subsist for many days in succession, was too meagre for the work in hand. Jackson, runs the story, groaned so audibly when Lee pronounced in favour of postponement, that Longstreet called the attention of the Commander-in-Chief to his apparent disrespect.

Be this as it may, had it been possible to adopt Jackson's advice, the Federal army would have been caught in the execution of a difficult manœuvre. On the morning of the 18th, about the very hour that the advance should have begun, Pope was informed by a spy that the Confederate army was assembled behind Clark's

Aug. 18.

[1] General George H. Gordon. *The Army of Virginia*, p. 9.

Mountain and the neighbouring hills; that the artillery horses were harnessed, and that the troops were moment-arily expecting orders to cross the river and strike his rear. He at once made preparations for retreat. The trains moved off to seek shelter behind the Rappahannock, and the army followed, leaving the cavalry in position, and marching as follows :—

Reno by Stevensburg to Kelly's Ford.
Banks and McDowell by Culpeper Court House and Brandy Station
    to the Rappahannock railway bridge.
Sigel by Rixeyville to Sulphur Springs.

The march was slow and halts were frequent. The long lines of waggons blocked every road, and on the morning of August 19 the troops were still at Aug. 19. some distance from the Rappahannock, in neither condition nor formation to resist a resolute attack.

The movement, however, was not discovered by the Con-federates until it had been more than four-and-twenty hours in progress. General Lee, on August 19, had taken his stand on Clark's Mountain, but the weather was unfavourable for observation. Late in the afternoon the haze lifted, and almost at the same moment the remaining tents of the Federal army, fifteen miles away to the north-west, sud-denly vanished from the landscape, and great clouds of dust, rising high above the woods, left it no longer doubtful that Pope had taken the alarm. It was too late to inter-fere, and the sun set on an army baffled of its prey. In the Confederate councils there was some dismay, among the troops much heart-burning. Every hour that was wasted brought nearer the junction of Pope and McClellan, and the soldiers were well aware that a most promising opportunity, which it was worth while living on green corn and apples to secure, had been allowed to slip. Nevertheless, the pursuit was prompt. By the light of the rising moon the advanced-guards plunged thigh-deep into the clear waters of the Aug. 20. Rapidan, and the whole army crossed by Raccoon and Somerville Fords. Stuart, with Robertson's and Fitzhugh Lee's brigades, pressed forward on the traces of the retreating foe. Near Brandy Station the Federal cavalry made a stubborn stand. The Confederates, covering a wide front, had become separated. Robertson had marched through Stevensburg, Fitzhugh Lee on Kelly's Ford, an interval of six miles dividing the two brigades; and when Robertson was met by Bayard's squadrons, holding a skirt of woods with dismounted men, it was several hours before a sufficient force could be assembled to force the road. Towards evening two of Fitzhugh Lee's regiments came up, and the Confederates were now concentrated in superior numbers. A series of vigorous charges, delivered by successive regiments on a front of fours, for the horsemen were confined to the road, hurried the retreating Federals across the Rappahannock; but the presence of infantry and guns near the railway bridge placed an effective barrier in the way of further pursuit. Before nightfall Jackson's advanced-guard reached Brandy Station, after a march of twenty miles, and Longstreet bivouacked near Kelly's Ford.

The Rappahannock, a broad and rapid stream, with banks high and well-timbered, now rolled between the hostile armies. Pope, by his timely retreat, had gained a position where he could be readily reinforced, and although the river, in consequence of the long drought, had much dwindled from its usual volume, his front was perfectly secure.

The situation with which the Confederate commander had now to deal was beset by difficulties. The delay from August 18 to August 20 had been most unfortunate. The Federals were actually nearer Richmond than the Army of Northern Virginia, and if McClellan, landing as Burnside had done at Aquia Creek, were to move due south through Fredericksburg, he would find the capital but feebly garrisoned. It was more probable, however, that he would reinforce Pope, and Lee held fast to his idea of crushing his enemies in detail. Aquia Creek was only thirty-five miles' march from the Rappahannock, but the disembarkation with horses, trains, and artillery must needs be a lengthy process, and it might still be possible, by skilful and swift

manœuvres, to redeem the time which had been already lost.
But the Federal position was very strong. Early on the
21st it was ascertained that Pope's whole army was massed
Aug. 21.   on the left bank of the Rappahannock, extending
          from Kelly's Ford to Hazel Run, and that a
powerful artillery crowned the commanding bluffs. To
turn the line of the river from the south was hardly
practicable. The Federal cavalry was vigilant, and Pope
would have quietly fallen back on Washington. A turning movement from the north was more promising, and
during the day Stuart, supported by Jackson, made
vigorous efforts to find a passage across the river. Covered
by a heavy fire of artillery, the squadrons drove in a
regiment and a battery holding Beverley Ford, and
spread their patrols over the country on the left bank. It
was soon evident, however, that the ground was unsuitable
for attack, and Stuart, menaced by a strong force of
infantry, withdrew his troopers across the stream. Nothing
further was attempted. Jackson went into bivouac near St.
James's Church, and Longstreet closed in upon his right.

The next morning, in accordance with Lee's orders to
'seek a more favourable place to cross higher up the river,
Aug. 22.   and thus gain the enemy's right,' Jackson, still
          preceded by Stuart, and concealing his march
as far as possible in the woods, moved towards the fords
near Warrenton Springs. Longstreet, meanwhile, marched
towards the bridge at Rappahannock Station, where the
enemy had established a *tête-de-pont*, and bringing his guns
into action at every opportunity, made brisk demonstrations
along the river.

Late in the afternoon, after an attack on his rear-guard
at Welford's Mill had been repulsed by Trimble, reinforced
by Hood, Jackson, under a lowering sky, reached the ruined
bridge at the Sulphur Springs. Only a few of the enemy's
cavalry had been descried, and he at once made preparations
to effect the passage of the Rappahannock. The 13th
Georgia dashed through the ford, and occupied the
cottages of the little watering-place. Early's brigade and
two batteries crossed by an old mill-dam, a mile below, and

took post on the ridge beyond. But heavy rain had begun to fall; the night was closing in; and the river, swollen by the storms in the mountains, was already rising. The difficulties of the passage increased every moment, and the main body of the Valley army was ordered into bivouac on the western bank. It was not, however, the darkness of the ford or the precarious footing of the mill-dam that held Jackson back from reinforcing his advanced-guard, but the knowledge that these dangerous roadways would soon be submerged by a raging torrent. Early was, indeed, in peril, but it was better that one brigade should take its chance of escape than that one half the column should be cut off from the remainder. Next morning the Aug. 23. pioneers were ordered to repair the bridge, while Longstreet, feinting strongly against the *tête-de-pont*, gave Pope occupation. Early's troops, under cover of the woods, moved northward to the protection of a creek named Great Run, and although the Federal cavalry kept close watch upon him, no attack was made till nightfall. This was easily beaten back; and Jackson, anxious to keep the attention of the enemy fixed on this point, sent over another brigade. At dawn on the 24th, however, as the Aug. 24. Federals were reported to be advancing in force, the detachment was brought back to the Confederate bank. The men had been for two days and a night without food or shelter. It was in vain that Early, after the bridge had been restored, had requested to be withdrawn. Jackson sent Lawton to reinforce him with the curt message: 'Tell General Early to hold his position;' and although the generals grumbled at their isolation, Pope was effectually deluded into the conviction that a serious attack had been repulsed, and that no further attempt to turn his right was to be immediately apprehended. The significance of Jackson's action will be seen hereafter.

While Jackson was thus mystifying the enemy, both Longstreet and Stuart had been hard at work. The former, after an artillery contest of several hours' duration, had driven the enemy from his *tête-de-pont* on the railway, and had burnt the bridge. The latter, on the morning of the

22nd, had moved northward with the whole of the cavalry, except two regiments, and had ridden round the Federal right. Crossing the Rappahannock at Waterloo Bridge and Hart's Mills, he marched eastward without meeting a single hostile scout, and as evening fell the column of 1,500 men and two pieces of artillery clattered into Warrenton. The troopers dismounted in the streets. The horses were fed and watered, and while the officers amused themselves by registering their names, embellished with fantastic titles, at the hotel, Stuart's staff, questioning the throng of women and old men, elicited important information. None of the enemy's cavalry had been seen in the vicinity for some days, and Pope's supply trains were parked at Catlett's Station, on the Orange and Alexandria Railway, ten miles south-east. After an hour's rest the force moved on, and passing through Auburn village was caught by the same storm that had cut off Early. The narrow roads became running streams, and the creeks which crossed the line of march soon rose to the horses' withers. But this was the very condition of the elements most favourable for the enterprise. The enemy's vedettes and patrols, sheltering from the fury of the storm, were captured, one after another, by the advanced-guard, and the two brigades arrived at Catlett's Station without the Federals receiving the least notice of their approach.

A moment's halt, a short consultation, a silent movement forward, and the astonished sentinels were overpowered. Beyond were the encampments and the trains, guarded by 1,500 infantry and 500 horsemen. The night was dark—the darkest, said Stuart, that he had ever known. Without a guide concerted action seemed impossible. The rain still fell in torrents, and the raiders, soaked to the skin, could only grope aimlessly in the gloom. But just at this moment a negro was captured who recognised Stuart, and who knew where Pope's baggage and horses were to be found. He was told to lead the way, and Colonel W. H. F. Lee, a son of the Commander-in-Chief, was ordered to follow with his regiment. The guide led the column towards the headquarter tents. 'Then there mingled with the noise of the rain upon the canvas and the roar of the wind in the forest the rushing sound of many horsemen, of loud voices, and clashing sabres.' One of Pope's staff officers, together with the uniform and horses of the Federal commander, his treasure chest, and his personal effects, fell into the hands of the Confederates, and the greater part of the enemy's troops, suddenly alarmed in the deep darkness, dispersed into the woods. Another camp was quickly looted, and the 1st and 5th Virginia Cavalry were sent across the railway, riding without accident, notwithstanding the darkness, over a high embankment with deep ditches on either side. But the Federal guards had now rallied under cover, and the attack on the railway waggons had to be abandoned. Another party had taken in hand the main object of the expedition, the destruction of the railway bridge over Cedar Run. The force which should have defended it was surprised and scattered. The timbers, however, were by this time thoroughly saturated, and only a few axes had been discovered. Some Federal skirmishers maintained a heavy fire from the opposite bank, and it was impossible to complete the work. The telegraph was more easily dealt with; and shortly before daylight on the 23rd, carrying with him 300 prisoners, including many officers, Stuart withdrew by the light of the blazing camp, and after a march of sixty miles in six-and-twenty hours, reached the Sulphur Springs before evening.

The most important result of this raid was the capture of Pope's dispatch book, containing most detailed information as to his strength, dispositions, and designs; referring to the reinforcements he expected, and disclosing his belief that the line of the Rappahannock was no longer tenable. But the enterprise had an indirect effect upon the enemy's calculations, which was not without bearing on the campaign. Pope believed that Stuart's advance on Catlett's Station had been made in connection with Jackson's attempt to cross at Sulphur Springs; and the retreat of the cavalry, combined with that of Early, seemed

STONEWALL JACKSON

to indicate that the movement to turn his right had been
definitely abandoned.

The Federal commander was soon to be undeceived.
Thrice had General Lee been baulked. The enemy, who
should have been annihilated on August 19, had gained six
days' respite. On the 20th he had placed himself behind
the Rappahannock. On the 22nd the rising waters forbade
Jackson's passage at the Sulphur Springs; and now, on the
afternoon of the 24th, the situation was still unchanged.
Disregarding Longstreet's demonstrations, Pope had marched
northward, keeping pace with Jackson, and his whole force
was concentrated on the great road which runs from the
Sulphur Springs through Warrenton and Gainesville to
Washington and Alexandria. He had answered move by
countermove. Hitherto, except in permitting Early to recross the river, he had made no mistake, and he had
gained time. He had marched over thirty miles, and
executed complicated manœuvres, without offering the Confederates an opening. His position near the Sulphur
Springs was as strong as that which he had left on the
lower reaches near the railway bridge. Moreover, the correspondence in his dispatch book disclosed the fact that a
portion at least of McClellan's army had landed at Aquia
Creek, and was marching to Bealtown; [1] that a strong force,
drawn from the Kanawha Valley and elsewhere, was assembling at Washington; and that 150,000 men might
be concentrated within a few days on the Rappahannock.
Lee, on learning McClellan's destination, immediately
asked that the troops which had been retained at Richmond
should be sent to join him. Mr. Davis assented, but it was
not till the request had been repeated and time lost that
the divisions of D. H. Hill and McLaws', two brigades of
infantry, under J. G. Walker, and Hampton's cavalry

[1] Between August 21 and 25 Pope received the following reinforcements
for the Army of the Potomac, raising his strength to over 80,000 men:

Third Corps.	Heintzleman	Hooker's Division Kearney's "	10,000
Fifth Corps.	Porter	Morell's " Sykes' "	10,000
Pennsylvania Reserves.	Reynolds		8,000

brigade were ordered up. Yet these reinforcements only
raised Lee's numbers to 75,000 men, and they were from
eighty to a hundred miles distant by an indifferent railroad.

Nor was it possible to await their arrival. Instant
action was imperative. But what action was possible ? A
defensive attitude could only result in the Confederate army
being forced back by superior strength; and retreat on
Richmond would be difficult, for the Federals held the
interior lines. The offensive seemed out of the question.
Pope's position was more favourable than before. His
army was massed, and reinforcements were close at hand.
His right flank was well secured. The ford at Sulphur
Springs and the Waterloo Bridge were both in his possession; north of the Springs rose the Bull Run Mountains, a
range covered with thick forest, and crossed by few roads;
and his left was protected by the march of McClellan's
army corps from Aquia Creek. Even the genius of a
Napoleon might well have been baffled by the difficulties in
the way of attack. But there were men in the Confederate
army to whom overwhelming numbers and strong positions
were merely obstacles to be overcome.

On August 24 Lee removed his headquarters to Jefferson,
where Jackson was already encamped, and on the same
evening, with Pope's captured correspondence before them,
the two generals discussed the problem. What occurred
at this council of war was never made public. To use
Lee's words : ' A plan of operations was determined on ; '
but by whom it was suggested there is none to tell us.
' Jackson was so reticent,' writes Dr. McGuire, ' that it was
only by accident that we ever found out what he proposed to
do, and there is no staff officer living (1897) who could throw
any light on this matter. The day before we started to march
round Pope's army I saw Lee and Jackson conferring together. Jackson—for him—was very much excited, drawing
with the toe of his boot a map in the sand, and gesticulating
in a much more earnest way than he was in the habit
of doing. General Lee was simply listening, and after
Jackson had got through, he nodded his head, as if acced-

ing to some proposal. I believe, from what occurred afterwards, that Jackson suggested the movement as it was made, but I have no further proof than the incident I have just mentioned.'[1] It is only certain that we have record of few enterprises of greater daring than that which was then decided on; and no matter from whose brain it emanated, on Lee fell the burden of the responsibility; on his shoulders, and on his alone, rested the honour of the Confederate arms, the fate of Richmond, the independence of the South; and if we may suppose, so consonant was the design proposed with the strategy which Jackson had already practised, that it was to him its inception was due, it is still to Lee that we must assign the higher merit. It is easy to conceive. It is less easy to execute. But to risk cause and country, name and reputation, on a single throw, and to abide the issue with unflinching heart, is the supreme exhibition of the soldier's fortitude.

Lee's decision was to divide his army. Jackson, marching northwards, was to cross the Bull Run Mountains at Thoroughfare Gap, ten miles as the crow flies from the enemy's right, and strike the railway which formed Pope's line of supply. The Federal commander, who would meanwhile be held in play by Longstreet, would be compelled to fall back in a north-easterly direction to save his communications, and thus be drawn away from McClellan. Longstreet would then follow Jackson, and it was hoped that the Federals, disconcerted by these movements, might be attacked in detail or forced to fight at a disadvantage. The risk, however, was very great.

An army of 55,000 men was about to march into a region occupied by 100,000,[2] who might easily be reinforced to 150,000; and it was to march in two wings,

---

[1] Letter to the author.

[2] Pope, 80,000; Washington and Aquia Creek, 20,000. Lee was well aware, from the correspondence which Stuart had captured, if indeed he had not already inferred it, that Pope had been strictly enjoined to cover Washington, and that he was dependent on the railway for supplies. There was not the slightest fear of his falling back towards Aquia Creek to join McClellan.

separated from each other by two days' march. If Pope were to receive early warning of Jackson's march, he might hurl his whole force on one or the other. Moreover, defeat, with both Pope and McClellan between the Confederates and Richmond, spelt ruin and nothing less. But as Lee said after the war, referring to the criticism evoked by manœuvres, in this as in other of his campaigns, which were daring even to rashness, 'Such criticism is obvious, but the disparity of force between the contending forces rendered the risks unavoidable.'[1] In the present case the only alternative was an immediate retreat; and retreat, so long as the enemy was not fully concentrated, and there was a chance of dealing with him in detail, was a measure which neither Lee nor Jackson was ever willing to advise.

On the evening of the 24th Jackson began his preparations for the most famous of his marches. His troops were quietly withdrawn from before the Sulphur Springs, and Longstreet's division, unobserved by the Federals, took their place. Captain Boswell was ordered to report on the most direct and hidden route to Manassas Junction, and the three divisions—Ewell's, Hill's, and the Stonewall, now commanded by Taliaferro—assembled near Jefferson. Three days' cooked rations were to be carried in the haversacks, and a herd of cattle, together with the green corn standing in the fields, was relied upon for subsistence until requisition could be made on the Federal magazines. The troops marched light. Knapsacks were left behind. Tin cans and a few frying-pans formed the only camp equipment, and many an officer's outfit consisted of a few badly baked biscuits and a handful of salt.

Long before dawn the divisions were afoot. The men were hungry, and their rest had been short; but they were old acquaintances of the morning star, and to march while Aug. 25 the east was still grey had become a matter of routine. But as their guides led northward, and the sound of the guns, opening along the Rappahannock, grew fainter and fainter, a certain excitement began to pervade the column. Something mysterious was in the air.

[1] *The Army of Northern Virginia*, Colonel Allan, p. 200.

What their movement portended not the shrewdest of the
soldiers could divine ; but they recalled their marches in the
Valley and their inevitable results, and they knew instinctively that a surprise on a still larger scale was in contem-
plation. The thought was enough. Asking no questions, and
full of enthusiasm, they followed with quick step the leader
in whom their confidence had become so absolute. The flood
had subsided on the Upper Rappahannock, and the divisions
forded it at Hinson's Mill, unmolested and apparently unobserved. Without halting it pressed on, Boswell with a
small escort of cavalry leading the way. The march led first
by Amissville, thence north to Orleans, beyond Hedgeman's
River, and thence to Salem, a village on the Manassas Gap
Railroad. Where the roads diverged from the shortest line
the troops took to the fields. Guides were stationed by the
advanced-guard at each gap and gate which marked the
route. Every precaution was taken to conceal the movement.
The roads in the direction of the enemy were watched by
cavalry, and so far as possible the column was directed
through woods and valleys. The men, although they knew
nothing of their destination, whether Winchester, or
Harper's Ferry, or even Washington itself, strode on mile
after mile, through field and ford, in the fierce heat of the
August noon, without question or complaint. 'Old Jack'
had asked them to do their best, and that was enough to
command their most strenuous efforts.

Near the end of the day Jackson rode to the head of
the leading brigade, and complimented the officers on the
fine condition of the troops and the regularity of the
march. They had made more than twenty miles, and
were still moving briskly, well closed up, and without
stragglers. Then, standing by the wayside, he watched
his army pass. The sun was setting, and the rays
struck full on his familiar face, brown with exposure,
and his dusty uniform. Ewell's division led the way,
and when the men saw their general, they prepared
to salute him with their usual greeting. But as they
began to cheer he raised his hand to stop them, and the
word passed down the column, 'Don't shout, boys, the

Yankees will hear us;' and the soldiers contented themselves with swinging their caps in mute acclamation. When the next division passed a deeper flush spread over Jackson's face. Here were the men he had so often led to triumph, the men he had trained himself, the men of the Valley, of the First Manassas, of Kernstown, and M'Dowell. The Stonewall regiments were before him, and he was unable to restrain them; devotion such as theirs was not to be silenced at such a moment, and the wild battle-yell of his own brigade set his pulses tingling. For once a breach of discipline was condoned. 'It is of no use,' said Jackson, turning to his staff, 'you see I can't stop them;' and then, with a sudden access of intense pride in his gallant veterans, he added, half to himself, 'Who could fail to win battles with such men as these?'

It was midnight before the column halted near Salem village, and the men, wearied outright with their march of six-and-twenty miles, threw themselves on the ground by the piles of muskets, without even troubling to unroll their blankets. So far the movement had been entirely successful. Not a Federal had been seen, and none appeared during the warm midsummer night. Yet the soldiers were permitted scant time for rest. Once more they were aroused while the stars were bright; and, half awake, snatching what food they could, they stumbled forward through the darkness. As the cool breath of the morning rose about them, the dark forests of the Bull Run Moun-
Aug. 26. tains became gradually visible in the faint light of the eastern sky, and the men at last discovered whither their general was leading them. With the knowledge, which spread quickly through the ranks, that they were making for the communications of the boaster Pope, the regiments stepped out with renewed energy. 'There was no need for speech, no breath to spare if there had been —only the shuffling tramp of marching feet, the rumbling of wheels, the creak and clank of harness and accoutrements, with an occasional order, uttered under the breath, and always the same: " Close up, men! Close up!"' [1]

[1] *Battles and Leaders*, vol. ii., p. 533.

Through Thoroughfare Gap, a narrow gorge in the Bull
Run range, with high cliffs, covered with creepers and crowned
with pines on either hand, the column wound steadily
upwards; and, gaining the higher level, the troops looked
down on the open country to the eastward. Over a vast
area of alternate field and forest, bounded by distant
uplands, the shadows of the clouds were slowly sailing.
Issuing from the mouth of the pass, and trending a little
to the south-east, ran the broad high-road, passing through
two tiny hamlets, Haymarket and Gainesville, and climbing
by gentle gradients to a great bare plateau, familiar to
the soldiers of Bull Run under the name of Manassas
Plains. At Gainesville this road was crossed by another,
which, lost in dense woods, appeared once more on the
open heights to the far north-east, where the white buildings
of Centreville glistened in the sunshine. The second
road was the Warrenton and Alexandria highway, the
direct line of communication between Pope's army and
Washington, and it is not difficult to divine the anxiety
with which it was scrutinised by Jackson. If his march
had been detected, a far superior force might already
be moving to intercept him. At any moment the news
might come in that the Federal army was rapidly approaching; and even were that not the case, it seemed
hardly possible that the Confederate column, betrayed by
the dust, could escape the observation of passing patrols or
orderlies. But not a solitary scout was visible; no movement was reported from the direction of Warrenton; and
the troops pressed on, further and further round the
Federal rear, further and further from Lee and Longstreet.
The cooked rations which they carried had been consumed
or thrown away; there was no time for the slaughter and
distribution of the cattle; but the men took tribute from
the fields and orchards, and green corn and green apples
were all the morning meal that many of them enjoyed.
At Gainesville the column was joined by Stuart, who had
maintained a fierce artillery fight at Waterloo Bridge the
previous day; and then, slipping quietly away under cover
of the darkness, had marched at two in the morning to cover

Jackson's flank. The sun was high in the heavens, and still the enemy made no sign. Munford's horsemen, forming the advanced-guard, had long since reached the Alexandria turnpike, sweeping up all before them, and neither patrols nor orderlies had escaped to carry the news to Warrenton.

So the point of danger was safely passed, and thirteen miles in rear of Pope's headquarters, right across the communications he had told his troops to disregard, the long column swung swiftly forward in the noonday heat. Not a sound, save the muffled roll of many wheels, broke the stillness of the tranquil valley; only the great dust cloud, rolling always eastward up the slopes of the Manassas plateau, betrayed the presence of war.

Beyond Gainesville Jackson took the road which led to Bristoe Station, some seven miles south of Manassas Junction. Neither the success which had hitherto accompanied his movement, nor the excitement incident on his situation, had overbalanced his judgment. From Gainesville the Junction might have been reached in little more than an hour's march; and prudence would have recommended a swift dash at the supply depôt, swift destruction, and swift escape. But it was always possible that Pope might have been alarmed, and the railroad from Warrenton Junction supplied him with the means of throwing a strong force of infantry rapidly to his rear. In order to obstruct such a movement Jackson had determined to seize Bristoe Station. Here, breaking down the railway bridge over Broad Run, and establishing his main body in an almost impregnable position behind the stream, he could proceed at his leisure with the destruction of the stores at Manassas Junction. The advantages promised by this manœuvre more than compensated for the increased length of the march.

The sun had not yet set when the advanced-guard arrived within striking distance of Bristoe Station. Munford's squadrons, still leading the way, dashed upon the village. Ewell followed in hot haste, and a large portion of the guard, consisting of two companies, one of cavalry and one of infantry, was immediately captured.

A train returning empty from Warrenton Junction to Alexandria darted through the station under a heavy fire.[1] The line was then torn up, and two trains which followed in the same direction as the first were thrown down a high embankment. A fourth, scenting danger ahead, moved back before it reached the break in the road. The column had now closed up, and it was already dark. The escape of the two trains was most unfortunate. It would soon be known, both at Alexandria and Warrenton, that Manassas Junction was in danger. The troops had marched nearly five-and-twenty miles, but if the object of the expedition was to be accomplished, further exertions were absolutely necessary. Trimble, energetic as ever, volunteered with two regiments, the 21st Georgia and 21st North Carolina, to move on Manassas Junction. Stuart was placed in command, and without a moment's delay the detachment moved northward through the woods. The night was hot and moonless. The infantry moved in order of battle, the skirmishers in advance; and pushing slowly forward over a broken country, it was nearly midnight before they reached the Junction. Half a mile from the depôt their advance was greeted by a salvo of shells. The Federal garrison, warned by the fugitives from Bristoe Station, were on the alert; but so harmless was their fire that Trimble's men swept on without a check. The two regiments, one on either side of the railroad, halted within a hundred yards of the Federal guns. The countersign was passed down the ranks, and the bugles sounded the charge. The Northern gunners, without waiting for the onset, fled through the darkness, and two batteries, each with its full complement of guns and waggons, became the prize of the Confederate infantry. Stuart, coming up on the flank, rode down the fugitives. Over 300 prisoners were taken, and the remainder of the garrison streamed northward through the deserted camps. The results of

---

[1] The report received at Alexandria from Manassas Junction ran as follows: ' No. 6 train, engine Secretary, was fired into at Bristoe by a party of cavalry, some 500 strong. They had piled ties on the track, but the engine threw them off. Secretary is completely riddled by bullets.'

this attack more than compensated for the exertions the troops had undergone. Only 15 Confederates had been wounded, and the supplies on which Pope's army, whether it was intended to move against Longstreet or merely to hold the line of the Rappahannock, depended both for food and ammunition were in Jackson's hands.

The next morning Hill's and Taliaferro's divisions joined Trimble. Ewell remained at Bristoe; cavalry patrols were sent out in every direction, and Jackson, Aug. 27. riding to Manassas, saw before him the reward of his splendid march. Streets of warehouses, stored to overflowing, had sprung up round the Junction. A line of freight cars, two miles in length, stood upon the railway. Thousands of barrels, containing flour, pork, and biscuit, covered the neighbouring fields. Brand-new ambulances were packed in regular rows. Field-ovens, with the fires still smouldering, and all the paraphernalia of a large bakery, attracted the wondering gaze of the Confederate soldiery; while great pyramids of shot and shell, piled with the symmetry of an arsenal, testified to the profusion with which the enemy's artillery was supplied.

It was a strange commentary on war. Washington was but a long day's march to the north; Warrenton, Pope's headquarters, but twelve miles distant to the south-west; and along the Rappahannock, between Jackson and Lee, stood the tents of a host which outnumbered the whole Confederate army. No thought of danger had entered the minds of those who selected Manassas Junction as the depôt of the Federal forces. Pope had been content to leave a small guard as a protection against raiding cavalry. Halleck, concerned only with massing the whole army on the Rappahannock, had used every effort to fill the store-houses. If, he thought, there was one place in Virginia where the Stars and Stripes might be displayed in full security, that place was Manassas Junction; and here, as nowhere else, the wealth of the North had been poured out with a prodigality such as had never been seen in war. To feed, clothe, and equip the Union armies no expenditure was deemed extravagant. For the comfort and well-being of the individual soldier the purse-strings of the nation were freely loosed. No demand, however preposterous, was disregarded. The markets of Europe were called upon to supply the deficiencies of the States; and if money could have effected the re-establishment of the Union, the war would have already reached a triumphant issue. But the Northern Government had yet to learn that the accumulation of men, *matériel*, and supplies is not in itself sufficient for success. Money alone cannot provide good generals, a trained staff, or an efficient cavalry; and so on this August morning 20,000 ragged Confederates, the soldiers of a country which ranked as the poorest of nations, had marched right round the rear of the Federal army, and were now halted in undisturbed possession of all that made that army an effective force.

Few generals have occupied a position so commanding as did Jackson on the morning of August 27. His enemies would henceforward have to dance while he piped. It was Jackson, and not Pope, who was to dictate the movements of the Federal army. It was impossible that the latter could now maintain its position on the Rappahannock, and Lee's strategy had achieved its end. The capture of Manassas Junction, however, was only the first step in the campaign. Pope, to restore his communications with Alexandria, would be compelled to fall back; but before he could be defeated the two Confederate wings must be united, and the harder part of the work would devolve on Jackson. The Federals, at Warrenton, were nearer by five miles to Thoroughfare Gap, his shortest line of communication with Lee and Longstreet, than he was himself. Washington held a large garrison, and the railway was available for the transit of the troops. The fugitives from Manassas must already have given the alarm, and at any moment the enemy might appear.

If there were those in the Confederate ranks who considered the manœuvres of their leader overbold, their misgivings were soon justified.

A train full of soldiers from Warrenton Junction put back on finding Ewell in possession of Bristoe Station ; but a more determined effort was made from the direction of Alexandria. So early as seven o'clock a brigade of infantry, accompanied by a battery, detrained on the north bank of Bull Run, and advanced in battle order against the Junction.[1] The Federals, unaware that the depôt was held in strength, expected to drive before them a few squadrons of cavalry. But when several batteries opened a heavy fire, and heavy columns advanced against their flanks, the men broke in flight towards the bridge. The Confederate infantry followed rapidly, and two Ohio regiments, which had just arrived from the Kanawha Valley, were defeated with heavy loss. Fitzhugh Lee, who had fallen back before the enemy's advance, was then ordered in pursuit. The cars and railway bridge were destroyed ; and during the day the brigade followed the fugitives as far as Burke's Station, only twelve miles from Alexandria.

This feeble attack appears to have convinced Jackson that his danger was not pressing. It was evident that the enemy had as yet no idea of his strength. Stuart's cavalry watched every road ; Ewell held a strong position on Broad Run, barring the direct approach from Warrenton Junction, and it was determined to give the wearied soldiers the remainder of the day for rest and pillage. It was impossible to carry away even a tithe of the stores, and when an issue of rations had been made, the bakery set working, and the liquor placed under guard, the regiments were let loose on the magazines. Such an opportunity occurs but seldom in the soldier's service, and the hungry Confederates were not the men to let it pass. 'Weak and haggard from their diet of green corn and apples, one can well imagine,' says Gordon, 'with what surprise their eyes opened upon the contents of the sutlers' stores, containing an amount and

---

[1] These troops were sent forward, without cavalry, by order of General Halleck. O. R., vol. xii., part iii., p. 680. The Federal Commander-in-Chief expected that the opposition would be slight. He had evidently no suspicion of the length to which the daring of Lee and Jackson might have carried them.

variety of property such as they had never conceived. Then
came a storming charge of men rushing in a tumultuous
mob over each other's heads, under each other's feet,
anywhere, everywhere, to satisfy a craving stronger
than a yearning for fame.   There were no laggards in
that charge, and there was abundant evidence of the fruits of
victory.   Men ragged and famished clutched tenaciously
at whatever came in their way, whether of clothing or
food, of luxury or necessity.   Here a long yellow-haired,
barefooted son of the South claimed as prizes a tooth-
brush, a box of candles, a barrel of coffee ; while another,
whose butternut homespun hung round him in tatters,
crammed himself with lobster salad, sardines, potted game
and sweetmeats, and washed them down with Rhenish
wine.   Nor was the outer man neglected.   From piles of
new clothing the Southerners arrayed themselves in the
blue uniforms of the Federals.   The naked were clad, the
barefooted were shod, and the sick provided with luxuries
to which they had long been strangers.' [1]

The history of war records many extraordinary scenes,
but there are few more ludicrous than this wild revel at
Manassas.   Even the chagrin of Northern writers gives
way before the spectacle ; and Jackson must have smiled
grimly when he thought of the maxim which Pope had
promulgated with such splendid confidence : ' Let us study
the probable lines of retreat of our opponents, and leave
our own to take care of themselves ! '

It was no time, however, to indulge in reflections on
the irony of fortune.   All through the afternoon, while the
sharp-set Confederates were sweeping away the profits
which the Northern sutlers had wrung from Northern
soldiers, Stuart's vigilant patrols sent in report on report
of the Federal movements.   From Warrenton heavy
columns were hurrying over the great highroad to Gainesville, and from Warrenton Junction a large force of all
arms was marching direct on Bristoe.   There was news,
too, from Lee.   Despite the distance to be covered, and the

---

[1] *The Army of Virginia.*   General George H. Gordon.

proximity of the enemy, a trooper of the 'Black Horse,' a regiment of young planters which now formed Jackson's escort, disguised as a countryman, made his way back from headquarters, and Jackson learned that Longstreet, who had started the previous evening, was following his own track by Orleans, Salem, and Thoroughfare Gap.[1] It was evident, then, that the whole Federal army was in motion north-wards, and that Longstreet had crossed the Rappahannock. But Longstreet had many miles to march and Thorough-fare Gap to pass before he could lend assistance; and the movement of the enemy on Gainesville threatened to intervene between the widely separated wings of the Confederate army.

It was no difficult matter for Jackson to decide on the course to be adopted. There was but one thing to do, to retreat at once; and only one line of escape still open, the roads leading north and north-west from Manassas Junction. To remain at Manassas and await Lee's arrival would have been to sacrifice his command. 20,000 men, even with the protection of intrenchments, could hardly hope to hold the whole Federal army at bay for two days; and it was always possible that Pope, blocking Thoroughfare Gap with a portion of his force, might delay Lee for even longer than two days. Nor did it recommend itself to Jackson as sound strategy to move south, attack the Federal column approaching Bristoe, and driving it from his path to escape past the rear of the column moving to Gainesville. The exact position of the Federal troops was far from clear. Large forces might be encountered near the Rappahannock, and part of McClellan's army was known to be marching westward from Aquia Creek. Moreover, such a movement would have ac-centuated the separation of the Confederate wings, and a local success over a portion of the hostile army would have been but a poor substitute for the decisive victory which Lee hoped to win when his whole force was once more concentrated.

---

[1] 'Up to the night of August 28 we received,' says Longstreet, 'reports from General Jackson at regular intervals, assuring us of his successful operation, and of confidence in his ability to baffle all efforts of the enemy till we should reach him.'—*Battles and Leaders*, vol. ii., p. 517.

About three in the afternoon the thunder of artillery
was heard from the direction of Bristoe. Ewell had sent
a brigade along the railroad to support some cavalry on
reconnaissance, and to destroy a bridge over Kettle Run.
Hardly had the latter task been accomplished when a strong
column of Federal infantry emerged from the forest and
deployed for action. Hooker's division of 5,500 men, belonging to McClellan's army, had joined Pope on the same day
that Jackson had crossed the Rappahannock, and had been
dispatched northwards from Warrenton Junction as soon as
the news came in that Manassas Junction had been captured. Hooker had been instructed to ascertain the strength
of the enemy at Manassas, for Pope was still under the
impression that the attack on his rear was nothing more than
a repetition of the raid on Catlett's Station. Striking the
Confederate outposts at Kettle Run, he deployed his troops
in three lines and pushed briskly forward. The batteries on
both sides opened, and after a hot skirmish of an hour's
duration Ewell, who had orders not to risk an engagement
with superior forces, found that his flanks were threatened.
In accordance with his instructions he directed his
three brigades to retire in succession across Broad Run.
This difficult manœuvre was accomplished with trifling
loss, and Hooker, ascertaining that Jackson's whole corps,
estimated at 30,000 men, was near at hand, advanced no
further than the stream. Ewell fell back slowly to the Junction; and shortly after midnight the three Confederate
divisions had disappeared into the darkness. The torch
had already been set to the captured stores; warehouses,
trains, camps, and hospitals were burning fiercely, and
the dark figures of Stuart's troopers, still urging on the
work, passed to and fro amid the flames. Of the value of
property destroyed it is difficult to arrive at an estimate.
Jackson, in his official report, enumerates the various
items with an unction which he must have inherited
from some moss-trooping ancestor. Yet the actual quantity mattered little, for the stores could be readily replaced.
But the effect of their destruction on the Federal operations
was for the time being overwhelming. And of this de-

struction Pope himself was a witness. The fight with
Ewell had just ceased, and the troops were going into
bivouac, when the Commander-in-Chief, anxious to ascertain with his own eyes the extent of the danger to which
he was exposed, reached Bristoe Station. There, while
the explosion of the piles of shells resembled the noise of
a great battle, from the ridge above Broad Run he saw the
sky to the north-east lurid with the blaze of a vast confla-
gration ; and there he learned for the first time that it was no
mere raid of cavalry, but Stonewall Jackson, with his whole
army corps, who stood between himself and Washington.

For the best part of three days the Union general had
been completely mystified. Jackson had left Jefferson on
the 25th. But although his march had been seen by the
Federal signallers on the hills near Waterloo Bridge,[1] and
the exact strength of his force had been reported, his destination had been unsuspected. When the column was last
seen it was moving northward from Orleans, but the
darkness had covered it, and the measure of prolonging
the march to midnight bore good fruit. For the best
part of two days Jackson had vanished from his enemy's
view, to be found by Pope himself at Manassas Junction.[2]
Nevertheless, although working in the dark, the Federal
commander, up to the moment he reached Bristoe Station,
had acted with sound judgment. He had inferred from the
reports of his signalmen that Jackson was marching to
Front Royal on the Shenandoah ; but in order to clear up
the situation, on the 26th Sigel and McDowell were ordered
to force the passage of the Rappahannock at Waterloo
Bridge and the Sulphur Springs, and obtain information of
the enemy's movements. Reno, at the same time, was to

---

[1] Five messages were sent in between 8.45 A.M. and 11 A.M., but evidently
reached headquarters much later. O. R., vol. xii., part iii., pp. 654-5.

[2] There is a curious undated report on page 671, O. R., vol. xii., part iii.,
from Colonel Duffie, a French officer in the Federal service, which speaks of
a column passing through Thoroughfare Gap ; but, although the compilers
of the Records have placed it under the date August 26, it seems evident, as
this officer (see p. 670) was at Rappahannock Station on the 26th and 27th
(O. R., vol. xii., part. iii., p. 688), that the report refers to Longstreet's and
not Jackson's troops, and was written on August 28.

cross below the railway bridge and make for Culpeper. The
manœuvres, however, were not carried out as contemplated.
Only McDowell advanced; and as Lee had replaced Longstreet, who marched to Orleans the same afternoon, by
Anderson, but little was discovered.

It was evident, however, that the Confederates were
trending steadily northwards, and on the night of the 26th
Pope ordered his 80,000 Federals to concentrate in the
neighbourhood of Warrenton.   Reports had come in that
hostile troops had passed through Salem, White Plains, and
Thoroughfare Gap.[1] But it seemed improbable, both to
Pope and McDowell, the second in command, that more
was meant by this than a flank attack on Warrenton.
McDowell expressed his opinion that a movement round
the right wing in the direction of Alexandria was far too
hazardous for the enemy to attempt. Pope appears to
have acquiesced, and a line of battle near Warrenton, with
a strong reserve at Greenwich, to the right rear, was then
decided on.   Franklin's army corps from the Peninsula,
instead of proceeding to Aquia Creek, was disembarking at
Alexandria, and Halleck had been requested to push these
10,000 men forward with all speed to Gainesville. The
Kanawha regiments had also reached Washington, and
Pope was under the impression that these too would be sent
to join him. He had therefore but little apprehension for
his rear. The one error of judgment into which both Pope
and McDowell had been betrayed was in not giving Lee
due credit for audacity or Jackson for energy. That Lee
would dare to divide his army they had never conceived ;
that Jackson would march fifty miles in two days and
place his single corps astride their communications was an
idea which had they thought of they would have instantly
dismissed. Like the Austrian generals when they first
confronted Napoleon, they might well have complained that
their enemy broke every rule of the military art; and like
all generals who believe that war is a mere matter of precedent, they found themselves egregiously deceived.

[1] O. R., vol. xii., part iii., p. 672. Pope to Porter, p. 675. Pope to
Halleck, p. 684.

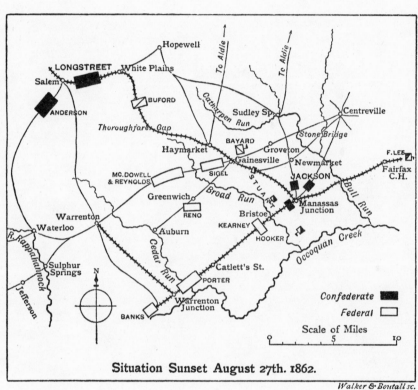

Situation Sunset August 27th. 1862.

Walker & Boutall sc.

L 2

The capture of Manassas, to use Pope's own words, rendered his position at Warrenton no longer tenable, and early on the 27th, the army, instead of concentrating on Warrenton, was ordered to move to Gainesville (from Gainesville it was easy to block Thoroughfare Gap); Buford's cavalry brigade was thrown out towards White Plains to observe Longstreet, and Hooker was dispatched to clear up the situation at Manassas. This move, which was completed before nightfall, could hardly have been improved upon. The whole Federal army was now established on the direct line of communication between Jackson and Lee, and although Jackson might still escape, the Confederates had as yet gained no advantage beyond the destruction of Pope's supplies. It seemed impossible that the two wings could combine east of the Bull Run Mountains. But on the evening of the 27th, after the conclusion of the engagement at Bristoe Station, Pope lost his head. The view he now took of the situation was absolutely erroneous. Ewell's retreat before Hooker he interpreted as an easy victory, which fully compensated for the loss of his magazines. He imagined that Jackson had been surprised, and that no other course was open to him than to take refuge in the intrenchments of Manassas Junction and await Lee's arrival. Orders were at once issued for a manœuvre which should ensure the defeat of the presumptuous foe. The Federal army corps, marching in three columns, were called up to Manassas, a movement which would leave Thoroughfare Gap unguarded save by Buford's cavalry. Some were to move at midnight, others ' at the very earliest blush of dawn.' ' We shall bag the whole crowd, if they are prompt and expeditious,' [1] said Pope, with a sad lapse from the poetical phraseology he had just employed.

And so, on the morning of the 28th, a Federal army once more set out with the expectation of surrounding Jackson, to find once more that the task was beyond their powers.

Aug. 28.

The march was slow. Pope made no movement from

[1] O. R. vol. xii., part ii., p. 72.

Bristoe Station until Hooker had been reinforced by Kearney and Reno; McDowell, before he turned east from Gainesville, was delayed by Sigel's trains, which crossed his line of march, and it was not till noon that Hooker's advanced-guard halted amid the still smouldering ruins on the Manassas plateau. The march had been undisturbed. The redoubts were untenanted. The woods to the north were silent. A few grey-coated vedettes watched the operations from far-distant ridges; a few stragglers, overcome perhaps by their Gargantuan meal of the previous evening, were picked up in the copses, but Jackson's divisions had vanished from the earth.

Then came order and counterorder. Pope was completely bewildered. By four o'clock, however, the news arrived that the railway at Burke's Station, within twelve miles of Alexandria, had been cut, and that the enemy was in force between that point and Centreville. On Centreville, therefore, the whole army was now directed; Hooker, Kearney, and Reno, forming the right wing, marched by Blackburn's Ford, and were to be followed by Porter and Banks; Sigel and Reynolds, forming the centre, took the road by New Market and the Stone Bridge; McDowell (King's and Ricketts' divisions), forming the left, was to pass through Gainesville and Groveton. But when the right wing reached Centreville, Pope was still at fault. There were traces of a marching column, but some small patrols of cavalry, who retreated leisurely before the Federal advance, were the sole evidence of the enemy's existence. Night was at hand, and as the divisions he accompanied were directed to their bivouacs, Pope sought in vain for the enemy he had believed so easy a prey.

Before his troops halted the knowledge came to him. Far away to the south-west, where the great Groveton valley, backed by the wooded mountains, lay green and beautiful, rose the dull booming of cannon, swelling to a continuous roar; and as the weary soldiers, climbing the slopes near Centreville, looked eagerly in the direction of the sound, the rolling smoke of a fierce battle was distinctly visible above the woods which bordered the Warrenton-Alexandria highway.

Across Bull Run, in the neighbourhood of Groveton, and still further westward, where the cleft in the blue hills marked Thoroughfare Gap, was seen the flash of distant guns. McDowell, marching northwards through Gainesville, had evidently come into collision with the enemy. Jackson was run to earth at last; and it was now clear that while Pope had been moving northwards on Centreville, the Confederates had been moving westward, and that they were once more within reach of Lee. But by what means, Pope might well have asked, had a whole army corps, with its batteries and waggons, passed through the cordon which he had planned to throw around it, and passed through as if gifted with the secret of invisibility?

The explanation was simple. While his enemies were watching the midnight glare above Manassas, Jackson was moving north by three roads; and before morning broke A. P. Hill was near Centreville, Ewell had crossed Bull Run by Blackburn's Ford, and Taliaferro was north of Bald Hill, with a brigade at Groveton, while Stuart's squadrons formed a screen to front and flank. Then, as the Federals slowly converged on Manassas, Hill and Ewell, marching unobserved along the north bank of Bull Run, crossed the Stone Bridge; Taliaferro joined them, and before Pope had found that his enemy had left the Junction, the Confederates were in bivouac north of Groveton, hidden in the woods, and recovering from the fatigue of their long night march.[1]

Jackson's arrangements for deceiving his enemy, for concealing his line of retreat, and for drawing Pope northward on Centreville, had been carefully thought out. The march from Manassas was no hasty movement to the rear. Taliaferro, as soon as darkness fell, had moved by New Market on Bald Hill. At 1 A.M. Ewell followed Hill to Blackburn's Ford; but instead of continuing the march on Centreville, had crossed Bull Run, and moving up stream, had joined Taliaferro by way of the Stone Bridge. Hill, leaving Centreville at 10 A.M.,

---

[1] A. P. Hill had marched fourteen miles, Ewell fifteen, and Taliaferro, with whom were the trains, from eight to ten.

marched to the same rendezvous. Thus, while the attention of the enemy was attracted to Centreville, Jackson's
divisions were concentrated in the woods beyond Bull
Run, some five or six miles west. The position in
which his troops were resting had been skilfully selected.
South of Sudley Springs, and north of the Warrenton
turnpike, it was within twelve miles of Thoroughfare
Gap, and a line of retreat, in case of emergency,
as well as a line by which Lee could join him, should
Thoroughfare Gap be blocked, ran to Aldie Gap, the
northern pass of the Bull Run Mountains. Established
on his enemy's flank, he could avoid the full shock of his
force should Lee be delayed, or he could strike effectively
himself; and it was to retain the power of striking that
he had not moved further northward, and secured his front
by camping beyond Catharpen Run. It was essential that
he should be prepared for offensive action. The object with
which he had marched upon Manassas had only been half
accomplished. Pope had been compelled to abandon the
strong line of the Rappahannock, but he had not yet been
defeated; and if he were not defeated, he would combine
with McClellan, and advance in a few days in overwhelming
force. Lee looked for a battle with Pope before he could
be reinforced, and to achieve this end it was necessary that
the Federal commander should be prevented from retreating further; that Jackson should hold him by the
throat until Lee should come up to administer the *coup
de grâce.*

It was with this purpose in his mind that Jackson
had taken post near Groveton, and he was now awaiting
the information that should tell him the time had come to
strike. But, as already related, the march of the Federals
on Manassas was slow and toilsome. It was not till
the morning was well on that the brigade of Taliaferro's
division near Groveton, commanded by Colonel Bradley
Johnson, was warned by the cavalry that the enemy was
moving through Gainesville in great strength. A skirmish
took place a mile or two north of that village, and Johnson,
finding himself menaced by far superior numbers, fell back

to the wood near the Douglass House. He was not followed. The Union generals, Sigel and Reynolds, who had been ordered to Manassas to ' bag ' Jackson, had received no word of his departure from the Junction; and believing that Johnson's small force was composed only of cavalry, they resumed the march which had been temporarily interrupted.

The situation, however, was no clearer to the Confederates. The enemy had disappeared in the great woods south-west of Groveton, and heavy columns were still reported coming up from Gainesville. During the afternoon, however, the cavalry captured a Federal courier, carrying McDowell's orders for the movement of the left and centre, which had been placed under his command, to Manassas Junction,[1] and this important document was immediately forwarded to Jackson.

' Johnson's messenger,' says General Taliaferro, ' found the Confederate headquarters established on the shady side of an old-fashioned worm-fence, in the corner of which General Jackson and his division commanders were profoundly sleeping after the fatigues of the preceding night, notwithstanding the intense heat of the August day. There was not so much as an ambulance at headquarters. The headquarters' train was back beyond the Rappahannock, at Jefferson, with remounts, camp equipage, and all the arrangements for cooking and serving food. All the property of the general, the staff, and the headquarters' bureau was strapped to the pommels and cantels of the saddles, and these formed the pillows of their weary owners. The captured dispatch roused Jackson like an electric shock. He was essentially a man of action. He rarely, if ever, hesitated. He never asked advice. He called no council to discuss the situation disclosed by this

[1] The order, dated 2 A.M., August 28, was to the following effect:—

' 1. Sigel's Corps to march from Gainesville to Manassas Junction, the right resting on the Manassas railroad.

' 2. Reynolds to follow Sigel.

' 3. King to follow Reynolds.

' 4. Ricketts to follow King; but to halt at Thoroughfare Gap if the enemy threatened the pass.'

King was afterwards, while on the march, directed to Centreville by the Warrenton-Alexandria road.

communication, although his ranking officers were almost at his side. He asked no conference of opinion. He made no suggestion, but simply, without a word, except to repeat the language of the message, turned to me and said: "Move your division and attack the enemy;" and to Ewell, "Support the attack." The slumbering soldiers sprang from the earth at the first murmur. They were sleeping almost in ranks; and by the time the horses of their officers were saddled, the long lines of infantry were moving to the anticipated battle-field.

'The two divisions, after marching some distance to the north of the turnpike, were halted and rested, and the prospect of an engagement on that afternoon seemed to disappear with the lengthening shadows. The enemy did not come. The Warrenton turnpike, along which it was supposed he would march, was in view, but it was as free from Federal soldiery as it had been two days before, when Jackson's men had streamed along its highway.' [1]

Jackson, however, was better informed than his subordinate. Troops were still moving through Gainesville, and, instead of turning off to Manassas, were marching up the turnpike on which so many eyes were turned from the neighbouring woods. King's division, while on the march to Manassas, had been instructed to countermarch and make for Centreville, by Groveton and the Stone Bridge. Ricketts, who had been ordered by McDowell to hold Thoroughfare Gap, was already engaged with Longstreet's advanced-guard, and of this Jackson was aware; for Stuart, in position at Haymarket, three miles north of Gainesville, had been skirmishing all day with the enemy's cavalry, and had been in full view of the conflict at the Gap. [2]

Jackson, however, knew not that one division was all that was before him. The Federal movements had covered

---

[1] *Battles and Leaders*, vol. ii., pp. 507, 508.

[2] Longstreet had been unable to march with the same speed as Jackson. Leaving Jefferson on the afternoon of August 26, he did not reach Thoroughfare Gap until 'just before night' on August 28. He had been delayed for an hour at White Plains by the Federal cavalry, and the trains of the army, such as they were, may also have retarded him. In two days he covered only thirty miles.

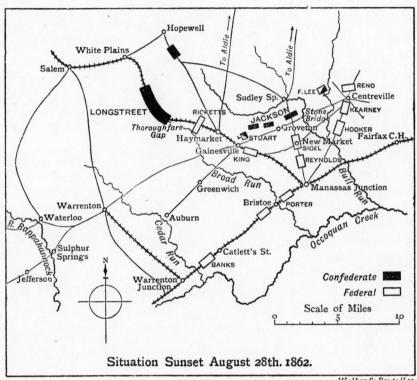

Hopewell

White Plains

Salem

LONGSTREET

Thoroughfare Gap

Haymarket

RICKETTS

Sudley Sp.

F. LEE

RENO

Centreville

JACKSON

Stone Bridge

KEARNEY

Groveton

HOOKER

STUART

Gainesville

New Market

SIGEL

Fairfax C.H.

KING

REYNOLDS

Broad Run

Greenwich

Manassas Junction

Bull Run

Warrenton

Waterloo

Auburn

Bristoe

PORTER

Occoquan Creek

R. Rappahannock

Cedar Run

Sulphur Springs

N

Catlett's St.

BANKS

Jefferson

Warrenton Junction

To Aldie

To Aldie

Confederate

Federal

Scale of Miles

0   5   10

Situation Sunset August 28th. 1862.

Walker & Boutall sc.

so wide an extent of country, and had been so well concealed by the forests, that it was hardly possible for
Stuart's patrols, enterprising as they were, to obtain
accurate information. Unaccustomed to such disjointed
marches as were now in progress across his front, Jackson
believed that King's column was the flank-guard of
McDowell's army corps. But, although he had been compelled to leave Hill near the Stone Bridge, in order to
protect his line of retreat on Aldie, he had still determined to
attack. The main idea which absorbed his thoughts is clear
enough. The Federal army, instead of moving direct from
Warrenton on Alexandria, as he had anticipated, had apparently taken the more circuitous route by Manassas, and if
Pope was to be fought in the open field before he could be
reinforced by McClellan, he must be induced to retrace his
steps. To do this, the surest means was a resolute attack on
King's division, despite the probability that it might be
strongly reinforced; and it is by no means unlikely that
Jackson deferred his attack until near sunset in order that,
if confronted by superior numbers, he might still be able
to hold on till nightfall, and obtain time for Longstreet to
come up.

Within the wood due north of the Dogan House, through
which ran an unfinished railroad, Ewell's and Taliaferro's
divisions, awaiting the propitious moment for attack, were
drawn up in order of battle. Eight brigades, and three
small batteries, which had been brought across country with
great difficulty, were present, and the remainder of the
artillery was not far distant.[1] Taliaferro, on the right, had
two brigades (A. G. Taliaferro's and the Stonewall) in first
line; Starke was in second line, and Bradley Johnson near
Groveton village. Ewell, on the left, had placed Lawton
and Trimble in front, while Early and Forno formed a
general reserve. This force numbered in all about 8,000
men, and even the skirmishers, thrown out well to the front,
were concealed by the undulations of the ground.

---

[1] Twenty pieces had been ordered to the front soon after the infantry
moved forward. The dense woods, however, proved impenetrable to all but
three horse-artillery guns, and one of these was unable to keep up.

The Federal division commanded by General King, although unprovided with cavalry and quite unsupported, was no unworthy enemy. It was composed of four brigades of infantry, led by excellent officers, and accompanied by four batteries. The total strength was 10,000 men. The absence of horsemen, however, placed the Northerners at a disadvantage from the outset.

The leading brigade was within a mile of Groveton, a hamlet of a few houses at the foot of a long descent, and the advanced-guard, deployed as skirmishers, was searching the woods in front. On the road in rear, with the batteries between the columns, came the three remaining brigades—Gibbon's, Doubleday's, and Patrick's—in the order named.

The wood in which the Confederates were drawn up was near a mile from the highway, on a commanding ridge, overlooking a broad expanse of open ground, which fell gently in successive undulations to the road. The Federals were marching in absolute unconsciousness that the enemy, whom the last reports had placed at Manassas, far away to the right, was close at hand. No flank-guards had been thrown out. General King was at Gainesville, sick, and a regimental band had just struck up a merry quickstep. On the open fields to the left, bathed in sunshine, there was not a sign of life. The whitewashed cottages, surrounded by green orchards, which stood upon the slopes, were lonely and untenanted, and on the edge of the distant wood, still and drooping in the heat, was neither stir nor motion. The troops trudged steadily forward through the dust; regiment after regiment disappeared in the deep copse which stands west of Groveton, and far to the rear the road was still crowded with men and guns. Jackson's time had come.

Two Confederate batteries, trotting forward from the wood, deployed upon the ridge. The range was soon found, and the effect was instantaneous. But the confusion in the Northern ranks was soon checked; the troops found cover inside the bank which lined the road, and two batteries, one with the advanced-guard and one from the centre of the column, wheeling into the fields to the left, came quickly into action. About the same moment Bradley Johnson became engaged with the skirmishers near Groveton.

The Confederate infantry, still hidden by the rolling ground, was forming for attack, when a Federal brigade, led by General Gibbon, rapidly deploying on the slopes, moved forward against the guns. It was Stuart's horse-artillery, so the Northerners believed, which had fired on the column, and a bold attack would soon drive back the cavalry. But as Gibbon's regiments came forward the Southern skirmishers, lying in front of the batteries, sprang to their feet and opened with rapid volleys; and then the grey line of battle, rising suddenly into view, bore down upon the astonished foe. Taliaferro, on the right, seized a small farmhouse near Gainesville, and occupied the orchard; the Stonewall Brigade advanced upon his left, and Lawton and Trimble prolonged the front towards the Douglass House. But the Western farmers of Gibbon's brigade were made of stubborn stuff. The Wisconsin regiments held their ground with unflinching courage. Both flanks were protected by artillery, and strong reinforcements were coming up. The advanced-guard was gradually falling back from Groveton; the rear brigades were hurrying forward up the road. The two Confederate batteries, over-powered by superior metal, had been compelled to shift position; only a section of Stuart's horse-artillery under Captain Pelham had come to their assistance, and the battle was confined to a frontal attack at the closest range. In many places the lines approached within a hundred yards, the men standing in the open and blazing fiercely in each other's faces. Here and there, as fresh regiments came up on either side, the grey or the blue gave way for a few short paces; but the gaps were quickly filled, and the wave once more surged forward over the piles of dead. Men fell like leaves in autumn. Ewell was struck down, and Taliaferro, and many of their field officers, and still the Federals held their ground. Night was settling on the field, and although the gallant Pelham, the boy soldier, brought a gun into action within seventy paces of Gibbon's line, yet

the front of fire, flashing redly through the gloom, neither
receded nor advanced. A flank attack on either side would
have turned the scale, but the fight was destined to end as
it had begun. The Federal commander, ignorant of the
enemy's strength, and reaching the field when the fight
was hottest, was reluctant to engage his last reserves.
Jackson had ordered Early and Forno, moving through
the wood west of the Douglass House, to turn the enemy's
right; but within the thickets ran the deep cuttings and
high embankments of the unfinished railroad; and the
regiments, bewildered in the darkness, were unable to
advance. Meanwhile the fight to the front had gradually
died away. The Federals, outflanked upon the left, and
far outnumbered, had slowly retreated to the road. The
Confederates had been too roughly handled to pursue.

The reports of the engagement at Groveton are singularly meagre. Preceded and followed by events of still
greater moment, it never attracted the attention it deserved.
On the side of the Union 2,800 men were engaged, on the
side of the Southerners 4,500, and for more than an hour
and a half the lines of infantry were engaged at the
very closest quarters. The rifled guns of the Federals undoubtedly gave them a marked advantage. But the men
who faced each other that August evening fought with a
gallantry that has seldom been surpassed. The Federals,
surprised and unsupported, bore away the honours. The
Western brigade, commanded by General Gibbon, displayed
a coolness and a steadfastness worthy of the soldiers
of Albuera. Out of 2,000 men the four Wisconsin and
Indiana regiments lost 750, and were still unconquered.
The three regiments which supported them, although it was
their first battle, lost nearly half their number, and the
casualties must have reached a total of 1,100. The Confederate losses were even greater. Ewell, who was shot
down in the first line, and lay long on the field, lost 725
out of 3,000. The Stonewall Brigade, which had by this time
dwindled to 600 muskets, lost over 200, including five field
officers; the 21st Georgia, of Trimble's brigade, 173
men out of 242; and it is probable that the Valley army on

this day was diminished by more than 1,200 stout soldiers. The fall of Ewell was a terrible disaster. Zealous and indefatigable, a stern fighter and beloved by his men, he was the most able and the most loyal of Jackson's generals. Taliaferro, peculiarly acceptable to his Virginia regiments as a Virginian himself, had risen from the rank of colonel to the command of a division, and his spurs had been well won. The battle of Groveton left gaps in Jackson's ranks which it was hard to fill, and although the men might well feel proud of their stubborn fight, they could hardly boast of a brilliant victory.

Strategically, however, the engagement was decisive. Jackson had brought on the fight with the view of drawing the whole Federal army on himself, and he was completely successful. The centre, marching on the Stone Bridge from Manassas Junction, heard the thunder of the cannon and turned westward; and before nightfall A. P. Hill's artillery became engaged with Sigel's advanced-guard. Pope himself, who received the intelligence of the engagement at 9.20 P.M., immediately issued orders for an attack on Jackson the next morning, in which the troops who had already reached Centreville were to take part. 'McDowell,' ran the order, 'has intercepted the retreat of the enemy, Sigel is immediately in his front, and I see no possibility of his escape.'

But Pope, full of the idea that Jackson had been stopped in attempting to retreat through Thoroughfare Gap, altogether misunderstood the situation. He was badly informed. He did not know even the position of his own troops. His divisions, scattered over a wide extent of country, harassed by Stuart's cavalry, and ignorant of the topography, had lost all touch with the Commander-in-Chief. Important dispatches had been captured. Messages and orders were slow in arriving, if they arrived at all. Even the generals were at a loss to find either the Commander-in-Chief or the right road. McDowell had ridden from Gainesville to Manassas in order to consult with Pope, but Pope had gone to Centreville. McDowell thereupon set out to rejoin his troops, but lost his way in the forest and went back to Manassas. From Ricketts Pope received no information whatever.[1] He was not aware that after a long skirmish at Thoroughfare Gap, Longstreet had opened the pass by sending his brigades over the mountains on either hand, threatening both flanks of the Federals, and compelling them to retire. He was not aware that King's division, so far from intercepting Jackson's retreat, had abandoned the field of Groveton at 1 A.M., and, finding its position untenable in face of superior numbers, had fallen back on Manassas; or that Ricketts, who had by this time reached Gainesville, had in consequence continued his retreat in the same direction.

Seldom have the baneful effects of dispersion been more strikingly illustrated, and the difficulty, under such circumstances, of keeping the troops in the hand of the Commander-in-Chief. On the morning of the 28th Pope had ordered his army to march in three columns on Manassas, one column starting from Warrenton Junction, one from Greenwich, and one from Buckland Mills, the roads which they were to follow being at their furthest point no more than seven miles apart. And yet at dawn on the 29th he was absolutely ignorant of the whereabouts of McDowell's army corps; he was but vaguely informed of what had happened during the day; and while part of his army was at Bald Hill, another part was at Centreville, seven miles north-east, and a third at Manassas and at Bristoe, from seven to twelve miles south-east. Nor could the staff be held to blame for the absence of communication between the columns. In peace it is an easy matter to assume that a message sent to a destination seven miles distant by a high-road or even country lanes arrives in good time. Seven miles in peace are very short. In war, in the neighbourhood of the enemy, they are very long. In peace, roads are easy to find. In war, it is the exception that they are found, even when messengers are provided with good maps

---

[1] Ricketts' report would have been transmitted through McDowell, under whose command he was, and as McDowell was not to be found, it naturally went astray.

and the country is thickly populated; and it is from war that the soldier's trade is to be learned.

Jackson's army corps bivouacked in the position they had held when the fierce musketry of Groveton died away. It was not till long after daybreak on the 29th that his cavalry patrols discovered that King's troops had disappeared, and that Longstreet's advanced-guard was already through Thoroughfare Gap. Nor was it till the sun was high that Lee learned the events of the previous evening, and these threw only a faint light on the general situation. But had either the Commander-in-Chief or his lieutenant, on the night of the 28th, known the true state of affairs, they would have had reason to congratulate themselves on the success of the plan which had been hatched on the Rappahannock. They had anticipated that should Jackson's movement on Manassas prove successful, Pope would not only fall back, but that he would fall back in all the confusion which arises from a hastily conceived plan and hastily executed manœuvres. They had expected that in his hurried retreat his army corps would lose touch and cohesion; that divisions would become isolated; that the care of his *impedimenta*, suddenly turned in a new direction, would embarrass every movement; and that the general himself would become demoralised.

The orders and counterorders, the marches and counter-marches of August 28, and the consequent dispersion of the Federal army, are sufficient in themselves to prove the deep insight into war possessed by the Confederate leaders.

Nevertheless, the risk bred of separation which, in order to achieve great results, they had deliberately accepted had not yet passed away. Longstreet had indeed cleared the pass, and the Federals who guarded it had retreated; but the main body of the Confederate army had still twelve miles to march before it could reach Jackson, and Jackson was confronted by superior numbers. On the plateau of Bull Run, little more than two miles from the field of Groveton, were encamped over 20,000 Federals, with the same number at Manassas. At Centreville, a seven miles' march, were 18,000; and at Bristoe Station, about the same distance, 11,000.

It was thus possible for Pope to hurl a superior force
against Jackson before Lee could intervene ; and although it
would have been sounder strategy, on the part of the Federal
commander, to have concentrated towards Centreville, and
have there awaited reinforcements, now fast coming up, he
had some reason for believing that he might still, unaided,
deal with the enemy in detail.   The high virtue of patience
was not his.   Ambition, anxiety to retrieve his reputation,
already blemished by his enforced retreat, the thought that
he might be superseded by McClellan, whose operations in
the Peninsula he had contemptuously criticised, all urged
him forward.   An unsuccessful general who feels instinctively that his command is slipping from him, and who sees
in victory the only hope of retaining it, seldom listens to the
voice of prudence.

So on the morning of the 29th Jackson had to do
with an enemy who had resolved to overwhelm him by
Aug. 29.   weight of numbers. Nor could he expect immediate
help.   The Federal cavalry still stood between
Stuart and Thoroughfare Gap, and not only was Jackson
unaware that Longstreet had broken through, but he was
unaware whether he *could* break through.   In any case, it
would be several hours before he could receive support, and
for that space of time his three divisions, worn with long
marching and the fierce fight of the previous evening, would
have to hold their own unaided.   The outlook, to all
appearance, was anything but bright.   But on the opposite
hills, where the Federals were now forming in line of battle,
the Valley soldiers had already given proof of their stubborn
qualities on the defensive.   The sight of their baptismal
battle-field and the memories of Bull Run must have gone
far to nerve the hearts of the Stonewall regiments, and
in preparing once more to justify their proud title the
troops were aided by their leader's quick eye for a position.
While it was still dark the divisions which had been
engaged at Groveton took ground to their left, and passing
north of the hamlet, deployed on the right of A. P. Hill.
The long, flat-topped ridge, covered with scattered copses
and rough undergrowth, which stands north of the War-

renton-Centreville road, commands the approaches from the south and east, and some five hundred yards below the crest ran the unfinished railroad.

Behind the deep cuttings and high embankments the Confederate fighting-line was strongly placed. The left, slightly thrown back, rested on a rocky spur near Bull Run, commanding Sudley Springs Ford and the road to Aldie Gap. The front extended for a mile and three-quarters south-west. Early, with two brigades and a battery, occupied a wooded knoll where the unfinished railroad crosses the highroad, protecting the right rear, and stretching a hand to Longstreet.

The infantry and artillery were thus disposed :—

Infantry.

Left.—A. P. Hill's Division. First and Second line : Three brigades. (Field, Thomas, Gregg.) Third line : Three brigades. (Branch, Pender, Archer.)

Centre.—Two brigades of Ewell's Division (now commanded by Lawton). (Trimble's and Lawton's.)

Right.—Taliaferro's Division (now commanded by Starke). First and Second line : Two brigades. Third line : Two brigades.

Force detached on the right : Two brigades of Ewell's Division (Early and Forno), and one battery.

Artillery.

16 guns behind the left,	On the ridge, five hundred yards
24 guns behind the right centre,	in rear of the fighting-line.

The flanks were secured by Stuart. A portion of the cavalry was placed at Haymarket to communicate as soon as possible with Longstreet. A regiment was pushed out towards Manassas, and on the left bank of Bull Run Fitzhugh Lee's brigade watched the approaches from Centreville and the north. Jackson's strength, deducting the losses of the previous day, and the numerous stragglers left behind during his forced marches, can hardly have exceeded 18,000 muskets, supported by 40 guns, all that there was room for, and some 2,500 cavalry. These numbers, however, were ample for the defence of the position which had been selected. Excluding the detached force on the extreme

right, the line occupied was three thousand yards in length,
and to every yard of this line there were more than five
muskets, so that half the force could be retained in third
line or reserve. The position was thus strongly held and
strong by nature. The embankments formed stout parapets,
the cuttings deep ditches.

Before the right and the right centre the green pastures,
shorn for thirteen hundred yards of all obstacles save a
few solitary cottages, sloped almost imperceptibly to the
brook which is called Young's Branch. The left centre and
left, however, were shut in by a belt of timber, from four
hundred to six hundred yards in width, which we may call
the Groveton wood. This belt closed in upon, and at one
point crossed, the railroad, and, as regards the field of fire,
it was the weakest point. In another respect, however, it
was the strongest, for the defenders were screened by the
trees from the enemy's artillery. The rocky hill on the
left, facing north-east, was a point of vantage, for an open
corn-field lay between it and Bull Run. Within the position,
behind the copses and undulations, there was ample cover
for all troops not employed on the fighting-line; and from
the ridge in rear the general could view the field from commanding ground.

Shortly after 5 A.M., while the Confederates were still
taking up their positions, the Federal columns were seen
5.15 A.M.   moving down the heights near the Henry House.
Jackson had ridden round his lines, and ordering
Early to throw forward two regiments east of the turnpike,
had then moved to the great battery forming in rear
of his right centre. His orders had already been issued.
The troops were merely to hold their ground, no general
counterstroke was intended, and the divisional commanders were to confine themselves to repulsing the
attack. The time for a strong offensive return had not
yet come.

The enemy advanced slowly in imposing masses.
Shortly after seven o'clock, hidden to some extent by the
woods, four divisions of infantry deployed in several lines
at the foot of the Henry Hill, and their skirmishers became

engaged with the Confederate pickets. At the same moment
three batteries came into action on a rise north-east of
Groveton, opposite the Confederate centre, and Sigel, supported by Reynolds, prepared to carry out his instructions,
and hold Jackson until the remainder of Pope's army should
arrive upon the field. At the end of July, Sigel's army corps
had numbered 13,000 men. Allowing for stragglers and
for casualties on the Rappahannock, where it had been
several times engaged, it must still have mustered 11,000.
It was accompanied by ten batteries, and Reynolds'
division was composed of 8,000 infantry and four batteries. The attack was thus no stronger than the defence,
and as the Federal artillery positions were restricted
by the woods, there could be little doubt of the result.
In other respects, moreover, the combatants were not
evenly matched. Reynolds' Pennsylvanians were fine
troops, already seasoned in the battles on the Peninsula, and commanded by such officers as Meade and
Seymour. But Sigel, who had been an officer in the
Baden army, had succeeded Frémont, and his corps was
composed of those same Germans whom Ewell had used so
hardly at Cross Keys. Many of them were old soldiers,
who had borne arms in Europe; but the stern discipline
and trained officers of conscript armies were lacking in
America, and the Confederate volunteers had little respect
for these foreign levies. Nor were Sigel's dispositions a
brilliant example of offensive tactics. His three divisions,
Schurz', Schenck's, and Steinwehr's, supported by Milroy's
independent brigade, advanced to the attack along a wide
front. Schurz, with two brigades, moving into the Groveton wood, assailed the Confederate left, while Milroy
and Schenck advanced over the open meadows which
lay in front of the right. Steinwehr was in reserve, and
Reynolds, somewhat to the rear, moved forward on the
extreme left. The line was more than two miles long;
the artillery, hampered by the ground, could render but
small assistance; and at no single point were the troops
disposed in sufficient depth to break through the front of
the defence. The attack, too, was piecemeal. Advancing

through the wood, Schurz' division was at once met by a sharp counterstroke, delivered by the left brigade (Gregg's South Carolina) of A. P. Hill's division, which drove the two Federal brigades apart. Reinforcements were sent in by Milroy, who had been checked on the open ground by the heavy fire of Jackson's guns, and the Germans rallied; but, after some hard fighting, a fresh counterstroke, in which Thomas' brigade took part, drove them in disorder from the wood; and the South Carolinians, following to the edge, poured heavy volleys into their retreating masses. Schenck, meanwhile, deterred by the batteries on Jackson's right, had remained inactive; the Federal artillery, such as had been brought into action, had produced no effect; Reynolds, who had a difficult march, had not yet come into action; and in order to support the broken troops Schenck was now ordered to close in upon the right. But the opportunity had already passed.

It was now 10.30 A.M., and Jackson had long since learned that Lee was near at hand. Longstreet's advanced-guard had passed through Gainesville, and the main body 10.15 A.M. was closing up. Not only had time been gained, but two brigades alone had proved sufficient to hold the enemy at arm's length, and the rough counter-strokes had disconcerted the order of attack. A fresh Federal force, however, was already approaching. The troops from Centreville, comprising the divisions of Hooker, Kearney, and Reno, 17,000 or 18,000 men, were hurrying over the Stone Bridge; and a second and more vigorous attack was now to be withstood. Sigel, too, was still capable of further effort. Bringing up Steinwehr's division, and demanding reinforcements from Reno, he threw his whole force against the Confederate front. Schenck, however, still exposed to the fire of the massed artillery, was unable to advance, and Milroy in the centre was hurled back. But through the wood the attack was vigorously pressed, and the fight raged fiercely at close quarters along the railway. Between Gregg's and Thomas' brigades a gap of over a hundred yards, as the men closed in upon the centre, had gradually opened. Opposite the gap was a deep cutting, and the Federals, covered by the wood, massed here unobserved in heavy force. Attack from this quarter was unexpected, and for a moment Hill's first line was in jeopardy. Gregg, however, had still a regiment in second line, and throwing it quickly forward he drove the enemy across the railroad. Then Hill, bringing up Branch from the third line, sent this fresh brigade to Gregg's support, and cleared the front.

The Germans had now been finally disposed of. But although Longstreet had arrived upon the ground, and was deploying in the woods on Jackson's right, thus relieving Early, who at once marched to support the centre, Jackson's men had not yet finished with the enemy. Pope had now taken over command; and besides the troops from Centreville, who had already reached the field, McDowell and Porter, with 27,000 men, were coming up from Manassas, and Reynolds had not yet been engaged. But it is one thing to assemble large numbers on the battle-field, another to give them the right direction.

In the direction of Gainesville high woods and rolling ridges had concealed Longstreet's approach, and the Federal patrols had been everywhere held in check by Stuart's squadrons. In ignorance, therefore, that the whole Confederate army was concentrated before him, Pope, anticipating an easy victory, determined to sweep Jackson from the field. But it was first necessary to relieve Sigel. Kearney's division had already deployed on the extreme right of the Federal line, resting on Bull Run. Hooker was on the left of Kearney and a brigade of Reno's on the left of Hooker. While Sigel assembled his shattered forces, these 10,000 fresh troops, led by some of the best officers of the Army of the Potomac, were ordered to advance against A. P. Hill. Reynolds, under the impression that he was fighting Jackson, was already in collision with Longstreet's advanced-guard; and McDowell and Porter, marching along the railway from Manassas, might be expected to strike the Confederate right rear at any moment. It was then with good

hope of victory that Pope rode along his line and explained
the situation to his generals.

But the fresh attack was made with no better concert
than those which preceded it.   Kearney, on the right, near
1 P.M.   Bull Run, was held at bay by Jackson's guns,
and Hooker and Reno advanced alone.

As the Federals moved forward the grey skirmishers fell
back through the Groveton wood, and scarcely had they
reached the railroad before the long blue lines came crashing
through the undergrowth. Hill's riflemen, lying down to
load, and rising only to fire, poured in their deadly volleys at
point-blank range.   The storm of bullets, shredding leaves
and twigs, stripped the trees of their verdure, and the long
dry grass, ignited by the powder sparks, burst into flames
between the opposing lines. But neither flames nor musketry
availed to stop Hooker's onset. Bayonets flashed through
the smoke, and a gallant rush placed the stormers on the
embankment.   The Confederates reeled back in confusion,
and men crowded round the colours to protect them.   But
assistance was at hand.   A fierce yell and a heavy volley,
and the regiments of the second line surged forward, driving
back the intruders, and closing the breach.   Yet the Federal
ranks reformed; the wood rang with cheers, and a fresh
brigade advanced to the assault. Again the parapet was
carried ; again the Southern bayonets cleared the front.
Hooker's leading brigade, abandoning the edge of the wood,
had already given ground. Reno's regiments, suffering fearful slaughter, with difficulty maintained their place ; and
Hill, calling once more upon his reserves, sent in Pender to
the counterstroke. Passing by the right of Thomas, who,
with Field, had borne the brunt of the last attack, Pender
crossed the railroad, and charged into the wood.   Many of
the men in the fighting-line joined in the onward movement.
The Federals were borne back; the brigades in rear were
swept away by the tide of fugitives ; the wood was cleared,
and a battery near by was deserted by the gunners.

Then Pender, received with a heavy artillery fire from
the opposite heights, moved boldly forward across the open.
But the counterstroke had been pushed too far. The line

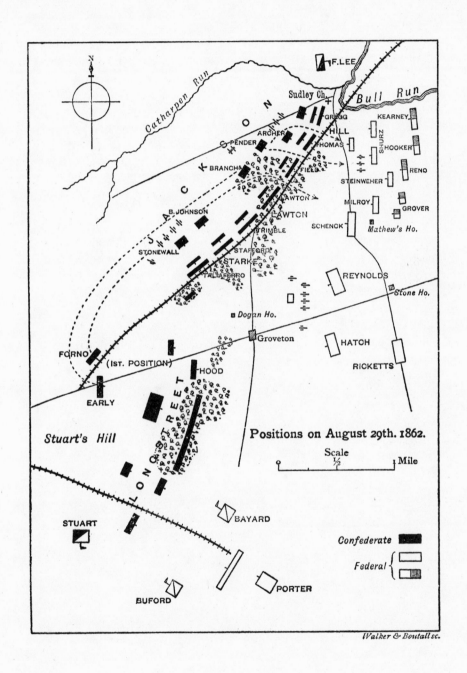

Positions on August 29th. 1862.

Scale ½ Mile

Confederate
Federal

F. LEE

Sudley Ch.
Bull Run

GREGG
KEARNEY
ARCHER
PENDER
HILL
THOMAS
SHURZ
HOOKER
BRANCHM
FIELD
RENO
STEINWEHER
LAWTON
MILROY
B. JOHNSON
LAWTON
GROVER
SCHENCK
Mathew's Ho.
TRIMBLE
STONEWALL
STAFFORD
STARKE
TALIAFERRO
REYNOLDS
Stone Ho.
Dogan Ho.
FORNO
Groveton
(IST. POSITION)
HATCH
HOOD
EARLY
RICKETTS
Stuart's Hill
STREET
LONG
STUART
BAYARD
PORTER
BUFORD

Walker & Boutall sc.

faltered; hostile infantry appeared on either flank, and as the Confederates fell back to the railroad, the enemy came forward in pursuit. Grover's brigade of Hooker's division had hitherto been held in reserve, sheltered by a roll of the land opposite that portion of the front which was held by **3 P.M.** Thomas. It was now directed to attack. 'Move slowly forward,' were the orders which Grover gave to his command, 'until the enemy opens fire. Then advance rapidly, give them one volley, and then the bayonet.' The five regiments moved steadily through the wood in a single line. When they reached the edge they saw immediately before them the red earth of the embankment, at this point ten feet high and lined with riflemen. There was a crash of fire, a swift rush through the rolling smoke, and the Federals, crossing the parapet, swept all before them. Hill's second line received them with a scattered fire, turned in confusion, and fled back upon the guns. Then beckoned victory to him who had held his reserves in hand. Jackson had seen the charge, and Forno's Louisianians, with a regiment of Lawton's, had already been sent forward with the bayonet.

In close order the counterstroke came on. The thinned ranks of the Federals could oppose no resolute resistance. Fighting they fell back, first to the embankment, where for a few moments they held their own, and then to the wood. But without supports it was impossible to rally. Johnson's and Starke's brigades swept down upon their flank, the Louisianians, supported by Field and Archer, against their front, and in twenty minutes, with a loss of one-fourth his numbers, Grover in his turn was driven beyond the Warrenton turnpike.

Four divisions, Schurz', Steinwehr's, Hooker's, and Reno's, had been hurled in succession against Jackson's front. Their losses had been enormous. Grover's brigade had lost 461 out of 2,000, of which one regiment, 283 strong, accounted for 6 officers and 106 men; three regiments of Reno's lost 530; and it is probable that more than 4,000 men had fallen in the wood which lay in front of Hill's brigades.

The fighting, however, had not been without effect on

the Confederates. The charges to which they had been exposed, impetuous as they were, were doubtless less trying than a sustained attack, pressed on by continuous waves of fresh troops, and allowing the defence no breathing space. Such steady pressure, always increasing in strength, saps the *moral* more rapidly than a series of fierce assaults, delivered at wide intervals of time. But such pressure implies on the part of the assailant an accumulation of superior force, and this accumulation the enemy's generals had not attempted to provide. In none of the four attacks which had shivered against Hill's front had the strength of the assailants been greater than that of his own division; and to the tremendous weight of such a stroke as had won the battles of Gaines' Mill or Cedar Run, to the closely combined advance of overwhelming numbers, Jackson's men had not yet been subjected.

The battle, nevertheless, had been fiercely contested, and the strain of constant vigilance and close-range fighting had told on the Light Division. The Federal skirmishers, boldly advancing as Pender's men fell back, had once more filled the wood, and their venomous fire allowed the defenders no leisure for repose.[1] Ammunition had already given out; many of the men had but two or three cartridges remaining, and the volunteers who ran the gauntlet to procure fresh supplies were many of them shot down. Moreover, nine hours' fighting, much of it at close range, had piled the corpses thick upon the railroad, and the ranks of Hill's brigades were terribly attenuated. The second line had already been brought up to fill the gaps, and every brigade had been heavily engaged.

It was about four o'clock, and for a short space the pressure on the Confederate lines relaxed. The continuous

---

[1] 'The Federal sharpshooters at this time,' says Colonel McCrady, of the Light Division, 'held possession of the wood, and kept up a deadly fire of single shots whenever any one of us was exposed. Every lieutenant who had to change position did so at the risk of his life. What was my horror, during an interval in the attack, to see General Jackson himself walking quickly down the railroad cut, examining our position, and calmly looking into the wood that concealed the enemy! Strange to say, he was not molested.'—*Southern Historical Society Papers*, vol. xiii., p. 27.

roar of the artillery dwindled to a fitful cannonade ; and
along the edge of the wood, drooping under the
4 P.M. heat, where the foliage was white with the dust of
battle, the skirmishers let their rifles cool. But the Valley
soldiers knew that their respite would be short. The Federal
masses were still marching and countermarching on the
opposite hills ; from the forest beyond long columns
streamed steadily to the front, and near the Warrenton
turnpike fresh batteries were coming into action.

Pope had ordered Kearney and Reno to make a fresh
attack. The former, one of the most dashing officers in
the Federal army, disposed his division in two lines. Reno,
in the same formation, deployed upon Kearney's right, and
with their flank resting on Bull Run the five brigades went
forward to the charge. The Confederate batteries, posted
on the ridge in rear, swept the open ground along the
stream ; but, regardless of their fire, the Federals came
rapidly to close quarters, and seized the railroad. When
Hill saw this formidable storm bursting on his
4.30 P.M. lines he felt that the supreme moment had arrived.
Would Gregg, on whose front the division of Reno was bearing down, be able to hold his own ? That gallant soldier,
although more than one half of his command lay dead or
wounded, replied, in answer to his chief's enquiry, that
his ammunition was almost expended, but that he had still
the bayonet. Nevertheless, the pressure was too heavy for
his wearied troops. Foot by foot they were forced back, and,
at the same moment, Thomas, Field, and Branch, still fighting desperately, were compelled to yield their ground. Hill,
anxiously looking for succour, had already called on Early.
The enemy, swarming across the railroad, had penetrated
to a point three hundred yards within the Confederate position. But the grey line was not yet shattered. The men of
the Light Division, though borne backwards by the rush,
still faced towards the foe ; and Early's brigade, supported
by two regiments of Lawton's division, advanced with
levelled bayonets, drove through the tumult, and opposed
a solid line to the crowd of Federals.

Once more the fresh reserve, thrown in at the propitious

moment, swept back numbers far superior to itself. Once
more order prevailed over disorder, and the cold steel
asserted its supremacy. The strength of the assailants was
already spent. The wave receded more swiftly than it
had risen, and through the copses and across the railroad
the Confederates drove their exhausted foe. General Hill
had instructed Early that he was not to pass beyond the
original front; but it was impossible to restrain the
troops, and not till they had advanced several hundred
yards was the brigade halted and brought back. The
5.15 P.M.   counterstroke was as completely successful as those
            that had preceded it. Early's losses were com-
paratively slight, those inflicted on the enemy very heavy,
and Hill's brigades were finally relieved. Pope abandoned
all further efforts to crush Jackson. Five assaults had
failed. 30,000 infantry had charged in vain through the
fatal wood; and of the 8,000 Federal casualties reported
on this day, by far the larger proportion was due to the
deadly fire and dashing counterstrokes of Jackson's
infantry.

While Pope was hurling division after division against
the Confederate left, Lee, with Longstreet at his side,
observed the conflict from Stuart's Hill, the wooded
eminence which stands south-west of Groveton. On this
wing, though a mile distant from Jackson's battle, both
Federals and Confederates were in force. At least one half
of Pope's army had gradually assembled on this flank.
Here were Reynolds and McDowell, and on the Manassas
road stood two divisions under Porter.

Within the woods on Stuart's Hill, with the cavalry on
his flank, Longstreet had deployed his whole force, with the
exception of Anderson, who had not yet passed Thoroughfare
Gap. But although both Pope and Lee were anxious to
engage, neither could bring their subordinates to the point.
Pope had sent vague instructions to Porter and McDowell,
and when at length he had substituted a definite order it
was not only late in arriving, but the generals found that it
was based on an absolutely incorrect view of the situation.
The Federal commander had no knowledge that Longstreet,

with 25,000 men, was already in position beyond his left. So close lay the Confederates that under the impression that Stuart's Hill was still untenanted, he desired Porter to move across it and envelop Jackson's right. Porter, suspecting that the main body of the Southern army was before him, declined to risk his 10,000 men until he had reported the true state of affairs. A peremptory reply to attack at once was received at 6.30, but it was then too late to intervene.

Nor had Lee been more successful in developing a counterstroke. Longstreet, with a complacency it is difficult to understand, has related how he opposed the wishes of the Commander-in-Chief. Three times Lee urged him forward. The first time he rode to the front to reconnoitre, and found that the position, in his own words, was not inviting. Again Lee insisted that the enemy's left might be turned. While the question was under discussion, a heavy force (Porter and McDowell) was reported advancing from Manassas Junction. No attack followed, however, and Lee repeated his instructions. Longstreet was still unwilling. A large portion of the Federal force on the Manassas road now marched northward to join Pope, and Lee, for the last time, bade Longstreet attack towards Groveton. 'I suggested,' says the latter, 'that the day being far spent, it might be as well to advance before night on a forced reconnaissance, get our troops into the most favourable positions, and have all things ready for battle the next morning. To this General Lee reluctantly gave consent, and orders were given for an advance to be pursued under cover of night, until the main position could be carefully examined. It so happened that an order to advance was issued on the other side at the same time, so that the encounter was something of a surprise on both sides.'[1] Hood, with his two Texan brigades, led the Confederates, and King's division, now commanded by Hatch, met him on the slopes of Stuart's Hill. Although the Federals, since 1 A.M. the same morning, had marched to Manassas and back again, the fight was spirited. Hood, however, was strongly supported, and the Texans pushed forward

[1] *Battles and Leaders*, vol. ii., p. 519.

a mile and a half in front of the position they had held since noon. Longstreet had now full leisure to make his reconnaissance. The ground to which the enemy had retreated was very strong. He believed it strongly manned, and an hour after midnight Hood's brigades were ordered to withdraw.

The firing, even of the skirmishers, had long since died away on the opposite flank. The battle was over, and the Valley army had been once more victorious. But when Jackson's staff gathered round him in the bivouac, 'their triumph,' says Dabney, 'bore a solemn hue.' Their great task had been accomplished, and Pope's army, harassed, starving, and bewildered, had been brought to bay. But their energies were worn down. The incessant marching, by day and night, the suspense of the past week, the fierce strife of the day that had just closed, pressed heavily on the whole force. Many of the bravest were gone. Trimble, that stout soldier, was severely wounded, Field and Forno had fallen, and in Gregg's brigade alone 40 officers were dead or wounded. Doctor McGuire, fresh from the ghastly spectacle of the silent battle-field, said, 'General, this day has been won by nothing but stark and stern fighting.' 'No,' replied Jackson, very quietly, 'it has been won by nothing but the blessing and protection of Providence.' And in this attitude of acknowledgment general and soldiers were as one. When the pickets had been posted, and night had fallen on the forest, officers and men, gathered together round their chaplains, made such preparations for the morrow's battle as did the host of King Harry on the eve of Agincourt.

NOTE

Students of war will note with interest the tactical details of the passage of the Rappahannock by the Army of Northern Virginia.

August 21.—FEDERALS.

In position behind the river from Kelly's Ford to Freeman's Ford. *Tête de pont* covering the railway bridge, occupied by a brigade.

CONFEDERATES.

Longstreet to Kelly's Ford.
Jackson to Beverley Ford.
Stuart to above Beverley Ford.
        Constant skirmishing and artillery fire.

August 22.—FEDERALS.

In position from Kelly's Ford to Freeman's Ford.
Bayard's cavalry brigade on right flank.
Buford's cavalry brigade at Rappahannock Station.

CONFEDERATES.

Jackson to Sulphur Springs.   Early crosses the river.
Longstreet to Beverley Ford and railway.
        Constant skirmishing and artillery fire.

August 23.—FEDERALS.

Pope abandons *tête de pont* and burns railway bridge.
Sigel moves against Early, but his advance is repulsed.
Army to a position about Warrenton, with detachments along the river, and a strong force at Kelly's Ford.

CONFEDERATES.

Early moves north to Great Run, and is reinforced by Lawton.
Stuart to Catlett's Station.
Longstreet demonstrates against railway bridge.

August 24.—FEDERALS.

Buford's and Bayard's cavalry to Waterloo.
Army to Waterloo and Sulphur Springs.

CONFEDERATES.

Jackson in the evening retires to Jefferson, and is relieved after
    dark opposite Sulphur Springs and Waterloo by Longstreet.
Anderson relieves Longstreet on the railway.
    Constant skirmishing and artillery fire all along the line.

August 25.—FEDERALS.

Pope extends his left down the river to Kelly's Ford, determining
    to receive attack at Warrenton should the Confederates cross.

CONFEDERATES.

Jackson moves north and crosses the river at Hinson's Mills.
Longstreet demonstrates at Waterloo, and Anderson at the Sulphur
    Springs.

August 26.—FEDERALS.

A reconnaissance in force, owing to bad staff arrangements, comes
    to nothing. At nightfall the whole army is ordered to con-
    centrate at Warrenton.

CONFEDERATES.

2 A.M. Stuart follows Jackson.
Late in the afternoon, Longstreet, having been relieved by
    Anderson, marches to Hinson's Mills.
Jackson captures Manassas Junction.
    Skirmishing all day along the Rappahannock.

August 27.—FEDERALS.

7 A.M. Hooker's division from Warrenton Junction to Bristoe
    Station.
8.30 A.M. Army ordered to concentrate at Gainesville, Buckland
    Mills, and Greenwich. Porter and Banks at Warrenton
    Junction.
3 P.M. Action at Bristoe Station.
6.30 P.M. Pope arrives at Bristoe Station.
Army ordered to march to Manassas Junction at dawn.

CONFEDERATES.

Jackson at Manassas Junction.
Longstreet to White Plains.

CHAPTER XVII

THE SECOND MANASSAS (*continued*)

DURING the night of August 30 the long line of camp-fires on the heights above Bull Run, and the frequent skirmishes along the picket line, told General Lee that his enemy had no intention of falling back behind the stream. And when morning broke the Federal troops were observed upon every ridge.

The Confederate leader, eager as he had been to force the battle to an issue on the previous afternoon, had now abandoned all idea of attack. The respite which Aug. 30. the enemy had gained might have altogether changed the situation. It was possible that the Federals had been largely reinforced. Pope and McClellan had been given time, and the hours of the night might have been utilised to bring up the remainder of the Army of the Potomac. Lee resolved, therefore, to await events. The Federal position was strong; their masses were well concentrated; there was ample space, on the ridges beyond Young's Branch, for the deployment of their numerous artillery, and it would be difficult to outflank them. Moreover, a contingent of fresh troops from Richmond, the divisions of D. H. Hill, McLaws, and Walker, together with Hampton's brigade of cavalry, and part of the reserve artillery, 20,350 men in all, had crossed the Rappahannock.[1] Until this force should join him he deter-

---

[1] D. H. Hill 7,000
McLaws 6,850
Walker 4,000
Hampton 1,500
Artillery 1,000
               20,350

mined to postpone further manœuvres, and to rest his army. But he was not without hope that Pope might assume the initiative and move down from the heights on which his columns were already forming. Aware of the sanguine and impatient temper of his adversary, confident in the *moral* of his troops, and in the strength of his position, he foresaw that an opportunity might offer for an overwhelming counterstroke.

Meanwhile, the Confederate divisions, still hidden in the woods, lay quietly on their arms. Few changes were made in the dispositions of the previous day. Jackson, despite his losses, had made no demand for reinforcements; and the only direct support afforded him was a battery of eighteen guns, drawn from the battalion of Colonel S. D. Lee, and established on the high ground west of the Douglass House, at right angles to his line of battle. These guns, pointing north-east, overlooked the wide tract of undulating meadow which lay in front of the Stonewall and Lawton's divisions, and they commanded a field of fire over a mile long. The left of the battery was not far distant from the guns on Jackson's right, and the whole of the open space was thus exposed to the cross-fire of a formidable artillery.

To the right of the batteries, Stuart's Hill was strongly occupied by Longstreet, with Anderson's division as general reserve; and this wing of the Confederate army was gradually wheeled up, but always under cover, until it was almost perpendicular to the line of the unfinished railroad. The strength of Lee's army at the battle of Manassas was hardly more than 50,000 of all arms. Jackson's command had been reduced by battle and forced marches to 17,000 men. Longstreet mustered 30,000, and the cavalry 2,500.

But numbers are of less importance than the confidence of the men in their ability to conquer,[1] and the spirit of the Confederates had been raised to the highest pitch. The keen

---

[1] Hood's Texans had a hymn which graphically expressed this truism :

  ' The race is not to him that's got
   The longest legs to run,
  Nor the battle to those people
   That shoot the biggest gun.'

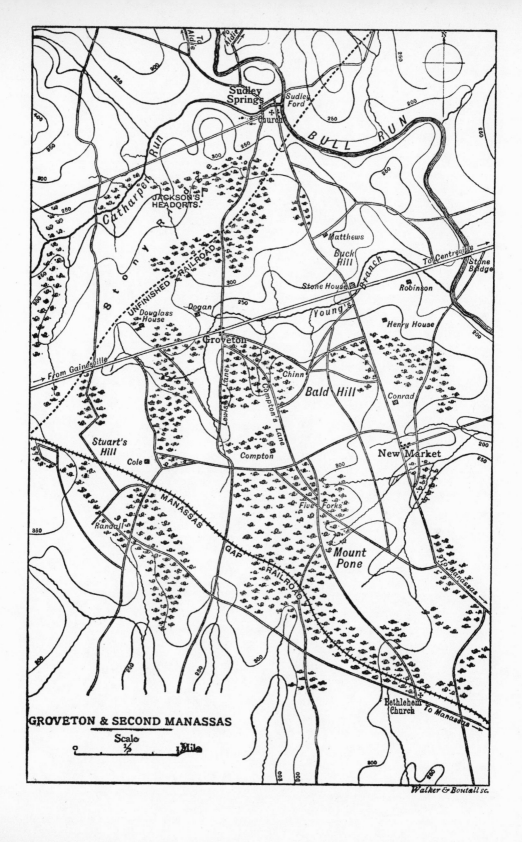

GROVETON & SECOND MANASSAS

Scale

0   ½   1 Mile

Walker & Boutall sc.

critics in Longstreet's ranks, although they had taken
no part in the Manassas raid, or in the battles of August 28
and 29, fully appreciated the daring strategy which had
brought them within two short marches of Washington. The
junction of the two wings, in the very presence of the
enemy, after many days of separation, was a manœuvre
after their own hearts. The passage of Thoroughfare
Gap revealed the difficulties which had attended the
operations, and the manner in which the enemy had been
outwitted appealed with peculiar force to their quick intelligence. Their trust in Lee was higher than ever; and
the story of Jackson's march, of the capture of Manassas,
of the repulse of Pope's army, if it increased their contempt for the enemy, inspired them with an enthusiastic
determination to emulate the achievements of their comrades. The soldiers of the Valley army, who, unaided
by a single bayonet, had withstood the five successive
assaults which had been launched against their position,
were supremely indifferent, now Longstreet was in line,
to whatever the enemy might attempt. It was noticed
that notwithstanding the heavy losses they had experienced Jackson's troops were never more light-hearted
than on the morning of August 30. Cartridge-boxes
had been replenished, rations had been issued, and for
several hours the men had been called on neither to march
nor fight. As they lay in the woods, and the pickets,
firing on the enemy's patrols, kept up a constant skirmish
to the front, the laugh and jest ran down the ranks, and
the unfortunate Pope, who had only seen ' the backs of his
enemies,' served as whetstone for their wit.

By the troops who had revelled in the spoils of Winchester Banks had been dubbed ' Old Jack's Commissary
General.' By universal acclamation, after the Manassas
foray, Pope was promoted to the same distinction ; and had
it been possible to penetrate to the Federal headquarters, the
mirth of those ragged privates would hardly have diminished. Pope was in an excellent humour, conversing
affably with his staff, and viewing with pride the martial
aspect of his massed divisions. Nearly his whole force

was concentrated on the hills around him, and Porter, who had been called up from the Manassas road, was already marching northwards through the woods. Banks still was absent at Bristoe Station, in charge of the trains and stores which had been removed from Warrenton ; but, shortly 10.15 A.M. after ten o'clock, 65,000 men, with eight-and-twenty batteries, were at Pope's disposal. He had determined to give battle, although Franklin and Sumner, who had already reached Alexandria, had not yet joined him ; and he anticipated an easy triumph. He was labouring, however, under an extraordinary delusion. The retreat of Hood's brigades the preceding night, after their reconnaissance, had induced him to believe that Jackson had been defeated, and he had reported to Halleck at daybreak : ' We fought a terrific battle here yesterday with the combined forces of the enemy, which lasted with continuous fury from daylight until dark, by which time the enemy was driven from the field, which we now occupy. The enemy is still in our front, but badly used up. We lost not less than 8,000 men killed and wounded, but from the appearance of the field the enemy lost at least two to one. The news has just reached me from the front that the enemy is retreating towards the mountains.'

If, in these days of long-range weapons, Napoleon's dictum still stands good, that the general who is ignorant of his enemy's strength and dispositions is ignorant of his trade, then of all generals Pope was surely the most incompetent. At ten o'clock on the morning of August 30, and for many months afterwards, despite his statement that he had fought ' the combined forces of the enemy ' on the previous day, he was still under the impression, so skilfully were the Confederate troops concealed, that Longstreet had not yet joined Jackson, and that the latter was gradually falling back on Thoroughfare Gap. His patrols had reported that the enemy's cavalry had been withdrawn from the left bank of Bull Run. A small reconnaissance in force, sent to test Jackson's strength, had ascertained that the extreme left was not so far forward as it had been yesterday ; while two of the Federal generals, reconnoitring beyond the turnpike, observed only a few skirmishers. On these negative reports Pope based his decision to seize the ridge which was held by Jackson. Yet the woods along the unfinished railroad had not been examined, and the information from other sources was of a different colour and more positive. Buford's cavalry had reported on the evening of the 29th that a large force had passed through Thoroughfare Gap. Porter declared that the enemy was in great strength on the Manassas road. Reynolds, who had been in close contact with Longstreet since the previous afternoon, reported that Stuart's Hill was strongly occupied. Ricketts, moreover, who had fought Longstreet for many hours at Thoroughfare Gap, was actually present on the field. But Pope, who had made up his mind that the enemy ought to retreat, and that therefore he must retreat, refused credence to any report whatever which ran counter to these preconceived ideas. Without making the slightest attempt to verify, by personal observation, the conclusions at which his subordinates had 12 noon. arrived, at midday, to the dismay of his best officers, his army being now in position, he issued orders for his troops to be 'immediately thrown forward in pursuit of the enemy, and to press him vigorously.'

Porter and Reynolds formed the left of the Federal army. These generals, alive to the necessity of examining the woods, deployed a strong skirmish line before them as they formed for action. Further evidence of Pope's hallucination was at once forthcoming. The moment Reynolds moved forward against Stuart's Hill he found his front overlapped by long lines of infantry, and, riding back, he informed Pope that in so doing he had had to run the gauntlet of skirmishers who threatened his rear. Porter, too, pushing his reconnaissance across the meadows west of Groveton, drew the fire of several batteries. But at this juncture, unfortunately for the Federals, a Union prisoner, recaptured from Jackson, declared that he had 'heard the rebel officers say that their army was retiring to unite with Longstreet.' So positively did the indications before him contradict this statement, that Porter, on sending the man

to Pope, wrote : ' In duty bound I send him, but I regard
him as either a fool or designedly released to give a wrong
impression.   No faith should be put in what he says.'   If
Jackson employed this man to delude his enemy, the ruse
was eminently successful.   Porter received the reply :
' General Pope believes that soldier, and directs you to
attack ; ' Reynolds was dismissed with a message that cavalry
would be sent to verify his report ; and McDowell was
ordered to put in the divisions of Hatch and Ricketts on
Porter's right.

During the whole morning the attention of the Confederates had been directed to the Groveton wood.   Beyond
the timber rose the hill north-east, and on this hill three or
four Federal batteries had come into action at an early
hour, firing at intervals across the meadows.   The Confederate guns, save when the enemy's skirmishers approached too close, hardly deigned to reply, reserving their
ammunition for warmer work.   That such work was to
come was hardly doubtful.   Troops had been constantly in
motion near the hostile batteries, and the thickets below
12.15 P.M. were evidently full of men.   Shortly after noon
the enemy's skirmishers became aggressive,
swarming over the meadows, and into the wood which had
seen such heavy slaughter in the fight of yesterday.   As
Jackson's pickets, extended over a wide front, gave slowly
back, his guns opened in earnest, and shell and shrapnel
flew fast over the open space.   The strong force of
skirmishers betrayed the presence of a line of battle not
far in rear, and ignoring the fire of the artillery, the
Confederate batteries concentrated on the covert behind
which they knew the enemy's masses were forming for
attack.   But, except the pickets, not a single man of
either the Stonewall or Lawton's division was permitted to
expose himself.   A few companies held the railroad, the
remainder were carefully concealed.   The storm was not
long in breaking.   Jackson had just ridden along his
lines, examining with his own eyes the stir in the Groveton wood, when, in rear of the skirmishers, advancing
over the highroad, appeared the serried ranks of the line

of battle. 20,000 bayonets, on a front which extended from Groveton to near Bull Run, swept forward against his front; 40,000, formed in dense masses on the slopes in rear, stood in readiness to support them; and numerous batteries, coming into action on every rising ground, covered the advance with a heavy fire.

Pope, standing on a knoll near the Stone House, saw victory within his grasp. The Confederate guns had been pointed out to his troops as the objective of the attack. Unsupported, as he believed, save by the scattered groups of skirmishers who were already retreating to the railroad, and assailed in front and flank, these batteries, he expected, would soon be flying to the rear, and the Federal army, in possession of the high ground, would then sweep down in heavy columns towards Thoroughfare Gap. Suddenly his hopes fell. Porter's masses, stretching far to right and left, had already passed the Dogan House; Hatch was entering the Groveton wood; Ricketts was moving forward along Bull Run, and the way seemed clear before them; when loud and clear above the roar of the artillery rang out the Confederate bugles, and along the whole length of the ridge beyond the railroad long lines of infantry, streaming forward from the woods, ran down to the embankment. 'The effect,' said an officer who witnessed this unexpected apparition, 'was not unlike flushing a covey of quails.'

Instead of the small rear-guard which Pope had thought to crush by sheer force of overwhelming numbers, the whole of the Stonewall division, with Lawton on the left, stood across Porter's path.

Reynolds, south of the turnpike, and confronting Longstreet, was immediately ordered to fall back and support the attack, and two small brigades, Warren's and Alexander's, were left alone on the Federal left. Pope had committed his last and his worst blunder. Sigel with two divisions was in rear of Porter, and for Sigel's assistance Porter had already asked. But Pope, still under the delusion that Longstreet was not yet up, preferred rather to weaken his left than grant the request of a subordinate.

Under such a leader the courage of the troops, however vehement, was of no avail, and in Porter's attack the soldiers displayed a courage to which the Confederates paid a willing tribute. Morell's division, with the two brigades abreast, arrayed in three lines, advanced across the meadows. Hatch's division, in still deeper formation, pushed through the wood on Morell's right. Nearer Bull Run were two brigades of Ricketts; and to Morell's left rear the division of regulars moved forward under Sykes.

Morell's attack was directed against Jackson's right. In the centre of the Federal line a mounted officer, whose gallant bearing lived long in the memories of the Stonewall division, rode out in front of the column, and, drawing his sabre, led the advance over the rolling grass-land. The Confederate batteries, with a terrible cross-fire, swept the Northern ranks from end to end. The volleys of the infantry, lying behind their parapet, struck them full in face. But the horse and his rider lived through it all. The men followed close, charging swiftly up the slope, and then the leader, putting his horse straight at the embankment, stood for a moment on the top. The daring feat was seen by the whole Confederate line, and a yell went up from the men along the railroad, ' Don't kill him! don't kill him!' But while the cry went up horse and rider fell in one limp mass across the earthwork, and the gallant Northerner was dragged under shelter by his generous foes.

With such men as this to show the way what soldiers would be backward? As the Russians followed Skobeleff's grey up the bloody slopes of Plevna, so the Federals followed the bright chestnut of this unknown hero, and not till the colours waved within thirty paces of the parapet did the charge falter. But, despite the supports that came thronging up, Jackson's soldiers, covered by the earthwork, opposed a resistance which no mere frontal attack could break. Three times, as the lines in rear merged with the first, the Federal officers brought their men forward to the assault, and three times were they hurled back, leaving hundreds of their number dead and wounded on the blood-

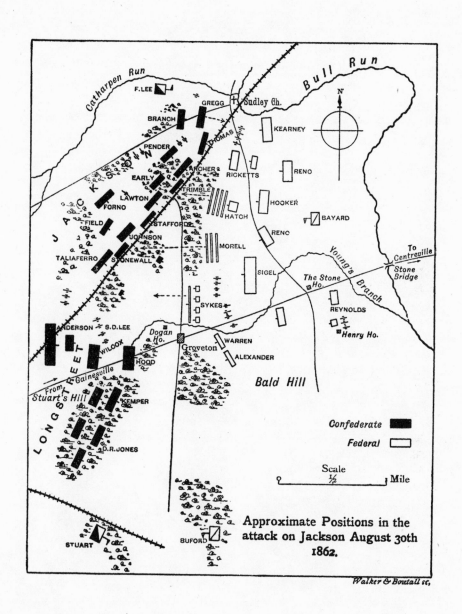

Catharpen Run

Bull Run

F. LEE

GREGG
Sudley Ch.
BRANCH
THOMAS
KEARNEY
PENDER
N
ARCHER
RICKETTS
RENO
EARLY
TRIMBLE
LAWTON
HOOKER
FORNO
HATCH
BAYARD
STAFFORD
FIELD
RENO
JOHNSON
MORELL
Young's Branch
To
Centreville
TALIAFERRO
STONEWALL
SIGEL
The Stone Ho.
Stone Bridge

SYKES
REYNOLDS
Henry Ho.
ANDERSON
S.D.LEE
Dogan Ho.
WILCOX
Groveton
WARREN
HOOD
ALEXANDER
From Gainesville
Stuart's Hill
KEMPER
Bald Hill

D.R.JONES

Confederate ▬
Federal ▭

Scale
½
Mile

STUART
BUFORD

Approximate Positions in the
attack on Jackson August 30th
1862.

JACKSON

LONGSTREET

Walker & Boutall sc,

soaked turf. One regiment of the Stonewall division, posted in a copse beyond the railroad, was driven in; but others, when cartridges failed them, had recourse, like the Guards at Inkermann, to the stones which lay along the railway-bed; and with these strange weapons, backed up by the bayonet, more than one desperate effort was repulsed. In arresting Garnett after Kernstown, because when his ammunition was exhausted he had abandoned his position, Jackson had lost a good general, but he had taught his soldiers a useful lesson. So long as the cold steel was left to them, and their flanks were safe, they knew that their indomitable leader expected them to hold their ground, and right gallantly they responded. For over thirty minutes the battle raged along the front at the closest range. Opposite a deep cutting the colours of a Federal regiment, for nearly half an hour, rose and fell, as bearer after bearer was shot down, within ten yards of the muzzles of the Confederate rifles, and after the fight a hundred dead Northerners were found where the flag had been so gallantly upheld.

Hill, meanwhile, was heavily engaged with Hatch. Every brigade, with the exception of Gregg's, had been thrown into the fighting-line; and so hardly were they pressed, that Jackson, turning to his signallers, demanded reinforcements from his colleague. Longstreet, in response to the call, ordered two more batteries to join Colonel Stephen Lee; and Morell's division, penned in that deadly cockpit between Stuart's Hill and the Groveton wood, shattered by musketry in front and by artillery at short range in flank, fell back across the meadows. Hatch soon followed suit, and Jackson's artillery, which during the fight at close quarters had turned its fire on the supports, launched a storm of shell on the defeated Federals. Some batteries were ordered to change position so as to rake their lines; and the Stonewall division, reinforced by a brigade of Hill's, was sent forward to the counter-attack. At every step the losses of the Federals increased, and the shattered divisions, passing through two regiments of regulars, which had been sent forward to support them, sought shelter in the woods. Then Porter and Hatch, under cover of their artillery, withdrew their infantry. Ricketts had fallen back before his troops arrived within decisive range. Under the impression that he was about to pursue a retreating enemy, he had found on advancing, instead of a thin screen of skirmishers, a line of battle, strongly established, and backed by batteries to which he was unable to reply. Against such odds attack would only have increased the slaughter.

It was after four o'clock. Three hours of daylight yet remained, time enough still to secure a victory. But the Federal army was in no condition to renew the attack. Worn with long marches, deprived of their supplies, and oppressed by the consciousness that they were ill-led, both officers and men had lost all confidence. Every single division on the field had been engaged, and every single division had been beaten back. For four days, according to General Pope, they had been following a flying foe. 'We were sent forward,' reported a regimental commander with quiet sarcasm, 'to pursue the enemy, who was said to be retreating; we found the enemy, but did not see them retreat.'

4.15 P.M.

Nor, had there been a larger reserve in hand, would a further advance have been permitted. The Stonewall division, although Porter's regiments were breaking up before its onset, had been ordered to fall back before it became exposed to the full sweep of the Federal guns. But the woods to the south, where Longstreet's divisions had been lying for so many hours, were already alive with bayonets. The grey skirmishers, extending far beyond Pope's left, were moving rapidly down the slopes of Stuart's Hill, and the fire of the artillery, massed on the ridge in rear, was increasing every moment in intensity. The Federals, just now advancing in pursuit, were suddenly thrown on the defensive; and the hand of a great captain snatched control of the battle from the grasp of Pope.

As Porter reeled back from Jackson's front, Lee had seen his opportunity. The whole army was ordered to advance to the attack. Longstreet, prepared since dawn for the counterstroke, had moved before the message

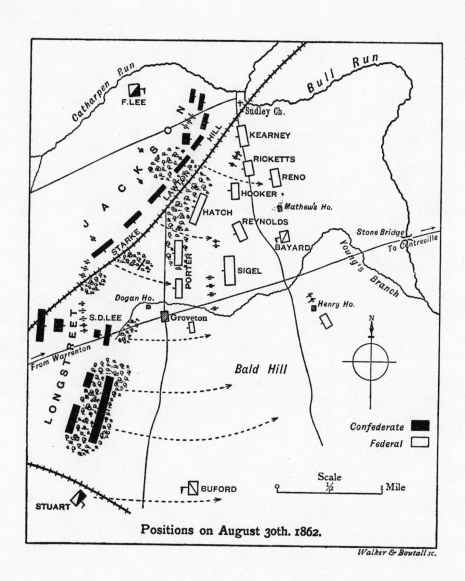

Catharpen Run

Bull Run

F. LEE

J A C K S O N

HILL

LAWTON

STARKE

Sudley Ch.

KEARNEY

RICKETTS

RENO

HOOKER

Mathew's Ho.

HATCH

REYNOLDS

BAYARD

PORTER

SIGEL

Stone Bridge

To Centreville

Young's Branch

Dogan Ho.

Henry Ho.

LONGSTREET

S. D. LEE

Groveton

From Warrenton

Bald Hill

N

Confederate

Federal

BUFORD

Scale
½
Mile

STUART

Positions on August 30th. 1862.

o 2

reached him, and the exulting yells of his soldiers were
now resounding through the forest. Jackson was desired
to cover Longstreet's left; and sending Starke and
Lawton across the meadows, strewn with the bloody *débris*
of Porter's onslaught, he instructed Hill to advance *en
échelon* with his left 'refused.' Anticipating the order,
the commander of the Light Division was already sweeping
through the Groveton wood.

The Federal gunners, striving valiantly to cover the
retreat of their shattered infantry, met the advance of the
Southerners with a rapid fire. Pope and McDowell exerted
themselves to throw a strong force on to the heights above
Bull Run; and the two brigades upon the left, Warren's
and Alexander's, already overlapped, made a gallant effort
to gain time for the occupation of the new position.

But the counterstroke of Lee was not to be withstood
by a few regiments of infantry. The field of Bull Run
had seen many examples of the attack as executed by
indifferent tacticians. At the first battle isolated brigades
had advanced at wide intervals of time. At the second
battle the Federals had assaulted by successive divisions.
Out of 50,000 infantry, no more than 20,000 had been
simultaneously engaged, and when a partial success had
been achieved there were no supports at hand to complete the victory. When the Confederates came forward it
was in other fashion; and those who had the wit to understand were now to learn the difference between mediocrity
and genius, between the half-measures of the one and
the resolution of the other. Lee's order for the advance embraced his whole army. Every regiment, every battery, and
every squadron was employed. No reserves save the artillery were retained upon the ridge, but wave after wave of
bayonets followed closely on the fighting-line. To drive
the attack forward by a quick succession of reinforcements, to push it home by weight of numbers, to pile
blow on blow, to keep the defender occupied along his
whole front, and to provide for retreat, should retreat be
necessary, not by throwing in fresh troops, but by leaving the enemy so crippled that he would be powerless

to pursue—such were the tactics of the Confederate leader.

The field was still covered with Porter's and Hatch's disordered masses when Lee's strong array advanced, and the sight was magnificent. As far as the eye could reach the long grey lines of infantry, with the crimson of the colours gleaming like blood in the evening sun, swept with ordered ranks across the Groveton valley. Batteries galloped furiously to the front; far away to the right fluttered the guidons of Stuart's squadrons, and over all the massed artillery maintained a tremendous fire. The men drew fresh vigour from this powerful combination. The enthusiasm of the troops was as intense as their excitement. With great difficulty, it is related, were the gunners restrained from joining in the charge, and the officers of the staff could scarcely resist the impulse to throw themselves with their victorious comrades upon the retreating foe.

The advance was made in the following order:
Wilcox' division, north of the turnpike, connected with Jackson's right. Then came Evans, facing the two brigades which formed the Federal left, and extending across the turnpike. Behind Evans came Anderson on the left and Kemper on the right. Then, in prolongation of Kemper's line, but at some interval, marched the division of D. R. Jones, flanked by Stuart's cavalry, and on the further wing, extending towards Bull Run, were Starke, Lawton, and A. P. Hill. 50,000 men, including the cavalry, were thus deployed over a front of four miles; each division was formed in at least two lines; and in the centre, where Anderson and Kemper supported Evans, were no less than eight brigades one in rear of the other.

The Federal advanced line, behind which the troops which had been engaged in the last attack were slowly rallying, extended from the Groveton wood to a low hill, south of the turnpike and east of the village. This hill was quickly carried by Hood's brigade of Evans's division. The two regiments which defended it, rapidly outflanked, and assailed by overwhelming numbers, were routed with the loss of nearly half their muster. Jackson's attack

through the Groveton wood was equally successful, but on
the ridge in rear were posted the regulars under Sykes;
and, further east, on Buck Hill, had assembled the remnants of four divisions.

Outflanked by the capture of the hill upon their left, and
fiercely assailed in front, Sykes's well-disciplined regiments,
formed in lines of columns and covered by a rear-guard of
skirmishers, retired steadily under the tremendous fire, preserving their formation, and falling back slowly across
Young's Branch.   Then Jackson, reforming his troops
along the Sudley road, and swinging round to the left,
moved swiftly against Buck Hill.   Here, in addition to the
infantry, were posted three Union batteries, and the artillery made a desperate endeavour to stay the counterstroke.

But nothing could withstand the vehement charge of
the Valley soldiers. 'They came on,' says the correspondent of a Northern journal, 'like demons emerging
from the earth.'   The crests of the ridges blazed with
musketry, and Hill's infantry, advancing in the very teeth
of the canister, captured six guns at the bayonet's point.
Once more Jackson reformed his lines ; and, as twilight
came down upon the battle-field, from position after
position, in the direction of the Stone Bridge, the divisions
of Stevens, Ricketts, Kearney, and Hooker, were gradually
pushed back.

On the Henry Hill, the key of the Federal position,
a fierce conflict was meanwhile raging.   From the high
ground to the south Longstreet had driven back several
brigades which, in support of the artillery, Sigel and
McDowell had massed upon Bald Hill.   But this position
had not been occupied without a protracted struggle.
Longstreet's first line, advancing with over-impetuosity,
had outstripped the second ; and before it could be supported was compelled to give ground under the enemy's
fire, one of the brigades losing 62 officers and 560
men.   Anderson and Kemper were then brought up;
the flank of the defenders was turned ; a counterstroke
was beaten back, ridge after ridge was mastered, the
edge of every wood was stormed ; and as the sun set

behind the mountains Bald Hill was carried.   During
this fierce action the division of D. R. Jones, leaving
the Chinn House to the left, had advanced against the
Henry Hill.   On the very ground which Jackson had
held in his first battle the best troops of the Federal
6 P.M.   army were rapidly assembling.   Here were
Sykes' regulars and Reynolds' Pennsylvanians ;
where the woods permitted batteries had been established ;
and Porter's Fifth Army Corps, who at Gaines' Mill and
Malvern Hill had proved such stubborn fighters, opposed
a strong front once more to their persistent foes.

Despite the rapid fire of the artillery the Southerners
swept forward with unabated vigour.   But as the attack was
pressed the resistance of the Federals grew more stubborn,
and before long the Confederate formation lost its strength.
The lines in rear had been called up.   The assistance of the
strong centre had been required to rout the defenders of Bald
Hill ; and although Anderson and Wilcox pressed forward
on his left, Jones had not sufficient strength to storm the
enemy's last position.   Moreover, the Confederate artillery
had been unable to follow the infantry over the broken
ground ; the cavalry, confronted by Buford's squadrons
and embarrassed by the woods, could lend no active aid,
and the Federals, defeated as they were, had not yet lost all
heart.   Whatever their guns could do, in so close a country,
to relieve the infantry had been accomplished ; and the
infantry, though continually outflanked, held together
with unflinching courage.   Stragglers there were, and
stragglers in such large numbers that Bayard's cavalry
brigade had been ordered to the rear to drive them back ;
but the majority of the men, hardened by months of discipline and constant battle, remained staunch to the
colours. The conviction that the battle was lost was no longer
a signal for ' the thinking bayonets ' to make certain of their
individual safety ; and the regulars, for the second time on
the same field, provided a strong nucleus of resistance.

Thrown into the woods along the Sudley-Manassas
road, five battalions of the United States army held the extreme left, the most critical point of the Federal line, until

a second brigade relieved them.   To their right Meade and
his Pennsylvanians held fast against Anderson and Wilcox;
and although six guns fell into the hands of the Confederate infantry, and four of Longstreet's batteries, which
had accompanied the cavalry, were now raking their
left, Pope's soldiers, as twilight descended upon the
field, redeemed as far as soldiers could the errors of
their general.   Stuart, on the right flank of the Confederate line, charged down the opposing cavalry [1] and
crossed Bull Run at Lewis' Ford; but the dark masses
on the Henry Hill, increased every moment by troops ascending from the valley, still held fast, with no hope indeed
of victory, but with a stern determination to maintain
their ground.   Had the hill been lost, nothing could have
saved Pope's army.   The crest commanded the crossings
of Bull Run.   The Stone Bridge, the main point of passage,
was not more than a mile northward, within the range of
artillery, and Jackson was already in possession of the
Matthew Hill, not fourteen hundred yards from the road
by which the troops must pass in their retreat.

The night, however, put an end to the battle.   Even the
Valley soldiers were constrained to halt.   It was impossible
in the obscurity to distinguish friend from foe.   The
7.30 P.M.   Confederate lines presented a broken front, here
pushed forward, and here drawn back; divisions, brigades,
and regiments had intermingled; and the thick woods, intervening at frequent intervals, rendered combination impracticable.   During the darkness, which was accompanied by heavy
rain, the Federals quietly withdrew, leaving thousands of

---

[1] This was one of the most brilliant cavalry fights of the war.   Colonel
Munford, of the 2nd Virginia, finding the enemy advancing, formed line
and charged, the impetuosity of the attack carrying his regiment through
the enemy's first line, with whom his men were thoroughly intermingled in
hand-to-hand conflict.   The Federals, however, who had advanced at a trot,
in four successive lines, were far superior in numbers; but the 7th and 12th
Virginia rapidly came up, and the charge of the 12th, constituting as it
were a last reserve, drove the enemy from the field.   The Confederates lost
5 killed and 40 wounded.   Munford himself, and the commander of the
First Michigan (Union) cavalry were both wounded by sabre-cuts, the latter
mortally.   300 Federals were taken prisoners, 19 killed, and 80 wounded.
Sabre, carbine, and revolver were freely used.

wounded on the field, and morning found them in position
on the heights of Centreville, four miles beyond Bull Run.

Pope, with an audacity which disaster was powerless to
tame, reported to Halleck that, on the whole, the results of
the battle were favourable to the Federal army. 'The
enemy,' he wrote, 'largely reinforced, assailed our position
early to-day. We held our ground firmly until 6 o'clock
P.M., when the enemy, massing very heavy forces on our
left, forced that wing back about half a mile. At dark we
held that position. Under all the circumstances, with
horses and men having been two days without food, and
the enemy greatly outnumbering us, I thought it best to
move back to this place at dark. The movement has been
made in perfect order and without loss. The battle was
most furious for hours without cessation, and the losses on
both sides very heavy. The enemy is badly whipped, and
we shall do well enough. Do not be uneasy. We will hold
our own here.'

Pope's actions, however, were invariably at variance
with Pope's words. At 6 P.M. he had ordered Franklin,
who was approaching Bull Run from Alexandria with
10,000 fresh troops, to occupy with his own command and
whatever other troops he could collect, the fortifications
round Centreville, and hold them 'to the last extremity.'
Banks, still at Bristoe Station, was told to destroy all the
supplies of which he was in charge, as well as the railway,
and to march on Centreville; while 30 guns and more
than 2,000 wounded were left upon the field. Nor were
Pope's anticipations as to the future to be fulfilled. The
position at Centreville was strong. The intrenchments
constructed by the Confederates during the winter of 1861
were still standing. Halleck had forwarded supplies; there
was ammunition in abundance, and 20,000 infantry under
Franklin and Sumner—for the latter also had come up from
Washington—more than compensated for the casualties of
the battle. But formidable earthworks, against generals
who dare manoeuvre, are often a mere trap for the un-
wary.

Before daylight Stuart and his troopers were in the saddle;

and, picking up many stragglers as they marched, came
within range of the guns at Centreville. Lee, accom-
Aug. 31.
panied by Jackson, having reconnoitred the position, determined to move once more upon the Federal rear.
Longstreet remained on the battle-field to engage the
attention of the enemy and cover the removal of the
wounded ; while Jackson, crossing not by the Stone Bridge,
but by Sudley Ford, was entrusted with the work of
forcing Pope from his strong position.

The weather was inclement, the roads were quagmires,
and the men were in no condition to make forced marches.
Yet before nightfall Jackson had pushed ten miles through
the mud, halting near Pleasant Valley, on the Little River
turnpike, five miles north-west of Centreville. During the
afternoon Longstreet, throwing a brigade across Bull Run to
keep the enemy on the *qui vive*, followed the same route. Of
these movements Pope received no warning, and Jackson's
proclivity for flank manœuvres had evidently made no
impression on him, for, in blissful unconsciousness that
his line of retreat was already threatened, he ordered all
waggons to be unloaded at Centreville, and to return to
Fairfax Station for forage and rations.

But on the morning of September 1, although his
whole army, including Banks, was closely concentrated
behind strong intrenchments, Pope had conceived
Sept. 1.
a suspicion that he would find it difficult to fulfil his
promise to Halleck that ' he would hold on.' The previous
night Stuart had been active towards his right and rear,
capturing his reconnoitring parties, and shelling his
trains. Before noon suspicion became certainty. Either
stragglers or the country people reported that Jackson was
moving down the Little River turnpike, and Centreville
was at once evacuated, the troops marching to a new position
round Fairfax Court House.

Jackson, meanwhile, covered by the cavalry, was advancing to Chantilly—a fine old mansion which the Federals
had gutted—with the intention of seizing a position whence
he could command the road. The day was sombre, and
a tempest was gathering in the mountains. Late in the

afternoon, Stuart's patrols near Ox Hill were driven in by
hostile infantry, the thick woods preventing the scouts from
ascertaining the strength or dispositions of the Federal force.
Jackson at once ordered two brigades of Hill's to feel the
enemy.   The remainder of the Light Division took ground
to the right, followed by Lawton; Starke's division held
the turnpike, and Stuart was sent towards Fairfax Court
House to ascertain whether the Federal main body was
retreating or advancing.

Reno, who had been ordered to protect Pope's flank, came
briskly forward, and Hill's advanced-guard was soon brought
to a standstill.   Three fresh brigades were rapidly deployed;
as the enemy pressed the attack a fourth was sent in, and
the Northerners fell back with the loss of a general and
many men. Lawton's first line became engaged at the same
time, and Reno, now reinforced by Kearney, made a vigorous
effort to hold the Confederates in check. Hays' brigade of
Lawton's division, commanded by an inexperienced officer,
was caught while 'clubbed' during a change of formation, and driven back in disorder ; and Trimble's brigade,
now reduced to a handful, became involved in the confusion.   But a vigorous charge of the second line restored
the battle. The Federals were beginning to give way.
General Kearney, riding through the murky twilight into
the Confederate lines, was shot by a skirmisher. The
hostile lines were within short range, and the advent
of a reserve on either side would have probably ended
the engagement.   But the rain was now falling in
torrents ; heavy peals of thunder, crashing through the
forest, drowned the discharges of the two guns which
Jackson had brought up through the woods, and the red
flash of musketry paled before the vivid lightning. Much
of the ammunition was rendered useless, the men were
unable to discharge their pieces, and the fierce wind
lashed the rain in the faces of the Confederates.   The
night grew darker and the tempest fiercer ; and as if by
mutual consent the opposing lines drew gradually apart.[1]

[1] It was at this time, probably, that Jackson received a message from a
brigade commander, reporting that his cartridges were so wet that he

On the side of the Confederates only half the force had been engaged. Starke's division never came into action, and of Hill's and Lawton's there were still brigades in reserve. 500 men were killed or wounded; but although the three Federal divisions are reported to have lost 1,000, they had held their ground, and Jackson was thwarted in his design. Pope's trains and his whole army reached Fairfax Court House without further disaster. But the persistent attacks of his indefatigable foe had broken down his resolution. He had intended, he told Halleck, when Jackson's march down the Little River turnpike was first announced, to attack the Confederates the next day, or

Sept. 2. 'certainly the day after.' The action at Chantilly, however, induced a more prudent mood; and, on the morning of the 2nd, he reported that 'there was an intense idea among the troops that they must get behind the intrenchments [of Alexandria]; that there was an undoubted purpose, on the part of the enemy, to keep on slowly turning his position so as to come in on the right, and that the forces under his command were unable to prevent him doing so in the open field. Halleck must decide what was to be done.' The reply was prompt, Pope was to bring his forces, 'as best he could,' under the shelter of the heavy guns.

Whatever might be the truth as regards the troops, there could be no question .but that the general was demoralised; and, preceded by thousands of stragglers, the army fell back without further delay to the Potomac. It was not followed except by Stuart. 'It was found,' says Lee, in his official dispatch, 'that the enemy had conducted his retreat so rapidly that the attempt to interfere with him was abandoned. The proximity of the fortifications around Alexandria and Washington rendered further pursuit useless.'

On the same day General McClellan was entrusted with the defence of Washington, and Pope, permitted to resign, was soon afterwards relegated to an obscure

feared he could not maintain his position. 'Tell him,' was the quick reply, ' to hold his ground; if his guns will not go off, neither will the enemy's.'

command against the Indians of the North-west. His errors had been flagrant. He can hardly be charged with want of energy, but his energy was spasmodic; on the field of battle he was strangely indolent, and yet he distrusted the reports of others. But more fatal than his neglect of personal reconnaissance was his power of self-deception. He was absolutely incapable of putting himself in his enemy's place, and time after time he acted on the supposition that Lee and Jackson would do exactly what he most wished them to do. When his supplies were destroyed, he concentrated at Manassas Junction, convinced that Jackson would remain to be overwhelmed. When he found Jackson near Sudley Springs, and Thoroughfare Gap open, he rushed forward to attack him, convinced that Longstreet could not be up for eight-and-forty hours. When he sought shelter at Centreville, he told Halleck not to be uneasy, convinced that Lee would knock his head against his fortified position. Before the engagement at Chantilly he had made up his mind to attack the enemy the next morning. A few hours later he reported that his troops were utterly untrustworthy, although 20,000 of them, under Franklin and Sumner, had not yet seen the enemy. In other respects his want of prudence had thwarted his best endeavours. His cavalry at the beginning of the campaign was effectively employed. But so extravagant were his demands on the mounted arm, that before the battle of Manassas half his regiments were dismounted. It is true that the troopers were still indifferent horsemen and bad horse-masters, but it was the fault of the commander that the unfortunate animals had no rest, that brigades were sent to do the work of patrols, and that little heed was paid to the physical wants of man and beast. As a tactician Pope was incapable. As a strategist he lacked imagination, except in his dispatches. His horizon was limited, and he measured the capacity of his adversaries by his own. He was familiar with the campaign in the Valley, with the operations in the Peninsula, and Cedar Run should have enlightened him as to Jackson's daring. But he had no conception that his adversaries would cheerfully accept great risks to achieve great ends; he had never dreamt of a general who would deliberately divide his army, or of one who would make fifty-six miles in two marches.

Lee, with his extraordinary insight into character, had played on Pope as he had played on McClellan, and his strategy was justified by success. In the space of three weeks he had carried the war from the James to the Potomac. With an army that at no time exceeded 55,000 men he had driven 80,000 into the fortifications of Washington.[1] He had captured 30 guns, 7,000 prisoners, 20,000 rifles, and many stand of colours; he had killed or wounded 13,500 Federals, destroyed supplies and material of enormous value; and all this with a loss to the Confederates of 10,000 officers and men.

So much had he done for the South; for his own reputation he had done more. If, as Moltke avers, the junction of two armies on the field of battle is the highest achievement of military genius,[2] the campaign against Pope has seldom been surpassed; and the great counter-stroke at Manassas is sufficient in itself to make Lee's reputation as a tactician. Salamanca was perhaps a more brilliant example of the same manœuvre, for at Salamanca Wellington had no reason to anticipate that Marmont would blunder, and the mighty stroke which beat 40,000 French in forty minutes was conceived in a few moments. Nor does Manassas equal Austerlitz. No such subtle manœuvres were employed as those by which Napoleon induced the Allies to lay bare their centre, and drew them blindly to their doom. It was not due to the skill of Lee that Pope weakened his left at the crisis of the battle.[3]

---

[1] Sumner and Franklin had become involved in Pope's retreat.

[2] Tried by this test alone Lee stands out as one of the greatest soldiers of all times. Not only against Pope, but against McClellan at Gaines' Mill, against Burnside at Fredericksburg, and against Hooker at Chancellorsville, he succeeded in carrying out the operations of which Moltke speaks; and in each case with the same result of surprising his adversary. None knew better how to apply that great principle of strategy, 'to march divided but to fight concentrated.'

[3] It may be noticed, however, that the care with which Longstreet's troops were kept concealed for more than four-and-twenty hours had much to do with Pope's false manœuvres.

But in the rapidity with which the opportunity was seized, in the combination of the three arms, and in the vigour of the blow, Manassas is in no way inferior to Austerlitz or Salamanca. That the result was less decisive was due to the greater difficulties of the battle-field, to the stubborn resistance of the enemy, to the obstacles in the way of rapid and connected movement, and to the inexperience of the troops. Manassas was not, like Austerlitz and Salamanca, won by veteran soldiers, commanded by trained officers, perfect in drill and inured to discipline.

Lee's strategic manœuvres were undoubtedly hazardous. But that an antagonist of different calibre would have met them with condign punishment is short-sighted criticism. Against an antagonist of different calibre, against such generals as he was afterwards to encounter, they would never have been attempted. ' He studied his adversary,' says his Military Secretary, ' knew his peculiarities, and adapted himself to them. His own methods no one could foresee—he varied them with every change in the commanders opposed to him. He had one method with McClellan, another with Pope, another with Hooker, another with Meade, and yet another with Grant.' Nor was the dangerous period of the Manassas campaign so protracted as might be thought. Jackson marched north from Jefferson on August 25. On the 26th he reached Bristoe Station. Pope, during these two days, might have thrown himself either on Longstreet or on Jackson. He did neither, and on the morning of the 27th, when Jackson reached Sudley Springs, the crisis had passed. Had the Federals blocked Thoroughfare Gap that day, and prevented Longstreet's passage, Lee was still able to concentrate without incurring defeat. Jackson, retreating by Aldie Gap, would have joined Longstreet west of the mountains; Pope would have escaped defeat, but the Confederates would have lost nothing.

Moreover, it is well to remember that the Confederate cavalry was in every single respect, in leading, horsemanship, training, and knowledge of the country, superior to the Federal. The whole population, too, was staunchly

Southern. It was always probable, therefore, that information would be scarce in the Federal camps, and that if some items did get through the cavalry screen, they would be so late in reaching Pope's headquarters as to be practically useless. There can be no question that Lee, in these operations, relied much on the skill of Stuart. Stuart was given a free hand. Unlike Pope, Lee issued few orders as to the disposition of his horsemen. He merely explained the manœuvres he was about to undertake, pointed out where he wished the main body of the cavalry should be found, and left all else to their commander. He had no need to tell Stuart that he required information of the enemy, or to lay down the method by which it was to be obtained. That was Stuart's normal duty, and right well was it performed. How admirably the young cavalry general co-operated with Jackson has already been described. The latter suggested, the former executed, and the combination of the three arms, during the whole of Jackson's operations against Pope, was as close as when Ashby led his squadrons in the Valley.

Yet it was not on Stuart that fell, next to Lee, the honours of the campaign. Brilliant as was the handling of the cavalry, impenetrable the screen it formed, and ample the information it procured, the breakdown of the Federal horse made the task comparatively simple. Against adversaries whose chargers were so leg-weary that they could hardly raise a trot it was easy to be bold. One of Stuart's brigadiers would have probably done the work as well as Stuart himself. But the handling of the Valley army, from the time it left Jefferson on the 25th until Longstreet reached Gainesville on the 29th, demanded higher qualities than vigilance and activity. Throughout the operations Jackson's endurance was the wonder of his staff. He hardly slept. He was untiring in reconnaissance, in examination of the country and in observation of the enemy, and no detail of the march escaped his personal scrutiny. Yet his muscles were much less hardly used than his brain. The intellectual problem was more difficult than the physical. To march his army fifty-six miles in two days was far simpler than to maintain it on Pope's flank until Longstreet came into line. The direction of his marches, the position of his bivouacs, the distribution of his three divisions, were the outcome of long premeditation. On the night of the 25th he disappeared into the darkness on the road to Salem, leaving the Federals under the conviction that he was making for the Valley. On the 26th he moved on Bristoe Station, rather than on Manassas Junction, foreseeing that he might be interrupted from the south-west in his destruction of the stores. On the 27th he postponed his departure till night had fallen, moving in three columns, of which the column marching on Centre-ville, whither he desired that the enemy should follow, was the last to move. Concentrating at Sudley Springs on the 28th, he placed himself in the best position to hold Pope fast, to combine with Longstreet, or to escape by Aldie Gap; and on the 29th the ground he had selected for battle enabled him to hold out against superior numbers.

Neither strategically nor tactically did he make a single mistake. His attack on King's division at Groveton, on the evening of the 28th, was purely frontal, and his troops lost heavily. But he believed King to be the flank-guard of a larger force, and under such circumstances turning move-ments were over-hazardous. The woods, too, prevented the deployment of his artillery; and the attack, in its wider aspect, was eminently successful, for the aim was not to defeat King, but to bring Pope back to a position where Lee could crush him. On the 29th his dispositions were admirable. The battle is a fine example of defensive tactics. The position, to use a familiar illustration, 'fitted the troops like a glove.' It was of such strength that, while the front was adequately manned, ample reserves remained in rear. The left, the most dangerous flank, was secured by Bull Run, and massed batteries gave protection to the right. The distribution of the troops, the orders, and the amount of latitude accorded to subordinate leaders, followed the best models. The front was so apportioned that each brigadier on the fighting-line had his own reserve, and each divisional general half his force in third line. The orders indicated that counterstrokes were not to be pushed so far as to involve the troops in an engagement with the enemy's reserves, and the subordinate generals were encouraged, without waiting for orders, and thus losing the occasion, to seize all favourable opportunities for counterstroke. The methods employed by Jackson were singularly like those of Wellington. A position was selected which gave cover and concealment to the troops, and against which the powerful artillery of a more numerous enemy was practically useless. These were the characteristics of Vimiera, Busaco, Talavera, and Waterloo. Nor did Jackson's orders differ from those of the great Englishman.

The Duke's subordinates, when placed in position, acted on a well-established rule. Within that position they had unlimited power. They could defend the first line, or they could meet the enemy with a counter-attack from a position in rear, and in both cases they could pursue. But the pursuit was never to be carried beyond certain defined limits. Moreover, Wellington's views as to the efficacy of the counterstroke were identical with those of Jackson, and he had the same predilection for cold steel. 'If they attempt this point again, Hill,' were his orders to that general at Busaco, 'give them a volley and charge bayonets; but don't let your people follow them too far.'

But it was neither wise strategy nor sound tactics which was the main element in Pope's defeat; neither the strong effort of a powerful brain, nor the judicious devolution of responsibility. A brilliant military historian, more conversant perhaps with the War of Secession than the wars of France, concludes his review of this campaign with a reference to Jackson as 'the Ney of the Confederate army.'[1] The allusion is obvious. So long as the victories of Napoleon are remembered, the name of his lieutenant will always be a synonym for heroic valour. But the valour of Ney was of a different type from that of Jackson. Ney's valour was animal, Jackson's was moral, and between the two there is a vast distinction. Before the

[1] Swinton. *Campaigns of the Army of the Potomac.*

enemy, when his danger was tangible, Ney had few rivals. But when the enemy was unseen and his designs were doubtful, his resolution vanished. He was without confidence in his own resources. He could not act without direct orders, and he dreaded responsibility. At Bautzen his timidity ruined Napoleon's combinations; in the campaign of Leipsic he showed himself incapable of independent command; and he cannot be acquitted of hesitation at Quatre Bras.

It was in the same circumstances that Ney's courage invariably gave way that Jackson's courage shone with the brightest lustre. It might appear that he had little cause for fear in the campaign of the Second Manassas, that he had only to follow his instructions, and that if he had failed his failure would have been visited upon Lee. The instructions which he received, however, were not positive, but contingent on events. If possible, he was to cut the railway, in order to delay the reinforcements which Pope was expecting from Alexandria; and then, should the enemy permit, he was to hold fast east of the Bull Run Mountains until Lee came up. But he was to be guided in everything by his own discretion. He was free to accept battle or refuse it, to attack or to defend, to select his own line of retreat, to move to any quarter of the compass that he pleased. For three days, from the morning of August 26 to the morning of August 29, he had complete control of the strategic situation; on his movements were dependent the movements of the main army; the bringing the enemy to bay and the choice of the field of battle were both in his hands. And during those three days he was cut off from Lee and Longstreet. The mountains, with their narrow passes, lay between; and, surrounded by three times his number, he was abandoned entirely to his own resources.

Throughout the operations he had been in unusually high spirits. The peril and responsibility seemed to act as an elixir, and he threw off much of his constraint. But as the day broke on August 29 he looked long and earnestly in the direction of Thoroughfare Gap, and when a messenger from Stuart brought the intelligence that Longstreet was through the pass, he drew a long breath and uttered a sigh of relief.[1] The period of suspense was over, but even on that unyielding heart the weight of anxiety had pressed with fearful force. For three days he had only received news of the main army at long and uncertain intervals. For two of these days his information of the enemy's movements was very small. While he was marching to Bristoe Station, Pope, for all he knew, might have been marching against Longstreet with his whole force. When he attacked King on the 28th the Federals, in what strength he knew not, still held Thoroughfare Gap; when he formed for action on the 29th he was still ignorant of what had happened to the main body, and it was on the bare chance that Longstreet would force the passage that he accepted battle with far superior numbers.

It is not difficult to imagine how a general like Ney, placed in Jackson's situation, would have trimmed and hesitated: how in his march to Manassas, when he had crossed the mountains and left the Gap behind him, he would have sent out reconnaissances in all directions, halting his troops until he learned the coast was clear; how he would have dashed at the Junction by the shortest route; how he would have forced his weary troops northward when the enemy's approach was reported; how, had he reached Sudley Springs, he would have hugged the shelter of the woods and let King's division pass unmolested; and, finally, when Pope's columns converged on his position, have fallen back on Thoroughfare or Aldie. Nor would he have been greatly to blame. Unless gifted with that moral fortitude which Napoleon ranks higher than genius or experience, no general would have succeeded in carrying Lee's design to a successful issue. In his unhesitating march to Manassas Junction, in his deliberate sojourn for four-and-twenty hours astride his enemy's communications, in his daring challenge to Pope's whole army at Groveton, Jackson displayed the indomitable courage characteristic of the greatest soldiers.

[1] Letter from Dr. Hunter McGuire.

As suggested in the first volume, it is too often overlooked, by those who study the history of campaigns,
that war is the province of uncertainty.   The reader
has the whole theatre of war displayed before him.   He
notes the exact disposition of the opposing forces at each
hour of the campaign, and with this in his mind's eye
he condemns or approves the action of the commanders.
In the action of the defeated general he usually often
sees much to blame; in the action of the successful
general but little to admire.   But his judgment is not
based on a true foundation.   He has ignored the fact
that the information at his disposal was not at the
disposal of those he criticises; and until he realises that
both generals, to a greater or less degree, must have
been groping in the dark, he will neither make just allowance for the errors of the one, nor appreciate the genius
of the other.

It is true that it is difficult in the extreme to ascertain
how much or how little those generals whose campaigns
have become historical knew of their enemy at any particular
moment.   For instance, in the campaign before us, we are
nowhere told whether Lee, when he sent Jackson to Manassas Junction, was aware that a portion of McClellan's
army had been shipped to Alexandria in place of Aquia; or
whether he knew, on the second day of the battle of Manassas, that Pope had been reinforced by two army corps from
the Peninsula.   He had certainly captured Pope's dispatch
book, and no doubt it threw much light on the Federal
plans, but we are not aware how far into the future this
light projected.   We do know, however, that, in addition to
this correspondence, such knowledge as he had was derived
from reports.   But reports are never entirely to be relied
on; they are seldom full, they are often false, and they are
generally exaggerated.   However active the cavalry, however
patriotic the inhabitants, no general is ever possessed of
accurate information of his enemy's dispositions, unless the
forces are very small, or the precautions to elude observation very feeble.   On August 28 Stuart's patrols covered
the whole country round Jackson's army, and during the

whole day the Federal columns were converging on Manassas. Sigel and Reynolds' four divisions passed through Gainesville, not five miles from Sudley Springs, and for a time were actually in contact with Jackson's outposts ; and yet Sigel and Reynolds mistook Jackson's outposts for reconnoitring cavalry. Again, when King's single division, the rear-guard of Pope's army, appeared upon the turnpike, Jackson attacked it with the idea that it was the flank-guard of a much larger force. Nor was this want of accurate intelligence due to lack of vigilance or to the dense woods. As a matter of fact the Confederates were more amply provided with information than is usually the case in war, even in an open country and with experienced armies.

But if, in the most favourable circumstances, a general is surrounded by an atmosphere which has been most aptly named ' the fog of war,' his embarrassments are intensified tenfold when he commands a portion of a divided army. Under ordinary conditions a general is at least fully informed of the dispositions of his own forces. But when between two widely separated columns a powerful enemy, capable of crushing each in turn, intervenes ; when the movements of that enemy are veiled in obscurity ; when anxiety has taken possession of the troops, and the soldiers of either column, striving hopelessly to penetrate the gloom, reflect on the fate that may have overtaken their comrades, on the obstacles that may delay them, on the misunderstandings that may have occurred—it is at such a crisis that the courage of their leader is put to the severest test.

His situation has been compared to a man entering a dark room full of assailants, never knowing when or whence a blow may be struck against him. The illustration is inadequate. Not only has he to contend with the promptings of his own instincts, but he has to contend with the instincts and to sustain the resolution of his whole army. It is not from the enemy that he has most to fear. A time comes in all protracted operations when the nervous energy of the best troops becomes exhausted, when the most daring shrink from further sacrifice, when the desire of self-preservation infects the stoutest veterans, and the will of the mass opposes a tacit resistance to all further effort. 'Then,' says Clausewitz, 'the spark in the breast of the commander must rekindle hope in the hearts of his men, and so long as he is equal to this he remains their master. When his influence ceases, and his own spirit is no longer strong enough to revive the spirit of others, the masses, drawing him with them, sink into that lower region of animal nature which recoils from danger and knows not shame. Such are the obstacles which the brain and courage of the military commander must overcome if he is to make his name illustrious.' And the obstacles are never more formidable than when his troops see no sign of the support they have expected. Then, if he still moves forward, although his peril increase at every step, to the point of junction ; if he declines the temptation, although overwhelming numbers threaten him, of a safe line of retreat ; if, as did Jackson, he deliberately confronts and challenges the hostile masses, then indeed does the soldier rise to the highest level of moral energy.

Strongly does Napoleon inveigh against operations which entail the division of an army into two columns unable to communicate ; and especially does he reprobate the strategy which places the point of junction under the very beard of a concentrated enemy. Both of these maxims Lee violated. The last because he knew Pope, the first because he knew Jackson. It is rare indeed that such strategy succeeds. When all has depended on a swift and unhesitating advance, generals renowned for their ardent courage have wavered and turned aside. Hasdrubal, divided from Hannibal by many miles and a Consular army, fell back to the Metaurus, and Rome was saved. Two thousand years later, Prince Frederick Charles, divided by a few marches and two Austrian army corps from the Crown Prince, lingered so long upon the Iser that the supremacy of Prussia trembled in the balance. But the character of the Virginian soldier was of loftier type. It has been remarked that after Jackson's death Lee never again attempted those great turning movements which had achieved his most brilliant victories.   Never again did he divide his army to unite it again on the field of battle.   The reason is not far to seek.   There was now no general in the Confederate army to whom he dared confide the charge of the detached wing, and in possessing one such general he had been more fortunate than Napoleon.[1]

[1] It is noteworthy that Moltke once, at Königgrätz, carried out the operation referred to ; Wellington twice, at Vittoria and Toulouse ; Napoleon, although he several times attempted it, and against inferior numbers, never, except at Ulm, with complete success.

CHAPTER XVIII

HARPER'S FERRY

THE Confederate operations in Virginia during the spring and summer of 1862 had been successful beyond expectation Sept. and almost beyond precedent. Within six months 1862. two great armies had been defeated; McClellan had been driven from the Peninsula, and Pope from the Rappahannock. The villages of Virginia no longer swarmed with foreign bayonets. The hostile camps had vanished from her inland counties. Richmond was free from menace; and in the Valley of the Shenandoah the harvest was gathered in without let or hindrance. Except at Winchester and Martinsburg, where the garrisons, alarmed by the news of Pope's defeat, were already preparing to withdraw; in the vicinity of Norfolk, and at Fortress Monroe, the invaders had no foothold within the boundaries of the State they had just now overrun; and their demoralised masses, lying exhausted behind the fortifications of Washington and Alexandria, were in no condition to resume the offensive. The North had opened the campaign in the early spring with the confident hope of capturing the rebel capital; before the summer was over it was questionable whether it would be able to save its own. Had the rival armies been equally matched in numbers and equipment this result would have hardly been remarkable. The Federals had had great difficulties to contend with—an unknown country, bad roads, a hostile population, natural obstacles of formidable character, statesmen ignorant of war, and generals at loggerheads with the Administration. Yet so superior were their numbers, so ample their resources, that even these disadvantages might have been overcome had the strategy of the Southern leaders been less admirable. Lee, Jackson, and Johnston had played the *rôle* of the defender to perfection. No attempt had been made to hold the frontier. Mobility and not earthworks was the weapon on which they had relied. Richmond, the only fortress, had been used as a 'pivot of operations,' and not merely as a shelter for the army. The specious expedient of pushing forward advanced-guards to harass or delay the enemy had been avoided; and thus no opportunity had been offered to the invaders of dealing with the defence in detail, or of raising their own *moral* by victory over isolated detachments. The generals had declined battle until their forces were concentrated and the enemy was divided. Nor had they fought except on ground of their own choice. Johnston had refused to be drawn into decisive action until McClellan became involved in the swamps of the Chickahominy. Jackson, imitating like his superior the defensive strategy of Wellington and Napoleon, had fallen back to a 'zone of manœuvre' south of the Massanuttons. By retreating to the inaccessible fastness of Elk Run Valley he had drawn Banks and Frémont up the Shenandoah, their lines of communication growing longer and more vulnerable at every march, and requiring daily more men to guard them. Then, rushing from his stronghold, he had dealt his blows, clearing the Valley from end to end, destroying the Federal magazines, and threatening Washington itself; and when the overwhelming masses he had drawn on himself sought to cut him off, he had selected his own battle-field, and crushed the converging columns which his skill had kept apart. The hapless Pope, too, had been handled in the same fashion as McClellan, Banks, Shields, and Frémont. Jackson had lured him forward to the Rapidan; and although his retreat had been speedy, Lee had completed his defeat before he could be efficiently supported. But, notwithstanding all that had been done, much yet remained to do.

It was doubtless within the bounds of probability that a second attempt to invade Virginia would succeed no

better than the first.   But it was by no means certain that
the resolution of the North was not sufficient to withstand a
long series of disasters so long as the war was confined to
Southern territory ; and, at the same time, it might well be
questioned whether the South could sustain, without foreign
aid, the protracted and exhausting process of a purely
defensive warfare.   If her tactics, as well as her strategy,
could be confined to the defensive ; that is, if her generals
could await the invaders in selected and prepared positions,
and if no task more difficult should devolve upon her
troops than shooting down their foes as they moved across
the open to the assault of strong intrenchments, then the
hope might reasonably be entertained that she might tire
out the North.   But the campaign, so far as it had progressed, had shown, if indeed history had not already made
it sufficiently clear, that opportunities for such tactics were
not likely to occur.   The Federal generals had consistently
refused to run their heads against earthworks.   Their
overwhelming numbers would enable them to turn any
position, however formidable ; and the only chance of
success lay in keeping these numbers apart and in preventing them from combining.

It was by strategic and tactical counterstrokes that the
recent victories had been won.   Although it had awaited
attack within its own frontier, the Army of Northern
Virginia had but small experience of defensive warfare.
With the exception of the actions round Yorktown, of
Cross Keys, and of the Second Manassas, the battles
had been entirely aggressive.   The idea that a small army,
opposed to one vastly superior, cannot afford to attack
because the attack is costly, and that it must trust
for success to favourable ground, had been effectually dis-
pelled.   Lee and Jackson had taught the Southerners
that the secret of success lies not in strong positions, but
in the concentration, by means of skilful strategy, of
superior numbers on the field of battle.   Their tactics had
been essentially offensive, and it is noteworthy that their
victories had not been dearly purchased.   If we compare
them with those of the British in the Peninsula, we shall

find that with no greater loss than Wellington incurred in the defensive engagements of three years, 1810, 1811, 1812, the Confederates had attacked and routed armies far larger in proportion than those which Wellington had merely repulsed.[1]

But if they had shown that the best defence lies in a vigorous offensive, their offensive had not yet been applied at the decisive point. To make victory complete it is the sounder policy to carry the war into hostile territory. A nation endures with comparative equanimity defeat beyond its own borders. Pride and prestige may suffer, but a high-spirited people will seldom be brought to the point of making terms unless its army is annihilated in the heart of its own country, unless the capital is occupied and the hideous sufferings of war are brought directly home to the mass of the population. A single victory on Northern soil, within easy reach of Washington, was far more likely to bring about the independence of the South than even a succession of victories in Virginia. It was time, then, for a strategic counterstroke on a larger scale than had hitherto been attempted. The opportunity was ripe. No great risk would be incurred by crossing the Potomac. There was no question of meeting a more powerful enemy. The Federals, recruited by fresh levies, would undoubtedly be numerically the stronger; and the Confederate equipment, despite the large captures of guns and rifles, was still deficient. But for deficiencies in numbers and in *matériel* the higher *moral* and the more skilful leading would make ample compensation. It might safely be inferred that the Northern soldiers would no longer display the cool confidence of Gaines' Mill or even of Malvern Hill. The places of the brave and seasoned soldiers who had fallen would

[1] Wellington's losses in the battles of these three years were 33,000. The Confederates lost 23,000 in the Valley and the Seven Days and 10,000 in the campaign against Pope. It is not to be understood, however, that the Duke's strategy was less skilful or less audacious than Lee's and Jackson's. During these three years his army, largely composed of Portuguese and Spaniards, was incapable of offensive tactics against his veteran enemies, and he was biding his time. It was the inefficiency of his allies and the miserable support he received from the English Government that prevented him, until 1813, from adopting a bolder policy.

be filled by recruits; and generals who had been out-
manœuvred on so many battle-fields might fairly be expected, when confronted once more with their dreaded
opponents, to commit even more egregious errors than
those into which they had already fallen.

Such were the ideas entertained by Lee and accepted by
the President, and on the morning of September 2, as soon

Sept. 2.   as it was found that the Federals had sought
            shelter under the forts of Alexandria, Jackson was
instructed to cross the Potomac, and form the advanced-
guard of the army of invasion. It may be imagined with
what feelings he issued his orders for the march on
Leesburg, above which lay an easy ford. For more than
twelve months, since the very morrow of Bull Run, he
had persistently advocated an aggressive policy.[1] The
fierce battles round Richmond and Manassas he had
looked upon as merely the prelude to more resolute efforts.
After he had defeated Banks at Winchester he had urged
his friend Colonel Boteler to inform the authorities that, if
they would reinforce him, he would undertake to capture
Washington. The message had been conveyed to Lee.
' Tell General Jackson,' was the reply of the Commander-
in-Chief, ' that he must first help me to drive these people
away from Richmond.'   This object had been now
thoroughly accomplished, and General Lee's decision to
redeem his promise was by none more heartily approved
than by the leader of the Valley army. And yet, though
the risks of the venture were small, the prospects of complete success were dubious. The opportunity had come,
but the means of seizing it were feeble. Lee himself was
buoyed up by no certain expectation of great results. In

---

[1] In Mrs. Jackson's Memoirs of her husband a letter is quoted from her
brother-in-law, giving the substance of a conversation with General Jackson
on the conduct of the war. This letter I have not felt justified in quoting.
In the first place, it lacks corroboration; in the second place, it contains
a very incomplete statement of a large strategical question; in the third
place, the opinions put in Jackson's mouth are not only contradictory, but
altogether at variance with his practice; and lastly, it attributes certain
ideas to the general—raising ' the black flag,' &c.—which his confidential staff
officers declare that he never for a moment entertained.

advocating invasion he confessed to the President that his troops were hardly fit for service beyond the frontier. 'The army,' he wrote, 'is not properly equipped for an invasion of the enemy's territory. It lacks much of the material of war, is feeble in transportation, the animals being much reduced, and the men are poorly provided with clothes, and in thousands of instances are destitute of shoes. . . . What concerns me most is the fear of getting out of ammunition.' [1]

This description was by no means over-coloured. As a record of military activity the campaign of the spring and summer of 1862 has few parallels. Jackson's division, since the evacuation of Winchester at the end of February, that is, in six months, had taken part in no less than eight battles and innumerable minor engagements; it had marched nearly a thousand miles, and it had long ago discarded tents. The remainder of the army had been hardly less severely tasked. The demands of the outpost service in front of Richmond had been almost as trying as the forced marches in the Valley, and the climate of the Peninsula had told heavily on the troops. From the very first the army had been indifferently equipped; the ill effects of hasty organisation were still glaring; the regimental officers had not yet learned to study the wants and comfort of their men; the troops were harassed by the ignorance of a staff that was still half-trained, and the commissariat officials were not abreast of their important duties. More than all, the operations against Pope, just brought to a successful issue, had been most arduous; and the strain on the endurance of the troops, not yet recovered from their exertions in the Peninsula, had been so great that a period of repose seemed absolutely necessary. It was not only that battle and sickness had thinned the ranks, but that those whose health had been proof against continued hardships, and whose strength and spirit were still equal to further efforts, were so badly shod that a few long marches over indifferent roads were certain to be more productive of casualties than a pitched battle. The want of

[1] O. R., vol. xix., part ii., pp. 590, 591.

boots had already been severely felt.[1] It has been said
that the route of the Confederate army from the Rappahannock to Chantilly might have been traced by the stains
of bloody feet along the highways; and if the statement
is more graphic than exact, yet it does not fall far short
of the truth. Many a stout soldier, who had hobbled
along on his bare feet until Pope was encountered and defeated, found himself utterly incapable of marching into
Maryland. In rear of the army the roads were covered
with stragglers. Squads of infantry, banding together for
protection, toiled along painfully by easy stages, unable
to keep pace with the colours, but hoping to be up in
time for the next fight; and amongst these were not a few
officers. But this was not the worst. Lax discipline and
the absence of soldierly habits asserted themselves with
the same pernicious effect as in the Valley. Not all the
stragglers had their faces turned towards the enemy, not all
were incapacitated by physical suffering. Many, without
going through the formality of asking leave, were making
for their homes, and had no idea that their conduct was
in any way peculiar. They had done their duty in more
than one battle, they had been long absent from their
farms, their equipment was worn out, the enemy had been
driven from Virginia, and they considered that they
were fully entitled to some short repose. And amongst
these, whose only fault was an imperfect sense of their
military obligations, was the residue of cowards and malin-
gerers shed by every great army engaged in protracted
operations.

Lee had been joined by the divisions of D. H. Hill,
McLaws, Walker, and by Hampton's cavalry, and the
strength of his force should have been 65,000 effectives.[2]
But it was evident that these numbers could not be long

---

[1] '1,000 pairs of shoes were obtained in Fredericktown, 250 pairs in
Williamsport, and about 400 pairs in this city (Hagerstown). They will
not be sufficient to cover the bare feet of the army.' Lee to Davis, September
12, 1862. O. R., vol. xix., part ii., p. 605.

[2] Calculated on the basis of the Field Returns dated July 20, 1862,
with the addition of Jackson's and Ewell's divisions, and subtracting the
losses (10,000) of the campaign against Pope.

maintained. The men were already accustomed to half-rations of green corn, and they would be no worse off in Maryland and Pennsylvania, untouched as yet by the ravages of war, than in the wasted fields of Virginia. The most ample commissariat, however, would not compensate for the want of boots and the want of rest, and a campaign of invasion was certain to entail an amount of hard marching to which the strength of the troops was hardly equal. Not only had the South to provide from her seven millions of white population an army larger than that of Imperial France, but from a nation of agriculturists she had to provide another army of craftsmen and mechanics to enable the soldiers to keep the field. For guns and gun-carriages, powder and ammunition, clothing and harness, gunboats and torpedoes, locomotives and railway plant, she was now dependent on the hands of her own people and the resources of her own soil; the organisation of those resources, scattered over a vast extent of territory, was not to be accomplished in the course of a few months, nor was the supply of skilled labour sufficient to fill the ranks of her industrial army. By the autumn of 1862, although the strenuous efforts of every Government department gave the lie to the idea, not uncommon in the North, that the Southern character was shiftless and the Southern intellect slow, so little real progress had been made that if the troops had not been supplied from other sources they could hardly have marched at all. The captures made in the Valley, in the Peninsula, and in the Second Manassas campaign proved of inestimable value. Old muskets were exchanged for new, smooth-bore cannon for rifled guns, tattered blankets for good overcoats. 'Mr. Commissary Banks,' his successor Pope, and McClellan himself, had furnished their enemies with the material of war, with tents, medicines, ambulances, and ammunition waggons. Even the vehicles at Confederate headquarters bore on their tilts the initials U.S.A.; many of Lee's soldiers were partially clothed in Federal uniforms, and the bad quality of the boots supplied by the Northern contractors was a very general subject of complaint in the

Southern ranks. Nor while the men were fighting were
the women idle. The output of the Government factories
was supplemented by private enterprise. Thousands of
spinning-wheels, long silent in dusty lumber-rooms, hum-
med busily in mansion and in farm; matrons and maids,
from the wife and daughters of the Commander-in-Chief
to the mother of the drummer-boy, became weavers and
seamstresses; and in every household of the Confederacy,
although many of the necessities of life—salt, coffee and
sugar—had become expensive luxuries, the needs of the
army came before all else.

But notwithstanding the energy of the Government
and the patriotism of the women, the troops lacked everything but spirit. Nor, even with more ample resources,
could their wants have been readily supplied. In
any case this would have involved a long halt in a secure
position, and in a few weeks the Federal strength would
be increased by fresh levies, and the *moral* of their defeated troops restored. But even had time been given
the Government would have been powerless to render substantial aid. Contingents of recruits were being drilled
into discipline at Richmond; yet they hardly exceeded
20,000 muskets; and it was not on the Virginia frontier
alone that the South was hard pressed. The Valley
of the Mississippi was beset by great armies; Alabama
was threatened, and Western Tennessee was strongly
occupied; it was already difficult to find a safe passage
across the river for the supplies furnished by the prairies
of Texas and Louisiana, and communication with Arkansas had become uncertain. If the Mississippi were
lost, not only would three of the most fertile States, as
prolific of hardy soldiers as of fat oxen, be cut off
from the remainder, but the enemy, using the river as
a base, would push his operations into the very heart of
the Confederacy. To regain possession of the great water-
way seemed of more vital importance than the defence of
the Potomac or the secession of Maryland, and now that
Richmond had been relieved, the whole energy of the Government was expended on the operations in Kentucky and

Tennessee. It may well be questioned whether a vigorous endeavour, supported by all the means available, and even by troops drawn from the West, to defeat the Army of the Potomac and to capture Washington, would not have been a more efficacious means to the same end ; but Davis and his Cabinet consistently preferred dispersion to concentration, and, indeed, the situation of the South was such as might well have disturbed the strongest brains. The sea-power of the Union was telling with deadly effect. Although the most important strategic points on the Mississippi were still held by Confederate garrisons, nearly every mile of the great river, from Cairo to New Orleans, was patrolled by the Federal gunboats ; and in deep water, from the ports of the Atlantic to the road-steads of the Gulf, the frigates maintained their vigilant blockade.

Even on the northern border there was hardly a gleam of light across the sky. The Federal forces were still for-midable in numbers, and a portion of the Army of the Potomac had not been involved in Pope's defeat. It was possible, therefore, that more skilful generalship than had yet been displayed by the Northern commanders might deprive the Confederates of all chance of winning a decisive victory. Yet, although the opportunity of meeting the enemy with a prospect of success might never offer, an inroad into Northern territory promised good results.

1. Maryland, still strong in sympathy with the South, might be induced by the presence of a Southern army to rise against the Union.

2. The Federal army would be drawn off westward from its present position ; and so long as it was detained on the northern frontier of Virginia nothing could be attempted against Richmond, while time would be secured for improv-ing the defences of the Confederate capital.

3. The Shenandoah Valley would be most effectively protected, and its produce transported without risk of interruption both to Lee's army and to Richmond.

To obtain such advantages as these was worth an effort, and Lee, after careful consideration, determined to cross the

Potomac. The movement was made with the same speed which had characterised the operations against Pope. It was of the utmost importance that the passage of the river should be accomplished before the enemy had time to discover the design and to bar the way. Stuart's cavalry formed the screen. On the morning after the battle of Chantilly, Fitzhugh Lee's brigade followed the retreating Federals in the direction of Alexandria. Hampton's brigade was pushed forward to Dranesville by way of Hunter's Mill. Robertson's brigade made a strong demonstration towards Washington, and Munford, with the 2nd Virginia, cleared out a Federal detachment which occupied Leesburg. Behind the cavalry the army marched unmolested and unobserved.[1] D. H. Hill's division was pushed forward as advanced-guard; Jackson's troops, who had been granted a

Sept. 6.
day's rest, brought up the rear, and on the morning of the 6th reached White's Ford on the Potomac. Through the silver reaches of the great river the long columns of men and waggons, preceded by Fitzhugh Lee's brigade, splashed and stumbled, and passing through the groves of oaks which overhung the water, wound steadily northward over the green fields of Maryland.

[1] The Army of Northern Virginia was thus organised during the Maryland campaign :—

Longstreet's	McLaws' Division		
	R. H. Anderson's Division		
	D. R. Jones' Division		
	J. G. Walker's Division	= 35,600	
	Evans' Brigade		
	Washington Artillery		
	S. D. Lee's Artillery battalion		
Jackson's	Ewell's (Lawton) Division		
	The Light (A. P. Hill) Division	= 16,800	
	Jackson's own (J. R. Jones) Division		
	D. H. Hill's Division	7,000	
Pendleton's Reserve Artillery, 4 battalions		1,000	
Stuart	Hampton's Brigade		
	Fitzhugh Lee's Brigade	= 4,000	
	Robertson's Brigade		
	3 H. A. batteries, Captain Pelham		
		Total	64,400

No allowance has been made for straggling. It is doubtful if more than 55,000 men entered Maryland.

The next day Frederick was occupied by Jackson,
Sept. 7. who was once more in advance; the cavalry at
Urbanna watched the roads to Washington, and
every city in the North was roused by the tidings that the
grey jackets had crossed the border. But although the
army had entered Maryland without the slightest difficulty, the troops were not received with the enthusiasm they
had anticipated. The women, indeed, emulating their Virginia sisters, gave a warm welcome to the heroes of so many
victories. But the men, whether terrorised by the stern rule
of the Federal Government, or mistrusting the power of
the Confederates to secure them from further punishment,
showed little disposition to join the ranks. It is possible
that the appearance of the Southern soldiery was not without effect. Lee's troops, after five months' hard marching
and hard fighting, were no delectable objects. With torn
and brimless hats, strands of rope for belts, and raw-hide
moccasins of their own manufacture in lieu of boots;
covered with vermin, and carrying their whole kit in Federal
haversacks, the ragged scarecrows who swarmed through
the streets of Frederick presented a pitiful contrast to
the trim battalions which had hitherto held the Potomac.
Their conduct indeed was exemplary. They had been
warned that pillage and depredations would be severely
dealt with, and all requisitions, even of fence-rails, were
paid for on the spot. Still recruits were few. The war-
worn aspect and indifferent equipment of the 'dirty darlings,' as more than one fair Marylander spoke of Jackson's
finest soldiers, failed to inspire confidence, and it was soon
evident that the western counties of Maryland had small
sympathy with the South.

There were certainly exceptions to the general absence
of cordiality. The troops fared well during their sojourn
in Frederick. Supplies were plentiful; food and clothing
were gratuitously distributed, and Jackson was presented
with a fine but unbroken charger. The gift was timely,
for 'Little Sorrel,' the companion of so many marches,
was lost for some days after the passage of the Potomac;
but the Confederacy was near paying a heavy price for

the 'good grey mare.' When Jackson first mounted her a band struck up close by, and as she reared the girth broke, throwing her rider to the ground. Fortunately, though stunned and severely bruised, the general was only temporarily disabled, and, if he appeared but little in public during his stay in Frederick, his inaccessibility was not due to broken bones. 'Lee, Longstreet, and Jackson, and for a time Jeb Stuart,' writes a staff officer, 'had their headquarters near one another in Best's Grove. Hither in crowds came the good people of Frederick, especially the ladies, as to a fair. General Jackson, still suffering from his hurt, kept to his tent, busying himself with maps and official papers, and declined to see visitors. Once, however, when he had been called to General Lee's tent, two young girls waylaid him, paralysed him with smiles and questions, and then jumped into their carriage and drove off rapidly, leaving him there, cap in hand, bowing, blushing, speechless. But once safe in his tent, he was seen no more that day.'[1] The next evening (Sunday) he went with his staff to service in the town, and slept soundly, as he admitted to his wife, through the sermon of a minister of the German Reformed Church.[2]

But it was not for long that the Confederates were permitted to repose in Frederick. The enemy had made no further reply to the passage of the Potomac beyond concentrating to the west of Washington. McClellan, who had superseded Pope, was powerless, owing to the inefficiency of his cavalry, to penetrate the cordon of Stuart's pickets, and to ascertain, even approximately, the dispositions of the invading force. He was still in doubt if the whole or only part of Lee's army had crossed

---

[1] 'Stonewall Jackson in Maryland.' Colonel H. K. Douglas. *Battles and Leaders*, vol. ii., p. 621.

[2] 'The minister,' says Colonel Douglas, 'was credited with much loyalty and courage, because he had prayed for the President of the United States in the very presence of Stonewall Jackson. Well, the general didn't hear the prayer, and if he had he would doubtless have felt like replying as General Ewell did, when asked at Carlisle, Pennsylvania, if he would permit the usual prayer for President Lincoln—"Certainly; I'm sure he needs it."'

into Maryland; and whether his adversary intended to attack Washington by the left bank of the Potomac, to move on Baltimore, or to invade Pennsylvania, were questions which he had no means of determining. This uncertainty compelled him to move cautiously, and on September 9 his advanced-guard was still twenty miles east of Frederick.

Nevertheless, the situation of the Confederates had become suddenly complicated. When the march into Maryland was begun, three towns in the Valley were held by the Federals. 3,000 infantry and artillery occupied Winchester. 3,000 cavalry were at Martinsburg; and Harper's Ferry, in process of conversion into an intrenched camp, had a garrison of 8,000 men. Lee was well aware of the presence of these forces when he resolved to cross the Potomac, but he believed that immediately his advance threatened to separate them from the main army, and to leave them isolated, they would be ordered to insure their safety by a timely retreat. Had it depended upon McClellan this would have been done. Halleck, however, thought otherwise; and the officer commanding at Harper's Ferry was ordered to hold his works until McClellan should open communication with him.

On arrival at Frederick, therefore, the Confederates, contrary to anticipation, found 14,000 Federals still established in their rear, and although Winchester had been evacuated,[1] it was clear that Harper's Ferry was to be defended. The existence of the intrenched camp was a serious obstacle to the full development of Lee's designs. His line of communication had hitherto run from Rapidan Station to Manassas Junction, and thence by Leesburg and Point of Rocks to Frederick. This line was within easy reach of Washington, and liable to be cut at any moment by the enemy's cavalry. Arrangements had therefore been already made to transfer the line to the Valley. There, sheltered by the Blue Ridge, the convoys of

[1] On the night of September 2. Lee's Report, O. R., vol. xix., part i., p. 139.

sick and wounded, of arms, clothing, and ammunition, could move in security from Staunton to Shepherdstown, and the recruits which were accumulating at Richmond be sent to join the army in Northern territory. But so long as Harper's Ferry was strongly garrisoned this new line would be liable to constant disturbance, and it was necessary that the post should either be masked by a superior force, or carried by a *coup de main*. The first of these alternatives was at once rejected, for the Confederate numbers were too small to permit any permanent detachment of a considerable force, and without hesitation Lee determined to adopt the bolder course. 25,000 men, he considered, would be no more than sufficient to effect his object. But 25,000 men were practically half the army, and the plan, when laid before the generals, was not accepted without remonstrance. Longstreet, indeed, went so far as to refuse command of the detachment. 'I objected,' he writes, 'and urged that our troops were worn with marching and were on short rations, and that it would be a bad idea to divide our forces while we were in the enemy's country, where he could get information, in six or eight hours, of any movement we might make. The Federal army, though beaten at the Second Manassas, was not disorganised, and it would certainly come out to look for us, and we should guard against being caught in such a condition. Our army consisted of a superior quality of soldiers, but it was in no condition to divide in the enemy's country. I urged that we should keep it in hand, recruit our strength, and get up supplies, and then we could do anything we pleased. General Lee made no reply to this, and I supposed the Harper's Ferry scheme was abandoned.' [1]

Jackson, too, would have preferred to fight McClellan first, and consider the question of communications afterwards; [2] but he accepted with alacrity the duty which his colleague had declined. His own divisions, reinforced by

---

[1] *Battles and Leaders*, vol. ii., p. 662.   [2] Dabney, vol. ii., p. 302.

those of McLaws, R. H. Anderson,[1] and Walker, were detailed for the expedition ; Harper's Ferry was to be invested on three sides, and the march was to begin at daybreak on September 10. Meanwhile, the remainder of the army was to move north-west to Hagerstown, five-and-twenty miles from Frederick, where it would alarm Lincoln for the safety of Pennsylvania, and be protected from McClellan by the parallel ranges of the Catoctin and South Mountains.

Undoubtedly, in ordinary circumstances, General Longstreet would have been fully justified in protesting against the dispersion of the army in the presence of the enemy. Hagerstown and Harper's Ferry are five-and-twenty miles apart, and the Potomac was between them. McClellan's advanced-guard, on the other hand, was thirty miles from Harper's Ferry, and forty-five from Hagerstown. The Federals were advancing, slowly and cautiously it is true, but still pushing westward, and it was certainly possible, should they receive early intelligence of the Confederate movements, that before Harper's Ferry fell a rapid march might enable them to interpose between Lee and Jackson. But both Lee and Jackson calculated the chances with a surer grasp of the several factors. Had the general in command of the Federal army been bold and enterprising, had the Federal cavalry been more efficient, or Stuart less skilful, they would certainly have hesitated before running the risk of defeat in detail. But so long as McClellan controlled the movements of the enemy, rapid and decisive action was not to be apprehended ; and it was exceedingly improbable that the scanty and unreliable information which he might obtain from civilian sources would induce him to throw off his customary caution. Moreover, only a fortnight previously the Federal army had been heavily defeated.[2]

Lee had resolved to woo fortune while she was in the

---

[1] Anderson was placed under McLaws' command.

[2] 'Are you acquainted with McClellan ?' said Lee to General Walker on September 8, 1862. 'He is an able general but a very cautious one. His enemies among his own people think him too much so. His army is in a very demoralised and chaotic condition, and will not be prepared for offensive operations—or he will not think it so—for three or four weeks.'—*Battles and Leaders*, vol. ii., pp. 605 and 606.

mood.   The movement against Harper's Ferry once
determined, it was essential that it should be carried out
Sept. 10.   with the utmost speed, and Jackson marched with
even more than ordinary haste, but without
omitting his usual precautions.   Before starting he asked
for a map of the Pennsylvania frontier, and made many
inquiries as to roads and localities to the north of
Frederick, whereas his route lay in the opposite direction.
'The cavalry, which preceded the column,' says Colonel
Douglas, 'had instructions to let no civilian go to the
front, and we entered each village we passed before the
inhabitants knew of our coming.   In Middletown two very
pretty girls, with ribbons of red, white, and blue floating
from their hair, and small Union flags in their hands,
rushed out of a house as we passed, came to the kerbstone,
and with much laughter waved their flags defiantly in the
face of the general.   He bowed, raised his hat, and turning
with his quiet smile to the staff, said, "We evidently have
no friends in this town."   Having crossed South Mountain
Sept. 11.   at Turner's Gap, the command encamped for the
night within a mile of Boonsboro' (fourteen miles
from Frederick).   Here General Jackson must determine
whether he would go to Williamsport or turn towards
Shepherdstown.   I at once rode into the village with a
cavalryman to make some inquiries, but we ran into a
Federal squadron, who without ceremony proceeded to make
war upon us.   We retraced our steps, and although we did
not stand upon the order of our going, a squad of them
escorted us out of the town with great rapidity.   Reaching
the top of the hill, we discovered, just over it, General
Jackson, walking slowly towards us, leading his horse.
There was but one thing to do.   Fortunately the chase had
become less vigorous, and with a cry of command to unseen
troops, we turned and charged the enemy.   They, suspecting trouble, turned and fled, while the general quickly
galloped to the rear.   As I returned to camp I picked up
the gloves which he had dropped in mounting, and took
them to him.   Although he had sent a regiment of
infantry to the front as soon as he went back, the only

allusion he made to the incident was to express the opinion that I had a very fast horse.

'The next morning, having learned that the Federal troops still occupied Martinsburg, General Jackson took the direct road to Williamsport. He then forded the Potomac, the troops singing, the bands playing "Carry me back to ole Virginny!" We marched on Martinsburg. General A. P. Hill took the direct turnpike, while Jackson, with the rest of his command, followed a side road, so as to approach Martinsburg from the west, and encamped four

Sept. 12. miles from the town. His object was to drive General White, who occupied Martinsburg, towards Harper's Ferry, and thus "corral" all the Federal troops in that military pen. As the Comte de Paris puts it, he " organised a grand hunting match through the lower Valley, driving all the Federal detachments before him and forcing them to crowd into the blind alley of Harper's Ferry."

'The next morning the Confederates entered Martinsburg. Here the general was welcomed with enthusiasm, and a great crowd hastened to the hotel to greet him. At first he shut himself up in a room to write dispatches, but the demonstration became so persistent that he ordered the door to be opened. The crowd, chiefly ladies, rushed in and embarrassed the general with every possible outburst of affection, to which he could only reply, "Thank you, you are very kind." He gave them his autograph in books and on scraps of paper, cut a button from his coat for a little girl, and then submitted patiently to an attack by the others, who soon stripped the coat of nearly all the remaining buttons. But when they looked beseechingly at his hair, which was thin, he drew the line, and managed to close the interview. These blandishments did not delay his movements, however, for in the afternoon he was off again, and his troops bivouacked on the banks of the Opequon.'[1]

[1] *Battles and Leaders*, vol. ii., pp. 622, 623. Major Hotchkiss relates that the ladies of Martinsburg made such desperate assaults on the mane and tail of the general's charger that he had at last to post a sentry over the stable.

On the 13th Jackson passed through Halltown and
Sept. 13.   halted a mile north of that village,[1] throwing out
pickets to hold the roads which lead south and
west from Harper's Ferry. Meanwhile, McLaws and
Walker had taken possession of the heights to the north
and east, and the intrenched camp of the Federals, which, in
addition to the garrison, now held the troops who had fled
from Martinsburg, was surrounded on every side. The
Federal officer in command had left but one brigade and
two batteries to hold the Maryland Heights, the long
ridge, 1,000 feet high, on the north shore of the Potomac,
which looks down on the streets of the little town. This
detachment, although strongly posted, and covered by
breastworks and abattis, was driven off by General
McLaws ; while the Loudoun Heights, a portion of the
Blue Ridge, east of the Shenandoah, and almost equally
commanding, were occupied without opposition by
General Walker. Harper's Ferry was now completely
surrounded. Lee's plans had been admirably laid and
precisely executed, and the surrender of the place was
merely a question of hours.

Nor had matters progressed less favourably elsewhere.
In exact accordance with the anticipations of Lee and
Jackson, McClellan, up till noon on the 13th, had received
no inkling whatever of the dangerous manœuvres which
Stuart so effectively concealed, and his march was very
slow. On the 12th, after a brisk skirmish with the
Confederate cavalry, his advanced-guard had occupied
Frederick, and discovered that the enemy had marched
off in two columns, one towards Hagerstown, the other
towards Harper's Ferry, but he was uncertain whether
Lee intended to recross the Potomac or to move northwards
into Pennsylvania. On the morning of the 13th, although
General Hooker, commanding the First Army Corps, took
the liberty of reporting that, in his opinion, ' the rebels had
no more intention of going to Pennsylvania than they had

---

[1] On September 10 he marched fourteen miles, on September 11 twenty,
on September 12 sixteen, and on September 13 twelve, arriving at Halltown
at 11 A.M.

of going to heaven,' the Federal Commander-in-Chief was still undecided, and on the Boonsboro' road only his cavalry was pushed forward. In four days McClellan had marched no more than five-and-twenty miles; he had been unable to open communication with Harper's Ferry, and he had moved with even more than his usual caution. But at noon on the 13th he was suddenly put into possession of the most ample information. A copy of Lee's order for the investment of Harper's Ferry, in which the exact position of each separate division of the Confederate army was laid down, was picked up in the streets of Frederick, and chance had presented McClellan with an opportunity unique in history.[1] He was within twenty miles of Harper's Ferry. The Confederates were more than that distance apart. The intrenched camp still held out, for the sound of McLaws' battle on the Maryland Heights was distinctly heard during the afternoon, and a resolute advance would have either compelled the Confederates to raise the siege, or have placed the Federal army between their widely separated wings.

But, happily for the South, McClellan was not the man for the opportunity. He still hesitated, and during the afternoon of the 13th only one division was pushed forward. In front of him was the South Mountain, the name given to the continuation of the Blue Ridge north of the Potomac, and the two passes, Turner's and Crampton's Gaps, were held by Stuart. No Confederate infantry, as Lee's order indicated, with the exception, perhaps, of a rear-guard, were nearer the passes than

[1] General Longstreet, in his *From Manassas to Appomattox*, declares that the lost order was sent by General Jackson to General D. H. Hill, 'but was not delivered. The order,' he adds, 'that was sent to General Hill from general headquarters was carefully preserved.' General Hill, however, in *Battles and Leaders*, vol. ii., p. 570 (note), says: 'It was proper that I should receive that order through Jackson, and not through Lee. I have now before me (1888) the order received from Jackson. My adjutant-general swore affidavit, twenty years ago, that no order was received at our office from General Lee.' Jackson was so careful that no one should learn the contents of the order that the copy he furnished to Hill was written by his own hand. The copy found by the Federals was wrapped round three cigars, and was signed by Lee's adjutant-general.

the Maryland Heights and Boonsboro'.[1] The roads
were good and the weather fine, and a night march of
twelve miles would have placed the Federal advanced-
guards at the foot of the mountains, ready to force the
Gaps at earliest dawn. McClellan, however, although his
men had made no unusual exertions during the past few
days, preferred to wait till daylight.

Nevertheless, on the night of the 13th disaster
threatened the Confederates. Harper's Ferry had not
yet fallen, and, in addition to the cavalry, D. H. Hill's
division was alone available to defend the passes. Lee,
however, still relying on McClellan's irresolution, determined to hold South Mountain, thus gaining time for
the reduction of Harper's Ferry, and Longstreet was
ordered back from Hagerstown, thirteen miles west of
Boonsboro', to Hill's assistance.

On the same night Jackson, at Halltown, opened communications with McLaws and Walker, and on the next
Sept. 14. morning (Sunday) he made the necessary arrangements to ensure combination in the attack. The
Federal lines, although commanded by the Maryland and
Loudoun Heights to the north and east, opposed a strong
front to the south and west. The Bolivar Heights, an open
plateau, a mile and a quarter in length, which has the
Potomac on the one flank and the Shenandoah on the other,
was defended by several batteries and partially intrenched.
Moreover, it was so far from the summits occupied by
McLaws and Walker that their guns, although directed
against the enemy's rear, could hardly render effective aid ;
only the extremities of the plateau were thoroughly exposed to fire from the heights.

In order to facilitate communication across the two
great rivers Jackson ordered a series of signal stations to
be established, and while his own batteries were taking up
their ground to assail the Bolivar Heights he issued his
instructions to his colleagues. At ten o'clock the flags on
the Loudoun Heights signalled that Walker had six rifled
guns in position. He was ordered to wait until McLaws,

[1] For the lost order, see Note at end of chapter.

who was employed in cutting roads through the woods, should have done the same, and the following message explained the method of attack :—

'General McLaws,—If you can, establish batteries to drive the enemy from the hill west of Bolivar and on which Barbour's House is, and from any other position where he may be damaged by your artillery. Let me know when you are ready to open your batteries, and give me any suggestions by which you can operate against the enemy. Cut the telegraph line down the Potomac if it is not already done. Keep a good look-out against a Federal advance from below. Similar instructions will be sent to General Walker. I do not desire any of the batteries to open until all are ready on both sides of the river, except you should find it necessary, of which you must judge for yourself. I will let you know when to open all the batteries.

'T. J. JACKSON,
'*Major-General Commanding.*' [1]

About half-past two in the afternoon McLaws reported that his guns were up, and a message 'to fire at such positions of the enemy as will be most effective,' followed the formal orders for the co-operation of the whole force.

'Headquarters, Valley District,
Sept. 14, 1862.

'**1.** To-day Major-General McLaws will attack so as to sweep with his artillery the ground occupied by the enemy, take his batteries in reverse, and otherwise operate against him as circumstances may justify.

'**2.** Brigadier-General Walker will take in reverse the battery on the turnpike, and sweep with his artillery the ground occupied by the enemy, and silence the batteries on the island of the Shenandoah should he find a battery (*sic*) there.

'**3.** Major-General A. P. Hill will move along the left bank of the Shenandoah, and thus turn the enemy's left flank and enter Harper's Ferry.

[1] Report of Signal Officer, O. R., vol. xix., part i., p. 958.

' 4. Brigadier-General Lawton will move along the turnpike for the purpose of supporting General Hill, and otherwise operating against the enemy to the left of General Hill.

' 5. Brigadier-General Jones will, with one of his brigades and a battery of artillery, make a demonstration against the enemy's right ; the remaining part of his division will constitute the reserve and move along the turnpike.

 ' By order of Major-General Jackson,
      ' Wm. L. Jackson,
    ' *Acting Assistant Adjutant-General.*' [1]

Jackson, it appears, was at first inclined to send a flag of truce, for the purpose of giving the civilian population time to get away, should the garrison refuse to surrender ; but during the morning heavy firing was heard to the northward, and McLaws reported that he had been obliged to detach troops to guard his rear against McClellan. The batteries were therefore ordered to open fire on the Federal works without further delay.

According to General Walker, Jackson, although he was aware that McClellan had occupied Frederick, not over twenty miles distant, could not bring himself to believe that his old classmate had overcome his prudential instincts, and attributed the sounds of battle to a cavalry engagement. It is certain that he never for a single moment anticipated a resolute attempt to force the passages of the South Mountain, for, in reply to McLaws, he merely instructed him to ask General D. H. Hill to protect his rear, and to communicate with Lee at Hagerstown. Had he entertained the slightest suspicion that McClellan was advancing with his whole force against the passages of the South Mountain, he would hardly have suggested that Hill should be asked to defend Crampton's as well as Turner's Gap.

With full confidence, therefore, that he would have time to enforce the surrender of Harper's Ferry and to join Lee on the further bank of the Potomac, the progress of

[1] Report of Signal Officer, O. R., vol xix., part i., p. 659.

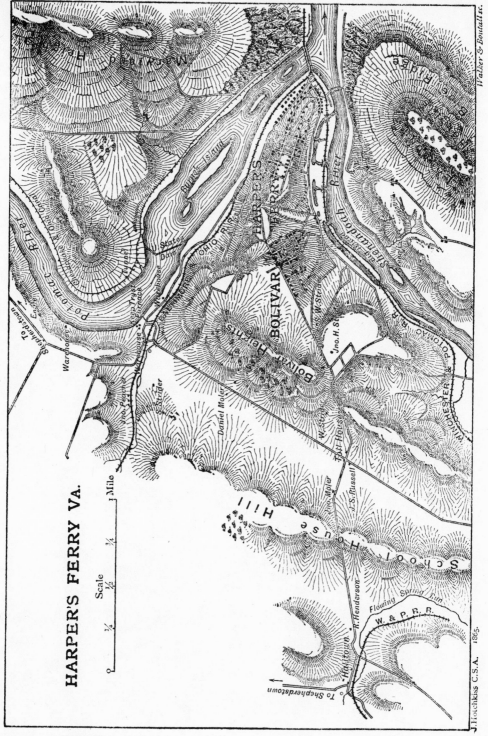

HARPER'S FERRY VA.

Scale

¼   ½   ¾   1 Mile

J. Hotchkiss C.S.A. 1865.

Walker & Boutall sc.

his attack was cautious and methodical. 'The position in front of me,' he wrote to McLaws, 'is a strong one, and I desire to remain quiet, and let you and Walker draw attention from Furnace Hill (west of Bolivar Heights), so that I may have an opportunity of getting possession of the hill without much loss.' It was not, then, till the artillery had been long in action, and the fire of the enemy's guns had been in some degree subdued, that the infantry was permitted to advance. Although the Federal batteries opened vigorously on the lines of skirmishers, the casualties were exceedingly few. The troops found cover in woods and broken ground, and before nightfall Hill had driven in the enemy's pickets, and had secured a knoll on their left flank which afforded an admirable position for artillery. Lawton, in the centre, occupied a ridge over which ran the Charlestown turnpike, brought his guns into action, and formed his regiments for battle in the woods. Jones' division held the Shepherdstown road on Lawton's left, seized Furnace Hill, and pushed two batteries forward.

No attempt was made during this Sunday evening to storm the Bolivar Heights; and yet, although the Confederate infantry had been hardly engaged, the enemy had been terribly shaken. From every point of the compass, from the lofty crests which looked down upon the town, from the woods towards Charlestown, from the hill to westward, a ceaseless hail of shells had swept the narrow neck to which the garrison was confined. Several guns had been dismounted. More than one regiment of raw troops had dispersed in panic, and had been with difficulty rallied. The roads were furrowed with iron splinters. Many buildings had been demolished, and although the losses among the infantry, covered by their parapets, had been insignificant, the batteries had come almost to their last round.

During the night Jackson made preparations for an early assault. Two of A. P. Hill's brigades, working their way along the bank of the Shenandoah, over ground which the Federal commander had considered impassable, established themselves to the left rear of the Bolivar Heights. Guns were brought up to the knoll which Hill

R 2

had seized during the afternoon; and ten pieces, which Jackson had ordered to be taken across the Shenandoah by Keyes' Ford, were placed in a position whence they could enfilade the enemy's works at effective range. Lawton and Jones pushed forward their lines until they could hear voices in the intrenchments; and a girdle of bayonets, closely supported by many batteries, encircled the hapless Federals. The assault was to be preceded by a heavy bombardment, and the advance was to be made as soon as Hill's guns ceased fire.

All night long the Confederates slept upon their arms, waiting for the dawn. When day broke, a soft silver mist, rising from the broad Potomac, threw its protecting folds over Harper's Ferry. But the Southern gunners knew the direction of their targets; the clouds were rent by the passage of screaming shells, and as the sun, rising over the Loudoun Heights, dispersed the vapours, the whole of Jackson's artillery became engaged. The Federal batteries, worked with stubborn courage, and showing a bold front to every fresh opponent, maintained the contest for an hour; but, even if ammunition had not failed them, they could not have long withstood the terrible fire which took them in front, in flank, and in reverse.[1] Then, perceiving that the enemy's guns were silenced, Hill ordered his batteries to cease fire, and threw forward his brigades against the ridge. Staunch to the last, the Federal artillerymen ran their pieces forward, and opened on the Confederate infantry. Once more the long line of Jackson's guns crashed out in answer, and two batteries, galloping up to within four hundred yards of the ridge, poured in a destructive fire over the heads of their own troops. Hill's brigades, when the artillery duel recommenced, had halted at the foot of the slope. Beyond, over the bare fields, the way was obstructed by felled timber, the lopped branches of which were closely interlaced, and above the abattis rose the line of breastworks. But before the charge was sounded

Sept. 15.

---

[1] The ten guns which had been carried across the Shenandoah were specially effective. Report of Colonel Crutchfield, Jackson's chief of artillery. O. R., vol. xix., part i., p. 962.

the Confederate gunners completed the work they had so
well begun.   At 7.30 A.M. the white flag was hoisted,
and with the loss of no more than 100 men Jackson had
captured Harper's Ferry with his artillery alone.

The general was near the church in the wood on the
Charlestown road, and Colonel Douglas was sent forward
to ascertain the enemy's purpose.   ' Near the top of the
hill,' he writes, ' I met General White (commanding the
Federals), and told him my mission.   Just then General
Hill came up from the direction of his line, and on his
request I conducted them to General Jackson, whom I
found sitting on his horse where I had left him.   He
was not, as the Comte de Paris says, leaning against a
tree asleep, but exceedingly wide-awake. . . .   The surrender was unconditional, and then General Jackson turned
the matter over to General A. P. Hill, who allowed General
White the same liberal terms that Grant afterwards gave
Lee at Appomattox.   The fruits of the surrender were
12,520 prisoners, 13,000 small arms, 73 pieces of artillery,
and several hundred waggons.

' General Jackson, after a brief dispatch to General
Lee announcing the capitulation, rode up to Bolivar and
down into Harper's Ferry.   The curiosity in the Union
army to see him was so great that the soldiers lined the
sides of the road.   Many of them uncovered as he passed,
and he invariably returned the salute.   One man had an
echo of response all about him when he said aloud:
" Boys, he's not much for looks, but if we'd had him we
wouldn't have been caught in this trap." ' [1]

The completeness of the victory was marred by the
escape of the Federal cavalry.   Under cover of the night
1,200 horsemen, crossing the pontoon bridge, and passing
swiftly up the towpath under the Maryland Heights, had
ridden boldly beneath the muzzles of McLaws' batteries,
and, moving north-west, had struck out for Pennsylvania.
Yet the capture of Harper's Ferry was a notable exploit,
although Jackson seems to have looked upon it as a mere
matter of course.

[1] *Battles and Leaders*, vol. ii., pp. 625-7.

'Through God's blessing,' he reported to Lee at eight
o'clock, 'Harper's Ferry and its garrison are to be surrendered. As Hill's troops have borne the heaviest part of the
engagement, he will be left in command until the prisoners
and public property shall be disposed of, unless you direct
otherwise. The other forces can move off this evening so
soon as they get their rations. To what point shall they
move ? I write at this time in order that you may be
apprised of the condition of things. You may expect to
hear from me again to-day, after I get more information
respecting the number of prisoners, &c.' [1]

Lee, with D. H. Hill, Longstreet, and Stuart, was
already falling back from the South Mountain to Sharpsburg, a little village on the right bank of the Antietam
Creek ; and late in the afternoon Jackson, Walker, and
McLaws were ordered to rejoin without delay.[2] September
14 had been an anxious day for the Confederate Commander-in-Chief. During the morning D. H. Hill, with
no more than 5,000 men in his command, had seen the
greater part of McClellan's army deploy for action in
the wide valley below and to the eastward of Turner's Gap.
Stuart held the woods below Crampton's Gap, six miles
south, with Robertson's brigade, now commanded by the
gallant Munford ; and on the heights above McLaws had
posted three brigades, for against this important pass, the
shortest route by which the Federals could interpose between
Lee and Jackson, McClellan's left wing, consisting of 20,000
men under General Franklin, was steadily advancing.

The positions at both Turner's and Crampton's Gaps
were very strong. The passes, at their highest points,
are at least 600 feet above the valley, and the slopes steep,
rugged, and thickly wooded. The enemy's artillery had

[1] O. R., vol. xix., part i., p. 951. General Longstreet (*From Manassas to
Appomattox*, p. 233) suggests that Jackson, after the capitulation of Harper's
Ferry, should have moved east of South Mountain against McClellan's rear.
Jackson, however, was acquainted neither with McClellan's position nor
with Lee's intentions, and nothing could have justified such a movement
except the direct order of the Commander-in-Chief.

[2] 'The Invasion of Maryland,' General Longstreet, *Battles and Leaders*,
vol. ii., p. 666.

little chance. Stone walls, running parallel to the crest, gave much protection to the Southern infantry, and loose boulders and rocky scarps increased the difficulties of the ascent. But the numbers available for defence were very small; and had McClellan marched during the night he would probably have been master of the passes before mid-day. As it was, Crampton's Gap was not attacked by Franklin until noon; and although at the same hour the advanced-guard of the Federal right wing had gained much ground, it was not till four in the evening that a general attack was made on Turner's Gap. By this time Long-street, after a march of thirteen miles, had reached the battle-field;[1] and despite the determination with which the attack was pressed, Turner's Gap was still held when darkness fell.

The defence of Crampton's Gap had been less successful. Franklin had forced the pass before five o'clock, and driving McLaws' three brigades before him, had firmly established himself astride the summit. The Confederate losses were larger than those which they had inflicted. McClellan reports 1,791 casualties on the right, Franklin 533 on the left. McLaws' and Munford's loss was over 800, of whom 400 were captured. The number of killed and wounded in Hill's and Longstreet's commands is unknown; it probably reached a total of 1,500, and 1,100 of their men were marched to Frederick as prisoners. Thus the day's fighting had cost the South 3,400 men. Moreover, Long-street's ammunition column, together with an escort of 600 men, had been cut up by the cavalry which had escaped from Harper's Ferry, and which had struck the Hagerstown road as it marched northward into Pennsyl-

---

[1] The order for the march had been given the night before ('The Invasion of Maryland,' General Longstreet, *Battles and Leaders*, vol. ii., p. 666), and there seems to have been no good reason, even admitting the heat and dust, that Longstreet's command should not have joined Hill at noon. The troops marched 'at daylight' (5 A.M.), and took ten hours to march thirteen miles. As it was, only four of the brigades took part in the action, and did so, owing to their late arrival, in very disjointed fashion. Not all the Confederate generals appear to have possessed the same 'driving power' as Jackson.

vania. Yet, on the whole, Lee had no reason to be chagrined with the result of his operations. McClellan had
acted with unexpected vigour. But neither in strategy nor
in tactics had he displayed improvement on his Peninsular
methods. He should have thrown the bulk of his army
against Crampton's Gap, thus intervening between Lee and
Jackson; but instead of doing so he had directed 70,000
men against Turner's Gap. Nor had his attack on Hill
and Longstreet been characterised by resolution. The
advanced-guard was left unsupported úntil 2 P.M., and
not more than 30,000 men were employed throughout
the day. Against this number 8,000 Confederates had
held the pass. Cobb, one of McLaws' brigadiers, who
commanded the defence at Crampton's Gap, though driven
down the mountain, had offered a stout resistance to superior
forces; and twenty-four hours had been gained for Jackson.
On the other hand, in face of superior numbers, the position at Turner's Gap had become untenable; and during
the night Hill and Longstreet marched to Sharpsburg.

This enforced retreat was not without effect on the
moral of either army. McClellan was as exultant as he was
credulous. 'I have just learned,' he reported to Halleck at
8 A.M. on the 15th, 'from General Hooker, in advance, that the enemy is making for Shepherdstown in a perfect panic; and that General Lee last night
stated publicly that he must admit they had been shockingly
whipped. I am hurrying forward to endeavour to press
their retreat to the utmost.' Then, two hours later : ' Information this moment received completely confirms the rout
and demoralisation of the rebel army. It is stated that
Lee gives his losses as 15,000. We are following as rapidly
as the men can move.' [1] Nor can it be doubted that
McClellan's whole army, unaccustomed to see their antagonists give ground before them, shared the general's
mood.[2] Amongst the Confederates, on the other hand,
there was some depression. It could not be disguised that

Sept. 15.

---

[1] O. R. vol. xix., pp. 294, 295.
[2] 'The *moral* of our men is now restored.' McClellan to Halleck
after South Mountain. O. R., vol. xix., part ii., p. 294.

a portion of the troops had shown symptoms of demoralisation. The retreat to the Antietam, although effectively screened by Fitzhugh Lee's brigade of cavalry, was not effected in the best of order. Many of the regiments had been broken by the hard fighting on the mountain; men had become lost in the forest, or had sought safety to the rear; and the number of stragglers was very large. It was not, then, with its usual confidence that the army moved into position on the ridge above the Antietam Creek. General Longstreet, indeed, was of opinion that the army should have recrossed the Potomac at once. 'The moral effect of our move into Maryland had been lost by our discomfiture at South Mountain, and it was evident we could not hope to concentrate in time to do more than make a respectable retreat, whereas by retiring before the battle [of Sharpsburg] we could have claimed a very successful campaign.'[1] So spake the voice of prudence. Lee, however, so soon as he was informed of the fall of Harper's Ferry, had ordered Jackson to join him, resolving to hold his ground, and to bring McClellan to a decisive battle on the north bank of the Potomac.

Although 45,000 men—for Lee at most could count on no more than this number, so great had been the straggling—were about to receive the attack of over 90,000, Jackson, when he reached Sharpsburg on the morning of the 16th, heartily approved the Commander-in-Chief's decision, and it is worth while to consider the reasons which led them to disagree with Longstreet.

1. Under ordinary conditions, to expect an army of 45,000 to wrest decisive victory from one of 90,000 well-armed enemies would be to demand an impossibility. The defence, when two armies are equally matched, is physically stronger than the attack, although we have Napoleon's word for it that the defence has the harder task. But that the inherent strength of the defence is so great as to enable the smaller force to annihilate its enemy is contrary to all the teaching of history. By making good use of favourable ground, or by constructing substantial works,

[1] *Battles and Leaders*, vol. ii., pp. 666, 667.

the smaller force may indeed stave off defeat and gain
time.   But it can hope for nothing more.   The records of
warfare contain no instance, when two armies were of
much the same quality, of the smaller army bringing the
campaign to a decisive issue by defensive tactics.   Wellington and Lee both fought many defensive battles with inferior
forces.   But neither of them, under such conditions, ever
achieved the destruction of their enemy.   They fought
such battles to gain time, and their hopes soared no
higher.   At Talavera, Busaco, Fuentes d'Onor, where
the French were superior to the allies, Wellington repulsed
the attack, but he did not prevent the defeated armies
taking the field again in a few days.   At the Wilderness,
Spotsylvania, the North Anna, and Cold Harbour, the great
battles of 1864, Lee maintained his ground, but he did
not prevent Grant moving round his flank in the direction
of Richmond.   At the Second Manassas, Jackson stood fast
for the greater part of two days, but he would never have
driven Pope across Bull Run without the aid of Longstreet.
Porter at Gaines' Mill held 55,000 men with 35,000 for
more than seven hours, but even if he had maintained his
position, the Confederate army would not have become a
mob of fugitives.   No; except on peculiarly favourable
ground, or when defending an intrenched camp, an army
matched with one of equal efficiency and numerically
superior, can never hope for decisive success.   So circum-
stanced, a wise general will rather retreat than fight, and
thus save his men for a more favourable opportunity.[1]

But Lee and Jackson had not to deal with ordinary
conditions.   Whatever may have been the case in the
Peninsula and in the Valley, there can be no question but
that the armies in Maryland were by no means equal in

---

[1] Before Salamanca, for instance, because Marmont, whose strength was
equal to his own, was about to be reinforced by 4,000 cavalry, Wellington
had determined to retreat.   It is true, however, that when weaker than Masséna, whom he had already worsted, by 8,000 infantry and 3,800 sabres, but
somewhat stronger in artillery, he stood to receive attack at Fuentes
d'Onor.   Yet Napier declares that it was a very audacious resolution.   The
knowledge and experience of the great historian told him that to pit 32,000
infantry against 40,000 was to trust too much to fortune.

quality. The Federals were far more accustomed to retreat than advance. For several months, whether they were engaged on the Shenandoah, on the Chickahominy, on the Rappahannock, or on Bull Run, they had been invariably outmanoeuvred. Their losses had been exceedingly severe, not only in battle, but from sickness and straggling. Many of their bravest officers and men had fallen. With the exception of the Second and Sixth Army Corps, commanded by Sumner and by Franklin, by far the greater part of the troops had been involved in Pope's defeat, and they had not that trust in their leaders which promises a strong offensive. While at Washington the army had been reinforced by twenty-four regiments of infantry, but the majority of these troops had been but lately raised; they knew little of drill; they were commanded by officers as ignorant as themselves, and they had never fired a musket. Nor were the generals equal in capacity to those opposing them. 'If a student of history,' says a Northern officer, 'familiar with the characters who figured in the War of Secession, but happening to be ignorant of the battle of Antietam, should be told the names of the men who held high commands there, he would say that with anything like equality of forces the Confederates must have won, for their leaders were men who made great names in the war, while the Federal leaders were, with few exceptions, men who never became conspicuous, or became conspicuous only through failure.'[1] And the difference in military capacity extended to the rank and file. When the two armies met on the Antietam, events had been such as to confer a marked superiority on the Southerners. They were the children of victory, and every man in the army had participated in the successes of Lee and Jackson. They had much experience of battle. They were supremely confident in their own prowess, for the fall of Harper's Ferry had made more than amends for the retreat from South Mountain, and they were supremely confident in their leaders. No new regiments weakened

[1] *The Antietam and Fredericksburg*, General Palfrey, p. 53.

the stability of their array. Every brigade and every regiment could be depended on. The artillery, which had been but lately reorganised in battalions, had, under the fostering care of General Pendleton, become peculiarly efficient, although the *matériel* was still indifferent ; and against Stuart's horsemen the Federal cavalry was practically useless.

In every military attribute, then, the Army of Northern Virginia was so superior to the Army of the Potomac that Lee and Jackson believed that they might fight a defensive battle, outnumbered as they were, with the hope of annihilating their enemy. They were not especially favoured by the ground, and time and means for intrenching were both wanting ; but they were assured that not only were their veterans capable of holding the position, but, if favoured by fortune, of delivering a counterstroke which should shiver the Army of the Potomac into a thousand fragments.

2. By retreating across the Potomac, in accordance with General Longstreet's suggestion, Lee would certainly have avoided all chances of disaster. But, at the same time, he would have abandoned a good hope of ending the war. The enemy would have been fully justified in assuming that the retrograde movement had been made under the compulsion of his advance, and the balance of *moral* have been sensibly affected in favour of the Federals. If the Potomac had once been placed between the opposing forces, McClellan would have had it in his power to postpone an encounter until his army was strongly reinforced, his raw regiments trained, and his troops rested. The passage of the river, it is true, had been successfully forced by the Confederates on September 5. But it by no means followed that it could be forced for the second time in face of a concentrated enemy, who would have had time to recover his *moral* and supply his losses. McClellan, so long as the Confederates remained in Maryland, had evidently made up his mind to attack. But if Maryland was evacuated he would probably content himself with holding the line of the Potomac ; and, in view of the relative strength of the two armies, it would be an

extraordinary stroke of fortune which should lay him open to assault. Lee and Jackson were firmly convinced that it was the wiser policy to give the enemy no time to reorganise and recruit, but to coerce him to battle before he had recovered from the defeat which he had sustained on the heights above Bull Run. To recross the Potomac would be to slight the favours of fortune, to abandon the initiative, and to submit, in face of the vast numbers of fresh troops which the North was already raising, to a defensive warfare, a warfare which might protract the struggle, but which must end in the exhaustion of the Confederacy. McClellan's own words are the strongest justification of the views held by the Southern leaders :—

'The Army of the Potomac was thoroughly exhausted and depleted by the desperate fighting and severe marching in the unhealthy regions of the Chickahominy and afterwards, during the second Bull Run campaign; its trains, administrative services and supplies were disorganised or lacking in consequence of the rapidity and manner of its removal from the Peninsula, as well as from the nature of its operations during the second Bull Run campaign.

'Had General Lee remained in front of Washington (south of the Potomac) it would have been the part of wisdom to hold our own army quiet until its pressing wants were fully supplied, its organisation was restored, and its ranks were filled with recruits—in brief, until it was prepared for a campaign. But as the enemy maintained the offensive, and crossed the Upper Potomac to threaten or invade Pennsylvania, it became necessary to meet him at any cost, notwithstanding the condition of the troops, to put a stop to the invasion, to save Baltimore and Washington, and throw him back across the Potomac. Nothing but sheer necessity justified the advance of the Army of the Potomac to South Mountain and Antietam in its then condition. The purpose of advancing from Washington was simply to meet the necessities of the moment by frustrating Lee's invasion of the Northern States, and when that was accomplished, to push with the utmost rapidity the work of reorganisation and supply, so that a new campaign might be promptly inaugurated with the army in condition to prosecute it to a successful termination without intermission.' [1]

And in his official report, showing what the result of a Confederate success might well have been, he says : ' One battle lost and almost all would have been lost.   Lee's army might have marched as it pleased on Washington, Baltimore, Philadelphia, or New York.   It could have levied its supplies from a fertile and undevastated country, extorted tribute from wealthy and populous cities, and nowhere east of the Alleghanies was there another organised force to avert its march.' [2]

3. The situation in the West was such that even a victory in Maryland was exceedingly desirable.   Confederate movements in Tennessee and Kentucky had won a measure of success which bade fair to open up a brilliant opportunity.   Should the Federals be defeated in both the theatres of war, the blow would be felt throughout the length and breadth of the Northern States ; and, in any case, it was of the utmost importance that all McClellan's troops should be retained in the East.

So, when the tidings came of Jackson's victory at Harper's Ferry, both armies braced themselves for the coming battle, the Confederates in the hope that it would be decisive of the war, the Federals that it would save the capital.   But the Confederates had still a most critical time before them, and Lee's daring was never more amply illustrated than when he made up his mind to fight on the Antietam.   McClellan's great army was streaming through the passes of the South Mountain. At Rohrersville, six miles east of the Confederate bivouacs, where he had halted as soon as the cannonade at Harper's Ferry ceased, Franklin was still posted with 20,000 men.   From their battle-field at Turner's Gap, ten miles from Sharpsburg, came the 70,000 which composed the right and centre ; and on the banks of the Antietam but 15,000 Southerners were in position. Jack-

---

[1] *Battles and Leaders*, vol. ii., p. 554.
[2] O. R., vol. xix., part i., p. 65.

son had to get rid of his prisoners, to march seventeen miles, and to ford the Potomac before he could reach the ground. Walker was twenty miles distant, beyond the Shenandoah; and McLaws, who would be compelled by Franklin's presence near Rohrersville to cross at Harper's Ferry and follow Jackson, over five-and-twenty. Would they be up before McClellan attacked? Lee, relying on McClellan's caution and Jackson's energy, answered the question in the affirmative.

The September day wore on. The country between the South Mountain and Sharpsburg, resembling in every characteristic the Valley of the Shenandoah, is open and gently undulating. No leagues of woodland, as in Eastern Virginia, block the view. The roads run through wide corn-fields and rolling pastures, and scattered copses are the only relics of the forest. It was not yet noon when the Federal scouts appeared among the trees which crown the left bank of the Antietam Creek. 'The number increased, and larger and larger grew the field of blue until it seemed to stretch as far as the eye could see. It was an awe-inspiring spectacle,' adds Longstreet, ' as this grand force settled down in sight of the Confederates, shattered by battles and scattered by long and tedious marches.' [1] But when night fell upon the field the only interchange of hostilities had been a brief engagement of artillery. McClellan's advance, owing to the difficulty of passing his great army through the mountains, and to the scarcity of roads, had been slow and tedious; in some of the divisions there had been unnecessary delay; and Lee had so disposed his force that the Federal commander, unenlightened as to the real strength of his adversary, believed that he was opposed by 50,000 men.

Nor was the next morning marked by any increase of activity. McClellan, although he should have been well aware

Sept. 16. that a great part of the Confederate army was still west of the Potomac, made no attack. ' It was discovered,' he reports, ' that the enemy had changed the position of some of his batteries. The masses of

[1] *Battles and Leaders*, vol. ii., p. 667.

his troops, however, were still concealed behind the opposite heights. It was afternoon before I could move the
troops to their positions for attack, being compelled to
spend the morning in reconnoitring the new position taken
up by the enemy, examining the ground, and finding fords,
clearing the approaches, and hurrying up the ammunition
and supply trains.'[1]

Considering that McClellan had been in possession of the
left bank of the Antietam since the forenoon of the previous
day, all these preliminaries might well have been completed
before daylight on the 16th. That a change in the dispositions of a few batteries, a change so unimportant as to
pass unnoticed in the Confederate reports, should have
imposed a delay, when every moment was precious, of
many hours, proves that Lee's and Jackson's estimate of
their opponent's character was absolutely correct. While
McClellan was reconnoitring, and the guns were thunder-
ing across the Antietam, Jackson and Walker crossed
the Potomac, and reported to Lee in Sharpsburg.[2]
Walker had expected to find the Commander-in-Chief
anxious and careworn. 'Anxious no doubt he was; but
there was nothing in his look or manner to indicate it.
On the contrary, he was calm, dignified, and even cheerful. If he had had a well-equipped army of a hundred
thousand veterans at his back, he could not have
appeared more composed and confident. On shaking
hands with us, he simply expressed his satisfaction with
the result of our operations at Harper's Ferry, and
with our timely arrival at Sharpsburg ; adding that with
our reinforcements he felt confident of being able to hold
his ground until the arrival of the divisions of R. H.
Anderson, McLaws, and A. P. Hill, which were still behind,
and which did not arrive till next day.'[3]

Yet the reinforcements which Jackson and Walker
had brought up were no considerable addition to Lee's

---

[1] O. R., vol. xix., part i., p. 55.
[2] According to Jackson's staff officers he himself reported shortly after
daylight.
[3] *Battles and Leaders*, vol. ii., p. 675.

strength. Jones' division consisted of no more than 1,600 muskets, Lawton's of less than 3,500. Including officers and artillery, therefore, the effectives of these divisions numbered about 5,500. A. P. Hill's division appears to have mustered 5,000 officers and men, and we may add 1,000 for men sick or on detached duties. The total should undoubtedly have been larger. After the battle of Cedar Run, Jackson had 22,450 effectives in his ranks. His losses in the operations against Pope, and the transfer of Robertson's cavalry to Stuart, had brought his numbers down by 5,787 ; but on September 16, including 70 killed or wounded at Harper's Ferry, they should have been not less than 16,800. In reality they were only 11,500. We have not far to look for the cause of this reduction. Many of the men had absented themselves before the army crossed into Maryland ; and if those who remained with the colours had seen little fighting since Pope's defeat, they had had no reason to complain of inactivity. The operations which resulted in the capture of Harper's Ferry had been arduous in the extreme. Men who had taken part in the forced marches of the Valley campaign declared that the march from Frederick to Harper's Ferry surpassed all their former experiences. In three-and-a-half days they had covered over sixty miles, crossing two mountain ranges, and fording the Potomac. The weather had been intensely hot, and the dust was terrible. Nor had the investment of Harper's Ferry been a period of repose. They had been under arms during the night which preceded the surrender, awaiting the signal to assault within a few hundred yards of the enemy's sentries. As soon as the terms of capitulation were arranged they had been hurried back to the bivouac, had cooked two days' rations, and shortly after midnight had marched to the Potomac, seventeen miles away. This night march, coming on the top of their previous exertions, had taxed the strength of many beyond endurance. The majority were badly shod. Many were not shod at all. They were ill-fed, and men ill-fed are on the highroad to hospital. There were stragglers, then, from every company in the command. Even the Stonewall

Brigade, though it had still preserved its five regiments, was reduced to 300 muskets ; and the other brigades of Jackson's division were but little stronger. Walker's division, too, although less hardly used in the campaign than the Valley troops, had diminished under the strain of the night march, and mustered no more than 3,500 officers and men at Sharpsburg. Thus the masses of troops which McClellan conceived were hidden in rear of D. H. Hill and Longstreet amounted in reality to some 10,000 effective soldiers.

It was fortunate, indeed, that in their exhausted condition there was no immediate occasion for their services on September 16. The shadows grew longer, but yet the Federals made no move ; even the fire of the artillery died away, and the men slept quietly in the woods to north and west of the little town. Meanwhile, in an old house, one of the few which had any pretensions to comfort in Sharpsburg, the generals met in council. Staff officers strolled to and fro over the broad brick pavement; the horses stood lazily under the trees which shaded the dusty road ; and within, Lee, Jackson, and Longstreet pored long and earnestly over the map of Maryland during the bright September afternoon. But before the glow of a lovely sunset had faded from the sky the artillery once more opened on the ridge above, and reports came in that the Federals were crossing the Antietam near Pry's Mill. Lee at once ordered Longstreet to meet this threat with Hood's division, and Jackson was ordered into line on the left of Hood. No serious collision, however, took place during the evening. The Confederates made no attempt to oppose the passage of the Creek. Hood's pickets were driven in, but a speedy reinforcement restored the line, and except that the batteries on both sides took part the fighting was little more than an affair of outposts. At eleven o'clock Hood's brigades were withdrawn to cook and eat. Jackson's division filled their place; and the night, although broken by constant alarms, passed away without further conflict. The Federal movements had clearly exposed their intention of attacking, and had even revealed the point which they would first assail.

McClellan had thrown two army corps, the First under Hooker, and the Twelfth under Mansfield, across the Antietam; and they were now posted, facing southward, a mile and a half north of Sharpsburg, concealed by the woods beyond Jackson's left.

NOTE

The essential paragraphs of the lost order ran as follows :—

' The army will resume its march to-morrow, taking the Hagerstown road.   General Jackson's command will form the advance, and after passing Middletown, with such portions as he may select, take the route towards Sharpsburg, cross the Potomac at the most convenient point, and by Friday night (September 12) take possession of the Baltimore and Ohio Railroad, capture such of the enemy as may be at Martinsburg, and intercept such as may attempt to escape from Harper's Ferry.

' General Longstreet's command will pursue the same road as far as Boonsboro', where it will halt with the reserve, supply, and baggage trains of the army.

' General McLaws, with his own division and that of General Anderson, will follow General Longstreet; on reaching Middletown he will take the route to Harper's Ferry, and by Friday morning (September 12) possess himself of the Maryland Heights and endeavour to capture the enemy at Harper's Ferry and vicinity.

' General Walker with his division . . . will take possession of the Loudoun Heights, if practicable by Friday morning (September 12), . . . He will as far as practicable co-operate with General McLaws and General Jackson in intercepting the retreat of the enemy.

' General D. H. Hill's division will form the rear-guard of the army, pursuing the road taken by the main body.

' General Stuart will detach a squadron of cavalry to accompany the commands of Generals Longstreet, Jackson, and McLaws, and, with the main body of the cavalry, will cover the route of the army and bring up all stragglers.

' The commands of Generals Jackson, McLaws and Walker, after accomplishing the objects for which they have been detached, will join the main body at Boonsboro' or Hagerstown.'

The second paragraph was afterwards modified by General Lee so as to place Longstreet at Hagerstown.

CHAPTER XIX

SHARPSBURG

IT is a curious coincidence that not only were the numbers of the opposing armies at the battle of Sharpsburg almost identical with those of the French and Germans at the 1862. battle of Wörth, but that there is no small resemSept. 17. blance between the natural features and surrounding scenery of the two fields. Full in front of the Confederate position rises the Red Hill, a spur of the South Mountain, wooded, like the Vosges, to the very crest, and towering high above the fields of Maryland, as the Hochwald towers above the Rhineland. The Antietam, however, is a more difficult obstacle than the Sauerbach, the brook which meanders through the open meadows of the Alsatian valley. A deep channel of more than sixty feet in width is overshadowed by forest trees; and the ground on either bank ascends at a sharp gradient to the crests above. Along the ridge to the west, which parts the Antietam from the Potomac, and about a mile distant from the former stream, runs the Hagerstown turnpike, and in front of this road there was a strong position. Sharpsburg, a village of a few hundred inhabitants, lies on the reverse slope of the ridge, extending in the direction of the Potomac, and only the church steeples were visible to the Federals. Above the hamlet was the Confederate centre. Here, near a limestone boulder, which stood in a plot which is now included in the soldiers' cemetery, was Lee's station during the long hours of September 17, and from this point he overlooked the whole extent of his line of battle. A mile northward, on the Hagerstown pike, his left centre was marked by a square white building, famous under the name of the Dunkard Church, and backed by a long dark wood. To the right, a mile southward, a bold spur, covered with scattered trees, forces the Antietam westward, and on this spur, overlooking the stream, he had placed his right.

Between the Hagerstown pike and the Antietam the open slopes, although not always uniform, but broken, like those on the French side of the Sauerbach, by long ravines, afforded an admirable field of fire. The lanes which cross them are sunk in many places below the surface : in front of Sharpsburg the fields were divided by low stone walls ; and these natural intrenchments added much to the strength of the position. Nor were they the only advantages. The belt of oaks beyond the Dunkard Church, the West Wood, was peculiarly adapted for defence. Parallel ledges of outcropping limestone, both within the thickets and along the Hagerstown road, rising as high as a man's waist, gave good cover from shot and shell ; the trees were of old growth, and there was little underwood. To the north-east, however, and about five hundred yards distant across the fields, lay the East Wood, covering the slopes to the Antietam, with Poffenberger's Wood beyond ; while further to the left, the North Wood, extending across the Hagerstown pike, approached the Confederate flank. The enemy, if he advanced to the attack in this quarter of the field, would thus find ample protection during his march and deployment ; and in case of reverse he would find a rallying-point in the North and Poffenberger's Woods, of which Hooker was already in possession. In the space between the woods were several small farms, surrounded by orchards and stone fences ; and on the slope east of the Dunkard Church stood a few cottages and barns.

Access to the position was not easy. Only a single ford, near Snaveley's house, exists across the Antietam, and this was commanded by the bluff on the Confederate right. The stone bridges, however, for want of time and means to destroy them, had been left standing. That nearest the confluence of the Antietam and the Potomac,

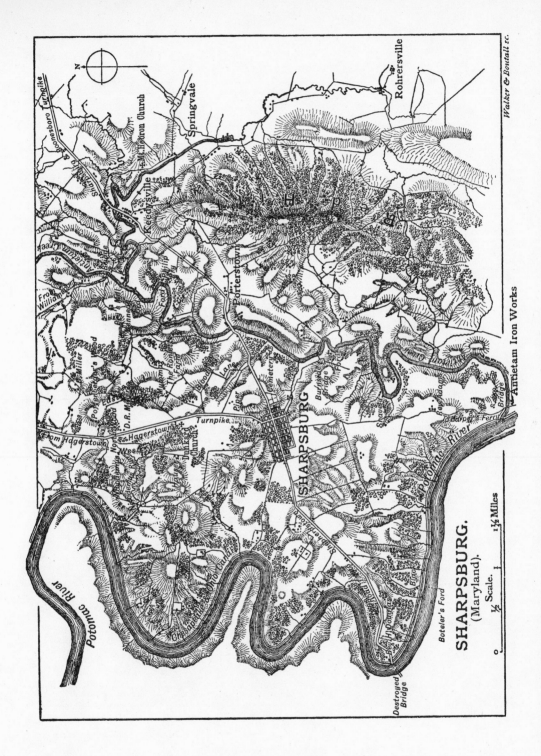

SHARPSBURG.
(Maryland).

Scale. 1 : ½ : 1¼ Miles

at the Antietam Iron-works, by which A. P Hill was
expected, was defended by rifle-pits and enfiladed by artillery.   The next, known as the Burnside Bridge, was completely overlooked by the heights above.   That opposite
Lee's centre could be raked throughout its length ; but the
fourth, at Pry's Mill, by which Hooker and Mansfield had
already crossed, was covered both from view and fire.
Roads within the position were numerous.   The Hagerstown
turnpike, concealed for some distance on either side of
Sharpsburg by the crest of the ridge, was admirably
adapted for the movement of reserves, and another broad
highway ran through Sharpsburg to the Potomac.

The position, then, in many respects, was well adapted
to Lee's purpose.   The flanks were reasonably secure.
The right rested on the Antietam.   The left was more open ;
but the West Wood formed a strong *point d'appui*, and
beyond the wood a low ridge, rising above Nicodemus Run,
gave room for several batteries ; while the Potomac was so
close that the space available for attack on this flank
was much restricted.   The ground could thus be held
by a comparatively small number of men, and a large
reserve set free for the counterstroke.   The great draw-
back was that the ridge east of the Antietam, although
commanded by the crest which the Confederates occupied,
would permit McClellan to deploy the whole of his powerful
artillery, and in no place did the range exceed two thousand
yards.   In case of retreat, moreover, the Potomac, two
hundred yards from shore to shore, would have to be crossed
by a few deep fords,[1] of which only one was practicable
for waggons.   These disadvantages, however, it was impossible to avoid ; and if the counterstroke were decisive,
they would not be felt.

The left of the position was assigned to Jackson, with
Hood in third line.   Next in order came D. H. Hill.
Longstreet held the centre and the right, with Walker
in reserve behind the flank.   Stuart, with Fitzhugh Lee's

---

[1] Two fords, behind the left and centre, were examined by Major Hotchkiss during the battle by Jackson's order, and were reported practicable for
infantry.

brigade and his four guns, was between the West Wood
and the Potomac.   Munford's two regiments of cavalry,
reinforced by a battery, held the bridge at the Antietam
Iron-works, and kept open the communication with
Harper's Ferry ; and twenty-six rifled pieces of the reserve
artillery were with D. H. Hill.   From the Nicodemus
Run to the bluff overhanging the Burnside Bridge is just
three miles, and for the occupation of this front the following troops were at Lee's disposal :—

		Men	Guns
Jackson {	Jones' Division	} 5,500	16[1]
	Ewell's Division (General Lawton) . .		
Longstreet {	D. R. Jones' Division	} 8,000	50
	Hood's Division (detached to Jackson) .		
	Evans' Brigade		
	D. H. Hill's Division	5,000	26
	Walker's Division	3,500	12
Stuart {	Fitzhugh Lee's Brigade	} 2,500	4
	Munford's Brigade		
Reserve Artillery		1,000	26
		25,500	134

On the far side of the Potomac the Shepherdstown
Ford was protected by the remainder of the reserve
artillery, with an infantry escort ; but so small was the
force whose retreat was thus secured that nearly every
man was required in the fighting-line.   Except the divisions
of Hood and Walker, 5,500 men all told, there was no
immediate reserve.

But at daybreak on the 17th the troops which had
been left at Harper's Ferry were rapidly coming up.
McLaws and Anderson, who had started before midnight,
were already nearing the Potomac ; Hampton's cavalry
brigade was not far behind, and orders had been dispatched to A. P. Hill.   But could these 13,000 bayonets
be up in time—before Hooker and Mansfield received strong
support, or before the Burnside Bridge was heavily
attacked ?   The question was indeed momentous.   If the
Federals were to put forth their whole strength without

[1] The majority of Jackson's guns appear to have been left behind,
the teams having broken down, at Harper's Ferry.

delay, bring their numerous artillery into action, and
press the battle at every point, it seemed hardly possible that
defeat could be averted.   McClellan, however, who had
never yet ventured on a resolute offensive, was not likely,
in Lee's judgment, to assault so strong a position as that
held by the Confederates with whole-hearted energy, and it
was safe to calculate that his troops would be feebly
handled.   Yet the odds were great.   Even after the arrival
of the absent divisions[1] no more than 35,000 infantry,
4,000 cavalry, and 194 guns would be in line, and the
enemy's numbers were far superior.   McClellan had
called in Franklin from Rohrersville, and his muster roll
was imposing.

	Men	Guns
First Corps—Hooker	14,856	40
Second Corps—Sumner	18,813	42
Fifth Corps—Porter	12,930	70
Sixth Corps—Franklin	12,300	36
Ninth Corps—Burnside	13,819	35
Twelfth Corps—Mansfield	10,126	36
Cavalry—Pleasanton	4,320	16
	87,164	275

In comparison with the masses arrayed between the
Red Hill and the Antietam, the Confederate army was but
a handful.

Notwithstanding McClellan's caution, the opening of the
battle was not long delayed.   Before sunrise the desultory
firing of the pickets had deepened to the roar of
battle.   Hooker, who had been ordered to begin
5 A.M.
the attack, forming his troops behind the North Wood,
directed them on the Dunkard Church, which, standing on rising ground, appeared the key of the position.
Jackson had already thrown back his two divisions at
nearly a right angle to the Confederate front.   His

	Men	Guns
[1] A. P. Hill's Division	5,000	18
McLaws' Division	4,500	24
R. H. Anderson's Division	3,500	18
Hampton's Cavalry Brigade	1,500	—
	14,500	60

right, which connected with the left of D. H. Hill, and resting on the western edge of the East Wood extended as far as the Miller House, was held by Lawton, with two brigades in front and one in second line.   West of the Hagerstown turnpike, and covering the ground as far as the Nicodemus Farm, was Jones' division ; the Stonewall and Jones' brigades in front, Taliaferro's and Starke's along the edge of the wood in rear.   Three guns stood upon the turnpike; the remainder of the artillery (thirteen) guns was with Stuart on the high ground north of Nicodemus Run.   Hood, in third line, stood near the Dunkard Church; and on Hood's right were three of Longstreet's batteries under Colonel Stephen Lee.

The ground which Jackson had been ordered to occupy was not unfavourable for defence, although the troops had practically no cover except the rail-fences and the rocky ledges.   There was a wide and open field of fire, and when the Federal skirmishers appeared north of the Miller House the Confederate batteries, opening with vigour at a range of eight hundred yards, struck down sixteen men at the first salvo.   This fire, and the stubborn resistance of the pickets, held the enemy for some time in check ; but Hooker deployed six batteries in reply, and after a cannonade of nearly an hour his infantry advanced.   From the cover of the woods, still veiled by the morning mist, the Federals came forward in strong force.   Across the dry ploughed land in Lawton's front the fight grew hot, and on the far side of the turnpike the meadows round the Nicodemus Farm became the scene of a desperate struggle.   Hooker had sent in two divisions, Meade on the left and Doubleday on the right, while a third under Ricketts acted in close support of Meade.[1]   The attack was waged with the dash and energy which had earned for Hooker the sobriquet of 'Fighting Joe,' and the troops he commanded had already proved their mettle on many murderous fields.   Meade's Pennsylvanians, together with the Indiana and Wisconsin

[1] Doubleday's Division consisted of Phelps', Wainwright's, Patrick's, and Gibbon's brigades ; Rickett's Division of Duryea's, Lyle's, and Hartsuff's ; and Meade's Pennsylvania Division of Seymour's, Magilton's, and Anderson's.

regiments, which had wrought such havoc in Jackson's ranks at Grovetown, were once more bearing down upon his line.   Nor were the tactics of the leaders ill-calculated to second the valour of the troops.   Hooker's whole army corps of 12,500 men was manœuvred in close combination. The second line was so posted as to render quick support. No portion of the front was without an adequate reserve in rear.   The artillery was used in mass, and the flanks were adequately guarded.

The conflict between soldiers so well matched was not less fierce than when they had met on other fields. Hooker's troops had won a large measure of success at South Mountain three days previously, and their blood was up.   Meade, Gibbon, and Ricketts were there to lead them, and the battle opened with a resolution which, if it had infected McClellan, would have carried the Sharpsburg ridge ere set of sun.   Stubborn was the resistance of Jackson's regiments, unerring the aim of his seasoned riflemen ; but the opposing infantry, constantly rein-forced, pressed irresistibly forward, and the heavy guns beyond the Antietam, finding an opening between the woods, swept the thin grey line from end to end.   Jones' division, after fighting for three-quarters of an hour on the meadows, fell back to the West Wood ; General Jones was carried wounded from the field, and the guns on the turnpike were abandoned.   So tremendous was

6.30 A.M.   the fire, that the corn, said Hooker, over thirty acres was cut as close by the bullets as if it had been reaped with the sickle, and the dead lay piled in regular ranks along the whole Confederate front. Never, he added, had been seen a more bloody or dismal battle-field.   To the east of the turnpike Lawton's division, strengthened at the critical moment by the brigade in second line, held Meade in check, and with a sharp counter-stroke drove the Pennsylvanians back upon their guns. But Gibbon, fighting fiercely in the centre by the Miller House, brought up a battery in close support of his first line, and pressed heavily on the West Wood until the Confederate skirmishers, creeping through the maize, shot down the gunners and the teams;[1] and Starke, who had succeeded Jones, led the Valley regiments once more into the open field. The battle swayed backwards and forwards under the clouds of smoke; the crash of musketry, reverberating in the woods, drowned the roar of the artillery; and though hundreds were shot down at the shortest range neither Federal nor Confederate flinched from the dreadful fray. Hooker sent in a fresh brigade, and Patrick, reinforcing Gibbon with four regiments, passed swiftly to the front, captured two colours, and made some headway. But again the Virginians rallied, and Starke, observing that the enemy's right had become exposed, led his regiments forward to the charge. Doubleday's division, struck fiercely in front and flank, reeled back in confusion past the Miller House, and although the gallant Starke fell dead, the Confederates recovered the ground which they had lost. Jackson's men had not been left unaided. Colonel Lee's guns had themselves to look to, for along the whole course of the Antietam McClellan's batteries were now in action, sweeping the Sharpsburg ridge with a tremendous fire; but Stuart, west of the Nicodemus Farm, had done much to embarrass Hooker's operations. Bringing his artillery into action, for the ground was unsuited to cavalry, he had distracted the aim of the Federal gunners, and, assailing their infantry in flank, had compelled Doubleday to detach a portion of his force against him. Jackson, with supreme confidence in the ability of his men to hold their ground, had not hesitated to reinforce Stuart with Early's brigade, the strongest in his command; but before Doubleday was beaten back, Early had been recalled.

It was now half-past seven. The battle had been in progress nearly three hours, and Hooker's attack had been repulsed. But fresh troops were coming into action from the north and north-east, and Lawton's and Jones' divisions were in no condition to withstand a renewed assault. No less than three officers in succession had led the latter. Not one single brigade in either

7.30 A.M.

---

[1] This battery of regulars, 'B' 4th U. S. Artillery, lost 40 officers and men killed and wounded, besides 33 horses. O. R., vol. xix., part i., p. 229.

division was still commanded by the officer who brought it into action, and but few regiments. Of 4,200 infantry,[1] 1,700 had already fallen. Never had Jackson's soldiers displayed a spirit more akin to that of their intrepid leader, and their fierce courage was not to be wasted. Reinforcements were close at hand. Early's brigade, 1,100 strong,[2] was moving across from Nicodemus Run into the West Wood. Hood brought his Texans, 1,800 muskets, to the relief of Lawton ; and on Hood's right, but facing eastward, for Ricketts was working round Jackson's right, three of D. H. Hill's brigades, hitherto hidden under cover, came rapidly into line. Lawton's division, nearly half the command being killed or wounded, was withdrawn to the Dunkard Church ; but on the skirt of the West Wood the heroic remnant of the Valley regiments still held fast among the limestone ledges.

The 8,500 infantry which McClellan had sent to Hooker's assistance formed the Twelfth Army Corps, commanded by Mansfield ; and with these men, too, Jackson's soldiers were well acquainted.[3] They were the men who had followed Banks and Shields from Kernstown to Winchester, from Port Republic to Cedar Run ; and the Valley army had not yet encountered more determined foes. Their attack was delivered with their wonted vigour. Several regiments, moving west of the turnpike, bore down on the West Wood. But coming into action at considerable intervals, they were roughly handled by Jones' division, now commanded by Colonel Grigsby, and protected by the rocks ; and Stuart's artillery taking them in flank they were rapidly dispersed. East of the highroad the battle raged with still greater violence. Hood and his Texans, as Lawton's brigades passed to the rear, dashed across the corn-field against Meade and Ricketts, driving back the infantry on the batteries, and shooting down the

---

[1] Early's brigade had not yet been engaged.

[2] One small regiment was left with Stuart.

[3] Mansfield's corps consisted of two divisions, commanded by Crawford (two brigades) and Greene (three brigades). The brigadiers were Knipe, Gordon, Tynedale, Stainbrook, Goodrich.

gunners.   But the Federal line remained unbroken, and
Mansfield's troops were already moving forward.   Crawford's brigade, and then Gordon's, struck the Texans in
front, while Greene, working round the East Wood, made
a resolute onslaught on D. H. Hill.   The struggle was
long and bloody.   The men stood like duellists, firing and
receiving the fire at fifty or a hundred paces.   Crawford
lost 1,000 men without gaining a foot of ground ; but
Gordon turned the scale, and Hood's brigades were
gradually forced back through the corn-field to the
Dunkard Church. A great gap had now opened in Jackson's
line.   Jones' division, its flank uncovered by Hood's
retreat, found itself compelled to seek a new position.
D. H. Hill's brigades, in the same plight, gave ground
towards Sharpsburg ; and Greene, following in pursuit,
actually crossed the turnpike, and penetrated the West
Wood ; but neither Hooker nor Mansfield were able to
support him, and unassisted he could make no progress.

At this moment, as if by common consent, the firing
ceased on this flank of the battle ; and as McClellan's
9 A.M.   Second Army Corps, led by Sumner, advanced
to sustain the First and Twelfth, we may stand
by Jackson near the Dunkard Church, and survey the
field after four hours' fighting.

Assailed in front by superior numbers, and enfiladed
by the batteries beyond the Antietam, the Confederate
left had everywhere given back.   The East Wood was in
possession of the enemy.   Their right occupied the Miller
House ; their centre, supported by many batteries, stood
across the corn-field ; while the left, thrust forward,
was actually established on the edge of the West Wood,
some five hundred yards to northward of the church.
But if Jackson had yielded ground, he had exacted a fearful
price.   The space between the woods was a veritable
slaughter-pen, reeking under the hot September sun, where
the blue uniforms lay thicker than the grey.   The First
Army Corps had been cut to pieces.   It had been beaten
in fair fight by Jackson's two divisions, counting at the
outset less than half its numbers, and aided only by

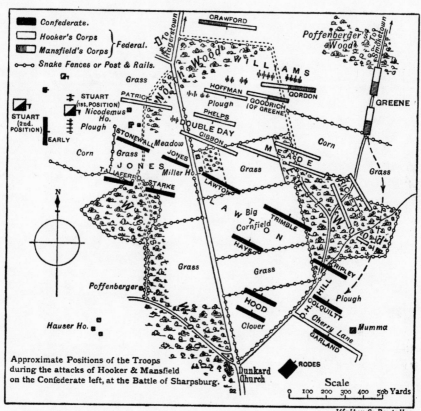

Approximate Positions of the Troops
during the attacks of Hooker & Mansfield
on the Confederate left, at the Battle of Sharpsburg.

Scale

Walker & Boutall sc.

the cavalry. It had lost in killed and wounded over 100 officers and 2,400 men. Hooker himself had been struck down, and as far as the Antietam the field was covered with his stragglers. The Twelfth Corps had suffered hardly less severely; and Mansfield himself, an old man and a gallant soldier, was dying of his wounds. His batteries indeed remained in action, pouring shot and shell on the West Wood and the Dunkard Church; but his infantry, reduced by more than 1,500 rifles, could do no more than hold their ground.

Nor was the exhaustion of the enemy the only advantage which the Confederates had gained by the slaughter of 4,000 men. The position to which Jackson had retired was more favourable than that from which he had been driven. The line, no longer presenting a weak angle, was almost straight, and no part of the front was open to enfilade. Stuart and his artillery, withdrawn to a more favourable position, secured the left. D. H. Hill on the right, though part of his force had given way, still held the Roulette House and the sunken road, and the troops in the West Wood were well protected from the Northern batteries. The one weak point was the gap occupied by Greene's Federals, which lay between Grigsby's regiments in the northern angle of the West Wood and Hood's division at the Dunkard Church. The enemy, however, showed no signs of making good his opportunity; Early's brigade was close at hand, and Lee had promised further reinforcements.

A glance southward showed that there was no reason for despair. Over all the field lay the heavy smoke of a great artillery battle. From near the Dunkard Church to the bluff overhanging the Antietam, a distance of two miles, battery on battery was in line. Here were Longstreet's artillery under Stephen Lee, together with the six-and-twenty guns of Cutts' reserve battalion, forty-eight guns in all; the divisional batteries of D. H. Hill, and the Washington artillery of New Orleans,[1] and in addition to these eighty guns others were in action above the Burnside Bridge. An array even more formidable crowned the opposite

[1] Both D. H. Hill and the Washington artillery had sixteen guns each.

T 2

crest; but although the Confederate batteries, opposed by larger numbers and heavier metal, had suffered terribly, both in men and in *matériel*, yet the infantry, the main strength of the defence, was still intact.[1] The cliffs of the Red Hill, replying to the rolling thunder of near 300 guns, gave back no echo to the sharper crack of musketry. Save a few skirmishers, who had crossed the Sharpsburg Bridge, not one company of McClellan's infantry had been sent into action south of the Dunkard Church. Beyond the Antietam, covering the whole space between the river and the hills, the blue masses were plainly to be seen through the drifting smoke; some so far in the distance that only the flash of steel in the bright sunshine distinguished them from the surrounding woods; others moving in dense columns towards the battle:

> Standards on standards, men on men;
> In slow succession still.

But neither by the Sharpsburg nor yet by the Burnside Bridge had a single Federal regiment crossed the stream; Lee's centre and right were not even threatened, and it was evident his reserves might be concentrated without risk at whatever point he pleased.

Walker's division was therefore withdrawn from the right, and McLaws, who had reached Sharpsburg shortly after sunrise, was ordered to the front. G. T. Anderson's brigade was detached from D. H. Hill; and the whole force was placed at Jackson's disposal. These fresh troops, together with Early's regiments, not yet engaged, gave 10,000 muskets for the counterstroke, and had Hooker and Mansfield been alone upon the field the Federal right wing would have been annihilated. But as the Confederate reserves approached the Dunkard Church, Sumner, whom McClellan

---

[1] 'Our artillery,' says General D. H. Hill, ' could not cope with the superior weight, calibre, range, and number of the Yankee guns; hence it ought only to have been used against masses of infantry. On the contrary, our guns were made to reply to the Yankee guns, and were smashed up or withdrawn before they could be effectually turned against massive columns of attack.' After Sharpsburg Lee gave orders that there were to be no more ' artillery duels ' so long as the Confederates fought defensive battles

had ordered to cross Pry's Bridge with the Second Army Corps, threw three divisions against the West Wood and the Roulette House.   In three lines, up the slope from the Antietam. at sixty yards distance and covering a wide front, came Sedgwick on the right, French on the left, and Richardson to the left rear.   So orderly was the advance of those 18,000 Northerners, and so imposing their array, that even the Confederate officers watched their march with admiration, and terrible was the shock with which they renewed the conflict.

Sedgwick, emerging from the East Wood, moved directly over the corn-field, crossed the turnpike, and entering the West Wood to northward of the point still held by Greene, swept through the timber, and with a portion of his advanced brigade reached the further edge.   Greene, at the same moment, moved upon the Dunkard Church, and Early, who with the fragments of Jones' division was alone within the wood, marched rapidly in the same direction. Attacked suddenly in flank from behind a ridge of rock Greene's regiments were driven back; and then Early, observing Sedgwick's third line pushing across the turnpike, reformed his troops for further action.   Greene, for the moment, had been disposed of, but a more formidable attack was threatening.   Sedgwick's 6,000 muskets, confronted only by some 600[1] of the Valley soldiers under Grigsby, were thronging through the wood, and a change of front southward would have sent them sweeping down the Confederate line.   Early could hardly have withstood their onset; Hood was incapable of further effort, and D. H. Hill was heavily pressed by French.   But Jackson's hand still held the reins of battle.   During the fierce struggle of the morning he had remained on the edge of the West Wood, leaving, as was his wont, the conduct of the divisions to his subordinates, but watching his enemy with a glance that saw beyond the numbers arrayed against him.   He had already demanded reinforcements from General Lee; and in anticipation of their speedy arrival

[1] Letter of Jackson's Adjutant-General. *Memoirs of W. N. Pendleton, D.D.*, p. 216.

their orders had been already framed. They had not been called for to sustain his front, or to occupy a new position. Despite the thronging masses of the Federals, despite the fact that his line was already broken, attack, and attack only, was in Jackson's mind, and the reserves and the opportunity arrived together. A staff officer was dispatched to direct Walker, on the left, to sustain the Texans, to clear the West Wood, and to place a detachment in the gap between the Dunkard Church and the batteries of Colonel Lee;[1] while Jackson himself, riding to meet McLaws, ordered him 'to drive the enemy back and turn his right.' Anderson's brigade was sent to support McLaws, and Semmes' brigade of McLaws' division was detached to strengthen Stuart.

Forming into line as they advanced, McLaws and Walker, leaving the Dunkard Church on their right, and moving swiftly through the wood, fell suddenly on Sedgwick's flank. Early joined in the *mêlée*, and 'the result,' says Palfrey, a Northern general who was present on the field, 'was not long doubtful. Sedgwick's fine division was at the mercy of their enemy. Change of front was impossible. In less time than it takes to tell it the ground was strewn with the bodies of the dead and wounded, while the unwounded were moving off rapidly to the north. Nearly 2,000 men were disabled in a moment.'[2] And the impetus of the counterstroke was not yet spent. Gordon's brigade of the Twelfth Corps had been dispatched to Sedgwick's help, but McLaws had reformed his troops, and after a short struggle the Confederates drove all before them.

Confusion reigned supreme in the Federal ranks. In vain their powerful artillery, firing case and canister with desperate energy, strove to arrest the rush of the pursuing infantry. Out from the West Wood and across the cornfield the grey lines of battle, preceded by clouds of skirmishers, pressed forward without a check, and the light batteries, plying whip and spur, galloped to the front in

---

[1] Sharpsburg. By Major-General J. G. Walker, C.S.A. *Battles and Leaders*, vol. ii., pp. 677, 678.

[2] *Memoirs*, p. 572. *The Antietam and Fredericksburg*, p. 87.

close support. Hope rose high. The Southern yell, peal-
ing from ten thousand throats, rang with a wild note of
anticipated triumph, and Jackson, riding with McLaws,
followed with kindling gaze the progress of his counterstroke
attack. 'God,' he said to his companion, as the shells fell
round them and the masses of the enemy melted away like
the morning mist, 'has been very kind to us this day.'

But the end was not yet. Sedgwick's brigades, flying to the north-east, rallied under the fire of their
batteries, and as the Confederates advanced upon the East
Wood, they found it already occupied by a fresh brigade.
Smith's division of the Sixth Corps had been sent forward
by McClellan to sustain the battle, and its arrival saved
his army from defeat. Once more the corn-field became
the scene of a furious struggle, the Southerners fighting
for decisive victory, the Federals for existence. So impetuous was McLaws' attack that the regiments on his left,
although checked by the fences, drove in a battery and dashed
back the enemy's first line; but the weight of the artillery
in front of the North Wood, supported by a portion of
Smith's division, prevented further advance, and a Federal
brigade, handled with rare judgment, rushed forward to
meet the assailants in the open. Sharp was the conflict,
for McLaws, a fine soldier, as daring as he was skilful,
strove fiercely to complete the victory; but the fight
within the woods and the swift pursuit had broken the
order of his division. Brigade had mingled with brigade,
regiment with regiment. There were no supports; and
the broken ranks, scourged by the terrible cross-fire of
many batteries, were unable to withstand the solid impact
of the Federal reserve. Slowly and sullenly the troops
fell back from the deadly strife. The enemy, no less
exhausted, halted and lay down beyond the turnpike;
and while the musketry once more died away to northward
of the Dunkard Church, Jackson, rallying his brigades,
re-established his line along the edge of the West Wood.

Near the church was a portion of Walker's division.
Further north were two of McLaws' brigades; then Armistead, who had been sent forward from Sharpsburg, and

then Early. A brigade of McLaws' division formed the
second line, and Anderson was sent back to D. H. Hill.
Hood also was withdrawn, and the survivors of Jones'
division, many of whom had shared in the counter-
attack, were permitted to leave the front. Their rifles
were no longer needed, for from half-past ten
10.30 A.M. onwards, so far as the defence of the Confederate left was concerned, the work was done. For many
hours the West Wood was exposed to the concentrated fire
of the Federal artillery; but this fire, although the range
was close, varying from six to fifteen hundred yards, had
little effect. The shattered branches fell incessantly among
the recumbent ranks, and the shells, exploding in the foliage,
sent their hissing fragments far and wide; yet the losses,
so more than one general reported, were surprisingly small.

But although the enemy's infantry had been repulsed,
no immediate endeavour was made by the Confederates to
initiate a fresh counterstroke. When Lee sent McLaws
and Walker to Jackson's aid, he sent in his last reserve, for
A. P. Hill had not yet reached the field, and R. H. Anderson's
division had already been taken to support the centre.
Thus no fresh troops were available, and the Federal right
was strong. At least fifteen batteries of artillery were in
position along the edge of the North Wood, and they were
powerfully supported by the heavy guns beyond the stream.

Yet the infantry so effectively protected was only
formidable by reason of its numbers. The First Corps and
the Twelfth no longer existed as organised bodies.[1] Sedgwick's division of the Second Corps was still more shattered.
Only Smith's division was effective, and General McClellan,
acting on the advice of Sumner, forbade all further
attack. Slocum's division of the Sixth Corps, which
reached the East Wood at twelve o'clock, was ordered
to remain in rear as support to Smith. The Confederate
left wing, then, had offered such strenuous resistance that
eight divisions of infantry, more than half of McClellan's
army, lay paralysed before them for the remainder of

---

[1] It was not until two o'clock that even Meade's Pennsylvanians were
reformed.

the day. 30,500 infantry, at the lowest calculation,[1] and probably 100 guns, besides those across the Antietam, had been massed by the Federals in this quarter of the field. Jackson's numbers, even after he had been reinforced by McLaws and Walker, at no time approached those arrayed against him, and 19,400 men, including Stuart and three brigades of Hill, and 40 guns, is a liberal estimate of his strength.[2] The losses on both sides had been exceedingly heavy. Nearly 13,000 men,[3] including no less than fifteen generals and brigadiers, had fallen within six hours. But although the Confederate casualties were not greatly exceeded by those of the enemy, and were much larger in proportion to their strength, the Federals had lost more than mere numbers. The *moral* of the troops had suffered, and still more the *moral* of the leaders. Even

[1] Hooker	. . . . . .	11,000
Mansfield	. . . . .	8,500
Sedgwick	. . . . .	6,000
Smith .	. . . . .	5,000
		30,500

[2] Lawton	. . . . .	3,600
Jones .	. . . . .	1,800
Hood .	. . . . .	2,000
Stuart .	. . . . .	1,500
G. T. Anderson	. . . .	1,000
Walker .	. . . . .	3,500
McLaws	. . . . .	4,500
D. H. Hill (3 brigades) .	. . .	1,500
		19,400

[3] The Federals engaged against Jackson lost in five and a half hours 7,000 officers and men. During the seven hours they were engaged at Gravelotte the Prussian Guard and the Saxon Army Corps lost 10,349; but 50,000 infantry were in action. The percentage of loss (20) was about the same in both cases. The Confederate losses up to 10.30 A.M. were as follows:

Jones	. . . . .	700
Lawton .	. . . .	1,334
Hood .	. . . .	1,002
McLaws .	. . . .	1,119
Walker .	. . . .	1,012
Anderson	. . . .	87
D. H. Hill (estimate)	. . . .	500
		5,754 (29 p.c.)

Sumner, bravest of men, had been staggered by the fierce assault which had driven Sedgwick's troops like sheep across the corn-field, nor was McClellan disposed to push matters to extremity.

Over in the West Wood, on the other hand, discouragement had no place. Jackson had not yet abandoned hope of sweeping the enemy from the field. He was disappointed with the partial success of McLaws' counterstroke. It had come too late. The fortuitous advance of Smith's division, at the very crisis of the struggle, had, in all human probability, rescued the Federal right from a terrible defeat. Had McLaws been able to reach the East Wood he would have compelled the hostile batteries to retreat; the Federal infantry, already shattered and disorganised, could hardly have held on, and the line would have been broken through. But although one opportunity had been lost, and he was once more thrown on the defensive, Jackson's determination to make the battle decisive of the war was still unshaken. His judgment was never clearer. Shortly before eleven o'clock his medical director, appalled by the number of wounded men sent back from the front, and assured that the day was going badly, rode to the West Wood in order to discuss the advisability of transferring the field hospitals across the Potomac. Dr. McGuire found Jackson sitting quietly on 'Little Sorrel' behind the line of battle, and some peaches he had brought with him were gratefully accepted. He then made his report, and his apprehensions were not made less by the weakness of the line which held the wood. The men, in many places, were lying at intervals of several yards; for support there was but one small brigade, and over in the corn-fields the overwhelming strength of the Federal masses was terribly apparent. Yet his imperturbable commander, apparently paying more attention to the peaches than to his subordinate's suggestions, replied by pointing to the enemy and saying quietly, 'Dr. McGuire, they have done their worst.'

Meanwhile, the tide of battle, leaving Jackson's front and setting strongly southwards, threatened to submerge the Confederate centre. French's division of Sumner's corps, two brigades of Franklin's, and afterwards Richardson's division, made repeated efforts to seize the Dunkard Church, the Roulette Farm, and the Piper House. From before ten until one o'clock the battle raged fiercely about

1 P.M. the sunken road which was held by D. H. Hill, and which witnessed on this day such pre-eminence of slaughter that it has since been known by the name of the 'Bloody Lane.' Here, inspired by the unyielding courage of their leaders, fought the five brigades of D. H. Hill, with R. H. Anderson's division and two of Walker's regiments; and here Longstreet, confident as always, controlled the battle with his accustomed skill. The Confederate artillery was by this time overpowered, for on each battery in turn the enemy's heavy ordnance had concentrated an overwhelming fire, and the infantry were supported by no more than a dozen guns. The attack was strong, but the sunken road, fortified by piles of fence-rails, remained inviolable. Still the Confederate losses were enormous, and defeat appeared a mere question of time; at one moment, the enemy under French had actually seized the wood near the Dunkard Church, and was only dispossessed by a desperate counterstroke. Richardson, who advanced on French's right, and at an appreciable interval of time, was even more successful than his colleague. The 'Bloody Lane,' already piled with dead, and enfiladed from a height to the north-west, was carried by a brilliant charge; and when the Roulette Farm, a strong defensive post, was stormed, Longstreet fell back to the turnpike through the wreck of the artillery. But at this critical juncture the Federals halted. They had not been supported by their batteries. Richardson had received a mortal wound, and a succession of rough counterstrokes had thinned their ranks. Here, too, the musketry dwindled to a spattering fire, and the opposing forces, both reduced to the defensive, lay watching each other through the long hours of the afternoon. A threat of a Federal advance from the Sharpsburg Bridge came to nothing. Four batteries of regulars, preceded by a force of infantry, pushed across the stream and came into action on either side of

the Boonsboro' road ; but on the slopes above, strongly
protected by the walls, Evans' brigade stood fast ; Lee sent
up a small support, and the enemy confined his movements
to a demonstration.

Still further to the south, however, the battle blazed out
at one o'clock with unexpected fury. The Federal attack,
recoiling first from Jackson and then from Longstreet,
swung round to the Confederate right ; and it seemed
as if McClellan's plan was to attempt each section of
Lee's line in succession. Burnside had been ordered
to force the passage of the bridge at nine o'clock, but
either the difficulty of the task, or his inexperience in
handling troops on the offensive, delayed his movements ;
and when the attack was made, it was fiercely met by four
Confederate brigades. At length, well on in the afternoon,
three Federal divisions crowned the spur, and, driving
Longstreet's right before them, made good their footing on the ridge. Sharpsburg was below them ; the Southern
infantry, outflanked and roughly handled, was falling back
in confusion upon the town ; and although Lee had assembled
a group of batteries in the centre, and regiments were
hurrying from the left, disaster seemed imminent. But
strong assistance was at hand. A. P. Hill, who had forded
the Potomac and crossed the Antietam by the lower bridge,
after a forced march of seventeen miles in eight hours from
Harper's Ferry,[1] attacked without waiting for orders, and
struck the Federals in flank with 3,000 bayonets. By this
brilliant counterstroke Burnside was repulsed and the
position saved.

Northern writers have laid much stress on this attack.
Had Burnside displayed more, or A. P. Hill less, energy,
the Confederates, they assert, could hardly have escaped
defeat. It is certainly true that Longstreet's four
brigades had been left to bear the brunt of Burnside's
assault without further support than could be rendered by
the artillery. They were not so left, however, because it
was impossible to aid them. Jackson's and Longstreet's

---

[1] Hill received his orders at 6.30 A.M. and marched an hour later,
reaching the battle-field about 3.30 P.M.

troops, despite the fiery ordeal through which they had
passed, were not yet powerless, and the Confederate leaders
were prepared for offensive tactics. A sufficient force to
sustain the right might have been withdrawn from the left
and centre ; but Hill's approach was known, and it was considered inadvisable to abandon all hold of the means for
a decisive counterstroke on the opposite flank. Early in
the afternoon Longstreet had given orders for an advance.
Hood's division, with full cartridge-boxes, had reappeared
upon the field. Jones' and Lawton's divisions were close
behind; the batteries had replenished their ammunition, and
if Longstreet was hardly warranted in arranging a general
counter-attack on his own responsibility, he had at least full
confidence in the ability of the troops to execute it. ' It
seemed probable,' he says, ' that by concealing our movements under cover of the (West) wood, we could draw our
columns so near to the enemy to the front that we would have
but a few rods to march to mingle our ranks with his ; that
our columns, massed in goodly numbers, and pressing
heavily upon a single point, would give the enemy much
trouble and might cut him in two, breaking up his battle
arrangements at Burnside Bridge.' [1]

The stroke against the centre was not, however, to
be tried. Lee had other views, and Jackson had been
already ordered to turn the Federal right. Stuart, reinforced by a regiment of infantry and several light batteries,
was instructed to reconnoitre the enemy's position, and
if favourable ground were found, he was to be supported
by all the infantry available. ' About half-past twelve,'
says General Walker, ' I sought Jackson to report that
from the front of my position in the wood I thought I had
observed a movement of the enemy, as if to pass through
the gap where I had posted Colonel Cooke's two regiments.
I found Jackson in rear of Barksdale's brigade, under an
apple tree, sitting on his horse, with one leg thrown
carelessly over the pommel of his saddle, plucking and
eating the fruit. Without making any reply to my
report, he asked me abruptly : " Can you spare me a

[1] *From Manassas to Appomattox*, pp. 256, 257.

regiment and a battery?" . . . adding that he wished to make up, from the different commands on our left, a force of four or five thousand men, and give them to Stuart, with orders to turn the enemy's right and attack him in the rear; that I must give orders to my division to advance to the front, and attack the enemy as soon as I should hear Stuart's guns, and that our whole left wing would move to the attack at the same time. Then, replacing his foot in the stirrup, he said with great emphasis, "We'll drive McClellan into the Potomac."

'Returning to my command, I repeated General Jackson's order to my brigade commanders and directed them to listen to the sound of Stuart's guns. We all confidently expected to hear the welcome sound by two o'clock at least, and as that hour approached every ear was on the alert. Napoleon at Waterloo did not listen more intently for the sound of Grouchy's fire than did we for Stuart's. Two o'clock came, but nothing was heard of Stuart. Half-past two, and then three, and still Stuart made no sign.

'About half-past three a staff officer of General Longstreet's brought me an order to advance and attack the enemy in my front. As the execution of this order would have materially interfered with Jackson's plans, I thought it my duty before beginning the movement to communicate with General Longstreet personally. I found him in rear of the position in which I had posted Cooke in the morning, and upon informing him of Jackson's intentions, he withdrew his order.

'While we were discussing this subject, Jackson himself joined us with the information of Stuart's failure to turn the Federal right, for the reason that he found it securely posted on the Potomac. Upon my expressing surprise at this statement, Jackson replied that he also had been surprised, as he had supposed the Potomac much further away; but he remarked that Stuart had an excellent eye for topography, and it must be as he represented. "It is a great pity," he added; "we should have driven McClellan into the Potomac." '[1]

[1] *Battles and Leaders*, vol. ii., pp. 679, 680.

That a counterstroke which would have combined a
frontal and flank attack would have been the best chance
of destroying the Federal army can hardly be questioned.
The front so bristled with field artillery, and the ridge
beyond the Antietam was so strong in heavier ordnance,
that a purely frontal attack, such as Longstreet suggested,
was hardly promising; but the dispositions which baffled
Stuart were the work of a sound tactician. Thirty rifled
guns had been assembled in a single battery a mile north
of the West Wood, where the Hagerstown turnpike ascends
a commanding ridge, and the broad channel of the Potomac
is within nine hundred yards. Here had rallied such
portions of Hooker's army corps as had not dispersed, and
here Mansfield's two divisions had reformed; and although
the infantry could hardly have opposed a resolute resistance
the guns were ready to repeat the lesson of Malvern Hill.
Against the rifled pieces the light Confederate smooth-
bores were practically useless. Stuart's caution was fully
justified, and the sun sank on an indecisive battle.

' The blessed night came, and brought with it sleep and
forgetfulness and refreshment to many; but the murmur
of the night wind, breathing over fields of wheat and
clover, was mingled with the groans of the countless
sufferers of both armies. Who can tell, who can even
imagine, the horrors of such a night, while the unconscious
stars shone above, and the unconscious river went rippling
by?'[1] Out of 130,000 men upon the ground, 21,000
had been killed or wounded, more than sixteen per cent.;
and 25,000 of the Federals can hardly be said to have
been engaged.

The losses of the Confederate left have already been
enumerated. Those of the centre and the right, although
A. P. Hill reported only 350 casualties, had hardly been
less severe. In all 9,500 officers and men, one-fourth of
the total strength, had fallen, and many of the regiments
had almost disappeared.[2] The 17th Virginia, for in-

[1] General Palfrey. *The Antietam and Fredericksburg.*
[2] 'One does not look for humour in a stern story like this, but the
Charleston Courier account of the battle contains the following statement:

stance, of Longstreet's command, took into battle 9
officers and 46 men; of these 7 officers and 24 men were
killed or wounded, and 10 taken prisoners, leaving 2
officers and 12 men to represent a regiment which was
over 1,000 strong at Bull Run.   Yet as the men sank down
to rest on the line of battle, so exhausted that they could
not be awakened to eat their rations; as the blood cooled
and the tension on the nerves relaxed, and even the officers,
faint with hunger and sickened with the awful slaughter,
looked forward with apprehension to the morrow, from one
indomitable heart the hope of victory had not yet vanished.
In the deep silence of the night, more oppressive than the
stunning roar of battle, Lee, still mounted, stood on the
highroad to the Potomac, and as general after general
rode in wearily from the front, he asked quietly of each,
'How is it on your part of the line?' Each told the
same tale: their men were worn out; the enemy's numbers
were overwhelming; there was nothing left but to retreat
across the Potomac before daylight.   Even Jackson had
no other counsel to offer.   His report was not the less impressive for his quiet and respectful tone.   He had had to
contend, he said, against the heaviest odds he had ever met.
Many of his divisional and brigade commanders were dead
or wounded, and his loss had been severe.   Hood, who
came next, was quite unmanned.   He exclaimed that he
had no men left. 'Great God!' cried Lee, with an excitement he had not yet displayed, 'where is the splendid
division you had this morning?' 'They are lying on
the field, where you sent them,' was the reply, 'for
few have straggled. My division has been almost wiped
out.'

After all had given their opinion, there was an appalling
silence, which seemed to last for several minutes, and then
General Lee, rising erect in his stirrups, said, 'Gentlemen,
we will not cross the Potomac to-night.   You will go to
your respective commands, strengthen your lines; send

"They [the Confederates] fought until they were cut to pieces, and then retreated only because they had fired their last round!"' General Palfrey,
The Antietam and Fredericksburg.

two officers from each brigade towards the ford to collect
your stragglers and get them up. Many have come in. I
have had the proper steps taken to collect all the men who
are in the rear. If McClellan wants to fight in the morning, I will give him battle again. Go!' Without a word
of remonstrance the group broke up, leaving their great
commander alone with his responsibility, and, says an eye-
witness, 'if I read their faces aright, there was not one but
considered that General Lee was taking a fearful risk.'[1]
So the soldiers' sleep was undisturbed. Through the
September night they lay beside their arms, and from the
dark spaces beyond came the groans of the wounded and
the nameless odours of the battle-field. Not often has the
night looked down upon a scene more terrible. The moon,
rising above the mountains, revealed the long lines of men
and guns, stretching far across hill and valley, waiting for
the dawn to shoot each other down, and between the armies
their dead lay in such numbers as civilised war has seldom
seen. So fearful had been the carnage, and comprised
within such narrow limits, that a Federal patrol, it is
related, passing into the corn-field, where the fighting had
been fiercest, believed that they had surprised a whole
Confederate brigade. There, in the shadow of the woods,
lay the skirmishers, their muskets beside them, and there, in
regular ranks, lay the line of battle, sleeping, as it seemed,
the profound sleep of utter exhaustion. But the first man
that was touched was cold and lifeless, and the next, and
the next; it was the bivouac of the dead.

When the day dawned the Confederate divisions, reinforced by some 5,000 or 6,000 stragglers, held the same
position as the previous evening, and over
Sept. 18. against them, seen dimly through the mist, lay
the Federal lines. The skirmishers, crouching behind the
shattered fences, confronted each other at short range; the
guns of both armies were unlimbered, and the masses of
infantry, further to the rear, lay ready for instant conflict.
But not a shot was fired. The sun rose higher in the

[1] Communicated by General Stephen D. Lee, who was present at the
conference.

heavens; the warm breath of the autumn morning rustled in the woods, but still the same strange silence prevailed. The men spoke in undertones, watching intently the movements of staff officers and orderlies; but the ranks lay as still as the inanimate forms, half hidden by the trodden corn, which lay so thickly between the lines; and as the hours passed on without stir or shot, the Southern generals acknowledged that Lee's daring in offering battle was fully justified. The enemy's aggressive strength was evidently exhausted; and then arose the question, Could the Confederates attack? It would seem that the possibility of a great counterstroke had already been the subject of debate, and that Lee, despite the failure of the previous evening, and Jackson's adverse report, believed that the Federal right might be outflanked and overwhelmed. 'During the morning,' writes General Stephen D. Lee, 'a courier from headquarters came to my battalion of artillery with a message that the Commander-in-Chief wished to see me. I followed the courier, and on meeting General Lee, he said, " Colonel Lee, I wish you to go with this courier to General Jackson, and say that I sent you to report to him." I replied, " General, shall I take my batteries with me ? " He said, " No, just say that I told you to report to him, and he will tell you what he wants." I soon reached General Jackson. He was dismounted, with but few persons round him. He said to me, " Colonel Lee, I wish you to take a ride with me," and we rode to the left of our lines with but one courier, I think. We soon reached a considerable hill and dismounted. General Jackson then said, " Let us go up this hill, and be careful not to expose yourself, for the Federal sharpshooters are not far off." The hill bore evidence of fierce fight the day before.[1] A battery of artillery had been on it, and there were wrecked caissons, broken wheels, dead bodies, and dead horses around. General Jackson said : " Colonel, I wish you to take your glasses and carefully examine the Federal line of battle." I did so, and saw a remarkably strong line of battle, with more troops than I knew General Lee had. After locating the

---

[1] Evidently the ridge which had been held by Stuart on the 17th.

different batteries, unlimbered and ready for action, and noting the strong skirmish line, in front of the dense masses of infantry, I said to him, "General, that is a very strong position, and there is a large force there.' He said, "Yes. I wish you to take fifty pieces of artillery and crush that force, which is the Federal right. Can you do it?" I can scarcely describe my feelings as I again took my glasses, and made an even more careful examination. I at once saw such an attempt must fail. More than fifty guns were unlimbered and ready for action, strongly supported by dense lines of infantry and strong skirmish lines, advantageously posted. The ground was unfavourable for the location of artillery on the Confederate side, for, to be effective, the guns would have to move up close to the Federal lines, and that, too, under fire of both infantry and artillery. I could not bring myself to say all that I felt and knew. I said, "Yes, General; where will I get the fifty guns?" He said, "How many have you?" I replied, "About twelve out of the thirty I carried into the action the day before." (My losses had been very great in men, horses, and carriages.) He said, "I can furnish you some, and General Lee says he can furnish some." I replied, "Shall I go for the guns?" "No, not yet," he replied. "Colonel Lee, can you crush the Federal right with fifty guns?" I said, "General, I can try. I can do it if anyone can." He replied, "That is not what I asked you, sir. If I give you fifty guns, can you crush the Federal right?" I evaded the question again and again, but he pressed it home. Finally I said, "General, you seem to be more intent upon my giving you my technical opinion as an artillery officer, than upon my going after the guns and making the attempt." "Yes, sir," he replied, "and I want your positive opinion, yes or no." I felt that a great crisis was upon me, and I could not evade it. I again took my glasses and made another examination. I waited a good while, with Jackson watching me intently.

'I said, "General, it cannot be done with fifty guns and the troops you have near here." In an instant he said, "Let us ride back, Colonel." I felt that I had

positively shown a lack of nerve, and with considerable
emotion begged that I might be allowed to make the
attempt, saying, " General, you forced me to say what I
did unwillingly. If you give the fifty guns to any other
artillery officer, I am ruined for life. I promise you I will
fight the guns to the last extremity, if you will only let me
command them." Jackson was quiet, seemed sorry for
me, and said, " It is all right, Colonel. Everybody knows
you are a brave officer and would fight the guns well," or
words to that effect. We soon reached the spot from which
we started. He said, " Colonel, go to General Lee, and
tell him what has occurred since you reported to me.
Describe our ride to the hill, your examination of the
Federal position, and my conversation about your crushing
the Federal right with fifty guns, and my forcing you to
give your opinion."

'With feelings such as I never had before, nor ever
expect to have again, I returned to General Lee, and gave
a detailed account of my visit to General Jackson, closing
with the account of my being forced to give my opinion as
to the possibility of success. I saw a shade come over
General Lee's face, and he said, " Colonel, go and join
your command."

'For many years I never fully understood my mission
that day, or why I was sent to General Jackson. When
Jackson's report was published of the battle, I saw that
he stated, that on the afternoon of September 17, General
Lee had ordered him to move to the left with a view
of turning the Federal right, but that he found the enemy's
numerous artillery so judiciously posted in their front, and
so near the river, as to render such an attempt too hazardous to undertake. I afterwards saw General J. E. B.
Stuart's report, in which he says that it was determined,
the enemy not attacking, to turn the enemy's right on
the 18th. It appears General Lee ordered General
Jackson, on the evening of the 17th, to turn the enemy's
right, and Jackson said that it could not be done. It
also appears from Stuart's report, and from the incident I
relate, that General Lee reiterated the order on the 18th,

and told Jackson to take fifty guns, and crush the Federal right. Jackson having reported against such attempt on the 17th, no doubt said that if an artillerist, in whom General Lee had confidence, would say the Federal right could be crushed with fifty guns, he would make the attempt.

'I now have the satisfaction of knowing that the opinion which I was forced to give on September 18 had already been given by Jackson on the evening of September 17, and that the same opinion was reiterated by him on September 18, and confirmed by General J. E. B. Stuart on the same day. I still believe that Jackson, Stuart, and myself were right, and that the attempt to turn the Federal right either on the 17th or on the 18th would have been unwise.

'The incident shows General Lee's decision and boldness in battle, and General Jackson's delicate loyalty to his commanding general, in convincing him of the inadvisability of a proposed movement, which he felt it would be hazardous to undertake.' [1]

The Federal left, protected by the Antietam, was practically inaccessible; and on receiving from the artillery officers' lips the confirmation of Jackson's report, Lee was fain to relinquish all hope of breaking McClellan's line. The troops, however, remained in line of battle; but during the day information came in which made retreat imperative. The Federals were being reinforced. Humphreys' division, hitherto held back at Frederick by orders from Washington, had marched over South Mountain; Couch's division, which McClellan had left to observe Harper's Ferry, had been called in; and a large force of militia was assembling on the Pennsylvania border. Before evening, therefore, Lee determined to evacuate his position, and during the night the Army of Northern Virginia, with all its trains and artillery, recrossed the Potomac at Boteler's Ford.

---

[1] Communicated to the author. The difficulties in the way of the attack, of which Jackson was aware on the night of the 17th, probably led to his advising retreat when Lee asked his opinion at the conference (*ante*, pp. 259, 260).

Such was the respect which the hard fighting of the Confederates had imposed upon the enemy, that although the rumbling of heavy vehicles, and the tramp of the long columns, were so distinctly audible in the Federal lines that they seemed to wakeful ears like the steady flow of a river, not the slightest attempt was made to interfere. It was not till the morning of the 19th that a Federal battalion, reconnoitring towards Sharpsburg, found the ridge and the town deserted; and although Jackson, who was one of the last, except the cavalry scouts, to cross the river, did not reach the Virginia shore till eight o'clock, not a shot was fired at him.

Nor were the trophies gathered by the Federals considerable. Several hundred badly wounded men were found in Sharpsburg, and a number of stragglers were picked up, but neither gun nor waggon had been left upon the field. The retreat, despite many obstacles, was as successfully as skilfully executed. The night was very dark, and a fine rain, which had set in towards evening, soon turned the heavy soil into tenacious mud; the ford was wide and beset with boulders, and the only approach was a narrow lane. But the energetic quartermaster of the Valley army, Major Harman, made light of all difficulties, and under the immediate supervision of Lee and Jackson, the crossing was effected without loss or misadventure. Just before nightfall, however, under Sept. 19. cover of a heavy artillery fire, the Federals pushed a force of infantry across the ford, drove back the two brigades, which, with thirty pieces of artillery, formed the Confederate rear-guard, and captured four guns. Emboldened by this partial success, McClellan ordered Porter to put three brigades of the Fifth Army Corps across the river the next morning, and reconnoitre towards Winchester.

The news of the disaster to his rear-guard was long in reaching Lee's headquarters. His army had not yet recovered from the confusion and fatigue of the retreat. The bivouacs of the divisions were several miles from the river, and were widely scattered. The generals were ignorant of each other's dispositions. No arrangements had been made to support the rear-guard in case of emergency. The greater part of the cavalry had been sent off to Williamsport, fifteen miles up stream, with instructions to cross the Potomac and delay the enemy's advance by demonstration. The brigadiers had no orders; many of the superior generals had not told their subordinates where they would be found; and the commander of the rear-guard, General Pendleton, had not been informed of the strength of the infantry placed at his disposal. On the part of the staff, worn out by the toils and anxieties of the past few days, there appears to have been a general failure; and had McClellan, calculating on the chances invariably offered by an enforced retreat, pushed resolutely forward in strong force, success might possibly have followed.

Lee, on receiving Pendleton's report, long after midnight, sent off orders for Jackson to drive the enemy back. Sept. 20. When the messenger arrived, Jackson had already ridden to the front. He, too, had received news of the capture of the guns; and ordering A. P. Hill and Early,[1] who were in camp near Martinsburg, to march at once to Shepherdstown, he had gone forward to reconnoitre the enemy's movements. When Lee's courier found him he was on the Shepherdstown road, awaiting the arrival of his divisions, and watching, unattended by a single aide-de-camp, the advance of Porter's infantry. He had at once grasped the situation. The Confederates were in no condition to resist an attack in force. The army was not concentrated. The cavalry was absent. No reconnaissance had been made either of lines of march or of positions. The roads were still blocked by the trains. The men were exhausted by their late exertions, and depressed by their retreat, and the straggling was terrible. The only chance of safety lay in driving back the enemy's advanced-guard across the river before it could be reinforced; and the chance was seized without an instant's hesitation.

The Federals advanced leisurely, for the cavalry which

[1] Commanding Ewell's division, *vice* Lawton, wounded at Sharpsburg.

should have led the way had received its orders too late to reach the rendezvous at the appointed hour, and the infantry, compelled to reconnoitre for itself, made slow progress. Porter's leading brigade was consequently not more than a mile and a half from the river when the Light Division reported to Jackson. Hill was ordered to form his troops in two lines, and with Early in close support to move at once to the attack. The Federals, confronted by a large force, and with no further object than to ascertain the whereabouts of the Confederate army, made no attempt to hold their ground. Their left and centre, composed mainly of regulars, withdrew in good order. The right, hampered by broken country, was slow to move; and Hill's soldiers, who had done much at Sharpsburg with but little loss, were confident of victory. The Federal artillery beyond the river included many of their heavy batteries, and when the long lines of the Southerners appeared in the open, they were met by a storm of shells. But without a check, even to close the gaps in the ranks, or to give time to the batteries to reply to the enemy's fire, the Light Division pressed forward to the charge. The conflict was short. The Northern regulars had already passed the ford, and only a brigade of volunteers was left on the southern bank. Bringing up his reserve regiment, the Federal general made a vain effort to prolong his front. Hill answered by calling up a brigade from his second line; and then, outnumbered and outflanked, the enemy was driven down the bluffs and across the river. The losses in this affair were comparatively small. The Federals reported 340 killed and wounded, and of these a raw regiment, armed with condemned Enfield rifles, accounted for no less than 240. Hill's casualties were 271. Yet the engagement was not without importance. Jackson's quick action and resolute advance convinced the enemy that the Confederates were still dangerous; and McClellan, disturbed by Stuart's threat against his rear, abandoned all idea of crossing the Potomac in pursuit of Lee.

The losses at Sharpsburg may be here recorded.

Jones' Division—1,800.

The Stonewall Brigade, 250 strong . . .	88
Taliaferro's Brigade	173
Starke's Brigade	287
Jones' Brigade	152

700 (38 p.c.)

Ewell's (Lawton) Division—3,600.

Lawton's Brigade, 1,150 strong . . .	567
Early's Brigade, 1,200 strong	194
Trimble's Brigade, 700 strong	237
Hays' Brigade, 550 strong	336

1,334 (47 p.c.)

The Light Division—3,000.

Branch's Brigade	104
Gregg's Brigade	165
Archer's Brigade	105
Pender's Brigade	30
Field's Brigade (not engaged)	—
Thomas' Brigade (at Harper's Ferry) . . .	—

404

Artillery (Estimated)	50

Total, 2,488 (209 officers).

D. H. Hill's Division—3,500.

Rodes' Brigade	203
Garland's Brigade (estimated)	300
Anderson's Brigade	302
Ripley's Brigade (estimated)	300
Colquitt's Brigade (estimated)	300

1,405

McLaws' Division—4,500.

Kershaw's Brigade	355
Cobb's Brigade	156
Semmes' Brigade	314 [1]
Barksdale's Brigade	294

1,119

---

[1] Semmes' four regiments, engaged in Jackson's counterstroke, reported the following percentage of loss. 53rd Georgia, 30 p.c.; 32nd Virginia, 45 p.c.; 10th Georgia, 57 p.c; 15th Virginia, 58 p.c.

D. R. JONES' DIVISION—3,500.

Toombs' Brigade (estimated)	125
Drayton's Brigade (estimated)	400
Anderson's Brigade	87
Garnett's Brigade	99
Jenkins' Brigade	210
Kemper's Brigade (estimated) . . .	120
	1,041

WALKER'S DIVISION—3,500.

Walker's Brigade	825
Ransom's Brigade	187
	1,012

HOOD'S DIVISION—2,000.

Laws' Brigade	454
Hood's Brigade	548
	1,002
Evans' Brigade, 250 strong	200

R. H. ANDERSON'S DIVISION—3,500.

Featherston's Brigade	304
Mahone's Brigade	76
Pryor's Brigade	182
Armistead's Brigade	35
Wright's Brigade	203
Wilcox' Brigade	221
	1,021

ARTILLERY.

Colonel S. D. Lee's Battalion	85
Washington Artillery	34
Cavalry, &c. &c. (estimated) . . .	143
	262

Grand total, 9,550.

ARMY OF THE POTOMAC.

First Corps—Hooker	2,590
Second Corps—Sumner	5,138
Fifth Corps—Porter	109
Sixth Corps—Franklin	439
Ninth Corps—Burnside	2,349
Twelfth Corps—Mansfield . . .	1,746
Cavalry Division, &c.	39
(2,108 killed)	12,410 [1]

[1] For the losses in various great battles, see Note at end of volume.

With Porter's repulse the summer campaign of 1862 was closed. Begun on the Chickahominy, within thirty miles of Richmond, it ended on the Potomac, within seventy miles of Washington; and six months of continuous fighting had brought both belligerents to the last stage of exhaustion. Falling apart like two great battleships of the older wars,

> The smoke of battle drifting slow a-lee,

hulls rent by roundshot, and scuppers awash with blood, but with the colours still flying over shattered spars and tangled shrouds, the armies drew off from the tremendous struggle. Neither Confederates nor Federals were capable of further effort. Lee, gathering in his stragglers, left Stuart to cover his front, and fell back towards Winchester. McClellan was content with seizing the Maryland Heights at Harper's Ferry, and except the cavalry patrols, not a single Federal soldier was sent across the river.

Reorganisation was absolutely imperative. The Army of the Potomac was in no condition to undertake the invasion of Virginia. Not only had the losses in battle been very large, but the supply train, hurriedly got together after Pope's defeat, had broken down; in every arm there was great deficiency of horses; the troops, especially those who had been engaged in the Peninsula, were half-clad and badly shod; and, above all, the army was very far from sharing McClellan's conviction that Sharpsburg was a brilliant victory. The men in the ranks were not so easily deceived as their commander. McClellan, relying on a return drawn up by General Banks, now in command at Washington, estimated the Confederate army at 97,000 men, and his official reports made frequent mention of Lee's overwhelming strength.[1]

[1] Mr. Lincoln had long before this recognised the tendency of McClellan and others to exaggerate the enemy's strength. As a deputation from New England was one day leaving the White House, a delegate turned round and said: 'Mr. President, I should much like to know what you reckon to be the number the rebels have in arms against us.' Without a moment's hesitation Mr. Lincoln replied: 'Sir, I have the best possible reason for knowing the number to be one million of men, for whenever one of our generals engages

The soldiers knew better. They had been close enough to
the enemy's lines to learn for themselves how thin was the
force which manned them. They were perfectly well aware
that they had been held in check by inferior numbers, and
that the battle on the Antietam, tactically speaking, was no
more of a victory for the North than Malvern Hill had been
for the South. From dawn to dark on September 18 they
had seen the tattered colours and bright bayonets of the
Confederates still covering the Sharpsburg ridge; they had
seen the grey line, immovable and defiant, in undisputed
possession of the battle-ground, while their own guns were
silent and their own generals reluctant to renew the fight.
Both the Government and the people expected McClellan to
complete his success by attacking Lee in Virginia. The Confederates, it was said—and men based their opinions on
McClellan's reports—had been heavily defeated, not only at
Antietam, but also at South Mountain; and although the
Army of the Potomac might be unfit for protracted operations, the condition of the enemy must necessarily be far
worse.

Such arguments, however, were entirely inapplicable to
the situation. The Confederates had not been defeated at
all, either at South Mountain or Sharpsburg; and although
they had eventually abandoned their positions they had
suffered less than their opponents. The retreat, however,
across the Potomac had undoubtedly shaken their *moral*.
' In a military point of view,' wrote Lee to Davis on September 25, ' the best move, in my opinion, the army could
make would be to advance upon Hagerstown and endeavour
to defeat the enemy at that point. I would not hesitate
to make it even with our diminished numbers did the
army exhibit its former temper and condition, but, as
far as I am able to judge, the hazard would be great and
reverse disastrous.' [1]   But McClellan was not more cheerful. ' The army,' he said on the 27th, ' is not now in a

a rebel army he reports that he has encountered a force twice his strength.
Now I know we have half a million soldiers, so I am bound to believe that
the rebels have twice that number.'

[1] O. R., vol. xix., part ii., p. 627.

condition to undertake another campaign nor to bring on
another battle, unless great advantages are offered by some
mistake of the enemy, or pressing military exigencies render
it necessary.' So far from thinking of pursuit, he thought
only of the defence of the Potomac, apprehending a renewed
attempt to enter Maryland, and by no means over-confident
that the two army corps which he had at last sent to Harper's
Ferry would be able to maintain their position if attacked.[1]
Nor were the soldiers more eager than their commander to
cross swords with their formidable enemy. 'It would be
useless,' says General G. H. Gordon, who now commanded a
Federal division, ' to deny that at this period there was a
despondent feeling in the army,' and the Special Corre-
spondents of the New York newspapers, the 'World' and
'Tribune,' confirm the truth of this statement. But the
clearest evidence as to the condition of the troops is furnished in the numerous reports which deal with straggling.
The vice had reached a pitch which is almost inconceivable. Thousands and tens of thousands, Federals as well
as Confederates, were absent from their commands.

'The States of the North,' wrote McClellan, ' are
flooded with deserters and absentees. One corps of this
army has 13,000 men present and 15,000 absent ; of this
15,000, 8,000 probably are at work at home.' [2] On September 23, General Meade, who had succeeded to the command of Hooker's corps, reported that over 8,000 men,
including 250 officers, had quitted the ranks either before or
during the battle of Antietam ; adding that ' this terrible
and serious evil seems to pervade the whole body.' [3] The
Confederates, although the privations of the troops during
the forced marches, their indifferent equipment, and the
deficiencies of the commissariat were contributory causes,
had almost as much reason to complain. It is said that
in the vicinity of Leesburg alone over 10,000 men were
living on the citizens. Jackson's own division, which took
into action 1,600 effectives on September 17 and lost 700,
had 3,900 present for duty on September 30 ; Lawton's

---

[1] O. R., vol. xix., part i., p. 70.
[2] Ibid., part ii., p. 365.   [3] Ibid., p. 348.

division rose from 2,500 to 4,450 during the same period;
and the returns show that the strength of Longstreet's and
Jackson's corps was only 37,992 on September 22, but 52,019
on October 1.[1] It is thus evident that in eight days the army
was increased by more than 14,000 men, yet only a few conscripts had been enrolled. Lee's official reports and correspondence allude in the strongest terms to the indiscipline
of his army. 'The absent,' he wrote on September 23, 'are
scattered broadcast over the land;' and in the dispatches of
his subordinates are to be found many references to the
vagrant tendencies of their commands.[2] A strong provost
guard was established at Winchester for the purpose of collecting stragglers. Parties of cavalry were sent out to protect
the farms from pillage, and to bring in the marauders as
prisoners. The most stringent regulations were issued as to
the preservation of order on the march, the security of
private property, and the proper performance of their duties
by regimental and commissariat officers. On September 23,
General Jones reported from Winchester that the country
was full of stragglers, that he had already sent back 5,000 or
6,000, and that the numbers of officers amongst them was
astonishing.[3] The most earnest representations were made
to the President, suggesting trial of the offenders by
drumhead court-martial, and ordinary police duties became
the engrossing occupation of every general officer.

It can hardly be said, then, that the Confederates had
drawn much profit from the invasion of Maryland. The
capture of Harper's Ferry made but small amends for

---

[1] O. R., vol. xix., part ii., pp. 621, 639.

[2] General orders, Sept. 4; Lee to Davis, Sept. 7; Lee to Davis, Sept. 13;
special orders, Sept. 21; circular order, Sept. 22; Lee to Davis, Sept. 23;
Lee to Secretary of War, Sept. 23; Lee to Pendleton, Sept. 24; Lee to
Davis, Sept. 24; Lee to Davis, Sept. 28; Lee to Davis, Oct. 2; O. R., vol.
xix., part ii. *See also* Report of D. H. Hill, O. R., vol. xix., part i., p. 1026.
Stuart to Secretary of War, Oct. 13. On Sept. 21, Jackson's adjutant-
general wrote, 'We should have gained a victory and routed them, had it
not been for the straggling. We were twenty-five thousand short by this
cause.' *Memoirs of W. N. Pendleton, D.D.*, p. 217. It is but fair to say that
on September 13 there was a camp of 900 barefooted men at Winchester, and
'a great many more with the army.' Lee to Quarter-Master-General, O. R.,
vol. xix., part ii., p. 614.

[3] O. R., vol. xix., part ii., p. 629.

the retreat into Virginia; and the stubborn endurance of Sharpsburg, however remarkable in the annals of war, had served no useful purpose beyond crippling for the time being the Federal army. The battle must be classed with Aspern and Talavera; Lee's soldiers saved their honour, but no more. The facts were not to be disguised. The Confederates had missed their mark. Only a few hundred recruits had been raised in Maryland, and there had been no popular outbreak against the Union Government. The Union army had escaped defeat; Lincoln had been able to announce to the Northern people that Lee's victorious career had at length been checked; and 12,000 veteran soldiers, the flower of the Southern army, had fallen in battle. Had General Longstreet's advice been taken, and the troops withdrawn across the Potomac after the fall of Harper's Ferry, this enormous loss, which the Confederacy could so ill afford, would certainly have been avoided. Yet Lee was not ill-satisfied with the results of the campaign, nor did Jackson doubt the wisdom of accepting battle on the Antietam.

The hazard was great, but the stake was greater. To achieve decisive success in war some risk must be run. 'It is impossible,' says Moltke, 'to forecast the result of a pitched battle;' but this is no reason that pitched battles, if there is a fair prospect of success, should be shirked. And in the Sharpsburg campaign the Confederates had un-doubtedly fair prospects of success. If the lost order had not fallen into McClellan's hands, Lee in all probability would have had ample time to select his battlefield and concentrate his army; there would have been no need of forced marches, and consequently much less straggling. Both Lee and Jackson counted on the caution of their opponent. Both were surprised by the unwonted vigour he displayed, especially at South Mountain and in the march to Sharpsburg. Such resolution in action, they were aware, was foreign to his nature. 'I cannot understand this move of McClellan's,' was Jackson's remark, when it was reported that the Federal general had boldly advanced against the strong position on South Mountain. But neither Lee nor Jackson was aware that McClellan had exact information of their dispositions, and that the carelessness of a Confederate staff officer had done more for the Union than all the Northern scouts and spies in Maryland. Jackson had been disposed to leave a larger margin for accidents than his commander. He would have left Harper's Ferry alone, and have fought the Federals in the mountains;[1] and he was probably right, for in the Gettysburg campaign of the following year, when Lee again crossed the Potomac, Harper's Ferry was ignored, although occupied by a strong garrison, and neither in advance nor retreat were the Confederate communications troubled. But as to the wisdom of giving battle on the Antietam, after the fall of Harper's Ferry, there was no divergence of opinion between Lee and his lieutenant. They had no reason to respect the Union army as a weapon of offence, and very great reason to believe that McClellan was incapable of wielding it. Their anticipations were well founded. The Federal attack was badly designed and badly executed. If it be compared with the German attack at Wörth, the defects of McClellan, the defects of his subordinates, the want of sound training throughout the whole army, become at once apparent. On August 6, 1870, there was certainly, early in the day, much disjointed fighting, due in great part to the difficulties of the country, the absence of the Crown Prince, and the anxiety of the generals to render each other loyal support. But when once the Commander-in-Chief appeared upon the field, and, assuming direction of the battle, infused harmony into the operations, the strength and unity of the attack could hardly have been surpassed. Almost at the same moment 30,000 men were launched against McMahon's front, 25,000 against his right, and 10,000 against his left. Every battalion within sound of the cannon participated in the forward movement; and numerous batteries, crossing the stream which corresponds with the Antietam, supported the infantry at the closest range. No general hesitated to act on his own responsibility. Everywhere there was

[1] Dabney, vol. ii., p. 302

co-operation, between infantry and artillery, between division and division, between army corps and army corps; and such co-operation, due to a sound system of command, is the characteristic mark of a well-trained army and a wise leader. At Sharpsburg, on the other hand, there was no combination whatever, and even the army corps commanders dared not act without specific orders. There was nothing like the close concert and the aggressive energy which had carried the Southerners to victory at Gaines' Mill and the Second Manassas. The principle of mutual support was utterly ignored. The army corps attacked in succession and not simultaneously, and in succession they were defeated. McClellan fought three separate battles, from dawn to 10 A.M. against Lee's left; from 10 A.M. to 1 P.M. against his centre; from 1 to 4 P.M. against his right. The subordinate generals, although, with a few exceptions, they handled their commands skilfully, showed no initiative, and waited for orders instead of improving the opportunity. Only two-thirds of the army was engaged; 25,000 men hardly fired a shot, and from first to last there was not the slightest attempt at co-operation. McClellan was made aware by his signallers on the Red Hill of every movement that took place in his opponent's lines, and yet he was unable to take advantage of Lee's weakness. He had still to grasp the elementary rule that the combination of superior numbers and of all arms against a single point is necessary to win battles.

The Northern infantry, indeed, had not fought like troops who own their opponents as the better men. Rather had they displayed an elasticity of spirit unsuspected by their enemies; and the Confederate soldiers, who knew with what fierce courage the attack had been sustained, looked on the battle of Sharpsburg as the most splendid of their achievements. No small share of the glory fell to Jackson. Since the victory of Cedar Run, his fame, somewhat obscured by Frayser's Farm and Malvern Hill, had increased by leaps and bounds, and the defence of the West Wood was classed with the march to Manassas Junction, the three days' battle about Groveton, and the swift seizure of Harper's Ferry. On October 2, Lee proposed to the President that the Army of Northern Virginia should be organised in two army corps, for the command of which he recommended Longstreet and Jackson. 'My opinion,' wrote Lee, 'of General Jackson has been greatly enhanced during this expedition. He is true, honest, and brave; has a single eye to the good of the service, and spares no exertion to accomplish his object.'[1] On October 11, Jackson received his promotion as Lieutenant-General, and was appointed to the Second Army Corps, consisting at that date of his own division, the Light Division, Ewell's, and D. H. Hill's, together with Colonel Brown's battalion of artillery; a force of 1,917 officers, 25,000 men, and 126 guns.

Jackson does not appear to have been unduly elated by his promotion, for two days after his appointment he wrote to his wife that there was no position in the world equal to that of a minister of the Gospel, and his letter was principally concerned with the lessons he had learned from the sermon of the previous Sunday.[2] The soldiers of

[1] O. R., vol. xix., part ii., p. 643.

[2] About this time he made a successful appearance in a new *rôle*. In September, General Bradley T. Johnson was told off to accompany Colonel Garnet Wolseley, the Hon. Francis Lawley, Special Correspondent to the *Times*, and Mr. Vizetelly, Special Correspondent of the *Illustrated London News*, round the Confederate camps. 'By order of General Lee,' he says, 'I introduced the party to General Jackson. We were all seated in front of General Jackson's tent, and he took up the conversation. He had been to England, and had been greatly impressed with the architecture of Durham Cathedral and with the history of the bishopric. The Bishops had been Palatines from the date of the Conquest, and exercised semi-royal authority over their bishopric.

'There is a fair history of the Palatinate of Durham in Blackstone and Coke, but I can hardly think that General Jackson derived his information from those two fountains of the law. Anyhow, he cross-examined the Englishmen in detail about the cathedral and the close and the rights of the bishops, &c. &c. He gave them no chance to talk, and kept them busy answering questions, for he knew more about Durham than they did.

'As we rode away, I said: "Gentlemen, you have disclosed Jackson in a new character to me, and I've been carefully observing him for a year and a half. You have made him exhibit *finesse*, for he did all the talking to keep you from asking too curious or embarrassing questions. I never saw anything like it in him before." We all laughed, and agreed that the general had been too much for the interviewers.'—*Memoirs*, pp. 530-1.

the Second Army Corps, however, did not allow him to forget his greatness. In their bivouacs by the clear waters of the Opequon, with abundance of supplies and with ample leisure for recuperation, the troops rapidly regained their strength and spirit. The reaction found vent in the most extravagant gaiety. No circumstance that promised entertainment was permitted to pass without attention, and the jest started at the expense of some unfortunate wight, conspicuous for peculiarity of dress or demeanour, was taken up by a hundred voices. None were spared. A trim staff officer was horrified at the irreverent reception of his nicely twisted moustache, as he heard from behind innumerable trees : 'Take them mice out o' your mouth ! take 'em out—no use to say they ain't there, see their tails hanging out!' Another, sporting immense whiskers, was urged 'to come out o' that bunch of hair! I know you're in there! I see your ears a-working!' So the soldiers chaffed the dandies, and the camp rang with laughter ; fun and frolic were always in the air, and the fierce fighters of Sharpsburg behaved like schoolboys on a holiday. But when the general rode by the men remembered the victories they had won and to whom they owed them, the hardships they had endured, and who had shared them ; and the appearance of 'Little Sorrel' was the sure precursor of a scene of the wildest enthusiasm. The horse soon learned what the cheers implied, and directly they began he would break into a gallop, as if to carry his rider as quickly as possible through the embarrassing ordeal. But the soldiers were not to be deterred by their commander's modesty, and whenever he was compelled to pass through the bivouacs the same tribute was so invariably offered that the sound of a distant cheer, rolling down the lines of the Second Army Corps, always evoked the exclamation : 'Boys, look out ! here comes old Stonewall or an old hare!' 'These being the only individuals,' writes one of Jackson's soldiers, ' who never failed to bring down the whole house.'

Nothing could express more clearly the loyalty of the soldiers to their general than this quaint estimate of his

x 2

popularity. The Anglo-Saxon is averse to the unrestrained
display of personal affection; and when his natural reluctance is overborne by irrepressible emotion, he attempts
to hide it by a jest. So Jackson's veterans laughed
at his peculiarities, at his dingy uniform, his battered cap,
his respect for clergymen, his punctilious courtesy, and his
blushes. They delighted in the phrase, when a distant yell
was heard, 'Here's "Old Jack" or a rabbit!' They delighted more in his confusion when he galloped through the
shouting camp. 'Here he comes,' they said, 'we'll make
him take his hat off.' They invented strange fables of
which he was the hero. 'Stonewall died,' ran one of the
most popular, ' and two angels came down from heaven to
take him back with them. They went to his tent. He
was not there. They went to the hospital. He was not
there. They went to the outposts. He was not there.
They went to the prayer-meeting. He was not there. So
they had to return without him; but when they reported
that he had disappeared, they found that he had made a
flank march and reached heaven before them.' Another
was to the effect that whereas Moses took forty years to
get the children of Israel through the wilderness, ' " Old
Jack" would have double-quicked them through in three
days on half rations!'

But, nevertheless, beneath this affectation of hilarity
lay a deep and passionate devotion; and two incidents
which occurred at this time show the extent of this
feeling, and at least one reason for its existence. 'On
October 8th,' writes Major Heros von Borcke, adjutant-
general of the cavalry division, 'I was honoured with
the pleasing mission of presenting to Stonewall, as a slight
token of Stuart's high regard, a new uniform coat, which
had just arrived from the hands of a Richmond tailor.
Starting at once, I reached the simple tent of our great
general just in time for dinner. I found him in his old
weather-stained coat, from which all the buttons had been
clipped by the fair hands of patriotic ladies, and which,
from exposure to sun, rain, and powder-smoke, and by
reason of many rents and patches, was in a very unseemly

condition. When I had despatched more important matters, I produced General Stuart's present in all its magnificence of gilt buttons and sheeny facings and gold lace, and I was heartily amused at the modest confusion with which the hero of many battles regarded the fine uniform, scarcely daring to touch it, and at the quiet way in which at last he folded it up carefully and deposited it in his portmanteau, saying to me, "Give Stuart my best thanks, Major; the coat is much too handsome for me, but I shall take the best care of it, and shall prize it highly as a souvenir. And now let us have some dinner." But I protested emphatically against the summary disposition of the matter of the coat, deeming my mission indeed but half executed, and remarked that Stuart would certainly ask how the coat fitted, and that I should take it as a personal favour if he would put it on. To this with a smile he readily assented, and having donned the garment, he escorted me outside the tent to the table where dinner had been served in the open air. The whole of the staff were in a perfect ecstasy at their chief's brilliant appearance, and the old negro servant, who was bearing the roast turkey to the board, stopped in mid career with a most bewildered expression, and gazed in such wonderment at his master as if he had been transfigured before him. Meanwhile, the rumour of the change ran like electricity through the neighbouring camps, the soldiers came running by hundreds to the spot, desirous of seeing their beloved Stonewall in his new attire; and the first wearing of a new robe by Louis XIV., at whose morning toilette all the world was accustomed to assemble, never created half the excitement at Versailles that was roused in the woods of Virginia by the investment of Jackson in the new regulation uniform.'[1]

The second incident is less amusing, but was not less appreciated by the rank and file. Riding one morning near Front Royal, accompanied by his staff, Jackson was stopped by a countrywoman, with a chubby child on either side, who inquired anxiously for her son Johnnie, serving, she said, 'in Captain Jackson's company.' The

[1] *Memoirs of the Confederate War*, vol. i.

general, with the deferential courtesy he never laid aside, introduced himself as her son's commanding officer, but begged for further information as to his regiment. The good dame, however, whose interest in the war centred on one individual, appeared astonished that 'Captain Jackson' did not know her particular 'Johnnie,' and repeated her inquiries with such tearful emphasis that the young staff officers began to smile. Unfortunately for themselves, Jackson heard a titter, and turning on them with a scathing rebuke for their want of manners, he sent them off in different directions to discover Johnnie, giving them no rest until mother and son were brought together.

But if the soldiers loved Jackson for his simplicity, and respected him for his honesty, beyond and above was the sense of his strength and power, of his indomitable will, of the inflexibility of his justice, and of the unmeasured resources of his vigorous intellect. It is curious even after the long lapse of years to hear his veterans speak of their commander. Laughter mingles with tears; each has some droll anecdote to relate, each some instance of thoughtful sympathy or kindly deed; but it is still plain to be seen how they feared his displeasure, how hard they found his discipline, how conscious they were of their own mental inferiority. The mighty phantom of their lost leader still dominates their thoughts; just as in the battles of the Confederacy his earthly presentment dominated the will of the Second Army Corps. In the campaign which had driven the invaders from Virginia, and carried the Confederate colours to within sight of Washington, his men had found their master. They had forgotten how to criticise. His generals had learned to trust him. Success and adulation had not indeed made him more expansive. He was as reticent as ever, and his troops—'the foot-cavalry' as they were now called—were still marched to and fro without knowing why or whither. But men and officers, instead of grumbling when they were roused at untimely hours, or when their marches were prolonged, without apparent necessity, obeyed with alacrity, and amused themselves by wondering what new surprise the general was preparing. 'Where are you going?' they were asked as they were turned out for an unexpected march: 'We don't know, but "Old Jack" does,' was the laughing reply. And they had learned something of his methods. They had discovered the value of time, of activity, of mystery, of resolution. They discussed his stratagems, gradually evolving, for they were by no means apparent at the time, the object and aim of his manœuvres; and the stirring verses, sung round every camp-fire, show that the soldiers not only grasped his principles of warfare, but that they knew right well to whom their victories were to be attributed.

STONEWALL JACKSON'S WAY

Come, stack arms, men, pile on the rails;
   Stir up the camp-fires bright;
No matter if the canteen fails,
   We'll make a roaring night.
Here Shenandoah brawls along,
There lofty Blue Ridge echoes strong,
To swell the Brigade's roaring song
   Of Stonewall Jackson's way.

We see him now—the old slouched hat,
   Cocked o'er his eye askew;
The shrewd dry smile—the speech so pat,
   So calm, so blunt, so true.
The 'Blue-Light Elder' knows them well:
Says he, 'That's Banks—he's fond of shell;
Lord save his soul! we'll give him——' well,
   That's Stonewall Jackson's way.

Silence! ground arms! kneel all! caps off!
   Old Blue-Light's going to pray;
Strangle the fool that dares to scoff!
   Attention! it's his way!
Appealing from his native sod,
In formâ pauperis to God,
'Lay bare thine arm—stretch forth thy rod,
   Amen!' That's Stonewall's way.

He's in the saddle now! Fall in!
   Steady, the whole Brigade!
Hill's at the Ford, cut off!—we'll win
   His way out, ball and blade.
What matter if our shoes are worn?
What matter if our feet are torn?
Quick step! we're with him before morn!
   That's Stonewall Jackson's way.

The sun's bright lances rout the mists
   Of morning—and, by George!
There's Longstreet struggling in the lists,
   Hemmed in an ugly gorge.
Pope and his columns whipped before—
'Bayonets and grape!' hear Stonewall roar;
'Charge, Stuart! pay off Ashby's score!'
   That's Stonewall Jackson's way.

Ah! maiden, wait and watch and yearn
   For news of Stonewall's band;
Ah! widow, read with eyes that burn
   The ring upon thy hand.
Ah! wife, sew on, pray on, hope on,
Thy life shall not be all forlorn;
The foe had better ne'er been born
   That gets in Stonewall's way.

NOTE

Jackson's Strength and Losses, August–September 1862.

Strength at Cedar Run, August 9 :

Winder's (Jackson's own) Division (estimate) . . .	3,000
Ewell's Division [1]	5,350
Lawton's Brigade [2]	2,200
A. P. Hill's (the Light) Division [3]	12,000
Robertson's Cavalry Brigade [4] (estimate) . . .	1,200
	23,750

Losses at Cedar Run :

Winder's Division	718	
Ewell's Division	195	
The Light Division	381	1,314
Cavalry, &c.	20	
		22,436

Losses on the Rappahannock, August 20–24 . . .	100	
Losses at Bristoe Station and Manassas Junction, August 26, 27	300	
Losses at Groveton, August 28 :		
Stonewall Division (estimate) . . . 441 }	1,200	4,000
Ewell's Division . . . . . 759 }		
Stragglers and sick (estimate)	1,200	
Cavalry transferred to Stuart	1,200	

Strength at Second Manassas, August 29 and 30 . . .	18,436

Losses :

Taliaferro's Division	416	
Ewell's Division	364	2,387
The Light Division	1,507	
Loss at Chantilly, September 1		500
Should have marched into Maryland . . .		15,549

---

[1] Report of July 31, O. R., vol. xii., part iii., p. 965.

[2] Report of August 20, O. R., vol. xii., part iii., p. 966. (Not engaged at Cedar Run.)

[3] Report of July 20, O. R., vol. xi., part iii., p. 645. ($3\frac{1}{2}$ regiments had been added.)

[4] Four regiments.

Strength at Sharpsburg:

Jones' Division 2,000		
Ewell's Division 4,000	11,800 [1]	
The Light Division 5,000		
(1 Brigade left at Harper's Ferry) 800		

Loss at Harper's Ferry   62

Losses at Sharpsburg:

Jones' Division 700	
Ewell's Division 1,334	2,438
The Light Division 404	

Strength on September 19   9,300

The Report of September 22, O. R., vol. xiv., part ii., p. 621, gives :

Jackson's own Division 2,553	
Ewell's Division 3,290	
The Light Division 4,777	
	10,620 [2]

[1] 3,866 sick and straggling since August 28 = 21 p.c.
[2] Over 1,300 stragglers had rejoined.

CHAPTER XX

FREDERICKSBURG

WHILE the Army of Northern Virginia was resting in the Valley, McClellan was preparing for a winter campaign.

1862. He was unable, however, to keep pace with the im-
October. patience of the Northern people. Not only was he determined to postpone all movement until his army was properly equipped, his ranks recruited, his cavalry remounted, and his administrative services reorganised, but the military authorities at Washington were very slow in meeting his demands. Notwithstanding, then, the orders of the President, the remonstrances of Halleck, and the clamour of the press, for more than five weeks after the battle of Sharpsburg he remained inactive on the Potomac. It may be that in the interests of the army he was perfectly right in resisting the pressure brought to bear upon him. He was certainly the best judge of the temper of his troops, and could estimate more exactly than either Lincoln or Halleck the chances of success if he were to encounter Lee's veterans on their native soil. However this may be, his inaction was not in accordance with the demands of the political situation. The President, immediately the Confederates retired from Maryland, had taken a step which changed the character of the war. Hitherto the Northerners had fought for the restoration of the Union on the basis of the Constitution, as interpreted by themselves. Now, after eighteen months of conflict, the Constitution was deliberately violated. For the clause which forbade all interference with the domestic institutions of the several States, a declaration that slavery should no longer exist within the boundaries

of the Republic was substituted, and the armies of the
Union were called upon to fight for the freedom of the
negro.

In the condition of political parties this measure was
daring. It was not approved by the Democrats, and many
of the soldiers were Democrats ; or by those—and they
were not a few—who believed that compromise was the
surest means of restoring peace ; or by those—and they
were numerous—who thought the dissolution of the Union
a smaller evil than the continuance of the war. The opposition was very strong, and there was but one means of
reconciling it—vigorous action on the part of the army,
the immediate invasion of Virginia, and a decisive victory.
Delay would expose the framers of the measure to the
imputation of having promised more than they could
perform, of wantonly tampering with the Constitution, and
of widening the breach between North and South beyond
all hope of healing.

In consequence, therefore, of McClellan's refusal to move
forward, the friction between the Federal Government and
their general-in-chief, which, so long as Lee remained in
Maryland, had been allayed, once more asserted its baneful
influence ; and the aggressive attitude of the Confederates
did not serve to make matters smoother. Although the
greater part of October was for the Army of Northern
Virginia a period of unusual leisure, the troops were not
altogether idle. As soon as the stragglers had been
brought in, and the ranks of the divisions once more
presented a respectable appearance, various enterprises
were undertaken. The Second Army Corps was entrusted with the destruction of the Baltimore and Ohio
Railway, a duty carried out by Jackson with characteristic thoroughness. The line from Harper's Ferry
to Winchester, as well as that from Manassas Junction to Strasburg, were also torn up ; and the spoils of the
late campaign were sent south to Richmond and Staunton.
These preparations for defensive warfare were not, however,
so immediately embarrassing to the enemy as the action
of the cavalry. Stuart's three brigades, after the affair at

Boteler's Ford, picketed the line of the Potomac from the North Mountain to the Shenandoah, a distance of forty miles : Hampton's brigade at Hedgesville, Fitzhugh Lee's at Shepherdstown, Munford's at Charlestown, and head-quarters near Leetown.

On October 8 General Lee, suspecting that McClellan was meditating some movement, ordered the cavalry to cross the Potomac and reconnoitre. Selecting 600 men from each of his brigades, with General Hampton, Colonels W. H. F. Lee and W. E. Jones in command, and accompanied by four horse-artillery guns, Stuart ren-

Oct. 9. dezvoused on the night of the 9th at Darkes-ville. As the day dawned he crossed the Potomac at McCoy's Ford, drove in the Federal pickets, and broke up a signal station near Fairview. Marching due north, he reached Mercersburg at noon, and Chambersburg, forty-six miles from Darkesville, at 7 P.M. on October 10. Chambersburg, although a Federal supply depôt of some importance, was without a garrison, and here 275 sick and

Oct. 10. wounded were paroled, 500 horses requisitioned, the wires cut, and the railroad obstructed ; while the machine shops, several trains of loaded cars, and a large quantity of small arms, ammunition, and clothing was de-

Oct. 11. stroyed. At nine the next morning the force marched in the direction of Gettysburg, moving round the Federal rear. Then, crossing the mountains, it turned south through Emmittsburg, passed the Monocacy near Frederick, and after a march of ninety miles since leaving Chambersburg reached Hyattstown at daylight on the

Oct. 12. 12th. Here, on the road which formed McClellan's line of communication with Washington, a few waggons were captured, and information came to hand that 4,000 or 5,000 Federal troops were near Poolesville, guarding the fords across the Potomac. Moving at a trot through the woods, the column, leaving Poolesville two or three miles to the left, made for the mouth of the Monocacy. About a mile and a half from that river an advanced-guard of hostile cavalry, moving eastward, was encountered and driven in. Colonel Lee's men were dismounted, a gun was brought into action, and under cover of this screen, posted on a high crest, the main body made a dash for White's Ford. The point of passage, although guarded by about 100 Federal riflemen, was quickly seized, and Stuart's whole force, together with the captured horses, had completed the crossing before the enemy, advancing in large force from the Monocacy, was in a position to interfere.

This brilliantly conducted expedition was as fruitful of results as the ride round McClellan's army in the previous June. The information obtained was most important. Lee, besides being furnished with a sufficiently full report of the Federal dispositions, learned that no part of McClellan's army had been detached to Washington, but that it was being reinforced from that quarter, and that therefore no over-sea expedition against Richmond was to be apprehended. Several hundred fine horses from the farms of Pennsylvania furnished excellent remounts for the Confederate troopers. Prominent officials were brought in as hostages for the safety of the Virginia citizens who had been thrown into Northern prisons. Only a few scouts were captured by the enemy, and not a man was killed. The distance marched by Stuart, from Darkesville to White's Ford, was one hundred and twenty-six miles, of which the last eighty were covered without a halt. Crossing the Potomac at McCoy's Ford about 6 A.M. on October 10, he had recrossed it at White's Ford, between 1 and 2 P.M. on October 12; he was thus for fifty-six hours inside the enemy's lines, and during the greater part of his march within thirty miles of McClellan's headquarters near Harper's Ferry.

It is often the case in war that a well-planned and boldly executed enterprise has a far greater effect than could possibly have been anticipated. Neither Lee nor Stuart looked for larger results from this raid than a certain amount of plunder and a good deal of intelligence. But skill and daring were crowned with a more ample reward than the attainment of the immediate object.

In the first place, the expedition, although there was little fighting, was most destructive to the Federal cavalry.

McClellan had done all in his power to arrest the raiders. Directly the news came in that they had crossed the Potomac, troops were sent in every direction to cut off their retreat. Yet so eminently judicious were Stuart's precautions, so intelligent the Maryland soldiers who acted as his guides, and so rapid his movements, that although constant reports were received by the Federal generals as to the progress and direction of his column, the information came always too late to serve any practical purpose, and his pursuers were never in time to bar his march. General Pleasanton, with such cavalry as could be spared from the picket line, marched seventy-eight miles in four-and-twenty hours, and General Averell's brigade, quartered on the Upper Potomac, two hundred miles in four days. The severity of the marches told heavily on these commands, already worn out by hard work on the outposts; and so many of the horses broke down that a period of repose was absolutely necessary to refit them for the field. Until his cavalry should have recovered it was impossible for McClellan to invade Virginia.

In the second place, neither the Northern Government nor the Northern people could forget that this was the second time that McClellan had allowed Stuart to ride at will round the Army of the Potomac. Public confidence in the general-in-chief was greatly shaken; and a handle was given to his opponents in the ranks of the abolitionists, who, because he was a Democrat, and had much influence with the army, were already clamouring for his removal.

The respite which Stuart had gained for Virginia was not, however, of long duration. On October 26, McClellan, having ascertained by means of a strong reconnaissance in force that the Confederate army was still in the vicinity of Winchester, commenced the passage of the Potomac. The principal point of crossing was

Oct. 26. near Berlin, and so soon as it became evident that the Federal line of operations lay east of the Blue Ridge, Lee ordered Longstreet to Culpeper Court House. Jackson, taking post on the road between Berryville and Charlestown, was to remain in the Valley.

On November 7 the situation was as follows :—

ARMY OF THE POTOMAC.

First Corps	Warrenton.
Second Corps . . .	Rectortown.
Third Corps	Between Manassas Junction and Warrenton.
Fifth Corps	White Plains.
Ninth Corps	Waterloo.
Eleventh Corps . . .	New Baltimore.
Cavalry Division . . .	Rappahannock Station and Sperryville.
Line of Supply . . .	Orange and Alexandria and Manassas Railways.
Twelfth Corps . . .	Harper's Ferry and Sharpsburg.

ARMY OF NORTHERN VIRGINIA.

First Corps	Culpeper Court House.
Second Corps. . . .	Headquarters, Millwood.
Cavalry Division . . .	Hampton's and Fitzhugh Lee's Brigades on the Rappahannock. Munford's Brigade with Jackson.
Lines of Supply . . .	Staunton—Strasburg. Staunton—Culpeper Court House. Richmond—Gordonsville.

Nov. 7.   On this date the six corps of the Army of the Potomac which were assembled between the Bull Run Mountains and the Blue Ridge numbered 125,000 officers and men present for duty, together with 320 guns.

The returns of the Army of Northern Virginia give the following strength :—

		Guns	
First Army Corps . .	31,939	112	(54 short-range smooth-bores)
Second Army Corps .	31,794	123	(53 ,, ,,)
Cavalry Division . .	7,176	4	
Reserve Artillery . .	900	36	(20 ,, ,,)
	71,809	275	

The Confederates were not only heavily outnumbered by the force immediately before them, but along the Potomac, from Washington westward, was a second hostile army, not indeed so large as that commanded by McClellan, but larger by several thousands than that commanded by

Lee. The Northern capital held a garrison of 80,000 ; at Harper's Ferry were 10,000 ; in the neighbourhood of Sharpsburg over 4,000 ; along the Baltimore and Ohio Railroad 8,000. Thus the total strength of the Federals exceeded 225,000 men. Yet in face of this enormous host, and with Richmond only weakly garrisoned behind him, Lee had actually separated his two wings by an interval of sixty miles. He was evidently playing his old game, dividing his army with a view to a junction on the field of battle.

Lincoln, in a letter of advice with which he had favoured McClellan a few days previously, had urged the importance of making Lee's line of supply the first objective of the invading army. 'An advance east of the Blue Ridge,' he said, 'would at once menace the enemy's line of communications, and compel him to keep his forces together ; and if Lee, disregarding this menace, were to cut in between the Army of the Potomac and Washington, McClellan would have nothing to do but to attack him in rear.' He suggested, moreover, that by hard marching it might be possible for McClellan to reach Richmond first.

The Confederate line of communications, so the President believed, ran from Richmond to Culpeper Court House, and McClellan's advanced-guards, on November 7, were within twenty miles of that point. Lee, however, had altogether failed to respond to Mr. Lincoln's strategical pronouncements. Instead of concentrating his forces he had dispersed them ; and instead of fearing for his own communications, he had placed Jackson in a position to interfere very seriously with those of his enemy.

Mr. Lincoln's letter to McClellan shows that the lessons of the war had not been altogether lost upon him. Generals Banks and Pope, with some stimulus from Stonewall Jackson, had taught him what an important part is played by lines of supply. He had mastered the strategical truism that an enemy's communications are his weakest point. But there were other considerations which had not come home to him. He had overlooked the possi-

bility that Lee might threaten McClellan's communications
before McClellan could threaten his; and he had yet to
learn that an army operating in its own country, if proper
forethought be exercised, can establish an alternative line
of supply, and provide itself with a double base, thus
gaining a freedom of action of which an invader, bound,
unless he has command of the sea, to a single line, is generally
deprived.

The President appears to have thought that, if Lee
were cut off from Richmond, the Army of Northern Virginia
would be reduced to starvation, and become absolutely powerless. It never entered his head that the astute commander
of that army had already, in anticipation of the very movement which McClellan was now making, established a second
base at Staunton, and that his line of supply, in case of
necessity, would not run over the open country between
Richmond and Gordonsville, but from Staunton to Culpeper,
behind the ramparts of the Blue Ridge.

Lee, in fact, accepted with equanimity the possibility of
the Federals intervening between himself and Richmond.
He had already, in the campaign against Pope, extricated
himself from such a situation by a bold stroke against his
enemy's communications; and the natural fastness of the
Valley, amply provided with food and forage, afforded
facilities for such a manœuvre which had been altogether
absent before the Second Manassas. Nor was he of Mr.
Lincoln's opinion, that if the Army of Northern Virginia
cut in between Washington and McClellan it would be a
simple operation for the latter to about face and attack the
Confederates in rear. He knew, and Mr. Lincoln, if he
had studied Pope's campaign, should have known it too,
that the operation of countermarching, if the line of communication has been cut, is not only apt to produce
great confusion and great suffering, but has the very
worst effect on the *moral* of the troops. But Lee had
that practical experience which Mr. Lincoln lacked, and
without which it is but waste of words to dogmatise on
strategy. He was well aware that a large army is a cumbrous machine, not readily deflected from the original

direction of the line of march; [1] and, more than all, he had
that intimate acquaintance with the soldier in the ranks,
that knowledge of the human factor, without which no
military problem, whether of strategy, tactics, or organisation, can be satisfactorily solved. McClellan's task, therefore, so long as he had to depend for his supplies on a
single line of railway, was not quite so simple as Mr.
Lincoln imagined.

Nevertheless, on November 7 Lee decided to unite
his army. As soon as the enemy advanced from Warrenton, Jackson was to ascend the Valley, and crossing the
Blue Ridge at Fisher's Gap, join hands with Longstreet, who would retire from Madison Court House to the
vicinity of Gordonsville. The Confederates would then be
concentrated on McClellan's right flank should he march on
Richmond, ready to take advantage of any opportunity for
attack; or, if attack were considered too hazardous, to
threaten his communications, and compel him to fall back
to the Potomac.

The proposed concentration, however, was not immediately carried out. In the first place, the Federal advance
came to a sudden standstill; and, in the second place,
Jackson was unwilling to abandon his post of vantage behind
the Blue Ridge. It need hardly be said that the policy of
manœuvring instead of intrenching, of aiming at the
enemy's flank and rear instead of barring his advance
directly, was in full agreement with his views of war; and
it appears that about this date he had submitted proposals
for a movement against the Federal communications. It
would be interesting indeed to have the details of his design,
but Jackson's letter-book for this period has unfortunately
disappeared, nor did he communicate his ideas to any of his
staff. Letters from General Lee, however, indicate that
the manœuvre proposed was of the same character as

[1] On November 1 the Army of the Potomac (not including the Third
Corps) was accompanied by 4,818 waggons and ambulances, 8,500 transport
horses, and 12,000 mules. O. R., vol. xix., part i., pp. 97–8. The train of
each army corps and of the cavalry covered eight miles of road, or fifty
miles for the whole.

that which brought Pope in such hot haste from the
Rappahannock to Bull Run, and that it was Jackson's suggestion which caused the Commander-in-Chief to reconsider
his determination of uniting his army.

'As long as General Jackson,' wrote Lee to the Secretary
of War on November 10, 'can operate with safety, and
secure his retirement west of the Massanutton Mountains,
I think it advantageous that he should be in a position to
threaten the enemy's flank and rear, and thus prevent his
advance southward on the east side of the Blue Ridge.
General Jackson has been directed accordingly, and should
the enemy descend into the Valley, General Longstreet will
attack his rear, and cut off his communications. The enemy
apparently is so strong in numbers that I think it prefer-
able to baffle his designs by manœuvring, rather than
resist his advance by main force. To accomplish the latter
without too great a risk and loss would require more than
double our present numbers.'[1]

His letter to Jackson, dated November 9, ran as
follows: 'The enemy seems to be massing his troops along
the Manassas Railroad in the vicinity of Piedmont, which
gives him great facilities for bringing up supplies from
Alexandria. It has occurred to me that his object may be
to seize upon Strasburg with his main force, to intercept
your ascent of the Valley. . . . This would oblige you to
cross into the Lost River Valley, or west of it, unless you
could force a passage through the Blue Ridge; hence my
anxiety for your safety. If you can prevent such a movement of the enemy, and operate strongly on his flank and
rear through the gaps of the Blue Ridge, you would certainly
in my opinion effect the object you propose. A demonstration of crossing into Maryland would serve the same
purpose, and might call him back to the Potomac. As my
object is to retard and baffle his designs, if it can be accomplished by manœuvring your corps as you propose, it will
serve my purpose as well as if effected in any other way.
With this understanding, you can use your discretion, which
I know I can rely upon, in remaining or advancing up the

[1] O. R., vol. xix., part ii., p. 711.

Valley. Keep me advised of your movements and intentions; and you must keep always in view the probability of an attack upon Richmond from either north or south, when a concentration of force will become necessary.' [1]

Jackson's plan, however, was not destined to be tried. McClellan had issued orders for the concentration of his army at Warrenton. His troops had never been in better condition. They were in good spirits, well supplied and admirably equipped. Owing to the activity of his cavalry, coupled with the fact that the Confederate horses were at this time attacked by a disease which affected both tongue and hoof, his information was more accurate than usual. He knew that Longstreet was at Culpeper, and Jackson in the Valley. He saw the possibility of separating the two wings of the enemy's forces, and of either defeating Longstreet or forcing him to fall back to Gordonsville, and he had determined to make the attempt.

On the night of November 7, however, at the very moment when his army was concentrating for an advance against Longstreet, McClellan was ordered to hand over his command to General Burnside. Lincoln had yielded to the insistence of McClellan's political opponents, to the rancour of Stanton, and the jealousy of Halleck. But in sacrificing the general who had saved the Union at Sharpsburg he sacrificed the lives of many thousands of his soldiers. A darker day than even the Second Manassas was in store for the Army of the Potomac. McClellan was not a general of the first order. But he was the only officer in the United States who had experience of handling large masses of troops, and he was improving every day. Stuart had taught him the use of cavalry, and Lee the value of the initiative. He was by no means deficient in resolution, as his march with an army of recently defeated men against Lee in Maryland conclusively proves; and although he had never won a decisive victory, he possessed, to a degree which was never attained by any of his successors, the confidence and affection of his troops. But deplorable

[1] O. R., vol. xix., part ii., p. 705.

as was the weakness which sanctioned his removal on the eve
of a decisive manœuvre, the blunder which put Burnside in
his place was even more so.   The latter appears to have
been the *protégé* of a small political faction.   He had many
good qualities.   He was a firm friend, modest, generous,
and energetic.   But he was so far from being distinguished
for military ability that in the Army of the Potomac it was
very strongly questioned whether he was fit to command
an army corps.   His conduct at Sharpsburg, where he had
been entrusted with the attack on the Confederate right,
had been the subject of the severest criticism, and by not a
few of his colleagues he was considered directly responsible
for the want of combination which had marred McClellan's
plan of attack.   More than once Mr. Lincoln infringed his
own famous aphorism, ' Never swap horses when crossing a
stream,' but when he transferred the destinies of the Army
of the Potomac from McClellan to Burnside he did more—
he selected the weakest of his team of generals to bear
the burden.

At the same time that McClellan was superseded,
General FitzJohn Porter, the gallant soldier of Gaines'
Mill and Malvern Hill, probably the best officer in the Army
of the Potomac, was ordered to resign command of the
Fifth Army Corps, and to appear before a court-martial
on charges of incompetency and neglect of duty at the
Second Manassas.   The fact that those charges were
preferred by Pope, and that Porter had been allowed to
retain his command through the campaign in Maryland,
were hardly calculated to inspire the army with confidence in
either the wisdom or the justice of its rulers ; and it was
the general opinion that his intimate friendship with
McClellan had more to say to his trial than his alleged
incompetency.

Burnside commenced his career by renouncing the
enterprise which McClellan had contemplated.   Longstreet
was left unmolested at Culpeper ; and, in order to free the
communications from Jackson, the Federal army was
marched eastward along the Rappahannock to Falmouth, a
new line of supply being established between that village

and Aquia Creek, the port on the Potomac, six hours' sail from Washington.

Lee had already foreseen that Jackson's presence in the Valley might induce the Federals to change their line of operations. Fredericksburg, on the south side of the Rappahannock, and the terminus of the Richmond and Potomac Railroad, had consequently been garrisoned by an infantry regiment and a battery, while three regiments of cavalry patrolled the river. This force, however, was not posted on the Rappahannock with a view of retarding the enemy's advance, but merely for observation. Lee, at this date, had no intention of concentrating at Fredericksburg. The Federals, if they acted with resolution, could readily forestall him, and the line of the North Anna, a small but difficult stream, thirty-six miles south, offered peculiar advantages to the defence.

The Federal march was rapid. On November 15 the Army of the Potomac left Warrenton, and the advanced-guard reached Falmouth on the afternoon of the 17th. General Sumner, in command, observing the weakness of the Confederate garrison, requested permission from Burnside to cross the Rappahannock and establish himself on the further bank. Although two army corps were at hand, and the remainder were rapidly closing up, Burnside refused, for the bridges had been broken, and he was unwilling to expose part of his forces on the right bank with no means of retreat except a difficult and uncertain ford. The same day, part of Longstreet's corps and a brigade of cavalry were sent to Fredericksburg ; and on the 19th, Lee, finding that the Federals had left Warrenton, ordered Longstreet to concentrate his whole force at Fredericksburg, and summoned Jackson from the Valley to Orange Court House.

Jackson, meanwhile, had moved to Winchester, probably with the design of threatening the enemy's garrisons on the Potomac, and this unexpected movement had caused much perturbation in the North. Pennsylvania and Maryland expected nothing less than instant invasion. The merchant feared for his strong-box, the farmer for his herds; plate was once more packed up; railway presidents demanded further protection for their lines; generals begged for reinforcements, and, according to the 'Times' Correspondent, it was 'the universal belief that Stonewall Jackson was ready to pounce upon Washington from the Shenandoah, and to capture President, Secretaries, and all.' But before apprehension increased to panic, before Mr. Lincoln had become infected by the prevailing uneasiness, the departure of the Confederates from the Valley brought relief to the affrighted citizens.

On November 22 Jackson bade farewell to Winchester. His headquarters were not more than a hundred yards from Dr. Graham's manse, and he spent his last evening with his old friends. 'He was in fine health and fine spirits,' wrote the minister's wife to Mrs. Jackson. 'The children begged to be permitted to sit up to see " General Jackson," and he really seemed overjoyed to see them, played with them and fondled them, and they were equally pleased. I have no doubt it was a great recreation to him. He seemed to be living over last winter again, and talked a great deal about the hope of getting back to spend this winter with us, in the old room, which I told him I was keeping for you and him. He certainly has had adulation enough to spoil him, but it seems not to affect or harm him at all. He is the same humble, dependent Christian, desiring to give God all the glory, looking to Him alone for a blessing, and not thinking of himself.'

So it was with no presage that this was the last time he would look upon the scenes he loved that Jackson moved southward by the Valley turnpike. Past Kernstown his columns swept, past Middletown and Strasburg, and all the well-remembered fields of former triumphs; until the peaks of the Massanuttons threw their shadows across the highway, and the mighty bulk of the noble mountains, draped in the gold and crimson of the autumn, once more re-echoed to the tramp of his swift-footed veterans. Turning east at New Market, he struck upwards by the familiar road; and then, descending the narrow pass, he forded the

Shenandoah, and crossing the Luray valley vanished in the forests of the Blue Ridge. Through the dark pines of Fisher's Gap he led his soldiers down to the Virginia plains, and the rivers and the mountains knew him no more until their dead returned to them.

On the 26th the Second Army Corps was at Madison Court House. The next day it was concentrated at Orange Court House, six-and-thirty miles from Fredericksburg. In eight days, two being given to rest, the troops had Nov. 27. marched one hundred and twenty miles, and with scarce a straggler, for the stern measures which had been taken to put discipline on a firmer basis, and to make the regimental officers do their duty, had already produced a salutary effect.

On Jackson's arrival at Orange Court House he found the situation unchanged. Burnside, notwithstanding that heavy snow-storms and sharp frosts betokened the approach of winter, the season of impassable roads and swollen rivers, was still encamped near Falmouth. The difficulty of establishing a new base of supplies at Aquia Creek, and some delay on the part of the Washington authorities in furnishing him with a pontoon train, had kept him idle; but he had not relinquished his design of marching upon Richmond. His quiescence, however, together with the wishes of the President, had induced General Lee to change his plans. The Army of Northern Virginia, 78,500 strong, although, in order to induce the Federals to attack, it was not yet closely concentrated, was ready to oppose in full force the passage of the Rappahannock, and Nov. 29. all thought of retiring to the North Anna had been abandoned. On November 29, therefore, Jackson was ordered forward, and while the First Army Corps occupied a strong position in rear of Fredericksburg, with an advanced detachment in the town, the Second was told off to protect the lower reaches of the Rappahannock. Ewell's division, still commanded by Early, was posted at Skinker's Neck, twelve miles south-east of Fredericksburg, a spot which afforded many facilities for crossing; D. H. Hill's at Port Royal, already menaced by Federal gunboats, six miles further down stream; A. P. Hill's and Taliaferro's (Jackson's own) at Yerby's House and Guiney's Station, five and nine miles respectively from Longstreet's right; and Stuart, whose division was now increased to four brigades, watched both front and flanks.

The Rappahannock was undoubtedly a formidable obstacle. Navigable for small vessels as far as Fredericksburg, the head of the tide water, it is two hundred yards wide in the neighbourhood of the city, and it increases in width and depth as it flows seaward. But above Falmouth there are several easy fords; the river banks, except near Fredericksburg, are clad with forest, hiding the movements of troops; and from Falmouth downward, the left bank, under the name of the Stafford Heights, so completely commands the right that it was manifestly impossible for the Confederates to prevent the enemy, furnished with a far superior artillery, from making good the passage of the stream. A mile west of Fredericksburg, however, extending from Beck's Island to the heights beyond the Massaponax Creek, runs a long low ridge, broken by ravines and partially covered with timber, which with some slight aid from axe and spade could be rendered an exceedingly strong position. Longstreet, who occupied this ridge, had been ordered to intrench himself; gun-pits had been dug on the bare crest, named Marye's Hill, which immediately faces Fredericksburg; a few shelter-trenches had been thrown up, natural defences improved, and some slight breastworks and abattis constructed along the outskirts of the woods. These works were at extreme range from the Stafford Heights; and the field of fire, extending as far as the river, a distance varying from fifteen hundred to three thousand yards, needed no clearing. Over such ground a frontal attack, even if made by superior numbers, had little chance of success.

But notwithstanding its manifest advantages the position found no favour in the eyes of Jackson. It could be easily turned by the fords above Falmouth—Banks', United States, Ely's, and Germanna. This, however, was a minor disqualification compared with the restrictions in the way of offensive action. If the enemy should cross at Fredericksburg, both his flanks would be protected by the river, while his numerous batteries, arrayed on the Stafford Heights, and commanding the length and the breadth of the battle-field, would make counterstroke difficult and pursuit impossible. To await attack, moreover, was to allow the enemy to choose his own time and place, and to surrender the advantages of the initiative. Burnside's communications were protected by the Rappahannock, and it was thus impracticable to manoeuvre against his most vulnerable point, to inflict on him a surprise, to compel him to change front, and, in case he were defeated, to cut him off from his base and deprive him of his supplies. The line of the North Anna, in Jackson's opinion, promised far greater results. The Federals, advancing from Fredericksburg, would expose their right flank and their communications for a distance of six-and-thirty miles; and if they were compelled to retreat, the destruction of their whole army was within the bounds of possibility. 'I am opposed,' he said to General D. H. Hill, 'to fighting on the Rappahannock. We will whip the enemy, but gain no fruits of victory. I have advised the line of the North Anna, but have been overruled.' [1]

So the days passed on. The country was white with snow. The temperature was near zero, and the troops, their blankets as threadbare as their uniforms, without greatcoats, and in many instances without boots, shivered beneath the rude shelters of their forest bivouacs. Fortunately there was plenty of work. Roads were cut through the woods, and existing tracks improved. The river banks were incessantly patrolled. Fortifications were constructed at Port Royal and Skinker's Neck, and the movements of the Federals, demonstrating now here and now there, kept the whole army on the alert. Nor were Jackson's men deprived of all excitement. He had the satisfaction of reporting to General Lee that D. H. Hill, with the aid of Stuart's horse-artillery, had frustrated two attempts of the Federal gunboats to pass up the river at Port Royal;

[1] Dabney, vol. ii., p. 355. From *Manassas to Appomattox*, p. 299.

and that the vigilance of Early at Skinker's Neck had caused the enemy to abandon the design which he had apparently conceived of crossing at that point.

But more vigorous operations were not long postponed. On December 10, General Burnside, urged by the impatience of the Northern press, determined to advance, and the next morning, at 3 A.M., the signal guns of the Confederates gave notice that the enemy was in motion. One hundred and forty Federal guns, many of large calibre, placed in epaulments on the Stafford Heights, frowned down upon Fredericksburg, and before the sun rose the Federal bridge builders were at work on the opposite shore. The little city, which had been deserted by the inhabitants, was held by Barksdale's Mississippi brigade of McLaws' division, about 1,600 strong, and the conduct of this advanced detachment must have done much to inspirit the troops who watched their prowess from the ridge in rear. A heavy fog hung upon the water, and not until the bridge was two-thirds completed, and shadowy figures became visible in the mist, did the Mississippians open fire. At such close quarters the effect was immediate, and the builders fled. Twice, at intervals of half an hour, they ventured again upon the deserted bridge, and twice were they driven back. Strong detachments were now moved forward by the Federals to cover the working parties, and artillery began to play upon the town. The Southerners, however, securely posted in rifle-pits and cellars, were not to be dislodged ; and at ten o'clock Burnside ordered the heavy batteries into action. Every gun which could be brought to bear on Fredericksburg discharged fifty rounds of shot and shell. To this bombardment, which lasted upwards of an hour, Longstreet's artillery could make no reply. Yet though the effect on the buildings was appalling, and flames broke out in many places, the defenders not only suffered little loss, but at the very height of the cannonade repelled another attempt to complete the bridge.

After a delay of several hours General Hooker, commanding the advance, called for volunteers to cross the river in boats. Four regiments came forward. The pon-

Dec. 11.

toons were manned, and though many lives were lost during the transit, the gallant Federals pushed quickly across; others followed, and Barksdale, who had no orders to hold the place against superior strength, withdrew his men from the river bank. About 4.30 P.M., three bridges being at last established, the enemy pushed forward, and the Mississippians, retiring in good order, evacuated Fredericksburg. A mile below, near the mouth of Hazel Run, the Confederate outposts had been driven in, and three more bridges had been thrown across. Thus on the night of the 11th the Federals, who were now organised in three Grand Divisions, each of two army corps, had established their advanced-guards on the right bank of the Rappahannock, and, under cover of the batteries on the Stafford Heights, could rapidly and safely pass over their great host of 120,000 men.[1]

Burnside had framed his plan of attack on the assumption that Lee's army was dispersed along the Rappahannock. His balloon had reported large Confederate bivouacs below Skinker's Neck, and he appears to have believed that Lee, alarmed by his demonstrations near Port Royal, had posted half his army in that neighbourhood. Utterly unsuspicious that a trap had been laid for him, he had resolved to take advantage of this apparently vicious distribution, and, crossing rapidly at Fredericksburg, to defeat the Confederate left before the right could lend support. Port Royal is but eighteen miles from Fredericksburg, and in prompt action, therefore, lay his only hope of success. Burnside, however, after the successful establishment of his six bridges, evinced the same want of resolution which had won him so unenviable a reputation at Sharpsburg. The long hours of darkness slipped peacefully away; no unusual sound broke the silence of the night, and all was still along the Rappahannock. It was not till the next morning, December 12, that the army began to cross, and the movement, made difficult by a dense fog, was by no means energetic. Four of the six army corps were transferred during the

Dec. 12.

---

[1] The three Grand Divisions were commanded by Sumner, Hooker, and Franklin.

day to the southern bank; but beyond a cavalry reconnaissance, which was checked by Stuart, there was no
fighting, and to every man in the Federal ranks it was
perfectly plain that the delay was fatal.

Lee, meanwhile, with ample time at his disposal and
full confidence in the wisdom of his dispositions, calmly
awaited the development of his adversary's plans. Jackson
brought up A. P. Hill and Taliaferro at noon, and posted
them on Longstreet's right; but it was not till that hour,
when it had at last become certain that the whole Federal
army was crossing, that couriers were dispatched to call
in Early and D. H. Hill. Once more the Army of Northern
Virginia was concentrated at exactly the right moment on
the field of battle.[1]

Like its predecessor, December 13 broke dull and calm,
and the mist which shrouded river and plain hid from each
Dec. 13. other the rival hosts. Long before daybreak the
Federal divisions still beyond the stream began
to cross; and as the morning wore on, and the troops near
Hazel Run moved forward from their bivouacs, the rumbling of artillery on the frozen roads, the loud words of
command, and the sound of martial music came, muffled
by the fog, to the ears of the Confederates lying expectant
on the ridge. Now and again the curtain lifted for a
moment, and the Southern guns assailed the long dark
columns of the foe. Very early had the Confederates taken
up their position. The ravine of Deep Run, covered with
tangled brushwood, was the line of demarcation between
Jackson and Longstreet. On the extreme right of the
Second Corps, and half a mile north of the marshy valley
of the Massaponax, where a spur called Prospect Hill juts
down from the wooded ridge, were fourteen guns under
Colonel Walker. Supported by two regiments of Field's
brigade, these pieces were held back for the present within
the forest which here clothed the ridge. Below Prospect
Hill, and running thence along the front of the position,
the embankment of the Richmond and Potomac Railroad
formed a tempting breastwork. It was utilised, however,

[1] Lord Wolseley. *North American Review*, vol. 149, p. 282.

only by the skirmishers of the defence. The edge of the
forest, one hundred and fifty to two hundred yards in rear,
looked down upon an open and gentle slope, and along the
brow of this natural glacis, covered by the thick timber,
Jackson posted his fighting-line. To this position it was
easy to move up his supports and reserves without exposing
them to the fire of artillery; and if the assailants should
seize the embankment, he relied upon the deadly rifles of his
infantry to bar their further advance up the ascent beyond.

The Light Division supplied both the first and second
lines of Jackson's army corps. To the left of Walker's
guns, posted in a shelter-trench within the skirts of the wood,
was Archer's brigade of seven regiments, including two of
Field's, the left resting on a coppice that projected beyond
the general line of forest. On the further side of this
coppice, but nearer the embankment, lay Lane's brigade,
an unoccupied space of six hundred yards intervening
between his right and Archer's left. Between Lane's right
and the edge of the coppice was an open tract two hundred
yards in breadth. Both of these brigades had a strong skirmish line pushed forward along and beyond the railroad.
Five hundred yards in rear, along a road through the woods
which had been cut by Longstreet's troops, Gregg's South
Carolina brigade, in second line, covered the interval between
Archer and Lane. To Lane's left rear lay Pender's
brigade, supporting twelve guns posted in the open, on the
far side of the embankment, and twenty-one massed in a
field to the north of a small house named Bernard's Cabin.
Four hundred yards in rear of Lane's left and Pender's
right was stationed Thomas's brigade of four regiments.[1]

It is necessary to notice particularly the shape, size,
and position of the projecting tongue of woodland which

[1] The dispositions were as follows:—

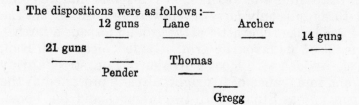

broke the continuity of Hill's line. A German officer on Stuart's staff had the day previous, while riding along the position, remarked its existence, and suggested the propriety of razing it; but, although Jackson himself predicted that there would be the scene of the severest fighting, the ground was so marshy within its depths, and the undergrowth so dense and tangled, that it was judged impenetrable and left unoccupied—an error of judgment which cost many lives. General Lane had also recognised the danger of leaving so wide a gap between Archer and himself, and had so reported, but without effect, to his divisional commander.

The coppice was triangular in shape, and extended nearly six hundred yards beyond the embankment. The base, which faced the Federals, was five hundred yards long. Beyond the apex the ground was swampy and covered with scrub, and the ridge, depressed at this point to a level with the plain, afforded no position from which artillery could command the approach to or issue from this patch of jungle. A space of seven hundred yards along the front was thus left undefended by direct fire.

Early, who with D. H. Hill had marched in shortly after daybreak, formed the right of the third line, Taliaferro the left. The division of D. H. Hill, with several batteries, formed the general reserve, and a portion of Early's artillery was posted about half a mile in rear of his division, in readiness, if necessary, to relieve the guns on Prospect Hill.

Jackson's line was two thousand six hundred yards in length, and his infantry 30,000 strong, giving eleven rifles to the yard; but nearly three-fourths of the army corps, the divisions of Early, Taliaferro, and D. H. Hill, were in third line and reserve. Of his one hundred and twenty-three guns only forty-seven were in position, but the wooded and broken character of the ground forbade a further deployment of his favourite arm. His left, near Deep Run, was in close touch with Hood's division of Longstreet's army corps; and in advance of his right, already protected by the Massaponax, was Stuart with two brigades and his horse-

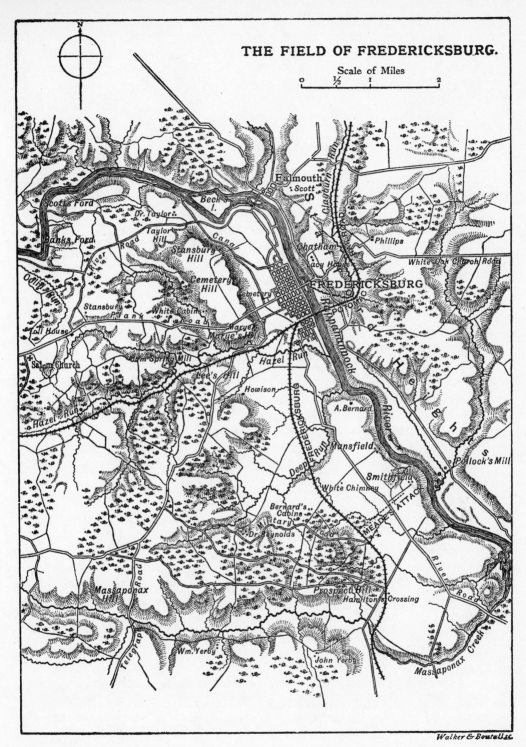

THE FIELD OF FREDERICKSBURG.

Scale of Miles

Walker & Boutall sc.

artillery. One Whitworth gun, a piece of great range and large calibre, was posted on the wooded heights beyond the Massaponax, north-east of Yerby's House.

Jackson's dispositions were almost identical with those which he had adopted at the Second Manassas. His whole force was hidden in the woods; every gun that could find room was ready for action, and the batteries were deployed in two masses. Instead, however, of giving each division a definite section of the line, he had handed over the whole front to A. P. Hill. This arrangement, however, had been made before D. H. Hill and Early came up, and with the battle imminent a change was hazardous. In many respects, moreover, the ground he now occupied resembled that which he had so successfully defended on August 29 and 30. There was the wood opposite the centre, affording the enemy a covered line of approach; the open fields, pasture and stubble, on either hand; the stream, hidden by timber and difficult of passage, on the one flank, and Longstreet on the other. But the position at Fredericksburg was less strong for defence than that at the Second Manassas, for not only was Jackson's line within three thousand yards—a long range but not ineffective—of the heavy guns on the Stafford Heights, but on the bare plain between the railway and the river there was ample room for the deployment of the Federal field-batteries. At the Second Manassas, on the other hand, the advantages of the artillery position had been on the side of the Confederates.

Nevertheless, with the soldiers of Sharpsburg, ragged indeed and under-fed, but eager for battle and strong in numbers, there was no reason to dread the powerful artillery of the foe; and Jackson's confidence was never higher than when, accompanied by his staff, he rode along his line of battle. He was not, however, received by his soldiers with their usual demonstrations of enthusiastic devotion. In honour of the day he had put on the uniform with which Stuart had presented him; the old cadet cap, which had so often waved his men to victory, was replaced by a head-dress resplendent with gold lace; 'Little Sorrel' had been deposed in favour of a more imposing charger; and

the veterans failed to recognise their commander until
he had galloped past them. A Confederate artillery-man
has given a graphic picture of his appearance when the
fight was at its hottest :—

'A general officer, mounted upon a superb bay horse
and followed by a single courier, rode up through our guns.
Looking neither to the right nor the left, he rode straight to
the front, halted, and seemed gazing intently on the enemy's
line of battle. The outfit before me, from top to toe, cap,
coat, top-boots, horse and furniture, were all of the new
order of things. But there was something about the man
that did not look so new after all. He appeared to be an
old-time friend of all the turmoil around him. As he had
done us the honour to make an afternoon call on the
artillery, I thought it becoming in someone to say something on the occasion. No one did, however, so, although
a somewhat bashful and weak-kneed youngster, I plucked
up courage enough to venture to remark that those big
guns over the river had been knocking us about pretty
considerably during the day. He quickly turned his head,
and I knew in an instant who it was before me. The
clear-cut, chiselled features ; the thin, compressed and determined lips ; the calm, steadfast eye ; the countenance to
command respect, and in time of war to give the soldier
that confidence he so much craves from a superior officer,
were all there. He turned his head quickly, and looking me
all over, rode up the line and away as quickly and silently
as he came, his little courier hard upon his heels ; and
this was my first sight of Stonewall Jackson.'

From his own lines Jackson passed along the front,
drawing the fire of the Federal skirmishers, who were
creeping forward, and proceeded to the centre of the
position, where, on the eminence which has since borne
the name of Lee's Hill, the Commander-in-Chief, surrounded by his generals, was giving his last instructions. It
was past nine o'clock. The sun, shining out with almost
September warmth, was drawing up the mist which
hid the opposing armies ; and as the dense white folds
dissolved and rolled away, the Confederates saw the broad

plain beneath them dark with more than 80,000 foes. Of these the left wing, commanded by Franklin, and composed of 55,000 men and 116 guns, were moving against the Second Corps ; 30,000, under Sumner, were forming for attack on Longstreet, and from the heights of Stafford, where the reserves were posted in dense masses, a great storm of shot and shell burst upon the Confederate lines. ' For once,' says Dabney, ' war unmasked its terrible proportions with a distinctness hitherto unknown in the forest-clad landscapes of America, and the plain of Fredericksburg presented a panorama that was dreadful in its grandeur.' It was then that Longstreet, to whose sturdy heart the approach of battle seemed always welcome, said to Jackson, ' General, do not all those multitudes of Federals frighten you ?' ' We shall very soon see whether I shall not frighten them ; ' and with this grim reply the commander of the Second Corps rode back to meet Franklin's onset.

The Federals were already advancing. From Deep Run southward, for more than a mile and a half, three great lines of battle, accompanied by numerous batteries, moved steadily forward, powerful enough, to all appearance, to bear down all opposition by sheer weight of numbers. ' On they came,' says an eye-witness, ' in beautiful order, as if on parade, their bayonets glistening in the bright sunlight ; on they came, waving their hundreds of regimental flags, which relieved with warm bits of colouring the dull blue of the columns and the russet tinge of the wintry landscape, while their artillery beyond the river continued the cannonade with unabated fury over their heads, and gave a background of white fleecy smoke, like midsummer clouds, to the animated picture.'

And yet that vast array, so formidable of aspect, lacked that moral force without which physical power, even in its most terrible form, is but an idle show. Not only were the strength of the Confederate position, the want of energy in the preliminary movements, the insecurity of their own situation, but too apparent to the intelligence of the regimental officers and men, but they mistrusted their

9 A.M. appears in the left margin beside "great lines of battle...batteries"

commander. Northern writers have recorded that the Army of the Potomac never went down to battle with less alacrity than on this day at Fredericksburg.

Nor was the order of attack of such a character as to revive the confidence of the troops. Burnside, deluded by the skill with which Jackson had hidden his troops into the belief that the Second Army Corps was still at Port Royal, had instructed Franklin to seize the ridge with a single division, and Meade's 4,500 Pennsylvanians were sent forward alone, while the remainder of the Grand Division, over 50,000 strong, stood halted on the plain, awaiting the result of this hopeless manœuvre.[1] Meade advanced in three lines, each of a brigade, with skirmishers in front and on the flank, and his progress was soon checked. No sooner had his first line crossed the Richmond road than the left was assailed by a well-directed and raking artillery fire.

Captain Pelham, commanding Stuart's horse-artillery, had galloped forward by Jackson's orders with his two rifled guns, and, escorted by a dismounted squadron, had come into action beyond a marshy stream which ran through a tangled ravine on the Federal flank. So telling was his fire that the leading brigade wavered and gave ground; and though Meade quickly brought up his guns and placed his third brigade *en potence* in support, he was unable to continue his forward movement until he had brushed away his audacious antagonist. The four Pennsylvania batteries were reinforced by two others; but rapidly changing his position as often as the Federal gunners found his range, for more than half an hour Pelham defied their efforts, and for that space of time arrested the advance of Meade's 4,500 infantry. One of his pieces was soon disabled; but with the remaining gun, captured from the enemy six months before, he maintained the unequal fight until his limbers were empty, and he received peremptory orders from Stuart to withdraw.

On Pelham's retirement, Franklin, bringing several batteries forward to the Richmond road, for more than

---

[1] Franklin's Grand Division consisted of the 42,800 men, and 12,000 of Hooker's Grand Division had reinforced him.

half an hour subjected the woods before him to a heavy
cannonade, in which the guns on the Stafford Heights
played a conspicuous part. Hidden, however, by the thick
timber, Jackson's regiments lay secure, unharmed by the
tempest that crashed above them through the leafless
branches; and, reserving their fire for the hostile infantry,
his guns were silent. The general, meanwhile, according
to his custom, had walked far out into the fields to reconnoitre for himself, and luck favoured the Confederacy
on this day of battle. Lieutenant Smith was his only
companion, and a Federal sharpshooter, suddenly rising
from some tall weeds two hundred paces distant, levelled
his rifle and fired. The bullet whistled between their
heads, and Jackson, turning with a smile to his aide-
de-camp, said cheerfully : ' Mr. Smith, had you not better
go to the rear ? They may shoot you.' Then, having
deliberately noted the enemy's arrangements, he returned
11.15 A.M. to his station on Prospect Hill. It was past
eleven before Meade resumed his advance.
Covered by the fire of the artillery, his first line was within
eight hundred yards of Jackson's centre, when suddenly
the silent woods awoke to life. The Confederate batteries,
pushing forward from the covert, came rapidly into action,
and the flash and thunder of more than fifty guns revealed
to the astonished Federals the magnitude of the task they
had undertaken. From front and flank came the scathing
fire ; the skirmishers were quickly driven in, and on the closed
ranks behind burst the full fury of the storm. Dismayed
and decimated by this fierce and unexpected onslaught,
Meade's brigades broke in disorder and fell back to the
Richmond road.

For the next hour and a half an artillery duel, in which
over 400 guns took part, raged over the whole field, and the
Confederate batteries, their position at last revealed, engaged
with spirit the more numerous and powerful ordnance
of the enemy. Then Franklin brought up three divisions
to Meade's support; and from the smouldering ruins of
Fredericksburg, three miles to the northward, beyond the
high trees of Hazel Run, the deep columns of Sumner's

Grand Division deployed under the fire of Longstreet's
guns. Sumner's attack had been for some time in progress
before Franklin was in readiness to co-operate. The
battle was now fully developed, and the morning mists
had been succeeded by dense clouds of smoke, shrouding
hill and plain, through which the cannon flashed redly, and
the defiant yells of Longstreet's riflemen, mingled with their
rattling volleys, stirred the pulses of Jackson's veterans.
As the familiar sounds were borne to their ears, it was seen
that the dark lines beyond the Richmond road were moving
forward, and the turn of the Second Corps had come.

It was one o'clock, and Jackson's guns had for the
moment ceased their fire. Meade's Pennsylvanians had
rallied. Gibbon's division had taken post on their right;
Birney and Newton were in support; and Doubleday, facing

1 P.M.   south, was engaged with Stuart's dismounted
          troopers. Twenty-one guns on the right, and
thirty on the left, stationed on the Richmond road, a
thousand yards from the Confederate position, formed a
second tier to the heavier pieces on the heights, and
fired briskly on the woods. Preceded by clouds of skirmishers, Meade and Gibbon advanced in column of brigades
at three hundred paces distance, the whole covering
a front of a thousand yards; and the supporting divisions
moved up to the Richmond road.

When the Federals reached the scene of their former
repulse, Jackson's guns again opened; but without the
same effect, for they were now exposed to the fire of the
enemy's batteries at close range. Even Pelham could do
but little; and the artillery beyond the railroad on Hill's
left was quickly driven in.

Meade's rear brigade was now brought up and deployed
on the left of the first, in the direction of the Massaponax,
thus further extending the front.

The leading brigade made straight for the tongue of
woodland which interposed between Lane and Archer. As
they neared the Confederate line, the Pennsylvanians,
masked by the trees, found that they were no longer
exposed to fire, and that the coppice was unoccupied.

Quickly crossing the border, through swamp and undergrowth they pushed their way, and, bursting from the
covert to the right, fell on the exposed flank of Lane's
brigade. The fight was fierce, but the Southerners were
compelled to give ground, for neither Archer nor Gregg
was able to lend assistance.

Meade's second brigade, though following close upon
the first, had, instead of conforming to the change of
direction against Lane's flank, rushed forward through the
wood. Two hundred paces from the embankment it came
in contact with Archer's left, which was resting on the very
edge of the coppice. The Confederates were taken by surprise. Their front was secured by a strong skirmish line;
but on the flank, as the thickets appeared impenetrable,
neither scouts nor pickets had been thrown out, and the
men were lying with arms piled. Two regiments, leaping
to their feet and attempting to form line to the left, were
broken by a determined charge, and gave way in disorder.
The remainder, however, stood firm, for the Federals,
instead of following up their success in this direction,
left Archer to be dealt with by the third brigade of
the division, which had now reached the railroad, and
swept on towards the military road, where Gregg's brigade
was drawn up within the forest. So thick was the cover,
and so limited the view, that General Gregg, taking the
advancing mass for part of Archer's line retiring, restrained the fire of his men. The Federals broke upon his
right. He himself fell mortally wounded. His flank regiment, a battalion of conscripts, fled, except one company,
without firing a shot. The two regiments on the opposite
flank, however, were with great readiness turned about, and
changing front inwards, arrested the movement of the
enemy along the rear.

The Federals had now been joined by a portion of the
first brigade, inspirited by their victory over Lane, and the
moment, to all appearance, seemed critical in the extreme
for the Confederates. To the left rear of the attacking
column, Meade's third brigade was held in check by
Walker's batteries and the sturdy Archer, who, notwith-

standing that a strong force had passed beyond his flank, and had routed two of his regiments, still resolutely held his ground, and prevented his immediate opponents from joining the intruding column.   To the right rear, opposite Pender, Gibbon's division had been checked by the fire of the great battery near Bernard's Cabin; two of his brigades had been driven back, and the third had with difficulty gained the shelter of the embankment.   So from neither left nor right was immediate support to be expected by Meade's victorious regiments.   But on the Richmond road were the divisions of Birney and Newton, with Doubleday's and Sickles' not far in rear, and 20,000 bayonets might have been thrown rapidly into the gap which the Pennsylvanians had so vigorously forced.   Yet Jackson's equanimity was undisturbed. The clouds of smoke and the thick timber hid the fighting in the centre from his post of observation on Prospect Hill, and the first intimation of the enemy's success was brought by an aide-de-camp, galloping wildly up the slope.   'General,' he exclaimed in breathless haste, 'the enemy have broken through Archer's left, and General Gregg says he must have help, or he and General Archer will both lose their position.'   Jackson turned round quietly, and without the least trace of excitement in either voice or manner, sent orders to Early and Taliaferro, in third line, to advance with the bayonet and clear the front.   Then, with rare self-restraint, for the fighting instinct was strong within him, and the danger was so threatening as to have justified his personal interference, he raised his field-glasses and resumed his scrutiny of the enemy's reserves on the Richmond road. His confidence in his lieutenants was not misplaced. Early's division, already deployed in line, came forward with a rush, and the Stonewall Brigade, responding with alacrity to Jackson's summons, led the advance of Taliaferro.

1.45 P.M.

The counterstroke was vigorous.   Meade's brigades had penetrated to the heart of the Confederate position, but their numbers were reduced to less than 2,000 bayonets; in the fierce fighting and dense thickets they had lost all semblance of cohesion, and not a single regiment had supported them. The men looked round in vain for help, and the forest around them resounded with the yells of the Confederate reinforcements. Assailed in front and flank by a destructive fire, the Pennsylvanians were rapidly borne back. Hill's second line joined in Early's advance. Gibbon was strongly attacked. Six brigades, sweeping forward from the forest, dashed down the slopes, and in a few moments the broken remnants of the Federal divisions were dispersing in panic across the plain. As the enemy fled the Confederate gunners, disregarding the shells of Franklin's batteries, poured a heavy fire into the receding mass; and although instructions had been given that the counterstroke was not to pass the railroad, Hoke's and Atkinson's brigades,[1] carried away by success and deaf to all orders, followed in swift pursuit. Some of Birney's regiments, tardily coming forward to Meade's support, were swept away, and the yelling line of grey infantry, shooting down the fugitives and taking many prisoners, pressed on towards the Richmond road. There the remainder of Birney's division was drawn up, protected by the breast-high bank, and flanked by artillery; yet it seemed for a moment as if the two Confederate brigades would carry all before them.

The troops of Meade and Gibbon were streaming in confusion to the rear. Two batteries had been abandoned, and before Hoke's onset the left of Birney's infantry gave ground for fifty yards. But the rash advance had reached its climax. Unsupported, and with empty cartridge-boxes, the Southerners were unable to face the fire from the road; sixteen guns had opened on them with canister; and after suffering heavy losses in killed, wounded, and prisoners, they withdrew in disorder but unpursued.

The success of the Second Army Corps was greater than even Jackson realised. Meade and Gibbon had lost 4,000 officers and men; and it was not till late in the afternoon that they were rallied on the river bank. The casualties in Birney's division swelled the total to 5,000, and the Confederate counterstroke had inflicted a

[1] Of Early's Division.

heavier blow than the tale of losses indicates. Not only the troops which had been engaged, but those who had witnessed their defeat, who had seen them enter the enemy's position, and who knew they should have been supported, were much disheartened. At 2.30 P.M., soon after the repulse of Hoke and Atkinson, Burnside, having just witnessed the signal failure of a fourth assault on Longstreet, sent an urgent order to Franklin to renew his attack. Franklin made no response. He had lost all confidence both in his superior and his men, and he took upon himself to disobey.

2.30 P.M.

On the Confederate side Taliaferro and Early, with part of the Light Division, now held the railway embankment and the skirt of the woods. D. H. Hill was brought up into third line, and the shattered brigades of A. P. Hill were withdrawn to the rear. During the rest of the afternoon the skirmishers were actively engaged, but although Jackson's victorious soldiery long and eagerly expected a renewal of the assault, the enemy refused to be again tempted to close quarters.

On the left, meanwhile, where the battle still raged, the Confederates were equally successful. Against an impregnable position 40,000 Northerners were madly hurled by the general of Mr. Lincoln's choice. By those hapless and stout-hearted soldiers, sacrificed to incompetency, a heroism was displayed which won the praise and the pity of their opponents. The attack was insufficiently prepared, and feebly supported, by the artillery. The troops were formed on a narrow front. Marye's Hill, the strongest portion of the position, where the Confederate infantry found shelter behind a stout stone wall, and numerous batteries occupied the commanding ground in rear, was selected for assault. Neither feint nor demonstration, the ordinary expedients by which the attacker seeks to distract the attention and confuse the efforts of the defence, was made use of; and yet division after division, with no abatement of courage, marched in good order over the naked plain, dashed forward with ever-thinning ranks, and then, receding sullenly before the storm of fire, left, within a hundred yards of the stone wall, a long line of writhing forms to mark the limit of their advance.

Two army corps had been repulsed by Longstreet with fearful slaughter when Meade and Gibbon gave way before Jackson's counterstroke, and by three o'clock nearly one-half of the Federal army was broken and demoralised. The time appeared to have come for a general advance of the Confederates. Before Fredericksburg, the wreck of Sumner's Grand Division was still clinging to such cover as the ground afforded. On the Richmond road, in front of Jackson, Franklin had abandoned all idea of the offensive, and was bringing up his last reserves to defend his line. The Confederates, on the other hand, were in the highest spirits, and had lost but few.

3 P.M.

General Lee's arrangements, however, had not included preparation for a great counterstroke, and such a movement is not easily improvised. The position had been occupied for defensive purposes alone. There was no general reserve, no large and intact force which could have moved to the attack immediately the opportunity offered. ' No skill,' says Longstreet, ' could have marshalled our troops for offensive operations in time to meet the emergency. My line was long and over broken country, so much so that the troops could not be promptly handled in offensive operations. Jackson's corps was in mass, and could he have anticipated the result of my battle, he would have been justified in pressing Franklin to the river when the battle of the latter was lost. Otherwise, pursuit would have been as unwise as the attack he had just driven off. It is well known that after driving off attacking forces, if immediate pursuit can be made, so that the victors can go along with the retreating forces pell-mell, it is well enough to do so ; but the attack should be immediate. To follow a success by counter-attack against the enemy in position is problematical.' [1]

Moreover, so large was the battle-field, so limited the view by reason of the woods, and with such ease had the

---

[1] *Battles and Leaders*, vol. iii., pp. 82-3.

Federal attacks been repulsed, that General Lee was
unaware of the extent of his success.   Ignorant, too, as he
necessarily was, of the mistrust and want of confidence in
its leaders with which the Federal army was infected, he
was far from suspecting what a strong ally he had in the
hearts of his enemies; while, on the other hand, the
inaccessible batteries on the Stafford Heights were an
outward and visible token of unabated strength.

Jackson, however, although the short winter day was
already closing in, considered that the attempt was worth
making.   About 3 P.M. he had seen a feeble attack on the
Confederate centre repulsed by Hood and Pender, and
about the same time he received information of Longstreet's success.

Franklin, meanwhile, was reforming his lines behind the
high banks of the Richmond road, and the approach of his
reserves, plainly visible from the Confederate position,
seemed to presage a renewed attack.   ' I waited some time,'
says Jackson, ' to receive it, but he making no forward
movement, I determined, if prudent, to do so myself.   The
artillery of the enemy was so judiciously posted as to make
an advance of our troops across the plain very hazardous ;
yet it was so promising of good results, if successfully
executed, as to induce me to make preparations for the
attempt.   In order to guard against disaster, the infantry
was to be preceded by artillery, and the movement postponed until late in the afternoon, so that if compelled
to retire, it would be under cover of the night.' [1]

Jackson's decision was not a little influenced by Stuart,
or rather by the reports which Stuart, who had sent out
staff officers to keep the closest watch on the enemy's
movements, had been able to furnish of the demoralised
condition of a great part of Franklin's force.   The cavalry
general, as soon as he verified the truth of these reports in
person, galloped off to confer with Jackson on Prospect Hill,
and a message was at once sent to Lee, requesting permission for an advance.   A single cannon shot was to be the
signal for a general attack, which Stuart, striking the

[1] *Jackson's Reports*, O. R., vol. xxi., p. 634.

enemy in flank, was to initiate with his two brigades and the lighter guns.

'Returning to our position,' to quote Stuart's chief of staff, 'we awaited in anxious silence the desired signal; but minute after minute passed by, and the dark veil of the winter night began to envelop the valley, when Stuart, believing that the summons agreed upon had been given, issued the order to advance. Off we went into the gathering darkness, our sharpshooters driving their opponents easily before them, and Pelham with his guns, pushing ahead at a trot, giving them a few shots whenever the position seemed favourable, and then again pressing forward. This lasted about twenty minutes, when the fire of the enemy's infantry began to be more and more destructive, and other fresh batteries opened upon us. Still all remained silent upon our main line. Our situation had become, indeed, a critical one, when a courier from General Jackson galloped up at full speed, bringing the order for Stuart to retreat as quickly as he could to his original position.'

Under cover of the night this retrograde movement was effected without loss; and the cavalry, as they marched back, saw the camp-fires kindling on the skirts of the forest, and the infantry digging intrenchments by the fitful glare.

The Second Corps had not come into action. Jackson had issued orders that every gun, of whatever calibre or range, which was not disabled should be brought to the front and open fire at sunset; and that as soon as the enemy showed signs of wavering, the infantry should charge with fixed bayonets, and sweep the invaders into the river. Hood's division, which had been temporarily placed at his disposal, was instructed to co-operate.[1] It appears, however, that it had not been easy, in the short space of daylight still available, to remedy the confusion into which the Confederates had been thrown by Meade's attack and their own counterstroke. The divisions were to some extent mixed up. Several regiments had been broken, and the ammunition of both infantry and artillery needed replenishment.

Advance and Retreat. Lieutenant-General J. B. Hood, p. 50.

Moreover, it was difficult in the extreme to bring the batteries forward through the forest; and, when they eventually arrived, the strength of the Federal position was at once revealed. Franklin's line was defended by a hundred and sixteen field pieces, generally of superior metal to those of the Confederates, and the guns on the Stafford Heights, of which at least thirty bore upon Jackson's front, were still in action. As the first Confederate battery advanced, this great array of artillery, which had been for some time comparatively quiet, reopened with vigour, and, to use Jackson's words, 'so completely swept our front as to satisfy me that the proposed movement should be abandoned.'

But he was not yet at the end of his resources. A strong position, which cannot be turned, is not always impregnable. If the ground be favourable, and few obstacles exist, a night attack with the bayonet, especially if the enemy be exhausted or half-beaten, has many chances of success; and during the evening Jackson made arrangements for such a movement. 'He asked me,' says Dr. McGuire, 'how many yards of bandaging I had, and when I replied that I did not know the exact number, but that I had enough for another fight, he seemed a little worried at my lack of information and showed his annoyance. I repeated rather shortly, "I have enough for another battle," meaning to imply that this was all that it was necessary for him to know. I then asked him : "Why do you want to know how much bandaging I have ? " He said: "I want a yard of bandaging to put on the arm of every soldier in this night's attack, so that the men may know each other from the enemy." I told him I had not enough cotton cloth for any such purpose, and that he would have to take a piece of the shirt tail of each soldier to supply the cloth, but, unfortunately, half of them had no shirts ! The expedient was never tried. General Lee decided that the attack would be too hazardous.' [1]

That night both armies lay on their arms. Burnside,

[1] Letter to the author.

notwithstanding that he spent several hours amongst the troops before Fredericksburg, and found that both officers and men were opposed to further attack, decided to renew the battle the next day. His arrangements became known to Lee, an officer or orderly carrying dispatches having strayed within the Confederate outposts,[1] and the Southern generals looked forward, on the morning of the 14th, to a fresh attack, a more crushing repulse, and a general counterstroke.

Such cheerful anticipations, however, so often entertained by generals holding a strong defensive position, are but seldom realised, and Fredericksburg was no exception. The Confederates spent the night in diligent preparation. Supplies of ammunition were brought up and distributed, the existing defences were repaired, abattis cut and laid, and fresh earthworks thrown up. Jackson, as usual on the eve of battle, was still working while others rested. Until near midnight he sat up writing and dispatching orders; then, throwing himself, booted and spurred, on his camp bed, he slept for two or three hours, when he again arose, lighted his candle, and resumed his writing. Before four o'clock he sent to his medical director to inquire as to the condition of General Gregg. Dr. McGuire reported that his case was hopeless, and Jackson requested that he would go over and see that he had everything he wished. Somewhat against his will, for there were many wounded who required attention, the medical officer rode off, but scarcely had he entered the farmhouse where Gregg was lying, than he heard the tramp of horses, and Jackson himself dismounted on the threshold. The brigadier, it appears, had lately fallen under the ban of his displeasure; but from the moment his condition was reported, Jackson forgot everything but the splendid services he had rendered on so many hard-fought fields; and in his anxiety that every memory should be effaced which might embitter his last moments, he had followed Dr. McGuire to his bedside.

The interview was brief, and the dying soldier was

[1] *From Manassas to Appomattox*, p. 316.

A A

the happier for it ; but the scene in that lonely Virginian homestead, where, in the dark hours of the chill December morning, the life of a strong man, of a gallant comrade, of an accomplished gentleman, and of an unselfish patriot—for Gregg was all these—was slowly ebbing, made a deeper impression on those who witnessed it than the accumulated horrors of the battle-field. Sadly and silently the general and his staff officer rode back through the forest, where the troops were already stirring round the smouldering camp-fires. Their thoughts were sombre. The Confederacy, with a relatively slender population, could ill spare such men as Gregg. And yet Jackson, though yielding to the depression of the moment, and deploring the awful sacrifices which the defence of her liberties imposed upon the South, was in no melting mood. Dr. McGuire, when they reached headquarters, put a question as to the best means of coping with the overwhelming numbers of the enemy. 'Kill them, sir! kill every man!' was the reply of the stern soldier who but just now, with words of tender sympathy and Christian hope, had bade farewell to his dying comrade.

But on December 14, as on the morrow of Sharpsburg, the Confederates were doomed to disappointment. 'Darkness still prevailed,' writes Stuart's chief of the staff, 'when we mounted our horses and again hastened to Prospect Hill, the summit of which we reached just in time to see the sun rising, and unveiling, as it dispersed the haze, the long lines of the Federal army, which once more stood in full line of battle between our own position and the river. I could not withhold my admiration as I looked down upon the well-disciplined ranks of our antagonists, astonished that these troops now offering so bold a front should be the same whom not many hours since I had seen in complete flight and disorder. The skirmishers of the two armies were not much more than a hundred yards apart, concealed from each other's view by the high grass in which they were lying, and above which, from time to time, rose a small cloud of blue smoke, telling that a shot had been fired. As the boom of artillery began

Dec. 14.

to sound from different parts of the line, and the attack might be expected every minute, each hastened to his post.'

But though the skirmishing at times grew hotter, and the fire of the artillery more rapid, long intervals of silence succeeded, until it at length became apparent to the Confederates that the enemy, though well prepared to resist attack, was determined not to fight outside his breastworks. Burnside, indeed, giving way to the remonstrances of his subordinates, had abandoned all idea of further aggressive action, and unless Lee should move forward, had determined to recross the Potomac.

The next morning saw the armies in the same positions, and the Federal wounded, many of whom had been struck down nearly forty-eight hours before, still lying untended between the hostile lines. It was not till now that Burnside admitted his defeat by sending a flag of truce with a request that he might be allowed to bury his dead.[1]

Dec. 15.

The same night a fierce storm swept the valley of the Rappahannock, and the Army of the Potomac repassed the bridges, evading, under cover of the elements, the observation of the Confederate patrols.

The retreat was effected with a skill which did much credit to the Federal staff. Within fourteen hours 100,000 troops, with the whole of their guns, ambulances, and ammunition waggons, were conveyed across the Rappahan-

---

[1] 'When the flag of truce,' says Major Hotchkiss, 'was received by General Jackson, he asked me for paper and pencil, and began a letter to be sent in reply; but after writing a few lines he handed the paper back, and sent a personal message by Captain Smith.'

Captain Smith writes: 'The general said to me, before I went out to meet Colonel Sumner, representing the Federals: "If you are asked who is in command of your right, do not tell them I am, and be guarded in your remarks." It so happened that Colonel Sumner was the brother-in-law of Colonel Long, an officer on General Lee's staff. While we were together, another Federal officer named Junkin rode up. He was the brother or cousin of Jackson's first wife, and I had known him before the war. After some conversation, Junkin asked me to give his regards to General Jackson, and to deliver a message from the Rev. Dr. Junkin, the father of his first wife. I replied, "I will do so with pleasure when I meet General Jackson." Junkin smiled and said: "It is not worth while for you to try to deceive us. We know that General Jackson is in front of us."

nock; but there remained on the south bank sufficient evidence to show that the Army of the Potomac had not escaped unscathed. When the morning broke the dead lay thick upon the field; arms and accoutrements, the *débris* of defeat, were strewed in profusion on every hand, and the ruined houses of Fredericksburg were filled with wounded. Burnside lost in the battle 12,647 men.

LEFT ATTACK—FRANKLIN.

First Corps	Meade's Division	1,853
	Gibbon's Division	1,267
	Doubleday's Division	214
Third Corps	Birney's Division	950
	Sickles' Division	100
Sixth Corps	Newton's Division	63
	Total . .	4,447

CENTRE.

Brook's Division	197
Howe's Division	186
Total . .	383

RIGHT ATTACK—SUMNER AND HOOKER.

Second Corps	Hancock's Division	2,032
	Howard's Division.	914
	French's Division	1,160
Ninth Corps	Burns' Division	27
	Sturgis' Division	1,007
	Getty's Division	296
Third Corps	Whipple's Division	129
Fifth Corps	Griffin's Division	926
	Sykes' Division	228
	Humphrey's Division	1,019
Engineers and Reserve Artillery, &c.		79
	Total . .	7,817
Grand Total (including 877 officers) . .		12,647
		(589 prisoners).

The Confederates showed 5,309 casualties out of less than 30,000 actually engaged.

LEFT WING—LONGSTREET.

First Corps {	Ransom's Division	535
	McLaws' Division	858
	Anderson's Division	159
Artillery		37

(1,224 on December 12.)   Total . . 1,589

CENTRE.

First Corps {	Pickett's Division	54
	Hood's Division	251

Total . . 305

RIGHT WING—JACKSON.

Light Division	2,120
Early's Division	932
D. H. Hill's Division	173
Taliaferro's Division	190

Total (including 500 captured) . . 3,415

No attempt was made by the Confederates to follow the enemy across the Rappahannock. The upper fords were open; but the river was rising fast, and the Army of the Potomac, closely concentrated and within a few miles of Aquia Creek, was too large to be attacked, and too close to its base to permit effective manœuvres, which might induce it to divide, against its line of communications. The exultation of the Southern soldiers in their easy victory was dashed by disappointment. Burnside's escape had demonstrated the fallacy of one of the so-called rules of war. The great river which lay behind him during the battle of Fredericksburg had proved his salvation instead of—as it theoretically should—his ruin. Over the six bridges his troops had more lines of retreat than is usually the case when roads only are available; and these lines of retreat were secure, protected from the Confederate cavalry by the river, and from the infantry and artillery by the batteries on the Stafford Heights. Had the battle been fought on the North Anna, thirty-six miles from Fredericksburg, the result might have been very different. A direct counterstroke would possibly have been no more practicable

than on the Rappahannock, for the superior numbers of the
enemy, and his powerful artillery, could not have been disregarded.   Nor would a direct pursuit have been a certain
means of making success decisive ; the rear of a retreating
army, as the Confederates had found to their cost at Malvern
Hill, is usually its strongest part.   But a pursuit directed
against the flanks, striking the line of retreat, cutting off
the supply and ammunition trains, and blocking the roads,
a pursuit such as Jackson had organised when he drove
Banks from the Valley, if conducted with vigour, seldom
fails in its effect.   And who would have conducted such an
operation with greater skill and energy than Stuart, at the
head of his 9,000 horsemen ?   Who would have supported
Stuart more expeditiously than the ' foot-cavalry ' of the
Second Army Corps ?

Lee's position at Fredericksburg, strong as it might
appear, was exceedingly disadvantageous.   A position which
an army occupies with a view to decisive battle should
fulfil four requirements :—

1. It should not be too strong, or the enemy will not
attack it.

2. It should give cover to the troops both from view and
fire from artillery, and have a good field of fire.

3. It should afford facilities for counterstroke.

4. It should afford facilities for pursuit.

Of these Lee's battle-field fulfilled but the first and
second.   It would have been an admirable selection if the
sole object of the Confederates had been to gain time, or to
prevent the enemy establishing himself south of the Rappahannock; but to encompass the destruction of the enemy's
whole army it was as ill adapted as Wellington's position at
Torres Vedras, at Busaco, or at Fuentes d'Onor.   But while
Wellington in taking up these positions had no further end
in view than holding the French in check, the situation of
the Confederacy was such that a decisive victory was eminently desirable.   Nothing was to be gained by gaining time.
The South could furnish Lee with no further reinforcements.   Every able-bodied man was in the service of his
country ; and it was perfectly certain that the Western

armies, although they had been generally successful during the past year, would never be permitted by Mr. Davis to leave the valley of the Mississippi.

The Army of Northern Virginia was not likely to be stronger or more efficient. Equipped with the spoils of many victories, it was more on a level with the enemy than had hitherto been the case. The ranks were full. The men were inured to hardships and swift marches; their health was proof against inclement weather, and they knew their work on the field of battle. The artillery had recently been reorganised. During the Peninsular campaign the batteries had been attached to the infantry brigades, and the indifferent service they had often rendered had been attributed to the difficulty of collecting the scattered units, and in handling them in combination. Formed into battalions of four or six batteries a large number of guns was now attached to each of the divisions, and each army corps had a strong reserve; so that the concentration of a heavy force of artillery on any part of a position became a feasible operation. The cavalry, so admirably commanded by Stuart, Hampton, and the younger Lees, was not less hardy or efficient than the infantry, and the *moral* of the soldiers of every arm, founded on confidence in themselves not less than on confidence in their leaders, was never higher.

'After the truce had been agreed upon,' says Captain Smith, 'litter-bearers to bring away the dead and wounded were selected from the command of General Rodes. When they had fallen in, General Rodes said to them : " Now, boys, those Yankees are going to ask you questions, and you must not tell them anything. Be very careful about this." At this juncture one of the men spoke up, and said, " General, can't we tell them that we whipped them yesterday ? " Rodes replied, laughing : " Yes, yes ! you can tell them that." Immediately another man spoke up: " General, can't we tell them that we can whip them to-morrow and the day after ? " Rodes again laughed, and sent those incorrigible jokers off with : " Yes, yes! go on, go on ! Tell them what you please." '

The Army of the Potomac, on the other hand, was not

likely to become weaker or less formidable if time were
allowed it to recuperate.   It had behind it enormous
reserves.   60,000 men had been killed, wounded, or captured
since the battle of Kernstown, and yet the ranks were as
full as when McClellan first marched on Richmond.   Many
generals had disappeared ; but those who remained were
learning their trade ; and the soldiers, although more familiar
with defeat than victory, showed little diminution of martial
ardour.   Nor had the strain of the war sapped the resources
of the North.   Her trade, instead of dwindling, had actually
increased ; and the gaps made in the population by the
Confederate bullets were more than made good by a
constant influx of immigrants from Europe.

It was not by partial triumphs, not by the slaughter of
a few brigades, by defence without counterstroke, by
victories without pursuit, that a Power of such strength and
vitality could be compelled to confess her impotence.
Whether some overwhelming disaster, a Jena or a Waterloo,
followed by instant invasion, would have subdued her stubborn spirit is problematical.   Rome survived Cannæ, Scot-
land Flodden, and France Sedan.   But in some such ' crowning mercy ' lay the only hope of the Confederacy, and had
the Army of the Potomac, ill-commanded as it was, been
drawn forward to the North Anna, it might have been utterly
destroyed.   Half-hearted strategy, which aims only at repulsing the enemy's attack, is not the path to ' king-making
victory ; ' it is not by such feeble means that States secure
or protect their independence.   To occupy a position where
Stuart's cavalry was powerless, where the qualities which
made Lee's infantry so formidable—the impetuosity of their
attack, the swiftness of their marches—had no field for
display, and where the enemy had free scope for the employment of his artillery, his strongest arm, was but to postpone
the evil day.   It had been well for the Confederacy if
Stonewall Jackson, whose resolute strategy had but one aim,
and that aim the annihilation of the enemy, had been the
supreme director of her councils.   To paraphrase Mahan :
' The strategic mistake (in occupying a position for which
pursuit was impracticable) neutralised the tactical advantage

gained, thus confirming the military maxim that a strategic mistake is more serious and far-reaching in its effects than an error in tactics.'

Lee, however, was fettered by the orders of the Cabinet; and Mr. Davis and his advisers, more concerned with the importance of retaining an area of country which still furnished supplies than of annihilating the Army of the Potomac, and relying on European intervention rather than on the valour of the Southern soldier, were responsible for the occupation of the Fredericksburg position. In extenuation of their mistake it may, however, be admitted that the advantages of concentration on the North Anna were not such as would impress themselves on the civilian mind, while the surrender of territory would undoubtedly have embarrassed both the Government and the supply department. Moreover, at the end of November, it might have been urged that if Burnside were permitted to possess himself of Fredericksburg, it was by no means certain that he would advance on Richmond; establishing himself in winter quarters, he might wait until the weather improved, controlling, in the meantime, the resources and population of that portion of Virginia which lay within his reach.

Nevertheless, as events went far to prove, Mr. Davis would have done wisely had he accepted the advice of the soldiers on the spot. His strategical glance was less comprehensive than that of Lee and Jackson. In the first place, they knew that if Burnside proposed going into winter quarters, he would not deliberately place the Rappahannock between himself and his base, nor halt with the great forest of Spotsylvania on his flank. In the second place, there could be no question but that the Northern Government and the Northern people would impel him forward. The tone of the press was unmistakable; and the very reason that Burnside had been appointed to command was because McClellan was so slow to move. In the third place, both Lee and Jackson saw the need of decisive victory. With them questions of strategic dispositions, offering chances of such victory, were of more importance than questions

of supply or internal politics. They knew with what rapidity
the Federal soldiers recovered their *moral*; and they
realised but too keenly the stern determination which
inspired the North. They had seen the hosts of invasion
retire in swift succession, stricken and exhausted, before
their victorious bayonets. Thousands of prisoners had been
marched to Richmond; thousands of wounded, abandoned
on the battle-field, had been paroled; guns, waggons and
small arms, enough to equip a great army, had been captured;
and general after general had been reduced to the ignominy
that awaits a defeated leader. Frémont and Shields had
disappeared; Banks was no longer in the field; Porter was
waiting trial; McDowell had gone; Pope had gone, and
McClellan; and yet the Army of the Potomac still held its
ground, the great fleets still kept their stations, the capture
of Richmond was still the objective of the Union Government, and not for a single moment had Lincoln wavered
from his purpose.

It will not be asserted that either Lee or Jackson
fathomed the source of this unconquerable tenacity.
They had played with effect on the fears of Lincoln;
they had recognised in him the motive power of the
Federal hosts; but they had not yet learned, for the
Northern people themselves had not yet learned it, that
they were opposed by an adversary whose resolution was
as unyielding as their own, who loved the Union even as
they loved Virginia, and who ruled the nation with the
same tact and skill that they ruled their soldiers.

In these pages Mr. Lincoln has not been spared. He
made mistakes, and he himself would have been the last to
claim infallibility. He had entered the White House with
a rich endowment of common-sense, a high sense of duty,
and an extraordinary knowledge of the American character;
but his ignorance of statesmanship directing arms was great,
and his military errors were numerous. Putting these aside,
his tenure of office during the dark days of '61 and '62
had been marked by the very highest political sagacity; his
courage and his patriotism had sustained the nation in its
distress; and in spite of every obstacle he was gradually

bringing into being a unity of sympathy and of purpose, which in the early days of the war had seemed an impossible ideal. Not the least politic of his measures was the edict of emancipation, published after the battle of Sharpsburg. It was not a measure without flaw. It contained paragraphs which might fairly be interpreted, and were so interpreted by the Confederates, as inciting the negroes to rise against their masters, thus exposing to all the horrors of a servile insurrection, with its accompaniments of murder and outrage, the farms and plantations where the women and children of the South lived lonely and unprotected. But if the edict served only to embitter the Southerners, to bind the whole country together in a still closer league of resistance, and to make peace except by conquest impossible, it was worth the price. The party in the North which fought for the re-establishment of the Union had carried on the war with but small success. The tale of reverses had told at last upon recruiting. Men were unwilling to come forward ; and those who were bribed by large bounties to join the armies were of a different character to the original volunteer. Enthusiasm in the cause was fast diminishing when Lincoln, purely on his own initiative, proclaimed emancipation, and, investing the war with the dignity of a crusade, inspired the soldier with a new incentive, and appealed to a feeling which had not yet been stirred. Many Northerners had not thought it worth while to fight for the re-establishment of the Union on the basis of the Constitution. If slavery was to be permitted to continue they preferred separation ; and these men were farmers and agriculturists, the class which furnished the best soldiers, men of American birth, for the most part abolitionists, and ready to fight for the principle they had so much at heart. It is true that the effect of the edict was not at once apparent. It was not received everywhere with acclamation. The army had small sympathy with the coloured race, and the political opponents of the President accused him vehemently of unconstitutional action. Their denunciations, however, missed the mark. The letter of the Constitution, as Mr. Lincoln clearly saw, had ceased to be regarded, at least by the great bulk of the people, with superstitious reverence.

They had learned to think more of great principles than of political expedients; and if the defence of their hereditary rights had welded the South into a nation, the assertion of a still nobler principle, the liberty of man, placed the North on a higher plane, enlisted the sympathy of Europe, and completed the isolation of the Confederacy.

But although Lee and Jackson had not yet penetrated the political genius of their great antagonist, they rated at its true value the vigour displayed by his Administration, and they saw that something more was wanting to wrest their freedom from the North than a mere passive resistance to the invader's progress. Soon after the battle of Fredericksburg, Lee went to Richmond and laid proposals for an aggressive campaign before the President. 'He was assured, however,' says General Longstreet, 'that the war was virtually over, and that we need not harass our troops by marches and other hardships. Gold had advanced in New York to two hundred premium, and we were told by those in the Confederate capital that in thirty or forty days we would be recognised (by the European Powers) and peace proclaimed. General Lee did not share this belief.' [1]

So Jackson, who had hoped to return to Winchester, was doomed to the inaction of winter quarters on the Rappahannock, for with Burnside's repulse operations practically ceased. The Confederate cavalry, however, did not at once abandon hostilities. On December 18, Hampton marched his brigade as far as the village of Occoquan, bringing off 150 prisoners and capturing a convoy; and on December 26 Stuart closed his record for 1862 by leading 1,800 troopers far to the Federal rear. After doing much damage in the district about Occoquan and Dumfries, twenty miles from Burnside's headquarters, he marched northward in the direction of Washington, and penetrated as far as Burke's Station, fifteen miles from Alexandria. Sending a telegraphic

Dec. 18.

Dec. 26.

[1] *Battles and Leaders*, vol. iii., p. 84.

message to General Meigs, Quartermaster-General at Washington, to the effect that the mules furnished to Burnside's army were of such bad quality that he was embarrassed in taking the waggons he had captured into the Confederate lines, and requesting that a better class of animal might be supplied in future, he returned by long marches through Warrenton to Culpeper Court House, escaping pursuit, and bringing with him a large amount of plunder and many prisoners. From the afternoon of December 26 to nightfall on December 31 he rode one hundred and fifty miles, losing 28 officers and men in skirmishes with detachments of the Federal cavalry. He had contrived to throw a great part of the troops sent to meet him into utter confusion by intercepting their telegrams, and answering them himself in a manner that scattered his pursuers and broke down their horses.

Near the end of January, Burnside made a futile attempt to march his army round Lee's flank by way of Ely's and Germanna Fords. The weather, however, was inclement ; the roads were in a fearful condition, and the troops experienced such difficulty in movement, that the operation, which goes by the name of the ' Mud Campaign,' was soon abandoned.

On January 26, Burnside, in consequence of the strong 1863. representations made by his lieutenants to the Jan. 26. President, was superseded. General Hooker, the dashing fighter of the Antietam, replaced him in command of the Army of the Potomac, and the Federal troops went into winter quarters about Falmouth, where, on the opposite shore of the Rappahannock, within full view of the sentries, stood a row of finger-posts, on which the Confederate soldiers had painted the taunting legend, ' This way to Richmond ! '

CHAPTER XXI

THE ARMY OF NORTHERN VIRGINIA

' In war men are nothing; it is the man who is everything. The general is the head, the whole of an army. It was not the Roman army that conquered Gaul, but Cæsar; it was not the Carthaginian army that made Rome tremble in her gates, but Hannibal; it was not the Macedonian army that reached the Indus, but Alexander; it was not the French army that carried the war to the Weser and the Inn, but Turenne; it was not the Prussian army which, for seven years, defended Prussia against the three greatest Powers of Europe, but Frederick the Great.' So spoke Napoleon, reiterating a truth confirmed by the experience of successive ages, that a wise direction is of more avail than overwhelming numbers, sound strategy than the most perfect armament; a powerful will, invigorating all who come within its sphere, than the spasmodic efforts of ill-regulated valour.

Even a professional army of long standing and old traditions is what its commander makes it; its character sooner or later becomes the reflex of his own; from him the officers take their tone; his energy or his inactivity, his firmness or vacillation, are rapidly communicated even to the lower ranks; and so far-reaching is the influence of the leader, that those who record his campaigns concern themselves but little as a rule with the men who followed him. The history of famous armies is the history of great generals, for no army has ever achieved great things unless it has been well commanded. If the general be second-rate the army also will be second-rate. Mutual confidence is the basis of success in war, and unless the troops have implicit trust in the resolution and resources of their chief, hesitation and half-heartedness are sure to mark their actions. They may fight with their accustomed courage; but the eagerness for the conflict, the alacrity to support, the determination to conquer, will not be there. The indefinable quality which is expressed by the word *moral* will to some degree be affected. The history of the Army of the Potomac is a case in point.

Between the soldiers of the North and South there was little difference. Neither could claim a superiority of martial qualities. The Confederates, indeed, at the beginning of the war possessed a larger measure of technical skill; they were the better shots and the finer riders. But they were neither braver nor more enduring, and while they probably derived some advantage from the fact that they were defending their homes, the Federals, defending the integrity of their native land, were fighting in the noblest of all causes. But Northerner and Southerner were of the same race, a race proud, resolute, independent; both were inspired by the same sentiments of self-respect; *noblesse oblige*—the *noblesse* of a free people—was the motto of the one as of the other. It has been asserted that the Federal armies were very largely composed of foreigners, whose motives for enlisting were purely mercenary. At no period of the war, however, did the proportion of native Americans sink below seventy per cent.,[1] and at the beginning of 1863 it was much greater. As a matter of fact, the Union army was composed of thoroughly staunch soldiers.[2]

[1] See Note at end of chapter.

[2] 'Throughout New England,' wrote the Special Correspondent of an English newspaper, ' you can scarcely enter a door without being aware that you are in a house of mourning. Whatever may be said of Irish and German mercenaries, I must bear witness that the best classes of Americans have bravely come forth for their country. I know of scarcely a family more than one member of which has not been or is not in the ranks of the army. The maimed and crippled youths I meet on the highroad certainly do not for the most part belong to the immigrant rabble of which the Northern regiments are said to consist; and even the present conscription is now in many splendid instances most promptly and cheerfully complied with by the wealthy people who could easily purchase exemption, but who prefer to set a good example.' Letter from Rhode Island, the *Times*, August 8, 1863.

Nor was the alien element at this time a source of weakness. Ireland and Germany supplied the greater number of those who have been called 'Lincoln's hirelings;' and, judging from the official records, the Irish regiments at least were not a whit less trustworthy than those purely American. Moreover, even if the admixture of foreigners had been greater, the Army of the Potomac, for the reason that it was always superior in numbers, contained in its ranks many more men bred in the United States than the Army of Northern Virginia.[1] For the consistent ill-success of the Federals the superior marksmanship and finer horsemanship of the Confederates cannot, therefore, be accepted as sufficient explanation.

In defence the balance of endurance inclined neither to one side nor the other. Both Southerner and Northerner displayed that stubborn resolve to maintain their ground which is the peculiar attribute of the Anglo-Saxon. To claim for any one race a pre-eminence of valour is repugnant alike to good taste and to sound sense. Courage and endurance are widely distributed over the world's surface, and political institutions, the national conception of duty, the efficiency of the corps of officers, and love of country, are the foundation of vigour and staunchness in the field. Yet it is a fact which can hardly be ignored, that from Crécy to Inkermann there have been exceedingly few instances where an English army, large or small, has been driven from a position. In the great struggle with France, neither Napoleon nor his marshals, although the armies of every other European nation had fled before them, could boast of having broken the English infantry; and no soldiers have ever received a prouder tribute than the admission of a generous enemy, 'They never know when they are beaten.' In America, the characteristics of the parent race were as prominent in the Civil War as they had been in the Revolution. In 1861–65, the side that stood on the defensive, unless hopelessly outnumbered, was almost

---

[1] John Mitchell, the Irish Nationalist, said in a letter to the Dublin *Nation* that there were 40,000 Irishmen in the Southern armies. The *Times*, February 7, 1863.

invariably successful, just as it had been in 1776–82.
'My men,' said Jackson, 'sometimes fail to drive the
enemy from his position, but to hold one, never!' The
Federal generals might have made the same assertion with
almost equal truth. Porter had indeed been defeated at
Gaines' Mill, but he could only set 35,000 in line against
55,000; Banks had been overwhelmed at Winchester, but
6,500 men could hardly have hoped to resist more than
twice their strength; and Shields' advanced-guard at Port
Republic was much inferior to the force which Jackson
brought against it; yet these were the only offensive victories
of the '62 campaign. But if in defence the armies were
well matched, it must be conceded that the Northern attack
was not pressed with the same concentrated vigour as the
Southern. McClellan at Sharpsburg had more than twice
as many men as Lee; Pope, on the first day of the Second
Manassas, twice as many as Jackson; yet on both occasions the smaller force was victorious. But, in the first
place, the Federal tactics in attack were always feeble.
Lincoln, in appointing Hooker to command the Army
of the Potomac, warned him 'to put in all his men.'
His sharp eye had detected the great fault which had
characterised the operations of his generals. Their
assaults had been piecemeal, like those of the Confederates
at Malvern Hill, and they had been defeated in detail by
the inferior numbers. The Northern soldiers were strangers
to those general and combined attacks, pressed with unyielding resolution, which had won Winchester, Gaines'
Mill, and the Second Manassas, and which had nearly
won Kernstown. The Northern generals invariably kept
large masses in reserve, and these masses were never used.
They had not yet learned, as had Lee, Jackson, and Longstreet, that superior numbers are of no avail unless they
are brought into action, impelling the attack forward by
sheer weight, at the decisive point. In the second place, none
of the Federal leaders possessed the entire confidence either
of their generals or their troops. With all its affection
for McClellan, it may strongly be questioned whether his
army gave him credit for dash or resolution. Pope was

defeated in his first action at Cedar Run.   Banks at
Winchester, Frémont west of Staunton, had both been out-
manœuvred.   Burnside had against him his feeble conduct
at Sharpsburg.   Hence the Federal soldiers fought most of
their offensive battles under a terrible disadvantage.   They
were led by men who had known defeat, and who owed
their defeat, in great measure, to the same fault—neglect to
employ their whole force in combination.   Brave and unyielding as they were, the troops went into battle mistrustful
of their leader's skill, and fearful, from the very outset, that
their efforts would be unsupported ; and when men begin
to look over their shoulders for reinforcements, demoralisation is not far off.   It would be untrue to say that a
defeated general can never regain the confidence of
his soldiers ; but unless he has previous successes to
set off against his failure, to permit him to retain
his position is dangerous in the extreme.   Such was
the opinion of Jackson, always solicitous of the *moral* of his
command.   ' To his mind nothing ever fully excused failure,
and it was rarely that he gave an officer the opportunity of
failing twice.   "The service," he said, " cannot afford to
keep a man who does not succeed."   Nor was he ever
restrained from a change by the fear of making matters
worse.   His motto was, get rid of the unsuccessful man at
once, and trust to Providence for finding a better.'

Nor was the presence of discredited generals the only
evil which went to neutralise the valour of the Federal
soldiers.   The system of command was as rotten in the
Army of the Potomac as in the Armies of Northern Virginia
and of the Valley it was sound ; and the system of command plays a most important part in war.   The natural
initiative of the American, the general fearlessness of responsibility, were as conspicuous among the soldiers as in
the nation at large.   To those familiar with the Official
Records, where the doings of regiments and even companies
are preserved, it is perfectly apparent that, so soon as the
officers gained experience, the smaller units were as boldly
and efficiently handled as in the army of Germany under
Moltke.   But while Lee and Jackson, by every means in

their power, fostered the capacity for independent action, following therein the example of Napoleon,[1] of Washington, of Nelson, and of Wellington, and aware that their strength would thus be doubled, McClellan and Pope did their best to stifle it; and in the higher ranks they succeeded. In the one case the generals were taught to wait for orders, in the other to anticipate them. In the one case, whether troops were supported or not depended on the word of the commanding general; in the other, every officer was taught that to sustain his colleagues was his first duty. It thus resulted that while the Confederate leaders were served by scores of zealous assistants, actively engaged in furthering the aim of their superiors, McClellan, Pope, and Frémont, jealous of power reduced their subordinates, with few ex-ceptions, to the position of machines, content to obey the letter of their orders, oblivious of opportunity, and incapable of co-operation. Lee and Jackson appear to have realised the requirements of battle far more fully than their opponents. They knew that the scope of the commander is limited; that once his troops are committed to close action it is impossible for him to exert further control, for his orders can no longer reach them; that he cannot keep the whole field under observation, much less observe every fleeting opportunity. Yet it is by utilising opportunities that the enemy's strength is sapped. For these reasons the Confederate generals were exceedingly careful not to chill the spirit of enterprise. Errors of judgment were never considered in the light of crimes; while the officer who, in default of orders, remained inactive, or who, when his orders were manifestly inapplicable to a suddenly changed situation, and there was no time to have them altered, dared not act for himself, was not long retained in responsible command. In the Army of the Potomac, on the other hand, centralisation was the rule. McClellan

---

[1] In the opinion of the author, the charge of centralisation preferred against Napoleon can only be applied to his leading in his later campaigns. In his earlier operations he gave his generals every latitude, and he main-tained that loose but effective system of tactics, in which much was left to the individual, adopted by the French army just previous to the wars of the Revolution.

expected blind obedience from his corps commanders, and nothing more, and Pope brought Porter to trial for using his own judgment, on occasions when Pope himself was absent, during the campaign of the Second Manassas. Thus the Federal soldiers, through no fault of their own, laboured for the first two years of the war under a disadvantage from which the wisdom of Lee and Jackson had relieved the Confederates. The Army of the Potomac was an inert mass, the Army of Northern Virginia a living organism, endowed with irresistible vigour.

It is to be noted, too, as tending to prove the equal courage of North and South, that on the Western theatre of war the Federals were the more successful. And yet the Western armies of the Confederacy were neither less brave, less hardy, nor less disciplined than those in Virginia. They were led, however, by inferior men, while, on the other hand, many of the Northern generals opposed to them possessed unquestionable ability, and understood the value of a good system of command.

We may say, then, without detracting an iota from the high reputation of the Confederate soldiers, that it was not the Army of Northern Virginia that saved Richmond in 1862, but Lee; not the Army of the Valley which won the Valley campaign, but Jackson.

It is related that a good priest, once a chaplain in Taylor's Louisiana brigade, concluded his prayer at the unveiling of the Jackson monument in New Orleans with these remarkable words: 'When in Thine inscrutable decree it was ordained that the Confederacy should fail, it became necessary for Thee to remove Thy servant Stonewall Jackson.'[1] It is unnecessary, perhaps, to lay much forcible emphasis on the personal factor, but, at the same time, it is exceedingly essential that it should never be overlooked.

The Government which, either in peace or war, commits the charge of its armed forces to any other than the ablest and most experienced soldier the country can produce is but laying the foundation of national disaster. Had the

[1] *Bright Skies and Dark Shadows*, p. 294. H. M. Field, D.D.

importance of a careful selection for the higher commands been understood in the North as it was understood in the South, Lee and Jackson would have been opposed by foes more formidable than Pope and Burnside, or Banks and Frémont. The Federal Administration, confident in the courage and intelligence of their great armies, considered that any ordinary general, trained to command, and supported by an efficient staff, should be able to win victories. Mr. Davis, on the other hand, himself a soldier, who, as United States Secretary of War, had enjoyed peculiar opportunities of estimating the character of the officers of the old army, made no such mistake. He was not always, indeed, either wise or consistent; but, with few exceptions, his appointments were the best that could be made, and he was ready to accept the advice, as regarded selections for command, of his most experienced generals.

But however far-reaching may be the influence of a great leader, in estimating his capacity the temper of the weapon that he wielded can hardly be overlooked. In the first place, that temper, to a greater or less degree, must have been of his own forging,—it is part of his fame. 'No man,' says Napier, 'can be justly called a great captain who does not know how to organise and form the character of an army, as well as to lead it when formed.' In the second place, to do much with feeble means is greater than to do more with large resources. Difficulties are inherent in all military operations, and not the least may be the constitution of the army. Nor would the story of Stonewall Jackson be more than half told without large reference to those tried soldiers, subalterns and private soldiers as they were, whom he looked upon as his comrades, whose patriotism and endurance he extolled so highly, and whose devotion to himself, next to the approval of his own conscience, was the reward that most he valued.

He is blind indeed who fails to recognise the unselfish patriotism displayed by the citizen-soldiers of America, the stern resolution with which the war was waged; the tenacity of the Northerner, ill-commanded and con-

stantly defeated, fighting in a most difficult country and
foiled on every line of invasion; the tenacity of the
Southerner, confronting enormous odds, ill-fed, ill-armed,
and ill-provided, knowing that if wounded his sufferings
would be great—for drugs had been declared contraband of
war, the hospitals contained no anæsthetics to relieve the
pain of amputation, and the surgical instruments, which
were only replaced when others were captured, were worn
out with constant usage; knowing too that his women-folk
and children were in want, and yet never yielding to
despair nor abandoning hope of ultimate victory.   Neither
Federal nor Confederate deemed his life the most precious
of his earthly possessions.   Neither New Englander nor Virginian ever for one moment dreamt of surrendering, no matter
what the struggle might cost, a single acre of the territory,
a single item of the civil rights, which had been handed
down to him. ' I do not profess,' said Jackson, ' any romantic
sentiments as to the vanity of life.   Certainly no man has
more that should make life dear to him than I have, in the
affection of my home; but I do not desire to survive the
independence of my country.'   And Jackson's attitude was
that of his fellow-countrymen.   The words of Naboth,
' Jehovah forbid that I should give to thee the inheritance of
my forefathers,' were graven on the heart of both North and
South; and the unknown and forgotten heroes who fought
in the ranks of either army, and who fought for a principle,
not on compulsion or for glory, are worthy of the highest
honours that history can bestow.

Nor can a soldier withhold his tribute of praise to the
capacity for making war which distinguished the American
citizen.   The intelligence of the rank and file played an
important *rôle* in every phase of a campaign.   As skirmishers,—and modern battles, to a very great extent, are
fought out by lines of skirmishers—their work was admirable; and when the officers were struck down, or when
command, by reason of the din and excitement, became impossible, the self-dependence of the individual asserted itself
with the best effect.[1]   The same quality which the German

[1] The historical student may profitably compare with the American

training had sought to foster, and which, according to
Moltke,[1] had much to do with the victories of 1870, was in-
born in both Northerner and Southerner. On outpost and
on patrol, in seeking information and in counteracting the
ruses of the enemy, the keen intelligence of the educated
volunteer was of the utmost value. History has hitherto
overlooked the achievements of the ' scouts,' whose names so
seldom occur in the Official Records, but whose daring was
unsurpassed, and whose services were of vast importance. In the Army of Northern Virginia every commanding general had his own party of scouts, whose business
it was to penetrate the enemy's lines, to see everything and
to hear everything, to visit the base of operations, to inspect
the line of communications, and to note the condition and
the temper of the hostile troops. Attracted by a pure
love of adventure, these private soldiers did exactly the same
work as did the English Intelligence officers in the Peninsula, and did it with the same thoroughness and acuteness.
Wellington, deploring the capture of Captain Colquhoun
Grant, declared that the gallant Highlander was worth as
much to the army as a brigade of cavalry; Jackson had scouts
who were more useful to him than many of his brigadiers.
Again, in constructing hasty intrenchments, the soldiers
needed neither assistance nor impulsion. The rough cover
thrown up by the men when circumstances demanded it, on
their own volition, was always adapted to the ground, and
generally fulfilled the main principles of fortification. For
bridge-building, for road-making, for the destruction, the
repair, and even the making, of railroads, skilled labour was
always forthcoming from the ranks; and the soldiers
stamped the impress of their individuality on the tactics
of the infantry. Modern formations, to a very large extent, had their origin on American battle-fields. The men
realised very quickly the advantages of shelter; the advance
by rushes from one cover to another, and the gradually working up, by this method, of the firing-line to effective range—

soldier the Armies of Revolutionary France, in which education and intelligence were also conspicuous.
    [1] *Official Account of the Franco-German War*, vol. ii., p. 168.

the method which all experience shows to be the true one
—became the general rule.

That the troops had faults, however, due in great
part to the fact that their intelligence was not thoroughly
trained, and to the inexperience of their officers, it is impossible to deny.

' I agree with you,' wrote Lee in 1863, ' in believing that
our army would be invincible if it could be properly organised
and officered.   There were never such men in an army
before.   They will go anywhere and do anything if properly
led. But there is the difficulty—proper commanders. Where
can they be obtained? But they are improving—constantly
improving. Rome was not built in a day, nor can we expect
miracles in our favour.' [1]   Yet, taking them all in all, the
American rank and file of 1863, with their native characteristics, supplemented by a great knowledge of war, were in
advance of any soldiers of their time.

In the actual composition of the Confederate forces no
marked change had taken place since the beginning of the
war.   But the character of the army, in many essential
respects, had become sensibly modified. The men encamped
on the Rappahannock were no longer the raw recruits who
had blundered into victory at the First Manassas ; nor were
they the unmanageable divisions of the Peninsula.   They
were still, for the most part, volunteers, for conscripts in the
Army of Northern Virginia were not numerous, but they were
volunteers of a very different type from those who had fought
at Kernstown or at Gaines' Mill. Despite their protracted
absence from their homes, the wealthy and well-born privates
still shouldered the musket.   Though many had been promoted to commissions, the majority were content to set an example of self-sacrifice and sterling patriotism, and the regiments were thus still leavened with a large admixture of educated and intelligent men.   It is a significant fact that during
those months of 1863 which were spent in winter quarters
Latin, Greek, mathematical, and even Hebrew classes were
instituted by the soldiers.   But all trace of social distinction had long since vanished. Between the rich planter

---

[1] Lee to Hood, May 21, 1863; *Advance and Retreat*, p. 53.

and the small farmer or mechanic there was no difference either in aspect or habiliments. Tanned by the hot Virginia sun, thin-visaged and bright-eyed, gaunt of frame and spare of flesh, they were neither more nor less than the rank and file of the Confederate army; the product of discipline and hard service, moulded after the same pattern, with the same hopes and fears, the same needs, the same sympathies. They looked at life from a common standpoint, and that standpoint was not always elevated. Human nature claimed its rights. When his hunger was satisfied and, to use his own expression, 'he was full of hog and hominy,' the Confederate soldier found time to discuss the operations in which he was engaged. Pipe in mouth, he could pass in review the strategy and tactics of both armies, the capacity of his generals, and the bearing of his enemies, and on each one of these questions, for he was the shrewdest of observers, his comments were always to the point. He had studied his profession in a practical school. The more delicate moves of the great game were topics of absorbing interest. He cast a comprehensive glance over the whole theatre; he would puzzle out the reasons for forced marches and sudden changes of direction; his curiosity was great, but intelligent, and the groups round the camp-fires often forecast with surprising accuracy the manœuvres that the generals were planning. But far more often the subjects of conversation were of a more immediate and personal character. The capacity of the company cook, the quality of the last consignment of boots, the merits of different bivouacs, the prospect of the supply train coming up to time, the temper of the captain and subaltern—such were the topics which the Confederate privates spent their leisure in discussing. They had long since discovered that war is never romantic and seldom exciting, but a monotonous round of tiresome duties, enlivened at rare intervals by dangerous episodes. They had become familiar with its constant accompaniment of privations—bad weather, wet bivouacs, and wretched roads, wood that would not kindle, and rations that did not satisfy. They had learned that a soldier's worst enemy

may be his native soil, in the form of dust or mud; that
it is possible to march for months without firing a shot
or seeing a foe; that a battle is an interlude which breaks in
at rare intervals on the long round of digging, marching,
bridge-building, and road-making; and that the time of
the fiercest fire-eater is generally occupied in escorting mule-
trains, in mounting guard, in dragging waggons through
the mud, and in loading or unloading stores. Volunteering
for perilous and onerous duties, for which hundreds had
eagerly offered themselves in the early days, ere the
glamour of the soldier's life had vanished, had ceased
to be popular. The men were now content to wait
for orders; and as discipline crystallised into habit, they
became resigned to the fact that they were no longer
volunteers, masters of their own actions, but the paid
servants of the State, compelled to obey and powerless to
protest.

To all outward appearance, then, in the spring of 1863
the Army of Northern Virginia bore an exceedingly close
resemblance to an army of professional soldiers. It is true
that military etiquette was not insisted on; that more
license, both in quarters and on the march, was permitted
than would be the case in a regular army; that officers
were not treated with the same respect; and that tact,
rather than the strict enforcement of the regulations, was
the key-note of command. Nevertheless, taken as a whole,
the Confederate soldiers were exceedingly well-conducted.
The good elements in the ranks were too strong for those
who were inclined to resist authority, and the amount of
misbehaviour was wonderfully small. There was little
neglect of duty. Whatever the intelligence of the men
told them was necessary for success, for safety, or for
efficiency, was done without reluctance. The outposts
were seldom caught napping. Digging and tree-felling—
for the men had learned the value of making fortifications
and good roads—were taken as a matter of course. Nor
was the Southern soldier a grumbler. He accepted half-
rations and muddy camping-grounds without remonstrance;
if his boots wore out he made shift to march without

them ; and when his uniform fell to pieces he waited for the next victory to supply himself with a new outfit. He was enough of a philosopher to know that it is better to meet misery with a smile than with a scowl. Mark Tapley had many prototypes in the Confederate ranks, and the men were never more facetious than when things were at their worst. 'The very intensity of their sufferings became a source of merriment. Instead of growling and deserting, they laughed at their own bare feet, ragged clothes, and pinched faces ; and weak, hungry, cold, wet and dirty, with no hope of reward or rest, they marched cheerfully to meet the warmly clad and well-fed hosts of the enemy.'[1] Indomitable indeed were the hearts that beat beneath the grey jackets, and a spirit rising superior to all misfortune,

> That ever with a frolic welcome took
> The thunder and the sunshine,

was a marked characteristic of the Confederate soldier. Nor was it only in camp or on the march that the temper of the troops betrayed itself in reckless gaiety.[2] The stress of battle might thin their ranks, but it was powerless to check their laughter. The dry humour of the American found a fine field in the incidents of a fierce engagement. Nothing escaped without remark : the excitement of a general, the accelerated movements of the non-combatants, the vagaries of the army mule, the bad practice of the artillery—all afforded entertainment. And when the fight became hotter and the Federals pressed

[1] *Soldier Life in the Army of Northern Virginia.*

[2] General Longstreet relates an amusing story :—' One of the soldiers, during the investment of Suffolk (April 1863), carefully constructed and equipped a full-sized man, dressed in a new suit of improved "butternut" clothing ; and christening him Julius Cæsar, took him to a signal platform which overlooked the works, adjusted him to a graceful position, and made him secure to the framework by strong cords. A little after sunrise "Julius Cæsar" was discovered by some of the Federal battery officers, who prepared for the target so inviting to skilful practice. The new soldier sat under the hot fire with irritating indifference until the Confederates, unable to restrain their hilarity, exposed the joke by calling for "Three cheers for Julius Cæsar ! " The other side quickly recognised the situation, and good-naturedly added to ours their cheers for the old hero.'— *From Manassas to Appomattox.*

resolutely to the attack, the flow of badinage took a
grim and peculiar turn. It has already been related that
the Confederate armies depended, to a large degree, for
their clothing and equipments on what they captured.
So abundant was this source of supply, that the soldier had
come to look upon his enemy as a movable magazine of
creature comforts ; and if he marched cheerfully to battle,
it was not so much because he loved fighting, but that
he hoped to renew his wardrobe. A victory was much, but
the spoils of victory were more. No sooner, then, did the
Federals arrive within close range, than the wild yells of
the Southern infantry became mingled with fierce laughter
and derisive shouts. 'Take off them boots, Yank !' 'Come
out of them clothes ; we're gwine to have them !' 'Come on,
blue-bellies, we want them blankets !' 'Bring them rations
along ! You've got to leave them !'—such were the cries,
like the howls of half-famished wolves, that were heard along
Jackson's lines at Fredericksburg.[1] And they were not raised
in mockery. The battle-field was the soldier's harvest, and
as the sheaves of writhing forms, under the muzzles of their
deadly rifles, increased in length and depth, the men listened
with straining ears for the word to charge. The counterstroke was their opportunity. The rush with the bayonet
was never so speedy but that deft fingers found time to rifle
the haversacks of the fallen, and such was the eagerness for
booty that it was with the greatest difficulty that the troops
were dragged off from the pursuit. It is said that at Fredericksburg, some North Carolina regiments, which had re-

---

[1] 'During the truce on the second day of Fredericksburg,' says Captain
Smith, 'a tall, fine-looking Alabama soldier, who was one of the litter-bearers,
picked up a new Enfield rifle on the neutral ground, examined it, tested the
sights, shouldered it, and was walking back to the Confederate lines, when
a young Federal officer, very handsomely dressed and mounted, peremptorily
ordered him to throw it down, telling him he had no right to take it. The
soldier, with the rifle on his shoulder, walked very deliberately round the officer,
scanning him from head to foot, and then started again towards our lines.
On this the Federal lieutenant, drawing his little sword, galloped after him,
and ordered him with an oath to throw down the rifle. The soldier halted,
then walked round the officer once again, very slowly, looking him up and
down, and at last said, pointing to his fine boots : "I shall shoot you to-
morrow, and get them boots ; " then strode away to his command. The
lieutenant made no attempt to follow.'

pulsed and followed up a Federal brigade, were hardly to be restrained from dashing into the midst of the enemy's reserves, and when at length they were turned back their complaints were bitter. The order to halt and retire seemed to them nothing less than rank injustice. Half-crying with disappointment, they accused their generals of favouritism! 'They don't want the North Car'linians to git anything,' they whined. 'They wouldn't hev' stopped Hood's " Texicans "—they'd hev' let *them* go on! '

But if they relieved their own pressing wants at the expense of their enemies, if they stripped the dead, and exchanged boots and clothing with their prisoners, seldom getting the worst of the bargain, no armies—to their lasting honour be it spoken, for no armies were so destitute—were ever less formidable to peaceful citizens, within the border or beyond it, than those of the Confederacy. It was exceedingly seldom that wanton damage was laid to the soldier's charge. The rights of non-combatants were religiously respected, and the farmers of Pennsylvania were treated with the same courtesy and consideration as the planters of Virginia. A village was none the worse for the vicinity of a Confederate bivouac, and neither man nor woman had reason to dread the half-starved tatterdemalions who followed Lee and Jackson. As the grey columns, in the march through Maryland, swung through the streets of those towns where the Unionist sentiment was strong, the women, standing in the porches, waved the Stars and Stripes defiantly in their faces. But the only retort of ' the dust brown ranks' was a volley of jests, not always unmixed with impudence. The personal attributes of their fair enemies did not escape observation. The damsel whose locks were of conspicuous hue was addressed as ' bricktop' until she screamed with rage, and threatened to fire into the ranks ; while the maiden of sour visage and uncertain years was saluted as 'Ole Miss Vinegar ' by a whole division of infantry. But this was the limit of the soldier's resentment. At the same time, when in the midst of plenty he was not impeccable. For highway robbery and housebreaking he had no inclination, but he was by no means above petty larceny. Pigs and poultry, fruit, corn, vegetables and fence-rails, he looked upon as his lawful perquisites.

He was the most cunning of foragers, and neither stringent orders nor armed guards availed to protect a field of maize or a patch of potatoes; the traditional negro was not more skilful in looting a fowl-house;[1] he had an unerring scent for whisky or 'apple-jack;' and the address he displayed in compassing the destruction of the unsuspecting porker was only equalled, when he was caught *flagrante delicto*, by the ingenuity of his excuses. According to the Confederate private, the most inoffensive animals, in the districts through which the armies marched, developed a strange pugnacity, and if bullet and bayonet were used against them, it was solely in self-defence.

But such venial faults, common to every army, and almost justified by the deficiencies of the Southern commissariat, were more than atoned for when the enemy was met. Of the prowess of Lee's veterans sufficient has been said. Their deeds speak for themselves. But it was not the battle-field alone that bore witness to their fortitude. German soldiers have told us that in the war of 1870, when their armies, marching on Paris, found, to their astonishment, the great city strongly garrisoned, and hosts gathering in every quarter for its relief, a singular apathy took possession of the troops. The explanation offered by a great military writer is that 'after a certain period even the victor becomes tired of war;' and 'the more civilised,' he adds, 'a people is, the more quickly will this weakness become apparent.'[2] Whether this explanation be adequate is not easy to decide. The fact remains, however, that the Confederate volunteer was able to overcome that longing for home which chilled the enthusiasm of the German conscript. And this is the more remarkable, inasmuch as his career was not one of unchequered victory. In the spring of 1863, the Army of the Potomac, more numerous than ever, was still before

---

[1] Despite Lee's proclamations against indiscriminate foraging, 'the hens,' he said, 'had to roost mighty high when the Texans were about.'
[2] *The Conduct of War.* Von der Goltz.

him, firmly established on Virginian soil; hope of foreign intervention, despite the assurances of the politicians, was gradually fading, and it was but too evident that the war was far from over. Yet at no time during their two years of service had the soldiers shown the slightest sign of that discouragement which seized the Germans after two months. And who shall dare to say that the Southerner was less highly civilised than the Prussian or the Bavarian? Political liberty, freedom of speech and action, are the real elements of civilisation, and not merely education. But let the difference in the constitution of the two armies be borne in mind. The Confederates, with few exceptions, were volunteers, who had become soldiers of their own choice, who had assumed arms deliberately and without compulsion, and who by their own votes were responsible that war had been declared. The Germans were conscripts, a dumb, powerless, irresponsible multitude, animated, no doubt, by hereditary hatred of the enemy, but without that sense of moral obligation which exists in the volunteer. We may be permitted, then, to believe that this sense of moral obligation was one reason why the spirit of the Southerners rose superior to human weakness, and that the old adage, which declares that 'one volunteer is better than three pressed men,' is not yet out of date. Nor is it an unfair inference that the armies of the Confederacy, allied by the 'crimson thread of kinship' to those of Wellington, of Raglan, and of Clyde, owed much of their enduring fortitude to ' the rock whence they were hewn.'

And yet, with all their admirable qualities, the Southern soldiers had not yet got rid of their original defects. Temperate, obedient, and well-conducted, small as was the percentage of bad characters and habitual misdoers, their discipline was still capable of improvement. The assertion, at first sight, seems a contradiction in terms. How could troops, it may be asked, who so seldom infringed the regulations be other than well-disciplined? For the simple reason that discipline in quarters is an absolutely different quality from discipline in battle. No large body of

intelligent men, assembled in a just cause and of good
character, is likely to break out into excesses, or, if obedience
is manifestly necessary, to rebel against authority.   Subordination to the law is the distinguishing mark of all
civilised society.   But such subordination, however praise-
worthy, is not the discipline of the soldier, though it is often
confounded with it.   A regiment of volunteers, billeted in
some country town, would probably show a smaller list of
misdemeanours than a regiment of regulars.   Yet the latter
might be exceedingly well-disciplined, and the former have
no real discipline whatever.   Self-respect—for that is the
discipline of the volunteer—is not battle discipline, the
discipline of the cloth, of habit, of tradition, of constant
association and of mutual confidence.   Self-respect, excellent in itself, and by no means unknown amongst regular
soldiers, does not carry with it a mechanical obedience to
command, nor does it merge the individual in the mass, and
give the tremendous power of unity to the efforts of large
numbers.

It will not be pretended that the discipline of regular
troops always rises superior to privation and defeat.   It
is a notorious fact that the number of deserters from
Wellington's army in Spain and Portugal, men who
wilfully absented themselves from the colours and wan-
dered over the country, was by no means inconsiderable;
while the behaviour of the French regulars in 1870, and
even of the Germans, when they rushed back in panic
through the village of Gravelotte, deaf to the threats
and entreaties of their aged sovereign, was hardly in
accordance with military tradition.   Nevertheless, it is not
difficult to show that the Southerners fell somewhat short
of the highest standard.   They were certainly not incapable
of keeping their ranks under a hot fire, or of holding
their ground to the last extremity.   Pickett's charge at
Gettysburg is one of the most splendid examples of disciplined valour in the annals of war, and the endurance of
Lee's army at Sharpsburg has seldom been surpassed.   Nor
was the disorder into which the attacking lines were sooner
or later thrown a proof of inferior training.   Even in the

days of flint-lock muskets, the admixture of not only companies and battalions, but even of brigades and divisions, was a constant feature of fierce assaults over broken ground. If, under such conditions, the troops still press forward, and if, when success has been achieved, order is rapidly restored, then discipline is good ; and in neither respect did the Confederates fail. But to be proof against disorder is not everything in battle. It is not sufficient that the men should be capable of fighting fiercely ; to reap the full benefit of their weapons and their training they must be obedient to command. The rifle is a far less formidable weapon when every man uses it at his own discretion than when the fire of a large body of troops is directed by a single will. Precision of movement, too, is necessary for the quick concentration of superior forces at the decisive point, for rapid support, and for effective combination. But neither was the fire of the Confederate infantry under the complete control of their officers, nor were their movements always characterised by order and regularity. It was seldom that the men could be induced to refrain from answering shot with shot ; there was an extraordinary waste of ammunition, there was much unnecessary noise, and the regiments were very apt to get out of hand. It is needless to bring forward specific proof ; the admissions of superior officers are quite sufficient. General D. H. Hill, in an interesting description of the Southern soldier, speaks very frankly of his shortcomings. ' Self-reliant always, obedient when he chose to be, impatient of drill and discipline, he was unsurpassed as a scout or on the skirmish line. Of the shoulder-to-shoulder courage, bred of drill and discipline, he knew nothing and cared less. Hence, on the battle-field, he was more of a free lance than a machine. Who ever saw a Confederate line advancing that was not crooked as a ram's horn ? Each ragged rebel yelling on his own hook and aligning on himself ! But there is as much need of the machine-made soldier as of the self-reliant soldier, and the concentrated blow is always the most effective blow. The erratic effort of the Confederate, heroic though it was, yet failed to achieve the maximum result just because it was erratic. Moreover, two serious evils attended that excessive egotism and individuality which came to the Confederate through his training, association, and habits. He knew when a movement was false and a position untenable, and he was too little of a machine to give in such cases the whole-hearted service which might have redeemed the blunder. The other evil was an ever-growing one. His disregard of discipline and independence of character made him often a straggler, and by straggling the fruit of many a victory was lost.' [1]

General Lee was not less outspoken. A circular issued to his troops during the last months of the war is vir-tually a criticism on their conduct. 'Many opportunities,' he wrote, 'have been lost and hundreds of valuable lives uselessly sacrificed for want of a strict observance of discipline. Its object is to enable an army to bring promptly into action the largest possible number of men in good order, and under the control of their officers. Its effects are visible in all military history, which records the triumph of discipline and courage far more frequently than that of numbers and resources. The importance and utility of thorough discipline should be impressed on officers and men on all occasions by illus-trations taken from the experience of the instructor or from other sources of information. They should be made to understand that discipline contributes no less to their safety than to their efficiency. Disastrous surprises and those sudden panics which lead to defeat and the greatest loss of life are of rare occurrence among disciplined troops. It is well known that the greatest number of casualties occur when men become scattered, and especially when they retreat in confusion, as the fire of the enemy is then more deliberate and fatal. The experience of every officer shows that those troops suffer least who attack most vigorously, and that a few men, retaining their organisation and acting in concert, accomplish far more with smaller loss than a larger number scattered and disorganised.

[1] *Southern Historical Society Papers*, vol. xiii., p. 261.

' The appearance of a steady, unbroken line is more formidable to the enemy, and renders his aim less accurate and his fire less effective. Orders can be readily transmitted, advantage can be promptly taken of every opportunity, and all efforts being directed to a common end, the combat will be briefer and success more certain.

' Let officers and men be made to feel that they will most effectually secure their safety by remaining steadily at their posts, preserving order, and fighting with coolness and vigour. . . . Impress upon the officers that discipline cannot be attained without constant watchfulness on their part. They must attend to the smallest particulars of detail. Men must be habituated to obey or they cannot be controlled in battle, and the neglect of the least important order impairs the proper influence of the officer.' [1]

That such a circular was considered necessary after the troops had been nearly four years under arms establishes beyond all question that the discipline of the Confederate army was not that of the regular troops with whom General Lee had served under the Stars and Stripes ; but it is not to be understood that he attributed the deficiencies of his soldiers to any spirit of resistance on their part to the demands of subordination. Elsewhere he says : ' The greatest difficulty I find is in causing orders and regulations to be obeyed. This arises not from a spirit of disobedience, but from ignorance.' [2] And here, with his usual perspicacity, he goes straight to the root of the evil. When the men in the ranks understand all that discipline involves, safety, health, efficiency, victory, it is easily maintained ; and it is because experience and tradition have taught them this that veteran armies are so amenable to control. ' Soldiers,' says Sir Charles Napier, ' must obey in all things. They may and do laugh at foolish orders, but they nevertheless obey, not because they are blindly obedient, but because they know that to disobey is to break the backbone of their profession.'

---

[1] *Memoirs of General Robert E. Lee.* By A. L. Long, Military Secretary and Brigadier-General, pp. 685–6.

[2] *Memoirs, &c.,* p. 619. Letter dated March 21, 1863.

Such knowledge, however, is long in coming, even to the regular, and it may be questioned whether it ever really came home to the Confederates.

In fact, the Southern soldier, ignorant, at the outset, of what may be accomplished by discipline, never quite got rid of the belief that the enthusiasm of the individual, his goodwill and his native courage, was a more than sufficient substitute. ' The spirit which animates our soldiers,' wrote Lee, ' and the natural courage with which they are so liberally endowed, have led to a reliance upon those good qualities, to the neglect of measures which would increase their efficiency and contribute to their safety.'[1] Yet the soldier was hardly to blame. Neither he nor his regimental officers had any previous knowledge of war when they were suddenly launched against the enemy, and there was no time to instil into them the habits of discipline. There was no regular army to set them an example; no historic force whose traditions they would unconsciously have adopted; the exigencies of the service forbade the retention of the men in camps of instruction, and trained instructors could not be spared from more important duties.

Such ignorance, however, as that which prevailed in the Southern ranks is not always excusable. It would be well if those who pose as the friends of the private soldier, as his protectors from injustice, realised the mischief they may do by injudicious sympathy. The process of being broken to discipline is undoubtedly galling to the instincts of free men, and it is beyond question that among a multitude of superiors, some will be found who are neither just nor considerate. Instances of hardship must inevitably occur. But men and officers—for discipline presses as hardly on the officers as on the men—must obey, no matter at what cost to their feelings, for obedience to orders, instant and unhesitating, is not only the life-blood of armies but the security of States; and the doctrine that under any conditions whatever deliberate disobedience can be justified is treason to the commonwealth. It is to be remembered that the

[1] *Memoirs, &c.,* p. 684. By A. L. Long.

end of the soldier's existence is not merely to conduct himself as a respectable citizen and earn his wages, but to face
peril and privations, not of his own free will, but at the bid-
ding of others; and, in circumstances where his natural instincts assert themselves most strongly, to make a complete
surrender of mind and body. If he has been in the habit
of weighing the justice or the wisdom of orders before obeying them, if he has been taught that disobedience may be a
pardonable crime, he will probably question the justice of
the order that apparently sends him to certain death; if
he once begins to think; if he once contemplates the
possibility of disobedience; if he permits a single idea to
enter his head beyond the necessity of instant compliance,
it is unlikely that he will rise superior to the promptings
of his weaker nature. *Men must be habituated to obey or
they cannot be controlled in battle;* and the slightest interference with the habit of subordination is fraught,
therefore, with the very greatest danger to the efficiency
of an army.

It has been asserted, and it would appear that the idea
is widespread, that patriotism and intelligence are of vastly
more importance than the habit of obedience, and it was
certainly a very general opinion in America before the war.
This idea should have been effectually dissipated, at all
events in the North, by the battle of Bull Run. Nevertheless, throughout the conflict a predilection existed in favour
of what was called the ‘thinking bayonet;’ and the very
term ‘machine-made soldier,’ employed by General D. H.
Hill, proves that the strict discipline of regular armies
was not held in high esteem.

It is certainly true that the ‘thinking bayonet’ is by
no means to be decried. A man can no more be a good
soldier without intelligence and aptitude for his profession than he can be a successful poacher or a skilful
jockey. But it is possible, in considering the value of
an armed force, to rate too highly the natural qualities
of the individual in the ranks. In certain circumstances, especially in irregular warfare, where each
man fights for his own hand, they doubtless play a con-

spicuous part.   A thousand skilled riflemen, familiar with
the 'moving accidents by flood and field,' even if they have
no regular training and are incapable of precise manœuvres,
may prove more than a match for the same number of
professional soldiers.   But when large numbers are in
question, when the concentration of superior force at a
single point, and the close co-operation of the three arms,
infantry, artillery, and cavalry, decide the issue, then the
force that can manœuvre, that moves like a machine at the
mandate of a single will, has a marked advantage ; and
the power of manœuvring and of combination is conferred
by discipline alone.   'Two Mamelukes,' said Napoleon,
'can defeat three French horsemen, because they are better
armed, better mounted, and more skilful.   A hundred
French horse have nothing to fear from a hundred
Mamelukes, three hundred would defeat a similar number,
and a thousand French would defeat fifteen hundred
Mamelukes.   So great is the influence of tactics, order,
and the power of manœuvring.'

It may be said, moreover, that whatever may have been
the case in past times, the training of the regular soldier
to-day neither aims at producing mere machines nor has it
that effect.   As much attention is given to the development
of self-reliance in the rank and file as to making them subordinate.   It has long been recognised that there are many
occasions in war when even the private must use his wits ;
on outpost, or patrol, as a scout, an orderly, or when his
immediate superiors have fallen, momentous issues may
hang on his judgment and initiative ; and in a good army
these qualities are sedulously fostered by constant instruction in field duties.   Nor is the fear justified that the
strict enforcement of exact obedience, whenever a superior is present, impairs, under this system of training, the
capacity for independent action when such action becomes
necessary.   In the old days, to drill and discipline the
soldier into a machine was undoubtedly the end of all his
training.   To-day his officers have the more difficult task
of stimulating his intelligence, while, at the same time,
they instil the habits of subordination ; and that such task

may be successfully accomplished we have practical proof. The regiments of the Light Brigade, trained by Sir John Moore nearly a century ago on the system of to-day, proved their superiority in the field over all others. As skirmishers, on the outpost, and in independent fighting, they were exceedingly efficient; and yet, when they marched shoulder to shoulder, no troops in Wellington's army showed a more solid front, manœuvred with greater precision, or were more completely under the control of their officers.

Mechanical obedience, then, is perfectly compatible with the freest exercise of the intelligence, provided that the men are so trained that they know instinctively when to give the one and to use the other; and the Confederates, had their officers and non-commissioned officers been trained soldiers, might easily have acquired this highest form of discipline. As it was, and as it always will be with improvised troops, the discipline of battle was to a great degree purely personal. The men followed those officers whom they knew, and in whom they had confidence; but they did not always obey simply because the officer had the right to command; and they were not easily handled when the wisdom of an order or the necessity of a movement was not apparent. The only way, it was said by an Englishman in the Confederacy, in which an officer could acquire influence over the Southern soldiers was by his personal conduct under fire. 'Every ounce of authority,' was his expression, 'had to be purchased by a drop of my blood.'[1] Such being the case, it is manifest that Jackson's methods of discipline were well adapted to the peculiar constitution of the army in which he served. With the officers he was exceedingly strict. He looked to them to set an example of unhesitating obedience and the precise performance of duty. He demanded, too—and in this respect his own conduct was a model—that the rank and file should be treated with tact and consideration. He remembered that his citizen soldiers were utterly unfamiliar with the forms and customs of military life, that what to the regular would

_____
[1] _Three Months in the Southern States._ General Sir Arthur Fremantle, G.C.B.

be a mere matter of course, might seem a gross outrage to the man who had never acknowledged a superior. In his selection of officers, therefore, for posts upon his staff, and in his recommendations for promotion, he considered personal characteristics rather than professional ability. He preferred men who would win the confidence of others— men not only strong, but possessing warm sympathies and broad minds—to mere martinets, ruling by regulation, and treating the soldier as a machine. But, at the same time, he was by no means disposed to condone misconduct in the volunteers. Never was there a more striking contrast than between Jackson the general and Jackson off duty. During his sojourn at Moss Neck, Mr. Corbin's little daughter, a child of six years old, became a special favourite. ' Her pretty face and winsome ways were so charming that he requested her mother that she might visit him every afternoon, when the day's labours were over. He had always some little treat in store for her—an orange or an apple—but one afternoon he found that his supply of good things was exhausted. Glancing round the room his eye fell on a new uniform cap, ornamented with a gold band. Taking his knife, he ripped off the braid, and fastened it among the curls of his little playfellow.' A little later the child was taken ill, and after his removal from Moss Neck he heard that she had died. ' The general,' writes his aide-de-camp, ' wept freely when I brought him the sad news.' Yet in the administration of discipline Jackson was far sterner than General Lee, or indeed than any other of the generals in Virginia. 'Once on the march, fearing lest his men might stray from the ranks and commit acts of pillage, he had issued an order that the soldiers should not enter private dwellings. Disregarding the order, a soldier entered a house, and even used insulting language to the women of the family. This was reported to Jackson, who had the man arrested, tried by drum-head court-martial, and shot in twenty minutes.' [1] He never failed to confirm the sentences of death passed by courts-martial on deserters. It was in vain that his oldest

[1] *Bright Skies and Dark Shadows.* Rev. H. M. Field, D.D., p. 286.

friends, or even the chaplains, appealed for a mitigation of the extreme penalty. 'While he was in command at Winchester, in December 1861, a soldier who was charged with striking his captain was tried by court-martial and sentenced to be shot. Knowing that the breach of discipline had been attended with many extenuating circumstances, some of us endeavoured to secure his pardon. Possessing ourselves of all the facts, we waited upon the general, who evinced the deepest interest in the object of our visit, and listened with evident sympathy to our plea. There was moisture in his eyes when we repeated the poor fellow's pitiful appeal that he be allowed to die for his country as a soldier on the field of battle, and not as a dog by the muskets of his own comrades. Such solicitude for the success of our efforts did he manifest that he even suggested some things to be done which we had not thought of. At the same time he warned us not to be too hopeful. He said: "It is unquestionably a case of great hardship, but a pardon at this juncture might work greater hardship. Resistance to lawful authority is a grave offence in a soldier. To pardon this man would be to encourage insubordination throughout the army, and so ruin our cause. Still," he added, "I will review the whole case, and no man will be happier than myself if I can reach the same conclusions as you have done." The soldier was shot.' [1]

On another occasion four men were to be executed for desertion to the enemy. The firing party had been ordered to parade at four o'clock in the afternoon, and shortly before the hour a chaplain, not noted for his tact, made his way to the general's tent, and petitioned earnestly that the prisoners might even now be released. Jackson, whom he found pacing backwards and forwards, in evident agitation, watch in hand, listened courteously to his arguments, but made no reply, until at length the worthy minister, in his most impressive manner, said, 'General, consider your responsibility before the Lord. You are sending these men's souls to hell!' With a look of intense

[1] Communicated by the Rev. Dr. Graham.

disgust at such empty cant, Jackson made one stride forward, took the astonished divine by his shoulders, and saying, in his severest tones, ' That, sir, is my business— do you do yours! ' thrust him forcibly from the tent.

His severity as regards the more serious offences did not, however, alienate in the smallest degree the confidence and affection of his soldiers. They had full faith in his justice. They were well aware that to order the execution of some unfortunate wretch gave him intense pain. But they recognised, as clearly as he did himself, that it was some- times expedient that individuals should suffer. They knew that not all men, nor even the greater part, are heroes, and that if the worthless element had once reason to believe that they might escape the legitimate consequences of their crimes, desertion and insubordination would destroy the army. By some of the senior officers, however, his rigorous ideas of discipline were less favourably considered. They were by no means disposed to quarrel with the fact that the sentences of courts-martial in the Second Army Corps were almost invariably confirmed; but they objected strongly to the same measure which they meted out to the men being consistently applied to themselves. They could not be brought to see that neglect of duty, however trivial, on the part of a colonel or brigadier was just as serious a fault as desertion or insubordination on the part of the men ; and the conflict of opinion, in certain cases, had unfortunate results.

To those whose conduct he approved he was more than considerate. General Lane, who was under him as a cadet at Lexington, writes as follows :—

' When in camp at Bunker Hill, after the battle of Sharpsburg, where the gallant Branch was killed, I, as colonel commanding the brigade, was directed by General A. P. Hill to hold my command in readiness, with three days' rations, for detached service, and to report to General Jackson for further orders. That was all the information that Hill could give me. I had been in Jackson's corps since the battles round Richmond, and had been very derelict in not paying my respects to my old professor.

As I rode to his headquarters I wondered if he would recognise me. I certainly expected to receive his orders in a few terse sentences, and to be promptly dismissed with a military salute. He knew me as soon as I entered his tent, though we had not met for years. He rose quickly, with a smile on his face, took my hand in both of his in the warmest manner, expressed his pleasure at seeing me, chided me for not having been to see him, and bade me be seated. His kind words, the tones of his voice, his familiarly calling me Lane, whereas it had always been Mr. Lane at the Institute, put me completely at my ease. Then, for the first time, I began to love that reserved man whom I had always honoured and respected as my professor, and whom I greatly admired as my general.

'After a very pleasant and somewhat protracted conversation, he ordered me to move at once, and as rapidly as possible, to North Mountain Depôt, tear up the Baltimore and Ohio Railroad, and put myself in communication with General Hampton (commanding cavalry brigade), who would cover my operations. While we were there General Jackson sent a member of his staff to see how we were progressing. That night I received orders to move at once and quickly to Martinsburg, as there had been heavy skirmishing near Kerneysville. Next morning, when I reported to General Jackson, he received me in the same cordial, warm-hearted manner, complimented me on the thoroughness of my work, told me that he had recommended me for promotion to take permanent charge of Branch's brigade, and that as I was the only person recommended through military channels, I would be appointed in spite of the two aspirants who were trying to bring political influence to bear in Richmond in their behalf. When I rose to go he took my hand in both of his, looked me steadily in the face, and in the words and tones of friendly warmth, which can never be forgotten, again expressed his confidence in my promotion, and bade me good-bye, with a " God bless you, Lane ! " ' [1]

On the other hand, Jackson's treatment of those who

[1] *Memoirs*, pp. 536–7.

failed to obey his orders was very different.   No matter how
high the rank of the offender, Jackson never sought to screen
the crime.[1] No thought that the public rebuke of his principal
subordinates might impair their authority or destroy their
cordial relations with himself ever stayed his hand ; and
it may well be questioned whether his disregard of consequences was not too absolutely uncompromising.   Men who
live in constant dread of their chief's anger are not likely
to render loyal and efficient service, and the least friction in
the higher ranks is felt throughout the whole command.
When the troops begin taking sides and unanimity disap-
pears, the power of energetic combination at once deterio-
rates.   That Jackson was perfectly just is not denied ;
the misconduct of his subordinates was sometimes flagrant ;
but it may well be questioned whether to keep officers under
arrest for weeks, or even months, marching without their
swords in rear of the column, was wholly wise. There is but
one public punishment for a senior officer who is guilty of
serious misbehaviour, and that is instant dismissal. If
he is suffered to remain in the army his presence will
always be a source of weakness. But the question will
arise, Is it possible to replace him ? If he is trusted by his
men they will resent his removal, and give but half-
hearted support to his successor ; so in dealing with those in
high places tact and consideration are essential.   Even Dr.
Dabney admits that in this respect Jackson's conduct is
open to criticism.

As already related, he looked on the blunders of his
officers, if those blunders were honest, and due simply to
misconception of the situation, with a tolerant eye.   He
knew too much of war and its difficulties to expect that
their judgment would be unerring. He never made the
mistake of reprehending the man who had done his best
to succeed, and contented himself with pointing out,
quietly and courteously, how failure might have been
avoided. 'But if he believed,' says his chief of the

[1] The five regimental commanders of the Stonewall Brigade were once
placed under arrest at the same time for permitting their men to burn
fence-rails ; they were not released until they had compensated the farmer.

staff, 'that his subordinates were self-indulgent or contumacious, he became a stern and exacting master; . . . and during his career a causeless friction was produced in the working of his government over several gallant and meritorious officers who served under him. This was almost the sole fault of his military character: that by this jealousy of intentional inefficiency he diminished the sympathy between himself and the general officers next his person by whom his orders were to be executed. Had he been able to exercise the same energetic authority, through the medium of a zealous personal affection, he would have been a more perfect leader of armies.' [1]

This system of command was in all probability the outcome of deliberate calculation. No officer, placed in permanent charge of a considerable force, least of all a man who never acted except upon reflection, and who had a wise regard for human nature, could fail to lay down for himself certain principles of conduct towards both officers and men. It may be, then, that Jackson considered the course he pursued the best adapted to maintain discipline amongst a number of ambitious young generals, some of whom had been senior to himself in the old service, and all of whom had been raised suddenly, with probably some disturbance to their self-possession, to high rank. It is to be remembered, too, that during the campaigns of 1862 his pre-eminent ability was only by degrees made clear. It was not everyone who, like General Lee, discerned the great qualities of the silent and unassuming instructor of cadets, and other leaders, of more dashing exterior, with a well-deserved reputation for brilliant courage, may well have doubted whether his capacity was superior to their own.

Such soaring spirits possibly needed a tight hand; and, in any case, Jackson had much cause for irritation. With Wolfe and Sherman he shared the distinguished honour of being considered crazy by hundreds of self-sufficient mediocrities. It was impossible that he should have been ignorant, although not one word of complaint ever passed

[1] Dabney, vol. ii. pp. 519-20.

his lips, how grossly he was misrepresented, how he was caricatured in the press, and credited with the most extravagant and foolhardy ideas of war.   Nor did his subordinates, in very many instances, give him that loyal and ungrudging support which he conceived was the due of the commanding general.   More than one of his enterprises fell short of the full measure of success owing to the shortcomings of others; and these shortcomings, such as Loring's insubordination at Romney, Steuart's refusal to pursue Banks after Winchester, Garnett's retreat at Kernstown, A. P. Hill's tardiness at Cedar Run, might all be traced to the same cause—disdain of his capacity, and a misconception of their own position.   In such circumstances it is hardly to be wondered at if his wrath blazed to a white heat. He was not of a forgiving nature.   Once roused, resentment took possession of his whole being, and it may be questioned whether it was ever really appeased.   At the same time, the fact that Jackson lacked the fascination which, allied to lofty intellect, wins the hearts of men most readily, and is pre-eminently the characteristic of the very greatest warriors, can hardly be denied.   His influence with men was a plant of slow growth.   Yet the glamour of his great deeds, the gradual recognition of his unfailing sympathy, his modesty and his truth, produced in the end the same result as the personal charm of Napoleon, of Nelson, and of Lee.   His hold on the devotion of his troops was very sure : ' God knows,' said his adjutant-general, weeping the tears of a brave man, ' I would have died for him ! ' and few commanders have been followed with more implicit confidence or have inspired a deeper and more abiding affection.   Long years after the war a bronze statue, in his habit as he lived, was erected on his grave at Lexington.   Thither, when the figure was unveiled, came the survivors of the Second Army Corps, the men of Manassas and of Sharpsburg, of Fredericksburg and Chancellorsville, and of many another hard-fought field ; and the younger generation looked on the relics of an army whose peer the world has seldom seen.   When the guns had fired a salute, the wild rebel yell, the music which the great Virginian had loved so well, rang loud above his grave, and as the last reverberations died away across the hill, the grey-haired ranks stood still and silent. 'See how they loved him!' said one, and it was spoken with deepest reverence. Two well-known officers, who had served under Jackson, were sitting near each other on their horses. Each remarked the silence of the other, and each saw that the other was in tears. 'I'm not ashamed of it, Snowden!' 'Nor I, old boy,' replied the other, as he tried to smile.

When, after the unveiling, the columns marched past the monument, the old fellows looked up, and then bowed their uncovered heads and passed on. But one tall, gaunt soldier of the Stonewall Brigade, as he passed out of the cemetery, looked back for a moment at the life-like figure of his general, and waving his old grey hat towards it, cried out, 'Good-bye, old man, good-bye; we've done all we could for you; good-bye!'

It is not always easy to discern why one general is worshipped, even by men who have never seen him, while another, of equal or even superior capacity, fails to awaken the least spark of affection, except in his chosen friends. Grant was undoubtedly a greater soldier than McClellan, and the genius of Wellington was not less than that of Nelson. And yet, while Nelson and McClellan won all hearts, not one single private had either for Wellington or Grant any warmer sentiment than respect. It would be as unfair, however, to attribute selfishness or want of sympathy to either Wellington or Grant, as to insinuate that Nelson and McClellan were deliberate bidders for popularity. It may be that in the two former the very strength of their patriotism was at fault. To them the State was everything, the individual nothing. To fight for their country was merely a question of duty, into which the idea of glory or recompense hardly entered, and, indifferent themselves either to praise or blame, they considered that the victory of the national arms was a sufficient reward for the soldier's toils. Both were generous and open-handed, exerting themselves incessantly to provide for the comfort and well-being of their troops.

Neither was insensible to suffering, and both were just as capable of self-sacrifice as either Nelson or McClellan. But the standpoint from which they looked at war was too exalted. Nelson and McClellan, on the other hand, recognised that they commanded men, not stoics. Sharing with Napoleon the rare quality of captivating others, a quality which comes by nature or comes not at all, they made allowance for human nature, and identified themselves with those beneath them in the closest *camaraderie*. And herein, to a great extent, lay the secret of the enthusiastic devotion which they inspired.

If the pitiless dissectors of character are right we ought to see in Napoleon the most selfish of tyrants, the coldest and most crafty of charlatans. It is difficult, however, to believe that the hearts of a generation of hardy warriors were conquered merely by ringing phrases and skilful flattery. It should be remembered that from a mercenary force, degraded and despised, he transformed the Grand Army into the terror of Europe and the pride of France. During the years of his glory, when the legions controlled the destinies of their country, none was more honoured than the soldier. His interests were always the first to be considered. The highest ranks in the peerage, the highest offices of State, were held by men who had carried the knapsack, and when thrones were going begging their claims were preferred before all others. The Emperor, with all his greatness, was always ' the Little Corporal ' to his grenadiers. His career was their own. As they shared his glory, so they shared his reward. Every upward step he made towards supreme power he took them with him, and their relations were always of the most cordial and familiar character. He was never happier than when, on the eve of some great battle, he made his bivouac within a square of the Guard ; never more at ease than when exchanging rough compliments with the veterans of Rivoli or Jena. He was the representative of the army rather than of the nation. The men knew that no civilian would be preferred before them ; that their gallant deeds were certain of his recognition ; that their claims to the cross, to pension, and to promotion, would be as carefully considered as the claims of their generals. They loved Napoleon and they trusted him; and whatever may have been his faults, he was 'the Little Corporal,' the friend and comrade of his soldiers, to the end.

It was by the same hooks of steel that Stonewall Jackson grappled the hearts of the Second Army Corps to his own. His men loved him, not merely because he was the bravest man they had ever known, the strongest, and the most resolute, not because he had given them glory, and had made them heroes whose fame was known beyond the confines of the South, but because he was one of themselves, with no interests apart from their interests; because he raised them to his own level, respecting them not merely as soldiers, but as comrades, the tried comrades of many a hard fight and weary march. Although he ruled them with a rod of iron, he made no secret, either officially or privately, of his deep and abiding admiration for their self-sacrificing valour. His very dispatches showed that he regarded his own skill and courage as small indeed when compared with theirs. Like Napoleon's, his congratulatory orders were conspicuous for the absence of all reference to himself; it was always 'we,' not 'I,' and he was among the first to recognise the worth of the rank and file. 'One day,' says Dr. McGuire, 'early in the war, when the Second Virginia Regiment marched by, I said to General Johnston, "If these men will not fight, you have no troops that will." He expressed the prevalent opinion of the day in his reply, saying, "I would not give one company of regulars for the whole regiment." When I returned to Jackson I had occasion to quote General Johnston's opinion. "Did he say that?" he asked, "and of those splendid men?" And then he added: "The patriot volunteer, fighting for his country and his rights, makes the most reliable soldier upon earth." And his veterans knew more than that their general believed them to be heroes. They knew that this great, valiant man, beside whom all others, save Lee himself, seemed small and feeble, this mighty captain, who held the hosts of the enemy in the hollow of his hand, was the kindest and the most considerate of human beings. To them he was " Old Jack " in the same affectionate sense as he had been " Old Jack " to his class-mates at West Point. They followed him willingly, for they knew that the path he trod was the way to victory; but they loved him as children do their parents, because they were his first thought and his last.

In season and out of season he laboured for their welfare. To his transport and commissariat officers he was a hard master. The unfortunate wight who had neglected to bring up supplies, or who ventured to make difficulties, discovered, to his cost, that his quiet commander could be very terrible ; but those officers who did their duty, in whatever branch of the service they might be serving, found that their zeal was more than appreciated. For himself he asked nothing ; on behalf of his subordinates he was a constant and persistent suitor. He was not only ready to support the claims to promotion of those who deserved it, but in the case of those who displayed special merit he took the initiative himself : and he was not content with one refusal. His only difference with General Lee, if difference it can be called, was on a question of this nature. The Commander-in-Chief, it appears, soon after the battle of Fredericksburg, had proposed to appoint officers to the Second Army Corps who had served elsewhere. After some correspondence Jackson wrote as follows :—' My rule has been to recommend such as were, in my opinion, best qualified for filling vacancies. The application of this rule has prevented me from even recommending for the command of my old brigade one of its officers, because I did not regard any of them as competent as another of whose qualifications I had a higher opinion. This rule has led me to recommend Colonel Bradley T. Johnson for the command of Taliaferro's brigade. . . . I desire the interest of the service, and no other interest, to determine who shall be selected to fill the vacancies. Guided by this principle, I cannot go outside of my command for persons to fill vacancies in it, unless by so doing a more competent officer is secured. This same principle leads me to oppose having officers who have never served with me, and of whose qualifications I have no knowledge, forced upon me by promoting them to fill vacancies in my command, and advancing them over meritorious officers well qualified for the positions, and of whose qualifications I have had ample opportunities of judging from their having served with me.

'In my opinion, the interest of the service would be injured if I should quietly consent to see officers with whose qualifications I am not acquainted promoted into my command to fill vacancies, regardless of the merits of my own officers who are well qualified for the positions. The same principle leads me, when selections have to be made outside of my command, to recommend those (if there be such) whose former service with me proved them well qualified for filling the vacancies. This induced me to recommend Captain Chew, who does not belong to this army corps, but whose well-earned reputation when with me has not been forgotten.'

And as he studied the wishes of his officers, working quietly and persistently for their advancement, so he studied the wishes of the private soldiers. It is well known that artillerymen come, after a time, to feel a personal affection for their guns, especially those which they have used in battle. When in camp near Fredericksburg Jackson was asked to transfer certain field-pieces, which had belonged to his old division, to another portion of the command. The men were exasperated, and the demand elicited the following letter :—

'December 3, 1862.

'General R. E. LEE,
'Commanding Army of Northern Virginia.

'General,—Your letter of this date, recommending that I distribute the rifle and Napoleon guns " so as to give General D. H. Hill a fair proportion " has been received. I respectfully request, if any such distribution is to be made, that you will direct your chief of artillery or some other officer to do it ; but I hope that none of the guns which belonged to the Army of the Valley before it became part of the Army of Northern Virginia, after the battle of Cedar Run, will be taken from it. If since that time any artillery has improperly come into my command, I trust that it will be taken away, and the person in whose possession it may be found punished, if his conduct requires it. So careful was I to prevent an improper distribution of the artillery and other public property captured at Harper's Ferry, that I issued a written order directing my staff officers to turn over to the proper chiefs of staff of the Army of Northern Virginia all captured stores. A copy of the order is herewith enclosed.

'General D. H. Hill's artillery wants existed at the time he was assigned to my command, and it is hoped that the artillery which belonged to the Army of the Valley will not be taken to supply his wants.

'I am, General, your obedient servant,

'T. J. JACKSON, *Lieutenant-General.*'

No further correspondence is to be found on the subject, so it may be presumed that the protest was successful.

Jackson's relations with the rank and file have already been referred to, and although he was now commander of an army corps, and universally acknowledged as one of the foremost generals of the Confederacy, his rise in rank and reputation had brought no increase of dignity. He still treated the humblest privates with the same courtesy that he treated the Commander-in-Chief. He never repelled their advances, nor refused, if he could, to satisfy their curiosity; and although he seldom went out of his way to speak to them, if any soldier addressed him, especially if he belonged to a regiment recruited from the Valley, he seldom omitted to make some inquiry after those he had left at home. Never, it was said, was his tone more gentle or his smile more winning than when he was speaking to some ragged representative of his old brigade. How his heart went out to them may be inferred from the following. Writing to a friend at Richmond he said : 'Though I have been relieved from command in the Valley, and may never again be assigned to that important trust, yet I feel deeply when I see the patriotic people of that region under the heel of a hateful military despotism. There are all the hopes of those who have been with me from the commencement of the war in Virginia, who have repeatedly left their homes and families in the hands of the enemy, to brave the dangers of battle and disease; and there are those who have so devotedly laboured for the relief of our suffering sick and wounded.'

NOTE

Table showing the Nationality and Average Measurements of 346,744 Federal Soldiers examined for Military Service after March 6, 1863.

	Number.	Height. ft. in.	Chest at Inspiration. in.
United States　.　.	237,391	5　7·40	35·61
(69 per cent.)			
Germany　.　.　.	35,935	5　5·54	35·88
Ireland .　.　.　.	32,473	5　5·54	35·24
Canada .　.　.　.	15,507	5　5·51	35·42
England　.　.　.	11,479	5　6·02	35·41
France .　.　.　.	2,630	5　5·81	35·29
Scotland　.　.　.	2,127	5　6·13	35·97
Other nationalities, including Wales and five British Colonies .	9,202	—	—
	346,744		

Report of the Provost Marshal General, 1866, p. 698.

The Roll of the 35th Massachusetts, which may be taken as a typical Northern regiment, shows clearly enough at what period the great influx of foreigners took place. Of 104 officers the names of all but four—and these four joined in 1864—are pure English. Of the 964 rank and file of which the regiment was originally composed, only 50 bore foreign names. In 1864, however, 495 recruits were received, and of these over 400 were German immigrants.—*History of the 35th Regiment, Mass. Volunteers,* 1862-65.

CHAPTER XXII

WINTER QUARTERS

DURING the long interval which intervened between the battle of Fredericksburg and the next campaign, Jackson employed himself in preparing the reports of his battles, which had been called for by the Commander-in-Chief. They were not compiled in their entirety by his own hand. He was no novice at literary composition, and his pen, as his letter-book shows, was not that of an unready writer. He had a good command of language, and that power of clear and concise expression which every officer in command of a large force, a position naturally entailing a large amount of confidential correspondence, must necessarily possess. But the task now set him was one of no ordinary magnitude. Since the battle of Kernstown, the report of which had been furnished in April 1862, the time had been too fully occupied to admit of the crowded events being placed on record, and more than one-half of the division, brigade, and regimental commanders who had been engaged in the operations of the period had been killed. Nor, even now, did his duties permit him the necessary leisure to complete the work without assistance. On his requisition, therefore, Colonel Charles Faulkner, who had been United States Minister to France before the war, was attached to his staff for the purpose of collecting the reports of the subordinate commanders, and combining them in the proper form. The rough drafts were carefully gone over by the general. Every sentence was weighed ; and everything that might possibly convey a wrong impression was at once rejected ; evidence was called to clear up disputed points ;

1863.

no inferences or suppositions were allowed to stand ; truth was never permitted to be sacrificed to effect ; superlatives were rigorously excluded,[1] and the narratives may be unquestionably accepted as an accurate relation of the facts. Many stirring passages were added by the general's own pen; and the praise bestowed upon the troops, both officers and men, is couched in the warmest terms. Yet much was omitted. Jackson had a rooted objection to represent the motives of his actions, or to set forth the object of his movements. In reply to a remonstrance that those who came after him would be embarrassed by the absence of these explanations, and that his fame would suffer, he said : ' The men who come after me must act for themselves ; and as to the historians who speak of the movements of my command, I do not concern myself greatly as to what they may say.' To judge, then, from the reports, Jackson himself had very little to do with his success ; indeed, were they the only evidence available, it would be difficult to ascertain whether the more brilliant manœuvres were ordered by himself or executed on the initiative of others. But in this he was perfectly consistent. When the publisher of an illustrated periodical wrote to him, asking him for his portrait and some notes of his battles as the basis of a sketch, he replied that he had no likeness of himself, and had done nothing worthy of mention. It is not without interest, in this connection, to note that the Old Testament supplied him with a pattern for his reports, just as it supplied him, as he often declared, with precepts and principles applicable to every military emergency. After he was wounded, enlarging one morning on his favourite topic of practical religion, he turned to the staff officer in attendance, Lieutenant Smith, and asked him with a smile : ' Can you tell me where the Bible gives generals a model for their official reports of battles ? ' The aide-de-camp answered, laughing, that it never entered his mind to think of looking for such a thing

---

[1] The report of Sharpsburg, which Jackson had not yet revised at the time of his death, is not altogether free from exaggeration.

in the Scriptures. ' Nevertheless,' said the general, ' there
are such ; and excellent models, too.   Look, for instance,
at the narrative of Joshua's battles with the Amalekites ;
there you have one.   It has clearness, brevity, modesty ;
and it traces the victory to its right source, the blessing
of God.'

The early spring of 1863 was undoubtedly one of the
happiest seasons of a singularly happy life.   Jackson's
ambition, if the desire for such rank that would enable him
to put the powers within him to the best use may be so
termed, was fully gratified.   The country lad who, one-and-
twenty years ago, on his way to West Point, had looked on
the green hills of Virginia from the Capitol at Washington,
could hardly have anticipated a higher destiny than that
which had befallen him.   Over the hearts and wills of
thirty thousand magnificent soldiers, the very flower of
Southern manhood, his empire was absolute ; and such
dominion is neither the heritage of princes nor within the
reach of wealth.   The most trusted lieutenant of his great
commander, the strong right arm with which he had
executed his most brilliant enterprises, he shared with him
the esteem and admiration not only of the army but of the
whole people of the South.   The name he had determined,
in his lonely boyhood, to bring back to honour already
ranked with those of the Revolutionary heroes.   Even
his enemies, for the brave men at the front left rancour
to the politicians, were not proof against the attraction of
his great achievements.   A friendly intercourse, not always
confined to a trade of coffee for tobacco, existed between
the outposts ; ' Johnnies ' and ' Yanks ' often exchanged
greetings across the Rappahannock ; and it is related that
one day when Jackson rode along the river, and the
Confederate troops ran together, as was their custom, to
greet him with a yell, the Federal pickets, roused by the
sudden clamour, crowded to the bank, and shouted across
to ask the cause.   ' General Stonewall Jackson,' was the
proud reply of the grey-coated sentry.   Immediately, to
his astonishment, the cry, ' Hurrah for Stonewall Jackson ! '
rang out from the Federal ranks, and the voices of North

and South, prophetic of a time to come, mingled in acclamation of a great American.

The situation of the army, although the winter was unusually severe, was not without its compensations. The
country was covered with snow, and storms were frequent;
rations were still scarce,[1] for the single line of badly laid
rails, subjected to the strain of an abnormal traffic, formed
a precarious means of transport; every spring and pond
was frozen; and the soldiers shivered beneath their scanty
coverings.[2] Huts, however, were in process of erection, and
the goodwill of the people did something to supply the deficiencies of the commissariat.[3] The homes of Virginia
were stripped, and many—like Jackson himself, whose
blankets had already been sent from Lexington to his
old brigade—ordered their carpets to be cut up into
rugs and distributed amongst the men. But neither
cold nor hunger could crush the spirit of the troops.
The bivouacs were never merrier than on the bare hills
and in the dark pine-woods which looked down on the
ruins and the graves of Fredericksburg. Picket duty was

[1] On January 23 the daily ration was a quarter of a pound of beef, and
one-fifth of a pound of sugar was ordered to be issued in addition, but there
was no sugar! Lee to Davis, O. R., vol. xxi., p. 1110. In the Valley, during
the autumn, the ration had been one and one-eighth pound of flour, and one
and a quarter pounds of beef. On March 27 the ration was eighteen ounces
of flour, and four ounces of indifferent bacon, with occasional issues of rice,
sugar, or molasses. Symptoms of scurvy were appearing, and to supply
the place of vegetables each regiment was directed to send men daily to
gather sassafras buds, wild onions, garlic, &c., &c. Still 'the men are
cheerful,' writes Lee, 'and I receive no complaints.' O. R., vol. xxv.,
part ii., p. 687. On April 17 the ration had been increased by ten pounds of
rice to every 100 men about every third day, with a few peas and dried
fruits occasionally. O. R., vol. xxv., part ii., p. 730.

[2] On January 19, 1,200 pairs of shoes and 400 or 500 pairs of blankets
were forwarded for issue to men without either in D. H. Hill's division.
O. R., vol. xxi., p. 1097. In the Louisiana brigade on the same date, out
of 1,500 men, 400 had no covering for their feet whatever. A large number
had not a particle of underclothing, shirts, socks, or drawers; overcoats were
so rare as to be a curiosity; the 5th Regiment could not drill for want of
shoes; the 8th was almost unfit for duty from the same cause; the condition of the men's feet, from long exposure, was horrible, and the troops
were almost totally unprovided with cooking utensils. O. R., vol. xxi.,
p. 1098.

[3] O. R., vol. xxi., p. 1098.

light, for the black waters of the great river formed a secure
barrier against attack ; and if the men's stomachs were
empty, they could still feast their eyes on a charming landscape. 'To the right and left the wooded range extended
towards Fredericksburg on the one hand, and Port Royal
on the other ; in front, the far-stretching level gave full
sweep to the eye ; and at the foot of its forest-clad bluffs,
or by the margin of undulating fields, the Rappahannock
flowed calmly to the sea. Old mansions dotted this beautiful
land—for beautiful it was in spite of the chill influences of
winter, with its fertile meadows, its picturesque woodlands,
and its old roads skirted by long lines of shadowy
cedars.' [1]

The headquarters of the Second Army Corps were established at Moss Neck, on the terrace above the Rappahannock, eleven miles below Fredericksburg. After the retreat
of the Federals to Falmouth, the Confederate troops had reoccupied their former positions, and every point of passage
between Fredericksburg and Port Royal was strongly
intrenched and closely watched. At Moss Neck Jackson
was not only within easy reach of his divisions, but was
more comfortably housed than had usually been the case.
A hunting-lodge which stood on the lawn of an old and
picturesque mansion-house, the property of a gentleman
named Corbin, was placed at his disposal—he had declined
the offer of rooms in the house itself lest he should trespass
on the convenience of its inmates ; and to show the peculiar
constitution of the Confederate army, an anecdote recorded by his biographers is worth quoting. After his first
interview with Mrs. Corbin, he passed out to the gate,
where a cavalry orderly who had accompanied him was
holding his horse. 'Do you approve of your accommodation,
General ?' asked the courier. 'Yes, sir, I have decided to
make my quarters here.' 'I am Mr. Corbin, sir,' said the
soldier, 'and I am very pleased.'

The lower room of the lodge, hung with trophies of
the chase, was both his bedroom and his office ; while a
large tent, pitched on the grass outside, served as a mess-

[1] Cooke, p. 389.

room for his military family; and here for three long
months, until near the end of March, he rested from the
labour of his campaigns. The Federal troops, on the
snow-clad heights across the river, remained idle in their
camps, slowly recovering from the effects of their defeat
on the fields of Fredericksburg; the pickets had ceased to
bicker; the gunboats had disappeared, and ' all was quiet
on the Rappahannock.' Many of the senior officers in the
Confederate army took advantage of the lull in operations
to visit their homes; but, although his wife urged him to
do the same, Jackson steadfastly refused to absent himself
even for a few days from the front. In November, to his
unbounded delight, a daughter had been born to him. ' To
a man of his extreme domesticity, and love for children,'
says his wife, ' this was a crowning happiness; and yet, with
his great modesty and shrinking from publicity, he requested that he should not receive the announcement by
telegraph, and when it came to him by letter he kept the
glad tidings to himself—leaving his staff and those around
him in the camp to hear of it from others. This was to
him " a joy with which a stranger could not intermeddle,"
and from which even his own hand could not lift the veil
of sanctity. His letters were full of longing to see his little
Julia; for by this name, which had been his mother's, he
had desired her to be christened, saying, " My mother was
mindful of me when I was a helpless, fatherless child, and
I wish to commemorate her now." '

' How thankful I am,' he wrote, ' to our kind Heavenly
Father for having spared my precious wife and given us a
little daughter! I cannot tell how gratified I am, nor how
much I wish I could be with you and see my two darlings.
But while this pleasure is denied me, I am thankful it is
accorded to you to have the little pet, and I hope it may be
a great deal of company and comfort to its mother. Now,
don't exert yourself to write to me, for to know that you
were exerting yourself to write would give me more pain
than the letter would pleasure, *so you must not do it*. But
you must love your *esposo* in the mean time. . . . I expect
you are just now made up with that baby. Don't you wish

your husband wouldn't claim any part of it, but let you have the sole ownership? Don't you regard it as the most precious little creature in the world? Do not spoil it, and don't let anybody tease it. Don't permit it to have a bad temper. How I would love to see the darling little thing! Give her many kisses from her father.

'At present I am fifty miles from Richmond, and eight miles from Guiney's Station, on the railroad from Richmond to Fredericksburg. Should I remain here, I do hope you and baby can come to see me before spring, as you can come on the railway. Wherever I go, God gives me kind friends. The people here show me great kindness. I receive invitation after invitation to dine out and spend the night, and a great many provisions are sent me, including cakes, tea, loaf-sugar, &c., and the socks and gloves and handkerchiefs still come!

'I am so thankful to our ever-kind Heavenly Father for having so improved my eyes as to enable me to write at night. He continually showers blessings upon me ; and that *you* should have been spared, and our darling little daughter given us, fills my heart with overflowing gratitude. If I know my unworthy self, my desire is to live entirely and unreservedly to God's glory. Pray, my darling, that I may so live.'

Again to his sister-in-law : 'I trust God will answer the prayers offered for peace. Not much comfort is to be expected until this cruel war terminates. I haven't seen my wife since last March, and never having seen my child, you can imagine with what interest I look to North Carolina.'

But the tender promptings of his deep natural affection were stilled by his profound faith that ' duty is ours, consequences are God's.' The Confederate army, at this time as at all others, suffered terribly from desertion ; and one of his own brigades reported 1,200 officers and men absent without leave.

'Last evening,' he wrote to his wife on Christmas Day, ' I received a letter from Dr. Dabney, saying, "one of the highest gratifications both Mrs. Dabney and I could enjoy would be another visit from Mrs. Jackson," and he invites me to meet you there. He and Mrs. Dabney are very kind, but it appears to me that it is better for me to remain with my command so long as the war continues. . . . If all our troops, officers and men, were at their posts, we might, through God's blessing, expect a more speedy termination of the war. The temporal affairs of some are so deranged as to make a strong plea for their returning home for a short time ; but our God has greatly blessed me and mine during my absence, and whilst it would be a great comfort to see you and our darling little daughter, and others in whom I take a special interest, yet duty appears to require me to remain with my command. It is important that those at headquarters set an example by remaining at the post of duty.'

So business at headquarters went on in its accustomed course. There were inspections to be made, the deficiencies of equipment to be made good, correspondence to be conducted—and the control of 30,000 men demanded much office-work—the enemy to be watched, information to be sifted, topographical data to be collected, and the reports of the battles to be written. Every morning, as was his invariable habit during a campaign, the general had an interview with the chiefs of the commissariat, transport, ordnance, and medical departments, and he spent many hours in consultation with his topographical engineer. The great purpose for which Virginia stood in arms was ever present to his mind, and despite his reticence, his staff knew that he was occupied, day and night, with the problems that the future might unfold. Existence at headquarters to the young and high-spirited officers who formed the military family was not altogether lively. Outside there was abundance of gaiety. The Confederate army, even on those lonely hills, managed to extract enjoyment from its surroundings. The hospitality of the plantations was open to the officers, and wherever Stuart and his brigadiers pitched their tents, dances and music were the order of the day. Nor were the men behindhand. Even the heavy snow afforded them entertainment. Whenever a thaw took place they set themselves to making snow-

balls ; and great battles, in which one division was arrayed
against another, and which were carried through with the
pomp and circumstance of war, colours flying, bugles
sounding, and long lines charging elaborately planned intrenchments, were a constant source of amusement, except
to unpopular officers.   Theatrical and musical performances
enlivened the tedium of the long evenings ; and when, by
the glare of the camp-fires, the band of the 5th Virginia
broke into the rattling quick-step of 'Dixie's Land,' not the
least stirring of national anthems, and the great concourse
of grey-jackets took up the chorus, closing it with a yell

> That shivered to the tingling stars,

the Confederate soldier would not have changed places with
the President himself.

There was much social intercourse, too, between the different headquarters.   General Lee was no unfrequent
visitor to Moss Neck, and on Christmas Day Jackson's
aides-de-camp provided a sumptuous entertainment, at
which turkeys and oysters figured, for the Commander-in-
Chief and the senior generals.   Stuart, too, often invaded
the quarters of his old comrade, and Jackson looked forward
to the merriment that was certain to result just as much
as the youngest of his staff.   'Stuart's exuberant cheerful-
ness and humour,' says Dabney, 'seemed to be the happy
relief, as they were the opposites, to Jackson's serious and
diffident temper.   While Stuart poured out his " quips and
cranks," not seldom at Jackson's expense, the latter sat by,
sometimes unprepared with any repartee, sometimes blushing, but always enjoying the jest with a quiet and merry
laugh.   The ornaments on the wall of the general's quarters
gave Stuart many a topic of badinage.   Affecting to believe
that they were of General Jackson's selection, he pointed now
to the portrait of some famous race-horse, and now to the
print of some celebrated rat-terrier, as queer revelations of
his private tastes, indicating a great decline in his moral
character, which would be a grief and disappointment to
the pious old ladies of the South.   Jackson, with a quiet
smile, replied that perhaps he had had more to do with

race-horses than his friends suspected. It was in the midst of such a scene as this that dinner was announced, and the two generals passed to the mess-table. It so happened that Jackson had just received, as a present from a patriotic lady, some butter, upon the adornment of which the fair donor had exhausted her housewife's skill. The servants, in honour of General Stuart's presence, had chosen this to grace the centre of the board. As his eye fell upon it, he paused, and with mock gravity pointed to it, saying, "There, gentlemen! If that is not the crowning evidence of our host's sporting tastes. He even has his favourite game-cock stamped on his butter!" The dinner, of course, began with great laughter, in which Jackson joined, with as much enjoyment as any.'

Visitors, too, from Europe, attracted by the fame of the army and its leaders, had made their way into the Confederate lines, and were received with all the hospitality that the camps afforded. An English officer has recorded his experiences at Moss Neck :—

'I brought from Nassau a box of goods (a present from England) for General Stonewall Jackson, and he asked me when I was at Richmond to come to his camp and see him. I left the city one morning about seven o'clock, and about ten landed at a station distant some eight or nine miles from Jackson's (or, as his men called him, "Old Jack's") camp. A heavy fall of snow had covered the country for some time before to the depth of a foot, and formed a crust over the Virginian mud, which is quite as villainous as that of Balaclava. The day before had been mild and wet, and my journey was made in a drenching shower, which soon cleared away the white mantle of snow. You cannot imagine the slough of despond I had to pass through. Wet to the skin, I stumbled through mud, I waded through creeks, I passed through pine-woods, and at last got into camp about two o'clock. I then made my way to a small house occupied by the general as his headquarters. I wrote down my name, and gave it to the orderly, and I was immediately told to walk in.

'The general rose and greeted me warmly. I expected

to see an old, untidy man, and was most agreeably surprised and pleased with his appearance. He is tall, handsome, and powerfully built, but thin. He has brown hair and a brown beard. His mouth expresses great determination. The lips are thin and compressed firmly together; his eyes are blue and dark, with keen and searching expression. I was told that his age was thirty-eight, and he looks forty. The general, who is indescribably simple and unaffected in all his ways, took off my wet overcoat with his own hands, made up the fire, brought wood for me to put my feet on to keep them warm while my boots were drying, and then began to ask me questions on various subjects. At the dinner hour we went out and joined the members of his staff. At this meal the general said grace in a fervent, quiet manner, which struck me very much. After dinner I returned to his room, and he again talked for a long time. The servant came in and took his mattress out of a cupboard and laid it on the floor.

'As I rose to retire, the general said, " Captain, there is plenty of room on my bed, I hope you will share it with me ? " I thanked him very much for his courtesy, but said " Good-night," and slept in a tent, sharing the blankets of one of his aides-de-camp. In the morning at breakfast-time I noticed that the general said grace before the meal with the same fervour I had remarked before. An hour or two afterwards it was time for me to return to the station ; on this occasion, however, I had a horse, and I returned to the general's headquarters to bid him adieu. His little room was vacant, so I slipped in and stood before the fire. I then noticed my greatcoat stretched before it on a chair. Shortly afterwards the general entered the room. He said : " Captain, I have been trying to dry your greatcoat, but I am afraid I have not succeeded very well." That little act illustrates the man's character. With the care and responsibilities of a vast army on his shoulders he finds time to do little acts of kindness and thoughtfulness.'

With each of his staff officers he was on most friendly

terms; and the visitors to his camp, such as the English officer quoted above, found him a most delightful host, discussing with the ease of an educated gentleman all manner of topics, and displaying not the slightest trace of that awkwardness and extreme diffidence which have been attributed to him. The range and accuracy of his information surprised them. 'Of military history,' said another English soldier, 'he knew more than any other man I met in America; and he was so far from displaying the somewhat grim characteristics that have been associated with his name, that one would have thought his tastes lay in the direction of art and literature.' 'His chief delight,' wrote the Hon. Francis Lawley, who knew him well, 'was in the cathedrals of England, notably in York Minster and Westminster Abbey. He was never tired of talking about them, or listening to details about the chapels and cloisters of Oxford.'[1]

'General Jackson,' writes Lord Wolseley, 'had certainly very little to say about military operations, although he was intensely proud of his soldiers, and enthusiastic in his devotion to General Lee; and it was impossible to make him talk of his own achievements. Nor can I say that his speech betrayed his intellectual powers. But his manner, which was modesty itself, was most attractive. He put you at your ease at once, listening with marked courtesy and attention to whatever you might say; and when the subject of conversation was congenial, he was a most interesting companion. I quite endorse the statement as to his love for beautiful things. He told me that in all his travels he had seen nothing so beautiful as the lancet windows in York Minster.'

In his daily intercourse with his staff, however, in his office or in the mess-room, he showed to less advantage than in the society of strangers. His gravity of demeanour seldom wholly disappeared, his intense earnestness was in itself oppressive, and he was often absent and preoccupied. 'Life at headquarters,' says one of his staff officers, 'was decidedly dull. Our meals were often very

[1] *The Times*, June 11, 1863.

dreary. The general had no time for light or trivial conversation, and he sometimes felt it his duty to rebuke our thoughtless and perhaps foolish remarks. Nor was it always quite safe to approach him. Sometimes he had a tired look in his eyes, and although he never breathed a word to one or another, we knew that he was dissatisfied with what was being done with the army.' [1]

Intense concentration of thought and purpose, in itself an indication of a powerful will, had distinguished Jackson from his very boyhood. During his campaigns he would pace for hours outside his tent, his hands clasped behind his back, absorbed in meditation; and when the army was on the march, he would ride for hours without raising his eyes or opening his lips. It was unquestionably at such moments that he was working out his plans, step by step, forecasting the counter-movements of the enemy, and providing for every emergency that might occur. And here the habit of keeping his whole faculties fixed on a single object, and of imprinting on his memory the successive processes of complicated problems, fostered by the methods of study which, both at West Point and Lexington, the weakness of his eyes had made compulsory, must have been an inestimable advantage. Brilliant strategical manœuvres, it cannot be too often repeated, are not a matter of inspiration and of decision on the spur of the moment. The problems presented by a theatre of war, with their many factors, are not to be solved except by a vigorous and sustained intellectual effort. 'If,' said Napoleon, 'I always appear prepared, it is because, before entering on an undertaking, I have meditated for long and have foreseen what may occur. It is not genius which reveals to me suddenly and secretly what I should do in circumstances unexpected by others; it is thought and meditation.'

The proper objective, speaking in general terms, of all military operations is the main army of the enemy, for a campaign can never be brought to a successful conclusion until the hostile forces in the field have become demoralised

---

[1] Letter from Dr. Hunter McGuire.

E E 2

by defeat; but, to ensure success, preponderance of numbers is usually essential, and it may be said, therefore, that the proper objective is the enemy's main army when it is in inferior strength.

Under ordinary conditions, the first step, then, towards victory must be a movement, or a series of movements, which will compel the enemy to divide his forces, and put it out of his power to assemble even equal strength on the battle-field.

This entails a consideration of the strategic points upon the theatre of war, for it is by occupying or threatening some point which the enemy cannot afford to lose that he will be induced to disperse his army, or to place himself in a position where he can be attacked at a disadvantage. While his main army, therefore, is the ultimate objective, certain strategic points become the initial objectives, to be occupied or threatened either by the main body or detached forces. It is seldom, however, that these initial objectives are readily discovered; and it is very often the case that even the ultimate objective may be obscured.

These principles are well illustrated by the operations in the Valley of Virginia during the month of May and the first fortnight of June, 1862. After the event it is easy to see that Banks' army was Jackson's proper objective—being the principal force in the secondary theatre of war. But at the time, before the event, Lee and Jackson alone realised the importance of overwhelming Banks and thus threatening Washington. It was not realised by Johnston, a most able soldier, for the whole of his correspondence goes to show that he thought a purely defensive attitude the best policy for the Valley Army. It was not realised by Jackson's subordinates, for it was not till long after the battle of Winchester that the real purport of the operations in which they had been engaged began to dawn on them. It was not realised by Lincoln, by Stanton, or even by McClellan, for to each of them the sudden attack on Front Royal was as much of a surprise as to Banks himself; and we may be perfectly confident that none but a trained strategist, after a prolonged study of the map and the situation, would realise it now.

It is to be noted, too, that Jackson's initial objectives—the strategical points in the Valley—were invariably well selected. The Luray Gap, the single road which gives access across the Massanuttons from one side of the Valley to the other, was the most important. The flank position on Elk Run, the occupation of which so suddenly brought up Banks, prevented him interposing between Jackson and Edward Johnson, and saved Staunton from capture, was a second; Front Royal, by seizing which he threatened Banks at Strasburg in flank and rear, compelling him to a hasty retreat, and bringing him to battle on ground which he had not prepared, a third; and the position at Port Republic, controlling the only bridge across the Shenandoah, and separating Shields from Frémont, a fourth. The bearing of all these localities was overlooked by the Federals, and throughout the campaign we cannot fail to notice a great confusion on their part as regards objectives. They neither recognised what the aim of their enemy would be, nor at what they should aim themselves. It was long before they discovered that Lee's army, and not Richmond, was the vital point of the Confederacy. Not a single attempt was made to seize strategic points, and if we may judge from the orders and dispatches in the Official Records, their existence was never recognised. To this oversight the successive defeats of the Northern forces were in great part due. From McClellan to Banks, each one of their generals appears to have been blind to the advantages that may be derived from a study of the theatre of war. Not one of them hit upon a line of operations which embarrassed the Confederates, and all possessed the unhappy knack of joining battle on the most unfavourable terms. Moreover, when it at last became clear that the surest means of conquering a country is to defeat its armies, the true objective was but vaguely realised. The annihilation of the enemy's troops seems to have been the last thing dreamt of. Opportunities of crushing him in detail were neither sought for nor created. As General

Sheridan said afterwards : ' The trouble with the commanders of the Army of the Potomac was that they never
marched out to "lick " anybody ; all they thought of was
to escape being " licked " themselves.'

But it is not sufficient, in planning strategical combinations, to arrive at a correct conclusion as regards the objective.   Success demands a most careful calculation of ways
and means : of the numbers at disposal ; of food, forage, and
ammunition ; and of the forces to be detached for secondary
purposes.   The different factors of the problem—the
strength and dispositions of the enemy, the roads, railways, fortresses, weather, natural features, the *moral* of the
opposing armies, the character of the opposing general, the
facilities for supply—have each and all of them to be considered, their relative prominence assigned to them, and
their conflicting claims to be brought into adjustment.

For such mental exertion Jackson was well equipped.
He had made his own the experience of others. His
knowledge of history made him familiar with the principles
which had guided Washington and Napoleon in the selection of objectives, and with the means by which they
attained them. It is not always easy to determine the
benefit, beyond a theoretical acquaintance with the pheno-
mena of the battle-field, to be derived from studying the
campaigns of the great masters of war.   It is true that no
successful general, whatever may have been his practical
knowledge, has neglected such study ; but while many have
borne witness to its efficacy, none have left a record of the
manner in which their knowledge of former campaigns
influenced their own conduct.

In the case of Stonewall Jackson, however, we have
much evidence, indirect, but unimpeachable, as to the
value to a commander of the knowledge thus acquired.
The Maxims of Napoleon, carried in his haversack, were
constantly consulted throughout his campaigns, and this
little volume contains a fairly complete exposition, in
Napoleon's own words, of the grand principles of war.
Moreover, Jackson often quoted principles which are not
to be found in the Maxims, but on which Napoleon

consistently acted. It is clear, therefore, that he had studied the campaigns of the great Corsican in order to discover the principles on which military success is based ; that having studied and reflected on those principles, and the effect their application produced, in numerous concrete cases, they became so firmly imbedded in his mind as to be ever present, guiding him into the right path, or warning him against the wrong, whenever he had to deal with a strategic or tactical situation.

It may be noted, moreover, that these principles, especially those which he was accustomed to quote, were concerned far more with the moral aspect of war than with the material. It is a fair inference, therefore, that it was to the study of human nature as affected by the conditions of war, by discipline, by fear, by the want of food, by want of information, by want of confidence, by the weight of responsibility, by political interests, and, above all, by surprise, that his attention was principally directed. He found in the campaigns of Jena and of Austerlitz not merely a record of marches and manœuvres, of the use of intrenchments, or of the general rules for attack and defence ; this is the mechanical and elementary part of the science of command. What Jackson learned was the truth of the famous maxim that the moral is to the physical—that is, to armament and numbers—as three to one. He learned, too, to put himself into his adversary's place and to realise his weakness. He learned, in a word, that war is a struggle between two intellects rather than the conflict of masses ; and it was by reason of this knowledge that he played on the hearts of his enemies with such extraordinary skill.

It is not to be asserted, however, that the study of military history is an infallible means of becoming a great or even a good general. The first qualification necessary for a leader of men is a strong character, the second, a strong intellect. With both Providence had endowed Jackson, and the strong intellect illuminates and explains the page that to others is obscure and meaningless. With its innate faculty for discerning what is essential and for discarding unimportant details, it discovers most valuable lessons where ordinary men see neither light nor leading. Endowed with the power of analysis and assimilation, and accustomed to observe and to reflect upon the relations between cause and effect, it will undoubtedly penetrate far deeper into the actual significance and practical bearing of historical facts than the mental vision which is less acute.

Jackson, by reason of his antecedent training, was eminently capable of the sustained intellectual efforts which strategical conceptions involve. Such was his self-command that under the most adverse conditions, the fatigues and anxieties of a campaign, the fierce excitement of battle, his brain, to use the words of a great Confederate general, 'worked with the precision of the most perfect machinery.'[1] But it was not only in the field, when the necessity for action was pressing, that he was accustomed to seclude himself with his own thoughts. Nor was he content with considering his immediate responsibilities. His interest in the general conduct of the war was of a very thorough-going character. While in camp on the Rappahannock, he followed with the closest attention the movements of the armies operating in the Valley of the Mississippi, and made himself acquainted, so far as was possible, not only with the local conditions of the war, but also with the character of the Federal leaders. It was said that, in the late spring of 1862, it was the intention of Mr. Davis to transfer him to the command of the Army of the Tennessee, and it is possible that some inkling of this determination induced him to study the Western theatre.[2] Be this as it may, the general situation, military and political, was always in his mind, and despite the victory of Fredericksburg, the future was dark and the indications ominous.

According to the Official Records, the North, at the beginning of April, had more than 900,000 soldiers under

---

[1] General G. B. Gordon. *Introduction to Memoirs of Stonewall Jackson,* p. xiv.

[2] In April he wrote to his wife: ' There is increasing probability that I may be elsewhere as the season advances.' That he said no more is characteristic.

arms; the South, so far as can be ascertained, not more than 600,000. The Army of the Potomac was receiving constant reinforcements, and at the beginning of April, 130,000 men were encamped on the Stafford Heights. In the West, the whole extent of the Mississippi, with the exception of the hundred miles between Vicksburg and Port Hudson, was held by the Federals, and those important fortresses were both threatened by large armies, acting in concert with a formidable fleet of gunboats. A third army, over 50,000 strong, was posted at Murfreesboro', in the heart of Tennessee, and large detached forces were operating in Louisiana and Arkansas. The inroads of the enemy in the West, greatly aided by the waterways, were in fact far more serious than in the East; but even in Virginia, although the Army of the Potomac had spent nearly two years in advancing fifty miles, the Federals had a strong foothold. Winchester had been reoccupied. Fortress Monroe was still garrisoned. Suffolk, on the south bank of the James, seventy miles from Richmond, was held by a force of 20,000 men; while another small army, of about the same strength, occupied New Berne, on the North Carolina coast.

Slowly but surely, before the pressure of vastly superior numbers, the frontiers of the Confederacy were contracting; and although in no single direction had a Federal army moved more than a few miles from the river which supplied it, yet the hostile occupation of these rivers, so essential to internal traffic, was making the question of subsistence more difficult every day. Louisiana, Texas and Arkansas, the cattle-raising States, were practically cut off from the remainder; and in a country where railways were few, distances long, and roads indifferent, it was impossible, in default of communication by water, to accumulate and distribute the produce of the farms. Moreover, the dark menace of the blockade had assumed more formidable proportions. The Federal navy, gradually increasing in numbers and activity, held the highway of the ocean in an iron grip; and proudly though the Confederacy bore her isolation, men looked across the waters with dread foreboding, for the shadow of their doom was already rising from the pitiless sea.

If, then, his staff officers had some reason to complain of their chief's silence and abstraction, it was by no means unfortunate for the South, so imminent was the danger, that the strong brain was incessantly occupied in forecasting the emergencies that might occur.

But not for a single moment did Jackson despair of ultimate success. His faith in the justice of the Southern cause was as profound as his trust in God's good providence. He had long since realised that the overwhelming strength of the Federals was more apparent than real. He recognised their difficulties; he knew that the size of an army is limited to the number that can be subsisted, and he relied much on the superior *moral* and the superior leading of the Confederate troops. After long and mature deliberation he had come to a conclusion as to the policy to be pursued. 'We must make this campaign,' he said, in a moment of unusual expansion, 'an exceedingly active one. Only thus can a weaker country cope with a stronger; it must make up in activity what it lacks in strength. A defensive campaign can only be made successful by taking the aggressive at the proper time. Napoleon never waited for his adversary to become fully prepared, but struck him the first blow.'

On these principles Jackson had good reason to believe General Lee had determined to act;[1] of their efficacy he was convinced, and when his wife came to visit him at the end of April, she found him in good heart and the highest spirits. He not only anticipated a decisive result from the forthcoming operations, but he had seen with peculiar satisfaction that a more manly tone was pervading the Confederate army. Taught by their leaders, by Lee, Jackson, Stuart, and many others, of whose worth and valour they had received convincing proof, the Southern soldiers had begun to practise the clean and wholesome virtue of self-control. They had discovered that purity

---

[1] 'There is no better way of defending a long line than by moving into the enemy's country.' Lee to General Jones, March 21, 1863; O. R., vol. xxv., part ii., p. 680.

and temperance are by no means incompatible with
military prowess, and that a practical piety, faithful in
small things as in great, detracts in no degree from skill
and resolution in the field. The Stonewall Brigade
set the example. As soon as their own huts were
finished, the men, of their own volition, built a log
church, where both officers and men, without distinction of
rank, were accustomed to assemble during the winter
evenings ; and those rude walls, illuminated by pine torches
cut from the neighbouring forest, witnessed such scenes
as filled Jackson's cup of content to overflowing. A chaplain writes : ' The devout listener, dressed in simple grey,
ornamented only with three stars, which any Confederate
colonel was entitled to wear, is our great commander,
Robert Edward Lee. That dashing-looking cavalry-man,
with " fighting jacket," plumed hat, jingling spurs, and gay
decorations, but solemn, devout aspect during the service,
is " Jeb " Stuart, the flower of cavaliers—and all through
the vast crowd wreaths and stars of rank mingle with the
bars of the subordinate officers and the rough garb of the
private soldier. But perhaps the most supremely happy of
the gathered thousands is Stonewall Jackson.' ' One could
not,' says another, ' sit in that pulpit and meet the concentrated gaze of those men without deep emotion. I
remembered that they were the veterans of many a bloody
field. The eyes which looked into mine, waiting for the
Gospel of peace, had looked steadfastly upon whatever is
terrible in war. Their earnestness of aspect constantly
impressed me. . . . They looked as if they had come on
business, and very important business, and the preacher
could scarcely do otherwise than feel that he, too, had
business of moment there ! '

At this time, largely owing to Jackson's exertions,
chaplains were appointed to regiments and brigades, and
ministers from all parts of the country were invited to
visit the camps. The Chaplains' Association, which did a
good work in the army, was established at his suggestion,
and although he steadfastly declined to attend its meetings,

deeming them outside his functions, nothing was neglected, so far as lay within his power, that might forward the moral welfare of the troops.

But at the same time their military efficiency and material comforts received his constant attention. Discipline was made stricter, indolent and careless officers were summarily dismissed, and the divisions were drilled at every favourable opportunity. Headquarters had been transferred to a tent near to Hamilton's Crossing, the general remarking, ' It is rather a relief to get where there will be less comfort than in a room, as I hope thereby persons will be prevented from encroaching so much upon my time.' On his wife's arrival he moved to Mr. Yerby's plantation, near Hamilton's Crossing, but ' he did not permit,' she writes, ' the presence of his family to interfere in any way with his military duties. The greater part of each day he spent at his headquarters, but returned as early as he could get off from his labours, and devoted all his leisure time to his visitors—little Julia having his chief attention and his care. His devotion to his child was remarked upon by all who beheld the happy pair together, for she soon learned to delight in his caresses as much as he loved to play with her. An officer's wife, who saw him often during this time, wrote to a friend in Richmond that " the general spent all his leisure time in playing with the baby." '

But these quiet and happy days were soon ended. On April 29 the roar of cannon was heard once more at April 29. Guiney's Station, salvo after salvo following in quick succession, until the house shook and the windows rattled with the reverberations. The crash of musketry succeeded, rapid and continuous, and before the sun was high wounded men were brought in to the shelter of Mr. Yerby's outhouses. Very early in the morning a message from the pickets had come in, and after making arrangements for his wife and child to leave at once for Richmond, the general, without waiting for breakfast, had hastened to the front. The Federals were crossing the

Rappahannock, and Stonewall Jackson had gone to his last field.[1]

[1] The Army of the Potomac was now constituted as follows:—

Engineer Brigade.	
First Corps.	Reynolds.
Second Corps.	Couch.
Third Corps.	Sickles.
Divisions.	Birney. Berry. Whipple.
Fifth Corps.	Meade.
Sixth Corps.	Sedgwick.
Eleventh Corps.	Howard.
Divisions.	McLean. Von Steinwehr. Schurz.
Twelfth Corps.	Slocum.
Divisions.	Williams. Geary
Cavalry Corps.	Stoneman.
Divisions.	Pleasonton. Averell. Gregg.

NOTE

Headquarters, Second Corps, Army of N. Va. :
April 13, 1863.

General Orders, No. 26.

I. . . . .

II. Each division will move precisely at the time indicated in the order of march, and if a division or brigade is not ready to move at that time, the next will proceed and take its place, even if a division should be separated thereby.

III. On the march the troops are to have a rest of ten minutes each hour. The rate of march is not to exceed one mile in twenty-five minutes, unless otherwise specially ordered. The time of each division commander will be taken from that of the corps commander. When the troops are halted for the purpose of resting, arms will be stacked, ranks broken, and in no case during the march will the troops be allowed to break ranks without previously stacking arms.

IV. When any part of a battery or train is disabled on a march, the officer in charge must have it removed immediately from the road, so that no part of the command be impeded upon its march.

Batteries or trains must not stop in the line of march to water; when any part of a battery or train, from any cause, loses its place in the column, it must not pass any part of the column in regaining its place.

Company commanders will march at the rear of their respective companies; officers must be habitually occupied in seeing that orders are strictly enforced; a day's march should be with them a day of labour; as much vigilance is required on the march as in camp.

Each division commander will, as soon as he arrive at his camping-ground, have the company rolls called, and guard details marched to the front of the regiment before breaking ranks; and immediately afterwards establish his chain of sentinels, and post his pickets so as to secure the safety of his command, and will soon thereafter report to their headquarters the disposition made for the security of his camp.

Division commanders will see that all orders respecting their divisions are carried out strictly; each division commander before leaving an encampment will have all damages occasioned by his command settled for by payment or covered by proper certificates.

V. All ambulances in the same brigade will be receipted for by the brigade quartermaster, they will be parked together, and habitually kept together, not being separated unless the exigencies of the service require, and on marches follow in rear of their respective brigades.

Ample details will be made for taking care of the wounded;

those selected will wear the prescribed badge; **and** no other person belonging to the army will be permitted to take part in this important trust.

Any one leaving his appropriate duty, under pretext of taking care of the wounded, will be promptly arrested, and as soon as charges can be made out, they will be forwarded.

By command of Lieutenant-General Jackson,

A. S. PENDLETON,
Assistant Adjutant-General.

CHAPTER XXIII

CHANCELLORSVILLE

It has already been said that while the Army of Northern Virginia lay in winter quarters the omens did not point to decisive success in the forthcoming campaign. During the same period that Lincoln and Stanton, taught by successive disasters, had ceased to interfere with their generals, Jefferson Davis and Mr. Seddon, his new Secretary of War, had taken into their own hands the complete control of military operations. The results appeared in the usual form : on the Northern side, unity of purpose and concentration ; on the Southern, uncertainty of aim and dispersion. In the West the Confederate generals were fatally hampered by the orders of the President. In the East the Army of Northern Virginia, confronted by a mass of more than 130,000 foes, was deprived of three of Longstreet's divisions ; and when, at the end of April, it was reported that Hooker was advancing, it was absolutely impossible that this important detachment could rejoin in time to assist in the defence of the Rappahannock.

A full discussion of the Chancellorsville campaign does not fall within the scope of this biography, but in justice to the Southern generals—to Lee who resolved to stand his ground, and to Jackson who approved the resolution—it must be explained that they were in no way responsible for the absence of 20,000 veterans. Undoubtedly the situation on the Atlantic littoral was sufficiently embarrassing to the Confederate authorities. The presence of a Federal force at New Berne, in North Carolina, threatened the main line of railway by which Wilmington and Charleston communicated with Richmond, and these two ports were of the utmost

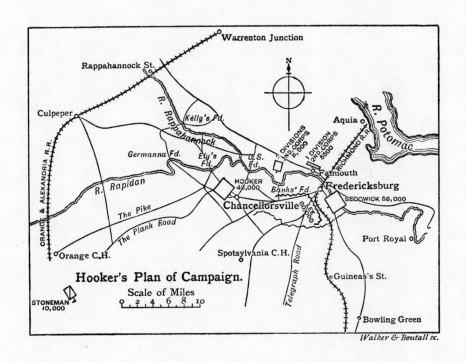

Hooker's Plan of Campaign.

Scale of Miles

importance to the Confederacy. So enormous were the profits arising from the exchange of munitions of war and medicines [1] for cotton and tobacco that English shipowners embarked eagerly on a lucrative if precarious traffic. Blockade-running became a recognised business. Companies were organised which possessed large fleets of swift steamers. The Bahamas and Bermuda became vast entrepôts of trade. English seamen were not to be deterred from a perilous enterprise by fear of Northern broadsides or Northern prisons, and despite the number and activity of the blockading squadrons the cordon of cruisers and gunboats was constantly broken. Many vessels were sunk, many captured, many wrecked on a treacherous coast, and yet enormous quantities of supplies found their way to the arsenals and magazines of Richmond and Atlanta. The railways, then, leading from Wilmington and Charleston, the ports most accessible to the blockade-runners, were almost essential to the existence of the Confederacy. Soon after the battle of Fredericksburg, General D. H. Hill was placed in command of the forces which protected them, and, at the beginning of the New Year, Ransom's division [2] was drawn from the Rappahannock to reinforce the local levies. A few weeks later [3] General Lee was induced by Mr. Seddon to send Longstreet, with the divisions of Hood and Pickett,[4] to cover Richmond, which was menaced both from Fortress Monroe and Suffolk.[5]

The Commander-in-Chief, however, while submitting to this detachment as a necessary evil, had warned General Longstreet so to dispose his troops that they could return to the Rappahannock at the first alarm. 'The enemy's position,' he wrote, 'on the sea-coast had been probably occupied merely for purposes of defence, it was likely that they were strongly intrenched, and nothing would be gained by attacking them.'

[1] Quinine sold in the South for one hundred dollars (Confederate) the ounce. O. R., vol. xxv., part ii., p. 79.

[2] 3,594 officers and men. Report of December 1. O. R., vol. xxi., p. 1082.

[3] Middle of February.

[4] Pickett, 7,165 ; Hood, 7,956—15,121 officers and men.

[5] Lee thought Pickett was sufficient. O. R., vol. xxi., p. 623.

The warning, however, was disregarded; and that Mr.
Seddon should have yielded, in the first instance, to the
influence of the sea-power, exciting apprehensions of sudden
attack along the whole seaboard of the Confederacy, may
be forgiven him.   Important lines of communication were
certainly exposed.   But when, in defiance of Lee's advice
that the divisions should be retained within easy reach of
Fredericksburg, he suggested to Longstreet the feasibility
of an attack on Suffolk, one hundred and twenty miles
distant from the Rappahannock, he committed an un-
pardonable blunder.

Had Jackson been in Longstreet's place, the Secretary's
proposal, however promising of personal renown, would
unquestionably have been rejected.   The leader who had
kept the main object so steadfastly in view throughout the
Valley campaign would never have overlooked the expressed
wishes of the Commander-in-Chief.   Longstreet, however,
brilliant fighting soldier as he was, appears to have miscon-
ceived the duties of a detached force.   He was already pre-
judiced in favour of a movement against Suffolk.   Before he
left for his new command, he had suggested to Lee that one
army corps only should remain on the Rappahannock, while
the other operated south of Richmond; and soon after his
arrival he urged upon his superior that, in case Hooker
moved, the Army of Northern Virginia should retire to the
North Anna.   In short, to his mind the operations of the
main body should be made subservient to those of the detached force; Lee, with 30,000 men, holding Hooker's
130,000 in check until Longstreet had won his victory and
could march north to join him.   Such strategy was not
likely to find favour at headquarters.   It was abundantly
evident, in the first place, that the Army of Northern
Virginia must be the principal objective of the Federals;
and, in the second place, that the defeat of the force of
Suffolk, if it were practicable, would have no effect whatever upon Hooker's action, except insomuch that his
knowledge of Longstreet's absence might quicken his resolution to advance.   Had Suffolk been a point vital to
the North the question would have assumed a different

shape. As it was, the town merely covered a tract of
conquered territory, the Norfolk dockyard, and the mouth
of the James River. The Confederates would gain little
by its capture ; the Federals would hardly feel its loss.
It was most improbable that a single man of Hooker's
army would be detached to defend a point of such
comparative insignificance, and it was quite possible that
Longstreet would be unable to get back in time to meet
him, even on the North Anna. General Lee, however,
anxious as ever to defer to the opinions of the man on the
spot, as well as to meet the wishes of the Government,
yielded to Longstreet's insistence that a fine opportunity
for an effective blow presented itself, and in the first week
of April the latter marched against Suffolk.

His movement was swift and sudden. But, as Lee had
anticipated, the Federal position was strongly fortified, with
the flanks secure, and Longstreet had no mind to bring
April 17. matters to a speedy conclusion. 'He could reduce
the place,' he wrote on April 17, 'in two or three
days, but the expenditure of ammunition would be very
large ; or he could take it by assault, but at a cost of 3,000
men.'

The Secretary of War agreed with him that the sacrifice
would be too great, and so, at a time when Hooker
was becoming active on the Rappahannock, Lee's lieutenant
was quietly investing Suffolk, one hundred and twenty
miles away.

From that moment the Commander-in-Chief abandoned
all hope that his missing divisions would be with him when
Hooker moved. Bitterly indeed was he to suffer for his selection of a commander for his detached force. The loss of
3,000 men at Suffolk, had the works been stormed, and
Hood and Pickett marched instantly to the Rappahannock,
would have been more than repaid. The addition of 12,000
fine soldiers, flushed with success, and led by two of the
most brilliant fighting generals in the Confederate armies,
would have made the victory of Chancellorsville a decisive
triumph. Better still had Longstreet adhered to his
original orders. But both he and Mr. Seddon forgot, as

Jackson never did, the value of time, and the grand principle of concentration at the decisive point.

Happily for the South, Hooker, although less flagrantly, was also oblivious of the first axiom of war. As soon as the weather improved he determined to move against Richmond. His task, however, was no simple one. On the opposite bank of the Rappahannock, from Banks' Ford to Port Royal, a distance of twenty miles, frowned line upon line of fortifications, protected by abattis, manned by a numerous artillery, against which it was difficult to find position for the Federal guns, and occupied by the victors of Fredericksburg. A frontal attack gave even less promise of success than in Burnside's disastrous battle. But behind Lee's earthworks were his lines of supply ; the Richmond Railway, running due south, with the road to Bowling Green alongside ; and second, the plank road, which, running at first due west, led past Chancellorsville, a large brick mansion, standing in a dense forest, to Orange Court House and the depôts on the Virginia Central Railroad.

At these roads and railways Hooker determined to strike, expecting that Lee would at once fall back, and give the Army of the Potomac the opportunity of delivering a heavy blow.[1] To effect his object he divided his 130,000 men into three distinct bodies. The cavalry, which, with the exception of one small brigade, had moved under General Stoneman to Warrenton Junction, was to march by way of Rappahannock Station, and either capturing or passing Culpeper and Gordonsville, to cut the Confederate communications, and should Lee retreat, to hold him fast.[2] General Sedgwick, with two army corps, the First and Sixth, forming the left wing of the army, was to cross the river below Fredericksburg, make a brisk demonstration of attack, and if the enemy fell back follow him rapidly down the Bowling Green and Telegraph roads. Then, while Lee's attention was thus attracted, the right wing,

[1] Hooker to Lincoln, April 12, O. R., vol. xxv., part ii., p. 199.

[2] The cavalry was to take supplies for six days, food and forage, depending on the country and on captures for any further quantity that might be required.

composed of the Fifth, Eleventh, and Twelfth Corps, with Pleasonton's brigade of cavalry, under Hooker's own command, would move up the Rappahannock to Kelly's Ford, push forward to the Rapidan, cross at Ely's and Germanna fords, and march upon Chancellorsville. The Third Corps was to remain concentrated on the Stafford Heights, ready to reinforce either wing as circumstances might require. The Second Corps was to leave one division on outpost at Falmouth, and to post two divisions on the north bank of the Rappahannock opposite Banks' Ford.

It will be observed that this design would place a wide interval between the two wings of the Federal army, thus giving the Confederates, although much inferior in numbers, the advantage of the interior lines.[1] Hooker, however, who knew the Confederate strength to a man, was confident that Lee, directly he found his position turned, and Stoneman in his rear, would at once retreat on Richmond. Yet he was not blind to the possibility that his great adversary, always daring, might assume the offensive, and attempt to crush the Federal wings in detail. Still the danger appeared small. Either wing was practically equal to the whole Confederate force. Sedgwick had 40,000, with the Third Corps, 19,000, and a division of the Second, 5,500, close at hand; Hooker 42,000, with two divisions of the Second Corps, 11,000, at Banks' Ford; the Third Corps could reinforce him in less than four-and-twenty hours; and Stoneman's 10,000 sabres, riding at will amongst Lee's supply depôts, would surely prevent him from attacking. Still precaution was taken in case the attempt were made. Sedgwick, if the enemy detached any considerable part of his force towards Chancellorsville, was ' to carry the works at all hazards, and establish his force on the Telegraph road.'[2] The right wing, ' if not strongly resisted, was to advance at all hazards, and secure a position uncovering

[1] From Franklin's Crossing below Fredericksburg, where Sedgwick's bridges were thrown, to Kelly's Ford is 27 miles; to Ely's Ford 19 miles, and to Chancellorsville 11 miles.

[2] O. R., vol. xxv., p. 268.

Banks' Ford.' [1]   Were the Confederates found in force near Chancellorsville, it was to select a strong position and await attack on its own ground, while Sedgwick, coming up from Fredericksburg, would assail the enemy in flank and rear.

Such was the plan which, if resolutely carried out, bade fair to crush Lee's army between the upper and the nether millstones, and it seems that the size and condition of his forces led Hooker to anticipate an easy victory. If the Army of the Potomac was not 'the finest on the planet,' as in an order of the day he boastfully proclaimed it, it possessed many elements of strength. Hooker was a strict disciplinarian with a talent for organisation. He had not only done much to improve the efficiency of his troops, but his vigorous measures had gone far to restore their confidence. When he succeeded Burnside a large proportion of the soldiers had lost heart and hope. The generals who had hitherto commanded them, when compared with Lee and Jackson, were mere pigmies, and the consciousness that this was the case had affected the entire army. The Official Records contain much justification of Jackson's anxiety that Burnside should be fought on the North Anna, where, if defeated, he might have been pursued. Although there had been no pursuit after the battle of Fredericksburg, no harassing marches, no continued retreat, with lack of supplies, abandoning of wounded, and constant alarms, the Federal regiments had suffered terribly in *moral*.

'The winter rains set in,' said Hooker, 'and all operations were for a while suspended, the army literally finding itself buried in mud, from which there was no hope of extrication before spring.

'With this prospect before it, taken in connection with the gloom and despondency which followed the disaster of Fredericksburg, the army was in a forlorn, deplorable condition. Reference to the letters from the army at this time, public and private, affords abundant evidence of its demoralisation ; and these, in their turn, had their effect upon the friends and relatives of the soldiers at

[1] O.R., vol. xxv., p. 274.

home. At the time the army was turned over to me desertions were at the rate of about two hundred a day. So anxious were parents, wives, brothers and sisters, to relieve their kindred, that they filled the express trains with packages of citizens' clothing to assist them in escaping from service. At that time, perhaps, a majority of the officers, especially those high in rank, were hostile to the policy of the Government in the conduct of the war. The emancipation proclamation had been published a short time before, and a large element of the army had taken sides antagonistic to it, declaring that they would never have embarked in the war had they anticipated the action of the Government. When rest came to the army, the disaffected, from whatever cause, began to show themselves, and make their influence felt in and out of the camps. I may also state that at the moment I was placed in command I caused a return to be made of the absentees of the army, and found the number to be 2,922 commissioned officers and 81,964 non-commissioned officers and privates. They were scattered all over the country, and the majority were absent from causes unknown.' [1]

In the face of this remarkable report it is curious to read, in the pages of a brilliant military historian, that ' armies composed of the citizens of a free country, who have taken up arms from patriotic motives . . . have constantly exhibited an astonishing endurance, and possessing a bond of cohesion superior to discipline, have shown their power to withstand shocks that would dislocate the structure of other military organisations.' [2] A force which had lost twenty-five per cent. of its strength by desertion, although it had never been pursued after defeat, would not generally be suspected of peculiar solidity. Nevertheless, the Northern soldiers must receive their due. Want of discipline made fearful ravages in the ranks, but, notwithstanding the defection of so many of their comrades, those that remained faithful displayed the best characteristics of their

[1] *Report of Committee on the Conduct of the War.*
[2] *Campaigns of the Army of the Potomac.* By William Swinton, p. 267.

race. The heart of the army was still sound, and only the influence of a strong and energetic commander was required to restore its vitality. This influence was supplied by Hooker. The cumbrous organisation of Grand Divisions was abolished. Disloyal and unsuccessful generals were removed. Salutary changes were introduced into the various departments of the staff. The cavalry, hitherto formed in independent brigades, was consolidated into a corps of three divisions and a brigade of regulars, and under a system of careful and uniform inspection made rapid improvement. Strong measures were taken to reduce the number of deserters. The ranks were filled by the return of absentees. New regiments were added to the army corps. The troops were constantly practised in field-exercises, and generals of well-deserved reputation were selected for the different commands. 'All were actuated,' wrote Hooker, 'by feelings of confidence and devotion to the cause, and I felt that it was a living army, and one well worthy of the Republic.'

On April 27, after several demonstrations, undertaken with a view of confusing the enemy, had been made at various points, the grand movement began.

The Confederate army still held the lines it had occupied for the past four months. Jackson's army corps extended from Hamilton's Crossing to Port Royal. McLaws' and Anderson's divisions occupied Lee's Hill and the ridge northward, and a brigade watched Banks' Ford. Stuart was with his main body, some 2,400 strong, at Culpeper, observing the great mass of Federal horsemen at Warrenton Junction, and the line of the Rappahannock was held by cavalry pickets.

The strength of the Army of Northern Virginia, so far as can be ascertained, did not exceed 62,000 officers and men.

Second Corps.

A. P. Hill's Division	11,500
Rodes' Division	9,500
Colston's (Jackson's own) Division	6,600
Early's Division	7,500
Artillery	2,100

First Corps.

Anderson's Division 8,100
McLaws' Division 8,600
Artillery 1,000

Cavalry.

Fitzhugh Lee's Brigade 1,500
W. H. F. Lee's Brigade (two regiments) . . . 900
Reserve Artillery 700
Add for reinforcements received since March 1, date
    of last return 4,000

                             Total . . 62,000
                            and 170 guns.

Thus the road to Richmond, threatened by a host of 130,000 men and 428 guns, was to be defended by a force of less than half the size. Ninety-nine generals out of a hundred would have considered the situation hopeless. The Confederate lines at Fredericksburg were certainly very strong, but it was clearly impossible to prevent the Federals outflanking them. The disparity in strength was far greater than at Sharpsburg, and it seemed that by sheer weight of numbers the Southern army must inevitably be driven back. Nor did it appear, so overwhelming were the Federal numbers, that counter-attack was feasible. The usual resource of the defender, if his adversary marches round his flank, is to strike boldly at his communications. Here, however, Hooker's communications with Aquia Creek were securely covered by the Rappahannock, and so great was his preponderance of strength, that he could easily detach a sufficient force to check the Confederates should they move against them.

Yet now, as on the Antietam, Lee and Jackson declined to take numbers into consideration. They knew that Hooker was a brave and experienced soldier, but they had no reason to anticipate that he would handle his vast masses with more skill than McClellan. That the Northern soldiers had suffered in *moral* they were well aware, and while they divined that the position they themselves had fortified might readily be made untenable, the fact that such was the case gave them small concern. They were agreed that the best measures of defence, if an opening offered, lay in a resolute offensive, and with Hooker in command it was not likely that the opportunity would be long delayed.

No thought of a strategic retreat, from one position to another, was entertained. Manœuvre was to be met by manœuvre, blow by counterblow.[1] If Hooker had not moved Lee would have forestalled him. On April 16 he had written to Mr. Davis : ' My only anxiety arises from the condition of our horses, and the scarcity of forage and provisions. I think it is all important that we should assume the aggressive by the 1st of May. . . . If we could be placed in a condition to make a vigorous advance at that time, I think the Valley could be swept of Milroy (commanding the Federal forces at Winchester), and the army opposite [Hooker's] be thrown north of the Potomac.'[2] Jackson, too, even after Hooker's plan was developed, indignantly repudiated the suggestion that the forthcoming campaign must be purely defensive. When some officer on his staff expressed his fear that the army would be compelled to retreat, he asked sharply, ' Who said that ? No, sir, we shall not fall back, we shall attack them.'

At the end of the month, however, Longstreet with his three divisions was still absent ; sufficient supplies for a forward movement had not yet been accumulated ;[3] two brigades of cavalry, Hampton's and Jenkins', which had been sent respectively to South Carolina and the Valley, had not rejoined,[4] and Hooker had already seized the initiative.

The first news which came to hand was that a strong force of all arms was moving up the Rappahannock in the

[1] ' The idea of securing the provisions, waggons, guns, of the enemy is truly tempting, and the idea has haunted me since December.' Lee to Trimble, March 8, 1862. O. R., vol. xxv., part ii., p. 658.

[2] O. R., vol. xxv., p. 725.

[3] ' From the condition of our horses and the amount of our supplies I am unable even to act on the defensive as vigorously as circumstances might require.' Lee to Davis, April 27, O. R., vol. xxv., p. 752.

[4] On April 20 Lee had asked that the cavalry regiments not needed in other districts might be sent to the Army of Northern Virginia. His request was not complied with until too late. O. R., vol. xxv., pp. 740, 741.

direction of Kelly's Ford. This was forwarded by Stuart on
April 28. the evening of April 28. The next the Federal
movements, which might have been morning
no more than a demonstration, became pronounced. Under
April 29. cover of a thick fog, pontoon bridges were laid
at Deep Run below Fredericksburg; Sedgwick's
troops began to cross, and were soon engaged with Jackson's
outposts; while, at the same time, the report came in that a
force of unknown strength had made the passage at Kelly's
Ford.

Lee displayed no perturbation. Jackson, on receiving
information of Sedgwick's movement from his outposts, had
sent an aide-de-camp to acquaint the Commander-in-Chief.
The latter was still in his tent, and in reply to the message
said: 'Well, I heard firing, and I was beginning to think
that it was time some of your lazy young fellows were
coming to tell me what it was about. Tell your good
general he knows what to do with the enemy just as well
as I do.'[1]

The divisions of the Second Army Corps were at once
called up to their old battle-ground, and while they were
on the march Jackson occupied himself with watching
Sedgwick's movements. The Federals were busily intrenching on the river bank, and on the heights behind
frowned the long line of artillery that had proved at
Fredericksburg so formidable an obstacle to the Confederate attack. The enemy's position was very strong,
and the time for counterstroke had not yet come. During
the day the cavalry was actively engaged between the
Rappahannock and the Rapidan, testing the strength of
the enemy's columns. The country was wooded, the
Federals active, and as usual in war, accurate information
was difficult to obtain and more difficult to communicate.
It was not till 6.30 P.M. that Lee received notice that
troops had crossed at Ely's and Germanna Fords at 2

[1] On March 12, before Hooker had even framed his plan of operations,
Lee had received information that the Federals, as soon as the state of the
roads permitted, would cross at United States, Falmouth, and some point
below; the attempt at Falmouth to be a feint. O. R., vol. xxv., part ii.,
p. 664.

P.M.   Anderson's division was at once despatched to Chancellorsville.

The next message, which does not appear to have been received until the morning of the 30th, threw more light on the situation. Stuart had made prisoners from the Fifth, the Eleventh, and the Twelfth Corps, and had ascertained that the corps commanders, Meade, Howard, and Slocum, were present with the troops. Anderson, moreover, who had been instructed to select and intrench a strong position, was falling back from Chancellorsville before the enemy's advance, and two things became clear :—

April 30.

1. That it was Hooker's intention to turn the Confederate left.

2. That he had divided his forces.

The question now to be decided was which wing should be attacked first. There was much to be said in favour of crushing Sedgwick. His numbers were estimated at 35,000 men, and the Confederates had over 60,000. Moreover, time is a most important consideration in the use of interior lines. The army was already concentrated in front of Sedgwick, whereas it would require a day's march to seek Hooker in the forest round Chancellorsville. Sedgwick's, too, was the smaller of the Federal wings, and his overthrow would certainly ruin Hooker's combinations. 'Jackson at first,' said Lee, 'preferred to attack Sedgwick's force in the plain of Fredericksburg, but I told him I feared it was as impracticable as it was at the first battle of Fredericksburg. It was hard to get at the enemy, and harder to get away if we drove him into the river, but if he thought it could be done, I would give orders for it.' Jackson asked to be allowed to examine the ground, but soon came to the conclusion that the project was too hazardous and that Lee was right. Orders were then issued for a concentration against Hooker, 10,000 men, under General Early, remaining to confront Sedgwick on the heights of Fredericksburg.

We may now turn to the movements of the Federals.

Hooker's right wing had marched at a speed which had

been hitherto unknown in the Army of the Potomac. At nightfall, on April 30, the three army corps, although they had been delayed by the Confederate cavalry, were assembled at Chancellorsville. In three days they had marched forty-six miles over bad roads, had forded breast-high two difficult rivers, established several bridges, and captured over a hundred prisoners.[1] Heavy reinforcements were in rear. The two divisions of the Second Corps had marched from Banks' Ford to United States Ford, six miles from Chancellorsville; while the Third Corps, ordered up from the Stafford Heights, was rapidly approaching the same point of passage. Thus, 70,000 men, in the highest spirits at the success of their manœuvres, were massed in rear of Lee's lines, and Hooker saw victory within his grasp.

'It is with heartfelt satisfaction,' ran his general order, 'that the commanding general announces to his army that the operations of the last three days have determined that our enemy must either ingloriously fly or come out from behind his defences, and give us battle on our own ground, where certain destruction awaits him. The operations of the Fifth, Eleventh, and Twelfth Corps have been a succession of splendid achievements.'

Hooker was 'skinning the lion while the beast yet lived,' but he had certainly much reason for congratulation. His manœuvres had been skilfully planned and energetically executed. The two rivers which protected the Confederate position had been crossed without loss; the Second and Third Corps had been brought into close touch with the right wing; Lee's earthworks were completely turned, and Stoneman's cavalry divisions, driving the enemy's patrols

---

[1] The troops carried eight days' supplies: three days' cooked rations with bread and groceries in the haversacks; five days' bread and groceries in the knapsacks; five days' 'beef on the hoof.' The total weight carried by each man, including sixty rounds of ammunition, was 45 lbs. The reserve ammunition was carried principally by pack mules, and only a small number of waggons crossed the Rappahannock. Four pontoon bridges were laid by the engineers. One bridge took three-quarters of an hour to lay; the other three, one and a half hour to lay, and an hour to take up. Each bridge was from 100 to 140 yards long. O. R., vol. xxv., pp. 215, 216.

before them, were already within reach of Orange Court
House, and not more than twenty miles from Gordonsville.
Best of all, the interval between the two wings—twenty-six
miles on the night of the 28th—was now reduced to eleven
miles by the plank road.

Two things only were unsatisfactory :—

1. The absence of information.

2. The fact that the whole movement had been observed
by the Confederate cavalry.

Pleasonton's brigade of horse had proved too weak for
the duty assigned to it.   It had been able to protect the
front, but it was too small to cover the flanks ; and at the
flanks Stuart had persistently struck.   Hooker appears to
have believed that Stoneman's advance against the Central
Railroad would draw off the whole of the Confederate
horse.   Stuart, however, was not to be beguiled from his
proper functions.   Never were his squadrons more skilfully
handled than in this campaign.   With fine tactical
insight, as soon as the great movement on Chancellorsville
became pronounced, he had attacked the right flank of the
Federal columns with Fitzhugh Lee's brigade, leaving only
the two regiments under W. H. F. Lee to watch Stoneman's
10,000 sabres.   Then, having obtained the information he
required, he moved across the Federal front, and routing
one of Pleasonton's regiments in a night affair near Spotsylvania Court House, he had regained touch with his own
army.   The results of his manœuvres were of the utmost
importance.   Lee was fully informed as to his adversary's
strength ; the Confederate cavalry was in superior strength
at the critical point, that is, along the front of the two
armies ; and Hooker had no knowledge whatever of what was
going on in the space between Sedgwick and himself. He was
only aware, on the night of April 30, that the Confederate
position before Fredericksburg was still strongly occupied.

The want, however, of accurate information gave him
no uneasiness.   The most careful arrangements had been
made to note and report every movement of the enemy the
next day.

No less than three captive balloons, in charge of skilled

observers, looked down upon the Confederate earthworks.[1] Signal stations and observatories had been established on each commanding height; a line of field telegraph had been laid from Falmouth to United States Ford, and the chief of the staff, General Butterfield, remained at the former village in communication with General Sedgwick. If the weather were clear, and the telegraph did not fail, it seemed impossible that either wing of the Federal army could fail to be fully and instantly informed of the situation of the other, or that a single Confederate battalion could change position without both Hooker and Sedgwick being at once advised.

Moreover, the Federal Commander-in-Chief was so certain that Lee would retreat that his deficiency in cavalry troubled him not at all. He had determined to carry out his original design. The next morning—May 1—the May 1. right wing was to move by the plank road and uncover Banks' Ford, thus still further shortening the line of communication between the two wings; and as the chief of the staff impressed on Sedgwick, it was 'expected to be on the heights west of Fredericksburg at noon or shortly after, or, if opposed strongly, at night.' Sedgwick, meanwhile, was 'to observe the enemy's movements with the utmost vigilance; should he expose a weak point, to attack him in full force and destroy him; should he show any symptom of falling back, to pursue him with the utmost vigour.' [2]

But Hooker was to find that mere mechanical precautions are not an infallible remedy for a dangerous situation. The Confederates had not only learned long since the importance of concealment, and the advantage of night marches, but in the early morning of May 1 the river mists rendered both balloons and observatories useless. Long before the sun broke through the fog, both McLaws and Jackson had joined Anderson at Tabernacle

[1] Balloons, which had been first used in the Peninsular campaign, were not much dreaded by the Confederates. 'The experience of twenty months' warfare has taught them how little formidable such engines of war are.' Special Correspondent of the *Times* at Fredericksburg, January 1, 1863.

[2] O. R., vol. xxv., p. 306.

Church, and a strong line of battle had been established at
the junction of the two roads, the pike and the plank,
which led east from Chancellorsville. The position was
favourable, running along a low ridge, partially covered
with timber, and with open fields in front. Beyond those
fields, a few hundred paces distant, rose the outskirts of
a great forest, stretching far away over a gently undulating
country. This forest, twenty miles in length from east to
west, and fifteen in breadth from north to south, has given
to the region it covers the name of the Wilderness of Spotsylvania, and in its midst the Federal army was now involved.
Never was ground more unfavourable for the manœuvres of
a large army. The timber was unusually dense. The groves
of pines were immersed in a sea of scrub-oak and luxuriant
undergrowth. The soil was poor. Farms were rare, and
the few clearings were seldom more than a rifle shot in
width. The woodland tracks were seldom travelled ;
streams with marshy banks and tortuous courses were met
at frequent intervals, and the only *débouchés* towards
Fredericksburg, the pike, the plank road, an unfinished
line of railway a mile south of their junction, and the
river road, about two miles north, were commanded from
the Confederate position.

When Jackson arrived upon the scene, Anderson, with
the help of Lee's engineers, had strongly intrenched the
whole front. A large force of artillery had
already taken post. The flanks of the line were
covered ; the right, which extended to near Duerson's Mill,
by Mott's Run and the Rappahannock ; the left, which
rested on the unfinished railroad not far from Tabernacle
Church, by the Massaponax Creek. For the defence of this
position, three miles in length, there were present 45,000
infantry, over 100 guns, and Fitzhugh Lee's brigade of
cavalry, a force ample for the purpose, and giving about
nine men to the yard. On the rolling ground eastward
there was excellent cover for the reserves, and from the
breastworks to the front the defiles, for such, owing to
the density of the wood, were the four roads by which
the enemy must approach, might be so effectively swept

8 A.M.

as to prevent him from deploying either artillery or infantry.

But Jackson was not disposed to await attack. Only 10,000 men remained in the Fredericksburg lines to confront Sedgwick, and if that officer acted vigorously, his guns would soon be heard in rear of the lines at Tabernacle Church. Work on the intrenchments was at once broken off, and the whole force was ordered to prepare for an immediate advance on Chancellorsville.

10.45 A.M.

Before eleven o'clock the rear brigades had closed up; and marching by the pike and the plank road, with a regiment of cavalry in advance, and Fitzhugh Lee upon the left, the Confederate army plunged resolutely into the gloomy depths of the great forest. Anderson's division led the way, one brigade on the pike, and two on the plank road; a strong line of skirmishers covered his whole front, and his five batteries brought up the rear. Next in order came McLaws, together with the two remaining brigades of Anderson, moving by the pike, while Jackson's three divisions were on the plank road. The artillery followed the infantry.

About a mile towards Chancellorsville the Federal cavalry was found in some force, and as the patrols gave way, a heavy force of infantry was discovered in movement along the pike. General McLaws, who had been placed in charge of the Confederate right, immediately deployed his four leading brigades, and after the Federal artillery, unlimbering in an open field, had fired a few rounds, their infantry advanced to the attack. The fight was spirited but short. The Northern regulars of Sykes' division drove in the Confederate skirmishers, but were unable to make ground against the line of battle. Jackson, meanwhile, who had been at once informed of the encounter, had ordered the troops on the plank road to push briskly forward, and the Federals, finding their right in danger of being enveloped, retired on Chancellorsville. Another hostile column was shortly afterwards met on the plank road, also marching eastward. Again there was a skirmish, and again Jackson, ordering a brigade to march

G G 2

rapidly along the unfinished railroad, had recourse to a
turning movement; but before the manœuvre was completed, the Federals began to yield, and all opposition
gradually melted away.   The following order was then sent
to McLaws :—

'Headquarters, Second Corps, Army of Northern Virginia,
2.30 P.M.   'May 1, 1863, 2.30 P.M. (received 4 P.M.).

'General,—The Lieutenant-General commanding directs
me to say that he is pressing up the plank road; also,
that you will press on up the turnpike towards Chancellorsville, as the enemy is falling back.
'Keep your skirmishers and flanking parties well out, to
guard against ambuscade.
'Very respectfully, your obedient servant,
'J. G. MORRISON,
'Acting Assistant Adjutant-General.' [1]

There was something mysterious in so easy a victory.
The enemy was evidently in great strength, for, on both
roads, heavy columns had been observed behind the lines
of skirmishers.   Several batteries had been in action;
cavalry was present; and the Confederate scouts reported
that a third column, of all arms, had marched by the river
road toward Banks' Ford, and had then, like the others, un-
accountably withdrawn.   The pursuit, therefore, was slow
and circumspect.   Wilcox' brigade, on the extreme right,
moved up the Mine road, in the direction of Duerson's
Mill; Wright's brigade, on the extreme left, followed Fitzhugh Lee's cavalry on the unfinished railroad; while the
main body, well closed up, still kept to the main highways.
At length, late in the afternoon, Hooker's tactics became
clear.   As Jackson's advanced-guards approached Chancel-
     5 P.M.   lorsville, the resistance of the Federal skirmishers,
               covering the retreat, became more stubborn.   From
the low ridge, fringed by heavy timber, on which the
mansion stands, the fire of artillery, raking every avenue of
approach, grew more intense, and it was evident that the
foe was standing fast on the defensive.

[1] O. R., vol. xxv., p. 764.

The Confederate infantry, pushing forward through the undergrowth, made but tardy progress; the cavalry patrols found that every road and bridle-path was strongly held, and it was difficult in the extreme to discover Hooker's exact position. Jackson himself, riding to the front to reconnoitre, nearly fell a victim to the recklessness he almost invariably displayed when in quest of information. The cavalry had been checked at Catherine Furnace, and were waiting the approach of the infantry. Wright's brigade was close at hand, and swinging round northwards, drove back the enemy's skirmishers, until, in its turn, it was brought up by the fire of artillery. Just at this moment Jackson galloped up, and begged Stuart to ride forward with him in order to find a point from which the enemy's guns might be enfiladed. A bridle-path, branching off from the main road to the right, led to a hillock about half a mile distant, and the two generals, accompanied by their staffs, and followed by a battery of horse-artillery, made for this point of vantage. 'On reaching the spot,' says Stuart's adjutant-general, ' so dense was the undergrowth, it was found impossible to find enough clear space to bring more than one gun at a time into position; the others closed up immediately behind, and the whole body of us completely blocked up the narrow road. Scarcely had the smoke of our first shot cleared away, when a couple of masked batteries suddenly opened on us at short range, and enveloped us in a storm of shell and canister, which, concentrated on so narrow a space, did fearful execution among our party, men and horses falling right and left, the animals kicking and plunging wildly, and everybody eager to disentangle himself from the confusion, and get out of harm's way. Jackson, as soon as he found out his mistake, ordered the guns to retire; but the confined space so protracted the operation of turning, that the enemy's cannon had full time to continue their havoc, covering the road with dead and wounded. That Jackson and Stuart with their staff officers escaped was nothing short of miraculous.' [1]

[1] *Memoirs of the Confederate War* Heros von Borcke.

Other attempts at reconnaissance were more successful. Before nightfall it was ascertained that Hooker was in strong force on the Chancellorsville ridge, along the plank road, and on a bare plateau to the southward called Hazel Grove. ' Here,' in the words of General Lee, ' he had assumed a position of great natural strength, surrounded on all sides by a dense forest, filled with a tangled undergrowth, in the midst of which breastworks of logs had been constructed, with trees felled in front, so as to form an almost impenetrable abattis. His artillery swept the few narrow roads, by which the position could be approached from the front, and commanded the adjacent woods. The left of his line extended from Chancellorsville towards the Rappahannock, covering the Bark Mill (United States) Ford, which communicated with the north bank of the river by a pontoon bridge. His right stretched westward along the Germanna Ford road (the pike) more than two miles. . . . As the nature of the country rendered it hazardous to attack by night, our troops were halted and formed in line of battle in front of Chancellorsville at right angles to the plank road, extending on the right to the Mine road, and to, the left in the direction of the Catherine Furnace.'

As darkness falls upon the Wilderness, and the fire of the outposts, provoked by every movement of the patrols, gradually dies away, we may seek the explanation of the Federal movements. On finding that his enemy, instead of 'ingloriously flying,' was advancing to meet him, and advancing with confident and aggressive vigour, Hooker's resolution had failed him. Waiting till his force was concentrated, until the Second and Third Corps had crossed at United States Ford, and were close to Chancellorsville, it was not till eleven o'clock on the morning of May 1 that he had marched in three great columns towards Fredericksburg. His intention was to pass rapidly through the Wilderness, secure the open ground about Tabernacle Church, and there, with ample space for deployment, to form for battle, and move against the rear of Marye's Hill.[1]

[1] O. R., vol. xxv., p. 324.

But before his advanced-guards got clear of the forest defiles they found the Confederates across their path, displaying an unmistakable purpose of pressing the attack. Hooker at once concluded that Lee was marching against him with nearly his whole force, and of the strength of that force, owing to the weakness of his cavalry, he was not aware. The news from the Stafford Heights was disquieting. As soon as the fog had lifted, about nine o'clock in the morning, the signal officers and balloonists had descried long columns of troops and trains marching rapidly towards Chancellorsville.[1] This was duly reported by the telegraph,[2] and it was correctly inferred to signify that Lee was concentrating against the Federal right. But at the same time various movements were observed about Hamilton's Crossing; columns appeared marching from the direction of Guiney's Station; there was much traffic on the railway, and several deserters from Lee's army declared, on being examined, that Hood's and Pickett's divisions had arrived from Richmond.[3] The statements of these men—who we may suspect were not such traitors as they appeared—were confirmed by the fact that Sedgwick, who was without cavalry, had noticed no diminution in the force which held the ridge before him.

It is easy, then, to understand Hooker's decision to stand on the defensive. With a prudent foresight which does him much credit, before he marched in the morning he had ordered the position about Chancellorsville, covering his lines of retreat to United States and Ely's Fords, to be reconnoitred and intrenched, and his front, as Lee said, was undoubtedly very strong. He would assuredly have done better had he attacked vigorously when he found the Confederates advancing. His sudden retrograde movement, especially as following the swift and successful manœuvres which had turned Lee's position, could not fail to have a discouraging effect upon the troops; and

[1] O. R., vol. xxv., pp. 323, 336.

[2] *Ibid.* p. 326. The telegraph, however, appears to have worked badly, and dispatches took several hours to pass from Falmouth to Chancellorsville.

[3] *Ibid.* p. 327.

if Sedgwick had been ordered to storm the Fredericksburg lines, the whole Federal force could have been employed, and the Confederates, assailed in front and rear simultaneously, must, to say the least, have been embarrassed. But in abandoning his design of crushing Lee between his two wings, and in retiring to the stronghold he had prepared, Hooker did what most ordinary generals would have done, especially one who had served on the losing side at Fredericksburg. He had there learned the value of intrenchments. He had seen division after division shatter itself in vain against a stone wall and a few gun-pits, and it is little wonder that he had imbibed a profound respect for defensive tactics. He omitted, however, to take into consideration two simple facts. First, that few districts contain two such positions as those of the Confederates at Fredericksburg; and, secondly, that the strength of a position is measured not by the impregnability of the front, but by the security of the flanks. The Fredericksburg lines, resting on the Rappahannock and the Massaponax, had apparently safe flanks, and yet he himself had completely turned them, rendering the whole series of works useless without firing a shot. Were Lee and Jackson the men to knock their heads, like Burnside, against stout breastworks strongly manned? Would they not rather make a wide sweep, exactly as he himself had done, and force him to come out of his works? Hooker, however, may have said that if they marched across his front, he would attack them *en route*, as did Napoleon at Austerlitz and Wellington at Salamanca, and cut their army in two. But here he came face to face with the fatal defect of the lines he had selected, and also of the disposition he had made of his cavalry. The country near Chancellorsville was very unlike the rolling plains of Austerlitz or the bare downs of Salamanca. From no part of the Federal position did the view extend for more than a few hundred yards. Wherever the eye turned rose the dark and impenetrable screen of close-growing trees, interlaced with wild vines and matted undergrowth, and seamed with rough roads, perfectly passable for troops, with which his enemies were far better acquainted than himself. Had Stoneman's cavalry been present, the squadrons, posted far out upon the flanks, and watching every track, might have given ample warning of any turning movement, exactly as Stuart's cavalry had given Lee warning of Hooker's own movement upon Chancellorsville. As it was, Pleasonton's brigade was too weak to make head against Stuart's regiments; and Hooker could expect no early information of his enemy's movements.

He thus found himself in the dilemma which a general on the defensive, if he be weak in cavalry, has almost invariably to face, especially in a close country. He was ignorant, and must necessarily remain ignorant, of where the main attack would be made. Lee, on the other hand, by means of his superior cavalry, could reconnoitre the position at his leisure, and if he discovered a weak point could suddenly throw the greater portion of his force against it. Hooker could only hope that no weak point existed. Remembering that the Confederates were on the pike and the plank road, there certainly appeared no cause for apprehension. The Fifth Corps, with its flank on the Rappahannock, held the left, covering the river and the old Mine roads. Next in succession came the Second Corps, blocking the pike. In the centre the Twelfth Corps, under General Slocum, covered Chancellorsville. The Third Corps, under Sickles, held Hazel Grove, with Berry's division as general reserve; and on the extreme right, his breastworks running along the plank road as far as Talley's Clearing, was Howard with the Eleventh Corps, composed principally of German regiments. Strong outposts of infantry had been thrown out into the woods; the men were still working in the intrenchments; batteries were disposed so as to sweep every approach from the south, the south-east, or the south-west, and there were at least five men to every yard of parapet. The line, however, six miles from flank to flank, was somewhat extensive, and to make certain, so far as possible, that sufficient numbers should be forthcoming to defend the position, at 1.55 on the morning of May 2, Sedgwick was instructed to send the First Army Corps to Chancellorsville. Before midnight, moreover, thirty-four guns, principally horse-artillery, together with a brigade of infantry, were sent from Falmouth to Banks' Ford.

Sedgwick, meantime, below Fredericksburg, had contented himself with engaging the outposts on the opposite ridge. An order to make a brisk demonstration, which Hooker had dispatched at 11.30 A.M., did not arrive, the telegraph having broken down, until 5.45 P.M., six hours later; and it was then too late to effect any diversion in favour of the main army.

Yet it can hardly be said that Sedgwick had risen to the height of his responsibilities. He knew that a portion at least of the Confederates had marched against Hooker, and the balloonists had early reported that a battle was in progress near Tabernacle Church. But instead of obeying Napoleon's maxim and marching to the sound of the cannon, he had made no effort to send support to his commander. Both he and General Reynolds[1] considered 'that to have attacked before Hooker had accomplished some success, in view of the strong position and numbers in their front, might have failed to dislodge the enemy, and have rendered them unserviceable at the proper time.'[2] That is, they were not inclined to risk their own commands in order to assist Hooker, of whose movements they were uncertain. Yet even if they had been defeated, Hooker would still have had more men than Lee.

[1] The following letter (O. R., vol. xxv., p. 337) is interesting as showing the state of mind into which the commanders of detached forces are liable to be thrown by the absence of information :—

'Headquarters, First Corps, May 1, 1863.

'Major-General Sedgwick,—I think the proper view to take of affairs is this : If they have not detached more than A. P. Hill's division from our front, they have been keeping up appearances, showing weakness, with a view of delaying Hooker, and tempting us to make an attack on their fortified position, and hoping to destroy us and strike for our depôt over our bridges. We ought therefore, in my judgment, *to know something of what has transpired on our right.*

'JOHN F. REYNOLDS, *Major-General.*'

[2] Dispatch of Chief of the Staff to Hooker, dated 4 P.M., May 1.   O. R., vol. xxv., p. 326.

429

CHAPTER XXIV

CHANCELLORSVILLE (*continued*)

AT a council of war held during the night at Chancellorsville House, the Federal generals were by no means unanimous as to the operations of the morrow. Some of the generals advised an early assault. Others favoured a strictly defensive attitude. Hooker himself wished to contract his lines so as to strengthen them; but as the officers commanding on the right were confident of the strength of their intrenchments, it was at length determined that the army should await attack in its present position.

Three miles down the plank road, under a grove of oak and pine, Lee and Jackson, while their wearied soldiers slept around them, planned for the fourth and the last time the overthrow of the great army with which Lincoln still hoped to capture Richmond. At this council there was no difference of opinion. If Hooker had not retreated before the morning—and Jackson thought it possible he was already demoralised—he was to be attacked. The situation admitted of no other course. It was undoubtedly a hazardous operation for an inferior force to assault an intrenched position; but the Federal army was divided, the right wing involved in a difficult and unexplored country, with which the Confederate generals and staff were more or less familiar, and an opportunity so favourable might never recur. 'Fortune,' says Napoleon, 'is a woman, who must be wooed while she is in the mood. If her favours are rejected, she does not offer them again.' The only question was where the attack should be delivered. Lee himself had reconnoitred the enemy's left. It was very strong, resting on the Rappahannock, and covered by a stream called Mineral Spring Run. Two of Jackson's staff officers had reconnoitred the front, and had pronounced it impregnable, except at a fearful sacrifice of life. But while the generals were debating, Stuart rode in with the reports of his cavalry officers, and the weak point of the position was at once revealed. General Fitzhugh Lee, to whose skill and activity the victory of Chancellorsville was in great part due, had discovered that the Federal right, on the plank road, was completely in the air; that is, it was protected by no natural obstacle, and the breastworks faced south, and south only. It was evident that attack from the west or north-west was not anticipated, and Lee at once seized upon the chance of effecting a surprise.

Yet the difficulties of the proposed operation were very great. To transfer a turning column to a point from which the Federal right might be effectively outflanked necessitated a long march by the narrow and intricate roadways of the Wilderness, and a division of the Confederate army into two parts, between which communication would be most precarious. To take advantage of the opportunity the first rule of war must be violated. But as it has already been said, the rules of war only point out the dangers which are incurred by breaking them; and, in this case, before an enemy on the defensive from whom the separation might be concealed until it is too late for him to intervene, the risks of dispersion were much reduced. The chief danger lay in this, that the two wings, each left to its own resources, might fail to act in combination, just as within the past twenty-four hours Hooker and Sedgwick had failed. But Lee knew that in Jackson he possessed a lieutenant whose resolution was invincible, and that the turning column, if entrusted to his charge, would be pushed forward without stop or stay until it had either joined hands with the main body, or had been annihilated.

Moreover, the battle of Fredericksburg had taught both armies that the elaborate constructions of the engineer are not the only or the most useful resources of fortification. Hooker had ordered his position to be intrenched in the hope that Lee and Jackson, following Burnside's example, would dash their divisions into fragments against them and thus become an easy prey. Lee, with a broader appreciation of the true tactical bearing of ditch and parapet, determined to employ them as a shelter for his own force until Jackson's movement was completed, and the time had come for a general advance. Orders were at once sent to General McLaws to cover his front, extending across the pike and the plank roads, with a line of breastworks; and long before daylight the soldiers of his division, with the scanty means at their disposal, were busy as beavers amongst the timber.

It only remained, then, to determine the route and the strength of the outflanking force; and here it may be observed that the headquarters staff appears to have neglected certain precautions for which there had been ample leisure. So long ago as March 19 a council of war had decided that if Hooker attacked he would do so by the upper fords, and yet the Wilderness, lying immediately south of the points of passage, had not been adequately examined. Had Jackson been on the left wing above Fredericksburg, instead of on the right, near Hamilton's Crossing, we may be certain that accurate surveys would have been forthcoming. As it was, the charts furnished to the Commander-in-Chief were untrustworthy, and information had to be sought from the country-people.

'About daylight on May 2,' says Major Hotchkiss, 'General Jackson awakened me, and requested that I
May 2. would at once go down to Catherine Furnace,
2.30 A.M. which is quite near, and where a Colonel Welford lived, and ascertain if there was any road by which we could secretly pass round Chancellorsville to the vicinity of Old Wilderness Tavern. I had a map, which our engineers had prepared from actual surveys, of the surrounding country, showing all the public roads, but with few details of the intermediate topography. Reaching Mr. Welford's, I aroused him from his bed, and soon learned that he himself had recently opened a road through the woods in that direction for the purpose of hauling cord-wood and iron ore to his furnace. This I located on the map, and having

asked Mr. Welford if he would act as a guide if it became necessary to march over that road, I returned to head-quarters. When I reached those I found Generals Lee and Jackson in conference, each seated on a cracker box, from a pile which had been left there by the Federals the day before. In response to General Jackson's request for my report, I put another cracker box between the two generals, on which I spread the map, showed them the road I had ascertained, and indicated, so far as I knew it, the position of the Federal army. General Lee then said, " General Jackson, what do you propose to do ? " He replied, " Go around here," moving his finger over the road which I had located upon the map. General Lee said, " What do you propose to make this movement with ? "   " With my whole corps," was the answer. General Lee then asked, " What will you leave me ? " " The divisions of Anderson and McLaws," said Jackson. General Lee, after a moment's reflection, remarked, " Well, go on," and then, pencil in hand, gave his last in-structions. Jackson, with an eager smile upon his face, from time to time nodded assent, and when the Com-mander-in-Chief ended with the words, " General Stuart will cover your movement with his cavalry," he rose and saluted, saying, " My troops will move at once, sir." [1] The necessary orders were forthwith dispatched.   The trains, parked in open fields to the rear, were to move to Todd's Tavern, and thence westward by interior roads ; the Second Army Corps was to march in one column, Rodes' division in front, and A. P. Hill's in rear ; the First Virginia Cavalry, with whom was Fitzhugh Lee, covered the front; squadrons of the 2nd, the 3rd, and the 5th were on the right ; Hotchkiss, accompanied by a squad of couriers, was to send back constant reports to General Lee ; the commanding officers were impressed with the im-portance of celerity and secrecy ; the ranks were to be kept well closed up, and all stragglers were to be bayoneted.

3.30 A.M.

---

[1] Letter to the author.   A letter of General Lee to Mrs. Jackson, which contains a reference to this council of war, appears as a Note at the end of the chapter.

The day had broken without a cloud, and as the troops began their march in the fresh May morning, the green vistas of the Wilderness, grass under foot, and thick foliage overhead, were dappled with sunshine. The men, comprehending intuitively that a daring and decisive movement was in progress, pressed rapidly forward, and General Lee, standing by the roadside to watch them pass, saw in their confident bearing the presage of success. Soon after the first regiments had gone by Jackson himself appeared at the head of his staff. Opposite to the Commander-in-Chief he drew rein, and the two conversed for a few moments. Then Jackson rode on, pointing in the direction in which his troops were moving. 'His face,' says an eyewitness, 'was a little flushed, as it was turned to General Lee, who nodded approval of what he said.' Such was the last interview between Lee and Jackson.

4.5 A.M.

Then, during four long hours, for the column covered at least ten miles, the flood of bright rifles and tattered uniforms swept with steady flow down the forest track. The artillery followed, the guns drawn by lean and wiry horses, and the ammunition waggons and ambulances brought up the rear. In front was a regiment of cavalry, the 5th Virginia, accompanied by General Fitzhugh Lee; on the flanks were some ten squadrons, moving by the tracks nearest the enemy's outposts; a regiment of infantry, the 23rd Georgia, was posted at the cross-roads near Catherine Furnace; and the plank road was well guarded until Anderson's troops came up to relieve the rear brigades of the Second Army Corps.

Meanwhile, acting under the immediate orders of General Lee, and most skilfully handled by McLaws and Anderson, the 10,000 Confederates who had been left in position opposite the Federal masses kept up a brisk demonstration. Artillery was brought up to every point along the front which offered space for action; skirmishers, covered by the timber, engaged the enemy's pickets, and maintained a constant fire, and both on the pike and the river road the lines of battle, disposed so as to give an impression of great strength, threatened instant assault. Despite all precautions, however, Jackson's movement did not escape the notice of the Federals. A mile north of Catherine Furnace the eminence called Hazel Grove, clear of timber, looked down the valley of the Lewis Creek, and 8 A.M. as early as 8 A.M. General Birney, commanding the Federal division at this point, reported the passage of a long column across his front.

The indications, however, were deceptive. At first, it is probable, the movement seemed merely a prolongation of the Confederate front; but it soon received a different interpretation. The road at the point where Jackson's column was observed turned due south; it was noticed that the troops were followed by their waggons, and that they were turning their backs on the Federal lines. Hooker, when he received Birney's report, jumped to the conclusion that Lee, finding the direct road to Richmond, through Bowling Green, 11 A.M. threatened by Sedgwick, was retreating on Gordonsville. About 11 A.M. a battery was ordered into action on the Hazel Grove heights. The fire caused some confusion in the Confederate ranks; the trains were forced on to another road ; and shortly after noon, General Sickles, commanding the Third Army Corps, was permitted by 12.15 P.M. Hooker to advance upon Catherine Furnace and to develop the situation. Birney's division moved forward, and Whipple's soon followed. This attack, which threatened to cut the Confederate army in two, was so vigorously opposed by Anderson's division astride the plank road and by the 23rd Georgia at the Furnace, that General Sickles was constrained to call for reinforcements. Barlow's brigade, which had hitherto formed the reserve of the Eleventh Corps, holding the extreme right of the Federal line, the flank at which Jackson was aiming, was sent to his assistance. Pleasonton's cavalry brigade followed. Sickles' movement, even before the fresh troops arrived, had met with some success. The 23rd Georgia, driven back to the unfinished railroad and surrounded, lost 300 officers and men. But word had been sent to Jackson's column, and Colonel Brown's artillery battalion, together with the brigades of Archer and Thomas, rapidly retracing their steps, checked the advance in front, while Anderson, manœuvring his troops with vigour, struck heavily against the flank. Jackson's train, thus effectively protected, passed the dangerous point in safety, and then Archer and Thomas, leaving Anderson to deal with Sickles, drew off and pursued their march.

These operations, conducted for the most part in blind thickets, consumed much time, and Jackson was already far in advance. Moving in a south-westerly direction, he had struck the Brock road, a narrow track which runs nearly due north, and crosses both the plank road and the pike at a point about two miles west of the Federal right flank. The Brock road, which, had Stoneman's three divisions of cavalry been present with the Federal army, would have been strongly held, was absolutely free and unobstructed. Since the previous evening Fitzhugh Lee's patrols had remained in close touch with the enemy's outposts, and no attempt had been made to drive them in. So with no further obstacle than the heat the Second Army Corps pressed on. Away to the right, echoing faintly through the Wilderness, came the sound of cannon and the roll of musketry; couriers from the rear, galloping at top speed, reported that the trains had been attacked, that the rear brigades had turned back to save them, and that the enemy, in heavy strength, had already filled the gap which divided the Confederate wings. But, though the army was cut in two, Jackson cast no look behind him. The battle at the Furnace made no more impression on him than if it was being waged on the Mississippi. He had his orders to execute; and above all, he was moving at his best speed towards the enemy's weak point. He knew—and none better—that Hooker would not long retain the initiative; that every man detached from the Federal centre made his own chances of success the more certain; and trusting implicitly in Lee's ability to stave off defeat, he rode northwards with redoubled assurance of decisive victory. Forward was the cry, and though the heat was stifling, and the dust, rising from the deep ruts on the unmetalled road, rose in dense clouds beneath the trees, and men dropped fainting in the ranks, the great column pushed on without a check.[1]

About 2 P.M., as the rear brigades, Archer and Thomas, after checking Sickles, were just leaving Welford's House, some six miles distant, Jackson himself had reached the plank road, the point where he intended to turn eastward against the Federal flank. Here he was met by Fitzhugh Lee, conveying most important and surprising information.

2 P.M.

The cavalry regiment had halted when it arrived on the plank road ; all was reported quiet at the front ; the patrols were moving northward, and, attended by a staff officer, the young brigadier had ridden towards the turnpike. The path they followed led to a wide clearing at the summit of a hill, from which there was a view eastward as far as Dowdall's Tavern. Below, and but a few hundred yards distant, ran the Federal breastworks, with abattis in front and long lines of stacked arms in rear; but untenanted by a single company. Two cannon were seen upon the highroad, the horses grazing quietly near at hand. The soldiers were scattered in small groups, laughing, cooking, smoking, sleeping, and playing cards, while others were butchering cattle and drawing rations. What followed is best told in General Fitzhugh Lee's own words.

'I rode back and met Jackson. "General," said I, "if you will ride with me, halting your columns here, out of sight, I will show you the great advantage of attacking down the old turnpike instead of the plank road, the enemy's lines being taken in reverse. Bring only one courier, as you will be in view from the top of the hill." Jackson assented. When we reached the eminence the picture below was still unchanged, and I watched him closely as he gazed on Howard's troops. His expression was one of intense interest. His eyes burnt with a brilliant glow, and his face was slightly flushed, radiant at the success of his flank movement. To the remarks made to him while the unconscious line of blue was pointed out

---

[1] There were three halts during the march of fourteen miles. Letter from Major Hotchkiss.

he made no reply, and yet during the five minutes he was on the hill his lips were moving. " Tell General Rodes," he said, suddenly turning his horse towards the courier, "to move across the plank road, and halt when he gets to the old turnpike. I will join him there." One more look at the Federal lines, and he rode rapidly down the hill.'

The cavalry, supported by the Stonewall Brigade, was immediately placed a short distance down the plank road, in order to mask the march of the column. At 4 P.M. Rodes was on the turnpike. Passing down it for about a mile, in the direction of the enemy's position, the troops were ordered to halt and form for battle. Not a shot had been fired. A few hostile patrols had been observed, but along the line of breastworks, watched closely by the cavalry, the Federal troops, still in the most careless security, were preparing their evening meal. Jackson, meanwhile, seated on a stump near the Brock road, had penned his last dispatch to General Lee.

'Near 3 P.M. May 2, 1863.

'General,—The enemy has made a stand at Chancellor's,[1] which is about two miles from Chancellorsville. I hope as soon as practicable to attack. I trust that an ever-kind Providence will bless us with great success.

'Respectfully,

'T. J. JACKSON, Lieutenant-General.

'The leading division is up, and the next two appear to be well closed.

'T. J. J.

'General R. E. Lee.'

25,000 men were now deploying in the forest within a mile of the Federal works, overlapping them both to north and south, and not a single general in the Northern army appears to have suspected their presence. The day had passed quietly at Chancellorsville. At a very early hour in

[1] Melzi Chancellor's house; otherwise Dowdall's Tavern.

H H 2

the morning Hooker, anticipating a vigorous attack, had ordered the First Army Corps, which had hitherto been acting with Sedgwick below Fredericksburg, to recross the Rappahannock and march to Chancellorsville. Averell's division of cavalry, also, which had been engaged near Orange Court House with W. H. F. Lee's two regiments, was instructed about the same time to rejoin the army as soon as possible, and was now marching by the left bank of the Rapidan to Ely's Ford. Anticipating, therefore, that he would soon be strongly reinforced, Hooker betrayed no uneasiness. Shortly after dawn he had ridden round his lines. Expecting at that time to be attacked in front only, he had no fault to find with their location or construction. 'As he looked over the barricades,' says General Howard, 'while receiving the cheers and salutes of the men, he said to me, "How strong! how strong!"' When the news came that a Confederate column was marching westward past Catherine Furnace, his attention, for the moment, was attracted to his right. At 10 A.M. he was still uncertain as to the meaning of Jackson's movement. As the hours went by, however, and Jackson's column disappeared in the forest, he again grew confident; the generals were informed that Lee was in full retreat towards Gordonsville, and a little later Sedgwick received the following :

'Chancellorsville, May 2, 1863, 4.10 P.M.

'General Butterfield,—The Major-General Commanding directs that General Sedgwick cross the river (*sic*) as soon as indications will permit,[1] capture Fredericksburg with everything in it, and vigorously pursue the enemy. We know that the enemy is fleeing, trying to save his trains. Two of Sickles' divisions are among them.
'J. H. VAN ALEN,
'*Brigadier-General and Aide-de-Camp.*'

'(Copy from Butterfield, at Falmouth, to Sedgwick, 5.50 P.M.).'

[1] Sedgwick had crossed the river on April 29 and 30.

At 4 o'clock, therefore, the moment Jackson's vanguard reached the old turnpike near Luckett's Farm, Hooker believed that all danger of a flank attack had passed away. His left wing was under orders to advance, as soon as a swamp to the front could be 'corduroyed,' and strike Lee in flank; while to reinforce Sickles, 'among the enemy's trains,' Williams' division of the Twelfth Corps was sent forward from the centre, Howard's reserve brigade (Barlow's) from the right, and Pleasonton's cavalry brigade from Hazel Grove.

The officers in charge of the Federal right appear to have been as unsuspicious as their commander. During the morning some slight preparations were made to defend the turnpike from the westward; a shallow line of rifle-pits, with a few epaulements for artillery, had been constructed on a low ridge, commanding open fields, which runs north from Dowdall's Tavern, and the wood beyond had been partially entangled. But this was all, and even when the only reserve of the Eleventh Army Corps, Barlow's brigade, was sent to Sickles, it was not considered necessary to make any change in the disposition of the troops. The belief that Lee and Jackson were retreating had taken firm hold of every mind. The pickets on the flank had indeed reported, from time to time, that infantry was massing in the thickets; and the Confederate cavalry, keeping just outside effective range, occupied every road and every clearing. Yet no attempt was made, by a strong reconnaissance in force, to ascertain what was actually going on within the forest; and the reports of the scouts were held to be exaggerated.

The neglect was the more marked in that the position of the Eleventh Army Corps was very weak. Howard had with him twenty regiments of infantry and six batteries; but his force was completely isolated. His extreme right, consisting of four German regiments, was posted in the forest, with two guns facing westward on the pike, and a line of intrenchments facing south. On the low hill eastward, where Talley's Farm, a small wooden cottage, stood in the midst of a wide clearing, were two more German regiments and two American. Then, near the junction of the roads, intervened a patch of forest, which was occupied by four regiments, with a brigade upon their left; and beyond, nearly a mile wide from north to south, and five or six hundred yards in breadth, were the open fields round the little Wilderness Church, dipping at first to a shallow brook, and then rising gradually to a house called Dowdall's Tavern. In these fields, south of the turnpike, were the breastworks held by the second division of the Eleventh Army Corps; and here were six regiments, with several batteries in close support. The 60th New York and 26th Wisconsin, near the Hawkins House at the north end of the fields, faced to the west; the remainder all faced south. Beyond Dowdall's Tavern rose the forest, dark and impenetrable to the view; but to the south-east, nearly two miles from Talley's, the clearings of Hazel Grove were plainly visible. This part of the line, originally entrusted to General Sickles, was now unguarded, for two divisions of the Third Corps were moving on the Furnace; and the nearest force which could render support to Howard's was Berry's division, retained in reserve north-east of Chancellorsville, three miles distant from Talley's Farm and nearly two from Howard's left.

The Confederates, meanwhile, were rapidly forming for attack. Notwithstanding their fatigue, for many of the brigades had marched over fifteen miles, the men were in the highest spirits. A young staff-officer, who passed along the column, relates that he was everywhere recognised with the usual greetings. 'Say, here's one of old Jack's little boys; let him by, boys!' 'Have a good breakfast this morning, sonny?' 'Better hurry up, or you'll catch it for gettin' behind.' 'Tell old Jack we're all a-comin'. Don't let him begin the fuss till we get there!' But on reaching the turnpike orders were given that all noise should cease, and the troops, deploying for a mile or more on either side of the road, took up their formation for attack. In front were the skirmishers of Rodes' division, under Major Blackford; four hundred yards in rear came the lines of battle, Rodes forming the first line ; [1] Colston, at two hundred yards distance, the second line ; A. P. Hill, part in line and part in column, the third. In little more than an hour-and-a-half, notwithstanding the dense woods, the formation was completed, and the lines dressed at the proper angle to the road.

5.45 p.m. Notwithstanding that the enemy might at any moment awake to their danger, not a single precaution was neglected. Jackson was determined that the troops should move forward in good order, and that every officer and man should know what was expected from him. Staff-officers had been stationed at various points to maintain communication between the divisions, and the divisional and brigade commanders had received their instructions. The whole force was to push resolutely forward through the forest. The open hill, about a thousand yards eastward, on which stood Talley's Farm, was to be carried at all hazard, for, so far as could be ascertained, it commanded, over an intervening patch of forest, the ridge which ran north from Dowdall's Tavern. After the capture of the heights at Talley's, if the Federals showed a determined front on their second line, Rodes was to halt under cover until the artillery could come up and dislodge them. Under no other circumstances was there to be any pause in the advance. A brigade of the first line was detailed to guard the right flank, a regiment the left ; and the second and third lines were ordered to support the first, whenever it might be necessary, without waiting for further instructions. The field hospital was established at the Old Wilderness Tavern.

The men were in position, eagerly awaiting the signal ; their quick intelligence had already realised the situation, and all was life and animation. Across the narrow clearing stretched the long grey lines, penetrating far into the forest on either flank ; in the centre, on the road, were four

---

[1] Rodes' brigades were formed in the following order :

....

∶ | ‾‾‾ ‾‾‾ ‾‾‾ ‾‾‾   ·········
     Iverson O'Neal Doles Colquitt
                        ‾‾‾‾ ∶
                       Ramseur

Napoleon guns, the horses fretting with excitement; far to the rear, their rifles glistening under the long shafts of the setting sun, the heavy columns of A. P. Hill's division were rapidly advancing, and the rumble of the artillery, closing to the front, grew louder and louder. Jackson, watch in hand, sat silent on 'Little Sorrel,' his slouched hat drawn low over his eyes, and his lips tightly compressed. On his right was General Rodes, tall, lithe, and soldierly, and on Rodes' right was Major Blackford.

'Are you ready, General Rodes?' said Jackson.

'Yes, sir,' said Rodes, impatient as his men.

'You can go forward, sir,' said Jackson.

A nod from Rodes was a sufficient order to Blackford, and the woods rang with the notes of a single bugle. Back came the responses from bugles to right and
6 P.M.   left, and the skirmishers, dashing through the wild undergrowth, sprang eagerly to their work, followed by the quick rush of the lines of battle. For a moment the troops seemed buried in the thickets; then, as the enemy's sentries, completely taken by surprise, fired a few scattered shots, and the guns on the turnpike came quickly into action, the echoes waked; through the still air of the summer evening rang the rebel yell, filling the forest far to north and south, and the hearts of the astonished Federals, lying idly behind their breastworks, stood still within them.

So rapid was the advance, so utterly unexpected the attack, that the pickets were at once over-run; and, crashing through the timber, driving before it the wild creatures of the forest, deer, and hares, and foxes, the broad front of the mighty torrent bore down upon Howard's flank. For a few moments the four regiments which formed his right, supported by two guns, held staunchly together, and even checked for a brief space the advance of O'Neal's brigade. But from the right and from the left the grey infantry swarmed round them; the second line came surging forward to O'Neal's assistance; the gunners were shot down and their pieces captured; and in ten minutes the right brigade of the Federal army, sub-

merged by numbers, was flying in panic across the clearing.
Here, near Talley's Farm, on the fields south of the turnpike and in the forest to the north, another brigade, hastily
changing front, essayed to stay the rout. But Jackson's
horse-artillery, moving forward at a gallop, poured in
canister at short range; and three brigades, O'Neal's,
Iverson's, and Doles', attacked the Northerners fiercely in
front and flank. No troops, however brave, could have
long withstood that overwhelming rush. The slaughter
was very great; every mounted officer was shot down, and
in ten or fifteen minutes the fragments of these hapless regiments were retreating rapidly and tumultuously towards
the Wilderness Church.

The first position had been captured, but there was
no pause in the attack. As Jackson, following the
artillery, rode past Talley's Farm, and gazed across the
clearing to the east, he saw a sight which raised high his
hopes of a decisive victory. Already, in the green corn-
fields, the spoils of battle lay thick around him. Squads
of prisoners were being hurried to the rear. Abandoned
guns, and waggons overturned, the wounded horses still
struggling in the traces, were surrounded by the dead and
dying of Howard's brigades. Knapsacks, piled in regular
order, arms, blankets, accoutrements, lay in profusion near
the breastworks; and beyond, under a rolling cloud of
smoke and dust, the bare fields, sloping down to the brook,
were covered with fugitives. Still further eastward, along
the plank road, speeding in wild confusion towards Chancellorsville, was a dense mass of men and waggons; cattle,
maddened with fright, were rushing to and fro, and on the
ridge beyond the little church, pushing their way through
the terror-stricken throng like ships through a heavy sea, or
breaking into fragments before the pressure, the irregular
lines of a few small regiments were moving hastily to the
front. At more than one point on the edge of the distant
woods guns were coming into action; the hill near Talley's
Farm was covered with projectiles; men were falling, and
the Confederate first line was already in some confusion.

Galloping up the turnpike, and urging the artillery for-

ward with voice and gesture, Jackson passed through the
ranks of his eager infantry; and then Rodes's division,
rushing down the wooded slopes, burst from the covert, and,
driving their flying foes before them, advanced against the
trenches on the opposite ridge.　Here and there the rush
of the first line was checked by the bold resistance of the
German regiments.　On the right, especially, progress was
slow, for Colquitt's brigade, drawn off by the pressure of
Federal outposts in the woods to the south, had lost touch
with the remainder of the division; Ramseur's brigade in
rear had been compelled to follow suit, and on this flank
the Federals were most effectively supported by their
artillery.　But Iverson, O'Neal, and Doles, hardly halting to
reform as they left the woods, and followed closely by the
second line, swept rapidly across the fields, dashed back
the regiments which sought to check them, and under a
hot fire of grape and canister pressed resolutely forward.

The rifle-pits on the ridge were occupied by the last
brigade of Howard's Army Corps.　A battery was in rear,
three more were on the left, near Dowdall's Tavern, and
many of the fugitives from Talley's Farm had rallied behind
the breastwork.　But a few guns and four or five thousand
rifles, although the ground to the front was clear and open,
were powerless to arrest the rush of Jackson's veterans.
The long lines of colours, tossing redly above the swiftly
moving ranks, never for a moment faltered; the men,
running alternately to the front, delivered their fire, stopped
for a moment to load, and then again ran on.　Nearer
and nearer they came, until the defenders of the trenches,
already half demoralised, could mark through the smoke-
drift the tanned faces, the fierce eyes, and the gleaming
bayonets of their terrible foes.　The guns were already
flying, and the position was outflanked; yet along the whole
length of the ridge the parapets still blazed with fire; and
while men fell headlong in the Confederate ranks, for a
moment there was a check.　But it was the check of a
mighty wave, mounting slowly to full volume, ere it falls in
thunder on the shrinking sands.　Running to the front with
uplifted swords, the officers gave the signal for the charge.

The men answered with a yell of triumph ; the second line, closing rapidly on the first, could no longer be restrained ; and as the grey masses, crowding together in their excitement, breasted the last slope, the Federal infantry, in every quarter of the field, gave way before them ; the ridge was abandoned, and through the dark pines beyond rolled the rout of the Eleventh Army Corps.

It was seven o'clock. Twilight was falling on the woods; and Rodes' and Colston's divisions had become so 7 p.m. inextricably mingled that officers could not find their men nor men their officers. But Jackson, galloping into the disordered ranks, directed them to press the pursuit. His face was aglow with the blaze of battle. His swift gestures and curt orders, admitting of no question, betrayed the fierce intensity of his resolution. Although the great tract of forest, covering Chancellorsville on the west, had swallowed up the fugitives, he had no need of vision to reveal to him the extent of his success. 10,000 men had been utterly defeated. The enemy's right wing was scattered to the winds. The Southerners were within a mile-and-a-half of the Federals' centre and completely in rear of their intrenchments; and the White House or Bullock road, only half-a-mile to the front, led directly to Hooker's line of retreat by the United States Ford. Until that road was in his possession Jackson was determined to call no halt. The dense woods, the gathering darkness, the fatigue and disorder of his troops, he regarded no more than he did the enemy's overwhelming numbers. In spirit he was standing at Hooker's side, and he saw, as clearly as though the intervening woods had been swept away, the condition to which his adversary had been reduced.

To the Federal headquarters confusion and dismay had come, indeed, with appalling suddenness. Late in the afternoon Hooker was sitting with two aides-de-camp in the verandah of the Chancellor House. There were few troops in sight. The Third Corps and Pleasonton's cavalry had long since disappeared in the forest. The Twelfth Army Corps, with the exception of two brigades, was already advancing against Anderson ; and only the trains and some artillery remained

within the intrenchments at Hazel Grove. All was going
well. A desultory firing broke out at intervals to the eastward, but it was not sustained ; and three miles to the south,
where, as Hooker believed, in pursuit of Jackson, Sickles
and Pleasonton were, the reports of their cannon, growing
fainter and fainter as they pushed further south, betokened
no more than a lively skirmish. The quiet of the Wilderness, save for those distant sounds, was undisturbed, and
men and animals, free from every care, were enjoying the
calm of the summer evening. It was about half-past
six. Suddenly the cannonade swelled to a heavier roar,
and the sound came from a new direction. All were
listening intently, speculating on what this might mean,
when a staff-officer, who had stepped out to the front
of the house and was looking down the plank road with
his glass, exclaimed : ' My God, here they come ! '
Hooker sprang upon his horse ; and riding rapidly down
the road, met the stragglers of the Eleventh Corps—men,
waggons, and ambulances, an ever-increasing crowd—
rushing in blind terror from the forest, flying they knew
not whither. The whole of the right wing, they said,
overwhelmed by superior numbers, was falling back on
Chancellorsville, and Stonewall Jackson was in hot pursuit.

The situation had changed in the twinkling of an eye.
Just now congratulating himself on the complete success
of his manœuvres, on the retreat of his enemies, on the
flight of Jackson and the helplessness of Lee, Hooker
saw his strong intrenchments taken in reverse, his army
scattered, his reserves far distant, and the most dreaded of
his opponents, followed by his victorious veterans, within a
few hundred yards of his headquarters. His weak point had
been found, and there were no troops at hand wherewith
to restore the fight. The centre was held only by the two
brigades of the Twelfth Corps at the Fairview Cemetery.
The works at Hazel Grove were untenanted, save by a few
batteries and a handful of infantry. The Second and Fifth
Corps on the left were fully occupied by McLaws, for Lee,
at the first sound of Jackson's guns, had ordered a vigorous
attack up the pike and the plank road. Sickles, with

20,000 men, was far away, isolated and perhaps surrounded, and the line of retreat, the road to United States Ford, was absolutely unprotected.

Messengers were despatched in hot haste to recall Sickles and Pleasonton to Hazel Grove. Berry's division, forming the reserve north-east of the Chancellor House, was summoned to Fairview, and Hays' brigade of the Second Corps ordered to support it. But what could three small brigades, hurried into position and unprotected by intrenchments, avail against 25,000 Southerners, led by Stonewall Jackson, and animated by their easy victory? If Berry and Hays could stand fast against the rush of fugitives, it was all that could be expected; and as the uproar in the dark woods swelled to a deeper volume, and the yells of the Confederates, mingled with the crash of the musketry, were borne to his ears, Hooker must have felt that all was lost. To make matters worse, as Pleasonton, hurrying back with his cavalry, arrived at Hazel Grove, the trains of the Third Army Corps, fired on by the Confederate skirmishers, dashed wildly across the clearing, swept through the parked artillery, and, breaking through the forest, increased the fearful tumult which reigned round Chancellorsville.

The gunners, however, with a courage beyond all praise, stood staunchly to their pieces; and soon a long line of artillery, for which two regiments of the Third Army Corps, coming up rapidly from the south, formed a sufficient escort, was established on this commanding hill. Other batteries, hitherto held in reserve, took post on the high ground at Fairview, a mile to the north-east, and, although Berry's infantry were not yet in position, and the stream of broken troops was still pouring past, a strong front of fifty guns opposed the Confederate advance.

But it was not the artillery that saved Hooker from irretrievable disaster.[1] As they followed the remnants of the Eleventh Army Corps, the progress of Rodes and Colston had been far less rapid than when they stormed forward

---

[1] Lieutenant-Colonel Hamlin, the latest historian of Chancellorsville, has completely disposed of the legend that these fifty guns repulsed a desperate attack on Hazel Grove.

past the Wilderness Church.   A regiment of Federal cavalry,
riding to Howard's aid by a track from Hazel Grove to the
plank road, was quickly swept aside ; but the deep darkness
of the forest, the efforts of the officers to re-form the ranks,
the barriers opposed by the tangled undergrowth, the difficulty of keeping the direction, brought a large portion of
the troops to a standstill.   At the junction of the White
House road the order to halt was given, and although a
number of men, pushing impetuously forward, seized a line
of log breastworks which ran north-west through the timber
below the Fairview heights, the pursuit was stayed in the
midst of the dense thickets.

      At this moment, shortly after eight o'clock, Jackson was
              at Dowdall's Tavern.   The reports from the front
8.15 P.M.   informed him that his first and second lines had
halted ; General Rodes, who had galloped up the plank
road to reconnoitre, sent in word that there were no
Federal troops to be seen between his line and the Fairview
heights ; and Colonel Cobb, of the 44th Virginia, brought
the news that the strong intrenchments, less than a mile
from Chancellorsville, had been occupied without resistance.

      There was a lull in the battle ; the firing had died
away, and the excited troops, with a clamour that was
heard in the Federal lines, sought their companies and
regiments by the dim light of the rising moon.   But
deeming that nothing was done while aught remained to
do, Jackson was already planning a further movement.
Sending instructions to A. P. Hill to relieve Rodes and
Colston, and to prepare for a night attack, he rode forward, almost unattended, amongst his rallying troops, and
lent his aid to the efforts of the regimental officers.   Intent
on bringing up the two divisions in close support of Hill,
he passed from one regiment to another.   Turning to
Colonel Cobb, he said to him : 'Find General Rodes, and
tell him to occupy the barricade [1] at once,' and then
added : 'I need your help for a time ; this disorder must be
corrected.   As you go along the right, tell the troops from
me to get into line and preserve their order.'

      [1] In the woods west of the Fairview Heights.

It was long, however, before the men could be assembled, and the delay was increased by an unfortunate
incident. Jackson's chief of artillery, pressing forward up
the plank road to within a thousand yards of Chancellorsville,
opened fire with three guns upon the enemy's position.
This audacious proceeding evoked a quick reply. Such
Federal guns as could be brought to bear were at once
turned upon the road, and although the damage done was
small, A. P. Hill's brigades, just coming up into line, were
for the moment checked; under the hail of shell and
canister the artillery horses became unmanageable, the
drivers lost their nerve, and as they rushed to the rear
some of the infantry joined them, and a stampede was only
prevented by the personal efforts of Jackson, Colston, and
their staff-officers. Colonel Crutchfield was then ordered to
cease firing; the Federals did the same; and A. P. Hill's
brigades, that of General Lane leading, advanced to the
deserted breastworks, while two brigades, one from Rodes'
division and one from Colston's, were ordered to guard the
roads from Hazel Grove.

These arrangements made, Jackson proceeded to join
his advanced line. At the point where the track to the
White House and United States ford strikes
8.45 P.M.   the plank road he met General Lane, seeking his
instructions for the attack. They were sufficiently brief:
' Push right ahead, Lane; right ahead ! ' As Lane galloped
off to his command, General Hill and some of his staff
came up, and Jackson gave Hill his orders. ' Press them;
cut them off from the United States Ford, Hill; press
them.' General Hill replied that he was entirely unac-
quainted with the topography of the country, and asked
for an officer to act as guide. Jackson directed Captain
Boswell, his chief engineer, to accompany General Hill,
and then, turning to the front, rode up the plank road,
passing quickly through the ranks of the 18th North Carolina of Lane's brigade. Two or three hundred yards eastward the general halted, for the ringing of axes and the words
of command were distinctly audible in the enemy's lines.
While the Confederates were re-forming, Hooker's

reserves had reached the front, and Berry's regiments, on the Fairview heights, using their bayonets and tin-plates for intrenching tools, piling up the earth with their hands, and hacking down the brushwood with their knives, were endeavouring in desperate haste to provide some shelter, however slight, against the rush that they knew was about to come.

After a few minutes, becoming impatient for the advance of Hill's division, Jackson turned and retraced his steps towards his own lines. 'General,' said an officer who was with him, 'you should not expose yourself so much.' 'There is no danger, sir, the enemy is routed. Go back and tell General Hill to press on.'

Once more, when he was only sixty or eighty yards from where the 18th North Carolina were standing in the trees, he drew rein and listened—the whole party, generals, staff-officers, and couriers, hidden in the deep shadows of the silent woods. At this moment a single rifle-shot rang out with startling suddenness.

A detachment of Federal infantry, groping their way through the thickets, had approached the Southern lines.

The skirmishers on both sides were now engaged, and the lines of battle in rear became keenly on the alert. Some mounted officers galloped hastily back to their commands. The sound startled the Confederate soldiers, and an officer of the 18th North Carolina, seeing a group of strange horsemen riding towards him through the darkness —for Jackson, hearing the firing, had turned back to his own lines—gave the order to fire.

The volley was fearfully effective. Men and horses fell dead and dying on the narrow track. Jackson himself received three bullets, one in the right hand, and two in the left arm, cutting the main artery, and crushing the bone below the shoulder, and as the reins dropped upon his neck, 'Little Sorrel,' frantic with terror, plunged into the wood and rushed towards the Federal lines. An overhanging bough struck his rider violently in the face, tore off his cap, and nearly unhorsed him; but recovering his seat, he managed to seize the bridle with his bleeding hand, and turned into the road. Here Captain Wilbourn, one of his staff-officers, succeeded in catching the reins ; and, as the horse stopped, Jackson leaned forward and fell into his arms. Captain Hotchkiss, who had just returned from a reconnais-sance, rode off to find Dr. McGuire, while Captain Wilbourn, with a small penknife, ripped up the sleeve of the wounded arm. As he was doing so, General Hill, who had himself been exposed to the fire of the North Carolinians, reached the scene, and, throwing himself from his horse, pulled off Jackson's gauntlets, which were full of blood, and bandaged the shattered arm with a handkerchief. ' General,' he said, ' are you much hurt ? ' ' I think I am,' was the reply, ' and all my wounds are from my own men. I believe my right arm is broken.'

To all questions put to him he answered in a perfectly calm and self-possessed tone, and, although he spoke no word of complaint, he was manifestly growing weaker. It seemed impossible to move him, and yet it was absolutely necessary that he should be carried to the rear. He was still in front of his own lines, and, even as Hill was speak-ing, two of the enemy's skirmishers, emerging from the thicket, halted within a few paces of the little group. Hill, turning quietly to his escort, said, ' Take charge of those men,' and two orderlies, springing forward, seized the rifles of the astonished Federals. Lieutenant Morrison, Jackson's aide-de-camp, who had gone down the road to reconnoitre, now reported that he had seen a section of artillery unlimbering close at hand. Hill gave orders that the general should be at once removed, and that no one should tell the men that he was wounded. Jackson, lying on Hill's breast, opened his eyes, and said, ' Tell them simply that you have a wounded Confederate officer.' Lieutenants Smith and Morrison, and Captain Leigh of Hill's staff, now lifted him to his feet, and with their aid he walked a few steps through the trees. But hardly had they gained the road when the Federal batteries, along their whole front, opened a terrible fire of grape and canister. The storm of bullets, tearing through the foliage, was for-tunately directed too high, and the three young officers,

laying the general down by the roadside, endeavoured to
shield him by lying between him and the deadly hail.　The
earth round them was torn up by the shot, covering them
with dust; boughs fell from the trees, and fire flashed from
the flints and gravel of the roadway.　Once Jackson
attempted to rise; but Smith threw his arm over him, holding him down, and saying, 'General, you must be still—it
will cost you your life to rise.'

After a few minutes, however, the enemy's gunners,
changing from canister to shell, mercifully increased their
range; and again, as the Confederate infantry came
hurrying to the front, their wounded leader, supported by
strong arms, was lifted to his feet.　Anxious that the men
should not recognise him, Jackson turned aside into the
wood, and slowly and painfully dragged himself through
the undergrowth.　As he passed along, General Pender,
whose brigade was then pushing forward, asked Smith
who it was that was wounded.　'A Confederate officer'
was the reply; but as they came nearer Pender, despite the
darkness, saw that it was Jackson.　Springing from his
horse, he hurriedly expressed his regret, and added that
his lines were so much disorganised by the enemy's artillery
that he feared it would be necessary to fall back.　'At this
moment,' says an eye-witness, 'the scene was a fearful one.
The air seemed to be alive with the shriek of shells and the
whistling of bullets; horses riderless and mad with fright
dashed in every direction; hundreds left the ranks and
hurried to the rear, and the groans of the wounded and dying
mingled with the wild shouts of others to be led again to
the assault.　Almost fainting as he was from loss of blood,
desperately wounded, and in the midst of this awful uproar,
Jackson's heart was unshaken.　The words of Pender
seemed to rouse him to life.　Pushing aside those who
supported him, he raised himself to his full height, and
answered feebly, but distinctly enough to be heard above
the din, "You must hold your ground, General Pender;
you must hold out to the last, sir."'

His strength was now completely gone, and he asked
to be allowed to lie down.　His staff-officers, however,

refused assent. The shells were still crashing through the forest, and a litter having been brought up by Captain Leigh, he was carried slowly towards Dowdall's Tavern. But before they were free of the tangled wood, one of the stretcher-bearers, struck by a shot in the arm, let go the handle. Jackson fell violently to the ground on his wounded side. His agony must have been intense, and for the first time he was heard to groan.

Smith sprang to his side, and as he raised his head a bright beam of moonlight made its way through the thick foliage, and rested upon his white and lacerated face. The aide-de-camp was startled by its great pallor and still-ness, and cried out, 'General, are you seriously hurt?' 'No, Mr. Smith, don't trouble yourself about me,' he replied quietly, and added some words about winning the battle first, and attending to the wounded afterwards. He was again placed upon the litter, and carried a few hundred yards, still followed by the Federal shells, to where his medical director was waiting with an ambulance.

Dr. McGuire knelt down beside him and said, 'I hope you are not badly hurt, General?' He replied very calmly but feebly, 'I am badly injured, doctor, I fear I am dying.' After a pause he went on, 'I am glad you have come. I think the wound in my shoulder is still bleeding.' The bandages were readjusted and he was lifted into the ambulance, where Colonel Crutchfield, who had also been seriously wounded, was already lying. Whisky and morphia were administered, and by the light of pine torches, carried by a few soldiers, he was slowly driven through the fields where Hooker's right had so lately fled before his impetuous onset. All was done that could ease his sufferings, but some jolting of the ambulance over the rough road was unavoidable; 'and yet,' writes Dr. McGuire, 'his uniform politeness did not forsake him even in these most trying circumstances. His complete control, too, over his mind, enfeebled as it was by loss of blood and pain, was wonderful. His suffering was intense; his hands were cold, his skin clammy. But not a groan escaped him—not a sign of suffering, except the slight corrugation of the brow, the fixed, rigid face, the thin lips, so tightly compressed that the impression of the teeth could be seen through them. Except these, he controlled by his iron will all evidence of emotion, and, more difficult than this even, he controlled that disposition to restlessness which many of us have observed upon the battle-field as attending great loss of blood. Nor was he forgetful of others. He expressed very feelingly his sympathy for Crutchfield, and once, when the latter groaned aloud, he directed the ambulance to stop, and requested me to see if something could not be done for his relief.

'After reaching the hospital, he was carried to a tent, and placed in bed, covered with blankets, and another drink of whisky and water given him. Two hours and a half elapsed before sufficient reaction took place to warrant an examination, and at two o'clock on Sunday morning I informed him that chloroform would be given him; I told him also that amputation would probably be required, and asked, if it was found necessary, whether it should be done at once. He replied promptly, "Yes, certainly, Dr. McGuire, do for me whatever you think best."

'Chloroform was then administered, and the left arm amputated about two inches below the shoulder. Throughout the whole of the operation, and until all the dressings were applied, he continued insensible. About half-past three, Colonel (then Major) Pendleton arrived at the hospital. He stated that General Hill had been wounded, and that the troops were in great disorder. General Stuart was in command, and had sent him to see the general. At first I declined to permit an interview, but Pendleton urged that the safety of the army and success of the cause depended upon his seeing him. When he entered the tent the general said, "Well, Major, I am glad to see you; I thought you were killed." Pendleton briefly explained the position of affairs, gave Stuart's message, and asked what should be done. Jackson was at once interested, and asked in his quick way several questions. When they were answered, he remained silent, evidently trying to think; he contracted his brow, set his mouth, and for some moments lay obviously endeavouring to concentrate his thoughts. For a moment we believed he had succeeded, for his nostrils dilated, and his eye flashed with its old fire, but it was only for a moment: his face relaxed again, and presently he answered, very feebly and sadly: "I don't know—I can't tell; say to General Stuart he must do what he thinks best." Soon after this he slept.'

So, leaving behind him, struggling vainly against the oppression of his mortal hurt, the one man who could have completed the Confederate victory, Pendleton rode wearily through the night. Jackson's fall, at so critical a moment, just as the final blow was to be delivered, had proved a terrible disaster. Hill, who alone knew his intention of moving to the White House, had been wounded by a fragment of shell as he rode back to lead his troops. Boswell, who had been ordered to point out the road, had been killed by the same volley which struck down his chief, and the subordinate generals, without instructions and without guides, with their men in disorder, and the enemy's artillery playing fiercely on the forest, had hesitated to advance. Hill, remaining in a litter near the line of battle, had sent for Stuart. The cavalry commander, however, was at some distance from the field. Late in the evening, finding it impossible to employ his command at the front, he had been detached by Jackson, a regiment of infantry supporting him, to take and hold Ely's Ford. He had already arrived within view of a Federal camp established at that point, and was preparing to charge the enemy, under cover of the night, when Hill's messenger recalled him.

When Stuart reached the front he found the troops still halted, Rodes and Colston reforming on the open fields near Dowdall's Tavern, the Light Division deployed within the forest, and the generals anxious for their own security.

So far the attack had been completely successful, but Lee's lack of strength prevented the full accomplishment of his design. Had Longstreet been present, with Pickett and Hood to lead his splendid infantry, the

Third Corps and the Twelfth would have been so hardly pressed that Chancellorsville, Hazel Grove, and the White House would have fallen an easy prize to Jackson's bayonets. Anderson, with four small brigades, was powerless to hold the force confronting him, and marching rapidly northwards, Sickles had reached Hazel Grove before Jackson fell. Here Pleasonton, with his batteries, was still in position, and Hooker had not yet lost his head. As soon as Birney's and Whipple's divisions had come up, forming in columns of brigades behind the guns, Sickles was ordered to assail the enemy's right flank and check his advance. Just before midnight the attack was made, in two lines of battle, supported by strong columns. The night was very clear and still; the moon, nearly full, threw enough light into the woods to facilitate the advance, and the tracks leading north-west served as lines of direction.

The attack, however, although gallantly made, gained no material advantage. The preliminary movements were plainly audible to the Confederates, and Lane's brigade, most of which was now south of the plank road, had made every preparation to receive it. Against troops lying down in the woods the Federal artillery, although fifty or sixty guns were in action, made but small impression; and the dangers of a night attack, made upon troops who are expecting it, and whose *moral* is unaffected, were forcibly illustrated. The confusion in the forest was very great; a portion of the assailing force, losing direction, fell foul of Berry's division at the foot of the Fairview heights, which had not been informed of the movement, and at least two regiments, fired into from front and rear, broke up in panic. Some part of the log breastworks which Jackson's advanced line had occupied were recaptured; but not a single one of the assailants, except as prisoners, reached the plank road. And yet the attack was an exceedingly well-timed stroke, and as such, although the losses were heavy, had a very considerable effect on the issue of the day's fighting. It showed, or seemed to show, that the Federals were still in good heart, that they were rapidly concentrating, and that the Confederates might be met by vigorous counter-strokes. 'The fact,' said Stuart in his official dispatch, 'that the attack was made, and at night, made me apprehensive of a repetition of it.'

So, while Jackson slept through the hours of darkness that should have seen the consummation of his enterprise, his soldiers lay beside their arms; and the Federals, digging, felling, and building, constructed a new line of parapet, protected by abattis, and strengthened by a long array of guns, on the slopes of Fairview and Hazel Grove. The respite which the fall of the Confederate leader had brought them was not neglected; the fast-spreading panic was stayed; the First Army Corps, rapidly crossing the Rappahannock, secured the road to the White House, and Averell's division of cavalry reached Ely's Ford. On the left, between Chancellorsville and the river, where a young Federal colonel, named Miles,[1] handled his troops with conspicuous skill, Lee's continuous attacks had been successfully repulsed, and at dawn on the morning of May 3 the situation of the Union army was far from unpromising. A gap of nearly two miles intervened between the Confederate wings, and within this gap, on the commanding heights of Hazel Grove and Fairview, the Federals were strongly intrenched. An opportunity for dealing a crushing counterblow—for holding one portion of Lee's army in check while the other was overwhelmed—appeared to present itself. The only question was whether the *moral* of the general and the men could be depended upon.

May 3.

In Stuart, however, Hooker had to deal with a soldier who was no unworthy successor of Stonewall Jackson. Reluctantly abandoning the idea of a night attack, the cavalry general, fully alive to the exigencies of the situation, had determined to reduce the interval between himself and Lee; and during the night the artillery was brought up to the front, and the batteries deployed wherever they could find room. Just before the darkness began to lift, orders were received from Lee that the assault was to be made as early as possible; and the right wing, swinging round in order to come abreast of the centre,

[1] Commander-in-Chief, U.S. Army, 1898.

became hotly engaged. Away to the south-east, across the hills held by the Federals, came the responding thunder of Lee's guns; and 40,000 infantry, advancing through the woods against front and flank, enveloped in a circle of fire a stronghold which was held by over 60,000 muskets.

It is unnecessary to describe minutely the events of the morning. The Federal troops, such as were brought into action, fought well; but Jackson's tremendous attack had already defeated Hooker. Before Sickles made his night attack from Hazel Grove he had sent orders for Sedgwick to move at once, occupy Fredericksburg, seize the heights, and march westward by the plank road; and, at the same time, he had instructed his engineers to select and fortify a position about a mile in rear of Chancellorsville. So, when Stuart pressed forward, not only had this new position been occupied by the First and Fifth Army Corps, but the troops hitherto in possession of Hazel Grove were already evacuating their intrenchments.

These dispositions sufficiently attest the demoralisation of the Federal commander. As the historian of the Army of the Potomac puts it: ' The movement to be executed by Sedgwick was precisely one of those movements which, according as they are wrought out, may be either the height of wisdom or the height of folly. Its successful accomplishment certainly promised very brilliant results. It is easy to see how seriously Lee's safety would be compromised if, while engaged with Hooker in front, he should suddenly find a powerful force assailing his rear, and grasping already his direct line of communication with Richmond. But if, on the other hand, Lee should be able by any slackness on the part of his opponent to engage him in front with a part of his force, while he should turn swiftly round to assail the isolated moving column, it is obvious that he would be able to repulse or destroy that column, and then by a vigorous return, meet or attack his antagonist's main body. In the successful execution of this plan not only was Sedgwick bound to the most energetic action, but Hooker also was engaged by every con-

sideration of honour and duty to so act as to make the
dangerous task he had assigned to Sedgwick possible.'[1]

But so far from aiding his subordinate by a heavy
counter-attack on Lee's front, Hooker deliberately abandoned the Hazel Grove salient, which, keeping asunder the
Confederate wings, strongly facilitated such a manœuvre;
and more than this, he divided his own army into two
portions, of which the rear, occupying the new position,
was actually forbidden to reinforce the front.

It is possible that Hooker contemplated an early retreat
of his whole force to the second position. If so, Lee and
Stuart were too quick for him. The cavalry commander,
as soon as it became light, and the hills and undulations
of the Wilderness emerged from the shadows, immediately
recognised the importance of Hazel Grove. The hill was
quickly seized; thirty pieces of artillery, established on the
crest, enfiladed the Federal batteries, facing west, on the
heights of Fairview; and the brigade on Stuart's extreme
right was soon in touch with the troops directed by General
Lee. Then against the three sides of the Federal position
the battle raged. From the south and south-east came
Anderson and McLaws, the batteries unlimbering on
every eminence, and the infantry, hitherto held back,
attacking with the vigour which their gallant commanders
knew so well how to inspire. And from the west, formed
in three lines, Hill's division to the front, came the Second
Army Corps. The men knew by this time that the leader
whom they trusted beyond all others had been struck down,
that he was lying wounded, helpless, far away in rear.
Yet his spirit was still with them. Stuart, galloping
along the ranks, recalled him with ringing words to their
memories, and as the bugles sounded the onset, it was
with a cry of 'Remember Jackson!' that his soldiers
rushed fiercely upon the Federal breastworks.

The advanced line, within the forest, was taken at the
first rush; the second, at the foot of the Fairview heights,
protected by a swampy stream, a broad belt of abattis, and

[1] *Campaigns of the Army of the Potomac*, pp. 241-2.

with thirty guns on the hill behind, proved far more formidable, and Hill's division was forced back. But Rodes and Colston were in close support. The fight was speedily renewed ; and then came charge and counter-charge ; the storm of the parapets ; the rally of the defenders ; the rush with the bayonet ; and, mowing down men like grass, the fearful sweep of case and canister. Twice the Confederates were repulsed. Twice they reformed, brigade mingled with brigade, regiment with regiment, and charged again in the teeth of the thirty guns.

On both sides ammunition began to fail ; the brushwood took fire, the ground became hot beneath the foot, and many wounded perished miserably in the flames. Yet still, with the tangled abattis dividing the opposing lines, the fight went on ; both sides struggling fiercely, the Federals with the advantage of position, the Confederates of numbers, for Hooker refused to reinforce his gallant troops. At length the guns which Stuart had established on Hazel Grove, crossing their fire with those of McLaws and Anderson, gained the upper hand over the Union batteries. The storm of shell, sweeping the Fairview plateau, took the breastworks in reverse ; the Northern infantry, after five hours of such hot battle as few fields have witnessed, began sullenly to yield, and as Stuart, leading the last charge, leapt his horse over the parapet, the works were evacuated, and the tattered colours of the Confederates waved in triumph on the hill.

'The scene,' says a staff-officer, 'can never be effaced from the minds of those that witnessed it. The troops were pressing forward with all the ardour and enthusiasm of combat. The white smoke of musketry fringed the front of battle, while the artillery on the hills in rear shook the earth with its thunder and filled the air with the wild shrieking of the shells that plunged into the masses of the retreating foe. To add greater horror and sublimity to the scene, the Chancellorsville House and the woods surrounding it were wrapped in flames. It was then that General Lee rode to the front of his advancing battalions. His presence was the signal for one of those uncontrollable outbursts of enthusiasm which none can appreciate who have not witnessed them.

' The fierce soldiers, with their faces blackened with the smoke of battle, the wounded, crawling with feeble limbs from the fury of the devouring flames, all seemed possessed of a common impulse. One long, unbroken cheer, in which the feeble cry of those who lay helpless on the earth blended with the strong voices of those who still fought, hailed the presence of the victorious chief.

' His first care was for the wounded of both armies, and he was among the foremost at the burning mansion, where some of them lay. But at that moment, when the transports of his troops were drowning the roar of battle with acclamations, a note was brought to him from General Jackson. It was handed to him as he sat on his horse near the Chancellorsville House, and unable to open it with his gauntleted hands, he passed it to me with directions to read it to him. I shall never forget the look of pain and anguish that passed over his face as he listened. In a voice broken with emotion he bade me say to General Jackson that the victory was his. I do not know how others may regard this incident, but for myself, as I gave expression to the thoughts of his exalted mind, I forgot the genius that won the day in my reverence for the generosity that refused its glory.'

Lee's reply ran :—

' General,—I have just received your note, informing me that you were wounded. I cannot express my regret at the occurrence. Could I have directed events, I should have chosen for the good of the country to be disabled in your stead.

' I congratulate you upon the victory, which is due to your skill and energy.

' Very respectfully, your obedient servant,

' R. E. LEE, *General.*'

Such was the tribute, not the less valued that it was couched in no exaggerated terms, which was brought to the bedside in the quiet hospital. Jackson was almost alone. As the sound of cannon and musketry, borne across the forest, grew gradually louder, he had ordered all those who had remained with him, except Mr. Smith, to return to the battle-field and attend to their different duties.

His side, injured by his fall from the litter, gave him much pain, but his thoughts were still clear, and his speech coherent. 'General Lee,' he said, when his aide-de-camp read to him the Commander-in-Chief's brief words, 'is very kind, but he should give the praise to God.'

During the day the pain gradually ceased; the general grew brighter, and from those who visited the hospital he inquired minutely about the battle and the troops engaged. When conspicuous instances of courage were related his face lit up with enthusiasm, and he uttered his usual 'Good, good,' with unwonted energy when the gallant behaviour of his old command was alluded to. 'Some day,' he said, 'the men of that brigade will be proud to say to their children, "I was one of the Stonewall Brigade."' He disclaimed all right of his own to the name Stonewall: 'It belongs to the brigade and not to me.' That night he slept well, and was free from pain.

Meanwhile the Confederate army, resting on the heights of Chancellorsville, preparatory to an attack upon Hooker's second stronghold, had received untoward news. Sedgwick, at eleven o'clock in the morning, had carried Marye's Hill, and, driving Early before him, was moving up the plank road. Wilcox' brigade of Anderson's division, then at Banks' Ford, was ordered to retard the advance of the hostile column. McLaws was detached to Salem Church. The Second Army Corps and the rest of Anderson's division remained to hold Hooker in check, and for the moment operations at Chancellorsville were suspended.

McLaws, deploying his troops in the forest, two hundred and fifty yards from a wide expanse of cleared ground, pushed his skirmishers forward to the edge, and awaited the attack of a superior force. Reserving his fire to close quarters, its effect was fearful. But the Federals pushed forward; a school-house occupied as an advanced post was captured, and at this point Sedgwick was within an ace of breaking through. His second line, however, had not yet deployed, and a vigorous counterstroke, delivered by two brigades, drove back the whole of his leading division in great disorder. As night fell the Confederates, careful not to expose themselves to the Union reserves, retired to the forest, and Sedgwick, like Hooker, abandoned all further idea of offensive action.

The next morning Lee himself, with the three remaining brigades of Anderson, arrived upon the scene. Sedgwick, who had lost 5,000 men the preceding day, had fortified a position covering Banks' Ford, and occupied it with over 20,000 muskets. Lee, with the divisions of McLaws, Anderson, and Early, was slightly stronger. The attack was delayed, for the Federals held strong ground, difficult to reconnoitre ; but once begun the issue was soon decided. Assailed in front and flanks, with no help coming from Hooker, and only a single bridge at Banks' Ford in rear, the Federals rapidly gave ground.

May 4.

Darkness, however, intensified by a thick fog, made pursuit difficult, and Sedgwick re-crossed the river with many casualties but in good order. During these operations, that is, from four o'clock on Sunday afternoon until after midnight on Monday, Hooker had not moved a single man to his subordinate's assistance.[1] So extraordinary a situation has seldom been seen in war : an army of 60,000 men, strongly fortified, was held in check for six-and-thirty hours by 20,000 ; while not seven miles away raged a battle on which the whole fate of the campaign depended.

Lee and Jackson had made no false estimate of Hooker's incapacity. Sedgwick's army corps had suffered so severely in men and in *moral* that it was not available for immediate service, even had it been transferred to Chancellorsville ; and Lee was now free to concentrate his whole force against the main body of the Federal army. His men, notwithstanding their extraordinary exertions, were confident of victory. 'As I sheltered myself,' says an

---

[1] It is but fair, however, to state that Hooker, during the cannonade which preceded the final assault at Chancellorsville, had been severely bruised by a fall of masonry.

eye-witness, 'in a little farmhouse on the plank road

May 5.   the brigades of Anderson's division came splash-
ing through the mud, in wild tumultuous spirits,
singing, shouting, jesting, heedless of soaking rags, drenched
to the skin, and burning again to mingle in the mad
revelry of battle.'[1]   But it was impossible to push forward,
for a violent rain-storm burst upon the Wilderness, and the
spongy soil, saturated with the deluge, absolutely precluded
all movement across country.   Hooker, who had already
made preparations for retreat, took advantage of the

May 6.   weather, and as soon as darkness set in put his
army in motion for the bridges.   By eight o'clock
on the morning of the 6th the whole force had crossed;
and when the Confederate patrols pushed forward, Lee
found that his victim had escaped.

The Army of the Potomac returned to its old camp on
the hills above Fredericksburg, and Lee reoccupied his
position on the opposite ridge.   Stoneman, who had scoured
the whole country to within a few miles of Richmond,
returned to Kelly's Ford on May 8.   The raid had effected
nothing.   The damage done to the railroads and canals was
repaired by the time the raiders had regained the Rappahannock.   Lee's operations at Chancellorsville had not
been affected in the very slightest degree by their presence
in his rear, while Stoneman's absence had proved the ruin
of the Federal army.   Jackson, who had been removed by
the Commander-in-Chief's order to Mr. Chandler's house,
near Guiney's Station, on the morning of May 5, was asked
what he thought of Hooker's plan of campaign.   His reply
was : 'It was in the main a good conception, an excellent
plan.   But he should not have sent away his cavalry ; that
was his great blunder.   It was that which enabled me to
turn him without his being aware of it, and to take him in
the rear.   Had he kept his cavalry with him, his plan
would have been a very good one.'   This was not his only
comment on the great battle.   Among other things, he said
that he intended to cut the Federals off from the United
States Ford, and, taking a position between them and the

[1] Hon. Francis Lawley, the *Times*, June 16, 1863.

river, oblige them to attack him, adding, with a smile,
'My men sometimes fail to drive the enemy from a
position, but they always fail to drive us away.' He
spoke of General Rodes, and alluded in high terms to his
splendid behaviour in the attack on Howard. He hoped
he would be promoted, and he said that promotion should
be made at once, upon the field, so as to act as an incentive
to gallantry in others. He spoke of Colonel Willis, who
had commanded the skirmishers, and praised him very
highly, and referred most feelingly to the death of Paxton,
the commander of the Stonewall Brigade, and of Captain
Boswell, his chief engineer. In speaking of his own share
in the victory he said : ' Our movement was a great success ;
I think the most successful military movement of my life.
But I expect to receive far more credit for it than I
deserve. Most men will think I planned it all from the
first ; but it was not so. I simply took advantage of circumstances as they were presented to me in the providence of God. I feel that His hand led me—let us give
Him the glory.'

It must always be an interesting matter of speculation
what the result would have been had Jackson accomplished
his design, on the night he fell, of moving a large part of
his command up the White House road, and barring the
only line of retreat left open to the Federals.

Hooker, it is argued, had two corps in position which
had been hardly engaged, the Second and the Fifth ; and
another, the First, under Reynolds, was coming up. Of
these, 25,000 men might possibly, could they have been
manœuvred in the forest, have been sent to drive Jackson
back. And, undoubtedly, to those who think more of numbers
than of human nature, of the momentum of the mass
rather than the mental equilibrium of the general, the fact
that a superior force of comparatively fresh troops was at
Hooker's disposal will be sufficient to put the success of
the Confederates out of court. Yet the question will
always suggest itself, would not the report that a victorious
enemy, of unknown strength, was pressing forward, in the
darkness of the night, towards the only line of retreat,

have so demoralised the Federal commander and the
Federal soldiers, already shaken by the overthrow of
the Eleventh Army Corps, that they would have thought
only of securing their own safety ?   Would Hooker, whose
tactics the next day, after he had had the night given him
in which to recover his senses, were so inadequate, have
done better if he had received no respite ?   Would the soldiers of the three army corps not yet engaged, who had
been witnesses of the rout of Howard's divisions, have
fared better, when they heard the triumphant yells of
the advancing Confederates, than the hapless Germans ?
'The wounding of Jackson,' says a most careful historian
of the battle, himself a participator in the Union disaster,
'was a most fortunate circumstance for the Army of
the Potomac.   At nine o'clock the capture or destruction
of a large part of the army seemed inevitable.   There was,
at the time, great uncertainty and a feeling akin to panic
prevailing among the Union forces round Chancellorsville; and when we consider the position of the troops
at this moment, and how many important battles
have been won by trivial flank attacks— how Richepanse
(attacking through the forest) with a single brigade ruined
the Austrians at Hohenlinden—we must admit that the
Northern army was in great peril when Jackson arrived
within one thousand yards of its vital point (the White
House) with 20,000 men and 50 cannon.' [1]   He must be a
great leader indeed who, when his flank is suddenly rolled
up and his line of retreat threatened, preserves sufficient
coolness to devise a general counterstroke.   Jackson had
proved himself equal to such a situation at Cedar Run, but
it is seldom in these circumstances that Providence sides
with the 'big battalions.'

The Federal losses in the six days' battles were heavy:
over 12,000 at Chancellorsville, and 4,700 at Fredericksburg, Salem Church, and Banks' Ford; a total of 17,287.
The army lost 13 guns, and nearly 6,000 officers and men
were reported either captured or missing.

The casualties were distributed as follows :—

[1] *Chancellorsville*, Lt.-Colonel A. C. Hamlin.

First Army Corps	135
Second ,, ...	1,925
Third ,, ...	4,119
Fifth ,, ...	700
Sixth ,, ...	4,590
Eleventh ,, ...	2,412
Twelfth ,, ...	2,822
Pleasonton's Cavalry Brigade	141
	16,844

The Confederate losses were hardly less severe. The killed and wounded were as under :—

SECOND ARMY CORPS.

A. P. Hill's Division	2,583
Rodes' ,, ...	2,178
Colston's ,, ...	1,868
Early's ,, ...	851
Anderson's ,, ...	1,180
McLaws' ,, ...	1,379
Artillery	227
Cavalry	11
Prisoners (estimated)	2,000
	12,277

But a mere statement of the casualties by no means represents the comparative loss of the opposing forces. Victory does not consist in merely killing and maiming a few thousand men. This is the visible result; it is the invisible that tells. The Army of the Potomac, when it retreated across the Rappahannock, was far stronger in mere numbers than the Army of Northern Virginia; but in reality it was far weaker, for the *moral* of the survivors, and of the general who led them, was terribly affected. That of the Confederates, on the other hand, had been sensibly elevated, and it is *moral*, not numbers, which is the strength of armies. What, after all, was the loss of 12,200 soldiers to the Confederacy? In that first week of May there were probably 20,000 conscripts in different camps of instruction, more than enough to recruit the depleted regiments to full strength. Nor did the slaughter of Chancellorsville diminish to any appreciable degree the vast hosts of the Union.

And yet the Army of the Potomac had lost more than all the efforts of the Government could replace. The Army of Virginia, on the other hand, had acquired a superiority of spirit which was ample compensation for the sacrifice which had been made. It is hardly too much to say that Lee's force had gained from the victory an increase of strength equivalent to a whole army corps of 30,000 men, while that of his opponent had been proportionately diminished. Why, then, was there no pursuit?

It has been asserted that Lee was so crippled by his losses at Chancellorsville that he was unable to resume operations against Hooker for a whole month. This explanation of his inactivity can hardly be accepted.

On June 16 and 18, 1815, at Quatre-Bras and Waterloo, the Anglo-Dutch army, little larger than that of Northern Virginia, lost 17,000 men; and yet on the 19th Wellington was marching in pursuit of the French; nor did he halt until he arrived within sight of Paris. And on August 28, 29, and 30, 1862, at Groveton and the Second Manassas, Stonewall Jackson lost 4,000 officers and men, one-fifth of his force, but he was not left in rear when Lee invaded Maryland. Moreover, after he had defeated Sedgwick, on the same night that Hooker was recrossing the Rappahannock, Lee was planning a final attack on the Federal intrenchments, and his disappointment was bitter when he learned that his enemy had escaped. If his men were capable of further efforts on the night of May 5, they were capable of them the next day; and it was neither the ravages of battle nor the disorganisation of the army that held the Confederates fast, but the deficiency of supplies, the damage done to the railways by Stoneman's horsemen, the weakness of the cavalry, and, principally, the hesitation of the Government. After the victory of Chancellorsville, strong hopes of peace were entertained in the South. Before Hooker advanced, a large section of the Northern Democrats, despairing of ultimate success, had once more raised the cry that immediate separation was better than a hopeless contest, involving such awful sacrifices, and it needed all Lincoln's strength to stem the tide of disaffection.

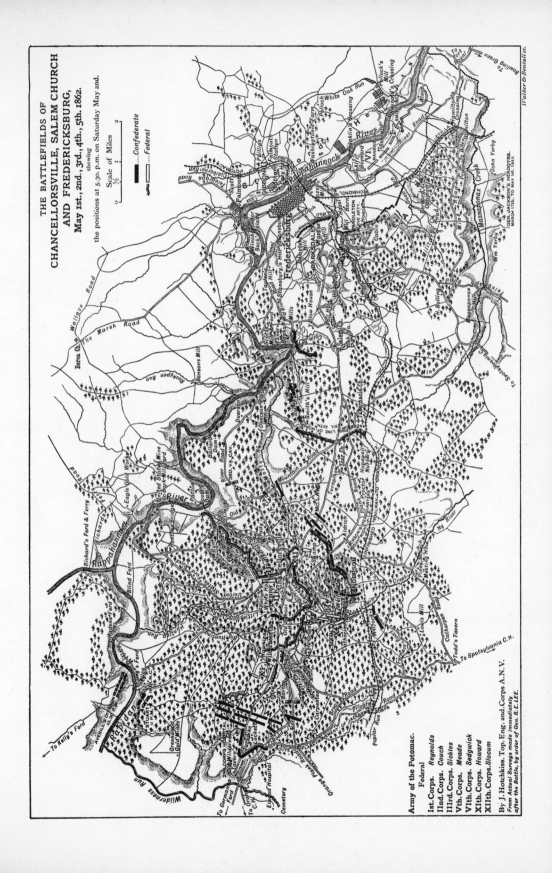

THE BATTLEFIELDS OF
CHANCELLORSVILLE, SALEM CHURCH
AND FREDERICKSBURG,
May 1st, 2nd, 3rd, 4th, 5th, 1862.

shewing
the positions at 5.30. p.m. on Saturday May 2nd.

......Confederate
......Federal

Scale of Miles
½   1   2

Army of the Potomac.
Federal

Ist. Corps.   Reynolds
IInd. Corps.   Couch
IIIrd. Corps. Sickles
Vth. Corps.   Meade
VIth. Corps.   Sedgwick
XIth. Corps.   Howard
XIIth. Corps. Slocum

By J. Hotchkiss. Top. Eng. 2nd. Corps A.N.V.
From Actual Surveys made immediately
after the Battle, by order of Gen. R. E. LEE.

GEN. JACKSON'S HEADQTRS.
MARCH 17TH. TO MAY 1ST. 1863.

The existence of this despondent feeling was well known to the Southern statesmen; and to such an extent did they count upon its growth and increase that they had over-looked altogether the importance of improving a victory, should the army be successful; so now, when the chance had come, they were neither ready to forward such an enterprise, nor could they make up their minds to depart from their passive attitude. But to postpone all idea of counterstroke until some indefinite period is as fatal in strategy as in tactics. By no means an uncommon policy, it has been responsible for the loss of a thousand oppor-tunities.

Had not politics intervened, a vigorous pursuit—not necessarily involving an immediate attack, but drawing Hooker, as Pope had been drawn in the preceding August, into an unfavourable situation, before his army had had time to recover—would have probably been initiated. It may be questioned, however, whether General Lee, even when Longstreet and his divisions joined him, would have been so strong as he had been at the end of April. None felt more deeply than the Commander-in-Chief that the absence of Jackson was an irreparable misfortune. 'Give him my affectionate regards,' he said to an aide-de-camp who was riding to the hospital; 'tell him to make haste and get well, and come back to me as soon as he can. He has lost his left arm, but I have lost my right.' 'Any victory,' he wrote privately, 'would be dear at such a price. I know not how to replace him.'

His words were prophetic. Exactly two months after Chancellorsville the armies met once more in the clash of battle. During the first two days, on the rolling plain round Gettysburg, a village of Pennsylvania, four Federal army corps were beaten in succession, but ere the sun set on the third Lee had to admit defeat.

And yet his soldiers had displayed the same fiery courage and stubborn persistence which had carried them victorious through the Wilderness. But his 'right arm' had not yet been replaced. 'If,' he said after the war, with unaccustomed emphasis, 'I had had Jackson at Gettysburg I should have won the battle, and a complete victory there would have resulted in the establishment of Southern independence.'

It was not to be. Chancellorsville, where 130,000 men were defeated by 60,000, is up to a certain point as much the tactical masterpiece of the nineteenth century as was Leuthen of the eighteenth. But, splendid triumph as it was, the battle bore no abiding fruits, and the reason seems very clear. The voice that would have urged pursuit was silent. Jackson's fall left Lee alone, bereft of his *alter ego*; with none, save Stuart, to whom he could entrust the execution of those daring and delicate manœuvres his inferior numbers rendered necessary ; with none on whose resource and energy he could implicitly rely. Who shall say how far his own resolution had been animated and confirmed at other crises by the prompting and presence of the kindred spirit? 'They supplemented each other,' said Davis, 'and together, with any fair opportunity, they were absolutely invincible.'

Many a fierce battle still lay before the Army of Northern Virginia; marvellous was the skill and audacity with which Lee manœuvred his ragged regiments in the face of overwhelming odds; fierce and unyielding were the soldiers, but with Stonewall Jackson's death the impulse of victory died away.

It is needless to linger over the closing scene at Guiney's Station. For some days there was hope that the patient would recover ; pneumonia, attributed to his fall from the May 7. litter as he was borne from the field, supervened, and he gradually began to sink. On the Thursday his wife and child arrived from Richmond ; but he was then almost too weak for conversation, and on Sunday morning it was evident that the end was near. May 10. As yet he had scarcely realised his condition. If, he said, it was God's will, he was ready to go, but he believed that there was still work for him to do, and that his life would be preserved to do it. At eleven o'clock Mrs. Jackson knelt by his side, and told him that he could not live beyond the evening. 'You are frightened, my child,' he replied, 'death is not so near; I may yet get well.' She fell upon the bed, weeping bitterly, and told him again that there was no hope. After a moment's pause, he asked her to call Dr. McGuire. 'Doctor,' he said, 'Anna tells me I am to die to-day; is it so?' When he was answered, he remained silent for a moment or two, as if in intense thought, and then quietly replied, 'Very good, very good; it is all right.'

About noon, when Major Pendleton came into the room, he asked, 'Who is preaching at headquarters to-day?' He was told that Mr. Lacy was, and that the whole army was praying for him. 'Thank God,' he said; 'they are very kind to me.' Already his strength was fast ebbing, and although his face brightened when his baby was brought to him, his mind had begun to wander. Now he was on the battle-field, giving orders to his men; now at home in Lexington; now at prayers in the camp. Occasionally his senses came back to him, and about half-past one he was told that he had but two hours to live. Again he answered, feebly but firmly, 'Very good; it is all right.' These were almost his last coherent words. For some time he lay unconscious, and then suddenly he cried out: 'Order A. P. Hill to prepare for action! Pass the infantry to the front! Tell Major Hawks——' then stopped, leaving the sentence unfinished. Once more he was silent; but a little while after he said very quietly and clearly, 'Let us cross over the river, and rest under the shade of the trees,' and the soul of the great captain passed into the peace of God.

NOTE I

[From General Lee's letter-book.]

Lexington, Va., 25th January, 1866.

MRS. T. J. JACKSON :—

MY DEAR MRS. JACKSON,—Dr. Brown handed me your note of the 9th, when in Richmond on business connected with Washington College. I have delayed replying since my return, hoping to have sufficient time to comply with your request. Last night I received a note from Mrs. Brown, enclosing one from Dr. Dabney, stating that the immediate return of his manuscript was necessary. I have not been able to open it ; and when I read it when you were here, it was for the pleasure of the narrative, with no view of remark or correction ; and I took no memoranda of what seemed to be errors. I have not thought of them since, and do not know that I can now recall them ; and certainly have no desire that my opinions should be adopted in preference to Dr. Dabney's. . . . I am, however, unable at this time to specify the battles to which my remark particularly refers. The opinion of Gen. Jackson, in reference to the propriety of attacking the Federal army under Gen. McClellan at Harrison's Landing, is not, I think, correctly stated. Upon my arrival there, the day after Gen. Longstreet and himself, I was disappointed that no opportunity for striking Gen. McClellan, on the retreat, or in his then position, had occurred, and went forward with Gen. Jackson alone, on foot ; and after a careful reconnaissance of the whole line and position, he certainly stated to me, at that time, the impropriety of attacking. I am misrepresented at the battle of Chancellorsville in proposing an attack in front, the first evening of our arrival. On the contrary, I decided against it, and stated to Gen. Jackson, we must attack on our left as soon as practicable ; and the necessary movement of the troops began immediately. In consequence of a report received about that time, from Gen. Fitz Lee, describing the position of the Federal army, and the roads which he held with his cavalry leading to its rear, Gen. Jackson, after some inquiry concerning the roads leading to the Furnace, undertook to throw his command entirely in Hooker's rear, which he accomplished with equal skill and boldness ; the rest of the army being moved to the left flank to connect with him as he advanced. I think there is some mistake, too, of a regiment of infantry being sent by him to the ford on the Rapidan, as described by Dr. Dabney. The cavalry was ordered to make such a demonstration. Gen. Stuart had proceeded to that part of the field to co-operate in Gen. Jackson's movement, and I always supposed it was his dismounted cavalry. As well as I now recollect, something is said by

Dr. Dabney as to Gen. Jackson's opinion as to the propriety of delivering battle at Sharpsburg. When he came upon the field, having preceded his troops, and learned my reasons for offering battle, he emphatically concurred with me. When I determined to withdraw across the Potomac, he also concurred; but said then, in view of all the circumstances, it was better to have fought the battle in Maryland than to have left it without a struggle. After crossing the Potomac, Gen. Jackson was charged with the command of the rear, and he designated the brigades of infantry to support Pendleton's batteries. I believed Gen. McClellan had been so crippled at Sharpsburg that he could not follow the Confederate army into Virginia immediately; but Gen. Stuart was ordered, after crossing the Potomac, to recross at once at Williamsport, threaten his right flank, and observe his movements. Near daylight the next morning, Gen. Pendleton reported to me the occurrence at Shepherdstown the previous evening, and stated that he had made a similar report to Gen. Jackson, who was lying near me on the same field. From his statement, I thought it possible that the Federal army might be attempting to follow us; and I sent at once to General Jackson to say that, in that event, I would attack it; that he must return with his whole command if necessary; that I had sent to Longstreet to countermarch the rest of the army; and that upon his joining me, unless I heard from him to the contrary, I should move with it to his support. Gen. Jackson went back with Hill's division, Gen. Pendleton accompanying him, and soon drove the Federals into Maryland with loss. His report, which I received on my way towards the river, relieved my anxiety, and the order of the march of the troops was again resumed. I have endeavoured to be as brief as possible in my statement, and with the single object of calling Dr. Dabney's attention to the points referred to, that he may satisfy himself as to the correctness of his own statements; and this has been done solely in compliance with your request. Other points may have attracted my attention in the perusal of the narrative; but I cannot now recall them, and do not know that those which have occurred to me are of importance. I wish I could do anything to give real assistance, for I am very anxious that his work should be perfect.

With feelings of great esteem and regard, I am,

Very truly yours,

(Signed) R. E. Lee.

The production of this letter is due to the kindness of Dr. Henry A. White, and of R. E. Lee, Esq., of Washington, youngest son of General Lee.

NOTE II

The following details, communicated to the author by one of Lee's generals, as to the formations of the Confederate infantry, will be found interesting:—

'Our brigades were usually formed of four or five regiments, each regiment composed of ten companies. Troops furnished by the same State were, as far as possible, brigaded together, in order to stimulate State pride, and a spirit of healthy emulation.

'The regiment was formed for attack in line two-deep, covered by skirmishers.

'The number of skirmishers, and the intervals between the men on the skirmish line, depended altogether on the situation. Sometimes two companies were extended as skirmishers; sometimes one company; sometimes a certain number of men from several companies. In rear of the skirmishers, at a distance ranging from three hundred to one hundred and fifty paces, came the remainder of the regiment.

'When a regiment or a brigade advanced through a heavily wooded country, such as the Wilderness, the point of direction was established, and the officers instructed to conform to the movements of the " guide company " or " guide regiment " as the case might be, the " guide" company or regiment governing both direction and alignment.

'The maintenance of direction under such circumstances was a very difficult matter. Our officers, however, were greatly assisted by the rank and file, as many of the latter were accomplished woodsmen, and accustomed to hunt and shoot in the dense forests of the South. Each regiment, moreover, was provided with a right and a left " general guide," men selected for their special aptitudes, being good judges of distance, and noted for their steadiness and skill in maintaining the direction.

'Then, again, the line of battle was greatly aided in maintaining the direction by the fire of the skirmishers, and frequently the line would be formed with a flank resting on a trail or woods-road, a ravine or watercourse, the flank regiment in such cases acting as the guide: (at Chancellorsville, Jackson's divisions kept direction by the turnpike, both wings looking to the centre.) In advancing through thick woods the skirmish line was almost invariably strengthened, and while the " line of battle," covered by the skirmishers, advanced in two-deep line, bodies in rear usually marched in columns of fours, prepared to come, by a " forward into line," to the point where their assistance might be desired. I never saw the compass used in wood-fighting. In all movements to attack it was the universal custom for the brigade commander to assemble both field and company officers to the " front and centre," and instruct them particularly as to the purpose of the movement, the method in which it was to be carried out, the point of direction, the guide regiment, the position of other brigades, &c., &c. Like action was also taken by the regimental commander when a regiment was alone.

'This precaution, I venture to think, is absolutely indispensable to an orderly and combined advance over any ground whatever, and, so far as my knowledge goes, was seldom omitted, except when haste was imperative, in the Army of Northern Virginia. Practical experience taught us that no movement should be permitted until every officer was acquainted with the object in view, and had received his instructions. I may add that brigade and regimental commanders were most particular to secure their flanks and to keep contact with other troops by means of patrols ; and, also, that in thick woods it was found to be of very great advantage if a few trustworthy men were detailed as orderlies to the regimental commander, for by this means he could most easily control the advance of his skirmishers and of his line of battle.

' N. H. HARRIS,
General, late Army of Northern Virginia.'

NOTE III

Before the campaign of 1864, the theatre of which embraced the region between the Rappahannock and Petersburg, including the Wilderness, corps of sharp-shooters, each 180 strong, were organised in many of the brigades of Lee's army. These 'light' troops undertook the outpost, advanced, flank, and rear guard duties. The men were carefully selected ; they were trained judges of distance, skilful and enterprising on patrol, and first-rate marksmen, and their rifles were often fitted with telescopic sights. In order to increase their confidence in each other they were subdivided into groups of fours, which messed and slept together, and were never separated in action. These corps did excellent service during the campaign of 1864.

CHAPTER XXV

THE SOLDIER AND THE MAN [1]

To the mourning of a sore-stricken nation Stonewall Jackson was carried to his rest. As the hearse passed to the Capitol, and the guns which had so lately proclaimed the victory of Chancellorsville thundered forth their requiem to the hero of the fight, the streets of Richmond were thronged with a silent and weeping multitude. In the Hall of Representatives, surrounded by a guard of infantry, the body lay in state; and thither, in their thousands, from the President to the maimed soldier, from the generals of the Valley army to wondering children, borne in their mothers' arms, the people came to look their last upon the illustrious dead. The open coffin, placed before the Speaker's chair, was draped in the Confederate standard; the State colours were furled along the galleries; and the expression on the face, firm and resolute, as if the spirit of battle still lingered in the lifeless clay, was that of a great conqueror, wise in council, mighty in the strife. But as the evening drew on the darkened chamber, hung with deep mourning, and resounding to the clash of arms, lost its sombre and martial aspect. Garlands of soft spring flowers, the tribute of the women of Virginia, rose high above the bier, and white pyramids of lilies, the emblems of purity and meekness, recalled the blameless life of the Christian soldier.

From Richmond the remains were conveyed to Lexington, and, under the charge of the cadets, lay for the night in the lecture-room of the Institute, which Jackson had quitted just two years before. The next morning he was buried, as he himself had wished, in the little cemetery above the town.

[1] Copyright 1898 by Longmans, Green, & Co.

Many were the mourners that stood around the grave, but they were few in number compared with those whose hearts were present on those silent hills. From the cities of the Atlantic coast to the far-off settlements of Texas the news that Stonewall Jackson had fallen came as a stunning blow. The people sorrowed for him with no ordinary grief, not as a great man and a good, who had done his duty and had gone to his reward, but as the pillar of their hopes and the sheet-anchor of the Confederate cause. Nor will those familiar with the further history of the Civil War, from the disaster of Gettysburg to the surrender at Appomattox, question the truth of this mournful presage. The Army of Northern Virginia became a different and less manageable instrument after Chancellorsville. Over and over again it failed to respond to the conceptions of its leader, and the failure was not due to the soldiers, but to the generals. Loyal and valiant as they were, of not one of his lieutenants could Lee say, as he had said of Jackson, ' Such an executive officer the sun never shone on. I have but to show him my design, and I know that if it can be done it will be done. No need for me to send or watch him. Straight as the needle to the pole he advances to the execution of my purpose.' [1]

These words have been quoted as an epitome of Jackson's military character. 'He was essentially,' says Swinton, ' an executive officer, and in that sphere he was incomparable ; but he was devoid of high mental parts, and destitute of that power of planning a combination, and of that calm, broad, military intelligence which distinguished General Lee.' [2] And this verdict, except in the South, has been generally accepted. Yet it rests on a most unsubstantial basis. Because Jackson knew so well how to obey it is asserted that he was not well fitted for independent command. Because he could carry out orders to the letter it is assumed that he was no master of strategy. Because his will was of iron, and his purpose, once fixed, never for a moment wavered, we are asked to believe that

[1] Hon. Francis Lawley, the *Times*, June 16, 1863.
[2] *Campaigns of the Army of the Potomac*, p. 289.

his mental scope was narrow. Because he was silent in
council, not eager in expressing his ideas, and averse to
argument, it is implied that his opinions on matters of
great moment were not worth the hearing. Because he was
shy and unassuming; because he betrayed neither in face
nor bearing, save in the heat of battle, any unusual power
or consciousness of power, it is hastily concluded that he was
deficient in the initiative, the breadth, and the penetration
which are the distinguishing characteristics of great generals.

In these pages, however, it has been made clear that
Jackson's quiet demeanour concealed a vivid imagination,
a fertile brain, and an extraordinary capacity for far-
reaching combinations. After he had once made up his
mind when and where to strike, it is true that his methods
of war were very simple, and his blows those of a sledge-
hammer. But simplicity of design and vigour of execution
are often marks of the very highest military ability.
'Genius,' says Napier, 'is not extravagant; it is ardent,
and it conceives great projects; but it knows beforehand
how to attain the result, and it uses the simplest means,
because its faculties are essentially calculating, industrious,
and patient. It is creative, because its knowledge is vast;
it is quick and peremptory, not because it is presumptuous,
but because it is well-prepared.' And Swinton's verdict
would have been approved by few of the soldiers of the
Civil War. It was not the verdict of Lee. Significant indeed was the cry of the great Confederate, the soul of truth
as of generosity, when Jackson was wounded: 'Could I
have directed events, I should have chosen, for the good of
the country, to have been disabled in your stead.' It was
not the verdict of the Southern people. 'No man,' it was
said by one who knew them well, 'had so magnificent
a prospect before him as General Jackson. Whether he
desired it or not, he could not have escaped being Governor
of Virginia, and also, in the opinion of competent judges,
sooner or later President of the Confederacy.'[1]   Nor
was it the verdict of the foe. 'Stonewall Jackson,'
wrote General Howard, commanding the Eleventh Corps

[1] Hon. Francis Lawley, the *Times*, June 11, 1863.

at Chancellorsville, 'was victorious. Even his enemies praise him ; but, providentially for us, it was the last battle he waged against the American Union. For, in bold planning, in energy of execution, which he had the power to diffuse, in indefatigable activity and moral ascendency, he stood head and shoulders above his *confrères*, and after his death General Lee could not replace him.' [1]

It can hardly be questioned that, at the time of his death, Jackson was the leader most trusted by the Confederates and most dreaded by the Federals. His own soldiers, and with them the whole population of the South, believed him capable of any task, invincible except by fate. It never, indeed, fell to Jackson's lot to lead a great army or to plan a great campaign. The operations in the Valley, although decisive in their results, were comparatively insignificant, in respect both of the numbers employed and of the extent of the theatre. Jackson was not wholly independent. His was but a secondary *rôle*, and he had to weigh at every turn the orders and instructions of his superiors. His hand was never absolutely free. His authority did not reach beyond certain limits, and his operations were confined to one locality. He was never permitted to cross the border, and ' carry the war into Africa.' Nor when he joined Lee before Richmond was the restraint removed. In the campaign against Pope, and in the reduction of Harper's Ferry, he was certainly entrusted with tasks which led to a complete severance from the main body, but the severance was merely temporary. He was the most trusted of Lee's lieutenants, but he was only a lieutenant. He had never the same liberty of action as those of his contemporaries who rose to historic fame—as Lee himself, as Johnston or Beauregard, as Grant, or Sherman, or as Sheridan—and consequently he had never a real opportunity for revealing the height and breadth of his military genius.

The Civil War was prolific of great leaders. The young American generals, inexperienced as they were in dealing with large armies, and compelled to improvise their tactics as they improvised their staff, displayed a talent for com-

---

[1] *Battles and Leaders*, vol. iii. p. 202.

mand such as soldiers more regularly trained could hardly
have surpassed. Neither the deficiencies of their material
nor the difficulties of the theatre of war were to be lightly
overcome ; and yet their methods displayed a refreshing
originality. Not only in mechanical auxiliaries did the
inventive genius of their race find scope. The principles
which govern civilised warfare, the rules which control the
employment of each arm, the technical and mechanical arts,
were rapidly modified to the exigencies of the troops and
of the country. Cavalry, intrenchments, the railway, the
telegraph, balloons, signalling, were all used in a manner
which had been hitherto unknown. Monitors and torpedoes
were for the first time seen, and even the formations of
infantry were made sufficiently elastic to meet the requirements of a modern battle-field. Nor was the conduct of the
operations fettered by an adherence to conventional practice.
From first to last the campaigns were characterised by
daring and often skilful manœuvres ; and if the tactics of
the battle-field were often less brilliant than the preceding
movements, not only are parallels to these tactics to be
found in almost every campaign of history, but they would
probably have escaped criticism had the opponent been
less skilful. But among the galaxy of leaders, Confederate
and Federal, in none had the soldiers such implicit confidence as in Stonewall Jackson, and than the Southern
soldiers, highly educated as many of them were, no better
judges of military capacity were ever known.

   Nevertheless, the opinion of the soldiers is no convincing
proof that Jackson was equal to the command of a large
army, or that he could have carried through a great campaign. Had Lee been disabled, it might be asked, would
Jackson have proved a sufficient substitute ?

   It has already been explained that military genius shows
itself first in character, and, second, in the application of
the grand principles of warfare, not in the mere manipula-
tion of armed masses. It cannot well be denied that Jackson
possessed every single attribute which makes for success in
war. Morally and physically he was absolutely fearless.
He accepted responsibility with the same equanimity that

he faced the bullets of the enemy. He permitted no obstacle to turn him aside from his appointed path, and in seizing an opportunity or in following up a victory he was the very incarnation of untiring energy. He had no moments of weakness. He was not robust, and his extraordinary exertions told upon his constitution. 'My health,' he wrote to his wife in January 1863, 'is essentially good, but I do not think I shall be able in future to stand what I have already stood;' and yet his will invariably rose superior to bodily exhaustion. A supreme activity, both of brain and body, was a prominent characteristic of his military life. His idea of strategy was to secure the initiative, however inferior his force; to create opportunities and to utilise them; to waste no time, and to give the enemy no rest. 'War,' he said, 'means fighting. The business of the soldier is to fight. Armies are not called out to dig trenches, to throw up breastworks, to live in camps, but to find the enemy and strike him; to invade his country, and do him all possible damage in the shortest possible time. This will involve great destruction of life and property while it lasts; but such a war will of necessity be of brief continuance, and so would be an economy of life and property in the end. To move swiftly, strike vigorously, and secure all the fruits of victory is the secret of successful war.'

That he felt to the full the fascination of war's tremendous game we can hardly doubt. Not only did he derive, as all true soldiers must, an intense intellectual pleasure from handling his troops in battle so as to outwit and defeat his adversary, but from the day he first smelt powder in Mexico until he led that astonishing charge through the dark depths of the Wilderness his spirits never rose higher than when danger and death were rife about him. With all his gentleness there was much of the old Berserker about Stonewall Jackson, not indeed the lust for blood, but the longing to do doughtily and die bravely, as best becomes a man. His nature was essentially aggressive. He was never more to be feared than when he was retreating, and where others thought only of strong defensive positions he looked persistently for the opportunity to attack. He was endowed, like Masséna, 'with that rare fortitude which seems to increase as perils thicken. When conquered he was as ready to fight again as if he had been conqueror.' 'L'audace, l'audace, et toujours l'audace' was the main-spring of all his actions, and the very sights and sounds of a stricken field were dear to his soul. Nothing had such power to stir his pulses as the rebel yell. 'I remember,' says a staff-officer, 'one night, at tattoo, that this cry broke forth in the camp of the Stonewall Brigade, and was taken up by brigades and divisions until it rang out far over field and wood. The general came hastily and bareheaded from his tent, and leaning on a fence near by, listened in silence to the rise, the climax, and the fall of that strange sere-nade, raising his head to catch the sound, as it grew fainter and fainter and died away at last like an echo among the mountains. Then, turning towards his tent, he muttered in half soliloquy, "That was the sweetest music I ever heard." '

Yet least of all was Jackson a mere fighting soldier, trusting to his lucky star and resolute blows to pull him through. He was not, indeed, one of those generals who seek to win victories without shedding blood. He never spared his men, either in marching or fighting, when a great result was to be achieved, and he was content with nothing less than the complete annihilation of the enemy. 'Had we taken ten sail,' said Nelson, 'and allowed the eleventh to escape, when it had been possible to have got at her, I could never have called it well done.' Jackson was of the same mind. 'With God's blessing,' he said before the Valley campaign, 'let us make thorough work of it.' When once he had joined battle, no loss, no suffering was permitted to stay his hand. He never dreamed of retreat until he had put in his last reserve. Yet his victories were won rather by sweat than blood, by skilful manœuvring rather than sheer hard fighting. Solicitous as he was of the comfort of his men, he had no hesitation, when his opportunity was ripe, of taxing their powers of endurance to the utter-most. But the marches which strewed the wayside with the footsore and the weaklings won his battles. The enemy, surprised and outnumbered, was practically beaten before a shot was fired, and success was attained at a trifling cost.

Yet, despite his energy, Jackson was eminently patient. He knew when to refuse battle, just as well as he knew when to deliver it. He was never induced to fight except on his own terms, that is, on his own ground, and at his own time, save at Kernstown only, and there the strategical situation forced his hand. And he was eminently cautious. Before he committed himself to movement he deliberated long, and he never attacked until he had ample information. He ran risks, and great ones, but in war the nettle danger must be boldly grasped, and in Jackson's case the dangers were generally more apparent than real. Under his orders the cavalry became an admirable instrument of reconnaissance. He showed a marked sagacity for selecting scouts, both officers and privates, and his system for obtaining intelligence was well-nigh perfect. He had the rare faculty, which would appear instinctive, but which is the fruit of concentrated thought allied to a wide knowledge of war, of divining the intention of his adversary and the state of his *moral*. His power of drawing inferences, often from seemingly unimportant trifles, was akin to that of the hunter of his native backwoods, to whom the rustle of a twig, the note of a bird, a track upon the sand, speak more clearly than written characters. His estimate of the demoralisation of the Federal army after Bull Run, and of the ease with which Washington might have been captured, was absolutely correct. In the middle of May, 1862, both Lee and Johnston, notwithstanding Jackson's victory over Milroy, anticipated that Banks would leave the Valley. Jackson thought otherwise, and Jackson was right. After the bloody repulse at Malvern Hill, when his generals reported the terrible confusion in the Confederate ranks, he simply stated his opinion that the enemy was retreating, and went to sleep again. A week later he suggested that the whole army should move against Pope, for McClellan, he said, would never dare to march on Richmond. At Sharpsburg, as the shells cut the trees to pieces in the West Wood, and the heavy

masses of Federal infantry filled the fields in front, he told
his medical director that McClellan had done his worst.
At Fredericksburg, after the first day's battle, he believed
that the enemy was already defeated, and, anticipating
their escape under cover of the darkness, he advised a night
attack with the bayonet. His knowledge of his adversary's
character, derived, in great degree, from his close observation
of every movement, enabled him to predict with astonishing
accuracy exactly how he would act under given circumstances.

Nor can he be charged in any single instance with
neglect of precautions by which the risks of war are diminished. He appears to have thought out and to have
foreseen—and here his imaginative power aided him—
every combination that could be made against him, and to
have provided for every possible emergency. He was never
surprised, never disconcerted, never betrayed into a false
manœuvre. Although on some occasions his success fell
short of his expectations, the fault was not his ; his strategy
was always admirable, but fortune, in one guise or another—
the indiscipline of the cavalry, the inefficiency of subordinates, the difficulties of the country—interfered with the full
accomplishment of his designs. But whatever could be
done to render fortune powerless that Jackson did. By
means of his cavalry, by forced marches, by the careful
selection of his line of march, of his camps, of his positions,
of his magazines, and lastly, by his consistent reticence, he
effectually concealed from the Federals both his troops and
his designs. Never surprised himself, he seldom failed to
surprise his enemies, if not tactically—that is, while they were
resting in their camps—at least strategically. Kernstown
came as a surprise to Banks, M'Dowell to Frémont. Banks
believed Jackson to be at Harrisonburg when he had
already defeated the detachment at Front Royal. At Cross
Keys and Port Republic neither Frémont nor Shields
expected that their flying foe would suddenly turn at bay.
Pope was unable to support Banks at Cedar Run till the
battle had been decided. When McClellan on the Chickahominy was informed that the Valley army had joined Lee

it was too late to alter his dispositions, and no surprise was ever more complete than Chancellorsville.

And the mystery that always involved Jackson's movements was undoubtedly the result of calculation. He knew the effect his sudden appearances and disappearances would have on the *moral* of the Federal generals, and he relied as much on upsetting the mental equilibrium of his opponents as on concentrating against them superior numbers. Nor was his view confined to the field of battle and his immediate adversary. It embraced the whole theatre of war. The motive power which ruled the enemy's politics as well as his armies was always his real objective. From the very first he recognised the weakness of the Federal position—the anxiety with which the President and the people regarded Washington—and on this anxiety he traded. Every blow struck in the Valley campaign, from Kernstown to Cross Keys, was struck at Lincoln and his Cabinet; every movement, including the advance against Pope on Cedar Run, was calculated with reference to the effect it would produce in the Federal councils; and if he consistently advocated invasion, it was not because Virginia would be relieved of the enemy's presence, but because treaties of peace are only signed within sight of the hostile capital.

It has been urged that the generals whom Jackson defeated were men of inferior stamp, and that his capacity for command was consequently never fairly tested. Had Grant or Sheridan, it is said, been pitted against him in the Valley, or Sherman or Thomas on the Rappahannock, his laurels would never have been won. The contention is fair. Generals of such calibre as Banks and Frémont, Shields and Pope, committed blunders which the more skilful leaders would undoubtedly have avoided; and again, had he been pitted against a worthy antagonist, Jackson would probably have acted with less audacity and greater caution. It is difficult to conceive, however, that the fact would either have disturbed his brain or weakened his resolution. Few generals, apparently, have been caught in worse predicaments than he was; first, when his army was near Harper's Ferry, and Frémont and Shields were converging on his

L L 2

rear; second, when he lay in the woods near Groveton, with no news from Longstreet, and Pope's army all around him; third, when he was marching by the Brock road to strike Hooker's right, and Sickles' column struck in between himself and Lee. But it was at such junctures as these that his self-possession was most complete and his skill most marked. The greater the peril, the more fixed became his purpose. The capacity of the opponent, moreover, cannot be accepted as the true touchstone of generalship. 'The greatest general,' said Napoleon, 'is he who makes the fewest mistakes,' *i.e.* he who neither neglects an opportunity nor offers one.

Thus tested Jackson has few superiors. During the whole of the two years he held command he never committed a single error. At Mechanicsville, and again at Frayser's Farm, the failure to establish some method of intercommunication left his column isolated; this, however, was a failure in staff duties, for which the Confederate headquarters was more to blame than himself. And further, how sure and swift was the retribution which followed a mistake committed within his sphere of action! What opportunity did Jackson miss? His penetration was unerring; and when, after he had marked his prey, did he ever hesitate to swoop? 'What seemed reckless audacity,' it has been well said by one of the greatest of Southern soldiers, 'was the essence of prudence. His eye had caught at a glance the entire situation, and his genius, with marvellous celerity and accuracy, had weighed all the chances of success or failure. While, therefore, others were slowly feeling their way, or employing in detail insufficient forces, Jackson, without for one moment doubting his success, hurled his army like a thunderbolt against the opposing lines, and thus ended the battle at a single blow.' [1]

But if Jackson never failed to take advantage of his

---

[1] General J. B. Gordon, Commanding 2nd Army Corps, Army of Northern Virginia. 'Jackson,' says one of his staff, 'never changed an order on the battlefield when he had once given it. I have seen Ewell, Early, A. P. Hill, and even Lee send an aide with an order, and in a few minutes send another messenger to recall or alter it.' Letter to the author.

opponent's blunders, it might be said that he sometimes laid himself open to defeat. Grant and Sheridan, had they been in place of Shields and Frémont, would hardly have suffered him to escape from Harper's Ferry; Sherman would probably have crushed him at the Second Manassas; Thomas would not have been surprised at Chancellorsville. But Jackson only pushed daring to its limits when it was safe to do so. He knew the men he had to deal with, and in whatever situation he might find himself he invariably reserved more than one means of escape.

On the field of battle his manœuvres were always sound and often brilliant. He never failed to detect the key-point of a position, or to make the best use of the ground. On the defensive his flanks were always strong and his troops concealed both from view and fire; on the offensive he invariably attacked where he was least expected. He handled the three arms, infantry, cavalry, and artillery, in the closest combination and with the maximum of effect. Except at Kernstown, where Garnett interfered, his reserve was invariably put in at exactly the right moment, and he so manipulated his command that he was always strongest at the decisive point. Nor did he forget that a battle is only half won where there is no pursuit, and whenever he held command upon the field, his troops, especially the cavalry, were so disposed that from the very outset the enemy's retreat was menaced. The soldiers, sharers in his achievements, compared his tactical leading with that of others, and gave the palm to Jackson. An officer of his staff, who served continuously with the Army of Northern Virginia, says: 'I was engaged in no great battle subsequent to Jackson's death in which I did not see the opportunity which, in my opinion, he would have seized, and have routed our opponents;'[1] and General Lane writes that on many a hard-fought field, subsequent to Chancellorsville, he heard his veterans exclaim: 'Oh for another Jackson!'

Until Jackson fell the Army of Northern Virginia, except when his advice was overruled, had never missed an opening. Afterwards it missed many. Gettysburg, which

---

[1] Major Hotchkiss, C.S.A.

should have been decisive of the war, was pre-eminently a battle of lost opportunities, and there are others which fall into the same category. It is a perfectly fair assumption, then, that Jackson, so unerring was his insight, would not only have proved an efficient substitute for Lee, but that he would have won such fame as would have placed him, as it placed his great commander, among the most illustrious soldiers of all ages. With any of his contemporaries, not even excepting Lee, he compares more than favourably. Most obedient of subordinates as he was, his strategical views were not always in accordance with those of his Commander-in-Chief. If Jackson had been in charge of the operations, the disastrous battle of Malvern Hill would never have been fought ; Pope would have been cut off from the Rappahannock ; McClellan would have found the whole Confederate army arrayed against him at South Mountain, or would have been attacked near Frederick ; and Burnside would have been encountered on the North Anna, where defeat would probably have proved his ruin. It is difficult to compare him with Lee. A true estimate of Lee's genius is impossible, for it can never be known to what extent his designs were thwarted by the Confederate Government. Lee served Mr. Davis ; Jackson served Lee, wisest and most helpful of masters. It would seem, however, that Jackson in one respect was Lee's superior. His courage, physical and moral, was not more brilliant or more steadfast ; his tactical skill no greater ; but he was made of sterner stuff. His self-confidence was supreme. He never doubted his ability, with God's help, to carry out any task his judgment approved. Lee, on the other hand, was oppressed by a consciousness of his own shortcomings. Jackson never held but one council of war. Lee seldom made an important movement without consulting his corps commanders. Jackson kept his subordinates in their place, exacting from his generals the same implicit obedience he exacted from his corporals. Lee lost the battle of Gettysburg because he allowed his second in command to argue instead of marching. Nor was that political courage, which Nelson declared is as necessary for a commander as military courage, a component part of Lee's character.[1] On assuming command of the Army of Northern Virginia, in spite of Mr. Davis' protestations, he resigned the control of the whole forces of the Confederacy, and he submitted without complaint to interference. Jackson's action when Loring's regiments were ordered back by the Secretary of War is sufficient proof that he would have brooked no meddling with his designs when once they had received the sanction of the Cabinet. At the same time, it must remain undetermined whether Jackson was equal to the vast responsibilities which Lee bore with such steadfast courage; whether he could have administered a great army, under the most untoward circumstances, with the same success; whether he could have assuaged the jealousies of the different States, and have dealt so tactfully with both officers and men that there should have been no friction between Virginians and Georgians, Texans and Carolinians.

It is probable that Jackson's temper was more akin to Grant's than Lee's. Grant had the same whole-hearted regard for the cause; the same disregard for the individual. He was just as ready as Jackson to place a recalcitrant subordinate, no matter how high his rank, under instant arrest, and towards the incompetent and unsuccessful he was just as pitiless. Jackson, however, had the finer intellect. The Federal Commander-in-Chief was unquestionably a great soldier, greater than those who overlook his difficulties in the '64 campaign are disposed to admit. As a strategist he ranks high. But Grant was no master of stratagem. There was no mystery about his operations. His manœuvres were strong and straightforward, but he had no skill in deceiving his adversary, and his tactics were not always of a high order. It may be questioned whether on the field of battle his ability was equal to that of Sherman, or of Sherman's great antagonist, Johnston. Elsewhere he was their superior. Both Sherman and Johnston were methodical rather than brilliant; patient, confident, and far-seeing as they were, strictly observant of the established principles of war, they were without a

[1] Lord Wolseley, *Macmillan's Magazine*, March, 1887.

touch of that aggressive genius which distinguished Lee, Grant, and Jackson.

Nevertheless, to put Jackson above Grant is to place him high on the list of illustrious captains. Yet the claim is not extravagant. If his military characteristics are compared with those of so great a soldier as Wellington, it will be seen that in many respects they run on parallel lines. Both had perfect confidence in their own capacity. ' I can do,' said Jackson, ' whatever I will to do ; ' while the Duke, when a young general in India, congratulated himself that he had learned not to be deterred by apparent impossibilities. Both were patient, fighting on their own terms, or fighting not at all. Both were prudent, and yet, when audacity was justified by the character of their opponent and the condition of his troops, they took no counsel of their fears. They were not enamoured of the defensive, for they knew the value of the initiative, and that offensive strategy is the strategy which annihilates. Yet, when their enemy remained concentrated, they were content to wait till they could induce him to disperse. Both were masters of ruse and stratagem, and the Virginian was as industrious as the Englishman. And in yet another respect they were alike. ' In issuing orders or giving verbal instruction, Jackson's words were few and simple ; but they were so clear, so comprehensive and direct, that no officer could possibly misunderstand, and none dared disobey.' [1] Exactly the same terms might be applied to Wellington. Again, although naturally impetuous, glorying in war, they had no belief in a lucky star ; their imagination was always controlled by common-sense, and, unlike Napoleon, their ambition to succeed was always subordinate to their judgment. Yet both, when circumstances were imperative, were greatly daring. The attacks at Groveton and at Chancellorsville were enterprises instinct with the same intensity of resolution as the storm of Badajos and Ciudad Rodrigo, the passage of the Douro, the great counterstroke of Salamanca. On the field of battle the one was not more vigilant nor imperturbable than the other, and both possessed a due

[1] General J. B. Gordon.

sense of proportion. They knew exactly how much they could effect themselves, and how much must be left to others. Recognising that when once the action had opened the sphere in which their authority could be exercised was very limited, they gave their subordinates a free hand, issuing few orders, and encouraging their men rather by example than by words. Both, too, had that 'most rare faculty of coming to prompt and sure conclusions in sudden exigencies—the certain mark of a master-spirit in war.'[1] At Bull Run, Jackson was ordered to support Evans at the Stone Bridge. Learning that the left was compromised, without a moment's hesitation he turned aside, and placed his brigade in the only position where it could have held its ground. At Groveton, when he received the news that the Federal left wing was retreating on Centreville across his front, the order for attack was issued almost before he had read the dispatch. At Chancellorsville, when General Fitz-hugh Lee showed him the enemy's right wing dispersed and unsuspecting, he simply turned to his courier and said, 'Let the column cross the road,' and his plan of battle was designed with the same rapidity as Wellington's at Salamanca or Assaye.

It has been already pointed out that Jackson's dispositions for defence differed in no degree from those of the great Duke. His visit to Waterloo, perhaps, taught the American soldier the value and importance of concealing his troops on the defensive. It was not, however, from Wellington that he learned to keep his plans to himself and to use every effort to mislead his adversary. Yet no general, not even Napoleon himself, brought about so many startling surprises as Wellington. The passage of the Douro, the storm of the frontier fortresses, the flank attack at Vittoria, the passage of the Adour, the passage of the Bidassoa—were each and all of them utterly unexpected by the French marshals; and those were by no means the only, or the most conspicuous, instances. Was ever general more surprised than Masséna, when pursuing his retreating foe through Portugal, in full anticipation of 'driving the leopards

[1] Napier.

into the sea,' he suddenly saw before him the frowning
lines of Torres Vedras, the great fortress which had sprung
from earth, as it were, at the touch of a magician's wand ?

The dispatches and correspondence of the generals who
were opposed to Wellington are the clearest evidence of his
extraordinary skill.   Despite their long experience, their
system of spies, their excellent cavalry, superior, during
the first years of the Peninsular War, both in numbers and
training, to the English, it was seldom indeed that the
French had more than the vaguest knowledge of his movements, his intentions, or his strength.   On no other theatre
of war—and they were familiar with many—had they encountered so mysterious an enemy.   And what was the result ?
Constantly surprised themselves, they at length hesitated
to attack even isolated detachments.   At Guinaldo, in 1812,
Marmont, with 30,000 soldiers, refused to assault a ridge
occupied by no more than 13,000.   The morning of Quatre-
Bras, when that important position was but thinly held,
even Ney was reluctant to engage.   In the judgment of
himself and his subordinates, who had met Wellington
before, the fact that there were but few red jackets to be
seen was no proof whatever that the whole allied army was
not close at hand, and the opportunity was suffered to
escape.   Other generals have been content with surprising
the enemy when they advanced against him ; Wellington
and Jackson sought to do so even when they were confined
to the defensive.

And in still another respect may a likeness be
found.   Jackson's regard for truth was not more scrupulous
than Wellington's.   Neither declined to employ every
legitimate means of deceiving their enemies, but both were
absolutely incapable of self-deception.   And this characteristic was not without effect on their military conduct.
Although never deterred by difficulties, they distinguished
clearly between the possible and the impossible.   To gain
great ends they were willing to run risks, but if their plans
are carefully considered, it will be seen that the margin left
to chance was small.   The odds were invariably in their
favour.   In conception as in execution obstacles were

resolutely faced, and they were constitutionally unable to close their eyes to contingencies that might prove ruinous. The promise of great results was never suffered to cajole them into ignoring the perils that might beset their path. Imagination might display in vivid colours the success that might accrue from some audacious venture, but if one step was obscure the idea was unhesitatingly rejected. Undazzled by the prospect of personal glory, they formed ' a true, not an untrue, picture of the business to be done,' and their plans, consequently, were without a flaw. Brilliant, indeed, were the campaigns of Napoleon, and astonishing his successes, but he who had so often deceived others in the end deceived himself. Accustomed to the dark dealings of intrigue and chicanery, his judgment, once so penetrating, became blunted. He believed what he wished to believe, and not that which was fact. More than once in his later campaigns he persuaded himself that the chances were with him when in reality they were terribly against him. He trusted to the star that had befriended him at Marengo and at Aspern; that is, he would not admit the truth, even to himself, that he had been overdaring, that it was fortune, and fortune alone, that had saved him from destruction, and Moscow and Vittoria, Leipsic and Waterloo, were the result.

But although there was a signal resemblance, both in their military characters as in their methods of war, between Wellington and Jackson, the parallel cannot be pushed beyond certain well-defined limits. It is impossible to compare their intellectual capacity. Wellington was called to an ampler field and far heavier responsibilities. Not as a soldier alone, but as financier, diplomatist, statesman, he had his part to play. While Napoleon languished on his lonely island, his great conqueror, the plenipotentiary of his own Government, the most trusted counsellor of many sovereigns, the adviser of foreign Administrations, was universally acknowledged as the mastermind of Europe. Nor was the mark which Wellington left on history insignificant. The results of his victories were lasting. The freedom of the nations was restored to them, and land and sea became the thoroughfares of peace. America, on the other hand, owes no single material benefit to Stonewall Jackson. In the cause of progress or of peace he accomplished nothing. The principle he fought for, the right of secession, lives no longer, even in the South. He won battles. He enhanced the reputation of American soldiers. He proved in his own person that the manhood of Virginia had suffered no decay. And this was all. But the fruits of a man's work are not to be measured by a mere utilitarian standard. In the minds of his own countrymen the memory of Wellington is hallowed not so much by his victories, as by his unfaltering honesty and his steadfast regard for duty, and the life of Stonewall Jackson is fraught with lessons of still deeper import.

Not only with the army, but with the people of the South, his influence while he lived was very great. From him thousands and ten thousands of Confederate soldiers learned the self-denial which is the root of all religion, the self-control which is the root of all manliness.[1] Beyond the confines of the camps he was personally unknown. In the social and political circles of Richmond his figure was unfamiliar. When his body lay in state the majority of those who passed through the Hall of Representatives looked upon his features for the first time. He had never been called to council by the President, and the members of the Legislature, with but few exceptions, had no acquaintance with the man who acted while they deliberated. But his fame had spread far and wide, and not merely the fame of his victories, but of his Christian character. The rare union of strength and simplicity, of child-like faith and the most fiery energy, had attracted the sympathy of the whole country, of the North as well as of the South ; and beyond the Atlantic, where with breathless interest the parent islands were watching the issue of the mighty conflict, it seemed that another Cromwell without Cromwell's ambition, or that another Wolfe with more than Wolfe's ability, had arisen among the soldiers of the youngest of nations. And this interest was intensified by his untimely end.

[1] See Note at end of volume.

When it was reported that Jackson had fallen, men murmured in their dismay against the fiat of the Almighty. 'Why,' they asked, 'had one so pure and so upright been suddenly cut down?' Yet a sufficient answer was not far to seek. To the English race, in whatever quarter of the globe it holds dominion, to the race of Alfred and De Montfort, of Bruce and Hampden, of Washington and Gordon, the ideal of manhood has ever been a high one. Self-sacrifice and the single heart are the attributes which it most delights to honour; and chief amongst its accepted heroes are those soldier-saints who, sealing their devotion with their lives, have won

> Death's royal purple in the foeman's lines.

So, from his narrow grave on the green hillside at Lexington, Jackson speaks with voice more powerful than if, passing peacefully away, in the fulness of years and honours, he had found a resting-place in some proud sepulchre, erected by a victorious and grateful commonwealth. And who is there who can refuse to listen? His creed may not be ours; but in whom shall we find a firmer faith, a mind more humble, a sincerity more absolute? He had his temptations like the rest of us. His passions were strong; his temper was hot; forgiveness never came easily to him, and he loved power. He dreaded strong liquor because he liked it; and if in his nature there were great capacities for good, there were none the less, had it been once perverted, great capacities for evil. Fearless and strong, self-dependent and ambitious, he had within him the making of a Napoleon, and yet his name is without spot or blemish. From his boyhood onward, until he died on the Rappahannock, he was the very model of a Christian gentleman:—

> E'en as he trod that day to God, so walked he from his birth,
> In simpleness, and gentleness, and honour, and clean mirth.

Paradox as it may sound, the great rebel was the most loyal of men. His devotion to Virginia was hardly surpassed by his devotion to his wife, and he made no secret of his absolute dependence on a higher power. Every action was a prayer, for every action was begun and ended in the name of the Almighty. Consciously and unconsciously, in deed as in word, in the quiet of his home and in the tumult of battle, he fastened to his soul those golden chains 'that bind the whole round earth about the feet of God.' Nor was their burden heavy. 'He was the happiest man,' says one of his friends, 'I ever knew,' and he was wont to express his surprise that others were less happy than himself.

But there are few with Jackson's power of concentration. He fought evil with the same untiring energy that he fought the North. His relations to his moral duties were governed by the same strong purpose, the same clear perception of the aim to be achieved, and of the means whereby it was to be achieved, as his manœuvres on the field of battle. He was always thorough. And it was because he was thorough—true, steadfast, and consistent, —that he reached the heroic standard. His attainments were not varied. His interests, so far as his life's work was concerned, were few and narrow. Beyond his religion and the army he seldom permitted his thoughts to stray. His acquaintance with art was small. He meddled little with politics. His scholarship was not profound, and he was neither sportsman nor naturalist. Compared with many of the prominent figures of history the range of his capacity was limited.

And yet Jackson's success in his own sphere was phenomenal, while others, perhaps of more pronounced ability, seeking success in many different directions, have failed to find it in a single one. Even when we contrast his recorded words with the sayings of those whom the world calls great —statesmen, orators, authors—his inferiority is hardly apparent. He saw into the heart of things, both human and divine, far deeper than most men. He had an extraordinary facility for grasping the essential and discarding the extraneous. His language was simple and direct, without elegance or embellishment, and yet no one has excelled him in crystallising great principles in a single phrase. The few maxims which fell from his lips are almost a complete summary of the art of war. Neither Frederick, nor Wellington, nor Napoleon realised more deeply the simple truths which ever since men first took up arms have been the elements of success; and not Hampden himself beheld with clearer insight the duties and obligations which devolve on those who love their country well, but freedom more.

It is possible that the conflicts of the South are not yet ended. In America men pray for peace, but dark and mysterious forces, threatening the very foundations of civic liberty, are stirring even now beneath their feet. The War of Secession may be the precursor of a fiercer and a mightier struggle, and the volunteers of the Confederacy, enduring all things and sacrificing all things, the prototype and model of a new army, in which North and South shall march to battle side by side. *Absit omen!* But in whatever fashion his own countrymen may deal with the problems of the future, the story of Stonewall Jackson will tell them in what spirit they should be faced. Nor has that story a message for America alone. The hero who lies buried at Lexington, in the Valley of Virginia, belongs to a race that is not confined to a single continent; and to those who speak the same tongue, and in whose veins the same blood flows, his words come home like an echo of all that is noblest in their history: 'What is life without honour? Degradation is worse than death. We must think of the living and of those who are to come after us, and see that by God's blessing we transmit to them the freedom we have ourselves inherited.'

NOTE I

Mr. W. P. St. John, President of the Mercantile Bank of New York, relates the following incident :—A year or two ago he was in the Shenandoah Valley with General Thomas Jordan, C.S.A., and at the close of the day they found themselves at the foot of the mountains in a wild and lonely place ; there was no village, and no house, save a rough shanty for the use of the 'track-walker' on the railroad. It was not an attractive place for rest, yet here they were forced to pass the night, and to sit down to such supper as might be provided in so desolate a spot. The unprepossessing look of everything was completed when the host came in and took his seat at the head of the table. A bear out of the woods could hardly have been rougher, with his unshaven hair and unkempt beard. He answered to the type of border ruffian, and his appearance suggested the dark deeds that might be done here in secret, and hidden in the forest gloom. Imagine the astonishment of the travellers when this rough backwoodsman rapped on the table and bowed his head. And such a prayer ! 'Never,' says Mr. St. John, ' did I hear a petition that more evidently came from the heart. It was so simple, so reverent, so tender, so full of humility and penitence, as well as of thankfulness. We sat in silence, and as soon as we recovered ourselves I whispered to General Jordan, " Who can he be ? " To which he answered, " I don't know, but he must be one of Stonewall Jackson's old soldiers." And he was. As we walked out in the open air, I accosted our new acquaintance, and after a few questions about the country, asked, " Were you in the war ? " " Oh, yes," he said with a smile, " I was out with Old Stonewall." '—*Southern Historical Society Papers*, vol. xix. p. 371.

NOTE II

List of Killed and Wounded (excluding Prisoners) in Great Battles

(The victorious side is given first)

Name of battle	Number of troops	Killed and wounded	Total	Total percentage	Percentage of victor
Blenheim, 1704 .	Allies, 56,000 . .	11,000	} 31,000	26	19
	French, 60,000 .	20,000			
Ramilies, 1706 .	Allies, 60,000 . .	3,600	} 11,600	9	6
	French, 62,000 .	8,000			
Oudenarde, 1708 .	Allies, 85,000 . .	10,000	} 20,000	11	11
	French, 85,000 .	10,000			
Malplaquet, 1709 .	Allies, 100,000 .	14,000	} 34,000	17	14
	French, 100,000 .	20,000			
Dettingen, 1743 .	Allies, 37,000 . .	2,350	} 9,350	9	6
	French, 60,000 .	7,000			
Fontenoy, 1745 .	French, 50,000 . .	6,000	} 13,300	14	12
	Allies, 40,000 .	7,300			
Prague, 1757 . .	Prussians, 64,000 .	12,000	} 22,000	17	18
	Austrians, 60,000 .	10,000			
Kollin, 1757 . .	Austrians, 53,000 .	8,000	} 19,000	21	15
	Prussians, 34,000 .	11,000			
Rosbach, 1757 .	Prussians, 22,000 .	541	} 4,541	6	2
	Allies, 46,000 .	4,000			
Leuthen, 1757 .	Prussians, 30,000 .	6,000	} 16,000	14	20
	Austrians, 80,000 .	10,000			
Breslau, 1757 . .	Austrians, 80,000 .	5,700	} 11,700	10	7
	Prussians, 30,000 .	6,000			
Zorndorf, 1758 .	Prussians, 32,760 .	12,000	} 32,000	38	37
	Russians, 52,000 .	20,000			
Hochkirch, 1758 .	Austrians, 90,000 .	6,000	} 14,000	10	8
	Prussians, 42,000 .	8,000			
Créfeld, 1758 . .	Allies, 33,000 . .	1,700	} 5,700	7	5
	French, 47,000 .	4,000			
Zullichau, 1759 .	Russians, 72,000 .	4,800	} 10,800	10	6
	Prussians, 27,500 .	6,000			
Kunnersdorf, 1759 .	Allies, 70,000 . .	14,000	} 31,000	27	20
	Prussians, 43,000 .	17,000			
Minden, 1759 . .	Allies, 37,000 . .	2,800	} 9,800	11	7
	French and Saxons, 52,000	7,000			

M M

Name of battle	Number of troops	Killed and wounded	Total	Total percentage	Percentage of victor
Torgau, 1760 . .	Prussians, 46,000 .	12,000	} 24,000	22	26
	Austrians, 60,000 .	12,000			
Leignitz, 1760 . .	Prussians, 30,000 .	3,000	} 8,000	12	10
	Austrians, 35,000 .	5,000			
Lonato and Castiglione, 1796	French, 44,000 .	7,000	} 17,000	18	15
	Austrians, 46,000 .	10,000			
Rivoli, 1797 . .	French, 18,000 .	4,500	} 14,500	30	25
	Austrians, 28,000 .	10,000			
Marengo, 1800 .	French, 28,000 .	5,000	} 13,000	22	17
	Austrians, 30,000 .	8,000			
Hohenlinden, 1800 .	French, 56,000 .	2,500	} 14,500	13	4
	Austrians, 50,000 .	12,000			
Austerlitz, 1805 .	French, 65,000 .	9,000	} 25,000	16	13
	Allies, 83,000 . .	16,000			
Jena, 1806 . .	French, 58,000 .	5,000	} 17,000	17	8
	Prussians, 40,000 .	12,000			
Auerstadt, 1806 .	French, 28,000 .	9,500	} 15,500	22	33
	Prussians, 45,000 .	6,000			
Eylau, 1807 . .	French, 70,000 .	20,000	} 42,000	33	28
	Russians, 63,500 .	22,000			
Heilsberg, 1807 .	Russians, 84,000 .	10,000	} 22,000	13	11
	French, 85,000 .	12,000			
Friedland, 1807 .	French, 75,000 .	10,000	} 34,000	23	13
	Russians, 67,000 .	24,000			
Vimiero, 1808 . .	English, 18,000 .	720	} 2,720	8	4
	French, 14,000 .	2,000			
Eckmühl, 1809 .	French, 65,000 .	7,000	} 15,000	10	10
	Austrians, 80,000 .	8,000			
Aspern, 1809 . .	Austrians, 75,000 .	20,000	} 45,000	26	26
	French, 95,000 .	25,000			
Wagram, 1809 .	French, 220,000 .	22,000	} 44,000	11	10
	Austrians, 150,000 .	22,000			
Talavera, 1809 .	English and Spanish, 53,000 . . .	7,200	} 15,500	14	13
	French, 56,000 .	8,300			
Albuera, 1811 . .	Allies, 32,000 . .	6,750	} 13,750	25	20
	French, 22,500 .	7,000			
Salamanca, 1812 .	Allies, 44,000 . .	5,000	} 15,000	16	11
	French, 47,000 .	10,000			
Borodino, 1812 .	French, 125,000 .	30,000	} 75,000	28	24
	Russians, 138,000 .	45,000			
Bautzen, 1813 .	French, 190,000 .	12,000	} 24,000	8	6
	Allies, 110,000 .	12,000			
Vittoria, 1813 . .	Allies, 83,000 . .	5,000	} 10,000	7	6
	French, 60,000 .	5,000			
Leipsic, 1813 . .	Allies, 290,000 .	42,000	} 92,000	20	14
	French, 150,000 .	50,000			

Name of battle	Number of troops	Killed and wounded	Total	Total percentage	Percentage of victor
Orthez, 1814	Allies, 37,000	2,250	} 6,050	7	6
	French, 40,000	3,800			
Toulouse, 1814	Allies, 52,000	4,650	} 10,550	11	9
	French, 38,000	5,900			
La Rothière, 1814	Allies, 80,000	6,500	} 12,500	10	8
	French, 40,000	6,000			
Montmirail, 1814	French, 25,000	2,000	} 5,000	7	8
	Allies, 39,000	3,000			
Laon, 1814	Allies, 60,000	2,000	} 9,000	8	3
	French, 52,000	7,000			
Ligny, 1815	French, 73,000	12,000	} 24,000	15	16
	Prussians, 86,000	12,000			
Quatre-Bras, 1815	Allies, 31,000	4,500	}. 8,700	16	14
	French, 21,500	4,200			
Waterloo, 1815	Allies, 100,000	20,000	} 42,000	24	20
	French, 70,000	22,000			
Alma, 1854	Allies, 51,000	3,400	} 9,100	10	6
	Russians, 35,000	5,700			
Inkermann, 1854	Allies, 15,700	3,287	} 13,787	15	21
	Russians, 68,000	10,500			
Magenta, 1859	Allies, 48,000	4,500	} 11,000	10	9
	Austrians, 60,000	6,500			
Solferino, 1859	Allies, 135,000	16,500	} 31,500	10	11
	Austrians, 160,000	15,000			
Bull Run, 1861	Confederates, 18,000	1,969	} 3,553	9	10
	Federals, 18,000	1,584			
Perryville, 1862	Federals, 27,000	3,700	} 6,900	16	—
	Confederates, 16,000	3,200			
Shiloh, 1862	Federals, 58,000	12,000	} 21,000	20	20
	Confederates, 40,000	9,000			
Seven Pines, 1862	Federals, 51,000	5,031	} 11,165	12	9
	Confederates, 39,000	6,134			
Gaines' Mill, 1862	Confederates, 54,000	8,000	} 13,000	14	14
	Federals, 36,000	5,000			
Malvern Hill, 1862	Federals, 80,000	2,800	} 8,300	5	3
	Confederates, 70,000	5,500			
Cedar Run, 1862	Confederates, 21,000	1,314	} 3,694	11	6
	Federals, 12,000	2,380			
Second Manassas, 1862	Confederates, 54,000	9,000	} 22,000	17	16
	Federals, 73,000	13,000			
Sharpsburg, 1862	Confederates, 41,000	9,500	} 21,910	17	23
	Federals, 87,000	12,410			
Fredericksburg, 1862	Confederates, 70,000	4,224	} 16,971	8	6
	Federals, 120,000	12,747			
Chickamauga, 1863	Confederates, 71,000	18,000	} 35,100	27	25
	Federals, 57,000	17,100			
Chancellorsville, 1863	Confederates, 62,000	10,000	} 24,000	12	17
	Federals, 130,000	14,000			

Name of battle	Number of troops	Killed and wounded	Total	Total percentage	Percentage of victor
Gettysburg, 1863 .	Federals, 93,000 .	19,000	} 37,000	24	20
	Confederates, 70,000	18,000			
Chattanooga, 1863 .	Federals, 60,000 .	5,500	} 8,500	8	9
	Confederates, 33,000	3,000			
Stone's River, 1863 .	Federals, 43,000 .	9,000	} 18,500	24	20
	Confederates, 37,712	9,500			
The Wilderness, 1864	Confederates, 61,000	11,000	} 26,000	14	18
	Federals, 118,000 .	15,000			
Spotsylvania Court House, 1864	Confederates, 50,000	8,000	} 25,000	16	16
	Federals, 100,000 .	17,000			
Cold Harbour, 1864 .	Confederates, 58,000	1,700	} 11,700	6	3
	Federals, 110,000 .	10,000			
Nashville, 1864 .	Federals, 55,000 .	3,000	} 6,500	6	5
	Confederates, 39,000	3,500			
Königgrätz, 1866 .	Prussians, 211,000 .	8,894	} 26,894	6	4
	Austrians, 206,000 .	18,000			
Wörth, 1870 . .	Germans, 90,000 .	10,642	} 18,642	13	11
	French, 45,000 .	8,000			
Spicheren, 1870 .	Germans, 37,000 .	4,871	} 8,871	13	13
	French, 29,000 .	4,000			
Colombey, 1870 .	Germans, 34,000 .	5,000	} 8,700	9	14
	French, 54,000 .	3,700			
Vionville, 1870 .	Germans, 70,000 .	15,800	} 32,800	19	22
	French, 98,000 .	17,000			
Gravelotte, 1870 .	Germans, 200,000 .	20,000	} 30,000	9	10
	French, 120,000 .	10,000			
Noisseville, 1870 .	Germans, 52,000 .	3,078	} 6,620	4	5
	French, 100,000 .	3,542			
Plevna, July 20, 1877	Turks, 20,000 . .	1,000	} 3,850	13	5
	Russians, 7,000 .	2,850			
Plevna, July 30, 1877	Turks, 20,000 . .	4,000	} 11,300	22	20
	Russians, 30,000 .	7,300			
Pelishat, August 31, 1877	Russians, 20,000 .	1,350	} 2,350	7	6
	Turks, 15,000 . .	1,000			
Lovtcha, 1877 . .	Russians, 20,000 .	1,500	} 3,500	14	7
	Turks, 5,000 . .	2,000			
Plevna, September 11, 1877	Turks, 35,000 . .	3,000	} 19,000	16	8
	Russians, 80,000 .	16,000			
Plevna, December 10, 1877	Russians, 24,000 .	2,000	} 8,000	17	8
	Turks, 20,000 . .	6,000			
Aladja Dagh, 1877 .	Russians, 60,000 .	1,450	} 5,950	6	2
	Turks, 35,000 . .	4,500			
Shipka, 1878 . .	Russians, 25,000 .	5,500	5,500	—	22
	Turks, 30,000 . .	—	—	—	—
Tel-el-Kebir, 1882 .	English, 17,000 .	439	} 3,439	9	2
	Egyptians, 25,000 .	3,000			

Although this return has been compiled from the most trustworthy sources, it can only be taken as approximately accurate.

BRITISH LOSSES

	Strength	Killed and wounded	Percentage
* Dettingen, 1743	12,000	821	6
* Fontenoy, 1745	16,600	4,002	24
Alexandria, 1801	12,000	1,521	12
* † Assaye, 1803	4,500	1,566	34
Coruña, 1809	14,500	1,000	6
* Talavera, 1809	20,500	6,250	30
* Albuera, 1811	8,200	3,990	48
Barossa, 1811	4,400	1,210	27
* Salamanca, 1812	26,000	3,386	13
* Quatre-Bras, 1815	12,000	2,504	20
* Waterloo, 1815	23,991	6,932	29
† Maharajpore, 1843	6,000	790	13
† Moodkee, 1845	9,000	874	9
† Ferozeshah, 1845	16,000	2,415	15
† Aliwal, 1846	10,500	580	5
† Sobraon, 1846	15,500	2,063	13
† Chillianwalla, 1849	15,000	2,388	15
* Alma, 1854	21,500	2,002	9
* Inkermann, 1854	7,464	2,357	31

* In those marked by an asterisk the force formed part of an allied army.
† In these battles Indian troops took part.

INDEX